'Benet Davetian's *Civility* will take you on a compelling social and psychological journey through the history of civility, from the Middle Ages to the present day. Essential reading for anyone interested in international standards and customs of courtesy, Davetian's perspective on the cross-cultural impact of civility practices is not only thorough and insightful, but also encouragingly optimistic.'

Louise Fox, etiquette coach and director of The Etiquette Leader

'Benet Davetian's magisterial yet highly readable study forms a worthy complement to Norbert Elias' classic discussion. The book includes many fascinating insights into the differences in civility practices between France, England, and the United States.'

William Outhwaite, professor of sociology, Newcastle University, author of *European Society* and *The Future of Society*, and co-editor of the *Blackwell Dictionary of Social Thought*

'This is an interesting and important piece of scholarship. It traces the evolution of civility across time and space, and finds that instead of being a monolithic concept, civility has taken different forms in France, England, and the United States. In this tour, Davetian takes us from the distant past to the present day, and also examines how the tide of civility may have crested, and may now be receding. A great read.'

A.R. Gillis, professor emeritus, Department of Sociology, University of Toronto, and author of 'Institutional dynamics and dangerous classes: Reading, writing, and arrest in 19th-century France,' *Social Forces*; 'So long as they both shall live: Marital dissolution and the decline of domestic homicide,' *American Journal of Sociology*; 'Crime and state surveillance,' *American Journal of Sociology*; and 'Literacy and the civilization of violence,' *Sociological Forum*

'Dr Davetian has accomplished an important goal with his book. He has meshed the personal and social into a text that gives meaning to what is usually dry theory. His academic credentials are impeccable but so are his feelings and emotions, his humanity, in regard to sociologic phenomena.'

Dr Arthur Janov, director, the Primal Center, Santa Monica, and author of *The Primal Scream*, *The Feeling Child*, and *Primal Healing*

'*Civility: A Cultural History* is impressive in both scope and depth, engaging in an innovative and substantial dialogue on the concept of civility. Well documented and erudite, Benet Davetian's book not only historicizes the development of civility but also locates the concept in today's society and offers a renewed perspective on crucial issues such as multiculturalism. I read *Civility* with great pleasure.'

Jean-François Côté, professor of sociology,
Université du Québec à Montréal, and author of
*Architecture d'un marcheur: Entretiens avec Wajdi Mouawad* and
*Le triangle d'Hermès: Poe, Stein, Warhol, figures de la modernité esthétique*

# CIVILITY: A CULTURAL HISTORY

Cut off in traffic? Bumped without apology on the subway? Forced to listen to a profane conversation in a public space? In today's Western societies, many feel that there has been a noticeable and marked decrease in mutual consideration in both public and private settings. Are we less civil now than in the past? Benet Davetian's masterful study *Civility: A Cultural History* responds to this question through a historical, social, and psychological discussion of the civility practices in three nations – England, France, and the United States.

Davetian's rich, multi-dimensional review of civility from 1200 to the present day provides an in-depth analysis of the social and personal psychology of human interaction and charts a new course for the study and understanding of civility and civil society. *Civility* addresses major topics in public discourse today regarding the ideals and practices of civility and the possibility of a future civility ethic capable of inspiring cooperation across cultural and national boundaries.

DR BENET DAVETIAN is chair and associate professor of sociology and anthropology at the University of Prince Edward Island (Canada) and director of the Civility Institute. He is listed in Canada's *Who's Who* for his accomplishments in literature and the social sciences.

BENET DAVETIAN

# Civility

## A Cultural History

UNIVERSITY OF TORONTO PRESS
Toronto Buffalo London

© University of Toronto Press Incorporated 2009
Toronto Buffalo London
www.utppublishing.com
Printed in Canada

ISBN 978-0-8020-9338-7 (cloth)
ISBN 978-0-8020-9722-4 (paper)

Printed on acid-free paper

---

**Library and Archives Canada Cataloguing in Publication**

Davetian, Benet, 1947–
  Civility : a cultural history / Benet Davetian.

  Includes bibliographical references and index.
  ISBN 978-0-8020-9338-7 (bound). – ISBN 978-0-8020-9722-4 (pbk.)

  1. Courtesy – Social aspects – History.   2. Courtesy – United States – History.   3. Courtesy – England – History.   4. Courtesy – France – History.   5. Courtesy – Europe – History.   I. Title.

  BJ1533.C9D39 2009      177'.109      C2008-907629-X

---

This book has been published with the help of a grant from the Canadian Federation for the Humanities and Social Sciences, through the Aid to Scholarly Publications Program, using funds provided by the Social Sciences and Humanities Research Council of Canada.

University of Toronto Press acknowledges the financial assistance to its publishing program of the Canada Council for the Arts and the Ontario Arts Council.

University of Toronto Press acknowledges the financial support for its publishing activities of the Government of Canada through the Book Publishing Industry Development Program (BPIDP).

# Contents

*Acknowledgments*  ix

1 Introduction  3

**Part I: The Genealogy of Western Courtesy and Civility**

2 From Barbarism to Courtly Manners  23

3 Secular Civility in the Renaissance  51

4 Shifts in Identity and Awareness: Protestantism and the Enlightenment  84

5 French Court Society, the French Revolution, and the Paradoxes of French Civility  98

6 England and the Victorian Ethic  141

7 The American Experience: Democracy and Informal Civility  211

**Part II: The Rise of the Late-Modern American Self**

8 Conformity, Opposition, and Identity  269

**Part III: The Multifaceted Anatomy of Civility**

9 Towards a Cultural Sociology of Civility  343

**Part IV: Contemporary French, American, and English Civility and Interaction**

10  A Comparative Field Study of France, America, and England   429

**Part V: Summing Up**

11  Civilizing and Recivilizing Processes   497

*Bibliography*   531

*Index*   573

# Acknowledgments

This work would not have been possible without the patient hospitality of citizens of the United States, England, and France. Over a period of many years, they gave of their time, their kindness, and their insights. I apologize to them for any statements that reveal any lack of understanding on my part.

I am also very grateful to two funding organizations that generously supported my research and made possible a project that would otherwise have been financially forbidding. I thank the British Commonwealth Association of Universities Fellowship Committee for their award (1998–2002) and the Social Sciences and Humanities Research Council of Canada for their fellowships (1998 to 2004). Additionally, I am grateful to the Canadian Centre for Ethics in Public Affairs (CCEPA) for a grant enabling me to study civility in the educational system (2007–8).

Many people contributed to the preparation of this work by offering insights and advice. Principal among these was Professor William Outhwaite of Newcastle University. His many patient readings of the manuscript left me grateful as well as enlightened. Many thanks also to Dr Anthony Synnott, who encouraged me during the later stages of the manuscript and kindly arranged for a pleasant and productive two-year stay at Concordia University in Montreal subsequent to my field research in Europe. I had some very good luck writing in some of the fine cafés and bistros of this wonderful cosmopolitan and multicultural world city.

No book can make it to market without the support and understanding of the administration of the university in which one teaches. Without course releases and other courtesies, an academic would be hard-pressed to complete a major manuscript in a timely way. I have been fortunate to have this support and am very grateful to the University of Prince Edward Island, Canada, a university located in one of the most civil regions of North America. I thank U.P.E.I. President H. Wade MacLauchlan; Dr Richard Kurial, Dean of Arts; Dr Vianne Timmons, former Vice-President Academic; Dr Katherine Schultz, Vice-President Research and Development; and Dr Rosemary Herbert, Vice-President Academic. Thanks are also due to the National Libraries of America, France, and England.

Nor can a book ever make it into the hands of the reader without the help of a compassionate and wise editor. This particular book owes its 'coming out' to Virgil Duff, Executive Editor of the University of Toronto Press. I am grateful to him for recognizing the work as worthy of publication and for his patience during the final revisions. Needless to say, I am also grateful to the anonymous referee-readers of the manuscript without whose input and critique this book would not have been what it is. I thank them for their time and contributions. And many thanks to James Leahy for his patient and expert copy editing.

Next, but certainly not any lesser, I owe fond gratitude to various individuals who have encouraged me to pursue my sociological themes. In random order they include Kurt Johansson, John Drysdale, John A. Hall, Charles Taylor, Stephen Turner, Susan Hoecker-Drysdale, Peter Wagner, Clara Khudaverdian, Arthur Janov, William Reimer, Frederick Lowey, Ronald B. Hatch, David Howes, Tom Trenton, Jean Mitchell, Udo Krautwurst, Henry Bissell, Linda Ghan, Matthew Keeping, William Weintraub, Neil Bissondath, Mamdouh ElGharib, Pearl Crichton, Joseph Kopachevsky, Henry Lustiger-Thaller, and the late Mordecai Richler. And special gratitude is owed to the late, great French-Canadian sociologist Professor Hubert Guindon, who so generously dispensed to us the valuable lessons he had learned while working with C. Wright Mills. Those of us who were fortunate enough to study with Guindon during our undergraduate years know for a fact that we would not have been able to accomplish what we did later on had it not been for the manner in which he inspired us with his devastating insights and mischievous humour.

Finally, the preparation of a work such as this takes a few years; that friends and family members continue to remember and love one, even though they have to put up with one's frequent hermetic withdrawals, is a great gift. I am thinking of a series of friends who are each very important to me. You know who you are, so I will not impose on you by mentioning your names. I thank you for your tolerant civility and loving friendship.

# CIVILITY: A CULTURAL HISTORY

# 1 Introduction

> I am sure that no traveler seeing things through author's spectacles can see them as they are.
> – Harriet Martineau, *How to Observe Manners and Morals*

The origins of this book are rooted in my childhood. My father worked for the United Nations, so we moved from one country to another every three or four years. I came to be fascinated by the manner in which people differed from one place to another. In the British school, we were sent to the principal if we were caught using a ballpoint instead of a fountain pen. In the American school, we were forbidden from using fountain pens. In the French school, we could use anything we wanted to just as long as we didn't forget to stand up when the teacher walked in. In England, we always had to leave a little food on the plate in order not to appear greedy. In France, we had to clean up our plate or face an ashen-faced hostess or host.

Early on, my father and mother admonished me to be extremely polite in all circumstances, even when the fault lay with the other. They both admired the English. But, that wasn't all of it. I came to discover that what was considered polite in one place differed from what was considered polite in another. Being polite in the manner of one country could get one in trouble in another one. I somehow managed to get along by imitating the mannerisms of the people who inhabited the country in which we were posted. Through such imitation I came to understand that while certain practices were universal, others were regional and local. Sometimes I felt embarrassed towards myself for being such a chameleon. I also wondered why it was that the way in which I moved and walked on the street differed as I went from London to Paris to New York to Salt Lake City to Montreal to Cairo. What was it about these places and people that made them so distinct? Why did my experience of others and myself change as I went from one culture to another?

Looking back, I'm grateful for this multinational, multicultural childhood. Being rootless, you learn to walk on the razor-sharp line that divides cultures. It's a tricky walk. You're part of it all, but you're also looking at it a little from the side. You begin noticing things that you might not were you fully colonized by the sacrosanct customs of your own folk.

A more recent origin for this book is located in another book I wrote, *The Seventh Circle* (1996). This work of documentary fiction, written with sociological rigour, focused on acts of ethnic rivalry, vengeance, genocide, and civil war. While I was pleased with the manner in which I managed to realistically describe the occurrence of these acts and the resentment and tension that were their root causes, I remained with two questions which I now realize are central to the development of an effective sociology of culture: 'Can a rigorous understanding of the anatomy of civility and incivility help prevent social cruelty? And, what roles do pride and shame play in social organization and minor and major conflicts?' As the reader will notice, these two questions form an integral part of this present work.

But 'why?' asks a colleague. 'Why are you writing a book on "civility"? Isn't it a tame topic?' Yes, it might sound tame at first glance ... a little like turning to the audience and saying, 'Gee folks, let's all get along. Peace and politeness to all.' That is, more or less, what journalists have been calling for over the past decade. Just an hour ago, I checked on google.com again to see how many entries contained the word 'incivility' or the word 'rudeness.' The count goes up every week. This time, over 3,500,000 in English and 150,000 in French. A lot of people seem concerned about the state of our face-to-face and group-to-group relations. As I write this, two national TV networks are in the middle of producing big-budget documentaries on rudeness. One of the networks interviewed me last week to ask me if I agreed that our civilization was disintegrating. I replied in the negative, and I hope that the reader will understand why I gave this response by the time he or she reaches the conclusion of this book.

My own motivations are different from those of journalists who warn that our ability to be civil with one another may be degenerating beyond easy repair. Although it goes without saying that I believe in the practice of civility and fairness and am saddened by the fact that financial and political double binds complicate the maintenance of an altruistic outlook, this book is not a preacher's manifesto. In fact, I am not at all sure that we can become a truly civil society unless we develop an in-depth understanding of civility *as well as* incivility. Our understanding of *civilizing processes* is not yet complete. Since the beginning of human history philosophers and priests have done their utmost to convince human beings to respect and get along with one another. P.M. Forni's (2002) eloquent and sensible book, *Choosing Civility*, is one of the more recent and inspiring additions to the literature. Yet, the fact that we still need convincing may be connected either to a stubborn and truculent human nature or, as I believe, to our lack of understanding of the 'anatomy of civility.' By this I mean the many ways in which a variety of interrelated factors and dimensions influence and shape the interaction rules and quirks of a given culture.

I undertook the research that went into the preparation of this work not because I wanted to convert readers, but because I was intrigued with a variety of issues. At the existential level, I wondered if we are continuing to build some sort of civil society that is at least as worthy as the one envisioned by our forefathers and foremothers or if we are becoming content to remain in a fragmented and disoriented society, not much aware anymore of our authentic possibilities. It is perhaps a question that many are asking, especially those who teach in universities where incoming students seem to have little knowledge of the peoples who lived in eras prior to their own.

Beyond this rather existential question I was interested in locating some of the innovations that might be necessary if we are to have a viable sociology of culture that is capable of explaining society at the micrological as well as macrological levels. Early on during my study I realized that only a multivariate analysis could protect me from losing my way and sliding into simplistic explanations. My chosen topic required a comparative and longitudinal study of political, economic, moral/religious, and psychological conditions during a variety of epochs. If I was to be able to somewhat coherently explain how civility was founded, how its philosophical and practical meanings were transformed over time, and how it came to form an integral part of our social and personal psychology, I would have to study a variety of topics, including emotions and communicative bonds and trust networks, religious beliefs and moral habituations, sexual norms, socialization customs, courtship and family organization, educational ideals, media, and, quite significantly, political practices and economic organization. I came to understand that these factors collectively form a 'process' that enfolds how people conceive of their personal identities, how they treat each other, and how they maintain and change their personal and communal ideals. Needless to say, I became convinced that every area in the social sciences would benefit from a historical and contemporary understanding of the complex factors that go into the formation of civility traditions. Certainly, this book now attempts to heal the long-standing rift between sociology and social psychology.

The complications (and opportunities) increase when we consider the fact that civility ideals and practices vary from one culture to the next. The development of a theoretically and empirically reliable definition of civility requires considerable cross-cultural knowledge and insight, for we need to select workable criteria of definitions that are not stunted by geocentric preferences. It is for this reason that this book is based on a substantial comparative study of civility in three nations that share common stages of economic and technological development: France, America, and England. I hope to demonstrate that there is an important connection between the habituations of the past and present preferences, while showing how new ideals entirely unconnected to historical habituations can additionally emerge when cultures arrive at points of 'critical shifts.' So, I have not only examined the civic history of these three nations (from 1200 till the present), but additionally studied them in a comparative contemporary context to more proficiently test my hypothesis that globalization of media and trade are not having a substantial levelling effect on cultures, not even on ones that share common economic capacities and political alliances.

In addition to the question 'Why is it that different cultures develop different standards and styles of civility?' I have addressed a more universal question: 'What is the anatomy of civility? What must we study and understand if we are to achieve a fairly scientific understanding of civility (and incivility) that is capable of reliably informing all social research?' This question is not inconsequential. It is my intention to demonstrate that a 'sociology of culture' that is historically as well as emotionally informed can provide substantially more reliable explanations of social organization and action than a sociology that is content to study social behaviour at the exclusion of the emotions and 'emotivations' that energize populations (Davetian 2005).

In brief, I have taken history into careful consideration before going on to discuss the various aspects of civility and how a comprehensive sociology of culture can arrive at a proficient understanding of how 'cultural mentalities' and 'cultural emotionalities' affect the civility habits of a culture. Thus, my work sets out to reveal the tripartite nature of civility and the civilizing process: their historical foundations; their dependence on moral, educational, and political values; and their very deep connection with human emotion.

Being a work on civility, this present volume is indebted to the seminal work produced by Norbert Elias in *The Civilizing Process* ([1939] 1978, 1982). Although my own work is not intended to provide a detailed presentation of Elias's body of work – as does Stephen Mennell's erudite account, *Norbert Elias – Civilization and the Human Self-Image* (1989) – I have included a fair amount of commentary on Elias's theory of social development and, in particular, his definition of the 'civilizing process' as a story of ever-increasing 'restraints.' I have also tried to broaden his theory in context of late-modern society in order to demonstrate why contemporary conditions now require more comprehensive explanations of civil society.

One major difference between this present work and the one produced by Elias is that my own study of the development of civility is not meant to argue for the benefits of what Elias termed *configurational sociology*. I take his argument for granted. The proposition that social organization and human agency are intimately linked has been adequately demonstrated by many contemporary sociological studies. What remains to be revealed is the dynamic emotional processes that connect these two spheres. This present work attempts to do that. It also aims to accomplish something that was not present in Elias's excellent treatment of the topic – it provides a thorough understanding of civility in cross-cultural perspective. Elias's conclusions were substantially influenced by his studies of the absolutist French monarchy. My own study not only includes a discussion of French society, but, additionally, extends the discussion to America and England; and it does so by taking all eras, including and following the medieval period, into consideration. I feel that this broader analysis of the anatomy of civility was somewhat absent in Elias's work. Elias's first concern was to show how civility and the monopolization of violence by the state were correlated. His first intention was not to produce a multi-dimensional and longitudinal account of civility. This limitation may have been due to the fact that he felt obliged to make a parallel statement regarding the art of social theorizing, for he wrote at a time when sociology offered not much more than two major theoretical alternatives: the structuralism of Parsonian sociology and the doctrinal certainty of classical Marxist theory. Elias had his hands full searching for a more unified conception of social organization and action, one that would accord interactive power to both society and individuals. So his work was meant not only to test his theory of civilizational development, but to also share his views regarding sociological perspective. This may have prevented him from going into further depth regarding his conception of *restraint* and *shame* and offering a theory and typology of civility that could serve for further research. I have attempted to provide these additional insights in this present work.

In brief, I have set out to produce a comprehensive account of civility from historical, sociological, and psychological points of view, while also providing a template for proficient field studies of civility and cultural ideology across ethnic and national boundaries. I have done so by addressing and hopefully achieving the following goals: (1) to describe how the Western civility and courtesy tradition was born at a time when the Western world was overwhelmed by violence and in sore need of communal reconstruction and cooperative restraint; (2) to explain how developments in civility practices were affected not only by the political, economic, and religious developments that led to the formation of civil institutions, but, just as importantly, by shifts in human awareness, knowledge, and sensibility; (3) to examine civility and courtesy in a cross-cultural context by grounding the study in historical as well as contemporary comparisons of the English, French, and American civility traditions; (4) to present a workable framework of analysis for civility research and a civility theory and topology that contributes to the design and implementation of further study; (5) to demonstrate how the political and economic habituations of a nation are mutually interactive with its emotional and motivational habituations; and (6) to propose, in my conclusion, that a useful, globally relevant theory of civility will have to go beyond our conception of manners, etiquette, and politeness and remain compatible with the emerging realization that civility and ethics may be mutually compatible within a system of interaction that posits no contradiction between loyalty to the well-being of the self and loyalty to the well-being of other selves. This process of interaction will require a thorough understanding of the social psychology of pride and shame. For want of a better term I call this process *eco-civility*.

In order to achieve the above goals without causing undue confusion on the reader's part, I have divided the book into five interconnected parts. The purpose and structure of those parts are explained below under the heading 'How This Book Is Organized.'

What do we mean when we speak of civility? Few of us living in contemporary cultures in which 'personal rights' are at the forefront of cultural politics stop to think of the roots of the words 'civility' and 'politeness.' The etymology of these words indicates that, at their inception, they were used to signify good 'citi-zenship.' 'Civility' derives from the Latin *civis*, *'the city,'* and politeness derives from the Greek *polis*, also *'the city.'* So, in the classical sense, civility and politeness are not just acts of friendliness, but also indications of how life is to be best lived in cities in which citizens are dependent on one another and the state for functional relations within complex social networks. As for manners, they are more than an indication of how one is to eat at table and greet others; they additionally serve as symbols of ideal character and social status.

For the purposes of this book, I have chosen a fairly universal definition that takes social order as well as personal sentiments into account. I have defined courtesy and civility as *the extent to which citizens of a given culture speak and act in ways that demonstrate a caring for the welfare of others as well as the welfare of the culture they share in common.* Such a definition permits us to study civility at both the private and public levels, in micro as well as macro contexts, and from the perspective of personal honour as well as public citizenship. At the international level, I have defined civility as *the degree to which states value each other's welfare and the preservation of world order enough to take the necessary steps to avoid misunderstanding, humiliation, injustice, and other acts that set in motion the need for acts of retribution.* Certainly the study of civility is also the study of cultural ideology, for different peoples continue to possess cultural mentalities and habituations that are distinct enough to cause misunderstandings and tensions.

Since certain chapters in this book include an analysis of conduct books from each of the cultures studied, it should be mentioned that the study of conduct books as indicators of cultural ideals is a nascent area in the sociology of culture. And, indeed, one does tread on delicate ground when trying to understand a nation from the behavioural models contained in the books of its philosophers, moralists, and trendsetters. There is always a variation between what is preached and what is eventually practised (just as there is between what actually happens in history and what is said to have happened). Even so, the writers of conduct books exert considerable short- and long-term influence on a culture's ideologies and practices. Moreover, conduct books are reliable historical records because they help reveal what is already being practised, since their writers are often given to complaining about those ongoing behaviours which they find unacceptable. For example, a Renaissance conduct book advising its adult readers not to spit at table is providing us with clear indication that some were indeed spitting at table; if they were not, it would not have been necessary to dispense the advice.

## Methodological and Theoretical Implications

While this work has somewhat of an encyclopedic nature, it also contains viewpoints and arguments regarding description, methodology, and theory.

At the descriptive level, I am trying to provide a more comprehensive representation of civility by going beyond Elias's theory of 'violence restraint.' I see civility as more than the absence of an undesired quality such as violence or corrosive behaviour. I hope to show through the combination of historical data, literary analysis, and insights from the fields of psychology and social psychology that civility is the endpoint of a series of emotional needs and traits that must be taken into consideration on their own merit if we are to understand both civility and incivility as interdependent as well as independent states of mind and heart. Here, I try to transcend binary thinking and affirm that civility is much more than the 'absence' of rudeness or the 'presence' of its polar opposite, politeness.

Very importantly, I am arguing at the methodological level that the duration of the period of time over which a given social practice is observed plays a very large role in the kind of explanations that emerge. In view of this, I have purposefully traced the story of civility as far back as the medieval age in order to allow myself to view the longest period of time possible for this particular Western tradition. The civility standards of the sixteenth, seventeenth, and eighteenth centuries would not be as understandable if one were not to be privy to the manner in which the civility tradition passed from the medieval theological ideal of 'virtue' to the later Renaissance secular ideal of 'consideration' for the comfort of others. Nor would we understand the moralizing of the Victorians in proper context were we not at once aware of the libertinism that preceded their era. I think that both Elias and Foucault approached social history with a similar preference for longitudinal insight (Spierenburg 2004).

Understandably, as Charles Tilly has eloquently argued in his book *Why?* (2006), the search for 'reasons' should be accompanied by an honest admission that the mere act of observing a process over a long historical time frame can easily turn into a form of storytelling. So, the realistic social scientist proceeds with her reasoning realizing that the story she is writing could be written differently. In the end, the degree to which a set of explanations are plausible depends on whether they follow a reasonable train of thought while leaving the reader with the impression that the explanations have engaged with what ordinary people were actually experiencing in the eras and locations included in the narrative. For Tilly, and also myself, a fairly workable answer to the question 'why' is found within a historical account that readily subjects itself to scrutiny from a variety of points of view: the political, the economic, the philosophical, and the psychological. It is only then that one succeeds in some measure, as Tilly points out, in 'rearranging the existing evidence in a new interpretation of mentalities and calculations that appears to be more consistent, economical, and/or plausible than the available interpretations' (1981:23). Such a narrative becomes even more credible when it is read in a long-range comparative mode. Too many social studies focus on one country and then make universal statements that collapse into inaccuracy when other cultures are introduced as controls. Thus, by asking 'why' a certain thing occurs and changes in one way rather than another *in a variety of countries*, despite the passing of centuries, we come that much closer to understanding the peculiarities of various geographic locations and cultural hubs in our own era.

Longitudinal studies provide us with an additional important advantage. They give us the opportunity of acquiring a more multi-dimensional understanding of the complex relationships between independent, intervening, and dependent variables. The long-range study allows us to notice far-reaching occurrences that emerge between supposed causes and supposed effects. Sometimes these 'interventions' surprise us and require us to rethink our understanding of the development of a given practice. This increases the depth and reliability of our analysis as well its theoretical outcomes. What is telescopic then becomes kaleidoscopic, revealing much that may have otherwise remained hidden. As A.R. Gillis (2004, 1996, 1989) has demonstrated, in a series of assiduous longitudinal studies of crime and deterrence, theoretical explanations can be too readily rejected or too readily accepted when the empirical evidence is drawn from a short or wrong period of time:

> Inability to find factual support for an argument may indicate that it is indeed unsupported by the data from a particular sample. At the very least this would clearly disprove the idea that the proposition will hold for *all* populations. It may even mean that the hypothesis will not hold in *any* population. However, failure to find supporting evidence can also occur when arguments are actually valid. For example, there may indeed be a relationship between the *concepts* in a proposition, but if there is weak correspondence between indicators and the concepts they are supposed to measure, there may be no observable association between the *variables* in the hypothesis. Thus, invalid measurement can nullify accurate propositions. (1996:75)

Gillis is arguing for studies of the longitudinal sort that not only take long stretches of history into consideration but also take careful note of how the initial and subsequent progression of a social development varies as one proceeds through time frames that are closely connected but characteristically and symbolically distinct from one another. Such variations can transform our understanding of the empirical evidence and lead us to a more profound understanding of the genesis and development of a social practice. As Gillis points out, 'Depending on the processes involved, the interval of time between cause and effect could range between nanoseconds and generations' (1996:76). And, indeed, an effect observed in the short range can become its polar opposite when observed further along the continuum of time. For example, the restraint of emotion in an emotionally violent culture may be considered a welcomed relief, while that same restraint might be considered a curse in an overly rational culture in which emotional expression has become stunted. Similarly, what is considered civil and uncivil can change depending on the historical era. Sometimes incivility becomes necessary as a defence against exclusionary civility rituals. Here, the incivility becomes, ironically enough, an affirmation of the civility of democratic equality. So what may seem incongruent in the short run may become credible when viewed in the long term; in fact, a given effect may dissipate and be replaced by an opposite effect if granted enough time.

Gillis (2004, 1989) demonstrates the viability of such sophisticated analysis in two further groundbreaking articles regarding state institutions and crime in nineteenth-century France. He shows that educational *as well as* policing institutions had a salient influence on crime rates. In 'Crime and State Surveillance in Nineteenth-Century France' (1989), Gillis uses time-series analysis to show that the long-range effect of France's establishment of two national police forces was indeed a decrease in major crimes between 1865 and 1913. Controlling for the fact that the sudden increase in police does correlate with increased reporting of crime, Gillis concedes that, despite increases in reporting of lesser crimes (a natural outcome of the presence of a large police force possessing the necessary manpower to survey the population and process complaints), major crimes decreased as a direct result of increased state surveillance. Yet, by extending his study to a host of other variables, he provides the additional and important insight that it was not the crime rate that led to increased policing but the broader interest of the state to repress 'dangerous classes' and limit political challenges to the state. The surveillance and reporting of crime was, therefore, a secondary outcome, preceded by a very salient intervening variable: the desire to control behaviour according to political standards.

Gillis has also discovered, in 'Institutional Dynamics and Dangerous Classes: Reading, Writing, and Arrest in Nineteenth-Century France' (2004), that the establishment of educational institutions given the mandate to produce conformity through a moral curriculum had a salient influence on crime rates. Yet, he specifies that the defining factor in change in crime rates was limited not to moral education in schools but to a by-product of education: the acquisition of 'literacy.' Not content to limit his research to the overall short-term crime rate, he investigates the literacy variable and discovers that as crime rates decreased in the literate population they increased in those portions of the population that remained illiterate. He suggests that public education and, importantly, literacy contributed to the creation of an educated literate class that came to believe that society was being threatened by a dangerous criminal underclass. This insight would not have been available had the study been limited to the time frame immediately following the establishment of a comprehensive police force, for it took time for educational institutions to dispense enough literacy for reliable data to emerge that showed a strong correlation between literacy and crime rates.

The reader will notice a similar 'constructive suspicion' in my own work. While I am not attempting to 'deconstruct' the historical and moral evidence, I am trying to show that first causes and intervening causes do differ from each other and are both worthy of being studied with a sharp eye for surprising contradictions and changes in outcome. The reader will notice this distinction in my re-evaluation of Weber's thesis regarding capitalism and my discussion of the manner in which the intervening movement of Romanticism facilitated capitalist consumption practices, thereby providing a counterbalance to the original Protestant ethic of self-denial and causing a reformation of our views on 'duty.'

Finally, at the theoretical level, I hope to argue that Norbert Elias's equating of civility with emotional restraint is problematic when applied to contemporary culture. It is very much based on the Freudian notion that the human being is in the grips of potentially destructive desires which, if not restrained, can lead to social chaos. Elias focused successfully on those eras in which the human body was being disciplined and restrained (repressed) for the purpose of facilitating central rule and the hegemony of a ruling class. Yet, had he extended his study to nations and eras in which a different, more expressive mode of interaction was favoured (despite the existence of a strong centralized state that exercised considerable authority and surveillance over its population) he might have revised his theory or, at least, refined and broadened it. In my own case, I have taken into account that there might have occurred a corresponding increase in human awareness and discernment, enough of an increase to require us to now update the classical conception of the human being as a potentially self-serving and other-destructive agent.

I have, in fact, discovered in my own study that both self-restraint and self-expression have opportunity costs. The nature and degree of these costs depend very much on location and historical situation. So, remaining aware of the dangers of favouring 'this or that,' I will be arguing that the study of civility (and incivility) is at once a study of the 'social bond' or, if you prefer, 'trust networks.' By consequence, the style of civil interaction (or the degree of politeness) is not sufficient indication of the stability and integration of a culture. Style is a time-specific reality. What is just as important is whether a given civility style is helping or hindering the culture from maintaining *a state of trust* between private and public practices as well as between ideological dialogues and actual practices. Thus, I will be arguing that the manner in which trust, distrust, pride, and embarrassment/shame are managed are the ultimate measures of a culture's civility ethos and an important variable in the construction of a locally and cross-culturally valid theory of contemporary civility.

**How This Book Is Organized**

In order to maintain coherence in a work covering three countries over an 800-year period, I have organized the contents of this book in five parts. While the text is longer than it might have been had I covered only one nation, I have in every chapter attempted to write in a manner that will prove coherent to academics as well as to members of the general public. Instructors who select this text as part of a one-semester course can count on it not taking much longer to read than some 250-page texts.

Cited text in this book has been selected to be part of the narrative. The reader who skims through these quoted passages and statements without considering them important parts of the continuous narrative will miss some salient points and be short-changed of the empirical foundations for some of my explanations. A complete reading, therefore, is the optimum method for using this particular book.

Throughout the narrative I have used the masculine form of the generic pronoun signifying otherness, although I remain conscious that it does not adequately represent the global human that transcends genders. I look forward to the day when all academics can agree on a substitute word and universalize its use. Sometimes, when grammatically appropriate, I have used the word 'they.' Users of languages that do not have masculine and feminine pronouns are very fortunate.

I have also tried to step out of the way and avoid irritating the reader through excessive uses of 'I.' I have instead used the word 'we,' trusting that the reader will not take it for the pretentious royal 'we.' I, of course, take full responsibility for all the material in the book since behind the 'we' is a single researcher. I revert to the 'I' in the concluding chapter of the book.

As mentioned above, the book is divided into five parts that are meant to be read consecutively. They are listed and explained below.

*Part I: The Genealogy of Western Courtesy and Civility (Chapters 2–7)*

In this first part, I have reviewed the development of Western civility by studying key courtesy and conduct books as well as important historical developments that occurred between the years 1200 and the close of the nineteenth century. I have started the narrative in the Middle Ages and examined how the Christian ethics of restraint and the Aristotelian virtue ethics were enlisted to legitimize the newly formed courts and create a certain communal cooperation between violent warriors who were threatening the stability of Europe (chapter 2). From there, I have proceeded to the Renaissance (chapter 3) and discussed its considerable effects on the development of a person-centred civility ethos that was not as dependent on theological dogma as were the courtesy ideals of the Middle Ages. I have supplemented this review with a section on the Protestant Reformation and the Enlightenment (chapter 4), watershed occurrences in Western history that substantially transformed morality and personal identity, facilitating the transformation of etiquette into civic ethics (civility). If there is a genesis to modern 'individualism' it is to be found in the Renaissance, the Protestant Reformation, and the Enlightenment.

From there I have moved to separate studies of the development of civility in France, England, and America prior to the twentieth century (chapters 5–7). I have used historical records, conduct books, literature, and a variety of artifacts that help us piece together the norms and practices of these three countries as they made their way from the thirteenth to the end of the nineteenth century. I attempt to show how the absolutist French monarchy followed by the French Revolution (chapter 5), the parliamentary system of England paralleled by the seminal influence of the Victorian movement (chapter 6), and the democratic communalism of the American federation of states (chapter 7) led to the formation of distinct national civility standards that are still observable today. During this narrative, I take particular note of how emotions were restrained and expressed in these three different cultures and how the consequences of such differences in emotional constitutions may be continuing to have a salient effect on the present civility practices of these countries.

*Part II: The Rise of the Late-Modern American Self (Chapter 8)*

In this second part, I have tried to further our understanding of the socio-psychology of present civility practices by making sense of the changes that have occurred in the twentieth and early twenty-first centuries and the manner in which they have impacted our standing conceptions of civility. During this era, many of the meanings and practices that were considered 'moral' were questioned as part of a broad cultural movement that revised social values in the interests of personal identity and social equity. These revisions have had an important effect not only on social relations and identity but also on the manner in which we theorize the social. In this chapter I have concentrated particularly on America because it has been at the forefront of the 'identity movement.' I have taken into account the rise of an 'oppositional self' in the 1960s and 1970s and the manner in which this has contributed to considerable moral permissiveness and informality in civil interactions; I have also described the rise of a subsequent 'therapeutic mentality' that has had considerable effects on private and public discourses. This focus on the American experience accomplishes two things: first, it helps us understand some of the contemporary American worry over incivility; second, it allows us to question why French and English civility practices were less affected by the 'cultural revolutions' that occurred in France and England during that same period. These insights contribute to the achievement of one of the core goals of this book: to shed light on what aspects maintain the civility tradition of a culture and what aspects perturb, weaken, and transform it.

*Part III: The Multifaceted Anatomy of Civility (Chapter 9)*

In this part of the book I have attempted to provide a comprehensive discussion of the various factors that need to be considered in the construction of a comprehensive and useful theory of civility. I have begun with a discussion of the important role played by human emotion in all situations involving social interaction and presented some cutting-edge research suggesting that a culture's civility and incivility are connected not only to its values and ideologies but also to the personal emotional biographies of its citizens. I have then reviewed and critiqued Norbert Elias's theory of *The Civilizing Process* ([1939] 1978, [1939] 1982, [1969] 1983) in light of some of the evidence that has emerged from my own comparative study. As part of my effort to provide as complete a picture as possible of the various dimensions that are involved in civility practices, I have reviewed our present understanding of the socialization process and how the 'presentation of self' involves complex processes very much affected by the emotions of pride, embarrassment, and shame. Following this, I have discussed how interactions and habituations vary as we cross over from one culture to another. I have specifically provided evidence demonstrating that cultures that value 'independence' differ markedly in their interaction habituations from cultures that value 'interdependence.' As part of my cross-cultural discussion, I have shown how a culture's relation to 'time, context, and space' has a salient influence on its cultural ideology and interaction preferences. Having shown that cultural ideologies and behaviour are intimately linked, I have then provided a comprehensive 'politeness theory' that reveals how different types of politeness are tied to a culture's preference for 'mutual association' or 'mutual distancing' between citizens. These preferences produce different face-saving and civility practices. Finally, I have provided a synthesis of the above knowledge through a discussion of how an understanding of the emotional nature of embarrassment and shame can help in the development of an emotionally informed sociology that is capable of explaining seminal transformations occurring in human relations at the personal, local, and global levels. I have concluded with a discussion of 'social bonds' and their seminal influence on private and public relations.

*Part IV: Contemporary French, American, and English Civility and Interaction (Chapter 10)*

This final part of the book is based on the previous parts as well as a comprehensive long-term field study carried out in the three countries of this study. I have begun by applying the historical, socio-psychological, and theoretical insights of preceding chapters and created a template for civility research. This template was used in my own comparative study of contemporary France, America, and England, discussed in this portion of the book. The field observations are organized around the following interconnected dimensions: civility styles and civil relations, state systems, family and childrearing, conceptions of self-esteem, education, media, conversation, courtship, work ethic, bureaucracy, and citizenship.

*Part V: Summing Up*

The final part of the book is a summary in which the various insights from previous chapters are brought together within a discussion of civility that is at once descriptive, analytical, and normative. Its chapter is, appropriately, entitled 'Civilizing and Recivilizing Processes.'

Here, I discuss the important role played by emotions in human interaction and suggest that the classical conception of the civilizing process

– the notion that civilization and anger restraint are synonymous – no longer serves to explain human interaction in an era when emotional expression and economic and technological proficiency need to somehow make peace with each other. Drawing upon the various strengths of the American, French, and English civility traditions, I suggest that cultures do not homogenize in late modernity but go through cycles of 'recivilizing' during which they may even borrow from and exchange the traits of one another. I hope to argue that the fact that civility practices are always in formation and reformation requires a sociology of culture that is capable of anticipating and observing change, certainly a sociology that is capable of being historically informed while remaining timely and immune to observational fatigue. During this argument I attempt to show that while the civility codes of England, America, and France can be summarized quite neatly, there are already ongoing changes in the most recent generations of these nations that require us to have frequent descriptive, analytical, and theoretical updates.

In this section, I also discuss the important roles played by embarrassment, shame, and national solidarity in civility and provide a comparative topology of American, French, and English civility/interaction practices.

At the normative level, I offer some thoughts on civility and its relationship with ethics in plural democracies. I discuss a civility standard that may be capable of transcending cultural habituations and cultural tensions. Drawing on what is known about the social psychology of human interaction, I propose that self-interested civility and other-interested civility can be mutually compatible if they are governed by a simple formula of ethics which I term *eco-civility*.

On a final note, it is regrettable that a systematic discussion of civility is still required after the passing of countless prophets, religions, and political systems. Something has prevented us from realizing an ideal social contract that substantially minimizes the discounting and demeaning of others. Despite the efforts of countless philosophers, social theorists, and scientists, the discussion of human sentiment and civility needs to continue in the hope that it will act as a sort of vaccine against the triumph of that which is mean-spirited. In this regard, one feels instructed by a quote from Amy Vanderbilt, who said, 'Good manners have much to do with emotions. To make them ring true, one must feel them, not merely exhibit them.' One also remains aware of the political uses of civility and the sobering observation of E.V. Lucas that 'there can be no defense like elaborate courtesy.' It is with such realistic foreknowledge of the uneasy tensions between true sentiment and ritual, between individual desire and communal mandates, that I share this work with you.

# Part I

# The Genealogy of Western Courtesy and Civility

The past is never dead. It's not even past.

– William Faulkner

# 2 From Barbarism to Courtly Manners

> ... abandon all evil vices: he is a miscreant and a hypocrite who thinks to gain God's love and glory through proud and boastful ways. No! It takes afflictions, fasting, prayer and true repentance ... Such are the arms with which a knight should arm himself if he wishes to love God and to be worthy and valiant.
>
> – Chrétien de Troyes, *Perceval*

## Introduction

Our contemporary Western understanding of *courtesy* and *civility* is founded on our experience of a democratic society in which all citizens are supposed to enjoy fair treatment before the law. The massive amount of literature that has recently appeared on the supposed waning of courtesy shows how much we have come to value democratic civility as a sign of civilized pro-social behaviour. Yet nostalgia for a supposedly more civil era distracts us from realizing that in a different time and place the outright disrespect, hatred, and exclusion of the 'other' was considered normal and vital for survival. Ironically, when Western *courtesy* first appeared as a social contract in Europe during the Middle Ages its practice had little to do with mutual consideration and everything to do with establishing and maintaining rigid differentiations between individuals possessing disparate amounts of military power, social prestige, and wealth. Nevertheless, it served to provide the foundation for a long tradition of civility founded on the belief that human interaction should be so conducted as to respect the safety and comfort of interactants. Thus, a knowledge of the origins of courtesy is very important if we are to understand the crucial role played by the restraint of violence in the development of later Western civility.

Although the early courtesy writings preached in favour of less violence, they were not meant to favour equality between citizens. In fact, the rationalization and maintenance of an inflexible social hierarchy were not at all in conflict with the highly influential Christian theology of the time. Social and economic inequality had already been morally legitimized in the earliest Church writings. These teachings had explained that, following the classical Golden Age, men and women had chosen their strongest warriors to represent them and then thanked them for their protective leadership by providing them with extraordinary social status and material rewards. It did not require a leap of imagination to take the next step and imbue the physically courageous post-Roman medieval champion or ruler with quasi-divine spiritual qualities. By the time of the absolutist French court, King Louis XIV was declaring with brazen confidence that obedience to God required obedience to the monarch.

At its conception in early medieval Christian Europe, therefore, courtesy was not a philosophy of generalized kindness but a process of deference and adulation intended to legitimize the rights claimed by the new chieftains of Europe (Bautier 1971, Brath 1930). Paying homage to these rulers in the form of goods, services, and oaths of loyalty formed the foundation of a strictly hierarchical feudal society and eventually led to the centralization of military and economic power and the establishment of a central state (Filmer 2001:109–21).

This emerging cult of courtesy also served to temper the acts of gratuitous cruelty that were destabilizing the formation of functioning protectorates. The brutality of the invading Teutonic hordes following the fall of the Roman Empire, and the sheer scope of the destruction they wrought, required an urgent joint secular and ecclesiastical project capable of rebuilding, reorganizing, and administrating the stricken communities. The new feudal order and its *cult of courtesy* helped mitigate the use of arbitrary brute force and facilitated the maintenance of a violence-tempering balance of power brokered by astute court counsellors who were adept in the arts of negotiation. The emergence of states that possessed the ability to control large populations would not have been possible without this initial control of tribal violence through the practice of diplomacy and reconciliation.

The new court counsellors who favoured diplomacy over confrontation were faced with two daunting tasks. On one hand, they had to convince the invading barbarians that they could deal with the towns they invaded through peaceful means that minimized loss of life. The clerics of the Church often successfully argued with the invading hordes to take booty but spare the population. This was a considerable achievement in diplomacy, considering that the invading hordes were habituated to making sport of the infants of the conquered by throwing them high up in the air and then catching them on their way down on the tip of their spears. And, on the other hand, Church leaders had to convince those Christian warriors who did step forward to protect vulnerable villages not to use their military might to dominate or plunder their new wards.

This fragile social contract became the foundation of feudalism, a system by which communally owned lands became transformed into estates governed by the most powerful protectors of a region. What originally determined whether a person would remain a serf or become a land-owning aristocrat of 'noble blood' was whether he had the military means and personal willingness to risk life in battle in return for lands, riches, and social status.

Although the Church had possessed very limited power in the days of Imperial Rome, its astute peace-brokering efforts now aligned it with the emerging chieftains, giving it more political and social influence than it had ever possessed. Although a feudalism based on aristocratic privilege was far different from the communalistic teachings of the early founders of Christianity, the Church managed to find a suitable and active role for its clerics during the medieval reorganization of western Europe. The new clerics were well disposed to fit into the new courts. In addition to possessing considerable knowledge of antiquity and the Latin language, they possessed valuable experience gained while preserving their ecclesiastical institution during centuries of political violence and turmoil. Privileged by the prior education of its curia and its vast monastic holdings of important classical texts, the Church became the originating point for the linguistic and religious creeds imposed on the new European protectorates. Latin became the language of educated people in the West, thereby helping establish Christianity as a common ideological bond capable of uniting rulers who might otherwise have remained in relentless open warfare with each other.

The construction of a functional standard of *civility*, however, took a long while to develop. The centralization of power in formally administrated courts required new alliances between the dominant ruler of a region and the lords who controlled specific localities. This was easier said than done. Although the loyalty of second-tier warlords and common warriors had to be bought through the granting of lands, these same land grants empowered their recipients and their armies, making them potential enemies of the central court. Whether or not an outlying estate cooperated with a regional chieftain or stood in opposition to him often depended on whether or not the estate needed protection from an enemy of its own; when such protection was no longer needed, estates tended to reassert their independence and ignore the directives sent down to them by central rulers. A. Luchaire (1902) describes the conditions that made the eventual adoption of a philosophy of 'restraint' and 'cooperation' necessary for communal survival:

> The inhabitants of each province formed a kind of little nation that abhorred all the others. The provinces were divided into a multitude of feudal estates whose owners fought each other incessantly. Not only the great lords, the barons, but also the smaller lords of the manor lived in desolate isolation and were uninterruptedly occupied in waging war against their 'sovereigns,' their equals, or their subjects. In addition, there was constant rivalry between town and town, village and village, valley and valley, and constant wars between neighbours that seemed to arise from the very multiplicity of these territorial units. (278)

Tension between the ruling monarchs and their outlying estates continued until certain military and economic developments weakened the ranks of the warrior nobility and facilitated the establishment of a strong central court. The introduction of money as a widespread currency of exchange and the invention of firearms weakened many of the nobles (*chevaliers*) who had ridden into war on horseback armed with swords and spears. A monarch could now free himself from the erratic loyalty of his outlying estates and assert his independence by putting together his own paid army of firearm-carrying foot soldiers. Moreover, the increasing use of money destabilized systems of barter, causing such an increase in prices that many of the lesser nobles were suddenly left with devalued fortunes; while the monarch continued taxing at current real monetary value, the lords were left collecting fixed land rents that no longer amounted to much in terms of buying power. Many were forced to sell off their properties and join the courts of monarchs as salaried courtiers whose survival now depended more than ever on the favours (and the moods) of the monarch (LeGoff [1964] 1988, Bautier 1971, Bloch [1940] 1961).

Such centralization of power required an ever-increasing restraint of aggression in interpersonal dealings. If a relatively small number of individuals were to take control over sizeable emerging states they had to not only keep a certain peace between themselves but also manage to keep their subjects from rebelling against their centralized authority. Military might was not sufficient to build such a controlled society; some ideological apparatus, capable of encouraging and rewarding restraint, was needed to strengthen and legitimize central rule. This ideological (and emotional) control was achieved through the development of complex codes of restraint and deference, supplemented by a state-imposed monopoly on the use of heavy ammunition. Carrying arms against the state became an act of treason, and gradually, with the further development of civil law, it also became a crime to use arms in personal or group conflicts not sanctioned by the state.

**The New Culture of Restraint**

In his seminal work *The Civilizing Process*, vol. 1 ([1939] 1978) and vol. 2 ([1939] 1982), Norbert Elias has convincingly argued that loyalty towards the emerging courts was achieved through a *'civilizing process'* requiring a curtailment and repression of certain impulses, drives, and behaviours and the cultivation of others. It would seem that a deftly executed ideological manoeuvre brought together the mercenary knights, the Christian Church, and the emerging monarchs. The principal aim of the early medieval *courtly literature* and *moral-political philosophy* was to address those of 'noble blood' and teach them to maintain their loyalty towards the Church and the monarchy through the adoption and practice of a new behavioural court ethic based on the restraint of violence and brutish self-interest.

Understandably, the warrior-knights did not adopt these new values of restraint without considerable resistance. Although the early courtesy literature represented the ideal knight as a caring and noble individual, he was, in reality, a fighter quite at ease with acts of extreme cruelty. Elias explains this lack of emotional restraint as the consequence of long periods in which no central authorities possessed the laws and networks of control necessary for the limitation and monopolization of violence. He, therefore, associates the rise of 'mutual consideration' between citizens with the rise of a central state capable of legislating the control of violence:

> Once the monopoly of physical power has passed to central authorities, not every strong man can afford the pleasure of physical attack. This is

now reserved to those few legitimized by the central authority (e.g. the police against the criminal), and to larger numbers only in exceptional times of war or revolution, in the socially legitimized struggle against internal or external enemies. ([1939] 1978:201–2)

This pressing need for restraint becomes even more understandable when one takes into account the volatile emotionalism of medieval populations. Medieval men and women were given to vacillating between joy and anger at the slightest provocation (Huizinga [1924] 1972). Such sudden mood swings were not restricted to conflict over territory but also permeated daily relationships between men and women. Beatings and rapes of women were not uncommon in a society in which women were supposed to defer to the authority of the military male (Luchaire 1902:374–9). Georges Duby (1981) also observes in his comprehensive study of the institutionalization of marriage in the Middle Ages that rape was not an uncommon occurrence, even in noble households (281). Similarly, Elias points to the considerable mistrust and distancing that existed between the genders in early court circles: a man's place was on the military field while a woman's domain was restricted to her 'ornamented chambers' ([1939] 1982:80). The medieval courtesy project thus had to temper conflict between warriors residing at court as well as between the warriors and the women of court.

Such a fragile public and private security was further threatened by a medieval worldview given to categorizing everything as either 'good' or 'bad,' 'wicked' or 'virtuous.' Such extremities of reaction were common, predisposing strangers to look upon one another with considerable suspicion. So, the project of establishing a workable code of civility capable of controlling an otherwise emotive population originated in the courts of the monarchs, where it became possible to adopt refined (non-aggressive) codes of behaviour in a relatively privileged and protected environment where cautious trust could be established through carefully cultivated alliances.

The restraints imposed by the earliest courtesy writers on the warriors who joined the new courts served to temper their aggression by assigning to the warriors certain moral qualities and obligations supposedly not within the reach or comprehension of the common population. In effect, the warrior was invited to dismount and enter the halls of court and abide by its protocols while remaining ready to take up his sword whenever required in the name of king and God. The warriors accepted this 'partial gentrification' because the life of a solitary knight was no longer viable; their loss of independence was compensated for by the status conferred on them by the new elitist courtesy codes.

Ecclesiastical rationalizations of social differentiation increased as clerics formed alliances with courts needing legitimacy and stability. Most medieval courtesy documents concentrated not on whether a strong monarchy was a worthy form of government, but on how the monarch and his entourage should maintain their *distinction* in relation to the rest of the population so as to be considered morally (and divinely) worthy of their privileges. The rationalization of power changed from the veneration of superior brute force to the veneration of force tempered by *virtuous being* and *bearing*; an aristocratic 'personality' and 'body' were in the making. For many centuries, this carefully designed comportment would remain the basis for distinction, separating those who were seen as exemplary members of society from those considered of lesser moral and social worth.

The social construction of this culture of courtesy, considerably dependent on the guidance of the Church, was facilitated by the daring claims of infallibility made by Church leaders. The genesis of the absolutist state is partially located in such theological supremacy. Although St Augustine had made the egalitarian promise that even the Bishop of Rome could be charged on counts of heresy if his pronouncements were found unsound, the medieval popes established a new curia given to making absolute statements regarding doctrine and Church policy (DeRosa 1988).

This adoption of a theology based on strict dogma seemed to coincide with the mentality of the times. The passage from the year 999 to the year 1000 terrified many because it had been predicted in the New Testament Book of Revelations (chapter 20) that, following a thousand years of Christianity, the devil would be let loose for a while. Expecting a cataclysmic upheaval, many prepared for the year 1000 with strong feelings of doom. A considerable amount of optimism was released when the devil did not appear at the turn of the millennium. And with this new hope came a strong need for social certainty. In his seminal work, *Medieval Civilization*, Jacques LeGoff ([1964] 1988) explains that this need for certitude predisposed people to look to the Church for guidance and accept its call for unity and obedience:

> It was a material and moral insecurity, for which, according to the Church, there was only one remedy: to rely on the solidarity of the group, of the communities of which one formed a part, and to avoid breaching this

solidarity by ambition and derogation ... Nothing that could be proposed was certain, except what had been vouchsafed for in the past ...The supreme authority was scripture, and, with it, the Fathers of the Church. (325–6)

Pope Gregory VII, a Tuscan who ascended to the papacy in 1078, responded to this need for moral certitude by making further claims of infallibility for the Church. Gregory argued that a priest did not need an emperor to seek God's forgiveness; an emperor, on the other hand, despite all his military might, needed a priest to plead for God's mercy on his behalf. Such theological supremacy was formalized by a change in the title given to the pope. While prior to Gregory the popes had been known as 'the Vicars of St Peter,' following Gregory's example they took to referring to themselves as the 'Vicars of Christ,' placing themselves on a level of prestige equal to if not greater than that assigned to kings (DeRosa 1988:78–80).

Pope Innocent III, who came to power in 1198, went far enough to declare that only the Church received the soul of God; the world of monarchs was simply a temporal domain vulnerable to the sins of the material world. Innocent's ultimate act of absolute theological authority was to declare that the Church was the central diocese of all Christianity and that every bishop was henceforth to be under the authority of the pope, who was to be considered the 'universal bishop.' At the Fourth Council in 1215, he passed decrees establishing a vertical hierarchical order proceeding up into the office of the Holy See. One of his decrees stated that every Catholic had to confess his sins to his local priest at least once a year; this commandment now gave special powers to priests, who acquired the ability to intercede with God on behalf of a person (as well as interceding in a person's life on behalf of God) (91–5). All members of the Church, including the nobility, became reliant on the clergy for guidance.

LeGoff ([1964] 1988) explains that one of the effects of medieval theology was the joining of physical valour and moral virtue. The Christian hero became the one with the most impressive exploits. And, sometimes, the moral goodness of his exploits became associated with his potential for going to the limits of human endurance, thereby explaining why the Christian monks of the epoch were called 'the athletes of Christ' (341–2). Extreme asceticism and self-mortification, combined with intense Christian scholarship, turned monasticism into a major force of the epoch. This monastic spirit is very much embedded in the English legend of King Arthur and the Holy Grail as well as the later French versions of the tale. The discipline and commitment required of the knight-champion is of messianic proportions: the knight must rise above his desires and abandon an inauthentic life in favour of spiritual wisdom. It is one of the most profound efforts in the history of Western civilization to recapture a long-lost union between nature and human action. So it would not be an exaggeration to say that the clerics became the *spiritual architects* of the new courts, not only out of a desire for power and influence, but also out of a need to create a mentality that would preserve Christian spirituality in civil society. Their role as emissaries helped them form a buffer zone between the monarch and his outlying estates, thereby investing them with the means and power to integrate canon law in courtly affairs.

The old Roman rules of good behaviour were revisited in many of the courtesy books of the Middle Ages. As early as the fourth century, St Ambrose, Bishop of Milan, had instructed priests to show modesty and shame *(verecundia)* in all their dealings (1984:131–2). In *De ordine palatii*, Archbishop Hincmar of Reims had similarly set down what he considered to be the function of the court and the responsibilities of its members. He called it a *scola*, or school. He did not mean this in terms of an ordinary school *(scolastici)* but in terms of a community of highly evolved men capable of teaching the younger members of court through their own disciplined behaviour *(disciplina id est correctio)* ([c. 806–82] 1885). Similar admonitions to clerics were handed down in the twelfth century from Petrus Alfonsi (*On Clerical Discipline*) and St Victor (*On the Education of Novices*) (Nicholls 1985:16, 36–8).

Thus, the behavioural codes of 'restraint' and 'self-discipline' that had for centuries been followed in the monastic orders were now injected into court culture. The role of the cleric as dispenser of knowledge, discipline, and virtue caused a marked change in the function of monastic scholars, who were now brought into the courts and given the duty of developing administrative systems. This *regale sacerdotium* (royal priesthood) transferred knowledge gained through religious textual scholarship to the business of the court and the training of court members. The instruction it dispensed followed the established Platonic curriculum, treating the humanities and sciences as mutually inclusive expressions of divinity. A strong emphasis was, therefore, placed on the transformation of knowledge into virtue. The 'beauty of proper bearing' *(Gratia decoris)* became as valued as the actual knowledge possessed by a person. This new valuation of 'manners' and 'the presentation of self' stood in contrast to the old Aristotelian tradition that valued the content of an argument for its own sake. This new development was, in effect, the birth of 'style,' an important element in the later development of etiquette, a practice that would eventually provoke the ire of many Puritanical Christian moralists.

Based on the *trivium*, the new scholasticism focused heavily on literary texts and the spiritual lessons that could be extracted from them. This reliance on the spiritual functions of knowledge led to a high valuation of personality and mannerisms as symbols of 'goodness' and 'nobility.' Lineage and title no longer provided sufficient assurance that a nobleman or a noblewoman would also be of noble spirit. Nor was victory on the battlefield any longer considered a complete measure of a person's moral worth. As important as the biography and military accomplishments of an aristocrat was his or her ability to *behave in noble ways*.

The new *curial* curriculum attempted to form a well-rounded individual through the transmission of certain qualities that included discipline and restraint *(disciplina)*, eloquence *(urbanitas)*, the harmonization of the attractive and the virtuous *(kalogathia)*, and an overall courteous demeanour *(curialitas)* that encompassed a variety of talents, including poise, humour, and humility (Jaegar 1965:127–75). Also considered important was the ability to have a *sensitive heart*; nobles were urged to be the opposite of peasants, who were considered crude, heartless, and unable to become worldly. The worship of the 'established' and the 'traditional' provided (intentionally or not) a perfect environment for the cultivation of a peasant class governed by respect for precedent and ready to accept the idea that the existence of a 'noble class' was divinely ordained and, therefore, unalterable. It also permitted the clergy to control the nobility to a certain extent by regularly citing excerpts from 'authoritative' Christian texts. Clerics developed the ability to rationalize their own involvement in worldly affairs by linking statesmanship with religious and moral virtue (LeGoff [1964] 1988:326).

It is understandable, therefore, that the early medieval courtesy tracts echoed Cicero's *De Officiis* and *Orator* and Aristotle's essays on the *golden mean*. The common recurring theme in this courtesy literature was the Judeo-Christian polarity between *good* and *evil* and the wise ruler's ability to tell one from the other. Cicero (1967) had expressed this golden mean as a coming together of various streams of thought and action:

Goodness as a whole arises from any one of four sources: it is to be found, first, in wisdom, which is the perception and knowledge of truth; secondly, in justice, which consists in preserving a fair relationship between men, giving to each his due and keeping one's word; thirdly in the greatness and strength of a courageous and invisible mind; and fourthly in observing that due order and sense of proportion in all words and actions which makes for moderation and reasonableness. (15–17)

Cicero's ideas are found in many medieval courtesy tracts, including Ramon Lull's *The Book of the Order of Chivalry* ([c. 1300] 1902), an important early medieval courtesy document that argued for a court culture that would be governed by qualities of justice, clemency, and peacemaking. *Moderation, prudence, love of justice,* and *valour* became the ideals of the new courtly personality. Modesty (*modestus*) became the cardinal virtue because it signified humility before a more superior divine being. Two of the virtues, however, required contradictory sentiments: *prudence* required a calculating and cunning spirit, while *valour* asked of the knight that he be as spiritual as he was fierce.

So, at its inception, *courtesy* was not simply a prescription for a set of mannerisms. It also consisted of a complex series of patterns of emotional restraint and disciplinary practices intended to hold back aggression and bring forth in its place behavioural regimes that were classified as *noble virtues*. A *courteous* person had to *desist* from doing and saying certain things while practising and expressing others. What we now consider simple *politeness* and *friendliness* were not sufficient in these courtly circles. There were also moral obligations. The term *noblesse oblige* refers to the duties of a noble person who was not allowed to adopt the mannerisms and vacillating attitudes attributed to the coarse peasant. In fact, what marked the European courtly culture was the coupling of the contemplative and the active to produce a refined and worldly personality.

This powerful ideology of differentiation was amply reflected in the literature of the period in which the peasant with some freehold land was frequently referred to as a *vilein*. Although the Roman root of the word was *villa* (a settlement of land), it took on derogatory connotations in post-Roman feudal society. The 'vile' peasant was seen to possess the crudity, the ingratitude, and the whole panoply of baser qualities opposed to courtly behavioural values. While court ideologues eventually conceded that noble birth did not automatically produce a noble soul, the personality of the peasant was considered set at birth. Boethius (c.

1149–52) wrote of the peasant: 'Whoever teaches an ass to play the harp uselessly wastes his effort. It is just so with you, vilein: I have taught you utterly in vain' (cited in Burnley 1998:90). The *vilein* was viewed to be lacking the tender heart and sensitivity required of the courtier, hopelessly unable to free himself from rusticity (*rusticas*). Even as late as the seventeenth and eighteenth centuries, many courtesy book writers warned that the lessons they dispensed were not to fall into the hands of the commoners.

Such elitist conceptions of nobility did not escape the criticism of monastic ideologues. In *Contra clericos aulicos* (c. 1072), Peter Damian attacked the obsessions of the new curial writers, accusing them of putting fancy names to old vices by sanctioning ambition under the guise of *urbanity* and submission under the pretence of *modesty*. Additional objections came from the court of Henry II in England: court critics John of Salisbury, Nigel Wireker, and Walter Map considered the *curialis* a corrupting rather than ennobling ethic. Certainly, some of the behavioural characteristics imposed on courtiers did not sit well with early Christian writings. Two of these were the talents of *hilaritas* or *iocunditas*, the ability to display humour and gaiety in the most trying circumstances. These social graces did not accord with a Biblical passage in Ecclesiastes 7.5 that pronounced: 'Gaiety dwells in the heart of the fool.'

These protests notwithstanding, adaptability in the face of adversity became the prime strength of the successful courtier. Such resilience was maintained through a balanced use of *courtesy* and *charm*. *Hilaritas* and *iocunditas* assured a discreet way out of the most troublesome situations – the art of the pointed *understatement* was perfected during this courtly age. Combined with *prudence*, these above qualities helped the courtier advance through the highly competitive and treacherous hierarchy at court.

The clerics who tried to temper the medieval world might have failed to bring about a certain sense of order in the courts had Christianity not warned of a judgment in the afterlife. Even William the Conqueror, who was known for never hesitating to cut down anyone who stood in the way of his ambitions, is purported to have confessed on his deathbed to a monk from his own Abbaye-aux-hommes. The dying monarch asked the monk to pray for divine mercy on his behalf. So, although outright communalism was not sought in the courtesy writings, the spiritual demands made of rulers had a tempering effect on outright barbaric violence. Left to their own devices and customs, pagan rulers might have produced quite a different (and perhaps more violent) social system.

**From Violence to Righteous Anger**

An important distinction needs be made between medieval aggression and anger, for while one was being discouraged the other was being accepted as a noble virtue. One of the shortcomings of Norbert Elias's magisterial review of the connection between violence restraint and the civilizing process is that he bases his theory on a broad definition of aggression. According to Elias, the civilizing process begins with the control of violence and aggression and the monopolization of military ordinance in the hands of a central state. This is accomplished through the social construction of mannerisms and rituals that restrain primary affects. Yet, by giving considerable attention to the growth of manners and rituals intended to decrease the possibilities of violent outcomes, Elias underemphasizes an important parallel development in which anger was becoming legitimized, recognized, and expressed. Certainly, no quarrel can be struck with the sensible conclusion that rational society required a limitation of armed confrontations. Yet, while violence and outright carnage were being curtailed through the authority of central courts, the emotion of anger was being refined and linked to honour. In certain situations, the expression of anger was even considered a useful and necessary virtue, proof of a noble spirit. So, the 'civilizing process' involved not only the curtailment of violence, but the development of *purposive anger*, an acceptable replacement to outright violence.

In fact, the monastics who took upon themselves the task of recivilizing Europe were faced with a dilemma. They could not categorically speak out against anger because anger was rationalized in the Bible. God's wrath descends upon humanity in numerous passages of the Holy Book, through direct intervention or through the zealous anger of the Biblical prophets. The virtuous man is allowed (maybe even expected) to be an angry man, considering the fact that he lives in a world of sins that insults his virtue. Psalms 4:5 advised: 'Grow angry, and do not sin.' Numerous other passages of both the Old and New Testaments value righteous anger (Psalms 139:21–2, Isaiah 13:9, Romans 2:5, Revelations 6:17). So, what the clerics needed to do in order to harmonize Christian theology with the emergence of a territorial aristocracy was to differentiate between anger that was a deadly sin and the type of anger that was *divinely justified* and *socially useful*. Even here, class distinctions played a major normative role. Just as courtesy rituals became reserved for those of noble birth, so did moral anger become the property of the nobility.

Anger against enemies had already been legitimized in the canonical writings and town charters. The practice of *clamour* (ritual anger), monastic maledictions, and the inclusion of curse clauses sealing tenth-century charters (e.g., 'whoever breaks this agreement will be cursed by God') legitimized purposive and religiously motivated anger (Little 1993). Similar representations of virtuous anger are found between the eighth and eleventh centuries in the Celtic tradition. Curses and maledictions were drafted to protect the virtuous from the ruses of those who would play unfairly and without honour. The killing of a priest, the stealing or desecration of church property, and the robbery and murder of travellers were some of the 'acts of disrespect' that justified personal and communal displays of anger and the drafting up of curses.

Thus, while patience and compassion were presented as virtues that would limit the use of *vengeful anger*, they were not in and of themselves prohibitions of the anger emotion. In fact, anger was considered a means by which outright violence could be avoided and honour maintained. Anger could signal to a transgressor that a revised social relationship was required and bring about reparatory behaviour that prevented outright physical violence. And, when practised by a ruler in response to quarrelsome parties in court, it could help restore harmony and reaffirm the authority and legitimacy of the monarch.

What the monastics did speak out against with considerable fervour was a *self-interested anger* bound neither to love of justice nor religious fervour. The trait of *debonereté* (debonair) does not initially appear as a body mannerism signifying elegance, but as a moral quality that restrains the noble individual from proceeding to vengeful acts once his anger has been satisfactorily expressed. The civilizing process here is not one of prohibition and complete repression but one of refinement and containment. In light of this earliest historical function, *debonereté* would be better explained as *goodness*, perhaps even *mercy*. And, indeed, great care was taken in the literature to distinguish between uncompromising self-interested anger and the anger that was motivated by commitment to virtue and honour within specified moral limits. The epic of *Raoul de Cambrai* (c. 1180) demonstrates the impasse created by an infernal circle of self-interested anger – deprived of all venues of compromise, the protagonist dies in the end, a victim of his own character flaw (Kay 1992).

Thus, anger expressed with measure was regarded as a sign of a lofty mind and worthy of great praise. The defending of honour through elaborate and public expressions of anger became a property of the aristocracy throughout the high Middle Ages and the Renaissance (Miller 1993). It placed potential opponents in a sort of 'trial by ordeal' that led to compromise and settlement. It also helped define and preserve ties of dependence in the feudal system (Bloch 1961). The *displeasure* (*ire, ira*) of the lord towards the vassal acted as a powerful socializing emotion that not only helped clarify the obligations of the feudal relationship, but also preserved it from degenerating into chaotic confrontations. Similarly, the fear of incurring royal displeasure had a powerful socializing effect on members at court who were increasingly dependent on the monarch's favour for their own survival (Head and Landes 1992).

And, here, once again, while the noble person was considered to possess the discernment required for distinguishing between free-floating and purposive honour-bound anger, the peasant was accused of remaining incapable of experiencing righteous or zealous anger. His anger was represented as animal-like rage, useless in terms of preserving social order and highly inefficient in times of war. He was neither an honourable citizen nor a useful warrior. When he did experience anger it was in the form of disorganized rage, driving him to pillage, rape, and mindless slaughter (Greenblatt 1983:1–29). Just as the peasant was considered incapable of feeling the nobler emotion of courtly love and the *lovesickness* that was a consequence of it (Wack 1990:60–70), so was he considered incapable of experiencing any morally legitimate emotion. Peasant fury in the 1200s and 1300s was likened to bestial rage, devoid of moral legitimacy. The Jacquerie peasant rebellion of 1358 was frequently referred to in the literature of the period as the doings of a murderous mob, incompetent militarily because of its lack of restraint and forethought (De Medeiros 1979:30–3).

The peasantry was ridiculed even when some of it members attempted to emulate the behaviour of chivalric society. It was thought that a peasant trying to act like a knight would only end up terrorizing the countryside, for he would remain fundamentally ignorant of the meaning of honour and true bravery. Chrétien de Troyes's *Perceval* ([1180–?] 1967) is written as a caution against coarse interpretations of noble motives. Perceval, the son of a peasant, has to undergo many tests before developing the spiritual maturity and restraint required of the knightly position he has chosen for himself. He must transcend his 'first' nature in order to comprehend the meaning of authentic service.

So, 'respect' and 'disrespect' in the medieval world have to be understood in context of feudal social relations and contracts and oaths of fealty and dependence (Bloch [1939–40] 1961). Codes of loyalty and specifications of duties prohibited people from attempting to compete with their superiors. A person's status had a definite place and price in the social order, and any insult directed at that status could require considerable sums to be paid in reparation; this was especially so in Celtic culture (Davies 1988:86–7).

Thus, the 'civilizing process' of which Elias speaks required not only a limitation of violence but also the appropriative act of defining what was acceptable and unacceptable anger. Had the medieval Christian courtesy literature required a complete repression of aggression it would have been very difficult to legitimize the emerging state's control of violence and the socialization of the knight as a pious servant ready to take up arms when required. Although the early courtesy writers referred to Christian canon to legitimize their claims, they struck a compromise between the earliest Christian call for a philosophy of 'neighbourly' love and a moral philosophy that elevated certain types of anger to the level of desired virtues. Coincidentally or intentionally, this allowed the emerging absolutist monarchs to dampen revolutionary rage while rationalizing their own aggressive campaigns as moral crusades. It also allowed, just as importantly, for subjects to use violence as a political tool. As Tilly (1986, [1995] 2005, 2003b, 2004, 2005a, 2005b) has amply documented in his various studies of collective violence and 'contention,' the restraint of free-ranging violence was itself a crucial step in the formation of political groups that used violence in purposive ways. So, while Elias focuses on the monopoly of violence on the part of the state, he underplays the continuing balancing relationship between the state which does give itself authority to exercise violence in order to prevent its occurrence (keeping order) and a citizenry which remains in a contentious relationship with the state in order to ensure that its interests are accommodated. Tilly notes this ongoing relationship and defines collective violence as a form of 'contentious politics' because it always involves 'relations of participants to governments' (2003b:26).

## Taming the Knight

Even the staunchest critics of the new courtly culture were powerless to stop its spread across Europe. The courts of various nations came to have more in common with each other's cultures than they did with their own populations. The French conquests of Britain ensured that many of the members of the British courts, if not of French origin, were fluent in French. Not only were nobles of various countries, including the Romanovs of Russia, now able to act in ways different from those of the commoners, they also possessed a language that the commoners did not.

The European nobility readily accepted the mannerisms and ideologies associated with *la courtoisie* because it realized that it could maintain its authoritative and privileged position vis-à-vis the commoners. Although *la courtoisie* entailed considerable spiritual idealism, it had a freezing effect on social mobility. A peasant attempting to behave like an aristocrat would have been laughed out of existence not only by the nobles but also by his fellow peasants; certainly, his priest would have chastised him for tampering with the divine order of things. It would not be until the late Renaissance, and then later yet after the French Revolution, that the values and mannerisms of the aristocracy would become increasingly available to a socially mobile population.

Another important function of *la courtoisie* was to provide aristocrats with a means for mutual recognition of their special status within a volatile court society. Through the practice of *calculated courtesy*, and its attendant behavioural protocols, a given courtier could determine who in court was of importance, or rising in importance, and who was falling out of favour. It was essential for a wise courtier to maintain his own prestige by cultivating relations with those of influence and avoiding contact with those whose careers were ailing.

As for clerics, they came to occupy a distinctly advantageous position. Positioning themselves as advisers to the monarch, they acquired a status equal to if not sometimes higher than that enjoyed by the military nobility. Bonizo, Bishop of Sutri (c. 1040), attempted to create a hierarchy of types in which he placed those who prayed (*oratores*) above the nobility (*pugnatores*) and the peasants (*agricultores*). He saw the duty of clerics as a noble and pious one: to teach and convince the king and his nobles that their mission was intended by God to be a benevolent one. Similarly, in his biography of King Robert the Pious (*Robert le Pieux; Epitoma vitae Regis Roberti Pii*), Helgaud de Fleury represents the monarch in mythical terms, describing him as a capable, courageous, wise, and benevolent leader who possesses an impeccable sense of honour (Bautier and Labory 1965).

Similar admonitions were made to courtiers and knights who were expected to be pious defenders of the weak, the poor, widows and orphans and, especially, not to engage in plunder or rape. The notion of deferring to the wants of another at the expense of one's own desires was a value that had already been preached to the monks by the early medieval church (Newhauser 1997:22–4). It was believed that avarice would lead to other vices, including mindless wrath and cruelty (93).

The concept of the warring knight as a faithful defender of royal interest was not an invention of the European Middle Ages. Kings' champions had existed as long as there had been chiefs and rulers – no one person can exercise forceful rule without the help of loyal and strong allies. But what was very particular to the Middle Ages was the appropriation of the warrior or knight as part of the medieval Christian world and the culture of *la courtoisie*. The behavioural models offered up by clerics to these potential aristocrats were based on the clerics' own knowledge of the myths surrounding the ancient *sancti milites* (saintly warriors). These saints had given equal importance to God, Church, and their fellow men and women, managing to navigate with ease between spiritual and temporal duties. Reading some of the early courtly literature one has the impression that what was expected of the king and his nobles was similar to what had been expected of the ancient Biblical prophets and saviours: a Messianic commitment to justice, a sympathetic and active relationship with the downtrodden, and a power of oratory capable of harmonizing wisdom with eloquence. All this was asked within a culture in which the majority of the population was enlisted for a pittance to produce a comfortable livelihood for precisely those who were supposed to be their benefactors and protectors.

One also notices in most of the medieval clerical tracts that the purpose of Church ideologues was not to draw the military monarch away from his role of conqueror and defender but to add a pious aspect to his political cunning. A monastic monarch would have been anathema to the clerics. This association between Christian virtue and military might runs through most of the early courtesy literature. In his widely circulated biography of William the Conqueror, Guillaume de Poitier (1070–1127) describes William as the perfect embodiment of the valiant knight (Davis and Chibnall 1998). John of Salisbury (1115–80) similarly idealizes the pious prince in *Policraticus, seu de nugis Curialium libri octo, & Epistolae*, a work completed during the reign of Henry II. Considering the king an emissary of the Church, he encourages the monarch to become proficient in literature and the arts so that he can better receive and use guidance from trusted members of court. As for the knight,

John represents him as a quasi-saintly personage entrusted with serving the king while tending to his own Christian faith. He criticizes quite severely the love of luxury and privilege of some knights and speaks out against the frivolity of courtly love (Nederman 1995).

The spiritual gravity of the knight's relationship to the realm is also the focus of Geoffrey of Monmouth's *History of the Kings of Britain* ([1138] 1973), in which the knights of the round table are represented as men devoted to their God, their king, and the ladies of their court. While the historical authenticity of the story remains to be established, the legend of King Arthur introduced the notion of *chivalry*, an ideal that was to become an important part of courtly literature and philosophy. Geoffrey made a considerable contribution to English folklore. While, until the appearance of his historical account, the French and German monarchies had both claimed that they were heirs to the legendary Charlemagne, Geoffrey's story of King Arthur allowed the English kings a celebrated place at the centre of a distinctly Celtic-English courtly literature. The Arthurian legends were subsequently transported to France, where they were refined and expanded.

Chrétien de Troyes's ([1180–?] 1967) classic tale of knighthood, *Perceval*, remains one of the most poignant illustrations of the new tough moral and spiritual standards that were being imposed on medieval knights. The poem follows the development of a knight from boyhood to manhood. It is a version of the Arthurian legend written from the point of view of an ordinary boy who, attracted by the glamour of knighthood, abandons his mother to go on the road and become a knight. The innocence and brash determination of the boy soon lead him to no good. Even though he is befriended by an experienced knight and taught the martial arts, he remains ignorant of the spiritual development necessary to become a knight with honour. When presented with a broken sword he is unable to mend it, for he does not yet possess the humility and compassion required for the acquisition of extraordinary powers. He erroneously believes that force will suffice him.

The story traces the many trials encountered by Perceval along his turbulent journey towards spiritual maturity. Only when he realizes the wisdom of the King Hermit's advice and puts it into practice does he beginning acquiring true power:

> Abandon all evil vices: he is a miscreant and a hypocrite who thinks to gain God's love and glory through proud and boastful ways. No! It takes afflictions, fasting, prayer and true repentance ... Such are the arms with

which a knight should arm himself if he wishes to love God and to be worthy and valiant. (1967:219)

His mentor further explains to him the nature of the knight's mission on earth and the spiritual meaning of the sword with which he is entrusted:

A knight's sword has two cutting edges: do you know why? It should be understood, I tell you truly, that one edge is for the defenses of the Holy Church, while the other should embody true earthly justice, protecting Christian people and upholding justice without trickery or covetousness. (213)

Only when Perceval understands the connection between honour, humility, and force does he emerge from his spiritual wasteland, a place in which pride stands in for love, and cruelty for compassion. Only then is he able to mend the sword. Perceval's success follows from this transformation of the secular (in which evil and good are polar opposites) into the spiritual (where the natural spirit of man is allowed to transcend earthly limitations and achieve the higher virtues of loyalty and love).

Somewhat less spiritual prescriptions for knighthood were offered by Étienne de Fougères, bishop of Rennes and Lisieux (1168–78), who, in *Livre des manières* (Book of Manners) ([c. 1350–1400] 1877), assigned a strong civic responsibility to the prince and his knights. Locating the nobility at the head of the feudal hierarchy, he admitted that the plight of the peasants was a sad one but offered the consolation that unfortunate peasants also occupied a divinely ordered station which they should accept with humility and patience. He reminded knights and nobles that one of their missions was to teach peasants to remain submissive in order to preserve the 'balance' of the realm.

Laudatory biographies of knights and kings, and the books of princely conduct that were addressed to them, found a receptive audience in medieval courts, where monarchs had learned the political value of maintaining an aristocracy safely tied to the court by complex rituals of dutiful courtesy. Not only did the writers of the courtly literature seek to socialize the nobility, they also sought to influence the behaviour of the monarch. Although they consistently lauded the monarch, they subtly cornered him into observing certain protocols and giving recognition to others when it was due them.

Those kings who fared best within this new court environment were those who were astute enough to know that a favour granted would eventually be returned manifold. In any case, there was no longer a great danger in giving awards of land and money in a centralized court system that possessed a paid army. Regardless of the real sentiments of his courtiers, the monarch rested secure in the knowledge that the top courtiers were always reminded by those of lower rank that they were governed by a rigid hierarchy and could fall down that hierarchy if they lost the favours of the king or his top advisers. A raised eyebrow or a subtle nod of the head on the part of the monarch was sufficient to build a courtier's career or bring it to a humiliating and tragic end. Thus, it suited a king to possess a court that actively and passionately argued for qualities of restraint, humility, and obedience. These psychological processes facilitated the social domination of courtiers and provided the monarch with an incentive to accomplish his goals through limited internal violence.

Court life did not remain altogether harmonious, however. No number of utopian courtesy books could eliminate the intense competition between courtiers. Life at court became so competitive that courtiers took to continuously measuring themselves against one another to determine which of them was closer to the king's favour. Courtiers poured over the lists of those who were allowed to enter the monarch's chambers – placement of one's name on the list became a major cause for celebration. So, a noble title, in and of itself, no longer guaranteed success in an increasingly complex court where the personality and social-political influence of the courtier now mattered as much as bloodline pedigree and military accomplishments. How well he or she did for himself increasingly depended on the ability to manage the *impressions* made on others.

Thus, through the influence of Christian courtly literature, the *ruffian* who had lived by his sword and counted the coins given him to fight for this or that lord was now brought face to face with the aesthetics of moral commitment and humility. *Chivalry* became the concept representing these codes and duties. The medieval use of the term – a derivative of *cheval* (horse) and *chevalier* (horseman) – was refined to include the ideal behavioural traits expected of all noblemen who worked in the service of their monarch. The primary qualities required of the knight-chevalier were courage, loyalty, moral discrimination, and outright toughness of character (Lacroix 1963). The knight was enlisted as a servant of God as well as monarch and expected to exhibit the highest Christian moral discernment even during his military exploits. The argument presented to him was that he would do better in combat if he went into it with noble ideals. These lofty ideals of sacrifice and devotion to the realm were the beginnings of a formal code of 'public honour' that would serve as a forerunner to *patriotism*.

Chrétien de Troyes's rendition of the Arthurian legend reveals the dilemma faced by the reformed Christian knight. Although he is required and encouraged to develop military prowess, he is also asked to humanize his military impulses through the adoption of Christian values that, if applied without any compromise, might altogether exclude the use of force. He is required to defeat the enemies of the realm, but to do so with humility and minimal bloodshed. The damaged sword in *Perceval* is the symbol of this unresolved polarity between the forces of aggression and restraint. The knight is being asked to reconcile these two antithetical aspects and develop a transcendental spirituality that places him and his sword in the service of a higher good.

This was a mystical project that managed to convince thousands of men to devote their swords and purses to the Crusades. Beginning in 1099, and continuing until 1270, the Crusades embodied the medieval attempt to reconcile the temporal with the divine. While they accomplished little and left thousands of nobles in ruin, they did represent the harnessing of the warrior mentality in the service of a theocratic experiment which, outside the Inquisition, has never since been equalled in Europe. The battle cry used by the French who organized the first crusade was '*Dieu le veut*' (God wants it) (Flori 2001).

Although it emerged at a time when the Church was strengthening its hold over dogma, the medieval courtesy literature differed in many ways from the older fatalistic genre of the epic in which heroes were at the mercy of supernatural forces. The chivalric literature gave its protagonist a considerable measure of self determination; the military knight lost in great measure his freedom to roam the countryside and pillage at will, but he was given a new freedom: the right to better his social and spiritual self.

**Courtly Love and Devotion**

*Courtesy* became an art to be learned in political and ecclesiastical circles as well as within love relationships between noble men and women. The transfer of courtly ideals into romantic relationships was not a frivolous project. An important way of socializing military leaders to limit their violence was to place them in frequent contact with women, who were considered to be less aggressive. The new courtly romances also allowed aristocrats to understand and deal with the marriages that were being contracted to unify warring parties. A fine distinction emerged between marriages arranged for political and economic reasons and passionate liaisons free from practical considerations.

The origins of medieval courtly love can be located in the classical period. The word 'love' (*amor*) originates from the word 'hook' (*amur*), alluding to the 'captivating' nature of love. The lover is 'hooked' by his love for the beloved and does his utmost to 'captivate' the object of his desires. The notion of sensual love for its own sake – as opposed to a means of procreation – was a major theme in Andreas Capellanus's *The Art of Courtly Love* ([1201–10] 1941), a popular book that became an important source of conduct reference in court circles right through the Italian Renaissance.

Capellanus believed, as had Ovid, that love between a man and woman who are married to each other is virtually impossible:

> Love cannot exert its power between two people who are married to each other. For lovers give each other everything freely, under no compulsion of necessity, but married people are in duty bound to give in to each other's desires and deny themselves to each other in nothing. (107)

For Capellanus, the ideal love was cloaked in secrecy and protected from the boredom of easy fulfillment; it required frustration, heightened passion, and devotion:

> If one has difficulty obtaining the embraces of one's lover and obtains them rarely, the lovers are bound to each other in more ardent chains of love and their souls are locked together in heavier and closer bonds of affection. (99)

For Capellanus, properly practised courtly love was an embodiment of integrity. His work reconfirmed the fundamental values of courtly literature: the rejection of avarice, the adherence to chastity for the sake of the beloved, a gallant respect for the love of others, avoidance of potential lovers of whom one would eventually be ashamed, avoidance of falsehood, the cultivation of discretion and secrecy, obedience to the wishes of the woman as proof of one's commitment to her love, a strong sense of modesty even under pressure, the avoidance of damaging gossip, and the practice of utmost politeness and consideration (81).

*Fin' amour* or *courtly love* differed from sensual love. In its purest form, it was not primarily intended for physical pleasure but was a means for the lover's own attainment of goodness, integrity, civic loyalty, and personal dignity. What effect such a veneration of purity must have had on the knights who appeared in the early courts is open to speculation. Of one thing we can be fairly certain: when the knight appears in medieval society, he is a mercenary who needs to look after his own interests. Many of the early knights had more of an emotional bond with their sword, their prized possession, than they did with the lord whom they served. What was needed to socialize the knight was a moral ideology capable of inspiring the knight's loyalty even during the absence of his lord. This was achieved by extending the knight's relationship with the lord to include members of the lord's family. To facilitate such an all-encompassing commitment, the lord's wife came to represent the lord in his absence. Often, she acted as the emotional and social link between the knight and his employer, thereby giving the first ladies at court considerable prestige in their entourage. The 'respect' and 'love' that the knight held for the wife of the lord, and, by extension, for other women in the court, further solidified the knight's commitment to the practice of *courtesy*, progressively defined as the general and continual consideration for the feelings and needs of others.

This 'gentrification' of the knight increased as knights moved into the larger extended households of the stronger rulers. Out of necessity they were forced to develop a certain *refinement* that permitted them to relate to the women of the household without causing them offence and disgust. As the central courts further distinguished themselves from the rural nobility and the rising class of tradesmen by adopting a standard of behaviour based on a refinement of the senses, women began to assume a more central role in courtly life. Deference towards women at court became part of a growing idealization of women as beings to be protected from the traits of the supposedly coarser male personality. The later 'gentlemanly conduct' of the eighteenth and nineteenth centuries comes not only from fair rules of combat and competition, but also from this earlier ethic of 'gentle' relations with the opposite gender. The function of the later eighteenth- and nineteenth-century 'salon hostess,' assigned the responsibility of keeping conversation between her guests amiable and non-conflicted, also emerges from this earlier recognition of the gentrifying influences of women at court.

The tradition of a knight asking a lady for a piece of her clothing (her 'colours') to take into combat with him is, therefore, not a Hollywood creation. It was a medieval custom, a manner of proving the knight's loyalty to his lord's household or to his beloved. In fact, the knight now had another face-saving consolation to rationalize his mercenary status. He could tell himself that he was serving the lord's household and carrying its 'colours,' not out of material obligation but *'par amour'* (out of love) and *'par honneur'* (out of honour). *Gallantry* became the readiness to act in the interests of others without consideration for self. And being allowed to be gallant indicated one's admittance into a privileged class that expected much more of its members *(noblesse oblige)* than it did of the general population.

Yet, this idealization of courtly virtues brought with it a series of consequences that created divisions and cliques. Along with courtly love came a negation of *humility* – others became potential rivals in the competition for the favours of the lord and/or his lady. The putting down of rivals created a climate of intrigue and conspiracy. This clique culture reached its peak during the later court of Versailles when intense infighting and corruption discredited the entire notion of a divinely ordained nobility. By the time of the revolution many French aristocrats no longer took seriously the rituals at court and performed them with tongue in cheek.

Another divisive effect of courtly devotion was the expectation of reward for supposedly 'selfless' service. This led to a continuing critique of the lord and a measuring of his generosity. Envy became a frequently experienced emotion for rising courtiers. There are indications in Eilhart von Oberge's German rendition of *Tristan and Isalde* that the 'saintliness' of the knight is complicated by involvement in worldly affairs. In order to survive, Tristan has to submit to the ways of a court that does not live up to the ideal that he himself has been asked to attain; as a result, he becomes cynical, deceitful, and cunning (Scaglione 1991:152–3). Thus, many courtiers became 'masters of disguise,' using stratagems when virtue on its own would not bring them the results they desired (154).

For all its paradoxical shortcomings courtly love did open the way for the democratization of culture and the creation of a later 'commoner's' courtesy. The romantic tales attributed to the courts became the material of Occitan lyrics composed by *troubadours* employed as court performers and entertainers at large. As they travelled from court to court they were occasionally invited to perform in the homes of rich merchants; gradually, the merchant classes learned and practised some of the ideals and mannerisms of court.

Travelling troubadours also helped spread the courtly ideals among regions and states. The ideal of *fin' amour* (pure love) was spread from the south of France to the north and then into other regions of Europe by troubadours who received encouragement and support from influential members of various courts. This early system of royal patronage set the stage for the artistic patronage relationships of the Renaissance. It also served as a model for the seventeenth- and eighteenth-century intellectual salons that were partial to receiving travelling intellectuals, artists, and musicians.

These new standards of chivalry also had important effects on the education of youth. Young men from noble families were prepared for a life of courtly service by being placed in the household of a lord under the tutelage of the women of the household. The young boy (page) or *damoiseau*, spent seven years with the women until, at the age of fourteen, he was declared a squire and given over into the care of the knights. He was then taught to use weapons, ride horseback, and become skilled at arts such as hawking. He was encouraged to write poetry, master the games of chess and backgammon, and become adept in the art of conversation. At the age of twenty-one the young man was knighted during an elaborate ceremony that included a special bath symbolizing purification (Lucas 1934 [1960]:128–9). These rituals raised female members of aristocratic households to influential social positions, giving them a substantial say in the gentrification of the male. The mixed-gender dances of the later Middle Ages, for example, served to channel aggressive energy into an art form, further contributing to the 'civilizing' of the male (Filmer 2001:1–16). Dance was to become a highly ritualized form of civil interaction by the time of the Renaissance (109–21).

Thus, although the culture of *courtoisie* was originally restricted to a privileged class, it eventually contributed to the spread of democratization. It now became possible for people of lower birth to achieve a certain amount of social mobility by learning and observing the behavioural codes of their 'social superiors.' Increasingly, knights who originated from ordinary families took to distinguishing themselves through valorous acts. The great military orders, such as the Knights of St John's of Jerusalem, the Knight Templars, and the Spanish orders of Alcantara, Calatrava, and St James of Compostella, provided men of humble origins the opportunity to learn and practise lofty ideals.

From Barbarism to Courtly Manners  49

And, in time, their families came to adopt heraldic shields that bore symbols, images, and mottoes representing their origins. Towards the later Middle Ages, many families who had no connection to the courts or religious orders had heralds of their own.

Norbert Elias has provided us with an erudite analysis of the gentrification of the knight and the later development of French court society (see chapter 5). As already mentioned, there are certain analytical problems with Elias's tendency to collapse 'violence' and 'anger' into one category. While his conception of restraint provides a coherent theory of civilization, the neatness of the theory can become problematic when applied to eras nearer to our own when anger was used as a 'recivilizing' mechanism. Elias concludes that the civilizing process is accompanied by an increasingly complex list of behaviours that are allowed or forbidden. While this analysis, based on the concept of a repressed subconscious, is in some part true, it does not explain why in certain eras what had been previously repressed has suddenly been freed with no permanent decivilizing effects. This theoretical problem is connected to the fact that Elias did not sufficiently consider that a group or nation could adopt civilized mannerisms and codes towards members of its own group while reserving its moral outrage (anger) for groups whom it considered a 'danger' to its own survival (Tilly 2005a). He viewed the Nazi era as a barbaric movement. Yet there was a paradox to the Nazi period – restraints on behaviour directed at a group considered as 'outsiders' were lifted, while immaculate codes of civility were maintained within the 'in-group.' This double-standard process, which Tilly terms 'durable inequality' (71–90), remains a part of all contemporary 'civilized societies.'

Elias might have given too much weight to the concept of 'repression' and, thereby, failed to see that as the 'civilizing process' goes beyond its function of state formation and monopolization of outright violence, it releases a certain cultural maturity that permits suspension of restraints without the loss of accumulated civilizational development. The works of Tilly (2005a, 2005b, 2003a, 1993a, 1993b, 1986), A.R. Gillis (2004:1303–31, 1989:307–41), and Gary Lafree (1994) show that a very important parallel to the monopolization of violence by the state during the 'civilizing process' is the rise of civil institutions. Rather than an imposition, civility becomes a settlement between a strong state and a contentious population. It is within this uneasy alliance that we see the birth of 'individualism' and the development of a culture that legitimizes the state according to the degree to which it recognizes the rights of the person.

So it would seem that the monopolization of violence by a strong ruler or state is the beginning of the control of free-floating violence; yet it is not the civilizing process itself, but, rather, a precondition for it. The civilizing process consists of a complex union of social practices and struggles, the resistance of the population towards central rule and a consequent heightened awareness of 'self' not being the least of them. As we hope to show in the next chapter, the rising awareness of the citizenry during the Renaissance had a salient influence on the development of secular civility ethics that were quite independent of the theological rationalizations of the medieval courtesy philosophers.

# 3 Secular Civility in the Renaissance

'I have set thee,' says the Creator to Adam 'in the midst of the world, that thou mayst the more easily behold and see all that is therein. I created thee a being neither heavenly nor earthly, neither mortal nor immortal only, that thou mightest be free to shape and to overcome thyself.
— Pico de Mirandola, *Oration on The Dignity of Man*

**Introduction**

The Renaissance was an important era in Western history because of its immense influence on the manner in which individuals conceived of their place in the universe and the way in which this conception facilitated the development of a civility tradition that was not as dependent on theological dogma. The subsequent Protestant Reformation and Enlightenment movements were facilitated by Renaissance interaction values because the Renaissance thinkers set the stage for a reversal in the ideologies that had kept absolutist monarchies in power. Although princes remained all-powerful in the Renaissance city-states, a new appreciation of individualism provided the rationale for a more secular and person-oriented civil society.

What marked the passage from medieval to Renaissance conceptions of ideal behaviour was the rift that was developing between blind faith and reason. Medieval conceptions of ideal being and bearing could not fully satisfy the new awareness that was being facilitated by advances in technology and trade. An educated university elite and a rising merchant class were demanding social philosophies capable of going beyond the medieval clerical dictum 'to love without measure.' Renaissance thinkers responded to a growing individualism by providing a modified view of humankind's place in the divine order. While God had stood at the centre of the universe in medieval culture, the thinkers of the Renaissance altered the theocratic paradigm by bringing humankind and the natural world into the centre of social philosophy. This new respect for the individual as a prime mover of reality was already evident in *The Divine Comedy* (1472), written in the vernacular Italian. Dante mercilessly condemns the religious luminaries of his time, stripping them of their earthly privileges and showing them in the afterlife as accountable as any other men. Such mistrust of clerical infallibility is also present in the works of Rabelais ([1532] 1939), who ridiculed the pretence of contrived virtue, favouring instead a natural civility based on an intuitive sense of personal honour. Rabelais's dictum, *Fay ce que tu vouldras* (do what thou wishes) (Bk 1, Ch. 57), implied that no rules of elaborate conduct were needed, provided a person possessed an unaffected sense of right and wrong. This marked the beginnings of a more secular notion of 'integrity,' one not limited to theological dogma.

This change in worldview accorded with developments in politics and economy. The rise of money economies and the increasing specialization of labour were producing an expansion in the social and economic networks of individuals, thereby broadening and complicating the process of citizenship and rendering medieval feudal theocracy an inadequate system of social organization.

Further facilitating transformations in the philosophy of civic obligations was the continuing tension between the aristocracy and the general population. As Elias ([1939] 1982) has pointed out in his analysis of state formation, the establishment of central rule would have been impossible without the existence of tensions between opposing classes. The rise of the post-Renaissance central state was made possible by the fact that the old military nobility and the rising new bourgeoisie had competitive interests but were unable to conclusively defeat each other during the Renaissance (173–4). Absolute monarchies eventually stepped in to bridge the gap:

> The antagonism between different parts of society certainly does not only take the form of conscious conflict. Plans and consciously adopted goals are far less decisive in producing tensions than anonymous figurational dynamics. To give one example, it is the dynamics of advancing monetarization and commercialization far more than the conscious attacks of bourgeois-urban circles, which push the bulk of the knightly feudal lords

downhill at the end of the Middle Ages. But however the antagonisms arising with the advance of the money network may be expressed in the plans and goals of individual people or groups, with them grows the tension between the urban classes who are gaining strength and the functionally weakening lords of the land. With the growth of this network and this tension, however, grows the room to maneuver of those who, having won the struggle between initially freely competing units, have become the central rulers of the whole – the kings, until finally, balanced between the bourgeoisie and the nobility, they attain their optimal strength in the form of the absolute monarchy. (175)

In *Renaissance and Revolution*, Joseph Anthony Mazzeo (1965) also describes the slow emergence of a centralized state, noting important changes in the

re-creation of ancient forms, in the growth of a civil bureaucracy, the decline of feudal military and economic structures, the rise of professional and mercenary armies, the development of advanced forms of diplomacy including the use of resident ambassadors, the keeping of administrative records in government, the secularization of political theory, and the more candid recognition among rulers of something like what we would call *raison d'état*. (5)

The development of new technologies and new trade routes was a decisive factor in the weakening of theological hegemony. The administrative talents of clerics no longer sufficed for the development of specialties as diverse as accounting, trade management, production planning, seafaring, and the study of foreign cultures and languages. Moreover, the new surplus of wealth contradicted the mentality of scarcity that had kept medieval populations in the service of their lay and ecclesiastical nobilities. The social and psychological effects of the rising materialism of the Renaissance cannot be understated, for the sudden availability of surplus transformed 'yearning' into 'desiring,' a more active and more present-oriented emotion that had a considerable transformative influence on personal identity (Baron 1966, Martines 1963, Von Martin 1944).

Paralleling the rise of Renaissance mercantilism was a growing liberalism in intellectual circles. Although Renaissance thinkers wisely avoided controversial confrontations with the Church, they managed to sidestep the restrictions of medieval dogma by revisiting the classics without overtly negating Christian faith. Even the most radical writers based their criticisms of existing theology on the need for a new purity of religious worship. Matteo Palmieri, who wrote seminal Renaissance texts putting forward ideas that a few years earlier might have been condemned by Rome, remained respectful of the theologians of his time. Vespasiano writes of Gianozzo Manetti, the translator of Aristotle: 'Added to his other virtues was a spirit of religion of which he always spoke with reverence' (Mazzeo 1965:50). Despite such circumspection, scholars, artists, and merchants were experimenting with formerly prohibited ideas and having a liberalizing effect that impacted even the curia of the Church.

As consequential as the accomplishments of the Renaissance scholars and artists were those of the statesmen and merchants. 'Wealth' (as capital available for saving, spending, and investing) increased during the Renaissance, setting in motion strong tensions between Christian ideology and the needs of merchants to maximize their profits. This left the Church itself in a precarious financial position, for canon law forbade it from making profits based on outright usury. Ecclesiastical institutions had to find ways of sanctifying profit without negating Christian principles; arguing for wealth was tantamount to arguing for the sanctity of the material world. Since Church philosophers such as St Augustine had cautioned against the evils of the City of Man, merchants and the Church had to find ways to circumvent this moral quandary without curtailing trade or invalidating the long-standing doctrinal credibility of Christianity.

One development that did have far-reaching democratizing effects was the invention of the modern printing press. The knowledge that for centuries had been denied the common people was put into their hands by virtue of a technical innovation that overwhelmed the long-standing ecclesiastical monopoly of texts. This caused a rise in individualism because rich merchants were now able to publish their memoirs during their own lifetime; many of these works argued for the sanctity of self-interest and social mobility. The mendicant philosophy of St Francis of Assisi was far from the minds of the new Renaissance writers, who tried to harmonize the teachings of the early courtesy writers with the new culture of affluence. Palmieri ([1528] 1944) gave his approval to family wealth and the accumulation of possessions in *Della vita civile*. Similarly, Alberti approved of wealth by cautioning that a man without a house and possessions was seriously jeopardizing his freedom (Gage 1968:23–5).

As for the Church, it took on a more worldly view of virtue, and some of the curia readily adapted to the Italian Renaissance love of luxury and sensuality. By the time of the High Renaissance, the salary of a cardinal of the Church was 3,500 times that of a servant (Burke 1986:224). Pope Alexander VI paraded his beautiful mistress in the Vatican in plain view of his cardinals. Having fathered nine illegitimate sons and bribed his way into the papacy, this member of the ruthless Borgia family used his daughter as a pawn in a series of dynastic arranged marriages. His son, Cesare Borgia, became one of the strongest and most feared *condottiere* (De Rosa 1988:144–6) and was the model used by Machiavelli ([1513] 1940) in his long essay on political power and governance, *The Prince*. Even so, the curia's growing ease with luxury did not alleviate the short-term financial problems of the Church. Although the Church needed financing it could not engage in trading – canon law forbade it from being entrepreneurial. Clerics found a way around this restriction by turning to the sale of deathbed absolutions and indulgences.

The Church had already been deriving a sizeable income through the sale of prayers offered for the soul of dead relatives who were believed to be in 'purgatory.' The idea of purgatory (introduced as doctrine in the eleventh century), a place of strict penance between heaven and hell in which some sinners spent time waiting for forgiveness, gave the Church the means to influence the families of the dead. Although people in purgatory would not be sent into hell, they could be indefinitely denied the right to ascend to heaven. For families who believed in heaven, hell, and purgatory, the possibility of their dead relatives interminably suspended between heaven and hell was a source of great anxiety. The Church responded to that anxiety by offering to say prayers on behalf of the dead so that their suffering might be minimized and their entry into heaven accelerated.

By the fifteenth century the Church possessed a large network of clerics and nuns visiting villages and towns and offering papal favours and indulgences for specified amounts of money. Although the considerable income derived from this business helped the Church fortify its tenuous position in Rome, it left the Church vulnerable to the upcoming critiques of Protestant reformers.

Yet, although the Church was left with no choice but to accept an alliance with the new merchant class, it retained considerable power because magnates realized that they had important administrative lessons to learn from the Church's long-standing expertise in managing its own assets. Moreover, they needed the Church's approval for their commercial activities. For the Christian merchant, it now became important to keep a clear conscience. His fear of the judgment after death required it. Conveniently, the Lateran Council of 1513 increased this anxiety by declaring that the soul was immortal. Contributions by merchants to ecclesiastical projects increased dramatically following this declaration. Cosimo de Medici is reported by Vespasiano to have confessed in 1439 to Pope Eugenius IV that he felt uneasy about the ways in which he had acquired his wealth. The pope advised Medici to 'unburden' his soul by building a monastery. He complied without complaint, bequeathing Italy with one of its minor architectural wonders (Gage 1968:49).

Thus, means were being found to rationalize mercantilism. Although the banknotes and promissory notes of the Medici Bank carried the words 'In Christ We Trust' printed on all notes, the Medicis did charge interest but under a different name, referring to it as 'administrative costs on an account.'

What eventually marked Renaissance mercantilism and differentiated it from medieval trade was the emergence of a hedonism that welcomed the joys of spending. In a speech given in 1427, the demagogue Stefano Porcari passionately affirmed the moral legitimacy of wealth:

> Let us contemplate the needs of private life. Whence are our houses and palaces procured ...? From riches! Whence come our clothes ...? Whence the meals for us and our children? From riches! Whence the means to educate our children and make them virtuous ...? From riches ...! These consecrated churches with their decorations, the walls, the towers, the defenses ...your places and dwellings, the most noble buildings, the bridges, the streets, with what have you built them, whence do you obtain the means of preserving them, if not from riches? (cited in Gage 1968:56)

Porcari was presenting the accumulation of wealth and its wise administration as a mechanism of 'common welfare.' And in so doing he was advancing the legitimacy of the paternalistic ruler. Pier Candido Decembrio at the court of Filippo Maria Visconti, Pandolfo Decembrio at the Este court, and Pontano at Naples were similarly passionate proponents of wealth. And, at the papal court, the Christian philosopher Lapo da Castiglionchio went to great pains to explain that Christ's poverty was a circumstance of history and really not in need of emulation by the pope or the curia (Hay 1961:151). So, although much of the Renaissance literature referred to the classics as well as to Christian theology, there was a tendency to extract and recombine classical and religious ideas so that the new, highly competitive mercantile environment could be made legitimate, intelligible, and manageable (Sombart 1915, Von Martin 1944).

This information is important to our understanding of civility during the Renaissance because the changing material circumstances of society caused a substantial transformation in what was considered civil and uncivil behaviour. For example, a vital part of wealth acquisition during the Renaissance became its flaunting in public. The exhibition of wealth was intended to help manage the impressions left on others and inform them of the wealth-owner's status, success, and political power. The public religious festivals and jubilees gave wealthy people ample opportunities to display their fortunes in public; surviving letters and records show that the funerals and marriages of the wealthy became lavish public events (Brucker 1969:122–3). Local fairs and jousting tournaments provided further opportunities for the display of wealth and the affirmation of the sanctity and good name of the wealthy family.

One need only examine artifacts to see the enormous change that occurred in the display of the body in the Renaissance. Although Elias ([1939] 1978) repeatedly focuses on the 'rising threshold of shame' in relation to bodily functions and a heightened sense of disgust towards them (65–6, 80), there occurred a radical transformation in the manner in which the body was adorned and presented in private and public. The theological climate of the medieval era had exercised a stronghold over the body. Until the fourteenth century the high valuation placed on modesty (spiritual and sexual) had affected the clothing worn by men and women. Both genders wore long and loose tunics that covered the entire body. Colours of fabrics were monochromatic and style was austere. But with the Renaissance, the entire medieval conception of modesty (*modestus* – 'keeping within measure') became liberalized. Clothing became colourful and ornamentation profuse and detailed. Particularly telling of the new mercantilism and love of flair and sensuality was the manner in which both men's and women's clothing accentuated the shape of the body without embarrassment: short, fitted jackets, tight hose, and prominent codpieces for men, and tight busts and décolletages for women (Laver 1969).

Brucker (1969) perceptively suggests that there was something quite tactical in these bodily displays of fortune: 'By indulging in extravagance and display, patricians were announcing their release from the restraints imposed by egalitarianism; they were emphasizing their special, exalted place in Florentine society' (124).

Indeed, there was something quite individualistic about the new interactive codes. The diaries and letters of wealthy families of the epoch reveal the new enjoyment of conspicuous spending and the sense of personal power released by spending. Giovanni Rucellai (d. 1481), a prosperous Florentine merchant, wrote in his journal: 'I think I've done myself more honour by having spent money than by having earned it. Spending gave me a deeper satisfaction ... the rich man must be generous, for liberality is the most noble and attractive virtue which he can possess' (cited in Brucker 1969:124).

Thus, *style* emerged as a valued part of personality and reputation. While medieval courtly literature had preached restraint, prudence, modesty, and decorum, the high valuation placed on *aesthetics* during the Renaissance made personal verbal and bodily *eloquence* virtues in and of themselves. The showing of the *adorned self* became a means for the affirmation of the worth of the self. Elias saw the Renaissance as a time of increasing psychological restraints. We hesitate to categorically state the same because a relative freeing of the human body was occurring. While the code of manners was becoming more complex and sophisticated, many other aspects of life, sensuality included, were being released from the restraints of a totalizing medieval theology.

**Humanism, Aesthetics, and Individualism**

A major characteristic of Renaissance thought was the search for interconnection and synthesis. Renaissance thinkers resisted the dogmas of the medieval Church and sought to bring together what had previously seemed exclusive modes of recognizing and describing experience. While there emerged competing explanations of humankind's place in the universe and the degree to which destiny was determined by providence, there was unity in the high valuation placed on *eloquence*. This respect for creative self-expression signalled a new appreciation of humankind's ability to break free of original sin.

So, while the superstitions and fatalistic cautions of the medieval age did not disappear altogether, Renaissance scholars and artists managed to avoid major confrontations with the Church; rather than attacking medieval theology, they returned to the classics in search of spiritual renewal. Poliziano, the celebrated poet who translated Greek works into Latin, expressed this renewed appreciation of the classical period when he admitted that 'I am not Cicero ... it is through Cicero that I have learnt how to be myself' (cited in Portoghesi 1972:27). He was voicing a growing recognition among Renaissance scholars and artists that they were in need of reacquiring the precision, eloquence, and sensuality of a bygone age.

Another development that affected civility norms was the manner in which the 'virtues' were analysed and discussed. Medieval courtly literature provided ample lists of the various virtues which, when taken together, made for an ideal individual. Renaissance thought, on the other hand, addressed the issue of 'virtue' itself, an inner quality not necessarily connected to the practice of a series of rituals, but, rather, a fountainhead of ethical comportment already contained in the human psyche. Renaissance works praised humankind and admired it instead of loathing its mortality. Men and women were not seen as passive recipients of divine will but as active participants in the fulfillment of God's plan on earth (Mazzeo 1965:53).

Even the notion of the hero was transformed during the Renaissance. In his major work, *De viris illustribus*, Petrarch treated the military and political champions of antiquity as central movers of history, contradicting St Augustine's view of history as a predestined journey controlled by divine forces. Petrarch's heroes possessed their own wills. Their virtue rested in their own perfection rather than in a manifestation of divine providence. Motivating their virtuous acts was their own personal quest for mortal glory. God did not necessarily appoint these heroes as chosen ones – they succeeded as a result of their own inner motivations. A human-centred intellectual tradition was emerging and it would be further refined through the works of the Protestant reformers and the thinkers of the Enlightenment (Lévi 2002).

Further facilitating the formation of a broadened public civility was the development of a vernacular language. Petrarch's *Rimes* were written in Italian. So was Boccaccio's *Decameron*, which retold stories of love, adventure, and the oddities of powerful people. These writers exemplified the 'educational acquaintance' favoured by Aristotle, who had explained that the 'universally educated' person was the one who was capable of practising critical thinking in as many fields as possible. The rising secular republicanism of the Renaissance thinkers was eloquently expressed by Gianfrancesco Pico de Mirandola (cited in Burckhardt [1860] 1944), who, in his famous *Speech on the Dignity of Man (Oratio de hominis dignitate)*, categorically denied the Church's medieval fatalism:

> 'I have set thee,' says the Creator to Adam 'in the midst of the world, that thou mayst the more easily behold and see all that is therein. I created thee

a being neither heavenly nor earthly, neither mortal nor immortal only, that thou mightest be free to shape and to overcome thyself. Thou mayst sink into a beast, and be born anew to the divine likeness. The brutes bring from their mother's body what they will carry with them as long as they live; the higher spirits are from the beginning, or soon after, what they will be for ever. To thee alone is given a growth and a development depending on thine own free will. Thou bearest in thee the germs of a universal life.' (215–16)

Pico's speech departed remarkably from medieval accounts of the Creation. For Pico, mankind was not condemned to eternal shame and suffering, but was given the opportunity of perfecting itself by divine mandate. Pico was representing an important theme of the Renaissance: man achieves dignity by choosing between the *higher* and *lower* levels of experience, thereby distinguishing himself as a being capable of discovering his own divinity. But the fact that he can err and choose lower levels of being and awareness is also indicative of his humanity – he is neither absolutely good nor absolutely evil. In Pico's universe, ambition forms a central part of human action. The outcome of such ambition is what determines the unfolding of a particular life; the individual remains free throughout to make or break himself.

What was remarkable about the Renaissance was that no serious clash occurred between the humanists and the Church. During the High Renaissance outstanding writers and artists were even rewarded with prestigious Church offices. Some classical scholars, such as Pietro Bembo, Girolamo Alexander, and Jacopo Sadoleto, were even appointed as cardinals (Ralph 1973:147).

Renaissance art also reflected the growing acceptance of the legitimacy of human agency and the human body. Byzantine art differed little from early Christian art. There was a frozen and almost superhuman dignity to the personages being depicted. Many of the Byzantine works had a triple purpose: to illustrate holy manuscripts, to tell the story of Christianity, and to 'illuminate' what otherwise might have been monotonous text. Evident in Byzantine painting was the domination of the body by the spirit. Many of the paintings show figures with oversized heads animated by piercing eyes and flattened bodies hidden behind garments. In effect, these paintings had a storytelling quality to them; elements of the paintings were juxtaposed to show events in different time frames; hence the lack of perspective in most Byzantine (and Romanesque) works. The eye had to travel from one detail to the next in order to reconstruct the story being told.

The art of the Renaissance, especially the High Renaissance (1500 onwards), provided a full representational image, complete with proper perspective. The use of perspective (the convergence of lines at a point of infinity in order to show all objects in proper proportion) made the viewer a central player in the image. The viewer could take any position desired and still see the picture in proper perspective and with little thematic change.

The participant aspect of perspective painting was emancipatory. Gazing into a picture, the viewer became conscious of himself as both the receiver of the image as well as a central player in its composition. This innovation replaced the symbolic representation of life with an actual and real space for the undistorted viewing of the corporeal and the secular. Men and women now dared to gaze on the creation as *they* saw it rather than as the way they imagined God saw it. This was a crucial development in the history of personal identity and the emergence of a self-centred psychological awareness that would have substantial effects on civility practices.

Renaissance humanism, however, did not argue for 'kindness' towards humans as much as it did for secular freedom. Many princes who committed the cruellest acts considered themselves devout humanists. The irony of the Renaissance lies in the fact that, precisely at a time when notions of individualism and secular liberty were taking root, class distinctions continued to be passionately maintained. Despite the existence of citizen assemblies, the city-states system fostered a culture in which strong princely rulers provided paternalistic leadership. Whether such rule produced tyranny or a benevolent administration was largely dependent on the personality of the prince who was in power. This paternalism was reminiscent of the ancient Roman tradition of paternal authority that granted total power to the father of a family, even the right to order his children's banishment from Rome. With this resurging paternalism came a broadening of administrative responsibility:

> The prince is to take everything into his charge, to maintain and restore churches and public buildings, to keep up the municipal police, to drain the marshes, to look after the supply of wine and corn; so to distribute the taxes that the people can recognize their necessity; he is to support the sick

and the helpless, and to give his protection and society to distinguished scholars, on whom his fame in after ages will depend. (Burckhardt [1860] 1944:6)

This new philosophy of 'efficacy' was also beginning to regulate the behaviour of rulers. Burckhardt explains that, increasingly, what mattered to the population was not the legitimacy of the ruler but his efficacy. There was a shift from the fixity of a feudal aristocracy towards a competitive political environment in which the fate of a ruler was considerably determined by his ability to manage and protect his interests. Ingenuity and the ability to promote self – accompanied by strong military and diplomatic resources – were required to rationalize and maintain authority within a highly competitive political environment. This accountability in the face of political reality appeared first in Italy because Italian rulers were not able, like their northern counterparts, to depend on the support of a strong feudal aristocracy and, therefore, had to prove themselves through their own talents. Although this facilitated tyranny and petty despotism, it also brought to power many exceptional men who managed to embody the Renaissance conception of the 'ideal prince.' The possibility of overthrowing one's predecessor prior to his natural death gave rise to the spirit of the 'public servant' type of politician who turned to his peers and the public for approval and support. We see here the emergence of 'public opinion' as a determining factor in the political longevity of a ruler. This had a certain democratizing effect, even though democracy itself was in its nascent stages and tyranny was rampant in some of the city-states.

The patrician nature of political organization was also reflected in the organization of the family. Just as important as a man's title and personal reputation as a citizen was the reputation and status of his family. The upholding of family values and the close surveillance of one's family history was of major concern during the Renaissance. Alberti ([c.1460] 1969), writing his partially autobiographical book *I libri della famiglia* set down four laws for a family that wished to be materially and morally successful: (1) respect the name of the family; (2) produce as many male children as possible; (3) avoid conflicts with other families; and (4) cultivate networks of friendship with other suitable families.

Family ties were of paramount importance, and a nobleman's family unit, *casato*, could easily comprise upwards of fifty people, including direct and indirect members of the family, protegés, servants, and slaves. The misbehaviour of one member could tarnish the reputation of the entire family. The rank of a person's family, therefore, often determined the type of life the person would have. In Florence and Tuscany, when a member of a family committed a crime or incurred a debt, other members of the family were also held accountable. This internalizing of commitment and responsibility towards members of the family led to a *blood-mutuality* that rationalized vendettas between families. The honour of the family became sacred – an honourable person conducted his affairs with integrity and remained ready to defend the reputation of his family, even if this required confrontational behaviour that did not accord with Christian virtues.

Within this climate of intense mercantile and political competition it became necessary for families to somehow balance the pragmatics of resource management with virtuous and just behaviour. Despite his recognition of the cruelties of the merchant patriciate, Alberti reassured that action combined with an intelligent management of spiritual and material resources would increase the health and longevity of a family:

> Fortune's cruel floods quickly submerge and destroy the family that throws itself upon those waves either by abandoning restraint and moderation in prosperity or by lacking a firm posture and a prudent self-control in the face of hostile storms. (30)

Alongside the pragmatics of resource and reputation management he placed the classical virtue of noble thought and action:

> Nobility of soul, we cannot but recognize, is itself sufficient to ascend and to possess the highest peaks: glorious praise, eternal flame, immortal glory. It seems undeniable that nothing is easier to acquire than this nobility, if only you seek it and value it. (29)

Thus, the practice of 'magnanimity' (Aristotle's *megalopsychia*) and 'calculated deference' became a means of imposing law, order, and meaning on what was becoming a chaotic and competitive society. In a volatile political and economic climate, it became important for a family to develop relationships with other families more powerful and influential than itself. *Fortuna* (fortune) could be extremely capricious in this new society. *Divine providence* had helped explain many unforeseen calamities during the theological Middle Ages. In the Renaissance, however, *chance* came to compete with the will of God. At the back of most powerful and wealthy men's minds was the fear of suddenly losing their fortune through erroneous business decisions or faulty political manoeuvrings. Such loss of wealth led to loss of political influence and then to a host of other misfortunes such as difficulty in finding the right marriage partners for one's children. In Florence, where respect for the new wealth was most intense, loss of wealth was rarely looked upon with sympathy; men who fell into poverty were even shunned by their own relatives. *Deference* became a means for promoting non-conflicted and profitable alliances. This quality was quite different from the *submissiveness* of the feudal vassal. A person now *deferred* to another in recognition of the other's identity and in order to avoid outright confrontation; this deference was more an act of alliance than of submission.

This transformation in the notion of virtue as an obligation to God into an obligation to community becomes quite understandable when viewed from the economic perspective. As we will argue in more detail in the chapter on the early roots of British parliamentarianism, the surplus of goods during the Renaissance surpassed the amount of gold and silver. Credit became introduced as a means of furthering economic activity and keeping up with rising demands for goods. As Charles Tilly (2005b) explains in *Trust and Rule*, 'networks of trust' had to be established in parallel with political regimes. These networks of trust brought together individuals who cooperated to verify and validate individuals worthy of trust and exclude those who were not (11–17). Thus, it was necessary for someone wishing to prosper in the new society of the Renaissance to develop a reputation as a person of upright standing. This was, in effect, a measure of that person's right to be included in mercantile networks of exchange, many of which were based on deferred payments. So, secular civility can, in a certain measure, be understood as a direct outcome of accelerating mercantilism. This is particularly noticeable in England in the sixteenth century (chapter 6).

The practice of 'deference,' placed in the hands of powerful individuals, became a formality and a tactic of discourse rather than a guarantee of consistent and incorruptible honour and sympathy. Cosimo de Medici was reported to maintain a very simple and humble merchant's demeanour during his daily affairs, but the palace he built at the Via Large was the most lavish in Florence. He was known to be quite merciless towards those who stood in his way while very loyal and deferential towards those who proved themselves trustworthy allies. Caution, mistrust, and aggressive competition were consequences of this new economic climate. And 'deference' was the behavioural tactic that the elites (and would-be elites) used to smoothen over hazardous situations and confirm their loyalty towards persons whom they considered useful allies or benefactors. Cosimo de Medici (cited in Gage 1968) reveals this spirit of calculation when he writes to one of his envoys, instructing him on how to become a master of the art of respect:

> I know that some time ago as a young man you were able to entertain two or three women at the same time, and I remind you that [dealing with Cardinals] is no greater effort or care, because it is enough to be discreet and do or say nothing that displeases those who trust you, seeking to gain with every man and lose with none. (192)

Receiving deferential treatment, however, was not a privilege enjoyed by every Italian citizen. Palmieri held little sympathy for the peasants and labourers who constituted at least one-third of Italian society in the mid-1400s. Unmoved by the sufferings of the destitute, he wrote:

> Let the working masses and the humblest sector of the middle classes struggle for the good of the Republic ... If the lowest order of society earn enough food to keep them going from day to day, then they have enough. (cited in Gage 1968:101)

As the guilds and communes lost their republican authority, the less influential were released from the status guaranteed them by the older corporate societies and were left to their own resources. For the man who was released into this new mercantile society without resources of his own, there remained only one option: to form alliances and 'bonds of obligation' with men who possessed the power and influence to help make his life livable. In effect, the powerful patriarchs of the newly emerging towns and cities had replaced the old feudal lords.

## Seminal Conduct Themes and Books of the Renaissance

Changes in political and economic circumstances during the Renaissance had important effects on courtesy and manners. The acceptance of materialism led to a heightened sense of bodily identity and an awareness and appreciation of 'style' and 'presentation of self.' There was a valuation of *dramaturgical artifice* that was quite distinct from the monastic severity of medieval courtesy. This new valuation of self-presentation brought with it a raised threshold of shame and a clearer demarcation between what was to be considered 'tasteful' and 'tasteless.' It goes without saying that any effort to watch one's manners, words, and expressions requires forethought. No behaviour can be censored or controlled without the actor keeping a keen eye on himself *and* others. That this self-surveillance was possible was not as much proof of how well repression had been imposed, but an indication of the degree to which human awareness had been freed from the limitations of a medieval theology founded on the monastic ideal of self-denial.

*Balancing Desire and Communal Survival:* The Prince

Niccolò di Bernardo die Machiavelli ([1513] 1940) understood the unique spirit of his times when he wrote *The Prince,* a precise meditation on the opportunities and limitations of power in a secular society.

Courtesy is not simply a practice composed of ideals and mannerisms. Implicit in any system of courtesy are political elements that regulate civil behaviour for the specific purpose of producing desired results. Many civility rituals are intended to increase the power and prestige of the practitioner or of those prescribing the rituals. Paralleling the Christian conception of courtesy as a celebration of mutual dignity and equality of spirit is a more utilitarian conception of civility, one that puts it in the service of power acquisition. Since Machiavelli attempted to provide advice on the ideal comportment of a prince, his work does qualify as conduct literature because it provided a set of behavioural guidelines intended to help an ambitious politician maintain his power and reputation while serving the state.

Moreover, his work is an excellent treatise on 'self-interest' and its limitations, for Machiavelli does not argue for unbridled self-interest but tries to show how the desire for self-gratification is one of the founding blocks of civil society and a means by which order (and civil discourse) can be preserved. His theory of a socially functional self-restraint is similar to the ideas contained in the conduct books that followed later as well as the theories of moral sentiments embedded in the writings of the Enlightenment social philosophers. His argument demonstrates how the desire for freedom from restraint will (if it is to be successful) demand that the beneficiary impose considerable restraints on himself in order to maintain the privilege of living with minimal restraints. It was Machiavelli's recognition of this paradox that makes *The Prince* such a difficult book to interpret. It is not only a book on power but also a treatise cautioning against the abuse of power.

Machiavelli speculated on what was 'possible' in human action and did it with a near total disregard for ecclesiastical dogma. It is surprising that *The Prince* did not provoke the hostility of the Church when it first appeared in print. The pope authorized its publication in 1531, and twenty-five more editions appeared over the next twenty years. It was not until the Inquisition of 1559 that the secular implications of the book were fully understood by the papal curia, and it was banned at the Council of Trent in 1564.

In a way, Machiavelli was one of the first 'utilitarians.' Trying to show the opportunities (and limitations) of self-interest, he reminded a potential ruler that, in the end, he would be constrained by the human nature of his subjects: 'Men will always be false to you unless they are compelled by necessity to be true' (chap. 23).

According to Machiavelli, the selfishness of a person will see to it that there exists an ordered environment in which to satisfy his needs. A man may wish to be the head of an institution, but he must first assure, by adjusting his reactions, that the society in which he lives does not fall into chaos, for chaos would mean the end of all institutions. It is this element of self-adjustment and self-restraint that distinguished Machiavelli's theory of socialization and interaction. Because the desire of the self and the will are limitless, individuals find means by which they impose limits on themselves in order to be able to enjoy a certain amount of satisfaction rather than none at all. By limiting desire one limits resistance from others against one's desires. So, in Machiavelli's scheme of things, self-restraint is not entirely imposed by outside ideologies and interests but is a natural occurrence in human relations. Regardless of whether a society supports or forbids outright violence, there is a point at which humans restrain their ambitions in the interests of individual and collective survival.

Herein lies our understanding of the rise of a secular 'courteous' citizen during the Renaissance. He is an individual who must balance self-interest, the interest of others, and the vicissitudes of unintended consequences. For Machiavelli, a 'publican civility' can flourish according to the realities of necessity; it need not be tied to an a priori religious conviction. He tries to demonstrate how a humanity burdened by infinite desire can actually develop spheres of thought, emotion, and action that even include public service. The *regulation of personal desire* becomes the process out of which emerges a dialogical and democratic public discourse.

Machiavelli's prince, therefore, becomes *princely* precisely because he accepts the inevitability of the fact that his own survival and happiness are connected to the public's acceptance of him. Flexibility becomes an adaptive mechanism and tempers the arrogance of ascribed privilege. Although, during his discussion of *fortuna*, Machiavelli admits that societies lose their flexibility and become self-destructive over time, he recognizes that, in the long run, a society's ultimate need is self-preservation. Surviving requires a compromising nature. It is when a culture can no longer accommodate compromise in the interests of survival that it goes into decline with leadership passing on to another culture – but the whole of humanity manages to survive due to cyclical regeneration and the indomitable human need for continuity.

This acceptance of 'contingency' was something quite new because it presented an alternative to providential assistance from the divine. Market and political forces complicated the concept of a divinely ordained reality – surprises and contradictions abounded everywhere. Like Hobbes, Machiavelli remained aware that beneath the surface of civilized behaviour remained the possibility of chaos and destruction. The admission of this contingency obscured the facile adoption of a perfect and stable conception of the human spirit, as was done in the earlier Christian and ecclesiastical courtly traditions. It required, instead, a citizen who possessed enough awareness to be able to turn back to himself in order to deal with his own imperfections. We see here the roots of a social code that requires particularly stringent restraints of impulse in the favour of foresight.

Unlike the courtesy literature of the Middle Ages, which coupled virtue with the search for divine salvation, the literature of the Renaissance increasingly tried to encourage the individual to deal with reality and social relations from the perspective of a personal honour that did not deny utilitarian realities. Honour required much more than obedience to prescribed virtues. It required a considerable amount of self-reflection. If a person was to be honourable in his dealings with others he had to continually practise a self-critique that would reveal his own desires, limitations, and weaknesses to himself. Thus, the increasing self-reflexivity of Renaissance culture was considerably responsible for the development of a consciousness that required self-regulation without substantial dependence on ecclesiastical directives. This *self-reflexivity* may have had a direct influence on the raising of the threshold of shame and embarrassment, powerful emotions in the controlling of social interaction. Yet, it would be an exaggeration to say that this raising of the shame threshold was based on increased repression of awareness.

*Balancing Courtesy and Integrity:* The Book of the Courtier

The tensions between the crudity of political life in an increasingly commercial network of social relations on the one hand, and the ideal of aesthetic excellence on the other, are noticeable in the content and tone of one of the seminal courtesy books of the Renaissance, *The Book of the Courtier* (*Il Cortegiano*) ([1529] 1974). Although medieval values of 'chivalry' had become nearly obsolete in the new urban mercantile climate, Baldassare Castiglione managed to revive the ideal of chivalric honour and style within the context of his era. *The Book of the Courtier* became one of the Renaissance's most widely read books and managed to leave an indelible imprint on the European aristocracies. Although briefly mentioned in Norbert Elias's *The Civilizing Process*, *The Book of the Courtier* is one of the most important milestones in the development of a Western courtesy and civility tradition and deserves a fairly detailed description.

Castiglione himself was born to the rank of count and educated in the humanist schools in Milan and Mantua. He travelled to England and Spain as an emissary and acted as Pope Clement III's representative at the court of Emperor Charles V. His book was the outcome of ten years of experience as a courtier with the Montefeltro family in the legendary court of Urbino. Castiglione was writing not only about the ideal courtier but also about his own fond recollections of life in the idyllic court of Guidobaldo Montefeltro, son of Federigo di Montefeltro, Duke of Urbino. Federigo was known as a man of very strong principles, even though he led brutal military campaigns. Presiding over a household of 500 people, he managed to create an environment in which *modesty* and *honesty* were considered cardinal virtues. He is reported to have never accepted the easy way out for himself; he refused a Church indulgence secured for him by an ally, preferring instead to fast with members of his household.

On matters of money, he was repeatedly quoted as admonishing that a man's word was far more important than his wealth. In regards to learning, he was very demanding of himself, and his library contained all the books necessary for an orderly acquisition of learning. In matters of art, he was not only a patron but also an expert – he had a master's knowledge of sculpture and was adept at communicating with painters and bringing out the best in them. As the paternalistic administrator-ruler of Urbino, he was intensely respected, to the point of reverence; men and women were known to kneel when he passed in the streets, an honour which was not automatically accorded to the nobility. He made Urbino one of the most vital courts in Italy. His son, Guidobaldo, continued his father's tradition; with his wife, Elisabetta Gonzaga, he provided Castiglione with an ideal setting for his book on the art of courtly behaviour.

Castiglione was writing at a time when gunpowder was decreasing the influence of the old nobility of the sword. So there is a wistful, ironic tone to the work. It is not only a book of conduct but also an autobiographical remembrance of Italy prior to the destabilizing invasion of the French (Burke 1995:34–5).

*The Book of the Courtier* is an excellent example of ideal discourse between men and women of honour. As impressive as the content of the dialogues is the fact that the speakers have found a pleasant and fair way of relating to one another. The tone of the work is in itself an important part of the author's message to the reader, who is given a double opportunity: to see courtiers in pleasant and meaningful discourse with one another and to hear each of them speak of the personal qualities necessary for the formation of an ideal courtier. There is something original here. Ideal mannerisms are not denied, but added to them now is the ideal of an opinionated and intelligent conversation that is not at all limited by ecclesiastical dogma or the artifice of aristocratic pretension. The dialogues begin when one of the guests suggests that in order to pass the time in some meaningful way the guests converse with one another and arrive at a consensus regarding what it means to be an 'ideal courtier.' The dialogues continue over a span of four evenings in the frequent presence of the Duchesse Elisabetta Gonzaga.

The predominant theme that repeatedly appears in the four books of *The Book of the Courtier* is the theme of 'honour.' The acceptance of virtue and honour is no longer a duty to God, but a responsibility towards the person's own self and the selves of those he or she encounters. This dual loyalty to self and others is noticeable in the manner in which the participants take great pains not to appear pedantic or insult one another with corrosive statements. There is an effort to reconcile the potentially incompatible motivations of duty towards the community at court and the need to be true to one's own self. The book was an important milestone in the personalizing (as opposed to theologizing) of communal duty.

Castiglione's treatment of courtesy differs considerably from that of his predecessors. Neither brute force nor the mixing of force and piety, qualities favoured by the medieval romances, are considered sufficient for the making of a courtier. The ideal courtier has to blend the graceful and the secular so as to become a courageous individual committed to justice, truth, and wise counsel. Certainly, he or she must not boast about his accomplishments or appear greedy for rewards. Discretion and self-dismissal, even in the presence of great personal worth and accomplishments, are the principal virtues of Castiglione's courtier.

*Grazia* (grace) and *gravitas* (dignity) assure a courtier that his speech will not seem affected or forced. The art of personality presentation is to remain unnoticeable, not because of deceitful motives but because of the natural 'bearing' appropriate to a refined courtier, a bearing designed not to cause offence to others. Castiglione admonishes his courtier to 'avoid affectation in every way possible ... so as to conceal all art and make whatever is done or said appear to be without effort and almost without any thought about it' (Book I, 43).

There is a strong affinity between Castiglione's preference for lack of ostentation (*sprezzatura*) and the Aristotelian ideal of the *golden mean*, an ideal that was the basis of Cicero's *Orator*, a work that urged men of proper bearing to exhibit a 'purposeful negligence' (*neglegentia diligens*) so as to give off the impression that ideas interested them more than the artifice of style (Burke 1969:11). This studied spontaneity (*all'improviso*) was also a cherished theme in Ovid, who advised young men at court to cultivate a casual look of neglect (*forma viros neglecta decet*) in order to exude self-confidence.

Petrarch and Alberti had affirmed their faith in the human will; Castiglione furthered their humanism by arguing that only through a disciplined application of *wilful intent* could the ideal courtier manage to consistently speak the type of truths that would allow him to become a trusted and useful adviser of the court. The questioning of self that appears later in the Protestant and Puritan writings is already present here in Castiglione's work, although it is remarkably free of religious references. Like Machiavelli, Castiglione is not speaking of the prescribed Christian 'virtues' but of 'virtue' as a state of being. He defines men of honour as 'those men who, even when they think they will not be observed or seen or recognized by anyone, show courage and are not careless of anything, however slight, for which they could be blamed' (Book I, 33).

What is particularly noteworthy about the courtiers quoted by Castiglione is their views on gender. Castiglione accords men and women of court similar responsibilities. The *donna di palazzo* is encouraged to share in her husband's interests in culture and the arts; she is identified as a gentle moderating force capable of bringing harmony and a pleasant disposition to the ambience of the court. As a tempering force in the court she is to be without equal, as was the Duchess Elisabetta Gonzaga, who occasionally stepped in to gently calm discussions whenever they risked becoming heated. An important section of the book involves dialogues between two women moderators and the men in the group during which participants discuss the role played by women in courtly power and intellectual debates. Only two of the men in the gathering believe that women occupy too powerful a position in court circles. The majority of the discussants agree that women and men have equal talents and deserve equal amounts of recognition.

Castiglione's political preferences are also evident in the dialogues. While he did not sanction the despotic regimes that were emerging in Italy, he did favour a monarchical system that would limit greed and administer equitable public policy through democratic assemblies. He explained that virtue could not exist without vice, nor justice without injustice, and considered the truly competent courtier as a stabilizing force in an imperfect world:

> I hold that the principal and true profession of the Courtier must be that of arms; which I wish him to exercise with vigor; and let him be known among the others as bold, energetic, and faithful to whomever he serves. (Book I, 32)

> Let the man we are seeking be exceedingly fierce, harsh, and always among the first, wherever the enemy is; and in every other place, humane, modest, reserved, avoiding ostentation above all things as well as that impudent praise of himself by which a man always arouses hatred and disgust in all who hear him. (33-4)

Like the earlier medieval writers, he considered the style of presentation as important as content: 'To separate thoughts from words is to separate soul from body: in neither case can it be done without destruction' (54). Form and content could not be separated: 'All this would be empty and of little moment if the thoughts expressed by the words were not fine, witty, acute, elegant, and solemn, according to the need' (55). Thus, for Castiglione wit is not to be developed through artificial manners or rigorous studies of conversational tactics, since it is the property of an intelligent mind and the outcome of discipline and commitment.

In Castiglione's ideal court, the courtier forms his self in conjunction with others who have influence over his behaviour. Even witty dialogue is a means by which the courtier can read the personality of others while developing and adjusting his own persona (Book II, 172–5). The ideal courtier must always proceed from some inner standard that protects him from being forced to act against his own conscience and self-interest. In effect, Castiglione is speaking of a 'quiet' confidence that needs not prove itself in every case.

*The Book of the Courtier* was presenting a new standard for courtly life. In addition to the respect and deference shown by courtiers towards their prince, all members of the court were to show mutual deference towards one another. Castiglione did not hold the ruler free from such a requirement: 'Among the many faults that we see in many of our princes nowadays, the greatest are ignorance and self-conceit' (Book IV, 290). He did not speak out against monarchy itself, but against the type of monarch whose rashness would make him unworthy of his position (303). As for the role of the courtier in court, he saw it as a delicate undertaking. The courtier was to be effortlessly discreet and affable while consciously ensuring that the ruler did not make decisions opposed to the welfare of the realm: 'You ought to obey your lord in all things profitable and honourable for him, not in those that will bring him harm and shame' (Book II, 117). And any opposition registered against the ruler had to be delivered with utmost tact: 'When he [the courtier] sees the mind of his prince inclined to a wrong action, he may dare to oppose him and in a gentle manner avail himself of the favor acquired by his good accomplishments, so as to dissuade him of every evil intent and bring him to the path of virtue' (Book IV, 289).

As for the courtier's family pedigree, it was best that he come from a noble family, mainly because someone of common rank might not be sufficiently motivated to develop the many qualities required of a competent courtier: 'The lowly born, they lack that spur, as well as that fear of dishonour, nor do they think themselves obliged to go beyond what was done by their forebears; whereas to the wellborn it seems a reproach not to attain at least to the mark set them by their ancestors' (Book 1, 28).

It is noteworthy that the Church is almost never mentioned in the entire text of *The Book of the Courtier*. When the publisher's censor examined the book, he removed the word *fortuna* (fortune or luck) because of its secular undertones and replaced it with the word 'God.' There is a remarkable degree of self-determination in Castiglione's text. Although he encourages the individual to learn from a master, he qualifies the master as someone of deservedly superior knowledge rather than someone who speaks in the name of authority.

The relevance of the work is best appreciated if we remember that Renaissance Italians were intensely involved in a dialogue between extremes. In art, for example, there was a tension between naturalism and idealism, order versus grace, and opulence versus simplicity. What distinguished the personages who appeared in Castiglione's work was their ability to understand the qualities of each extreme and their willingness to build a composite of an ideal courtier able to avoid excesses while being refined, discerning, and influential. This avoidance of extreme positions helped the courtier deal with a variety of rulers. He was able to remain unwavering when faced with two totally different rulers: one who only wished compliments, and another so arrogant and haughty as to reject both compliments and advice. The courtier was admonished not to forget his real task: to guide the undecided prince towards firm and realistic governance while encouraging the inflexible ruler to adopt a just and dialogical relationship with his subjects.

Castiglione's courtier was, therefore, not only a servant of the state, but a prime mover capable of influencing the course of history. Repeatedly, the notions of 'discipline' and 'honour' come up in the various passages of the book. Honour is presented not as unquestioning loyalty towards a lord or church, but as a 'sensible' attitude held by the courtier towards himself. 'Discipline' is not force over others, but a tempering influence on self. Here we have the emergence of an individuality that is quite different from the 'all for one' mentality of the Arthurian legends. The ideal Renaissance courtier recognizes that he is bound by codes of deference towards whomever he is serving; yet, at the same time, he remains loyal to his own sense of right and wrong and respects his own values during his interactions with his equals and superiors.

Peter Burke (1995), who has written a seminal book regarding the reception given to *The Book of the Courtier*, has discussed the ambiguity of the original work and the positive manner in which it was received in Italy and abroad precisely because of this ambiguity. Burke explains that Castiglione tried to show his readers how to act gracefully, something that is nearly impossible to teach through the dispensation of a set of rules; he did this by conveying the *sentiment* of grace through the manner in which he organized the content and tone of the dialogues of his characters. And he managed to do so without offending those at court who presumed to already know what he was teaching – the playful tone of the book kept it from sounding like a patronizing tome (32). It also softened the book's underlying purpose: to promote a model of rational and intellectual debate that excluded the need for violence.

Thus, due to his tactful writing style, Castiglione's book was widely welcomed and found its way into most European courts precisely because it presented a composite of a courtier that could be adapted to the particular court systems of different European monarchies. Not only was the book a treatise on the behaviour of an ideal courtier, it was also a meditation on the meaning of a graceful life, something of relevance to aristocrats. It was this idealization of 'grace' (*grazià*) and unaffected self-confidence that attracted members of the nobility, who began using the book as a behavioural guide. The ability to seem unaffected became the new measure of distinction.

Unlike Capellanus, who had written of a very distinct personality suited to a theologically governed knightly culture, Castiglione managed to write a work which was in many ways urbane, universal, and not limited to a particular epoch or region. In effect, he managed to build a bridge between the world of humanism and the world of courtly intrigue, finding some meeting point that could render the process of membership in court elites morally and aesthetically satisfying despite the rampant injustices of the rising absolutist monarchies. A series of works in Spain, Poland, Portugal, and France imitated the format of *The Book of the Courtier*, and the themes of honourable behaviour and a studied natural demeanour appeared frequently in the courtesy literature that followed Castiglione's work. By 1625, there were more than 900 courtesy works published in Europe and more than 800 written regarding the ideal Renaissance lady (Kelso 1929).

*Balancing Religious Creed and Personal Conscience:* The Colloquies

The Renaissance humanists attempted to avoid immutable categorizations, perhaps hoping that human awareness would increase through the confirmation of the creative will. Desiderius Erasmus (c. 1466–1536) personified this delicate Renaissance balance between the religious and the secular. Erasmus insisted that the Bible be put in the hands of ordinary laypeople so that they could read the message of the Gospels for themselves. His *Enrichiridion militis Christiani* (*Handbook of the Christian Soldier*) had enormous influence at the time of its third printing in 1515. He affirmed that a reading of the New Testament would provoke an inner change in the reader and guide him to the love of God and humanity. Believing that a 'religious' person was defined by his relationship to the word of God rather than by his allegiance to priests, he did not accord the clergy the right to stand between scriptures and the layperson. He felt that 'the philosophy of Christ' was sufficiently represented in the New Testament; thus, a person who consciously chose to live a moral life could chart his own path according to scripture and without clerical intervention.

He also believed that a culture could transform its practices and norms without falling into disorder. In *Colloquies* (1965), he freely permitted himself to comment on the mores and events of his time, agreeing with some while mercilessly criticizing others. He valued, for example, the ideal of loyalty embedded in the writings of monastics but wondered why celibacy was necessary for a virtuous life. He agreed with the maintenance of religious orders but heaped abuse on the misuse of power by existing orders. It took him forty years to write the *Colloquies*, in the process composing one of the most complete records of life in the Renaissance.

What makes the work an excellent representation of the best the Renaissance humanists had to offer is its unrelenting preoccupation with social reform and its refusal to align itself with any particular class or political group. Humanist intellectuals were increasingly carving out a social position for themselves by claiming the freedom to criticize the nobility as well as the common population. And, certainly, Erasmus made good use of this emerging intellectual freedom – writing with irony and outright ridicule, he facilitated the acceptance of a critical intellectual spirit and the recognition of ordinary individuals as thinking rational beings.

This movement away from categorical aristocratic behavioural standards had a democratizing effect. Yet, it required new specifications of ideal manners for the general population. A rising concern over manners and the corresponding importance accorded to *civility* among strangers marked a radical break with insular courtly conduct standards. Rather than training their readers to be ideal courtiers, the new courtesy writers focused on developing rules of public conduct. Erasmus's ([1530] 1558) *De civilitate morum puerilium* (*On Civility in*

*Boys*) radically departed from the format of medieval courtesy literature. Although the book was written for the son of a nobleman it did not pretend to be exclusively addressed to the nobility. While, like his predecessors, Erasmus criticized the coarseness (*rusticas*) of the peasant, he did not approve of the pretensions of the nobility. He addressed universal good manners as reflected in bodily carriage, gestures, dress, and facial expressions. He not only gave specific instructions on how one was to sit and behave at table, but promoted a civility based on consideration for the sensibilities of others. He paid little attention to social distinction, setting his work apart from the medieval courtesy writings and the works on *civilité* that were to follow in France. A universal standard was being sought, one capable of serving the rising merchant class.

The book was so popular that over thirty printings were made in the six years following its publication. It was translated into English in 1534 and subsequently into German. The French version underwent various translations in 1537, 1559, 1569, and 1673. Erasmus's work led to the Europeanization of the word *civilitate*: *civility* in English, *civilité* in French, *civiltà* in Italian, and *zivilität* in German.

*Manners for All Seasons:* The Galateo

Another book that had a far-reaching effect on European courtesy codes and manners was Giovanni Della Casa's *Il Galateo* ([1558] 1958). Unlike Castiglione, Della Casa had no interest in providing instructions for the formation of a perfect courtier. Even though some passages in the text mention and laud certain nobles, Della Casa states early on in his narrative that the elaborate interaction rituals and posing of those who consider themselves of high station are quite distasteful and to be avoided by truly well-mannered persons.

Rather than being a book on the noble virtues, *Galateo* is a practical guide to what a person must know and practise if he is not to *offend* others. Its most important difference from other courtesy books of the period lies in the rationale used for promoting circumspect manners. Manners are not presented as marks of aristocratic distinction but as practical devices meant to help a person do certain things and desist from doing others in order not to cause discomfort to other individuals. Public nudity, spitting in public, eating with one's mouth open, yawning, going to bed naked, urinating, and defecating in public – these have all taken on connotations of *embarrassment* and are being replaced by practices designed to hide primary physical functions from view. A *publican* civility is in the making.

The chapters of the text are fairly equally divided between the proper handling of physical functions and the rules to be followed when conversing. The author distinguishes between *etiquette*, which he admits can be pretentious and even hurtful to the sensibilities of others, and *civility*, which, when practised without hypocrisy, provides a person with the right frame of mind for remaining sensitive towards the feelings of others: 'It is certain that people who like to carry ceremonial to excess do so from empty-headedness and conceit, like the useless person they are ... But they are incapable of learning important things' (58).

Some of Della Casa's rules regarding bodily functions might appear quite evident to us. Yet, written just after the medieval period, they were necessary admonitions in a society increasingly concerned with concealing and refining the expression of bodily functions. Della Casa's advice to his young reader was given quite plainly:

> It is a repulsive habit to touch certain parts of the body in public, as some people do. (24)
> No polite person will prepare himself for the relief of nature while others are looking on. (24)
> It is bad manners, when you see something to nauseate you by the roadside, as sometimes happens, to turn to your companion and point it out to them. (24)
> Refrain as far as possible from making noises which grate upon the ear, such as grinding or sucking your teeth, making things squeak, or allowing rough stones or metal objects to scrape together and rasp. (25)
> When you have blown your nose, you should not open your handkerchief and inspect it ... such behaviour is nauseating. (26)
> When you are talking with someone, you should not approach him so close as to breathe in his face ... many people dislike the sensation of another's breath even if it is not tainted. (30)
> A man who knows how to behave will take care not to get his fingers so greasy as to dirty his napkin. (29)
> It is not polite to scratch yourself while seated at table. (98)
> It is also bad manners to clean up your teeth with your napkin. (98)

In all of the above examples there is a reaction against practices that must have existed at the time. Otherwise, there would have been no need to comment on them. The author's admonitions seem to indicate a new sense of 'disgust' that requires many practices to be veiled with the cloak of privacy: 'What disgusts the senses also upsets the mind' (92).

Della Casa's advice on the art of conversation is also based on a new aesthetic standard. Conversation is not meant to be a competitive mechanism; good conversation skills involve knowing the golden mean in the length of conversation, the speed at which one should be speaking, and the subjects that should be avoided in order not to bore one's audience. It is, for example, not right to speak of things at dinner that might upset others at table (41), nor is it appropriate to entertain others with boasts or self-flattery, nor to ridicule them in the interests of jest (62). Della Casa considers all vice and all absence of good manners as ugly and degrading. He does not refer to religious predispositions but to a human need for beauty and harmony, something that he considers natural and not dependent on religious doctrine.

The works of Della Casa and Erasmus differed from that of Castiglione in one important respect. While Castiglione was trying to compose a code for the ideal courtier – a personality quite distinct from the rest of the population – Erasmus and Della Casa were espousing conformity and amiability regardless of social station. Their purpose, in some important measure, was to develop a public civility that cut across class boundaries. Della Casa advises his reader: 'You should not set yourself against accepted customs but should discreetly observe them' (33). Elsewhere, he writes: 'You should not be uncouth or awkward but affable and friendly' (38). The other is the centre of attention, and all physical and speech mannerisms are to be directed at making the other remain within his comfort zone. Written a few hundred years before the English books on 'politeness,' *The Galateo* was to become the forerunner of the book on 'tact.' That it eventually became popular in England is no surprise. Della Casa's most important advice – 'Neither say or do anything to show dislike or disparagement of the other person present' (31) – would be heeded by the English conduct book writers (Bryson 1998).

Other conduct books of the Renaissance reveal this emerging trust in personal judgment. The medieval courtly literature had, in great measure, been ideological, seeking to establish political unity in a closed-off feudal hierarchy. There had been a tolerance of coarse manners in the general population that paralleled the categorical nature of medieval emotionalism and the aristocracy's conviction that only the higher sectors of society could learn to appreciate the new courtesy codes. Renaissance conduct books, however, began moving away from such elitist instruction, going to great pains to encourage people to desist from practising certain manners that they had been habituated to practising. What we would take for granted today was at that time a new code of emerging manners and one that would have a considerable effect on subsequent conceptions of ideal personality, embarrassment, and shame.

**Raising the Shame Threshold**

In *The Civilizing Process*, vol. 1, *The History of Manners* ([1939] 1978), Elias attributes to critical humanist thought an increasing intolerance of the coarseness of certain medieval manners as well as an allergy towards the exaggerated pretensions of nobles (70–7). 'Good manners' (that which is considered appropriate behaviour in public *and* private) are suddenly being described with much more specificity than during medieval times. The rules are becoming more numerous and more complex (78). For example, while medieval manners simply specified that a person should not appear greedy at table, the new codes of manners provided specific instructions on how this modesty was to be achieved: how meat should be picked with three fingers instead of the whole hand, how soup should be drunk in such a way as not to make noise, how food that had already touched one's hands should not be put in contact with the food of others.

The citizen was being asked to take distance from his own bodily functions and maintain a demarcation of privacy between himself and others. This notion of privacy could not have existed without a parallel increase in individuation and the development of a sense of 'disgust' towards some of the private functions of others. Civilized behaviour became not only defined by the practice of virtue, but also by the ability to feel and express disgust at the appropriate moments.

Noting the importance accorded to 'civility,' Elias observes that there was an increasing psychological pressure on the individual to notice the effect he was having on others. Through such observation a person learned to compare his own motives/behaviours with those of others and, through such a heightened process of reflective thought and observation, became more sensitive to the emotional reactions of others (78).

Now a question arises: why was such an assiduous examination of manners not made during the feudal period when the nobility very much needed to distinguish itself from the rest of the population? Part of the answer may lie in the fact that the feudal hierarchy was static and there was little mobility, so those at the top were fairly secure in their social positions. With the loosening of feudal ties, individuals of different social origins began having increased contact with one another. A new aristocracy was in formation, and specific codes of conduct were required to ensure that the old aristocracy did not become easily colonized by the behaviour of those moving up into its ranks. An additional explanation can be constructed by examining the use of private and public urban space during the Renaissance. With the waning of feudal estates, many individuals became travelling artisans, coming into more frequent contact with strangers and occupying common cramped quarters in inns and congested towns. It was not unusual for two individuals who had never met to be assigned the same bed in an inn. This new proximity between strangers must have required new rules regarding bodily functions, for what could be tolerated from a neighbour or family member might have proven irritating when practised by a stranger.

Elias states that this heightened sensitivity towards what was considered *distasteful* and *disgusting* had a strong effect on social conformity, for a person had to continuously survey himself to ensure that he was in line with whatever standard was in place in his social group:

> The question of uniform good behaviour becomes increasingly acute, particularly as the changed structure of the new upper class exposes each individual member to an unprecedented extent to the pressures of others and of social control ... Not abruptly but very gradually the code of behaviour becomes stricter and the degree of consideration expected of others becomes greater. The sense of what to do and what not to do in order not to offend or shock others becomes subtler, and in conjunction with the new power relationships the social imperative not to offend others becomes more binding, as compared to the preceding phase. (80)

Elias's general listing of the predominant areas of concern indicates this raising of the threshold of shame:

> Again and again we find the injunction to take one's allotted place and not to touch nose and ears at table. Do not put your elbow on the table, they often say. Show a cheerful countenance. Do not talk too much. There are frequent reminders not to scratch oneself or fall greedily on the food. Nor should one put a piece that one has had in one's mouth back into the communal dish; this, too, is often repeated. Not less frequent is the

instruction to wash one's hands before eating, or not to dip food into the saltcellar. Then it is repeated over and over again: do not clean your teeth with your knife. Do not spit on or over the table. Do not ask for more from a dish that has already been taken away. Do not let yourself go at table is a frequent command. Wipe your lips before you drink. Say nothing disparaging about the meal, nor anything that might irritate others. If you have dropped bread into the wine, drink it up or pour the rest away. Do not clean your teeth with the tablecloth. Do not offer others the remainder of your soup or the bread you have already bitten into. Do not blow your nose too noisily. Do not fall asleep at table. And so on. (65–6)

Thus, the reaction of personal embarrassment and shame required a public standard of behaviour, applied to the other as well as to one's self; disgust with the other was the flip side of self-restraint. Which behaviours were to be considered unacceptable in the other were in large part determined by those behaviours one had learned to accept as prohibitions applied to one's own self. Moreover, the maintenance of restraints on physical functions required considerable mental presence. A well-mannered person had to remain conscious of how his behaviour was affecting the responses of others. It is in this self-awareness that we find the common denominator of all courtesy and civility traditions: in order to consider the feelings and reactions of another towards one's own behaviour one has to be conscious of how one is behaving at any given instant. Such forethought allows an actor to collect information from a given experience and then use it to predict the reactions he may receive during future encounters. Of course, there must be some consistency of reaction if a person is to have a reliable indication of which of his behaviours are welcomed and which are not. And conduct manuals provided such consistency by informing large numbers of the population of changes in the behavioural code.

So, ironically, what Elias calls 'conformity' was facilitated by the new individualism of Renaissance culture. Without the self-awareness that accompanied self-interest, a person would have had a difficult time gauging the effects of his actions on others. The degree to which repression determines civility is a contentious issue, therefore. Surely, the bodily functions were being repressed out of view, but, concurrently, a great deal of human self-awareness, previously limited and censored by monastic ideology, was being given a new voice.

An important change thus occurred in the art and practice of courtesy during the Renaissance. Medieval courtesy codes were intended to decrease violence as well as legitimize a social order dependent on ascribed inequality. While such ideals of humility and loyalty contributed to the socialization of potential military rivals, there concurrently occurred a rationalization of temporal rule, positing the monarch as the earthly representation of divine will. The courtesy ideals of the Renaissance, on the other hand, were of a more secular and less absolutist nature. While belief in a deity was not abandoned, there appeared a new respect for personal agency.

This personalizing of ethics was a bold move in the direction of a modern secular society. It certainly proved inoffensive to the Protestants of the north, who insisted that personal salvation was not guaranteed by God and, consequently, needed to be earned through a continuing ethical relationship with other citizens who were similarly no longer able to count on the easy forgiveness of the Catholic confessional. In the Protestant communities, civility now acquired a religious function: to regulate the civic relationships of men and women so that the community might appear better in the eyes of a demanding God unwilling to provide easy assurances of salvation. While Catholic Italy and France managed to integrate the conservatism of the Church and the secularism of Renaissance civility and its high valuation of style, the severity of Protestant doctrine required a civility ethic particularly suited to the rigours of Protestant doctrine. Scholars and students of cross-cultural communication who minimize this seminal parting of ways between Protestant and Catholic civility rituals, and their underlying meanings and symbols, leave the origins and long-term effects of Catholic and Protestant civility unexplained.

# 4 Shifts in Identity and Awareness: Protestantism and the Enlightenment

> I consider looseness with words no less of a defect than looseness of the bowels.
>
> – John Calvin

### Protestantism and the Contingency of Personal Worth

Thinkers of the Renaissance placed a certain amount of responsibility on the individual for his actions and moral behaviour. Many of the writings of Renaissance thinkers favoured a personal morality that was not dependent on religious edict. This was an important transformation in worldview and it facilitated the massive cultural changes that occurred as a result of the Protestant Reformation and then the Enlightenment. Both historical developments had the effect of weakening the religious foundations of courtesy and transforming it into a practice of responsible secular citizenship. Our understanding of these changes is important if we are to appreciate how and why the French monarchy, the English monarchy, and the American republic came to differ so much from one another so as to require different civility practices.

The seeds of the Protestant movement were sown during the Renaissance, when the Roman Catholic Church lost a lot of its credibility (Baron 1966). Of the 300 bishops in Italy, the majority were nobles possessing no formal ecclesiastical training and had acquired their titles by paying a fee to the Church or to someone of influence. Most secular priests had no formal training in the priesthood and some begging friars had taken to misusing Church dogma to extort money from the poor. The churches of Italy had also become quite different from the solemn cathedrals of the north. Many had become gathering places for merchants. The painter Della Francesca captured this unlikely meeting of commerce and worship in his painting *Flagellation*, a scene showing merchants transacting business, seemingly unconcerned with an image of Christ's crucifixion placed prominently behind them.

Reaction against the corruption of the Catholic Church came from Italian as well as northern quarters. Writers began heaping abuse on nuns and monks, denigrating them as fornicators, liars, cheats, and drunkards. Although monastics had always been respected for their self-restraint and humility, the clerics of the Renaissance lost the trust of their congregations by becoming seduced by the new wealth. So tarnished became the image of the Church that the historian Francesco Guicciardini ([1528–30] [1857] 1965) wrote a fearless indictment of its lax morals:

> I know of no one who loathes the ambition, the avarice, and the sensuality of the clergy more than I – both because each of these vices is hateful in itself and because each and all are hardly suited to those who profess to live a life dependent upon God. Furthermore, they are such contradictory vices that they cannot coexist in a subject unless he be very unusual indeed. (48)

Guicciardini was against all forms of theological and political patriotism and might have sided with Martin Luther had he not been politically indebted to two popes.

Social or religious movements do not appear until established ideology has lost some credibility. Thus, although Protestantism appeared in the north, far from the centres of influence of the Roman Catholic Church, the history of Christianity might have been altogether different if the clerics of the Church had managed to maintain the ethical standards of the early monastics. It might have been more difficult for reformers like Martin Luther and John Calvin to argue for direct communication between man and God had the existing intervention of the clerics been more blameless.

Whether the Reformation was motivated by a desire for theological purity, or the desire to further facilitate mercantilism and make wealth acquisition a religiously viable end, the troubled state of the Roman Catholic Church facilitated the arrival of a new religious doctrine that added to existing restraints by demanding increased responsibility on the part of the individual towards the management of his religious faith. Securing the approval of others through a careful management of one's behaviour (and its dramaturgical possibilities) was no longer sufficient. The new Protestants also had to secure their own approval and the approval of God as best as they could imagine it in a very contingent theological paradigm. This had a profound influence on civility codes and rituals.

There is a substantial connection between the social and religious philosophy of an epoch, its political, economic, and moral conditions, and the manner in which individuals treat one another. Belief or disbelief in man's accountability to a supernatural force plays an important role in the formation of courtesy practices and standards. Citizens of a community, in which most people strongly believe that the world is created by a living God who holds individuals accountable for their actions, exhibit a double-edged deference towards one another: their treatment of one another is based on a recognition of their personal worth *as well as* a personification of their placement within a divine system managed by an active supreme being. Relations within such theological societies could be said to be *doubly deferential* or *triune*. The 'other' is not only a fellow citizen but also a spiritual sister or brother (a 'thou') who acts as a reminder of one's religious identity and duties. Members of a community are, therefore, in a relationship of mutual witnessing and considerable mutual surveillance for they feel themselves to be in the presence of a third all-seeing supernatural being.

The Protestant Reformation had a seminal influence on human relations and civility practices because it placed considerable spiritual responsibility on the individual. The removal of the Catholic confessional and the priest's power to speak to God on behalf of a person created a community in which citizens had to take over the ministerial functions previously reserved for the clergy.

This assumption of personal responsibility undoubtedly made for less artifice and a more grave interactive style. Protestantism insisted on deep self-reflection on the matter of behaviour and salvation. It, therefore, favoured 'sincerity' of thought and feeling. This movement away from the *performance* aspect of courtesy and towards the sincerity and authenticity of personally managed moral behaviour created a certain amount of resistance and criticism towards books such as Castiglione's *Il Corteganio* (Trilling 1971). Some Protestant works even ridiculed the medieval courtesy books (Starkey 1982:232–9). It is difficult to gauge how much of this resistance was connected to the waning of the ideal of courtliness and its implied aesthetics and how much of it was a defensive reaction to the invasion of Italian style and language in northern Europe. On the whole, however, those nations that were progressing towards absolute monarchies, such as Russia and France, continued to consider style and etiquette vital indicators of personal worth.

Unarguably, Protestantism had a new and important long-term influence on standing conceptions of propriety and impropriety. The Catholic Church had used the Augustinian dualistic conception of life to argue that the secular world was unreliable and that only devotion to the Church and its rituals could act as an effective insurance policy against the wiles of the devil. Man had been stuck between two formidable forces that were at odds: Good and Evil. When Martin Luther reacted against the Church's abuse of power, he realized that the central question that needed to be answered was the question of man's 'justification' in the eyes of God. Was God's gift of grace given a priori due to God's love of mankind, or was it to be earned on a case-by-case basis? By extension, had Christ died to set in motion an absolution of the sins of all Christians – an absolution that became effective upon the demonstration of total faith – or had Christ simply set an example that now needed to be replicated within an active and self-directed journey towards salvation? How was a sinner to earn God's favour without the confessional and the availability of absolutions and prayers administrated by priests who were supposedly capable of speaking to God on man's behalf? These were not trifling questions for a society that was passionately (and anxiously) obsessed with discovering and understanding God's purpose for mankind. This intense questioning of self would have an important effect on the reformation of social mores and citizenship ideals for it put tremendous pressure on the individual to map out a personal life that would be in accord with God's wishes.

It would be an understatement to say that the Protestant ideal was anything less than a strict mission entrusted to each member of the faith. John Calvin, who was far stricter than Martin Luther, denied the idea that salvation was a 'reward.' Since God stood outside humankind, God's decisions regarding human fate could not be analysed by human means nor tied to human covenants. Calvin ([Latin: 1536, French: 1541] 2001) found it ridiculous that a person would count on salvation simply because he had asked for it and been reassured by a cleric that it would be his. A person's decision to be faithful to God did not automatically put God in a contractual obligation to dispense salvation. God himself willed the fate of those He intended to save as well as those He meant to damn. If He chose to redeem a sinner or damn a righteous man it was a decision that was beyond human understanding, to be accepted as divine will. Such acceptance was the ultimate test of faith. In the absence of guarantees of salvation, man had to map out a pious and sincere life for himself. No ecclesiastical intermediaries could speak on his behalf, not for any price. Man was the sole arbiter of his relationship with God and, consequently, fully responsible for the outcome of his life.

Thus, according to Protestant doctrine, individuals could not possess foreknowledge of that for which they were predestined; all they could do was to perform at their best in order to increase their chances of salvation. It is hard to tell which came first, the desire for prosperity and a consequent break with Catholic ideology or the Protestant ascetic convictions which unintentionally (or intentionally) facilitated progress in the material world. At the outset, the main effect of Protestantism's removal of absolutions and indulgences was the rise of a strong *introspective individualism*, at times hopeful and at other times mired in morbid self-blame.

Calvin's theology also reunited God with the world. Although God was located outside the world, He remained its creator. So, accepting God was also an act of worldly acceptance. There was no longer any need for the monastic denigration of secular life. Protestants rejected the medieval Augustinian distinction between the 'sacred' and the 'secular,' believing, instead, that a person actually honoured God's creation by committing himself to good worldly works. Every person was, therefore, a potential member of God's priesthood. And God did not evaluate individuals by the grandeur of their work but by the sincerity of their motives. Godliness could be experienced in the most mundane tasks provided they were performed with God in mind and heart.

This communally grounded theology had a twofold effect. It liberated individuals to consider every secular activity that did not contravene Biblical prohibitions as potentially worthy of God's approval. It also placed secular activity under the scrutiny of religious ethics. In this manner, Protestantism imbued temporal life with a new mystic meaning. Calvin had declared that every person occupied a 'calling' chosen for him by God. Human dissatisfaction resulted from a person's non-acceptance of that which God wished him to do and where He wished him to be socially. If God assigned all men's callings, then no one calling could be considered superior to the next. This promoted a type of social equality that required courtesy practices based on a broad standard of tolerance, applicable to the interactions of individuals of varying social ranks. The courtesy a person gave and received was no longer a reflection of inherited privilege but of actual worldly involvement. And it could not be determined by the aesthetics of style. More important than mannerisms was the *character* of a person and the severity/sincerity of his religious intentions and practices. Calvin even warned against the superficiality of conversational competence when he stated: 'I consider looseness with words no less of a defect than looseness of the bowels.'

Emotional restraint had already been increasing during the Renaissance. The motive for this increase was the need to control aggression and also to provide courtiers, merchants, and republican politicians with the opportunity of observing the behaviour of their adversaries without revealing their own positions. This guardedness became transformed into an emotional reserve that went hand in hand with rational calculation. The Protestant movement furthered such restraint of emotions through its insistence on a serious and methodical relationship between personal conscience and divine guidance. There was a self-absorption that accompanied this continual search for the proper ways of seeking God's favour. This affected personal as well as communal relationships. A certain 'serious' (or perhaps 'dignified') Puritanism became embedded in even the most intimate personal relationships. Any comparison of Catholic and Protestant communities needs to take this transformation into account, for the varying emotional thresholds of Protestant and Catholic cultures and ideologies have important effects on the degree to which artifice and the aggrandizement of self and others become part of habitual civility rituals. Wit, in the Protestant sense, becomes the 'irony' of self-critique, a modified and tamer version of medieval 'moral anger.'

Protestant insistence on personal accountability also encouraged believers to think critically of one another. This 'mutual surveillance' cannot be sufficiently stressed, for it achieves its most radical form in the Puritan teachings in England and America.

Undoubtedly, the self-reflection of the Protestant doctrine facilitated the work of the Enlightenment thinkers, even though the Enlightenment occurred much later. In the interim, what did increase were the restraints put on the body and the mind, for Calvinistic Protestantism did not take kindly to sloth or the enjoyment of pleasure for its own sake. Whereas the Renaissance had attempted to free the human body from the domination of medieval theology, Protestantism delivered it back into servility, this time in the service of communal salvation. Although Calvin had asked in all irony, 'Is it faith to understand nothing, and merely submit your convictions implicitly to the Church?' he also warned that 'God preordained, for his own glory and the display of His attributes of mercy and justice, a part of the human race, without any merit of their own, to eternal salvation, and another part, in just punishment of their sin, to eternal damnation.' Delivered from the monastics of Catholicism, the Protestant was now required to be his own monk. It should not surprise us that a certain 'bodily hesitancy' (and even mistrust) entered into social relations and the relationship between a person and his physical body wherein lay his desires.

So, what has been termed 'Protestant guilt' in the popular literature might be better referred to as 'emotional hesitancy,' almost bordering on mistrust. After all, how could an individual fully trust his contemporaries when he remained painfully aware that any one of them could be damned without his being aware of it?

**The Enlightenment and the Civility of Tolerance**

Ernst Cassirer (1955) has aptly defined the project of the Enlightenment as a concentrated effort to formulate 'a new conception of the human being and (trace) its various meanings, its application and modifications' (228). The thinkers of the Enlightenment moved away from the study of divinity as a reality that stood outside man and concentrated instead on a study of humankind itself and the manner in which individuals used their faculties to perceive and deal with internal as well as external reality.

This bold project had a major influence on the morality and courtesy practices of the eighteenth, nineteenth, and twentieth centuries. The stage was set for a quantum shift from courtesy as a Christian virtue to civility as a social practice open to the vicissitudes of time and place. Certainly, the thinkers of the Enlightenment had a very important influence on events such as the French Revolution and the rise of an industrial state.

What was specifically (and importantly) at stake during the Enlightenment was a series of issues regarding mankind itself: the nature of consciousness, the reliability of thought, the manner in which humans arrived at social consensus, and the continuing and troubling question of good and evil. Underlying these issues was a desire on the part of the emerging philosophers and scientists to separate religion from the sphere of knowledge and relegate spirituality to the sphere of opinion and ideology. It was also the first formal use of the idea of *relativity* in the struggle against theological and political absolutism.

The philosophers of the seventeenth century who posited 'reason' as a sine qua non of human perception were putting forward a radical concept. Through the use of reason, mankind could find a measure of independence because reason gave a person the right to be critical and re-examine dogma. Through his 'method' (*la méthode*), René Descartes sought to understand the world by first finding what, if anything, in his own perceptions of reality was reliable. In an attempt to see if everything could be doubted, he set to questioning everything outside his own mind. Using this process of elimination, he arrived at the idea that the only thing of which he could be certain was the faculty he was using to do his doubting: his mind and its ability to reason. 'I think therefore I am,' *Cogito, ergo sum*, became the Cartesian dictum which separated the mind from the body and established a dualistic conception of the human being. What distinguished man was his ability to question blind obedience to 'faith' through the practice of reason. It was a new and impressive affirmation of individuation.

Determined to preserve the delineating line between person and environment, Descartes astutely distinguished between 'sense experience' and 'reason,' and argued that 'clarity' could keep the two realms from being mistaken for each other. What France acquired from Descartes (and abided loyally by it) was an insistence on the need for precision (*la précision*). On this matter of clarity and precision, Descartes (cited in Collinson, 1987) specified:

> I term that 'clear' that which is present and apparent to an attentive mind, in the same way that we see objects clearly when, being present in the regarding eye, they operate upon it with sufficient strength. But the distinct is that which is so precise and different from all other objects that contains nothing within itself but what is clear. (59)

John Locke ([1690] 1979) also addressed the subject of reality and perception. In *An Essay Concerning Human Understanding* Locke separated perceptions that came from the senses from those that were the actual symbolic representations of the immutable realities of the object world. A distinction was made between inner (person) and outer (social). By making this distinction Locke introduced a type of scepticism that could be used to question not only deductive reason but all perceptions. Locke's view of human knowledge implied that diversity (and contradiction) had to be accepted because a common reality could appear different to various viewers. In *A Letter Concerning Toleration* ([1689] 1983), appropriately published in the year of the signing of the English Bill of Rights, Locke urged that the essence of religious thought be retained minus the superstitions, intolerance, and dogma that had followed in the wake of the institutionalizing of religion. Locke affirmed that, in a climate of tolerance, individuals would respect the rights of others in the hope that those same others would respect their own rights through acts of reciprocity. Like Hobbes, Locke was searching for a 'civic personality' that could be set apart from the brutal realities of nature, a civility grounded in rationality. *The origins of English civility are deeply rooted in Locke's philosophy of human relations and human rights.* Good relations occur under the protection of desire restraint; human reason and mutual caretaking imply restraint of immediate self-centred pleasure-seeking in return for mutual harmony.

Locke also had considerable influence on French intellectuals; those parts of his philosophy that accepted scepticism as a healthy part of the reasoning process were very much of interest to members of the French intelligentsia who were struggling against the domination of existing institutions. Locke himself was considerably influenced by Montesquieu's criticisms of French society. Like Montesquieu, he believed that tolerance excluded all despotism. Many of the French who travelled to England and observed its political institutions came to admire Locke's ideas because they witnessed in limited practice some of the liberties of which he spoke. Voltaire himself was struck by the difference in life in England and France. England had religious tolerance, a relative freedom of press, a fairer taxation system that required nobles and clerics to pay taxes, a parliamentary system consisting of two houses, and a justice system that required warrants for arrests and a guarantee of early trials by jury. In his *Philosophical Letters on the English*, Voltaire ([1735] 1999) delivered a scathing criticism of the way affairs were conducted in France. No sentence of his better summarizes his opinion of the absolutist French government and the role of the clerics in the absolutist state than his cryptic cry: *'Crush the infamous thing!'* Although Voltaire crossed the boundaries of reason by indiscriminately extending his categorical criticism of Christianity to Judaism, his ultimate project was the encouragement of a monarchy that respected constitutional rights, a monarchy not very different from the one in England.

What particularly impressed Voltaire was Locke's deft negation of aristocratic notions of virtue. The exercise of virtue had been considered a means of censoring the selfish impulses of man in favour of a common good. Virtue was considered a restraint imposed on the animal nature of the human being. The divine right of kings had been rationalized by a mandate to exercise force in the interests of common survival. It was based on the Hobbesian conviction that men would not choose pro-social behaviours without strong state intervention. Locke, on the other hand, proposed that the best way to prevent self-interest from destroying social order was to accept it and let it be its own regulator. Reason would act as a natural restraining mechanism and make men aware of the consequences of their actions. Enlightened toleration of human nature, combined with the use of reason, would lead to self-regulation and social order, since self-interest would be tempered by a reasonable calculation of the consequences of outright brutal selfishness. In Locke's universe, the search for human rights becomes *a contract between all who require rights. The motive for preserving the rights of others, therefore, becomes an extension of one's own interest in preserving one's own rights.* Work becomes the great regulator of human passions. Through work, men learn to unite with one another to serve their own interests and use their reasoning powers to extract from nature those benefits that might otherwise be denied them if they remained solitary and without civil ties.

David Hume, writing in Scotland, further developed Locke's recognition of contingency by suggesting that it is only our observation of 'sufficient repetitions' that allows us to produce 'habitual' explanations for reality. A different set of repetitions, if sustained long enough, could completely alter understanding of objective reality. This was tantamount to negating the existence of an absolute external reality that could reliably be used for the formation of a code of morality based on an essential human nature. For Hume, much of reality perception was contingent on the subjective experience of the observer. New meanings could be created, thereby transforming former tendencies. It is ironic that postmodernists who critique the Enlightenment miss the fact that Hume may have been the first relativist. By grounding human studies in epistemological terms, he managed to negate the necessity for metaphysical explanations. In *A Treatise on Human Nature* ([1739] 1949) he stated that

> the common distinction betwixst the *moral* and *physical necessity* is without foundation. Our perceptions of our own ideas proceed in the exact same way we arrive at our perceptions of the external world – they follow the same rule of 'repetition' and 'habituated observation.' (171)

In Hume's non-deistic model, sympathy became a regulating mechanism and assured a certain measure of protection against outright injustice. He distinguished two types of moral phenomena: sympathy involving the taking on of the feelings of another (in itself a subjective and passionate act) and, on a more neutral level, 'moral judgments' (based on a relatively detached evaluation of the moral value of various objects in comparison with one another according to which was higher and lower) (Collinson 1987:83–5). This notion of a 'higher' moral judgment approximated some of the ideas developed by Kant. It also established a link between the virtues of politeness and the Enlightenment ideal of justice; to address another with politeness became a recognition of his worth and his rights to 'due process' (Kingwell 1993:363–87). This coupling of civility and civilizational worth (or superiority) was a subtext of historical and evolutionary social theory during the eighteenth and nineteenth centuries (Pagden 1988:33–45).

Hume was pointing to the viability of free choice. He questioned how something that was predetermined, such as natural order, could ever offer choice. Was choice not an essential aspect of freedom? And did freedom not prohibit predetermination? And what of divine law or natural law? Could they exist in the face of the contingent nature of human perception? Was a 'law' not simply a repeated reality that had become sufficiently observed to be accepted as a given? Hume facilitated acceptance of change by questioning the immutability of traditional customary behaviour. And, in explaining the relativity of perception, he further legitimized individualism, for if a reality could be perceived from different points of view then the holders of those points of view could possess considerably different characters yet deserve equal rights. Yet, this individualism, according to Hume, needed to be anchored in 'moral sentiments' that assured mutual recognition, liberty, and respect (Finlay 2004:369–91).

Echoing Locke, Anthony Shaftsbury ([1714] 1964) explained that self-interest was the basis of social structure; yet, he qualified this statement by asserting that the beneficial emotional effects of group association tempered the selfish impulse (3: 146). This belief in the ultimate viability of the pragmatics of human kindness was eventually reflected in English courtesy practices and much of the English literature of 'rights' denouncing inequality and suffering (Wollstonecraft [1790] 1970, Paine [1792] 1969, Godwin [1793] 1946).

This belief in the positive power of human sentiment seemed to suit the French *philosophes*, who were similarly interested in formulating a just civic society free from tyranny. Seeking an end to the ecclesiastical and monarchical domination of France, they were impressed with Locke's writings; French elite circles began adopting his empirical philosophy alongside Descartes's *rationalism*. So while the English and Scottish thinkers could manage by discussing how the individual and the social could be made to be more mutually supportive within the English political system, the French *philosophes* had to address the individual directly, in a bid to free him from France's *ancien régime*. This difference is crucial to our understanding of English *agreeability* and French *self-assertion*.

Jean-Jacques Rousseau's influence on the development of a French interactive style should not be underestimated. While the French have always confirmed Descartes's love of 'lucidity' and 'specificity' in their conversational style, they have been considerably influenced by Rousseau's call to emotional purity. Rousseau railed against the seventeenth-century belief in reason as a panacea for all social ills. Although he agreed with Locke's understanding of the primacy of sentiments, he remained unconvinced that reason itself would lead to a viable social order. In his *First Discourse, Discourses on the Sciences and Art* ([1750] 1964) Rousseau stood against all learning manifested in his time. He considered progress itself degenerative. He argued that since sites of knowledge were placed within a corrupt society, they could do little else but further the production of a corrupted cultural product. He held little hope that an unplanned society would produce a moral individual.

For Rousseau, the major task confronting humanity was to manage and control the individual's need for approval in a social setting. This was easier said than done: due to their search for approval and belonging, people developed an *amour propre* (self-love) that prevented them from distinguishing the difference between the way they actually were and the way they appeared to others. A reliable knowledge of self was further complicated in situations where the 'true consciousness' of the individual was contaminated by social obligations and the internalization of rules. While membership in a society meant the learning of inter-relatedness with others, it unfortunately also required the learning of tactics with which to deal with others: cunning, deceit, flattery, ostentation, and self-serving displays of talent and knowledge – precisely those qualities that prevented the creation of an equitable civil society.

Rousseau's uncompromising social critique identified *amour propre* as the origin of social inequality and discord. It was a psychological process that made a person feel that he had a right above others and a worth that was deserving of special recognition:

> He who in the civil order wants to preserve the primacy of the sentiments of nature does not know what he wants. Always in contradiction with himself, always floating between his inclinations and his duties, he will never be either man or citizen ... He will be one of these men of our days: a Frenchman, an Englishman, a *bourgeois*. ([1761] 1979:40)

Rousseau searched for a way out of this dilemma. In the *Social Contract* ([1762] 1968) he presented the *citizen* (as opposed to the person) as the highest ideal. He affirmed that the free and equal will of all citizens could, in an ideal situation, come together to form the *volonté général* (the general will). Anything else was simply an abuse of both person and citizen.

France was predisposed to sympathize with Rousseau's complaints that the 'pure person' had been subjugated by a social order built on inequity, privilege, narcissism, and violence. Voyages to the New World had already produced a body of literature and letters about the supposed 'purity' and 'innocence' of the Indians who lived in nature, undisturbed by the complexities and conflicts of European society. Secondary popular writers had also, in the wake of the rationalist onslaught of the seventeenth century, unabashedly argued in favour of the *wisdom of the heart*. There were mounting calls for *la sensibilité* (sensibility). Fairy tales, romances that featured tragic (and sometimes comic and pathetic) endings, and tales of adventure were sold in great quantities (Artz 1968). The fifty years preceding the French Revolution were emotionally troubling years for the French – famine, economic disasters, currency devaluation, and failed continental initiatives had left people in a sour mood. Literature provided a welcome relief. There was a flowering of confessional works and letters addressed to readers warning them of the evils of extreme rationality; in many of these tracts the simple life of the non-intellectual was held up as an ideal.

This seemingly paradoxical respect for the rational and the emotional must be taken into account in any study of French culture. In France, Cartesianism and sentimentalism found a way of co-existing. This had a considerable effect on French civility practices.

A nation enraged over centuries of inequity welcomed Descartes's individualism, Rousseau's communalism, and a popular literature favouring sentiments. This mixture of clarity, passion, and iconoclasm is found in the work of Voltaire, who, although a monarchist, fearlessly went up against the absolutist French state. His literary masterpiece *Candide* ([1758] 1992) ridiculed the ideas of Leibnitz, who had suggested that 'this was the best of all possible worlds.' Voltaire's work was a brutal criticism of the notion that all was for the best. Maddened by the callousness and paralysis of such unjustified optimism, Voltaire placed a series of characters in the most horrifying tragedies, all in the name of optimism. In effect, the work laughed in the face of clerics and aristocrats who seemed to remain unconcerned with the seething dissatisfaction of the population. Voltaire was attacking many homilies of the French system of privilege: its unbridled fantasies of expansion, its unjustified optimism, and its fascination with the superstition of divine rights.

A major effect of the ideals of the Enlightenment was a further heightening of personal awareness. Descartes's experiments in thought had necessitated a delay between thought and its observation. The statement 'I think therefore I am' was made plausible by the fact that the thinker was able to observe himself thinking. This self-awareness was also facilitated by changes in the education system; it now included rigorous studies of logic in the standard curriculum. This effect of *dédoublement* gradually permeated various social ranks as individuals became more aware of the manner in which they reasoned. This self-observation reached its summit in court society, where courtiers had to continually observe the actions and motivations of their adversaries and allies.

The sudden mood swings of the medieval age, the unbending mould of medieval theological dogma, and the celebratory narcissism of the Italian Renaissance were, therefore, modified through Protestant and Enlightenment self-reflection. By initiating a discussion regarding human nature and a politics based on 'rights' rather than canon law, the Enlightenment created the conditions necessary for the establishment of the modern liberal state. So, what we see occurring as we pass from the Middle Ages to the Renaissance and then into the Protestant Reformation and the Enlightenment is the placement of an ever-increasing responsibility on the individual to harmonize religiosity, adherence to civil contracts, and the exercise of personal conscience in social interactions, not a small feat for a continent with a violent history.

# 5 French Court Society, the French Revolution, and the Paradoxes of French Civility

*Celui qui a donné des rois aux hommes a voulu qu'on les respectât comme ses lieutenants, se réservant à lui seul le droit d'examiner leur conduite. Le volonté de Dieu est que quiconque est né sujet obéisse sans discernement.*

(He who has given kings to men intended them to be respected as his lieutenants, reserving only unto Himself the right to examine their conduct. The will of God is that whomever is born as a subject obey without discernment.)

– Louis XIV

## The Impasse between Divine Rights and Liberty

Although the Italians played a seminal role in the development of the Western civility tradition, it was during the reign of the French absolutist monarchs that civil etiquette became substantially associated with the preservation of privilege. The fact that egalitarian Protestantism was a minority movement in France allowed the French monarchs to adhere to an etiquette philosophy based on a social philosophy of distinction and superiority. In this chapter we would like to review the transition from etiquette to civility in France and discuss important aspects of French civil society prior to the twentieth century. This knowledge is crucial to our understanding of the important role played by court society in the development of Western civility as well as to our understanding of how England and America developed governance and civility traditions that substantially differed from the ones in France. We discuss these other two nations in chapters 6 and 7.

Indeed, democracy has come a long way since Louis XIV's chilling demand for absolute loyalty (quoted above). That his successor Louis XV made similar pronouncements, and that Louis XVI continued to favour divine aristocratic privilege, revealed the French monarchy's disconnection from the changes in human awareness that had resulted during the Renaissance, the Protestant Reformation, and the Enlightenment. It also revealed a particularly French characteristic of resisting those changes adopted by Anglo-Germanic countries. The forces that came together to produce the French Revolution were not only political and economic, but also intellectual and psychological.

As Norbert Elias has convincingly argued in *Court Society* ([1969] 1983), a growing body of literature promoting the logical imperatives of reason had altered the awareness of many literate individuals and placed their minds above blind obedience. The absolutist French state, however, was unable to change its core practices and adapt to France's need for institutions that favoured and facilitated free trade. Put simply, the *ancien régime* had outdated itself. The government's mounting national debt (a partial consequence of its support of the American Revolution), continuing censorship of the press, administrative ineptitude, and stultifying social inequalities robbed the monarchy of its credibility, despite its numerous attempts to reach compromises with dissatisfied factions. Although the bourgeoisie, nobility, and working class may have had incompatible desires and goals, they all had to face the fact that the French monarchy's claims to infallibility could no longer be justified on moral, political, or economic grounds. All three groups understood that when the monarch spoke of *le peuple* (the people) he was mainly referring to those aristocrats and functionaries who supported the monarchy and for whom were reserved the principal benefits of state.

Louis XIV's categorical warning (quoted above) was not only addressed to the general population, but, equally, to dissenting nobles. The declaration made by Louis XV was equally absolute:

> To attempt to establish such pernicious innovations as principles is to affront the magistrature, to betray its interests and to ignore the true, fundamental laws of the state, as if it were permissible to disregard the fact that in my person alone lies the sovereign power whose very nature is the spirit of counsel, justice and reason ... Legislative power is mine alone, without subordination or division ... Public order in its entirety emanates from me. I am its supreme guardian. My people are one with me, and the rights and interests of the nation – which some dare to make into a body

separate from the monarch – are of necessity united with my own and rest entirely in my hands. (Furet 1988:5–6)

When the aristocratic elites belatedly spoke in favour of the interests of the common population they spoke of it as some outside, untouchable periphery tucked safely away from the centre of power and social influence. The aristocracy had not gone through the transformation needed for it to acquire a new identity and credibility with the population. By the time the powder keg of the French Revolution exploded, every effort had been made to break down the social barricades erected by the aristocracy; few of the efforts had succeeded. Even compromise on the part of all parties might not have sufficed. France was in sore need of social and economic changes and it required new systems of political administration capable of accommodating such changes.

So, it was not dissatisfaction with *ancien régime* feudalism as such that triggered the revolution but the fact that the regime had been transformed into a lax form of its original version. In the old feudal system, the lord of an estate had considerable judicial and administrative rights over the estate and was, consequently, responsible for providing protection to those placed in his care. In a manner of speaking, he earned his keep. But this system of allegiance had been transformed when lands had been divided into small parcels and then further sectioned through inheritance. Sons of working serfs now owned plots that were too small to produce enough for their own families as well as for the lords who continued to exact payments over and above the taxes levied by the state. Moreover, the lord's own function had changed. He had lost much of his judicial authority as a result of the king's expansion of the state's judiciary powers. Many judicial issues were now regulated by court-appointed officials selected from the rising bourgeois sector. The feudal lord had become simply another citizen of the town, even though, out of respect, he was referred to as the 'first citizen.' Certainly, his military functions were for all practical purposes obsolete. The rise of money economies had decreased the power of the nobles by facilitating the king's amalgamation of economic and military power:

> He pays no longer for the services he needs, military, courtly, or administrative, by giving away parts of his property as the hereditary property of his servants ... At most he gives land or salaries for life, and then withdraws them so that the crown possessions are not reduced. (Elias [1939] 1978:221)

Such transformations in the power ratio between the nobility and the monarch created marked social differentiations within the French nobility. The court at Versailles had to accommodate a variety of interests: the *noblesse d'épée* (nobility of the sword), consisting of high nobles who had previously held considerable political influence at court due to the military achievements of their families, but who were now less influential than newcomers possessing astute political sense; the nobility of the robe, composed of newly appointed functionaries to whom were awarded (or sold) a noble title much to the consternation of the old nobility; and, finally, the rural nobility, which, being far from court, was left on the fringes with little or no political influence. The royal court had become the centre of *le monde* (the world). What mattered more than anything else was the social prestige of those who circulated in the corridors of that privileged world. One was either part of *le monde* or excluded from it.

By the seventeenth century, many of the lords had left the countryside out of sheer boredom and the need to secure prestige at the royal court; they returned to the countryside only to exact the rents owed to them or take an occasional rest from the rigours of life at court. Not being part of the daily life of the rural estate and the problems of its workers, they were more exacting and less personable. Alienated peasants began seeing their lords as uncaring predators tolerated by an inept state that lacked the coherence of the feudal order to which they had been habituated.

The bourgeoisie was similarly ill at ease. Although it had made significant gains in wealth and status, it remained cut off from the social privileges reserved for the high nobility. It might have accepted a trade-off between courtly prestige and the power it held in the state bureaucracy had the old nobility not demanded that the king cut back on his appointments of bourgeois functionaries. The continuing resistance of the nobility of the sword demonstrated to the bourgeoisie that it might not be any worse off following a massive political change (Rudé 1972).

The rising critical (and emotional) awareness of the French population also played a major role in the French Revolution. Absolute monarchy no longer seemed reasonable. François Furet (1988) notes the ironic fact that public criticism of the monarchy increased precisely when the state was making significant moves to curtail the feudal system:

> It mattered little that France was the last feudal country in Western Europe, as a result of the very activities of the administrative state, and that

it was also the country where criticism of the state by reason was the most systematic: suddenly the remains of feudalism – for example seigniorial rights, or the last serfs of the kingdom – were perceived as all the more oppressive precisely because they were residual. (16)

Along with the enfeeblement of the monarchy came haggling between aristocrats at court:

The king no longer reigned over them – he obeyed them: in this telescoping of absolute monarchy and aristocracy was forged the overall rejection of what was no longer, in actual fact, either absolute monarchy or aristocracy, but some thing born of the decadence of the two principles and still surviving on their complicity, at the expense of the people. (30)

The combined effect of the above-mentioned factors led to a series of swift developments causing the transformation of the Estates General into a National Assembly. By 1791, the newly formed Assembly had nationalized all Church lands, abolished the feudal system, put an end to censorship, ended the old divisions between provincial and local administrations, instituted legislation holding all citizens equal before the law, and created a strongly centralized government system that has survived to this day.

The French Revolution had a double effect that would play an important role in French modern governance and civil interactions. Having accomplished the political goals of the revolution, it then legitimized human action that remained independent of religious doctrine. If there is an important point of origin to Western secularism – better defined as the 'sovereignty of the people' – it is probably located in two separate events: the day when Martin Luther denied Catholic doctrine and the day when French revolutionaries took over the General Assembly of France and announced the start of a new era not at all dependent on the ideology of divine rights (Wallerstein 1996:56–7).

Elias has repeatedly explained that the rise of the central state played a key role in the limitation of violence. One cannot argue with this conclusion. Anthony Giddens (1985) has similarly described the state as a 'set of institutional forms of governance maintaining an administrative monopoly over a territory with demarcated boundaries (borders), its rule being sanctioned by law and direct control of the means of internal and external violence' (120). This heightened control of opposition and deviance was made possible by increasing 'internal pacification' (312).

By the time Louis XVI was forced to concede that the absolutist monarchy was no longer viable, an extensive state bureaucracy and policing force was fully operational and capable of centralizing information and surveillance in such a way as not only to control ongoing political protest but to anticipate possible future protests and make provision for their repression (Tilly 1986). As Jack Goody has argued in his seminal work on the connection between the development of writing and the organization of strong-state bureaucratic societies (1989), writing was as important to the formation of the central state as was the restraint of violence; it also played a seminal role in the organization and communications needed (i.e., pamphlets, letters) for the French Revolution (Markoff 1986:323–49). Both Elias and Foucault have managed to produce books that are some of the finest explanations of changes in practice over long periods (Spierenburg 2004).

## *Étiquette, Délicatesse,* and the Politics of Refinement

As Jorge Arditi (1988) has explained in *A Genealogy of Manners: Transformations of Social Relations in France and England from the Fourteenth to the Eighteenth Century*, the development of a strict code of manners was a crucial step in the development of a pacified social, political, and economic hierarchy. The aristocratic hierarchy that determined the rules of etiquette and manners was firmly installed in the absolutist court of France. So great was its influence that even the revolutionaries eventually settled on a republican civility standard that incorporated many of the interaction rituals of the aristocracy.

The gradual development of French civility rituals and values needs be understood in context of the social and political world of the French court. The relationship between the monarch and the nobility had changed with the progressive centralization of power. Along with centralization and a broadening bureaucratic surveillance apparatus, the notion of 'public welfare' had become a political weapon used by the monarch to control the power of the old nobility. Louis XIV had understood quite well that the power and status he accorded to his nobles had to be limited if they were to be prevented from uniting and organizing a common front against him. He was acutely aware that his own reign depended on the maintenance of tensions between the various nobles and social classes; outright elimination of a given class might have empowered another class and unleashed a unified force against his own position. By conferring new titles on bourgeois functionaries he succeeded in devaluing the power of members of the old nobility without actually eliminating them. They served their use: while members of the old nobility could no longer be a military threat to the monarch, they could help temper the rising power of the bourgeoisie.

That the nobility of the sword watched this reappropriation of power with dismay and mistrust is understandable. Aristocrats were pursuing the only identity available to them: membership in court society, the highest caste in the land. 'Prestige' was the ultimate good, placed even above wealth. An aristocrat could either seek a place in court or be left with no place at all. He or she had relatively little freedom to 'drop out' and prosper, because existing laws discouraged nobles from engaging in commercial activity. While members of the bourgeoisie also attempted to keep up appearances, they were expected and allowed to exercise a certain frugality and accumulate capital for further investments. Frugality on the part of an aristocrat, however, was condemned as unwillingness to fulfill the obligations of his or her position. *Noblesse oblige* referred not only to the personality traits required of an aristocrat who wished to be distinct from the rest of the population, but also to his or her duty to keep up appearances and support the aristocratic system. So while both groups sought power, the currencies they used for its acquisition were different: the bourgeoisie counted on its capital while the aristocracy traded with its social status (Elias [1969] 1983:111).

Elias explains the predicament of nobles with devalued fortunes who were, nevertheless, forced to keep up an aristocratic front:

> Their income from rent diminishes, but the compulsion to display gives them no honourable way to limit their consumption. They contract more debts, sell more land, their incomes fall further. To increase it by participating in lucrative commercial enterprise is both legally forbidden and personally degrading. It is equally degrading to reduce expenditures on household or display. The competitive pressure for status, prestige and power in society is no less strong than competition for capital and economic power in industrial societies. (73)

Elias astutely observes that this was not a society of conspicuous consumption, a description better suited to bourgeois society, as explained in Thorsten Veblen's (1899) *The Theory of the Leisure Class*, but one of prestige consumption. The value being fetishized was *magnificence*, a derivative of the Renaissance virtue of *magnanimity*. Sociability was a means for exercising power, but in a *grand* way. Max Weber (1922) has also suggested that 'luxury' is a means by which a person can affirm social power (1:1107). And power was obtained through the exercise of judgment in regards to one's own status as well as that of others; a successful aristocrat had to ensure that he did not attract enmity by outshining those of higher rank while making certain that he maintained a style of life that would outshine those of lower rank. A prince lived in a *palais*, a member of the nobility in a *hôtel*, and a member of the bourgeoisie in a *maison*. These specific demarcations in architectural classifications helped maintain differentiation and assignations of power and influence. The result of such gradations of status was a high valuation of *le grandeur* (splendour).

Thus, the courtesy rituals in the absolute court served to communicate to each member of the royal court the place that he occupied, the place he should not aspire to occupy without royal approval, and the place occupied by those who were the courtier's superiors or inferiors. Helping to reinforce the homogeneity of the system was the lingering presence of courtiers who had already lost important privileges and favours but retained the nominal permission to remain in court – they served to remind others of the dire consequences of non-compliance. So it is understandable that the early courtesy manuals preached deference to the will of the monarch. As importantly, it is equally understandable that post-revolutionary French society would continue to value hierarchy, despite proclamations of egalitarianism. Hierarchy was what had given form and splendour to France; the French were not about to abandon *in toto* the grandiose accomplishments of their monarchs. In fact, a series of secondary revolutions and social disturbances brought the French to the realization that some central form and authority would be needed, one strong enough to help them avoid the repetition of the bloody and painful years following the revolution. Violence and civility were, therefore, not in an alternating relationship with each other, but in a continual relationship of tension in which the presence of one affected and transformed and, sometimes, refined the other (Shephard 2006:593–603).

The practice of French court *étiquette*, therefore, was not simply restricted to a code of manners; it also required extensive advice on how to acquire and preserve a career at court. A good courtier who knew his politics insisted on the maintenance of formalities. He accepted the distance that was put between his superiors and himself, for this distance signified that he also had a right to affirm his own superiority over his inferiors. On more than one occasion visiting nobility from France were dismayed at the relative informality of their English and American hosts. *L'étiquette* (the manner in which one related with other courtiers and the king) became a tool for affirming one's own status, recognizing the status of others, and withholding undue recognition from those whose status was lower than one's own or about to become so.

Elias ([1939] 1982) notes that the new court society caused extreme 'sensitivity' because reactions could be judged immediately and taken personally to the detriment of the parties involved (273). A courtier made serious errors in protocol at the risk of his own status. 'Every mistake,' writes Elias, 'every careless step depresses the value of its perpetuator in courtly opinion; it may threaten his whole position at court' (272). The consequence of such careful social manoeuvring was generalized anxiety:

> The affairs, intrigues, conflicts over rank and favor knew no end. Everyone depended on everyone else, and all on the king. Each could harm each. He who rode high today was cast down tomorrow. There was no security. Everyone had to seek alliances with others whose stock was light, avoid unnecessary enmities, fight unavoidable enemies with cold calculation, and scrupulously maintain towards all others a degree of distance befitting their status. (104)

The common denominator in this courtly culture was 'psychological restraint.' Yet this restraint was quite different from the generalized emotional restraint that was increasingly becoming popular in England. It allowed for emotional outbursts, when those outbursts revealed the quick wit of the courtier. The sharpness of a courtier's tongue could be admired, provided he had a perfect command of the subtleties of the French language. That which was kept silent and hidden was as important as that which was expressed and revealed; similarly, that which was expressed with wit, if delivered too directly, could have been considered a faux pas, *une manqué de savoir vivre* (lack of discernment) if it was not aimed from an 'angle' that confirmed the ultimate noble worth of all participants in a conversation. The presence of civility, even within instances of nuanced insult, was a confirmation of class membership as much as it was a consideration for the ultimate dignity of the one who was at the receiving end of the wit.

Elias ([1969] 1983) explains that such emotional restraint and delicacy helped a courtier master three crucial talents:

1. *The art of observing people.* By carefully observing how other courtiers acted towards one another, a courtier was able to tell who was in favour with the king and who was losing his affection. Allegiances could be identified and decisions made regarding which associations were worth pursuing. By observing others in interaction and, just as importantly, by observing the king's behaviour towards specific individuals, the ambitious courtier could chart a useful course through the social minefield of the court.
2. *The art of dealing with people.* The art of diplomacy was born within courts, for it involved the restraining of personal emotions so that the intentions and character of the opponent (or ally) could be better understood and analysed. A courtier had to first understand his own intentions and then those of others. The selection of one form of behaviour over another was at the root of social relations at court. Emotional expression, therefore, took second place to calculated behaviour. It could be no other way because many of the courtiers spent their lives in court, and one wrong emotional outburst or insulting comment could earn a man or a woman an enemy for life.
3. *The discipline required for adhering to rational behaviour.* Outbursts could permanently damage a person's standing in court because they signified weakness and worry. Successful courtiers developed the art of distancing. They distanced themselves from their own emotions in order to understand and master them. And they also distanced themselves emotionally from other courtiers in order not to reveal their own minds. The quality of *délicatesse* refers to this indirect way of approaching one's allies and adversaries. If, for example, a courtier wanted to influence the opinions of someone close to the king, he needed to proceed delicately, speaking of many other non-related subjects that would first gain the trust of his listener. The intrigues that resulted from these behavioural protocols were legion (104–10). Failing to control one's emotions could ruin one's court career for 'true feelings' could give away one's 'trump card' and reveal one's 'weaknesses' (111).

Another important change occurred with the rise of absolute monarchies. Castiglione's courtier, who had managed his courtly relations based on personal grace, was now given different advice by seventeenth-century conduct writers. The courtier of the new absolutist courts was advised to be prudent, affable, and careful not to threaten the prince or monarch with impressive displays of knowledge. Survival in court, rather than self-realization, seemed to be the main theme of these later works (Burke 1995:120). Such restraint may have inhibited the development of a radical social conscience among courtiers, but it did serve to teach courtiers much about human psychology. It trained them to exercise forethought and methodically evaluate a statement or act before proceeding with it. *Sang froid* (cold-bloodedness) became the mark of self-control and political forethought.

The king played a central role in this highly contrived environment. His own use of *l'étiquette* was as necessary as those of his courtiers. With a single glance he could recognize a courtier and increase his or her prestige, or, by slightly turning his head away, signal to all present that the courtier was no longer in his favour. Even the size of the pensions he awarded his courtiers served to announce the level of their importance.

Elias has documented the bedroom rituals of the monarch in order to show how the feelings and conduct of individuals are shaped by the power structures of their society. Under Louis XIV, even the awakening of the king in the morning, an activity which in a non-aristocratic household would have been a fairly straightforward event, was treated as a means for not only seeing to the primary functions of the *levée* but also for establishing orders of rank:

> The king took his robe. The *maitre de la garderobe* pulled his nightshirt by the right sleeve, the first servant of the garderobe by the left; his day shirt was brought by the Lord Chamberlain or by one of the sons if he was present ... Meanwhile, the court was waiting in the great gallery on the garden side, that is, behind the king's bedroom, that ran the whole width of the middle part of the Chateau on the first floor. Such was the *lever of the king*. (84)

On occasion, the arrival of a high-ranking noble in the king's chambers in the morning required that the king's day shirt be first passed to the noble, who would then pass it back to the person normally entrusted with it. The Lord Chamberlain was allowed to pass the king's night shirt to no other than a prince. By the time of the court of Louis XVI these rituals had lost their primary function of getting the king dressed and had taken on the secondary function of determining the assignation of prestige (85). Many courtiers continued to perform the rituals with tongue in cheek, for even they realized that a new society was in the making outside the cloistered court at Versailles.

## From Etiquette to Civility: The Art of Conversing

The co-existence of the old and new nobilities created a considerable crisis in the French aristocratic system (Bitton 1969). Ironically, just as the monarch was facilitating social mobility, the standards of proper conduct were starting to become more rigorous than ever; democratization required new hierarchical standards of interaction to guard against a levelling effect (Elias [1969] 1983:78–116). More than ever before, French conduct standards took note of the Italian ideal of *sprezzatura* – the art of keeping interaction ambiguous enough to complicate mechanical imitation. Feeling their social position threatened from below by the arrival of educated members of the bourgeoisie, aristocrats adopted even more rigorous rules for themselves in a bid to maintain their social superiority (Billacois 1976, Bitton 1969, Stanton, 1980). In the days of Cardinal Richelieu, the primary quality that defined civil behaviour among the aristocracy was courtesy and deference; in theory, any act of insolence could be considered a crime against the state (Ranum 1980). What mattered more than anything else was the preservation of the image and influence of the social circle enclosing the old nobility. And, although the old nobility eventually lost its military might, it maintained a fetishistic obsession with pedigree; aristocrats continued to see themselves as members of a privileged and superior military caste (Schalk 1986).

At the turn of the seventeenth century, conduct books still addressed the nobility as a military institution. They listed the means by which reciprocity could be cultivated for the sake of preserving harmony and prestige. Although the appellation of *le gentilhomme* (gentleman) began appearing in some of the literature, the advice dispensed to the men of the aristocracy continued to be couched in military terms. Most of the advice in these manuals was designed to help a person of noble birth to deal with situations involving conflict between males without perturbing the homogeneous social circle.

In *Le gentilhomme* (1611), Nicolas Pasquier advised that a person of noble birth should gain admittance into the circle reserved for him by associating with the right people. Pasquier reminded his readers that the imperative of preserving the aristocratic social order stood above the personal needs of the courtier. In order to prosper, a courtier simply needed to carefully select the right company and ensure that his own behaviour did not perturb the cohesion of his social circle. There was a self-effacement implicit in this type of social membership, for the authority of the aristocratic circle was the force that bound its members together, much in the style of a military garrison.

This continual deference to the identity of the group was reaffirmed by François La Rochefoucauld ([1665] 1967), who advised in his book *Maximes* that an aristocrat needed to converse in such a way as to never reveal any desire to guide the conversation towards matters of personal interest to himself (193). This *indifférence* was not meant to denote a lack of interest but deference and self-restraint in favour of social cohesion. It was compatible with a social order in which the individual felt assured that his privileged status would be preserved as long as he deferred to the structure, identity, and rituals of his social group.

Within a few years of Pasquier's advice, however, the nobility was being forced to transform its values in order to remain credible. Military courage was no longer sufficient; nor was the readiness to submit to the rules and politics of *l'étiquette* enough indication of personal worth. The aristocracy was coming under considerable criticism and required a renewed definition of what it meant to possess a noble and cultured personality in a court that was increasingly receiving newly titled individuals.

Responding to the mood of the time, Nicolas Faret ([1630] 1970) argued in *L'honnête homme ou l'art de plaire à la cour* that the warrior mentality of the old nobles had become obsolete and distasteful (13–14). He called for the active education of the male in the art of interaction, advising his readers to seek out the company of women, whom Faret considered experts in the rules of polite interaction. A *délicatesse* of spirit permitting the integration of males and females was being idealized and it would play an important role in the various salons that would eventually be established outside the court of Versailles (Lougee 1976).

In the decade following the appearance of Faret's highly popular work, a series of manuals emerged giving conduct advice to women and affirming their increasing influence in French polite society (MacLean 1977). Du Bosc's *L'honnête femme* (1662) and Grenaille's *L'honnête fille* (1639) and *L'honnête veuve* (1640) were popular manuals in women's circles. The new *L'honnête homme* and *L'honnête femme* became a composite of aristocratic and upper bourgeois sensibilities (Mankin 1998:1206–8).

Although Faret's work was meant to advise his readers on how to succeed in court, it introduced many new concepts that would have long-range influences on French civility practices. Faret believed that the exaggerated calculations of courtly behaviour, and the intrigues and quarrels intended to secure advantageous positions at court, should be abandoned in favour of a more worldly civility. He explained that the conversations of men were too often connected to goals and reciprocal arrangements ([1630] 1970:89) and advised would-be courtiers to frequently leave court and seek the company of cultured women capable of instructing them and speaking on their behalf to influential others (90). Faret was reminding young men of the increasingly important political role played by women in French court society; a courtier who wished to remain in their favours and learn the art of gentle conversation did well to recognize and respect them for their intellectual virtues and political acumen (95).

Even though Faret was confirming the obsolescence of the military personality, he continued to stress the importance of maintaining the right alliances with members of court. Recognizing the pressures inherent in relations intended to establish and preserve reputation, he chose *pleasant conversation* as a source of relief for courtiers who were under pressure to continually measure and manage their careers at court. Conversation provided the courtier with a means for pleasing others and receiving their approval (67–70). Faret insisted that the principal task of a good conversationalist was to ensure that no *dissimulation* (dissimilitude or disagreement) took place within a conversation (72). The goal of the ideal conversation was *balanced reciprocity*.

Antoine de Courtin's (1671) *Nouveau traité de la civilité qui se pratique en France* also questioned the long-standing rituals of gesture and court etiquette that had distinguished the aristocracy. By attempting to discuss a new standard of distinction that could define French culture in general, Courtin recognized the new social mobility transforming France in the latter part of the seventeenth century. Rather than give specific advice on how a member of the nobility should handle situations at court, Courtin tried to teach his readers the rudiments of a general *civilité* applicable in all social situations. Recognizing that *l'étiquette*, in and of itself, could not adequately protect polite society from the corruptive influence of non-aristocratic factions capable of mimicking the latest etiquette rituals, he recommended that members of the elite develop a collective talent of *discernement*: the ability to see through the masks of others and determine their characters and motives (12).

On the matter of interaction, he reminded his readers that all conversations occurred between equals, a superior and an inferior, or an inferior and a superior (29). Courtin provided specific examples of the manner in which one was to comport oneself in the presence of individuals of various ranks (85). Unlike Faret, who favoured self-effacement in favour of the preservation of a homogeneous group, Courtin focused on an eclectic presentation of self in a socially mobile culture in which hierarchy was as important as ever (20).

This trend towards an open-ended code of civility was further elaborated in the work of le chevalier Méré ([1668] 1930). Since the court was increasingly frequented by the bourgeoisie, Versailles could no longer be considered the home of the elite. Consequently, Méré advised his readers to evade circles at court and expand their intellectual horizons by seeking civil company in other quarters such as the emerging intellectual salons where there was considerable freedom from the oppressive ceremonials of court (25, 122).

In this departure from the Renaissance conception of the courtier as an in-house adviser to the monarch, there is an abandonment of the standard of virtue as the hallmark of the noble. While *l'honnête homme* can be virtuous, it is altogether possible for an unjust man to be an *honnête homme*. What distinguishes the new civility is the ability to be agreeable and secure the approval of others. Méré presents his ideal type as someone able to excel in the art of agreeability, *les bienséances de la vie* (3:77). Gallantry, a quality associated with courtship between the sexes and behaviour in battle during the days of the old nobility, is no longer sufficient to navigate in high society. Additionally required is a worldliness that transcends the petty intrigues of courtship or war. The concept of *bienséance* (pleasantness) was now used to reintroduce aesthetics into behaviour. What counted as much as (or maybe even more) than what was being said was the manner in which it was being said.

Méré even advises his reader to learn the rudiments of human psychology so that he or she can better understand how to please others and receive their approval. He states that what ultimately counts in the social life of an individual are the feelings evoked in others by his behaviour or bearing (*comportement*). *L'honnête homme* must remain attentive to the reactions of others and use them as mirrors of his own comportment. Personal happiness is now dependent on creating a pleasing atmosphere around oneself through the cultivation of the pleasure of others. Conversations must avoid those political subjects and topics that might cause disagreement or, worse yet, boredom (3:119).

The elevation of pleasant and open-ended conversation to an art form needs be understood in relation to the waning political influence of the nobility. Beleaguered by the bourgeoisie's rising economic and political influence, aristocrats had to find some way of keeping at bay the lingering emptiness of their new lives. The ideal of *vraisemblance* embodied in Méré's work was an attempt to create mutual resemblance through the practice of a conversational ethic that created mutual identification and pleasure. The word itself needs be understood as a derivative of *vrai* (real) and *semblance* (appearance or semblance). *Vraisemblance* means to give the appearance of being real through whatever dramaturgical means are available. While it represents reality, it alters it through harmonizing and refining it according to existing social protocols. It requires forethought and the ability to express oneself as naturally as possible. It is the artifice of non-artifice – a practised naturalness.

It might seem that little had changed from the time that courtiers had to please the king at all costs. Yet, something important did change. The idea of a distinguished bearing of self was no longer limited to courtiers. A universal standard of nobility had been created through the promotion of a *civilité* that surpassed elaborate and oppressive rituals and gestures. As Méré himself observed with irony, the old notion of *l'honnête homme* as someone able to dance the right dances and participate in the right activities at court was now quite ridiculous when put to the test by sophisticated individuals who understood the universal worth of *subtlety* and *understatement* (1:48). It would seem that in the span of a few years, paralleling political, intellectual, and economic developments, the goal-oriented interaction rituals of an old nobility brought up on the rigid rules of political *étiquette* were no longer sufficient for dealing with the new emerging world of elite society. A sudden and concentrated attention was now paid to the art of conversation, the ultimate tool of distinction, for it depended on a mastery of a complicated language rich with nuances and subtle meanings. This important departure from the pragmatism of absolute court etiquette would play an important role in the formation of a modern French mentality mistrustful of bottom-line thinking and partial to style, wit, grandeur, and multi-layered communication.

Thus, the appellations of *l'honnête homme* and *l'honnête femme* cannot be literally translated as 'someone possessed of honesty (or unquestionable authenticity).' Rather, they were used to refer to persons who were able to operate in social situations without seeming affected, artificial, or cumbersome. *L'honnêteté* became synonymous with a practised authenticity that, ironically, required considerable theatrical agility.

All said, the new conduct writers were trying to block out the old military mentality of the warrior nobility as well as the petty greed of the merchants, whose business-focused conversations were now considered too goal-oriented to be termed civil (Huppart 1977). Aware that social classes were mixing, these courtesy writers called for a conversational style resistant to blind imitation. While the ritualized gestures of court etiquette could be imitated, authentic conversation could not. François de Caillères openly warned in 1690 that bourgeois pretensions were contaminating the nobility; he spoke out against the indiscriminate use of titles and homilies and called for a more rigorous civility ethic (1690:139). In *Du bon et du mauvais usage dans les manières de s'exprimer* (Proper usage in the manners of self expression) he wrote that *délicatesse* was the property of a select few and could be recognized through a person's ability to make proper use of the French language. He noted that there were remarkable differences between bourgeois and aristocratic speech. While he accepted the unavoidability of mutual influence, he cautioned that it should be the aristocrats who had the final say on the usage of a given word or phrase (1693:227–9).

This sensitivity to the manner in which things were expressed was intimately connected to the notion of *le bon goût* (good taste). While few of the conduct writers seemed to be able to specify its precise meaning, it was connected to the art of pleasing others while maintaining personal decorum; something in bad taste was that which upset another and perturbed social harmony. The faux pas was that which revealed someone's inability to put into practice the delicate rules of interaction; only a practised wit, expert at self-deprecation, could extricate himself from the ensuing embarrassment of the faux pas. Caillères was proposing that someone who had properly mastered the art of *politesse* and *discernement* would not need to resort to exaggerated expressions. He or she would possess sufficient *savoir vivre* and know how to navigate in social circles using appropriate body language and speech.

Thus, the new conversational style required speakers to demonstrate their noble status by avoiding self-aggrandizement. This deference to the goals of the social group and interactions based on notions of self-confirming equality has been described by Kenneth Burke in his theory of 'persuasion.' Conversations that do not depend on 'extraverbal' advantage provide speakers with the satisfaction of experiencing the actual process of talking (1950:269). This is the ultimate confirmation of privileged status, for leisure time is required for such purposeless, non-competitive talk. The satisfaction is possible because there is an a priori understanding that the speakers are equal to one another and of considerable worth. Thus, *parler comme il faut* (to speak as one should) was not simply a rule of rhetoric but a social contract confirming the exclusivity of the circle in which certain speakers found themselves. Obviously, radical change was antithetical to this social process. What counted was the cultivation and preservation of a civil environment capable of shutting out the more unpleasant aspects of the world.

The definitive advice on the art of conversation came from Madeleine de Scudéry, a prolific novelist and letter writer who specialized in works that included long passages of conversation. In *Conversations sur divers sujets* (1680) she categorically denied that conversations needed to have any practical end at all (1:2). The ultimate function of conversation was to contribute to sociability between equals; she even considered it useless to attempt to have proper conversations with people of a lower social status. Scudéry's novels were filled with voluminous records of conversations that seemed to exist for their own sake. Even so, they had an instructive quality to them; embedded in them were numerous dialogues in which speakers discussed what was to be said or avoided in proper speech (Aronson 1978). Although there was rarely any closure to these dialogues, they served to instruct readers on the delicate art of conveying meanings through subtlety.

Although a door that had been tightly shut between the aristocracy and the bourgeoisie had to be opened, a guardian was posted at that door – that guardian was a complex code of manners and social procedures. The high valuation of subtlety ensured a certain abhorrence towards embarrassing lapses in protocol, and this embarrassment was used as a means for censuring those who might contaminate aristocratic circles with habits and mannerisms brought up from the lower classes. Courtin remarked to his readers that a person of rank would be shocked at some of the habits and manners that were previously considered acceptable; there was a heightened sensitivity towards the faux pas.

Appearing five decades after Courtin's work, LaSalle's *Les règles de la bienséance et de la civilité chrétienne* (The rules of good conduct and Christian civility) ([1729] 1788) furthered the association between the observance of rules of manners and the development of personal refinement and discernment. Elias ([1939] 1978) has astutely observed that later editions of LaSalle's work included less specificity, as if what had been previously recommended had already been adopted and practised by members of high society as well as those arriving in its ranks (95).

As in the Renaissance, many of the manners prescribed were meant to hide from view what had come to be considered 'distasteful.' All the senses were enlisted in the increasing censorship of the physical body. The smell of the body, its nudity, the noises made at table, and the function of sleeping were restrained and controlled by specific prescriptions. For example, while in the sixteenth century sleeping nude was a general habit common to all classes, it was now forbidden to sleep without night clothes; similarly, the main bedroom was turned into a private place not to be shared by those not married to each other. New controls were also imposed on children who, with the rise of the single-family bourgeois household and the demise of the apprentice system, came under the direct socializing influence of their parents.

Elias contends that the development of 'manners' involved a certain 'detachment' from 'instinctual tendencies.' This detachment was achieved through the manipulation of anxiety:

> Society is gradually beginning to suppress the positive pleasure component in certain functions more and more strongly by the arousal of anxiety; or, more exactly, it is rendering this pleasure 'private' and 'secret' (i.e., suppressing it within the individual), while fostering the negatively charged effects – displeasure, revulsion, distaste – as the only feelings customary in society. (142)

Elias's analysis of manners is historically informed. During late medieval times books on manners were advising people not to spit on the table; by the time of the absolute French court, however, they were explaining the exact way a napkin should be placed on the knees – spitting by then was totally out of the question, unless one's mouth was in imminent danger of being scalded by hot food.

## Salon Culture: The New Bastion of Distinction

Manners were not the only social rituals enlisted to separate the elites from the common population. Having lost considerable political and economic influence, aristocrats found a new opportunity for acquiring distinction through the art of conversation, an activity that became assiduously practised in the *ruelles* or salons of the period. By setting themselves off from Versailles and its political rituals, these salons outlasted the reign of Louis XVI and became new centres of French social and political thought.

Two rules helped guide behaviour in these earlier salons: (1) participants were to consider themselves equal to one another. This was a considerable departure from the competitive, hierarchical attitudes at Versailles; (2) rather than competing among themselves, participants were to identify with one another by recognizing their superiority over the general population. This was done by demonstrating utmost refinement (*raffinement*) in conversations and avoiding distasteful confrontations. The hostesses of these salons were charged with moderating conversations so as to ensure that the cohesion of the group remained unthreatened. Needless to say, a good wit was highly valued during salon interactions, for it helped the speaker make controversial points while avoiding outright conflict. The illusion created within the salon was that it was free of hierarchy even though it was located in a hierarchical world. Participants were expected to be refined enough not to need to resort to ostentatious exhibitions of rank and artifice.

These conversation salons were extremely effective means for mythologizing and strengthening the ideal of noble behaviour within a rapidly industrializing world. Erving Goffman has explained that when the purpose of socializing becomes talk for its own sake, a boundary is automatically created between the talkers and the world, providing the conversants with the opportunity of developing ideas and values that increase their sense of identity. Goffman (1967) refers to such social gatherings as 'a little social system with its own boundary-maintaining tendencies ... a little patch of commitment and loyalty with its own heroes and its own villains' (113–14).

Goffman (1961) also assigns a 'euphoric' function to such conversational groups. At some point, the care taken by each member of the group not to threaten the sense of ease of other members creates moments of harmony and euphoria that confirm and solidify the identity of the group and its members (44). So, although they can be open-ended and avoid closure, conversations satisfy due to the fact that they are providing relief from utilitarian and restrictive standards. In fact, a phrase very current in mid-seventeenth-century France was *je ne sais quoi*. It expressed so perfectly the goals of an aristocratic elite determined to find some refined sentiment and superior worth that went beyond words and the bourgeois pragmatism of net monetary worth. *Je ne sais quoi* represented the exquisite feeling that arose when people in conversation suddenly found themselves in inexplicable sympathy with one another and quite pleased with the distinguished social circle that made such communion possible.

Although the salons of the seventeenth century continued to affirm the legitimacy of a monarchy and protected the privilege and status of aristocratic titles, their inclusion of members of the bourgeoisie and writers and philosophers eventually transformed them into centres for emerging radical Enlightenment thought (Lougee 1976). In an important passage in *Revolutionary France*, Furet (1988) provides us with the genesis of France's high valuation of writers and intellectuals. He notes how the prevailing political and social climate of the time helped salons establish a certain standard of *civil interaction* that was capable of crossing class boundaries and political agendas while welcoming free thinkers:

> The nobles of both Versailles and the capital read the same books as the cultured bourgeoisie, discussed Descartes and Newton, wept over the misfortunes of Prévost's *Manon Lescaut*, enjoyed Voltaire's *Lettres philosophiques*, d'Alembert's *Encyclopédie* or Rousseau's *Nouvelle Héloise*. The monarchy, the orders, the guilds, had separated the elites by isolating them in rival strongholds. In contrast, ideas gave them a meeting-point, with special privileged place: the salons, academies, Freemason's lodges, societies, cafés and theatres had woven an enlightened community with combined breeding, wealth and talent, and whose kings were the writers. An unstable and seductive combination of intelligence and rank, wit and snobbery, this world was capable of criticizing everything, including and not least itself; it was unwittingly presiding over a tremendous reshaping of ideas and values. (114)

Many of the intellectual salons were eventually held in the homes of successful bourgeois families. The renowned salons of Mme Geoffrion, Mlle Lespinasse, and Mme Necker were successful because of their relative informality and refreshing candour. Moreover, the absence of a presiding noble at these bourgeois salons gave more status to the intellectuals who attended. This suited many of them who had suffered slights in the salons of the nobility, where they had to defer to the ascribed aristocratic distinction of their host prior to being recognized for their own achievements (Picard 1943).

It was within these bourgeois salons where irritation with the priesthood was most evident. *L'incrédulité* (scepticism) was part and parcel of new intellectual discussions that attempted to create a revitalized French culture not dependent on clerical guidance. It was, in any event, unavoidable that the task of explaining social life was transferred from the clerics to the *philosophes*. This rise in popular philosophy accorded with the accelerating spirit of revolution, the new rational values of the bourgeoisie, and the seething anger of rural people towards their clergy (Magraw 1970:169–83). Popular philosophy could be modified to serve the needs of the moment; religious scripture could not. Popular philosophy gave France a tool for promoting a conversational ethic that was both courteous as well as self-affirming and not at all embarrassed with receiving or offering passionate opinion and criticism. The French continued to favour agreeability, but not at the expense of spontaneous, creative wit. A forced agreeability within a conversation otherwise offering the opportunity of creative disagreement would have defeated the spirit of post-revolutionary intellectual discourse.

**Post-Revolutionary France and the Reconciling of Sentimentality, Reason, and Style**

The French Revolution was a culmination in a series of developments. A majority of its supporters remained aware that they were not only changing a political system that had dominated them but also reaffirming the meaning of being French, a meaning which they felt had been perverted by the absolutism of the French monarchy. From the time of the 'reign of terror' of Robespierre till his demise in July 1794, a host of conduct books emerged specifying ideal civility practices between citizens who were, henceforth, to be considered equal and without differentiating distinctions. The appellation of *sieur, monsieur, and madame* were replaced with *citoyen(ne)* (citizen), and names were limited to their patronym forms without the use of aristocratic prefixes. The respectful '*vous*' form was replaced with the familiar '*tu*,' and the deferential body language and dress of courtiers ridiculed as a perversion of the authentic nature of free citizens.

The '*sans-culottes*' believed, not without cause, that tyrants had used elaborate civility practices, together with their exaggerated mannerisms, to keep their populations docile. Not only did the most radical of the revolutionary groups seek to eliminate the absolutist monarchy; they also found the civility practices that emanated from the court highly suspect (Rouvillois 2006:23–44). A marked change also occurred in clothing. The tight breeches worn by aristocrats were denigrated as pretentious and replaced with straight, loose trousers that represented the emerging work ethic. Women similarly began dressing in full-length, high-necked bodices reminiscent of the fashions favoured by the austere Elizabeth I. By the time Napoleon III took over France there were royal decrees specifying that men were to wear either the English gentleman's business suit, the military uniform, or the riding habit. Over the years the French would increasingly imitate the fashions coming from England, especially those which used elaborate stylistic ornamentation to hide the sexual contours of the woman's body while making for a larger-than-life body (Rubenstein 1995).

There was even a reaction against fancy clothing and make-up. Pellegrin (1989) reports in a detailed study of fashion in post-revolutionary France that one man was arrested in the Alpes-Maritimes region for overdressing on a Sunday, while another, in that same year, was arrested for underdressing on Sunday (73). By 1792 there was a complete reversal in the use of make-up. While make-up had been a vital part of daily grooming during the *ancien régime*, it could now be seen only on the faces of theatre performers. Politeness and all its accoutrements – perfume, luxury, fine speech, wit, irony – were now considered with extreme suspicion as remnants of a corrupt system. Gerlet (1793) even advised, in a conduct book written mainly for the use of children, that saying 'thank you' corrupted the mission of establishing unwavering equality between citizens (60–1).

Even worker–employer relations were put into question. The writer of a widely circulated republican conduct book declared that the use of the word 'domestic' for someone employed in a house was demeaning and should be replaced with the honorific of *homme ou femme de confiance* (a confidant) (Anonyme 1793:39).

Proponents of the 'anti-politesse' movement did not demand an end to civility but sought to define the basics of a civility ethic free from affectation and unjust distinctions, one built on a firm and simple foundation of decency and seriousness. This was as much a movement for 'anti-politeness' as it was for 'impoliteness.' The goals of these radicals were not substantially different from those of the moralists who would emerge in Victorian England to argue against the pretensions of etiquette – nor the goals of conduct writers in America who sought a particularly American democratic civility ethos free from Old World aristocratic influence. Yet, in France, the search for an abridged and egalitarian civility ethic ran into serious difficulties with the demise of the Jacobins in 1794. The civility (and incivility) practices they had favoured were now associated with the despised 'reign of terror' and were quickly abandoned by a well-established bourgeoisie that demanded a return to the old proprieties. Alexis de Tocqueville ([1856]

1995) worried about the turn taken by the revolution in *The Old Regime and the French Revolution*. Although he noted that the revolution had successfully eliminated a despotic monarchy, he suspected that it had then taken a wrong turn and distanced itself from its initial ideals of private and public liberty. After all, the first Republic had been toppled by Napoleon and the second had given way to his nephew Napoleon III.

Although the republican reaction against courtly traditions was carried out for a while through a practised 'gruffness' or 'anti-politeness' that scoffed at the mannerisms of the *ancien régime*, France did not altogether rid itself of the intricate civility rituals of the courts and the intellectual salons. Pride in French culture forbade the permanent abandonment of the aesthetic accomplishments of court society. Bonaparte's arrival at the political helm of France helped re-establish some of the classical practices, albeit within a more egalitarian social order. By 1795, the use of the formal *'vous'* was back in vogue, and, by 1800, France had embarked on a 'golden age' of bourgeois civility that would last for over a century and parallel, in some important aspects, the rise of middle-class Victorian politeness in England.

Many historians and writers have wondered why the post-revolutionary anti-distinction movement did not last. Certainly, its association with the 'reign of terror' did not contribute to its longevity. Yet, in addition to embarrassing associations, there was the question of the French temperament. Ernest Renan tried to explain that aristocratic civil styles particularly suited the needs of the French people. He suggested that the inborn sense of *courtoisie* of the French made them unsuitable republicans – the French excelled in the exquisite, appreciated that which was distinguished. These sentiments were further clarified in his now-famous classic lecture on the meaning of being a nation, delivered at the Sorbonne in 1882:

> A nation is a soul, a spiritual principle. Two things, which in truth are but one, constitute this soul or spiritual principle. One lies in the past, one in the present. One is the possession in common of a rich legacy of memories; the other is present-day consent, the desire to live together, the will to perpetuate the value of the heritage that one has received in an undivided form. Man, Gentlemen, does not improvise. The nation, like the individual, is the culmination of a long past of endeavours, sacrifice, and devotion. Of all cults, that of the ancestors is the most legitimate, for the ancestors have made us what we are. A heroic past, great men, glory (by which I

understand genuine glory), this is the social capital upon which one bases a national idea. To have common glories in the past and to have a common will in the present; to have performed great deeds together, to wish to perform still more – these are the essential conditions for being a people. One loves in proportion to the sacrifices to which one has consented, and in proportion to the ills that one has suffered. One loves the house that one has built and that one has handed down. The Spartan song – 'We are what you were; we will be what you are' – is, in its simplicity, the abridged hymn of every *patrie*. (cited in Eley and Suny 1996:41–55)

It would seem that Louis XIV had been the 'Sun King' and, despite his despotism, had left France with a legacy of grandeur. The French were not to abandon that grandeur nor their national love for grandiose monuments and rituals. By the early nineteenth century, *la politesse* (politeness) and all its nuanced interactions were fully in vogue. It had been transformed from an aristocratic to a bourgeois practice but remained, nevertheless, a distinct affirmation of French civilizational development. While it is not in the scope of this particular work to provide the many details on the massive movement against distinction and politeness that followed the French Revolution, it is interesting to note that, despite the most repressive measures (including the forbidding of the '*vous*' form, legislation against 'irony' and 'wit,' and the declaration of men and women as equal partners in the Republic), France managed to revert back to many of the proprieties it had developed over centuries of feudal rule.

By the late 1800s, Baronne Staffe, born a commoner with the name of Blanche Soyer, made her fortune and reputation with a series of conduct and etiquette manuals, the most famous of which was *Usage du monde* ([1891] 2007). Drawing on France's aristocratic etiquette heritage, and responding to the needs of a bourgeoisie keen on distinguishing itself through classical decorum despite the emergence of a brash industrial culture, she provided rules for nearly every social situation, even specifying what sort of conversation and just how much of it one should have during an outdoor picnic. Like many other French writers of the period, she affirmed that France had the right to favour elegance due to its privileged position as an originator of high culture. During that same *belle époque* (beautiful era) celebrated by Staffe there appeared no less than 500 substantial works on the art of *savoir vivre* (Rouvillois 2006:527–36). What differentiated these works from those that appeared during the golden age of Versailles was the detailed explanations they provided; it is as if the lack of first-hand knowledge regarding the subtleties of the old aristocracy's civility rituals made bourgeois families that much more keen to acquire unwavering guidelines.

This pride in a distinct French culture has transcended particular political eras. Every monarch and president has recognized it and supported it. Just five years prior to the revolution, Antoine de Rivarol restated the long-standing national pride in France's universal cultural mission: 'The time seems to have arrived when we can speak of a French world in the same manner in which we spoke of a Roman world.' Such sentiments of national perfection also moved Joseph De Maistre to state: 'Perhaps Europe only learns something well once the French have experienced it.' Victor Hugo, in turn, confessed his unconditional belief in the superiority of French civilization when he wrote: 'There is today in the universe only one literature that is truly alive, and that is French literature. Everywhere an idea appears, a French book has been created.' Even Voltaire, who railed against the injustices and the false pretenses of the nobility, admitted with great pride that the French language had become the universal language of the educated cadres of Europe.

And, indeed, the educated bourgeois cadres of French society required new conduct books that represented the accumulated civility traditions of French civilization. A whole slew of conduct books appeared, especially after 1860, when members of the small and middle bourgeoisie were increasingly in need of advice on how to behave in high society (*haute société*). Some of the titles listed by Rouvillois demonstrate that there was a massive return to the old ideal of *savoir vivre*. Rouvillois (2006) remarks with considerable insight that the appearance of manuals providing clear and precise behavioural instructions coincided with the formalization of the civil, penal, and commerce codes that gave all French citizens clear indications of their rights and obligations before the law (66–7).

Despite this reversion there were important lingering effects following the revolution, effects that were tied to the manner in which the French Enlightenment differed from its Anglican counterpart. While in the British Isles the Enlightenment was built on a base of rationality, science, and liberal capitalist theory, the Enlightenment in France was strongly individualistic and anti-clerical. Voltaire's ravings against the Catholic Church might not have found a suitably discontented audience in England, a country that had for long maintained parliamentary assemblies. In France, however, where public opinion was increasingly associating the excesses of the nobles of Versailles with the policies of the Catholic Church, Voltaire and other *philosophes* managed to light the embers of a growing passion for the secularization of society and the popularization of philosophy (Chadwick 1975). This set in motion the idea that a universal secular project of human awareness was not only possible but actually in the making. What remained to be accomplished in nineteenth-century France was the reconciliation of the discontents of post-revolutionary modernity with the accumulated heritage of French letters (Graña 1967), for literature had played a seminal role in mobilizing revolutionary fervour and helping the populace reject the polity of absolute power in favour of *a government of reason*.

Such respect for logic and ideas gave rise to a countermovement against rationality. While the French agreed with the Cartesian dictum that all things should be expressed with as much precision as possible, there were growing calls for a return to sentiment. *This seemingly paradoxical co-existence of the rational and the emotional must be taken into account in any study of French culture. On one hand, the French courtesy tradition teaches that a person should remain ambiguous in order not to cause offence; on the other hand, the logic of reason demands precision.* There is a paradoxical alliance born out of this contradiction between the authority of precision and the civility of ambiguity, between the worship of form and the search for freedom, between the meticulously polite and the self-affirmatively rude. The French know that, in order to be appreciated as a valuable gift given to another, politeness must be contrived so as to be imbued with the formality and gravity required to communicate to its beneficiary that an important compliment is being made. Yet the exchange must occur within a republican atmosphere.

So, French courtesy needs to be understood as the consequence of a cultural tradition that has been inspired by French courtly behaviour while remaining cautiously suspicious of inequality. Herein lies the paradoxical nature of French civility, an ethos that harmonizes self-affirming individualism with deferential behaviour. Refinement, discernment, style, lucidity, and a proper dose of sentimentality have left the French with a public interaction ritual that is at once complicated and simple. Where it differs substantially from English interaction practices is in its refusal to repress emotion during conversations. It also differs in its relationship to time, context, and space, important factors that will be more fully discussed in subsequent chapters.

What also changed substantially after the revolution was the aristocratic ideal that one had to appear pleasant at all times. After all, the revolution had been an act of singular insolence, hardly a pleasant event. The social functions of rudeness had already been demonstrated by the Jacobin movement; rudeness had not only helped revolutionaries deny the ascribed privilege of aristocrats but created a sense of class solidarity. To maintain *bienséance* after the revolution, therefore, required considerable trust and goodwill between citizens. Such trust was easy to share in salons habituated by regular members or in the bosom of family and well-known friends. But in the larger context of the anonymous streets, the etiquette of the nobles could no longer serve the needs of citizens encountering one another without the guarantee of complicity or reciprocity.

Warnings about the dangers of anonymity and the worship of pleasantness in anonymous company had been delivered in the works of Françoise Maintenon, the Marquise d'Aubigné (1772), who had warned that moral rectitude was in danger of disintegrating in polite society. Unlike Scudéry, Maintenon favoured a conversational style that would be economic, brief, and protected by a common-sense *méfiance* (suspicion or distrust). It would seem that the French heeded both Scudéry and Maintenon, using whichever conversational style they felt was most appropriate in a given situation. This tradition of opposites (sincerity and suspicion) may explain why moods can change quite quickly within a given conversation in France.

Alexis de Tocqueville ([1856] 1995) had a very insightful explanation for this *méfiance* (suspicion or distrust). He believed that the French Revolution had not succeeded in healing the animosities that had been generations in the making between those of privilege and those occupying ordinary stations in life:

> It was no easy task bringing together fellow citizens who had lived for many centuries aloof from, or even hostile to, each other and teaching them to co-operate in their own affairs. It had been far easier to estrange them than it now was to reunite them, and in so doing France gave the world a memorable example. Yet, when sixty years ago the various classes which under the old order had been isolated units in the social system came once again in touch, it was on their sore spots that they made contact and their first gesture was to fly at each other's throats. Indeed, even today, though class distinctions are no more, the jealousies and antipathies they caused have not died out. (107)

**The Ascension of Bourgeois Morality and Sentimentality**

Medieval doctrine had separated society into two camps: the noble and the common. The entire notion of a middle class placed as a buffer zone between the nobility and the common population was anathema to the medieval nobility. When economic developments brought forward a merchant population seeking adequate recognition of its status, a new class appeared, and its placement between the aristocracy and the common agricultural population gave it a political power that, although lower than that of the nobility, was higher than that of the working class. This merchant class, initially despised by the nobility, began acquiring freedoms that were not easily available to the nobles, who were stuck in court protocols, nor the poor, who were stuck in the misery of a daily struggle for existence. The social independence made possible by accumulated capital helped the *haute bourgeoisie* survive the revolution while steadily increasing its political and economic influence.

Elias ([1939] 1982) states that as 'contrasts' diminish 'varieties' increase (251). And it is this variation in class, opportunity, and potential courses of action that has the decisive influence on public manners in a republic. The lower ranks of French society were empowered to join in the revolution precisely because of a preceding blurring of contrasts between the nobility and the bourgeoisie. Although the efforts of the high bourgeoisie to imitate the higher nobility had not led to a complete levelling of identities, it had opened a channel for the downward dissemination of the nobility's expertise in the art of rational constraint and dramaturgical style; members of *la haute bourgeoisie* took to adding the article *de* to their names in imitation of the aristocracy. And a further channel of dissemination was opened between the bourgeoisie and the common population, permitting an upward flow of sentimentality. For the man on the street, restraint became not only a necessity within his own circle of contacts but a growing cultural practice that established a common denominator of citizenship.

All social classes remained aware that sentimentality and emotional expression were the hallmark of French culture and a necessary part of the new republicanism. The purity of the revolution had depended on a slew of emotional speeches and passionate actions that had broken the aristocratic protocol of *sang froid*. So, the rising bourgeoisie took care not to deny those aspects of aristocratic and French life that were laudable, while asserting their own identity as members of a viable social class with considerable power to influence public morality (Elias [1939] 1982:307).

A review of the genres that became popular between the 1600s and 1700s reveals a steadily rising emotionalism that eventually became an integral part of French culture. Previous to the revolution, class distinctions had not permitted the frequent staging of dramas that crossed class boundaries. With the pioneering work of Diderot, French popular theatre began serving the rising middle classes (Clark 1973). Quite different from classical tragedy, the new theatre concerned itself with domestic dramas and the fate of individuals caught in conflicted situations of love, loyalty, and betrayal. It was in these comedies and the dramas that outright public demonstrations of emotions became acceptable. The characters resisted their emotions, but, as the play progressed into its key scenes, the actors were allowed to weep, faint, and protest in anger (Ellis 1991). The themes of the courtly literature were replayed in some instances, but, more often than not, it was the common experiences of the people that were brought onto stage (Lowe 1982).

The novels of the period were even more given to sentimentalism for novelists could discuss the subtle emotions and secret thoughts of the self in a comprehensive way that could only be partially expressed on stage. Two novelists who best represented this flowering of emotion were Madame de Lafayette and Abbé Prévost. Their work was character oriented. There was little of the *novel of manners* that took great pains to establish mood through lengthy descriptions of nature and pleasant conversation. Instead, these writers concentrated on the 'self' of the character and its reactions in situations of moral and emotional conflict. What distinguished Madame de Lafayette, Abbé Prévost, and others of their temperament was their ability to delve into the motivations that lay at the root of psychological realities. Characters were allowed to reflect on their actions, thoughts, and feelings much in the style of a confessional. Whether the work was written in the first or third person, there was frequently a plot that placed the characters in situations that tested their moral and emotional constitutions. This affirmation of an a priori human sensibility that could co-exist with logic was a major turning point in human relations in France. The *cliché* had to be replaced with a statement capable of enlisting the emotional interest of the listener or respondent. This partiality to works of psychological depth continues to be visible in contemporary French novels and films in which a few characters hold the attention of their audience through long narrations and soul-searching conversations.

Thus, following the French Revolution, 'public spirit' or the 'will of the people' made available to a wider class of people the ability and right to give and expect civil responses. While civility in France was previously an honour accorded to someone of higher or equal social standing, it now became a right to which any man or woman could lay claim by affirming his or her free rights as a *citoyen(ne)*. This gradual expansion of the rights to civil treatment had already begun in the seventeenth century with the addition of *Monsieur* to the name of a bourgeois and *Maitre* to that of an artisan or lawyer. The appellation of *Citoyen(ne)* (citizen) additionally placed individual identity within a larger context of common fraternal public citizenship *(fraternité)*. The many cases documented in the court archives of the French legal system during the eighteenth and nineteenth centuries reveal that a sizeable number of them involved protests against insults and slander committed against the personal reputation of ordinary citizens (Haine 1996).

Napoleon Bonaparte recognized the new status of the 'common population.' In the manner of Louis XIV, who had elected the bourgeois Colbert as his first minister, Bonaparte took great care to support the new social mobility by appointing functionaries and generals who came from the common classes. Concurrently, he created a new caste of nobles, *la noblesse d'Empire* (nobility of the Empire). The Bourbon Restoration of 1814 did not disapprove of this return to aristocratic privilege and even returned the titles of aristocrats who had gone into exile following the revolution. Titles continued to be given out until the establishment of the Third Republic of 1870. Although the pre-revolutionary privileges of the aristocracy were never revived, the prestige of a noble title continued to be a source of both fascination and ridicule for the French. Even today, an aristocrat living within modest means receives particular respect in France.

Bonaparte's influence on the formation of modern France cannot be stressed enough. Admittedly, he developed a police state to secure the compliance of the population during the establishment of centralized rule. Yet the French were anxious to avoid another chaotic and bloody revolution that might leave Paris in shambles and degenerate its infrastructure. Beyond their need for stability, French citizens realized that Bonaparte's aggressive leadership was making France the world's most formidable power overseas. *La gloire* (glory), which has continued to be a cherished emotional experience in France, did not end with the demise of the absolute monarchy. It was, in fact, reconsecrated through Bonaparte's conquests and his ambitious development of the city of Paris. While his statues were taken down after his exile, his spirit continued to inspire France. His accomplishments also predisposed the French to expect grandeur from their subsequent leaders, moving the Comte de Rambuteau to remark in his *Mémoires* (1905) that Parisians needed frequent excitements – whether battlefield victories or new architectural projects – to satisfy their imaginations.

Also paralleling the revival of French cultural pride was a growing secularization of social values, a consequence of seventeenth-century rationalism and the ascension of the bourgeoisie. Large segments of the French population no longer considered the Church's aversion to worldly pursuits an adequate template for social life (Groethuysen 1927). The Church had discredited itself during the days of absolute rule and it no longer occupied a cherished place in the hearts of the French. The secularization of education and the broadening of non-religious topics taught in schools favoured a bourgeoisie that had previously not been a substantial part of the religious or aristocratic elites (Anderson 1975). This *laïque* morality accepted that a person could earn the respect of others through his own accomplishments and become worthy of enjoying the worldly comforts of such accomplishments. It also questioned the role of God in human affairs and civility, placing a particular responsibility on personal discernment. While it did not automatically embrace atheism, it called for a separation of church and state. This separation has continued to affect late-modern French government policy; the formation of religious associations is not a popular practice in France. Jean-Paul Sartre, an avowed atheist writing a hundred years later, attempted to explain the logic of France's laicism when he said that if God was found not to exist, we would develop the same norms of honesty, progress, and humanism.

This new secularism sought a self-generated 'authenticity' free from religious edict (Charme 1991:251–64, Price 1986:299–302, Magraw 1970:169–83). The spirit of this new secularism was expressed in *Religion de l'honnête homme*. Its author, Caraccioli, affirmed that, being a product of nature, man was already able to exercise a love of justice and an upright existence (as *honnête homme*) independently of religious dogma. The qualities needed for such an upright life were few: common sense, a clear conscience, and a respect for justice. A moral man was to neither neglect the affairs of the world nor indulge the flesh to excess. Frugality, attention to health, and respect for order in daily life became the virtues of this lay bourgeois morality (cited in Groethuysen 1927:291). This was what some scholars of French culture have called the *juste milieu* (Starzinger 1965, Spellman 1985, Adams, 2000).

Thus, the long journey from the seeking of *virtue* through self-abnegation to the seeking of *moral legitimacy* through involvement in the affairs of the world allowed the French bourgeoisie to acquire *laïque* (secular) as well as moral legitimacy (Poulet 1988). The revolution's valuation of *freedom* became transformed through bourgeois sensibility into a high valuation of social order. It was rationalized that social order was the means by which freedom could be protected. And enough chaos followed the revolution to make the love of centralized order a safety precaution against anarchy.

A major change also occurred in the morality of the family. Aristocratic marriages had often been arranged for convenience and marital infidelity had been a norm; the king himself was closer to his mistresses than to his wife. The location of the king's and queen's chambers at Versailles indicated their distanced and formal relationship (Elias [1969] 1983:41–60). Post-revolutionary morality placed on the bourgeois family the responsibility of building a home in which decency and affection between husband, wife, and children were of utmost priority. Babeau (1886) noted this shift from strict and distanced aristocratic relationships between parents and children to bourgeois relationships based on kindness and affection (301–2). Gaiffe (1910) noticed this same trend when he observed that many of the post-revolutionary plays staged in the theatres of Paris were written around family themes. Florian's plays included *The Good Mother*, *The Good Father*, *and The Happy Household*. Voltaire's *Enfant prodigue*, although based on the Biblical story of the prodigal son, had a message directed at the French family: a healing reunion between the father and the errant son.

The role of parents and children changed also. In his classic work, *Centuries of Childhood: A Social History of Family Life*, Philippe Ariès (1962) explains that, due to the demise of the apprentice system in Europe, parents were concerned that their children should not grow up to humiliate them 'with their ignorance and behaviour' (402). This preoccupation with the education (and health) of the child coincided with a decrease in the social networks of the father and mother and an increasing privatization of the family in middle-class circles (Price 1986:121–43). It was not the individualism of parents which created the family but the restriction of such (Ariès 1962:403). Through the restraining of the number of social contacts which the father and mother entertained with friends, servants, and clients, parents turned back into the family and developed increased intimacy with their children. By the late eighteenth century, the law of *primogeniture* (the awarding of inheritance to one favoured son at the exclusion of other children) had been banished; siblings were henceforth to be treated equally (403). This new approach to inheritance had an effect on the authority of the parent; the possessions of equal rights to inheritance by children placed a certain responsibility on the parent to act equitably in regards to the emotional life of the family. Ariès quotes Villele, who wrote to Polignac on 31 October

1824: 'Out of twenty well-to-do families, there is scarcely one which uses the power to favour the eldest or some other child. The bonds of subordination have been loosened everywhere to such an extent that in the family, the father considers himself obliged to humor his children' (403).

Even the architecture of homes changed, allowing for rooms that permitted additional privacy. Prior to that, servants had lived in very close quarters with their employers, sometimes sleeping in the same rooms or in beds placed in various parts of the house. Servants were now placed at a distance in servant quarters and bells installed to call them only when needed. The specification of rooms as 'bedrooms' and 'living rooms' and 'dining rooms' comes from this period of increasing privacy. In the courts of the sixteenth and seventeenth century it would have been virtually unthinkable for someone to spend time alone, for a person's identity was part of that of his social group; unannounced visits, communal living, and multiple conversations in shared rooms were not uncommon. The ideal of a private family was, therefore, a particularly middle-class invention (404).

## French Café Culture

The importance of the café in the formation of modern French civility practices and interaction cannot be stressed enough. By the nineteenth century, there existed enough cafés in Paris and France to allow French families to use the café appropriate to their social standing without feeling that they were compromising their social identity (Garrioch 1996).

Prior to the nineteenth century, the streets provided the working class with a carnivalesque environment that provided the poor with effective networks of communication and support (Magraw 1992). But with the rise of a pervasive state and organized policing methods designed to limit theft, prostitution, and civil violence, the streets came under the surveillance of the state and were gradually stripped of their former vitality. The working class had to create a functional space that it could call its own. It withdrew to the off-street public space of the café just as had the English poor withdrawn to the public house (the pub). In France, however, members of the bourgeoisie did not close themselves off in private clubs and private homes, as had the English, but joined a café culture capable of accommodating their own social class.

Although the meeting places of the working class had always disconcerted members of the middle class, who saw them as hotbeds of vice and corruption, the cafés of France managed to survive repeated attempts by the state to control and restrict their role as public interaction pathways. The café had always served as a place for the fermentation of political dissent. The French revolutionaries had used the cafés as strategic mechanisms to influence public opinion and as effective communications conduits for members of the revolutionary crowd. The governments that followed the revolution of 1789 remained aware of the potential political danger of cafés and realized that the drinking experience was a means of affirming group solidarity. As Hippolyte Taine remarked, 'Alcohol is the literature of the people.' Alcohol possessed the power to liberate people to have thoughts and emotions which otherwise might have remained restrained. So, the round of drinks, *la tournée*, was a coming together of people sharing common circumstances and sympathies; hence, Honoré de Balzac called the café *The Parliament of the People*.

Cafés were, in effect, a modified form of the elite intellectual salons. They facilitated intellectual discussion and the appreciation of ideas for their own sake. In his fascinating *Histoire des cafés de Paris*, François Fosca identifies the café as a forum that possessed the capacity to counteract political and social repression: 'Social equality constitutes the rule of the café. In a café the rich bore is rejected ... yet who would dare interrupt him in a salon? ... the café permits the affirmation of personality' (1934:213).

In *Public Drinking and Popular Culture in Eighteenth-Century Paris* (1988), Thomas Brennan is also of the opinion that cafés were not only respites from cramped housing conditions but networks of sociability that gave citizens the right to assemble and discuss current topics. The fact that political and ideological topics were being discussed in a public space, rather than in a drawing room, allowed discourse to be animated and free from the formalities that might have otherwise been observed in the private and cramped drawing room environment. When a law in 1851 tried to put cafés under strict government control, the lawyer-journalist Victor Hennequin denounced the crackdown, arguing that moral arguments were being used to impose political surveillance on the population (Haine 1996:10).

Paris, which had 4,500 cafés in 1840, came to possess nearly six times as many (22,000) only thirty years later. A 1909 survey assigned 1 café per 1,000 population in London, 3.75 per 1,000 in New York, and 11.25 per 1,000 in Paris (Jacquert 1912:757). With less than a hundred people per café, attendance in Paris cafés must have been quite regular for the owners to stay in business.

Contrary to the initial worries of the bourgeoisie, who had feared that café life would weaken the family, cafés and families actually complemented each other. The presence of women in the café acted as a tempering force. The private life of the family, which moralists feared would be comprised by the café, was in effect extended into the café. Since the more modest cafés were usually owned and operated by a husband and wife, they became suitable extensions of family life – owners often presided over weddings and acted as witnesses for legal transactions. It would seem, therefore, that the addition of this public space to the world of the working family helped stabilize it – a quarrel held in a café had a chance of occurring in the presence of familiar people who, although they practised considerable discretion, could step in and mediate if things started getting out of hand. The presence of families in a café also served to imbue public discourse with emotional expression, something which might not have occurred had domestic life been kept within the relative insulation of the home.

The co-existence of people from varied backgrounds and of various temperaments gave rise to a café etiquette designed to minimize violence. This etiquette was reflected in the interior design of the café. While prior to the eighteenth century cafés had consisted of one open space where a great number of people rubbed elbows and were always at risk of irritating one another, the nineteenth century cafés provided a choice between sitting at a table and standing at a counter. This separation of space allowed small groups to socialize without impinging on the space of others. A small group could initiate a discussion and then bring in people from the periphery to participate; meanwhile, a person was expected to observe café etiquette and not interrupt a conversation already in progress (Haine, 1996). Witty comments were the best admission ticket to an ongoing conversation. Jibes and remarks were not to be taken too seriously, nor was a person to press the point and request a fight to settle a point of honour. A sense of *savoir vivre* required the wounded party to come back with his own verbal *riposte* (a fencing term describing the exchange of blows of the sword). Conversation remained a competition of wits, and this verbal competition went a long way in avoiding potential violence. While personal reputation remained important and some café disagreements ended in court with accusations of unfair ruining of personal reputation, there was a marked absence of the duels that characterized the aristocracies of the seventeenth and eighteenth centuries (Kiernan 1988).

The principal point being made here is that while England became influenced by a strong middle-class moral ethic which affected the upper and lower classes, France responded positively to the working class's love of public entertainment and public gatherings and appropriated this friendliness in a cautious but substantial return to the streets. Sitting exposed to pedestrian traffic in a sidewalk café did not bother the bourgeoisie towards the end of the nineteenth century. The numbers of American writers and artists who travelled to Paris at the turn of the twentieth century, lured by the promises of café life, would require a volume in itself. One wonders if Ernest Hemingway would have been moved to describe Paris as 'a moveable feast' (1964) had Paris not had its cafés.

Whereas in England the Victorian middle classes colonized the working and upper classes with their particular morality of sensual prohibition and secrecy, in France, the working class gave to the nation one of its most sensual institutions: the café. The upper class obliged by sending down their own rituals of *style* and *discernement*. In a Paris metro today, when beggars enter a car to ask for money, they spend considerable time eloquently describing the circumstances that led them to requiring aid; some speak with a wit that would have made Louis XIV very proud of the legacy that he bequeathed to France.

## Authority and Liberty

What is being cautiously suggested here is that the French Revolution and its ensuing republicanism had a considerable effect on public interaction rituals in France, but not enough to eradicate the preceding culture of aristocracy and its civility rituals. The statement *se distinguer* (to distinguish oneself) dates back to the ascendancy of the bourgeoisie and its need to prove itself worthy of taking the helm in France. It also applies to the working class, who, following the revolution, believed that it needed no longer defer to social superiors. There was no real intention of permanently dropping the civility rituals of the aristocracy and adopting a simple, republican directness similar to the one adopted in America. The love of *raffinement* (refinement) complicated the adoption of a communication ethos based on directness of speech. Moreover, the claim of free citizenship was rationalized not only by the French constitution but by the accumulated international prestige of French civilization. While the Frenchman deferred to another, he was always quite partial to also deferring to his own special worth. If equality was to be preserved, then the recognition of distinction in another had to be accompanied by recognition of personal distinction. This acceptance of the paradox between self-affirmation and deference to the other may explain why the French have found no substantial contradiction between ethical behaviour and the valuation of elegance, nor an incompatibility between rudeness and extremely deferential behaviour. It certainly has facilitated the co-existence of an individualistic population and a highly centralized political and social system partial to vertical associations and their implicit rules of deference.

The thesis of this section of our argument might be evident to a francophile but perhaps less clear to individuals who have come to find France's adaptation to modernity a seemingly contradictory mix of individualism and deference to vertical authority. Geert Hofstede's (1983) seminal study of cultural characteristics reveals this paradox. While the French value individualism they also put a high valuation on deference to authority. France and Belgium are the only two countries in a list of fifty countries to demonstrate this paradoxical tendency. As we will argue in later chapters, this paradox has had a considerable effect on French civility and interaction rituals.

In this present section, we wish to consider how France's particular revolution, and the events that followed it, may have affected France's conception of liberty and civility. The words 'freedom,' 'liberty,' and 'democracy' are problematic words, for they do not mean the same things in various cultures. Constraining and defining these words in cultural context are the specific historical legacies of a nation and the manner in which citizens have reconciled their history with their present circumstances.

The revolution freed the French from three things: (1) a monarchy and an aristocracy that remained detached from the changing needs of France, (2) legislative practices that stood in the way of economic advancement, and (3) ascribed privileges that prevented members of the lower bourgeoisie and the working classes from bettering their lot. Liberty in France meant liberty from the particular tyranny of the French monarchy. The French Declaration of Rights differed from the one drafted in America. It is worth examining the text in order to locate those differences. Approved by the National Assembly of France on 26 August 1789, the declaration stated:

The representatives of the French people, organized as a National Assembly, believing that the ignorance, neglect, or contempt of the rights of man are the sole cause of public calamities and of the corruption of governments, have determined to set forth in a solemn declaration the natural, unalienable, and sacred rights of man, in order that this declaration, being constantly before all the members of the Social body, shall remind them continually of their rights and duties; in order that the acts of the legislative power, as well as those of the executive power, may be compared at any moment with the objects and purposes of all political institutions and may thus be more respected, and, lastly, in order that the grievances of the citizens, based hereafter upon simple and incontestable principles, shall tend to the maintenance of the constitution and redound to the happiness of all.

Considerable portions of the document were designed to free non-aristocrats from the tyranny of ascribed status and privileges. The French document was designed to decrease tyranny from the interior of the nation, while the American Declaration focused on the creation of a state that could remain free from colonial rule. There is a major difference here.

Article 1 of the French Declaration eliminated aristocratic privilege. Article 2, perhaps inspired by the writings of Rousseau, specified that the 'natural' rights of men could not be corrupted by the imposition of arbitrary laws. This article attempted to reverse the practice of the *lettres de cachet* that the king had used to detain and arrest whomever he wanted. Yet, law, in and of itself, if free from the interests of privileged elites, was to remain the means by which freedom could be preserved. Article 4 specified that, while liberty was to be preserved, the limits of liberty had to be specified at the levels of laws. Unlike the American Declaration of Rights, the French Declaration was not primarily seeking to protect individual freedom from state intervention but trying to establish a balance between self-interest and the preservation of the state and, by extension, French culture. This article was a troublesome one because it could be used to rationalize authoritarian rule if it was considered that the 'general good' of the country was at danger. Article 13 addressed the issues of taxes as they had existed in France prior to the drafting of the Declaration; aristocrats and the Church had been subject to different tax laws than those imposed on the rest of the population. Equality, however, demanded a standard tax-imposition system. Article 13 also established the basis by which a social welfare system could be rationalized. France's present comprehensive social services system is rooted in this original promise of social solidarity.

In some respects, therefore, the French and American Declarations were noticeably different in their definition of freedom. The American Declaration demanded freedom for the 'individual' while the French Declaration demanded freedom for 'society' under the generic appellation of 'man.' In attempting to draft a universal treatise against oppression, the French authors of the French Declaration of Rights left some power of discretion to future governments to determine to what extent freedom could be given to all without threatening the integrity of the nation. We would go far enough to suggest that, while the American Declaration sought to protect individual rights, the French Declaration sought to establish some understanding of an ideal collective social contract based on the *volonté générale* (the collective will).

There is no substantial contradiction between the above ideals and the fact that France supported Napoleon's rise to authoritarian rule. Napoleon arrived at a time when the revolution and the previous abuses of the absolute monarchy had left France in near shambles. Article 4 in the Declaration gave both Napoleon and the French a way of sanctioning strong rule without abandoning the principles of the revolution. It was *reasonable* to unite French citizens under some strong and universally effective central rule that would prevent the nation from fragmenting. If anything, the French constitutions and the original Declaration of Rights, by focusing on the welfare of the nation rather than the absolute freedom of the individual, set the foundation for a culture that could at once value liberty and equality while keeping a keen eye out for movements that might weaken the identity of the nation.

So, when Napoleon made his case to the French, he did not use divine rights as a rationalization for strong rule but promised to save France from chaos. His Napoleonic Code or *Code Civil* of 1804 replaced the 360 separate local codes that had existed prior to his rule. The code was created in order to assure the survival and cohesion of the 'general will' rather than the *carpe diem* freedom of every citizen in every conceivable situation. Americans who have never understood why the French legal system permitted itself to arrest and hold an individual until he could prove himself innocent (as compared to the Anglo-American system jury system which assumed a citizen was innocent unless proven guilty by the state) miss this salient difference between Anglo-American and French definitions of liberty. It is the liberty of the collective that is of concern. The Republic stands as the ultimate priority. The responsibility of the French judicial system is to establish probable cause, and it follows the deductive method of reasoning rather than the citing of specific precedents as is done in English common law.

Students of culture who cannot understand how the French could cheer Napoleon one day and then celebrate his demise the next, and then again welcome the arrival of the Prussians in Paris a few years later, miss an important distinction between fickleness and political astuteness. What mattered to the French, more than the short-term changes in political dominance, was the preservation of the nation and its traditions. It was a lesson learned during the aftermath of the revolution and its terror, and again during the devastating experiment of the Paris Commune that followed later in 1871, and, then again, a hundred years later, as France stepped back from the brink of yet another revolution during the labour and student unrest of May 1968.

From the historical point of view, there seems no irreconcilable paradox between the French search for individual identity and freedom and the search for reliable hierarchies capable of maintaining French civilization. The movement towards a central state had already begun in the time of Louis XV and XVI. While aristocrats had previously possessed considerable power in their own localities and been able to contest political decisions made in Versailles and Paris, they lost their power as the central court centralized policymaking within the jurisdiction of its own bureaucracy. When the revolution occurred, a central state bureaucracy was already in place. While the French managed to end the hegemony of the aristocratic-clerical state they did not manage, nor perhaps desire, to decentralize management of the nation.

This partiality to hierarchy also gave the French the continuing authority to hold the leader of the nation personally responsible for the ills of the nation. Napoleon, as well as Charles de Gaulle, were to complain that the French were never satisfied with their government. Perhaps that was the ultimate outcome of France's preservation of a conception of liberty and governance that did not exaggerate belief in the ability of isolated individuals to change the course of government. The French created a political system, let it do its work, and then held its leaders responsible for the outcomes. Changes in French republics have not been the result of fickleness, but a consequence of the demanding nature of the French electorate; the same population that cheered Napoleon when he first took the helm of France was to later remain silent the night that his second wife gave birth to his long-awaited heir.

It is not in the scope of this work to explain the many events and wars that occurred from the time Napoleon took over France until France finally rejected the restoration of the Bourbon monarchy and reverted to a republic. One thing is certain. The Declaration of Rights survived and gave French citizens a voice in their own politics. Despite the censorship of the Napoleonic regime and despite the brutality of the quashing of the revolts of the Paris Commune of the late nineteenth century, France managed to develop a system of government in which the leader of the government was given considerable political and oratory power while, at the same time, expected to practise a *noblesse oblige* and not turn to the expediency of fascism. President Charles de Gaulle, although he remained an autocratic figure in French politics and an outspoken defender of French culture, never reverted to totalitarian rule. Had he done so, his days would have been numbered, for, regardless of their respect for authority and tradition, the French were and are a highly individualistic culture. The main political difference between France and England and America is that the French conception of individuality is based on a preservation of accumulated culture. There is a bipolar sense of being French: one defers to cultural precedent as well as one's own sentiments; the demarcation line between the two is sometimes not clear to the untrained eye.

*Le juste milieu* of the French lies within this alliance between collective solidarity and individual aspiration. Imagination fills in when reality becomes too discouraging. But the order is never despised enough to warrant another corrective revolution. Had the need been there the second empire would have occurred with great difficulty. It was, in fact, during the second empire that the rising bourgeoisies and the revived aristocracy set about to formally carry over into modern France some of the practices of the civility traditions of the absolute monarchs. Despite countless tracts encouraging informality and lack of ritual, the French continued to accord tremendous importance to manners and protocol. As we will argue in Part IV of this book – when we discuss how 'time, context, and space' play an important role in civility rituals – this explains, in part, why France continues to maintain interaction rituals that are remarkably different from those of Anglo-American culture.

The English experience was different from the French one in one important aspect. While the French monarchy had been based on absolute rule as recently as the late eighteenth century, England had adopted parliamentary rule long before the French Revolution. This had permitted England to develop a conception of civil society that allowed the English monarchy to weather the storms of social change. It was also a conception of ideal governance that greatly influenced the manner in which the English developed an ethos of civility based on the high valuation of non-abrasive politeness.

# 6 England and the Victorian Ethic

> Comfortable people are kindly-tempered ... There must be peace, mutual forbearance, mutual help, and a disposition to make the best of everything ...
> – Samuel Smiles

## Harmonizing Monarchy and Liberty

The English political system had a considerable influence on the formation of a distinct English civility ethos. Although the French and the Americans chose to reject rule by monarchy, the English decided to remain with a constitutional monarchy tempered by an active parliament.

Despite the fact that England's history is a dizzying narrative of violence, riots, political plots, religious and international wars, and considerable exploitation of the poor (Tilly [1995] 2005), an outright English revolution was avoided due to steadily improving economic and judicial systems (Gilmour 1993). Although there were no less than 8,088 'contentious gatherings' in southeast England alone in a thirteen-year time period between 1758 and 1820 (Tilly [1995] 2005:xxv), the English state managed to avoid the overthrow of its monarchical base. An important innovation of the English system was the allocation of power to a landed gentry class that stood as a buffer zone between the peasants and a strong monarchy surveyed by an active parliament (Skocpol 1979:140).

A similar compromise was reached at the level of religion. The Anglican Church of England managed to chart a middle ground between papal absolutism and Presbyterian fervour, thereby preventing the type of secular anti-clerical backlash that occurred in France. Although

Elizabeth I returned England to Protestantism she was wise enough to retain some of the rituals of the Catholic faith: candlesticks, crucifixes, and clerical robes. The authorization of a Common Prayer Book in English in 1662 further allowed the common classes to have a direct experience with scripture and take an active part in public affairs.

These measures had their root in the changes made to the English state by Henry VII (1457–1509), who ushered in the Tudor dynasty by ending the dynastic struggles known as the War of the Roses. Henry VII succeeded in ending the medieval system of law in which local laws and customs dominated and in establishing a single state that ruled by royal decree. As early as the beginning of the sixteenth century, then, England had managed to build a state that was solvent and capable of managing a prosperous and united kingdom. This placed England at a distinct advantage when the early manifestations of the Industrial Revolution appeared on English soil.

Moreover, the political and religious tolerance of the Elizabethan period also had a marked effect on the British parliamentary system that came into its own shortly after the publication of the Authorized English version of the Bible. Parliament acquired particular legitimacy as a civil body representing all subjects when it intervened to end the rule of James II of the House of Stuart by passing the English Bill of Rights of 1689. Never again could a British monarch claim divine rights; nor could he or she override parliament to wage a personal war against personal political or religious opponents.

Most importantly, the bill protected the freedom of parliament (and its aristocratic members) by prohibiting a monarch from dissolving parliament; it also guarded against the danger of unrestricted royal appointments by specifying that there would be general elections every three years. Unlike in the French monarchy where nobles continued to be at the whim of an absolute monarch, the British nobility acquired a somewhat professional status that served it well when the Industrial Revolution began. Some of the clauses of the Bill of Rights additionally gave English citizens extraordinary judicial protection:

> That the pretended power of suspending of laws, or the execution of laws, by regal authority, without consent of parliament, is illegal. That it is the right of the subjects to petition the King, and all commitments and prosecutions for such petitioning are illegal. That the raising or keeping a standing army within the kingdom in time of peace, unless it be with consent of parliament, is against law. That the subjects which are protestants, may

have arms for their defence suitable to their conditions, and as allowed by law. That the freedom of speech, and debates or proceedings in parliament, ought not to be impeached or questioned in any court or place out of parliament. That excessive bail ought not to be required, nor excessive fines imposed; nor cruel and unusual punishments inflicted. That jurors ought to be duly impanelled and returned, and jurors which pass upon men in trials of high treason ought to be freeholders. That all grants and promises of fines and forfeitures of particular persons before conviction, are illegal and void. And that for redress of all grievances, and for the amending, strengthening and preserving of the laws, parliaments ought to be held frequently.

English parliamentary rule was, therefore, founded on an appreciation of the utility of liberty at the broader parliamentary level as well as within simple interactions among individuals. The English came to believe that there would always be a parliamentary solution capable of protecting all interests, moral as well as financial. This parliamentary liberty, and improving modes of production that steadily lowered the price of goods, helped stave off a massive republican revolt despite the fact that 'in 1873 four-fifths of the land was held by 7,000 individuals, peers prominent amongst them' (Briggs 1987:267). Elias's review of state formation would have benefited greatly if Britain had been the core of his study or an appreciable part of it. Since the Industrial Revolution did start in Britain, and since Britain managed to develop a state capable of accommodating capitalism, a study of the British state shows that what aided the formation of a gradually expanding democracy was the fact that both the forces of the state and the citizenry that had often stood in opposition to the policies of the state managed to take violent protest to a certain point and then stop and allow arbitration to complete the representational process. Thus, the development of a civilized state was not due solely to the monopoly of violence by the state but by the birth of institutions that represented non-military local pockets of civil society. In a manner of speaking, one could consider an alternate paradigm to the one that considers the prohibition and monopolization of violence as the precursor to civility; in an equal measure it was the state's readiness to decrease its use of violence towards its citizenry that permitted a bilateral development of civility (Braddick 2001).

Such compromise was not reached overnight. Civility was the consequence of many stand-offs between a repressive state and a contentious population. Tilly's excellent review of contentious politics and its role in the formation of the British modern state, *Popular Contention in Great Britain 1758–1834* ([1995] 2005), demonstrates that, precisely during the period when America and France were experiencing outright revolutions, the British state was managing to respond to popular uprisings with repressive authority. Involved in a massive military build-up for war with France, the English state had to take strong measures to ensure that the civilians who were being armed for the war would not use their armaments against the state. By the late 1700s the state had passed numerous laws prohibiting protest movements and contentious gatherings. Although this repression was hardly democratic, the non-violent (and violent) protests and petitions that emerged from such prohibition did serve to allow parliament and local magistrates to consider the validity of some of the claims of defendants. Paradoxically, repression through the passing of legislation opened up the way for 'offenders' to appear in court and be heard. Henceforth, the English avoided attacking the head of state and, instead, tried to bring about change through parliamentary legislation. English protest movements did not seek to topple the state but to bring about the 'protection or establishment of rights within the existing system. Hence the enormous eighteenth-century importance of "rights of freeborn Englishmen"' (Tilly 1993b:136).

Tilly has noticed this shift from revolution to civil protest, which for us represents the origins of civility in the English political arena:

> As the state's involvement (repressive or otherwise) in public contention iincreased, the forms of claim-making changed significantly ... [there was] a flowering of associational activity, public meetings, popular participation in elections, and direct efforts to influence the national state, especially through Parliament (212) ... Cosmopolitan, autonomous, modular collective action came to prevail over parochial, particular, bifurcated collective action. As a consequence, the frequency of direct attacks on persons and objects greatly declined. ([1995] 2005:221)

Tilly's study of the verbs used most often by organizers indicates that his definition of 'contentious protest' (protests that proceed to a certain point and then stop) is accurate in the sense of English politics. The verbs most frequently used by protestors were 'MEET, RESOLVE, RESOLVE, END' (220). And, indeed, uprisings were no longer restricted to random, localized violence but were calculatingly directed at the authorities who had the power to improve conditions. 'As is still true almost two centuries later,' writes Tilly, 'the organizers do their best to display unity of purpose, advertise their causes's worthiness, attract publicity, recruit donors, and draw the attention of public authorities' (220).

Political compromise, however, was not the most powerful agent of civility. Of equal importance was the influence of a booming mercantilism. Craig Muldrew's (1993, 1998, 2001) systematic and exhaustive analysis of sixteenth-century England provides us with a solid foundation for understanding the early origins of the English sense of fair play. Muldrew explains that beginning in the mid-1500s there was a sharp increase in textile production and continental trade. The growth of goods far surpassed the available supply of gold and silver, the main currencies of exchange. It became necessary to establish networks of credit. These entailed 'trust' as well as 'risk.' Muldrew points out some of the outcomes of these new ways of conducting trade:

> As credit networks became more complicated, and more obligations broken, it became important before entering into a contract to be able to make judgements about other people's honesty. The more reliable both parties in an agreement were in paying debts, delivering goods or in performing services, the more secure chains of credit became, and the greater the chance of general profit, future material security and general ease of life for all entangled in them. The result of this was that credit in social terms – the reputation of fair and honest dealing of a household and its members – became the currency of lending and borrowing. (1998:148)

Credit was, therefore, another word for the measurement of an individual's or household's trustworthiness. The measurement of the moral value of a 'neighbour' was their reputation for paying debts owed according to promises made. The 'keeping of the promise,' measured in medieval times as the keeping of oaths of fealty, was now transformed into respect for financial contracts. As Tilly explains, these new networks of credit served not only to validate a person's trustworthiness but also to exclude those who were considered worthy of distrust (2005b:15). Muldrew further specifies that this trustworthiness was connected not to wealth but to the ability of a household to use its good reputation to raise money when needed. The origins of the English class system not only are located in the monarchical form of government but are also deeply rooted in the division that developed between those who formed networks of trust based on credit worthiness and those they considered members of a proletariat incapable of possessing the moral fibre required to fulfill contracted financial obligations (1998:148–72). Muldrew explains that the saying 'paying on the nail' emanates from this period in England. Four bronze pillars with flat surfaces were erected in Bristol over the years, each with a flat surface. Downpayments and settlement of debts in cash were placed on the flat nail surfaces (106–7).

Thus, credit networks were citizen movements designed to compensate for a government that was not able to fully meet the demands of rising trade. While these networks had to affiliate themselves with the government's policing legal institutions in order to initiate and complete debt litigation, they remained private networks built on trust and on the high value placed on 'fair play.'

British individualism, therefore, was long in the making before the Victorian age. It was not only a confirmation of the rights possessed by citizens in a political system that was supposed to grant them due process, but also a reflection of the kingdom's disciplined approach to financial transactions and the honouring of debts. Here, trust becomes a two-way process between a citizenry and the state; the citizenry accepts to practise a civility of mutual trust and have faith in the state, in turn, to enforce punishments for breaches of such trusts (i.e., debtors' prisons). Margaret Levi has also explained that this trust between private and state institutions is a contingent one based on a mutual evaluation of trustworthiness and sincerity. The private sectors agree through a sort of 'contingent consent' with constraints and demands imposed by the state provided they feel that the state itself is trustworthy and consistent. This 'ethical reciprocity' becomes the foundation of a democratic society (1997:21). So, when political thinkers such as Thomas Paine spoke in support of the French Revolution, they did so because they wanted the French to acquire a sovereignty based on reasonable rights, something that they felt was already possessed by the English and their institutions (Tilly 1993b:136).

In his perceptive analysis of England, *The English: A Portrait of a People* (1998), British broadcaster and historian Jeremy Paxman suggests that the Anglican Church also played a seminal role in facilitating the preservation of English individualism:

> It is in the fight with Church and the State, first to get access to the Bible in their own language, and then to use the scriptures to establish their own relationships with one another and with authority, that we see the spirit of English individualism at work. It is one of the reasons that it has

never been necessary for the Englishman or Englishwoman to submerge their identity within the state. And it is one of the reasons that the country produced so many eccentrics. (114)

Paxman quotes the Bishop of Norwich as receiving the following advice from his predecessor: 'Welcome to Norfolk. If you want to lead someone in this part of the world, find out where they're going. And walk in front of them' (134). Alexis de Tocqueville (1958) similarly observed during his travels in England and Ireland that the 'spirit of individuality is the basis of the English character' (88). When De Tocqueville asked John Stuart Mill in conversation whether the English would eventually choose a centralized government, Mill replied without any hesitation:

> Our habits or the nature of our temperament do not in the least draw us towards general ideas; but centralization is based on general ideas; that is the desire for power to attend, in a uniform and general way, to present and future needs of society. We have never considered government from such a lofty point of view. (81)

Another factor that helped soften relations between the aristocracy and the rest of the population was the fact that the power of the English aristocracy was not displayed in a central court as was that of the French aristocracy at the court of Versailles. Most English aristocrats preferred to maintain their own mansions in the country and were, consequently, in closer sympathetic contact with the workers who took care of their lands than were their counterparts in France.

Brian Manning ([1976] 1991) has noted these fundamental differences between France and England in *The English People and the English Revolution*. He explains that it was the 'middle sort' of Englishmen who played a key role in changing England's political system (181–241). The landed gentry stood between the aristocracy and the urban middle and lower classes, serving as a tempering force; the fact that both the untitled gentry and the aristocracy shared the appellation of 'gentlemen' shows the unique class system that existed in England. Less antagonistic towards each other than the various factions of the French *ancien régime*, the English aristocracy, gentry, and middle classes found means for resolving conflicts through arbitration (Mingaux 1976). John Stuart Mill even suggested that the English were quite partial to their aristocracy and reluctant to topple it: 'The English, of all ranks and classes, are at bottom, in all their feelings, aristocratic. They have the conception of liberty, and set some value by it, but the very idea of equality is strange and offensive to them' (cited in Manning [1976] 1991:205).

Certainly, when Edmund Burke published *Reflections on the Revolution in France* he was not complaining of the fall of absolute monarchy but of the act of overthrowing a government by brutal force (Wallerstein 1996:59). So, while in France it was the monarch who controlled violence, in England it was a self-ruling government body that chose self-restraint in the interests of preserving unity and a continuing measure of independence at all levels (Elias and Dunning 1986:58). This talent of restraining the self has played a major role in British civil society. Moreover, it has helped preserve a national ethos based on the belief that the state and its citizens are continuously and mutually engaged in the fortification and preservation of individual liberties within a system in which the rule of law is highly respected.

**Early English Courtesy Literature**

English courtesy literature published prior to the eighteenth century followed themes similar to the ones in the French and Italian courtesy canons. Young Englishmen from well-to-do families who went on the 'grand tour' of Europe referred to these books and were inspired by them (Burnley 1998:74). Translations of Continental courtesy books were frequent and reached sizeable upper-class audiences. And, like the Continentals, the English valued the ability to be eloquent. The *art of speeche* was idealized in Chaucer's work and, to an even larger extent, in the writings of Walter Map (114–18). Yet, what seemed to attract the English the most, following the end of the twelfth century, was the literature of courtly love and its high valuation of 'sensitivity' (90, 148–51).

Like the writers of the late Renaissance, English courtesy authors considered good manners as an indication of good character. The ethical person remained sensitive to the reactions of others out of concern for the relationship he shared with them. The origins of English behavioural restraint may be found in this early imposition of strong controls on those practices connected to offensive or disturbing bodily expression. One has this impression from examining the contents of those Continental books that were most popular in England. Caxton translated Jacques Le Grand's *Book of Good Manners* in 1487 and Alexander Barclay published Domenico Mancini's *Mirror of Good Manners (Dequatuor virtutibus)* in 1523. Both works relied considerably on the medieval conception of Christian virtue as the foundation of proper behaviour, and both had substantial sections on the rudiments of good manners. Robert Peterson's translation of Della Casa's *Galateo* followed shortly after in 1576 (with a second translation in 1774 by the poet Richard Graves). The *Galateo* enjoyed a long shelf life and was referred to quite frequently during Victorian times. Its favouring of publican civility – as opposed to court etiquette – appealed very much to the English.

The books written by the English themselves spoke highly of a personal sensibility not dependent on noble title (Mason [1935] 1971:35). John Russell's *Boke of Nurture* (1450) associated an honourable personality with domestic values. Thomas Lupset's *Exhortations to Yonge Men* (1529) singled out virtue as the most important quality of a well-bred person, making no mention of behaviour at court. Thomas Elyot's *The Boke Named the Governour* (1531) restated Castiglione's republican message: honour and responsibility could be practised by anyone. Elyot, however, added a distinctly English theme: he preached in favour of an immutable natural and hierarchical order not dependent at all on the power of monarchs; *it was order rather than title that would preserve England*. The Tudor sovereigns understood this need for order in a realm marked by a violent history, and they preserved such order by employing capable individuals regardless of their social origins. This helped create a middle range of gentry and squires that contributed to the maintenance of social stability and civility in towns despite riots.

Thus, the early English courtesy documents tried to demonstrate how virtue, honour, and a humane consideration for others would produce a person adept in all social circumstances, even those involving competition and war. It is interesting to note that the use of the word 'gentleman,' an appellation not restricted to the person of the courtier or the knight, appears quite early in the English literature and is offered up as a quality that transcends a person's aristocratic or common background. *Gentlemanly* and *ladylike* conduct becomes a universal measure for the English civility ideal. Originally attributed to the aristocratic 'breed,' it is broadened into a national virtue.

By the seventeenth century, English courtesy books were defining how good manners helped develop a *gentleman* or *gentlewoman* capable of navigating the increasing complex social circles of a rapidly industrializing society that required considerable social acuity in social interactions (Borsay 2000:1302–3, Smuts 2001:301–11). Many of the conduct books written in that century preached against ostentatious and fashionable pretense, concentrating instead on a more simple conception of civility (Mason [1935] 1971:118–20). While many of these books equated nobility with lineage, they took care to mention that those from respectable professions could be considered noble provided they demonstrated the proper personal qualities (130). There was also a corresponding use of lower-class colloquial English in the speech patterns and writings of polite society (Taylor 1997, McIntosh [1976] 1986:1–10). Unlike the French, who preferred that changes in the French language be determined by the members of the elite Académie Française, England welcomed a national language that was accessible to all classes. The simplicity of modern English is connected to the various transformations experienced in English literature as writers standardized, clarified, and simplified usage.

Robert Brathwayt's *The English Gentleman* (1630) and its sister volume, *The English Gentlewoman* (1631), exemplified this English penchant for simplicity in communication and interaction rituals. Brathwayt preached against vanity and warned that the trappings of society could corrupt a young man's personality. *Moderation* was the guiding theme in these conduct manuals. Along with Richard Alstree's (1658) *The Whole Duty of Man* and *The Gentleman's Calling* (1660), Henry Peacham's (1622) *The Compleat Gentleman*, and the Frenchman Jean Gailhard's (1678) *The Compleat Gentleman*, they presented the art of conversation as vitally necessary to the social skills of the cultured individual, while cautioning that conversations should avoid becoming pretentious. Like Della Casa, who had written that 'ugly' habits, such as uncleanness and messy eating, should be avoided in order not to cause offence to others, the English conduct manuals treated manners as a set of behavioural rituals intended to minimize discomfort in social settings and simplify relations in order to avoid embarrassing situations. *While the French chose rituals of elaboration, the English developed a distinct philosophy of utility and simplicity.*

Moreover, writing under the shadow of the French and Italian courtesy writers, English conduct book writers tried to distinguish between appearance and sincere intent. Obadiah Walker's (1673) *Of Education, especially of Young Gentlemen* even took great pains to differentiate between 'etiquette' and 'good manners.' Walker warned his readers not to be seduced by the aristocratic manners of the French. For Walker, true civility depended not on slavishly following fashions or adopting the stylistic formalism of French courts, but on a consistent consideration for the persons of others. A 'gentleman' or 'gentlewoman' would not do or say anything that might be disrespectful of another. The ideals of cleanliness espoused in the book were intended to be an act of respect towards others, part and parcel of the ethic of 'gentility.'

This concern for manners was exemplified by the founding of the Society for the Reformation of Manners (1692), an institution that facilitated the publication of a slew of works arguing how manners and personal integrity were closely linked (Mason [1935] 1971:180–2). And, indeed, a genteel comportment required 'presence of mind' and 'tenacity.' Thus, what emerged in these later books on manners was a culture of psychological as well as bodily restraint – a kind of grace under pressure.

Along with advice on how to avoid disturbing or upsetting others came advice on how to best earn their approval in an increasingly anonymous society where first impressions counted for so much. As early as 1642, Peacham's *The Art of Living in London* was instructing readers on how to prosper socially in anonymous urban centres by turning the larger community to advantage through a studied presentation of self.

A similar transformation from medieval courtesy ideals to secular ideals was also occurring in the salon culture of England. While the early English salons had been patterned along the Renaissance salon exemplified in *The Book of the Courtier*, the Elizabethan salon became a centre for serious literary discussion and the promotion of literature (Tinker 1967). Perhaps the resistance of Continental style was connected to fears of rising French agnosticism; but there certainly was no resistance to the enjoyment of conversation for its own sake. The Blue Stockings Club, founded at the end of the eighteenth century, and the salons animated by the Countess of Pembroke and Mrs Montagu, received the best of English society, including Hannah More, an ardent moralist not given to ostentatious displays (83–8). By the time of the later salons, England had embraced a form of the Platonic Renaissance – the themes of love and loyalty were becoming exemplified in the relationships developed between salon intellectuals (Cassirer 1953).

As in France, these conversation circles gave rise to the art of letter writing, considered an intimate extension of the art of conversation. Letters permitted a person to enlarge his or her social circle and remain in courteous exchange with individuals of varying acquaintance. It also permitted the sharing of intimate information that might have otherwise remained censured in the context of a social gathering (Hornbeak 1934). This view of intimacy in correspondence was very similar to the French view that the *lettre intime* was itself a rare form of literature. Hannah More reveals the power of a letter to create and maintain sincerity and intimacy: 'What I want in a letter is a picture of my friend's mind, and the common sense of his life ... I want him to turn out the inside of his heart to me, without disguise, without appearing better than he is, without writing for a character' (cited in Tinker 1967:247).

Within the personal letters of the epoch we see a movement away from the rationalism of the period and towards a sentimentalism or sensibility based on 'sincerity of feeling.' This development would have an important influence on ensuing debates on civility and the Romanticism of some of the later Victorian values, beliefs, and practices.

And, indeed, the ideal of sentimental sincerity was a reaction against the toughness of spirit that was necessary for dealing with the new economic opportunities that were broadening the gap between the wealthy and the poor. The life of a labourer was brutish and short. Children were enlisted to carry coal in mines. The numbers of paupers wandering from borough to borough increased to epidemic proportions, aggravated by migrants escaping the potato famine of Ireland. The middle classes understood that some measure of relief for the poor would be required if massive revolt was to be avoided. Parishes began handing out relief funds to the poorest families. The number of charitable organizations administered by members of the upper and middle classes increased in direct proportion to the misery of the displaced.

The laws creating workhouses in which paupers were admitted and given clean sleeping accommodations and modest food in return for work were a consequence of the horror felt by well-off Victorians when faced with streets populated by people who seemed to come from another age. Pauperism was considered a social deviance – a mentality of helplessness that could become contagious if not controlled. Victorians distinguished between paupers who were considered undesirable personalities and the working poor who were respected for accepting their lot and managing as best they could. Sometimes, the distinction became blurred and some of the poor were classified as paupers. Having withdrawn from the squalor of the streets into their own homes, the middle classes now sought to clean up the streets and have them reflect their own economic and aesthetic identity. This, in effect, was the genesis of a modern state-administered social welfare system in England. It also created the English penchant for leaving socially disturbing realities out of private political discourse, giving the misleading impression that the English are resigned to a continuously decaying society (Paxman 1998). In *The Hanging Tree: Execution and the English People, 1770–1868* (1994), V.A.C. Gatrell explains that public hangings in England were very popular until they were outlawed in the mid-nineteenth century. Gatrell contends that it was not the executions per se that bothered the middle-class Victorians but the emotional reactions of the crowds that attended these public events. The unbridled passions of the scaffold crowd reflected the violence of the state and its ruthless justice; this certainly unsettled middle-class notions of civility and social welfare. A better alternative was to sequester criminals and the justice meted out to them away from view in penitentiaries (Ignatieff 1978). This notion of a 'civilized' criminal justice system remains with us even today when the issue of 'civilized torture' is considered in response to struggles against terror movements (Linklater 2007).

Double standards notwithstanding, what helped keep social classes in a relative degree of surface mutual sympathy was the people's pride in a monarchy that had withstood the tests of time while managing to make England a world leader. Practicality and pride, rather than docility, motivated the English to stay the course and to cautiously proceed with reform.

On a philosophical level, England accepted the Cartesian model of reason as the final arbiter of things, while, in France, the seventeenth century reaction against reason had predisposed citizens to move towards a paradoxical mix of sentimentality and Lockean utilitarianism. This mix suited the bourgeoisie in France for it needed to follow utilitarian goals while not losing sight of the politically emancipatory aspects of emotional expression. A nation that undergoes an outright national revolution, an event filled with very strong passions, does not easily give up the association formed in its collective consciousness between sentimentality, emotionalism, and the phenomenon of being a free person with full rights. In England, a nation that had not undergone a passionate revolution, an alternate way was found to affirm personal liberty: the act of being reasonable became the vaccine against the injustices that can emerge from emotional impulsiveness.

**From Regency Libertinism to Victorian Morality**

During a visit to London in 1897, Mark Twain remarked that, although English history was nearly two thousand years old, England had moved further ahead under the reign of Queen Victoria than it had during its two thousand years of existence. Such rapid development caused massive social, economic, and political transformations in the span of a few decades. Although the English were left feeling displaced and uncertain, they managed to develop a civility ethic that moved D.H. Lawrence to write: 'I don't like England very much, but the English *do* seem a rather lovable people. They have such a lot of gentleness' (cited in Paxman 1999:253).

Even the police, usually figures of coercive authority, were considered of gentle demeanour. In an 1883 article in the *Times*, the English bobby was personified as the best symbol of Victorian reasonableness:

> The policeman who is in foreign cities regarded as an enemy, not only by the criminal classes but by the working classes generally, and who in times of social disturbance is made the first victim of popular hatred, is in England rather the friend of the people than otherwise. (14 September 1883)

Paralleling such gentleness was considerable mercantile ambition. By grace of its incomparable merchant fleet and the economic head start it acquired as leader of the Industrial Revolution, England was successfully exporting its products globally and managing to colonize one-fourth of the world. Within its own borders, a comprehensive new railways system facilitated a massive migration to the urban centres, causing progress as well as degeneration. Some of these changes were so striking that someone born in the first decade of the nineteenth century might not have recognized the London of the late Victorian era.

So much change in such a short span of time left Victorians torn between the optimism of a rapidly developing industrial economy and worry over the social problems that came in its wake. Poverty, urban congestion, and a weakening of the traditional parish community challenged old certitudes (Briggs 1987:216–41). Matthew Arnold understood well the stress of managing massive unremitting change when he warned:

> For what wears out the life of mortal men?
> Tis that from change to change their being rolls;
> Tis that repeated shocks, again, again,
> Exhaust the energy of strongest souls. (1890, cited in Allen 1998:154)

Some Victorians, including the influential writer Thomas Babbington Macauley, welcomed the frenzied activity of industrial development; other Victorians waxed nostalgic over a former and more tranquil style of life. Tennyson warned that all this development and change would cripple human happiness. In *Nottingham and the Mining Country*, D.H. Lawrence (cited in Paxman 1999) commented in retrospect on the industrial landscape of Victorian times:

> The real tragedy of England, as I see it, is the tragedy of ugliness. The country is lovely; the man-made England is so vile ... The great crime which the moneyed classes and promoters of industry committed in the palmy Victorian days was the condemning of the workers to ugliness, ugliness, ugliness: meanness and formlessness and ugly surroundings, ugly ideals, ugly religion, ugly hope, ugly love, ugly clothes, ugly furniture, ugly houses, ugly relationships between workers and employers. (165)

Observing the squalor of the northern industrial cities, H.G. Wells (1934) observed:

> It is only because the thing was spread over a hundred years and not concentrated in a few weeks that history fails to recognize what sustained disaster, how much massacre, degeneration, and disablement of lives was due to the housing of people in the nineteenth century. (277)

These same conditions moved Friedrich Engels ([1892] 1952) to write *The Conditions of the Working Class in England*, a seminal work that energized and informed the works of Karl Marx. Tilly's more recent work, on the other hand, demonstrates that, despite the horrible working conditions in this new industrial complex, English workers managed to bring about a massive cultural revolution by steadily struggling for improved working conditions and trade unions ([1995] 2005).

As in any society experiencing rapid change there was considerable debate between conservative and forward-looking factions. It was an age of conformity as well as dissent, a time of prudish caution as well as love of novelty. The Victorian 'values' that have been reified in retrospective accounts were the outcomes of delicate compromises reached between opposing interests. On one hand were those who feared that industrialization would erode religious faith and cause social corruption. Disagreeing with them were those who remained confident that industrial society needed not be regulated by any absolute rules except those of the market.

Many feared the utilitarian spirit required by industrialization. John Stuart Mill (1833), in his essay 'Comparison of the Tendencies of French and English Intellect,' cautioned:

The English public think nobody worth listening to, except in so far as he tells them of something to be done, and not only that, but of something which can be done immediately. What is more, the only reasons they will generally attend to, are those founded on the specific good consequences to be expected from the adoption of the specific propositions. (804)

Mill was to worry about the 'utilitarian' mentality of the English in several other essays and books. He expressed the crisis of the new industrial society in *Spirit of the Age* (1831). Mill recognized that a new agent, 'the individual,' was rising through the ashes of nominal superficial religion and emerging in the industrial landscape unable to count on the certainties of the past while unprepared to declare himself thoughtfully and conclusively regarding the present and the future. This was an age of intense anxiety – many of the contraptions, the machines, and the towering factories belching smoke into previously pristine rural regions were all new apparitions that excited some Victorians while frightening many others. Compounding this worry over a rapidly changing lifestyle was the fear of revolution. Carlyle's (1797) account of the French Revolution had cautioned that it would require only a few developments to set off similar explosive unrest in England.

Compounding this uncertainty was the outrage felt by certain moralists over the libertinism of the earlier Regency period. High society in Regency England, led by the prince regent, who was notorious for his gluttony and love of lavish entertainment, favoured a toil-free pleasure-filled life (Priestley 1969). The regent's banquets made culinary history. At one feast prepared in the Brighton Pavilion, his French chef, Carême, served more than a hundred dishes (Murray 1998:179–85). The quantity and variety of food in the prince's own daily diet was astounding – when he died, he was so obese that his belly hung below his knees. Equally opulent was the Brighton Pavilion in which these sumptuous feasts were served. Although a tour of the pavilion today reveals a palace much more modest than the one at Versailles, what catches the eye is the impressive kitchen, which, during the life of the prince regent, contained every conceivable cooking convenience of the time.

The *high society* forming outside the Regency court was equally given to an energetic search for pleasure. French aristocrats who visited England were astounded by the amount of French dishes consumed during a single sitting in the houses of the wealthy. While the poor had to manage with frugal meals that rarely included meat, the nobility and the *nouveaux riches* followed a lifestyle that defined a good hostess by how much food she could waste when throwing a party. Gluttony became a sign of distinction for the aristocracy and the wealthy merchant class.

Nor was the ideal of marital fidelity as pervasive during the Regency as it was in the middle and late Victorian periods. Melville (1908, 1926) and Murray (1998) document that the keeping of mistresses was common in aristocratic circles, and no secret was made of such extra-marital liaisons. In fact, a mistress often enjoyed more favour than did a wife and was encouraged to develop her wit and charm. The candid writings of Harriette Wilson (1929), the most famous courtesan of the Regency, show the off-hand manner in which extra-marital relations were contracted and lived. Murray (1998) qualifies, however, that, in spite of the common acceptance of these liaisons among the upper classes, the Regency period was a transitional time between the 'licentious formality' of the eighteenth century and the 'Puritanism' of the nineteenth. Although adultery was assumed to always be present in certain aristocratic families, in which marriages were often still being contracted for political and economic ends, adultery was beginning to be considered a sin, especially in middle-class circles (146).

Some historians have attributed the reckless pursuit of pleasure and the new exhibitionism of the upper classes to a style set by the prince regent himself, who had little interest in economy, a partial interest in politics, and a total obsession with parties. Yet, one person cannot set the tone of an epoch or a social class; there were other forces influencing the behaviour of the aristocracy. There was a general denial of reality within the aristocracy during the reign of the prince regent that might help explain the quasi-desperate pursuit of pleasure and status. The colourful costumes worn at Regency functions, the gluttony, the maintenance of elaborate country mansions, the keeping of mistresses in plain view, the penchant for masked balls where anonymity facilitated promiscuous behaviour – all this stood in stark contrast to the violence, crime, and poverty that were afflicting the majority of the population. It was as if the upper classes were having one last fling before letting their successors settle down to the formulation of a workable and more sober society.

Middle-class Victorians took up the challenge with considerable ardour. They were faced with a dilemma. They could not sanction the immorality of the Regency's open celebration of pleasure and the aristocracy's withdrawal from reality; nor could they revert to a non-progressive ideology founded on medieval Christian virtues. The discipline and commercialism required by industrialization complicated the adoption of either solution. Once again, the English had to opt for the 'middle ground.'

A plethora of moral books and movements emerged in response to the numerous massive social displacements of industrialization. Hannah More's widely influential books – *Thoughts on the Importance of the Manners of the Great to General Society* (1788) and *Christian Morals* (1813) – together with William Wilberforce's *Practical View* (1797), addressed issues particular to a rapidly industrializing nation that possessed a dominant aristocracy substantially preoccupied with the goings on of its own exclusive social circles. Aristocrats were encouraged to improve themselves and act as an example to the rest of the nation. This idea of 'improvement' through moral rectitude was to become a central theme of the early Victorian epoch. It helped link *manners* with *ethical comportment*, echoing Edmund Burke's ([1796] 1991) passionate argument regarding the importance of manners in moral development:

> Manners are of more importance than laws. Upon them, in a great measure the laws depend. The law touches us but here and there, and now and then. Manners are what vex or soothe, corrupt or purify, exalt or debase, barbarize or refine us, by a constant, steady, uniform, insensible operation, like that of the air we breathe in. They give their whole form and colour to our lives. According to their quality, they aid morals, they supply them, or they totally destroy them. (242)

Moralists suggested that the middle and lower classes were in need of leadership from the aristocracy and would improve by applying the principles of self-betterment. They did not call for a revolt against the aristocracy but encouraged members of the upper class to reform themselves and stand as examples. Concurrently, they called for a return to religious virtue. Hannah More favoured Sunday schools as a means of controlling rising delinquency. The Methodist and anti-conformist movements had already awakened interest in social activism when More sounded her alarm. According to these movements, being a nominal Christian was not sufficient. Going to church only to fall asleep there was considered by reformers as an unfortunate left-over from a previous epoch of 'leisure' during which most men worried only about the pennies in their pockets and the food in their bellies. The Church of England responded to this moral revival by forming pious societies and charity groups designed to provide spiritual and material relief to the poor. In a bid to promote the integrity and stability of the family, it also began preaching against sexual libertinism, something that had been of less concern in the eighteenth century.

Associating the ruling classes with the notion of a 'public good' was unique to England and facilitated a later cooperative, non-revolutionary venture between the aristocracy and the middle classes, a venture that eventually drew in the working classes. In France, the aristocracy had bitterly withdrawn from the monarchy's bungling attempts at integrating the bourgeoisie within the administration of the state. As a consequence of this, the French did not view the aristocracy as a class to be emulated but one whose habits could lead to further subjugation. They adopted some of its stylistic and aesthetic mannerisms but rejected its downward condescension with their own brand of upwardly reactive publican pride. In England, however, although the aristocracy was considered suspect due to its proverbial sensual libertinism, the upper classes managed to extricate themselves from their bad reputation at the eleventh hour. The early Victorian saying 'A place for each, and to each his place' was the social compromise reached between the aristocracy and the rest of the nation in exchange for social certainty, order, and stability.

A fitting example of the moral literature that appeared in response to the gluttony and ornamentalism of the Regency period was Reverend Thomas Gisborne's (1794) *Enquiry into the Duties of Men in the Higher and Middle Classes*. He insisted that morality, manners, and honour were equally required for the development of a complete gentleman or gentlewoman capable of functioning in a society in which social mobility and mercantilism were on the rise. Gisborne espoused a moral imperative that would protect people against the corruptive influences of a fickle marketplace. Such warnings against the dangers of commercialism were also present in Lord Chesterfield's *Letters* (1774). Chesterfield made every effort to encourage the preservation of the persona of the traditional English gentleman despite the mercantilism of the period. Hugely popular at the time of its publication, the work advised its reader that, although he might end up as a merchant, he would morally prosper as long as he took care to acquire all the qualities and 'polite behaviour of a gentleman.'

Thus, the qualities attributed to the well-bred gentleman were being filtered down to the commercial classes and being presented as a national ideal. England was acquiring a national courtesy tradition no longer dependent on continental imports. A similar democratization was observable in English usage. The colloquialisms of the working classes were increasingly integrated into the novels and works of nonfiction, thereby creating a distinctly English publican language that was neither aristocratic nor bound by the lowest common linguistic denominator. This rapprochement between the aristocracy and the lower classes was accomplished in great part through the inclusion in novels of protagonists who had been in the service of the aristocracy and, having learned the language of the nobility, were now using their own version of *genteel speech* (McIntosh 1986:9–10, 82–3). The traditional English butler was such a personage, able to converse equally with his titled employers and his working-class staff. What continued, however, to keep classes distinctly separate from one another was the matter of 'accent.' To this day, a person's accent in England can limit his social mobility.

Travel abroad now became a fashion rather than a search for knowledge and education in Continental mannerisms, as had been the custom during the grand tours of the previous century. The same foreigners who had previously acted as models of perfect etiquette for the youth of the upper English classes were now considered as anomalies. So, the influence of the Italians and the French decreased in direct relation to the rising wealth of the English aristocracy and upper middle classes. Literature even appeared exposing the 'superficial' side of the Continental cult of elegance. The anonymously published *The Man of Manners* (c. 1735) observed that many of the elegant lacked proper manners and could scarcely conceal their crudity with their fine clothes.

**Reconciling Morality and Etiquette**

The tensions between 'the elegance of style' and 'the rigours of moral values' led to the publication of a number of quasi-evangelical works whose primary purpose was to preach against moral liberalism. Appearing antagonistically alongside these moral tracts was the 'etiquette book,' a secular product designed to teach the mannerisms of good society without substantial references to more profound issues of right and wrong. One genre tried to revive moral values in a society increasingly given to expedient commercial solutions, while the other contented itself with promoting the fashionable mannerisms of the day. Manners were valued in the morality conduct books, but only inasfar as they were reflections of a moral person. In fact, many evangelical moralists considered manners on their own (without strong principled action) the stuff of corruption and hypocrisy.

Two of the most important conduct books of the evangelic revival movement were Thomas Gisborne's (1797) *An Enquiry into the Duties of Men* and Mrs Hester Chapone's (1778) *Letters on the Improvement of the Mind*. Similar titles such as *A Father's Instructions to His Children* (1776), *A Father's Bequest to His Son* (1811), and *Female Excellence or, Hints to Daughters* (1840) all tried to establish a respect for principled behaviour. The foundation of their arguments was religious integrity. William Wilberforce (1797), in *A Practical View of the Prevailing Religious System*, blasted the aristocracy for amusing itself and the middle class for pursuing profit at all moral cost. He declared that the enemy of humanity was the spirit of the world and a rising atheism that favoured profit over devotion. Manners were to be the finishing touches of principled comportment rather than practices sufficient unto themselves. The ideal of *bearing* (Winchester College's motto of 1393: 'manners maketh man') was giving way to the ideal of moral conduct.

The elevation of morality as a measuring tool for social legitimacy permitted a rising middle class to lay claim to a distinction that might otherwise not have been available to it. It also permitted it to keep a watchful eye on the excesses of the aristocracy and the corruptive influences of industrial society.

Evangelists appear only when there is social incertitude. Industrialization had created large urban areas in which anonymity was rampant – new products, new fashions and habits, all threatened to undermine the fixity and permanence of previous religious standards. The reaction of the aristocracy and the middle class towards the anxieties unleashed by the Industrial Revolution was to turn inwards to their homes and their own social circles. Family and close friends henceforth represented the social network that would stand against the influences of an increasingly complex and corrupt public world fraught with crime, fraud, poverty, and violence. The aristocrats mistrusted the new world because they feared the threat of a future rise in the power of the lower classes. The growing middle class mistrusted the new industrialization because it threatened its desire to remain free of bad influence and the deviance that came in its wake.

Withdrawal from the streets was partially a way of establishing a zone of safety as well as differentiation in social rank. By not consorting with the working classes, who were much more at ease with street culture, the middle classes distanced themselves and found self-esteem in such separatism. The theory that people take to public places when their housing is poor does not take into account the reverse of that process: the well-off do not remain off the streets because they have superior housing, but, rather, because they do not wish to be associated with those who are on the street. In fact, the upper and middle classes were not homebound; they practised selective sociability and invited their guests to private functions at exclusive clubs (Houghton 1957, Briggs 1954).

A further interesting phenomenon occurred in connection with the home. Middle-class families reclaimed their children from the old apprentice system and took upon themselves the role of socializing them and instilling them with moral virtues intended to protect them from anonymous corruptive public influences. Although nannies and governesses were employed in the more affluent homes where children were sent off to boarding schools, parents more often than not kept a close watch on the moral development of their children. The middle-class family used its new freedom and status to make the conduct of family members the hallmark of the family's reputation. The lower working classes, whose families were often dispersed in separate quarters due to their work as domestics or apprentices, did not yet have this privilege.

This tendency to consider the behaviour of the child as the signature of the family was already a nascent idea in the seventeenth century. John Locke ([1693] 1892) had written in *How to Bring Up Your Children, Being Some Thoughts on Health Education and Health Care* that meticulous attention paid to the raising of a child would produce grown children who would later on have respect and affection for their parents. At a time when only one-fourth to one-third of infants survived to their first birthday and only half of children reached their fifteenth birthday, the child was becoming a precious commodity.

Adopting some of the practices of the past while rejecting others, Victorians sought a reliable moral culture capable of transcending the uncertainties of the new industrial society. The entire era should be remembered not only for its Victorian code of family morality but also for the environment in which this code came into being: an increasingly dense urban world in which many lived in terrible conditions. The child labour factories, workhouses, and the poorhouses so eloquently described in the works of Charles Dickens, together with the smog-filled streets of London, where thousands died every year from coal fumes, made for an urban setting in which those who could afford it began sequestering themselves from the streets. The countless scams and tricks of the street hucksters who preyed upon a gullible population unaccustomed to the new machines and concoctions coming off the industrial lines further justified the arguments of those calling for restraint and caution.

Yet, standing in stark contrast to the conduct books that warned of moral perils were the etiquette books. The original French use of the word *étiquette* refers to a processing of labelling or codifying. It literally means something that is attached or affixed to something. Historically, it referred to the announcements and rules that were nailed onto posts and walls in towns announcing new decisions and laws. They were, therefore, as changeable as the policies of the authorities who affixed them. It is no coincidence that the word eventually came to be applied in connection with 'fashions' of behaviour that were subject to change.

So there were important variations between early courtesy books intended for courtiers, conduct books intended for people seeking moral guidance in response to a changing environment, and etiquette books listing the rules of fashionable and proper social behaviour. Conduct books sought the development of a virtuous mentality capable of resisting bad influence by remaining true to Christian principles. Etiquette books, on the other hand, were content to describe how a person could appear socially distinguished through certain mannerisms and adherence to pre-established rituals of interaction.

The rules of etiquette (e.g., which type of visit warranted which type of introduction, which type of calling card was to be left under which circumstances, and which corner of the card was to be folded to signify which message) were already in existence within aristocratic circles. These guides were meant as much to inform a high society increasingly receiving merchants in its folds of the long-standing practices of the aristocracy as they were to provide aristocrats with encyclopedic replays of their own culture. Etiquette, the art of knowing how to conduct oneself in polite society in order to be in tandem with that society's rules of propriety and membership, was already part of an aristocrat's upbringing. Yet, for someone moving up in society, who had grown up in less auspicious social circles, the how-to book of etiquette allowed the learning of what may have not been known or observed before. So, when it first appeared, etiquette was a replay of the mannerisms already practised by those of higher social rank. Its basis was imitation rather than personal development. It was only later that moral issues were in some measure integrated in the etiquette manuals in a bid to arrive at a compromise with the moralists.

By their very nature, etiquette books were the means by which the upper classes colonized the social behaviour of the rising middle classes. Through such colonization the aristocracy reserved the right at any given moment to raise the stakes in upward mobility by changing the rules of etiquette. Generally, however, as pointed out by Leanore Davidoff (1973) in *The Best Circles: Society Etiquette and the Season*, mobility was allowed from the middle class into the upper echelons to accommodate a changing technology requiring cooperative links between a land economy and a machine economy.

So, while conduct books tried to instill in their readers a sense of social duty and honour, qualities that were considerably needed during a period in which many had taken to questionable conduct due to the lure of the new industrial economy, the etiquette book contented itself with listing the protocols that needed following and the decorum that needed preserving in different social situations involving people of varying ranks. Thus, two etiquette books published a few years apart could contain many discrepancies, depending on the changing whims of whichever group was socially ascendant.

Although these etiquette books did not preoccupy themselves with moral issues, they nevertheless taught protocols of behaviour designed to create the *appearance* that the feelings of the other were being taken into consideration. In the English etiquette books considerable pains were taken to describe rules of behaviour that were specifically meant not to cause emotional discomfort to the other. One rule of etiquette was to conceal one's own emotional suffering so as not to create uneasiness in another. 'Propriety' included the avoidance of the 'horror' of emotional embarrassment. This remains a central component in English courtesy practices, and we shall discuss its full contemporary connotations in a later chapter, where we analyse the social psychology of varying politeness rituals. It is interesting to note, meanwhile, that some writers, such as Tim Newton (1998), have suggested that emotional restraint was not only a civility practice in England but a means by which the requirements of a market economy could be rationalized and detached from personal sentiment (69–80).

**The Polite and Considerate Individual**

What facilitated the acceptance of etiquette books by the morally preoccupied middle classes was the fact that these books began responding to some of the moral fears of the population. It took a while for this compromise to occur. Marjorie Morgan (1994) has suggested that the type of courtesy rules eventually adopted in Victorian England differed from the ideas espoused by the early conduct and etiquette books. The early etiquette works were quite unconcerned with morality or social justice:

> Etiquette reinforced the social hierarchy by assuming that the supreme consideration in regulating conduct between people was rank. Hierarchy permeated social observances and human relations regarding such matters as filing into the dining-room, seating arrangements, visits of ceremony, introductions, acquaintances, intimacy and even the seemingly trivial question concerning whether it was proper to pass a decanter on a tray or by hand. (28)

According to Morgan, with the development of a broader conception of 'good society,' a boundary that increasingly included the rising middle classes, there occurred a shift from etiquette meant for high society to one that could be practised within the 'drawing rooms' of middle-class homes. And, along with these more simplified rules of etiquette, there occurred a compromise between the writers of conduct and etiquette books, with each accepting the validity of the other's propositions. Etiquette books began making passing reference to the need to combine good manners with good ethics, and conduct writers returned to considering manners a useful prerequisite for the development of a moral gentleman and gentlewoman (120–31).

Thus, morality and good manners met in the drawing rooms of the Victorians. The separation of family life from the public sphere made a quasi-religion out of home life. And, indeed, the Victorian penchant for great amounts of furniture and decorative items revealed a careful planning of home space to provide the comforts and aesthetic stimulation required by a family trying to surround itself with a pleasing environment to inure itself from a hard and squalid external world. The leader of the Victorian 'self-help' movement, Samuel Smiles ([1875] 1958), valued home life to such an extent that he equated having a happy life at home with the development of an overall positive mental attitude:

> The Art of Living is best exhibited in the Home. The first condition of a happy home, where good influence prevails over bad ones, is Comfort. Where there are carking cares, querulousness, untidiness, slovenliness, and dirt, there can be little comfort either for man or woman. The husband who has been working all day, expects to have something as a compensa-

tion for his toil. The least that his wife can do for him, is to make his house snug, clean, and tidy, against his home-coming at eve. (359)

Like many middle-class Victorians, Smiles believed that a comfortable and pleasing home was the best protection against the temptations of a corrupt world. A man who was comfortable at home would be less disposed to being drawn away from his family. Thus, the Victorian search for comfort in the home also had a moral component:

Comfortable people are kindly-tempered ... There must be peace, mutual forbearance, mutual help, and a disposition to make the best of everything ... Comfortable people are persons of common sense, discretion, prudence, and economy. They have a natural affinity for honesty and justice, goodness and truth. (361)

In *Propriety and Position* (1987), M. Curtin explains that the etiquette books that flooded the publishing market in England after the 1830s concentrated heavily on the manners to be used in the drawing rooms of families. Victorian architects now planned houses with separate rooms, each with its own separate functions: the drawing room, the smoking room, the reading room, the bedroom, the servant's room; all had protocols of behaviour. What might have been discussed in one room was considered inappropriate conversation in another. Middle-class men were busy working in an industrial and commercial complex that increasingly made demands on their time, yet their wives, who were encouraged to remain idle and in charge of their homes, were left taking on an active moral and social position in Victorian society. Propriety and a peaceful comportment became the rule of the home, and it was left to the woman of the house to protect these values. The Victorian family gathered and behaved with propriety whether a stranger was present or not. Much of this propriety was meant to teach children the manners and codes of conduct that were expected of them. Undoubtedly, this ongoing attention to manners and propriety between parents and their children established the foundation for an English ethic of politeness based on emotional restraint and deference, for opposition to the parent was considered a sign of ill-breeding.

While they now contained token sections on morality, the etiquette books of the period continued to primarily focus on the manners and protocols to be used within the family and during visits paid to other families. How and when a calling card was to be used, the precise manner in which tea was to be served, and times appropriate for different types of visits were all noted in detail. Curtin suggests that many of these books were also intended to build a moral image for the women of the household and preserve them from gossip that might have compromised their reputation. The Victorian woman was expected to possess infinite tact, be kind with her family as well as strangers, and remain generally responsible for the happiness of her household. This, of course, put her in a position of considerable power as well as saddling her with an overall social responsibility bordering on self-denial. It is not coincidental that most etiquette books of the period had a strong female orientation.

This idealization of the female as a duty-bound agent of domestic and sexual purity – in considerable contrast to late seventeenth-century and early eighteenth-century sexual mores – became entrenched in mainstream Victorian thought. Considered to be members of the weaker sex, and supposedly given to welcoming chastity as proof of personal breeding and honour, women were expected to be gracious and social but not possess intellectual ambitions that might act to the detriment of the comfort of their family. What occurred here – as had in Della Casa's relegation of physical functions to the backstage of social life – was that overt sexuality became associated with moral corruption. In previous epochs, wedding rituals had required the guests to accompany the bride and groom to their bedroom, then undress them and put them to bed. Such public displays of nudity or sexuality would have been totally horrifying to those Victorians who now came to equate sexual conservatism with ethics and sensible family values.

While conformity to the opinions of others continued to be important within the smaller circles of family and friends within urban settings, the anonymity of urban life gave rise to a second standard, driving underground many of the sexual improprieties forbidden to Victorian families of 'good standing.' Prostitution increased and a lucrative pornography market came into being. This does not at all mean that a sizeable number of Victorians partook of these illicit pleasures, but it allowed a minority who needed them to avail themselves of them. Those who stood against these practices were quick to form private and public groups that tried to rehabilitate 'fallen women.' So the accusation that the Victorians practised a double standard is misleading in our opinion. A more useful assessment would recognize that contrasting ideologies vied for control of public morality.

Nor was dress any longer an indicator of actual moral worth. Increased spending power permitted even people of low social rank (and those of questionable moral practice) to acquire the latest fashions. A person could dress 'up' or 'down' in relation to their social rank and gain access to public places which might otherwise have been forbidden them in a smaller community where their identity and status were known. Manners and fashion allowed a person to hide their actual moral identity and create a favourable impression.

The products and frivolities that arrived in the wake of industrialization generated great excitement. This celebration of the *new* created a spirit of *contagion* and *imitation* which sorely worried conduct writers. Their fears were partially justified. The rise of the industrial *wage earner* considerably weakened existing patterns of familial moral authority. Wage earning took people away from their communities and decreased the influence of parents, parish elders, and clergy. While morals had previously been taught within the closed circle of the family and the town community, a new breed of moralizers and trendsetters appeared in the hundreds of newspapers and journals that became readily available in all areas due to the railway system. News from one city could reach another within a matter of hours and be purchased and read by anyone. Journalists became the new priesthood. They could write whatever they believed in and whatever suited the purpose of profit-motivated publishers increasingly beholden to corporate advertisers. Sometimes, the resulting editorial content contradicted the values held by parents and educators. And with the flooding of the market with body care and luxury items, the printed journal became a guide to the new joys of spending.

So pervasive became the habit of *imitative spending* that cartoonists began satirizing the new conspicuous consumption. John Leech's (1: 1886) *Pictures of Life and Character* poignantly shows the growing dominance of *taste* and *trend* and the pretentious competitiveness provoked in people of all classes. And fashion journals, such as *La Belle Assemblée*, showed the public the latest 'fashionable looks.' English fashion designers had managed to design clothes, which unlike the products of expensive Parisian haute couture, were elegant as well as affordable. Increasing numbers of women of modest means fell under the spell of fashion. Lady Palmerston, a leading trendsetter, writing in *La Belle Assemblée* (1807), summarized the new fashion ethic with brutal candour:

> It is not the good taste of a dress that constitutes its merit, but solely the fancy of the moment. You are thought exceedingly handsome in a very

ugly fashion, if it be but new, and you are thought ridiculous in a very handsome fashion, if it be out of date. (2:125)

Being *out of date* became a major fear of the rising classes, much to the dismay of moralists, who understood that constant change could undermine fixed notions of right and wrong; the danger of the *love of novelty* lay precisely in the fact that *novelty*, by definition, was a tradition-breaker. As early as 1781, Reverend V. Knox, a prominent writer on education, had complained that 'the too high estimation of the ornamental qualification is injurious to the individual, and to [the] continuity' (158). And, indeed, the Regency period had produced a wealth of ornamental luxury products that were avidly collected by the idle rich. It was not ornament and fashion, per se, to which the nineteenth-century moralists objected but to the *deception* made possible by the new premium placed on appearance and commercial success (McKendrick and Plumb 1979).

As for 'politeness,' it was a by-product of appearance management; it did not necessarily reveal the actual sentiments of a person. Even though it could very well include authentic emotions of friendliness and respect, sincerity was not required in all polite reactions. Politeness had a double edge. On one hand it permitted civil contact between strangers, assuring a certain amiability that diminished the possibility of discord and embarrassment. On the other hand, it acted as a mark of distinction and created distancing without abrasive unpleasantness.

'Privacy,' a word used reverently in England ever since the rise of the Victorians, now helped rationalize the need for keeping certain aspects of one's life hidden from public view. The polite person was considered to at least understand the meaning of propriety and privacy. Being *civilized* in the English manner came to mean being *amiable, fair,* and *avoiding unpleasantness*, even in situations of potential conflict or suffering. This was quite different from the *raffinement* (refinement) espoused by French courtesy. English politeness was not simply a matter of personal *style*. Aesthetic embellishment took second place to a cult of *cautious amiability* bordering on *reserve*.

What we see occurring here is a progression from courtesy as virtue, to conduct as moral discipline, to politeness and etiquette as marks of a civic distinction reminiscent of aristocratic sensibility, and, finally, to the development of a public politeness ethos. That there was a middle-class moral reaction to the deceptions of a society increasingly given to valuing appearance is understandable. So a certain compromise was struck between the moralists who stood against deception and the pragmatists who considered it an unavoidable by-product of a socially coherent civilized society. Both sides realized that neither total sincerity nor total pretense could have served in the new English industrial society.

The moralists had believed that the best defence against deception was loyalty to virtue, resistance to vice, and a total *sincerity* in relations with others. This search for authenticity had been a major theme in the literature of the period (Guilhamet 1974). But sincerity, if applied without restriction, would have required individuals to reveal all their thoughts and emotions, even those that were offensively critical of others. A sincerity practised without discrimination would have led to social dissonance. Reacting to the single-mindedness of both camps, cartoonists were quick to portray individuals telling one another exactly what they thought: the promoter admitting to his client that he would like nothing better than to trick him, the guest telling his hostess that he was leaving the party not because of a painful attack of gout but because he was totally bored and then her replying that she was glad to be rid of him because he was indeed a total bore. The cartoons showed how impossible would be the adoption of sincerity in all social situations. Satire became a means for critiquing social insincerity, providing some relief from the formally established politeness ethos (Browning 1983).

The evangelical moralists also presented 'sincerity' as a means by which a person could reveal his true intentions in the perilously anonymous urban society. Yet, as Morgan (1994) astutely points out, a sincere person could not count on his own sincerity to reveal the intentions of others. Lacking knowledge of the background and activities of another person left everyone, sincere or not, with the problem of never being sure of public dealings (130). Loving thy brother as you would have him love you did not work very well in streets populated by hucksters and promoters, for these types were more interested in their potential victim's wallet than in his fraternity. Quacks and salesmen of dubious products (including health elixirs) had duped many, charging much but delivering little. Even evangelists realized that measures stronger than personal sincerity were needed. This came in the form of professionalization.

Medical doctors, lawyers, and accountants formed professional associations to control quackery and build an image based on *sincere service*. Professional bodies also began exercising a moral control over their memberships. The educational qualifications of a potential medical doctor or lawyer had to be accompanied by attestations of his personal integrity. In this way, professional bodies legitimized the personal ambitions of their members and reassured the public that membership was a sign of competence and honesty. In effect, a type of aristocratic honour became conferred on professionals and set them apart from merchants.

Unlike the merchant whose main motive was the creation of maximum profit, the professional became perceived as someone who not only practised his profession for the public good but upheld high ideals of morality. Alexander Carr-Saunders and P.A. Wilson's *The Professions* (1933), W.J. Reader's *Professional Men* (1966), and Magali Sarfatti-Larson's *The Rise of Professionalism* (1977) locate the nineteenth century as the starting point for the modern professional spirit. Of course, professions existed prior to the industrial age. Yet, the manner in which 'professionalism' was now presented implied a disinterested and expert practitioner enlisted in the service of public welfare. By the end of the nineteenth century, actors, clergymen, journalists, artists, writers, musicians, and engineers were included in the list of professions. This professional legitimacy brought about a *formalization* of integrity. The integral professional paid attention to form as well as substance, to manners as well as morals. This formalism gave professionals considerable social authority, producing a kind of aristocracy of 'experts.'

In effect, the English dealt with the insecurities of industrial life by arriving at a compromise between the aristocracy and the middle class. Elias ([1939] 1982) points to this compromise as a distinctly English quality, one which eliminated the need for a revolution and contributed to the establishment of a culture of restraint in which politeness was of paramount importance (309–10). The middle classes realized that they could with great difficulty remain a distinct social order without some measure of pretense. The aristocracy, for its part, accepted to temper its former amoralism and hedonism with a concern for public welfare and ethics. This commonality explains why, although there still continue to be great differences between the upper classes and the rest of the population (financial as well as educational and cultural), there remains a common citizenship felt by all classes that seems to resist the dislocations of advanced technology and the increasing influence of American media. The common denominator was and continues to be the democratization of politeness and the practice of a very special behavioural tool called 'tact.'

*Tact* required putting some distance between oneself and others. It was based on an agreement not to be overly direct with another, nor unduly impose on the privacy of the other. And tact did require some emotional reserve. Lord Chesterfield ([1774] 1969), in his letters to his son, cautions against the folly of being emotionally transparent:

> Beware, therefore, now that you are coming into the world, of these proferred friendships. Receive them with great civility, but with great incredulity too; and pay them with compliments but not with confidence. (32)

Like politeness, tact was a behavioural mechanism not dependent on wealth or title. It became a means by which a certain distance could be maintained in social contacts. It was a refinement of politeness, a conscious application of it. Anyone could practise tact if he or she understood its basic purpose. And in the urban setting where people did not know each other and were wary of the influence of strangers, tact became a way of preserving a public demeanour that permitted a sharing of civic space with a minimum of personal involvement or conflict. Retaining one's *poise* became a means by which both the other and the self could be treated with non-invasive deference and reserve.

The Duke of Wellington was practising tremendous restraint on the battlefield of Waterloo when he leafed through a fashion magazine while making jovial comments to his officers during the height of battle. This was not insensitivity but the desire to appear unruffled and display 'emotional steadiness' to officers who might have been sorely worried. It would have been quite *tactless* to openly admit the danger of the situation. Such loss of restraint would have also entailed a loss of nerve. The entire English notion of *keeping a stiff upper lip* refers not only to emotional restraint but the keeping of a stoic demeanour in face of adversity, suffering, and danger.

Extolling the virtues of tact, Lord Chesterfield cautioned against excessive self-revelation and considered it a dangerous practice that could irritate the neutral civil space between subjects. He advised:

> Of all things, banish the egotism out of your conversation, and never think of entertaining people with your own personal concerns or private affairs; though they are interesting to you, they are tedious and impertinent to everybody else; besides that, one cannot keep one's private affairs too secret. (34)

Tact also involved a consideration for the other's dignity, whether the other was of a higher or lower class than one's own. It required a certain 'depersonalization' of both interactants; it required identification with the other through common humanity rather than specific biography. Before tact could be exercised the other had to be recognized as someone to be protected from direct, discomforting observations. This did not mean that the desire to compete with, surpass, or even defraud others was eliminated. Nor did it put an end to razor-sharp conceit. Rather, it meant that a common agreement was established between citizens of various ranks to maintain a public spirit based on an active, uncompromisingly polite interactive style that, above all, sought to *pacify* potential aggression and emotion. Tact and subtlety ensured that nothing would be said that might create unease in the other. It also somehow gave rise to a cheery disposition buoyed by optimistic faith. That anger was frowned upon during this period is understandable. Children had to desist from expressing anger towards their parents because respect had to be maintained at all times – anger signified that the authority of the parent was being discounted and disrespected. When anger did need expressing in polite society, it was done through irony and icy comments; a cheery disposition could even mask anger.

Essayist Roger Rosenblatt shows this particularly English mix of courtesy, kindness, and compassion when discussing a scene from the film of Jane Austen's *Sense and Sensibility*:

> The pivotal scene in the film of Jane Austen's Emma occurs when Emma flings a witty insult in the direction of Miss Bates, a sweet-natured, simple-minded thing, by pointing out how boring the lady is ... But Knightly, Emma's severely critical friend, who loves her, tears into Emma later for her uncharacteristic act of cruelty ... Emma is shaken to the roots with shame. She knows how wrong she was. What Knightly and Austen are asserting is a connection between courtesy, kindness, and compassion. All the apparently superficial manners that propel Emma's small English universe are, when one probes to the roots, instruments of compassion. (1996)

Politeness and tact, therefore, as conceived in England, came to rest on a quasi-moral belief that public comfort was sacrosanct enough for individuals to desist from any extravagant homage to self that might be socially embarrassing, irritating, or hurtful to others. It is not surprising then that a citizen getting off a bus in England (outside the large cities, at least) turns to thank the driver; the act is performed to communicate to the driver that he or she is not taken for granted. It is the ultimate expression of 'modesty.' It is hardly surprising that Della Casa's utilitarian treatment of manners and tact was very popular in England.

Thus, a mutual colonization took place between the aristocracy and the middle class. The middle class accepted the premium placed by the aristocracy on *manners* and the aristocracy began moulding itself to middle-class concern with *morals*. While it is true that manners are usually transmitted from the upper to the lower classes, the melding of *etiquette* and *morality* created a two-directional flow of influence. While the etiquette books of the early nineteenth century dispensed the rules of manners with disregard for moral qualities such as sincerity, authenticity, and integrity, the etiquette books which appeared in the latter half of the century took special care to affirm the importance of *character* as well as *mannerism*. A series of books written anonymously revealed this compromise reached between manners and morals: *Talking and Debating: or Fluency of Speech Attained* (1856), *General Usage in Modern Polite Society* (1867), *Talk and Talkers* (1859), and *Modern Etiquette in Private and Public* (1871). These conduct books reflected the growing influence and power of the middle classes and an aristocracy in process of renewal and reform. A certain complicity between classes was created, and this complicity was made possible by the fact that England had distinguished itself on the international front through the practice of a distinctly English respect for rationality and order.

Yet, this respect for order and privacy did not mean that the Victorians were not given to favouring the imaginary regions of the mind and heart. In fact, the 'romanticizing' of life became a direct consequence of a civility system that needed some life-giving escape valve. This resistance against an overly rationalized industrial order had already begun in the eighteenth century when a 'cult of sensibility' had challenged the English preference for emotional reserve.

## From Eighteenth-Century Sentimentalism to Victorian Romanticism

Many explanations of the effects of Protestantism often gloss over its paradoxical effects on social interactions. Following Max Weber's (1930) seminal work on *The Protestant Ethic and the Spirit of Capitalism*, the social sciences have come to equate the rationalization of capitalist societies with the asceticism of Protestant doctrine. This theory, however, misses many of the events and changes in awareness that occurred between the origins of capitalism and its later manifestations. To ignore these intervening occurrences makes one prone to directly connecting the consequences of capitalism with its origins. This does not help us in any way understand the emotional basis of contemporary consumption-oriented societies. We are left to conclude that a religious doctrine degenerated into simple greed. We would propose a different explanation, one that is necessary to our understanding of civility in contemporary society and, certainly, vital to our understanding of the origins of Victorian romanticism and its effect on twentieth-century civil norms.

The Industrial Revolution created a dilemma for many Europeans who continued to remain obliged to the influences of a pious Protestantism founded on a high valuation of asceticism. Increased prosperity required justification for the use of products not previously considered essential. Such justification was especially needed for the consumption of ornamental products. Ministering to personal pleasure required some rational justification of pleasurable consumption if Protestant's high valuation of deep piety was not to be embarrassingly debunked.

Victorians were faced with the need to decide what role should be played by desire and emotion in the new society. Ironically, however, the ideologies of ascetic Protestantism had already helped create the conditions necessary for the acceptance of hedonism long before the Victorians were faced with their dilemma. Weber's focus on 'asceticism' as the foundation of capitalism underplays the later role played by personal imagination in the creation of sensuous consumption.

Protestantism had in some measure already sanctioned individualism when Protestant theologians had consigned to the individual the singularly personal act of moral self-evaluation; the elimination of the priest as an intermediary (and witness of the inner conscience of the individual) had the effect of separating the world of action (governed by communal standards and judgments) and the world of personal conscience (a realm considerably open to a person's sentimental and imaginative intervention). Although Protestant theologians specified that there should be no contradictions between the world of action and the realm of personal sentiment, there did develop a heightened private relationship between a person and his inner sentimental self.

A further justification for sentiment appeared during the eighteenth century when a 'cult of sensibility' mounted a considerable resistance towards the aesthetic barrenness of the governance of reason *and* the emotional stoicism of an aristocracy considered patently arrogant and corrupt. Sentimentality allowed a person to provide others with outward indications of the *benevolence, sincerity, and compassion* of his inner self despite the emotional limitations of a social dialogue based on reason and social propriety.

Anthony Ashley Cooper, Third Earl of Shaftesbury ([1714] 1964), rationalized the virtue and aesthetics of sentiments in *An Inquiry Concerning Virtue and Merit*:

> Of this even the wickedest Creature living must have a *Sense*. So that if there be any further meaning in this *Sense* of Right and Wrong; if in reality there be any *Sense* of this kind ... it must consist in real Antipathy or Aversion to *Injustice* or *Wrong*, and in a real Affection or Love towards *Equity* and *Right*, for its own sake, and on the account of its own natural Beauty and Worth. (42)

Shaftesbury's vindication of human goodness (and the ability to experience it as a sensory or emotional reality) stood in stark contrast to Bernard de Mandeville's amoral rationalization of a free-market economy in which both vice and virtue led to economic benefits. Shaftesbury's attack on utilitarianism struck a cord in the rising middle classes. While he did not attack mercantilism, he reassured that benevolence would limit its excesses.

A potent argument in favour of an innate sense of right and wrong had also been made by Adam Smith ([1759] 1982) in *The Theory of the Moral Sentiments*. Moral goodness had previously been rationalized in one of two ways: as a rule to be legislated or as a value that could be argued through reasonable dialogue. Neither argument took into account the possibility of an innate human moral sense. Smith, however, argued that people were born with this moral sense. Just as they possessed a natural preference for beauty and harmony, so did they *sense* right from wrong. Their *conscience*, a faculty that went beyond the law and rational argument, informed them of the morality of their actions. And *sympathy* (the recognition that different persons shared a natural fellowship of sentiment) motivated humans to seek order and cooperation.

Shaftesbury's and Smith's works had a profound (and lasting) influence on intellectual and artistic thought in England. Poets were enlisted to sing the praises of the ultimate benevolence of human nature. Sir William Jones, a member of Dr Johnson's Literary Club, concurred with Shaftesbury's optimistic faith in human goodness. In an essay entitled 'On the Arts Commonly Called Imitative' (1772), Jones called for a poetic tradition that would not content itself on imitating manners but be *passionately evocative*. The underlying belief of these calls for sensibility was the certainty that the heart contained its own rational moral principles and that a return to feeling would assure the expression of innate goodness (Mullan 1988). Such abiding faith in the ennobling effects of sentiments, even the melancholic kinds, moved the anonymous writer of a 1755 essay – aptly entitled 'Moral Weeping' – to state:

> Moral weeping is the sign of so noble a passion, that it may be questioned whether those are properly men, who never weep upon any occasion. They may pretend to be as heroical as they please, and pride themselves in a stoical insensibility; but this will never pass for virtue with the true judges of human nature. What can be more noble human than to have a tender sentimental feeling of our own and other's [sic] misfortunes? This degree of sensibility every man ought to wish to have for his own sake, as it disposes him to, and renders him more capable of practising [sic] all the virtues that promote his own welfare and own happiness.

Widely popular when it first appeared, Henry Mackenzie's ([1771] 1967) *A Man of Feeling* became the leading text of the new cult of sentimentality. Mackenzie merged sentiment and sensibility, considering them mutually reinforcing virtues. In his story, the hero, Harley, is made to suffer a series of episodes in which he remains benevolent despite the uncaring reactions of others. He helps the disadvantaged, suffers the pain of lost love, and, although he does not succeed according to worldly measures of success, he manages to remain of good heart. Mackenzie asked a profound question in his work: is unbending benevolence the mark of a virtuous man or simply the behaviour of a fool? What are to be the limits of disinterested altruistic behaviour? If Harley was indeed not a fool, then what was to be said about those who remained unresponsive to him? Was their preoccupation with their own interests to be judged as immoral? Were they to be held accountable for not responding to Harley with a warmness of heart equal to his own? Undoubtedly, readers of varying persuasions reached those conclusions that best suited their dispositions.

The call for sensibility should not predispose us to conclude that a major revolution in feeling occurred in the eighteenth century. Sentimentalism did not require self-affirmative, confrontational emotionalism. Although some writers worried about the increasing attention paid to sentimental friendships, and wondered whether this would decrease parental influence and the unity of the family, no major intergenerational conflict occurred. *The distinction between sentiments and primary emotions is an important one if we are to understand why the Victorians ended up mistrusting strong displays of emotion while maintaining a considerable respect for compassion.* A sensible person had access to some of his senses if not his primal emotional repertoire. He was able and willing to shed tears and show mortification when confronted with the plight of other individuals and the discomforting aspects of a rapidly changing world. Certainly, sentimentalism did begin reversing a process of emotional restraint that had been centuries in the making. And the cult of sensibility was supported by many mainstream writers known for their impetuous personalities (Jones 1993, Brissenden 1974). But, by and large, it did not cause an emotional uprising of the magnitude witnessed in the mid-twentieth century.

Sentimentality did not successfully bridge the boundary between social rituals and a sincere benevolent morality because it remained trapped in its own web of exaggeration and artifice. In retrospect, the *Princeton Encyclopedia of Poetry and Poetics* defines sentimentality as the presence of exaggerated emotion in a situation that does not warrant such a show of sentiment (Preminger 1974).

Being a dramatized show of feeling, sensibility could not successfully provide a guarantee of sustained communal solidarity. The fact that the sentimental person was 'demonstrating' his sensibility (as opposed to expressing an uncontrollable primary emotion) rendered the act suspect or, at least, tinged with self-love. Eleanor Sickels (1969) similarly observes, in *The Gloomy Egoist: Moods and Themes of Melancholy from Gray to Keats*, that sentimentality often involved indulging in emotions for their own sake (195). Many even experienced a distinct pleasure in feeling melancholic, for their melancholy confirmed to them that they were of a gentle and innocent disposition and, consequently, unsuited to the brutal utilitarianism of an uncaring world.

Regardless of its potential egoism, many in the eighteenth century came to consider sentimentality as a mark of sincerity. A person of *natural sentimentality* was considered honourable and emotionally responsive to the predicaments of others. As for those given to being sentimental, they rationalized their lack of stoicism as a moral resistance against the utilitarianism of reason and the amoralism of the old stoic aristocracy (Bredvold 1962).

Ironically, the justification of emotional exhibitionism as a moral quality established a credible link between Protestant ideology and the new cult of feeling. Although there was 'pleasure in pity,' pity itself was a moral act that was completely in keeping with the Protestant requirement of compassion (Aldridge 1949:139). And, although sentimentalists questioned the highly rational outcomes of Protestantism, their search for purity betrayed a particularly Protestant disposition towards idealism. It is difficult for us living in a culture in which a sudden outburst of tears (especially in public) is considered a sign of 'unresolved emotional issues' to imagine that members of parliament in the eighteenth century were given to openly weeping to demonstrate their sincerity, especially when a favoured bill was defeated by the opposition. The cult of sensibility accorded moral approval to people who allowed themselves to 'indulge in all the virtuousness of sorrow' and even 'a pleasing kind of distress' (Sickels 1969:103) because the alternative, emotional stoicism, became considered a sign of heartlessness. The open display of sentiments was some proof that the feeling capacities of the gentle classes had survived after centuries of restraints and controls imposed by political and ideological change, the last and least favoured of these being the rising influence of the industrialists and scientists.

This contrast between sentiment and the restraint and prudence of 'good sense' is most evident in Jane Austen's classic novel *Sense and Sensibility* ([1811] 1965). The two sisters who are the protagonists of the novel are polar opposites, even though neither finds ultimate satisfaction. Marianne lives through feverish emotion, valuing all that is sensational and picturesque. Her volatility is energized by a deep Rousseauian desire to be true to her primal nature; yet, there is an element of narcissism to her behaviour, for there seems to be a self-luxuriating side to her distress and her pleased impetuosity. Competing for her desire to be natural is her need to feel unique and different from her sister Elinor and everything that she represents. Elinor, on the other hand, is the embodiment of good middle-class sense and emotional restraint. When Marianne rationalizes an impropriety that she has committed with a potential suitor by saying that it could not have been wrong because she felt good during the experience, Elinor reminds her that the 'pleasantness' of an experience does not indicate its moral validity.

At stake is an oppositional relationship between self-gratification and the common sense required to remain within the good graces of moral society. Marianne chooses the path of the sentimental impulsive self, even though it leads her into troublesome situations. The roots of bohemianism are present in some moderate form in Marianne's approach to life, for she consistently searches for the ideal heart connection, the ideal person whose tastes will match hers, bringing about a perfect union of sensibilities. The two sisters are in fact the consequence of an existing polarity between common sense and sentiment. Marianne seems to drive Elinor to be more restrained than she might otherwise be, while Elinor's detached common sense provides Marianne with further justifications for pursuing a self-exploratory life. For Marianne, giving in to 'good sense' means giving in to a deadened personality. She cannot bear that alternative.

It was predictable that the cult of sensibility would lose its fervour following a growing suspicion that over-indulgence in sentiments had the paradoxical effect of creating a self-satisfaction that ironically led to a callousness of heart and to ethical passivity. J.M.S. Tompkins (1961) notes the narcissistic aspects of exaggerated sentimentality in his study *The Popular Novel in England, 1770–1880*:

> Again and again we find that enormity of self-congratulation with which the weeper at once luxuriates in the beguiling softness of tears and compliments himself on his capacity for shedding them, seeing in his mind's eye not only the object of his attention ... but himself in a suitable attribute of it. (101)

A considerable number of works appeared at the end of the eighteenth century denouncing sentimentality and its self-absorptive qualities (Rogers 1934:98–122, Aldridge 1949:76–87, Brissenden 1974). Twelve years after publishing *The Man of Feeling*, Mackenzie himself took to criticizing the unrestrained popularization of sentiment in the novels of the period:

> In the enthusiasm of sentiment there is much the same danger as in the enthusiasm of religion, of substituting certain impulses and feelings of what may be called a visionary kind, in the place of real practical duties, which in morals, as in theology, we might not improperly denominate *good works*. ([1785] 2003)

Hannah More ([1778] 1853) also delivered a scathing attack on sentimentality in a work urging women to resist the seduction of popular sentimental novels:

> The present age may be termed ... the age of sentiment, a word which, in the implication it now bears, was unknown to our plain ancestors. Sentiment is the varnish of virtue, to conceal the deformity of vice; and it is

not uncommon for the same persons to make a jest of religion, to break through the most solemn ties and engagements, to practice every art of latent fraud and open seduction, and yet to value themselves on speaking and writing *sentimentally*. (295)

More felt obliged, nevertheless, to redefine sentimentality in terms of a new imperative of authenticity, distinguishing between sentiments and principles. Sentiment was the virtue of ideas, while principle was the virtue of action. One could not exist without the other, not in an honest person. Realizing that goodness still required emotional expression, she rationalized authentic virtue by admitting that a certain amount of Romantic imagination could be considered virtuous provided that it was not cheapened by sensationalism:

> And enthusiasm is so far from being disagreeable, that a portion of it is perhaps necessary in an engaging woman. But it must be the enthusiasm of the heart, not of the senses. It must be the enthusiasm which grows up from a feeling mind, and is cherished by a virtuous education; not that which is compounded of irregular passions, and artificially refined by books of unnatural fiction and improbable adventure. I will even go so far as to assert, that a young woman cannot have any real greatness of soul, or the true elevation of principle, if she has not a tincture of what the vulgar would call Romance, but which persons of a certain way of thinking will discern to proceed from those fine feelings, and that charming sensibility, without which, though a woman may be worthy, yet she can never be amiable. (295)

It would seem that the same movement towards *sensibilité* that occurred in France was reproduced in some measure in England. There was one notable difference, however. France was Catholic and more disposed to tolerating sensuality and artifice. The French had certainly learned the aesthetic pleasures taught to them by Louis XIV, who had succeeded, through pomp and ceremony, to build an impressive cultural and artistic heritage for France. The French were less disposed to turn against sentimentality once it had been proven to no longer be a reliable indicator of moral worth. Despite the moralistic warnings of writers such as Madame de Maintenon (1772), the French managed to feel at ease with artifice and its softening strategies. Their acceptance of *vraisemblance* (the act of *appearing* real) took the edges off the search for an exact correlation between inner personal sentiment and outward expression.

Reading through the French literature, one has the impression that the goal of the French was not as much to formalize moral validation but to seek pleasure in sentimental interactions that helped confirm self-identity and the limitless ability of the self to express itself with dramaturgical subtlety. There is no indication that there was an overriding requirement that such exchanges should be rational, stoic, or restrained, all qualities more fittingly associated with Protestantism's and Anglicanism's distinct histories in England. Moreover, French laicism freed the French from having to evaluate every practice according to religious worth.

A key word in Hannah More's manifesto in favour of a tempered sentimentalism was the word 'romance.' It would seem that More recognized that, in a world governed by superficiality and corruption, a certain amount of imagination was needed to distance oneself and lead a principled life. Informed by the self-affirming emotiveness of the cult of sensibility, and their own disdain for the hegemony of utilitarianism, Romantics used personal sentiment and passionate judgment of existing social practices, hoping that they could reverse the cold-hearted bottom-line mentality of many of the *nouveaux riches*. While the disease of heartlessness had not changed, the enemy seemed to have done so – the old aristocracy was replaced by a new prospering middle class anxious to rationalize its new riches. A more Puritan solution to the dilemma of industrial expediency could not have been found, for Romanticism, despite its original allergy towards scienticism, reaffirmed the Protestant valuation of inner conscience and individualism. And it did so by assigning a quasi-spiritual value to the human *imagination*.

In a perceptive work entitled *The Romantic Ethic and the Spirit of Modern Consumerism* ([1987] 1993), Colin Campbell has argued that Puritanism carried within it the necessary conditions for the creation of a modern personality that was morally comfortable with hedonism. Campbell suggests that the emotional restraints imposed on children may have encouraged daydreaming, the necessary condition for the creation of a Romantic predisposition.

This romantic aspect of *daydreaming* is crucial to the understanding of the Romantic spirit that emerged in the Victorian era and which continues to have an effect on contemporary societies of consumption. Fantasy and imagination – discreet ways of thinking of what is either different from external reality, not readily available, or forbidden – created a certain personal satisfaction which habituated the person to feeling comfortable with pleasure, or, at least, desirous of experiencing it

(Addison 1961, Barfield 1954, Brown, 1991). So, the hedonism movement was not exclusively a product of the 1920s and 1960s – it was already rooted in the Romantic leanings of the Victorians. Moreover, imagination established the pre-conditions for social idealism. Imagining and sensing pleasure in the privacy of the daydream, the Romantic returned into the world anxious to find a concrete manifestation of his imagined desires and ideals. Campbell ([1987] 1993) astutely differentiates between eighteenth-century sentimentalism and nineteenth-century Romanticism by explaining that Romantics placed emphasis not on sentiment but on passion, believing in 'the centrality of the personal drama of conversion and salvation (in which each soul had a unique destiny)' (185).

Predictably, imagination – an act that could produce ideas that substantially differed from 'reality' – created dissatisfaction, since the idealist, in his search for a perfect vehicle for his imagination, was often disappointed by the utilitarian mentality that preached realism at all cost. T.E. Hulme (1962) has attributed this desire for social perfection to the legacy left behind by Utopian writers such as Rousseau:

> Romantics had been taught by Rousseau that man was basically good, that it was only bad laws and customs that had suppressed him. Remove all these and the infinite possibilities of man could have a chance ... Here is the root of all romanticism: that man, the individual, is an infinite reservoir of possibilities; and if you can so rearrange society by the destruction of oppressive order then these possibilities will get a chance and you will get Progress. (35–6)

Campbell ([1987] 1993) explains how this determination to create a world that could be worthy of the name 'progress' from a variety of perspectives – material, emotional, and spiritual – caused considerable excitement in artists, moving them to look on art as the only means of stimulating the imagination of those whose feelings had become lulled to sleep by the expediencies of modern living. Sensibility and the high valuation of the senses were, in a manner, the precursors of the Romantic movement, a self-defensive response to a rational industrial world (Hilles and Bloom 1965). Campbell ([1987] 1993) argues that, in rejecting the trappings of bourgeois society (house, furniture, carriages, and clothes), the Romantics were aware that they were committing themselves to an ethic of 'pleasure' and holding that as a valued means for self-expression (197). Disillusioned by the fact that the sentimentalists had operated using merely more elegant versions of existing social conventions of submission, the Romantics went to the other extreme and called for a sincerity that could limit bourgeois propriety and its undesirable muting of the human spirit. Towards the end of the eighteenth century it became important to determine the affable individual's moral values and his sense of discernment (Sheriff 1982:27–35).

In fact, what may have distinguished the Victorian civility practices is that they were based on a certain global vision of progress that facilitated the rise of liberalism despite the surface appearance of a staunchly conservative culture (Otter 2002:1–15).

## Self-Help: The Importance of Being Earnest

The period of 1840 to 1870, properly considered the mid-Victorian period, was a time of great confidence in English industrial institutions. During the thirty years between 1851 and 1881, 'the national product rose from £523 million (£25 per capita) to £1,051 million (£75 per capita)' (Briggs 1987:231). Anticipating this economic boom, Prince Albert opened the Great Exhibition of 1850 at the Crystal Palace, a gigantic glass greenhouse three times the length of Albert Hall that put on display the latest developments of science and industry. The exhibit elated middle-class Victorians for it seemed to confirm that their struggle for a good society built through rational industriousness and morality had been successful. Three-quarters of the products exhibited were made in England or in British territories. Working-class people also filed through the exhibition, impressed with the great products that they had helped manufacture; albeit they entered on days when the price of admission was lowered to be within their means.

To imagine the strain that people must have felt while they adjusted to the opportunities and limitations of industrial progress is to see a culture presented with contradictory advice: it is good to have manners but manners alone without morality are naught. It is good to be moral but how far can a moral person go if he is lacking in manners? It is good for the woman to be submissive and soft but can these same qualities not make her vain and unable to comprehend matters of intellect? It is desirable that a woman develop her intellect, but then what if she becomes too manly and loses her good heart?

Enough shocks hit the Victorians in the nineteenth century to make the use of traditional books on behaviour unsatisfactory. Charles Darwin published *On the Origin of Species* ([1859] 1995) and *The Descent of*

*Man* (1871), advancing the idea that human life followed the laws of a natural world that favoured the survival of the fittest. Other surprises were delivered by Thomas Henry Huxley's *The Physical Basis of Life* ([1868] 1893). Huxley questioned the whole notion of fixity, arguing that man consisted of an amalgamation of chemicals and liquids and air. Pious Victorians were left wondering about the whereabouts of the soul. Charles Lyell's *Principles of Geology* (1840) had already put into question the Biblical assurance that the earth was created six thousand years ago. Theology was rapidly becoming replaced by a national tradition of cause-and-effect thinking, most of it based on scientific rationalism.

Despite the jarring dislocations of industrialization, a violent revolution might have been considered unreasonable. On a philosophical level, England had not rejected the Cartesian model of reason as the final arbiter of things. The seventeenth-century reaction against reason had predisposed France to move towards a paradoxical mix of sentimentality and Lockean utilitarianism. This mix suited the bourgeoisie in France for it needed to follow utilitarian goals while not losing sight of the politically emancipatory aspects of emotional expression. A nation that undergoes an outright national revolution, an event filled with strong passions, does not easily give up the association formed in its collective consciousness between sentimentality, emotionalism, and the phenomenon of being a free person with full rights.

In England, however, the Victorians managed to use reason as a justification for many of the collective cultural values that they embraced, including that of emotional restraint. The widespread adoption of 'reasonableness' was a strong component of the new ethos of politeness. Ironically enough, the English adopted Descartes's separation of the mind and body and then tempered that severe disassociation with the sentimentality espoused by writers such as Hume and Smith. Pragmatism and the gentler feelings somehow became mutually compatible in England.

The historian Asa Briggs has labelled the Victorian project as the 'Age of Improvement' (1954). And improvement and self-help were the new catchwords of a middle class forced to reconcile the promises of industrialization with the misery surrounding them. Proponents of 'self-help' managed to equate helping the self with helping others in society. It was assumed that just as bad influence could be contagious, so could the setting of example become socially progressive and help the more unfortunate improve their lot. It was also a way adopted by middle-class Victorians of reassuring themselves that their project was not doomed to failure. Carlyle named this worry the 'terror of not succeeding' (1843:146). *Emulation* was the catchword now in a progressive society in which men and women were accomplishing unheard-of things.

To understand the incertitude facing the Victorians one has only to visualize a society in which, on one hand, great wealth was being created, while, on the other hand, a massive displacement was making survival nearly impossible for hundreds of thousands. The streets of London were disturbing reminders to the middle classes that their comfortable lifestyles were being won at a price. By the 1850s there were nearly 750,000 women working as servants in middle- and upper-class homes and a further 25,000 employed as governesses. These women helped remind more fortunate women that the most satisfactory career was that of a married woman. Work became the great 'protector,' whether it was the work of a husband or the work of a woman thrown back on her own means. And work accelerated the pace of life. In the 1860s, Frances Cobbe (1864) made the following comment about her own era compared with the early decades of the nineteenth century:

> That constant sense of being-driven – not precisely like 'dumb' cattle, but cattle who must read, write, and talk more in twenty-four hours than twenty-four hours will permit, can never been known to them [the people of 1800–30]. (482)

Indeed, the 'reserve' of the middle class was partially motivated by a desire not to be associated with the uncleanness and misery of the poor, who were living in terrible accommodations or no accommodations at all. In *Democracy in America* ([1884] 1994), Alexis de Tocqueville explained this English reserve as a particularly aristocratic defence mechanism against the dangers of social mixing:

> Aristocratic pride still being a very strong force with the English, and the boundaries of aristocracy having become doubtful, each man is constantly afraid lest advantage be taken of his familiarity. Not being able to judge at first sight the social position of the people he meets, he prudently avoids contact with them. He is afraid that some slight service rendered may draw him into an unsuitable friendship. He dreads civility and is as much anxious to avoid the demonstrative gratitude of a stranger as his hostility. (566)

One cannot stress enough the brilliance of Tocqueville's insight, for it demonstrates how a practice can become uncoupled from its original cause and take on a shape and purpose of its own long after it has outgrown its purposes. To understand the force of habituation is to realize that a sociology of culture needs to take two histories into account: the conscious and the forgotten.

It was within this climate of anxiety and worry that the Victorians turned to the idea of 'self-help,' the notion that a person was responsible for *improving* himself through whatever means were available. Overpowered by the contingency of industrial life, with its multiple seductions and displacements, a family had to exercise its duty: to work honestly, to never give up hope, and to press for the manifestation of an ideal culture governed by principled behaviour.

This social idealism accorded with the idealism of the Victorian scientists and engineers who saw a future blessed with technical progress. It was as if there were a concentrated effort to come up with reliable general laws in both the social and natural realms. Even Mill ([1865] 1961), who came to mistrust the mechanization of rationalism, wondered if the natural laws of science could be applied to human action and produce a set of universal laws capable of guiding social behaviour. Influenced by Auguste Comte, whom he introduced to England, he searched for a balance between optimism and anxiety, hope and disappointment, for he believed that even the more painful realizations of life could lead to a renewed commitment to duty and a revitalized practical morality.

That Victorian writers often communicated with a partially educated public experiencing the anxieties of uncertainty should not be overlooked. There were as many prophets as newspapers and journals. What mattered less than what a man believed in was whether he was able to adopt a belief and stand by it. This penchant for 'volitional action' had been a central theme of British literature and Evangelical Anglicanism. As literature was made popular and accessible to the middle class, themes of self-realization and personal responsibility emerged and supplemented the romances. English literature during the mid-nineteenth century played an important role in the creation of a public English personality (Taylor 1997:125).

Samuel Smiles's 'Self-Help' ([1859] 1958) became the behavioural bible of the period. Smiles believed that a man should be able to make something worthy of himself regardless of his social position. 'Perseverance' and 'energy' were sources of wealth in self-improvement. Smiles legitimized this optimistic view of a person's options in life by citing the biographies of successful men who had come from humble beginnings. In defence of the ambitious individual he wrote:

> It is energetic individualism which produces the most powerful effects upon the life and action of others, and really constitutes the best practical education. Schools, academies, and colleges, give but the merest beginnings of culture in comparison with it. Far more influential is the life-education daily given in our homes, in the streets, behind the counters, in workshops, at the loom and the plough, in counting-houses and manufactories, and in the busy haunts of men. This is the finishing instruction as markers of society, which Schiller designated 'the education of the human race,' consisting of action, conduct, self-culture, self-control. (39)

Smiles was championing a respect for work, any type of work, provided a person did his best to arrive at his utmost potential. He even considered easy riches a hindrance to self-realization: 'Riches are so great a temptation to ease and self-indulgence to which men are by nature prone, that the glory is all the greater of those who, born to ample fortunes, nevertheless take an active part in the work of their generation' (51). He swept aside the idea that failure can come to good, hard-working people: 'Men who are constantly lamenting their luck are in some way or other reaping the consequences of their neglect, misman-agement, improvidence, or want of application' (267). To further his argument, he quoted Dr Johnson, who had declared: 'All the complaints which are made of the world are unjust. I never knew a man of Merit neglected; it was generally his own fault that he failed at success' (266).

Smiles, however, did not address the fact that the jobs that were being created in the new industrial state were being made possible precisely by individuals who were spending their money on products without which they had managed quite well before. Like many moralists of the Victorian era he did not consider what Mandeville had realized in his *Fable of the Bees* ([1715] 1962) that virtue and vice were part of a system that required both for its economic survival, that for every miser a wastrel was needed to balance the available supply of cash.

The Victorian ethos attempted to connect personal health and virtue with public health and order. This was a key period in Western history because it transformed conceptions of the body. As Anthony Synnott (1993) explains in *The Body Social*, the end of the nineteenth century brought forth an acute 'medicalization of society.' Vaccination legislation and public health laws controlled the bodily freedom of individuals in the name of public welfare (26). So did the poorhouses, the shelters for unwed mothers, and the placement of illegitimate infants in the care of wet nurses far from the eyes and minds of the unfortunate child's family. The 'breach of promise' clause in marriage laws further ensured that a man who proposed marriage, seduced the potential bride, and then broke his promise of marriage would face consequences.

Smiles embodied the Victorian association between self-regulation and public welfare. He was also (intentionally or not) legitimizing the inequalities that had emerged as a result of the Industrial Revolution. Echoing the Victorians' horror of the idle pauper, he wrote, 'Labour is not only a necessity and a duty, but a blessing: only the idler feels it to be a curse' ([1859] 1958:59), and, again, 'There is no reason why the condition of the average workman should not be a useful honourable, respectable, and happy one' (284). On the poverty of the English labourer, he pronounced 'that this class would be otherwise than frugal, contented, intelligent, and happy is not the design of providence' (284). According to Smiles, a wise man should exhibit thrift and live below his means, regardless of his income. For a man barely able to put food on the table of his family it meant missing even more meals than were already being missed. In *Thrift* ([1875] 1958), Smiles criticized the working class for spending all its earnings and thereby limiting its opportunities for self-advancement. He was one of the earliest modern proponents of a 'culture of poverty' theory: 'The greater number of workmen possess little capital save their labour; and, as we have already seen, many of them uselessly and wastefully spend most of their earnings, instead of saving them and becoming capitalists' (99). Explaining the formula for wealth creation, he advised: 'It is the savings of individuals which compose the wealth – in other words, the well-being – of every nation ... every thrifty person may be regarded as a public benefactor, and every thriftless person as a public enemy' (2).

The Victorian uneasiness with hedonism is echoed in Smiles's advice regarding the socialization of youth: 'All work and no play makes Jack a dull boy; but all play and no work makes him something greatly worse. Nothing can be more hurtful to a youth than to have his world sodden with pleasure' ([1859] 1958:318). Elsewhere in the book, he asserts: 'The battle of life is, in most cases, fought uphill and to win it without a struggle were perhaps to win it without honour ... The school of Difficulty is the best school of moral discipline' (325). Regarding character, he states: 'That character is power is true in a much higher sense that knowledge is power. Mind without heart, intelligence without conduct, cleverness without goodness, are powers in their way, but they may be powers only for mischief' (362). Objecting to the cult of appearance and fashion, he declares: 'There is a dreadful ambition abroad for being "genteel." We keep up appearances, too often at the expense of honesty; and though we may not be rich, yet we must seem to be so. We must be "respectable" though only in the meanest sense – in mere vulgar outward show' (290).

Smiles's unwavering faith in the individual also reflected a growing disillusionment with government in the mid-Victorian era. Thrown back on their own resources to formulate some workable collective ethic, the Victorians came to value 'personal enthusiasm' as a socially cohesive force. It was this unwavering belief in the power of the person to improve himself that led to what has since become known as Victorian 'earnestness.'

Such earnestness, however, had consequences. Christopher Lane (2003) has observed in *Hatred and Civility: The Antisocial Life in Victorian England* – a perceptive psychoanalytical critique of Victorian evangelism – that one of the consequences of this single-minded commitment to 'social progress' was the censoring and mistrust of 'misanthropy.' While withdrawal from a corruptive society had been tolerated and even admired in the eighteenth century, the Victorian ethic of 'enthusiasm' rendered those who criticized from the margins highly suspect. Civility and the benevolent associations it produced were equated with social responsibility. The misanthrope was now seen as someone who stood in the way of cheerful progress, a mental aberration rather than a credible conscientious objector. Such obligatory sociability further contributed to the suppression of 'dangerous' emotions, leaving successive generations with the onerous task of reversing this code of enforced silence.

Smiles's enthusiasm found a large audience in America. His republican non-aristocratic presentation of self-worth and self-improvement appealed to Americans seeking a republican representation of ideal behaviour. Writing of authentic politeness, he stated: 'The inbred politeness which springs from right-heartedness and kindly feelings is of no exclusive rank or station. The mechanic who works at the bench may possess it, as well as the clergyman or the peer' ([1859] 1958:369). In support of the English practice of tact, he wrote: 'The gentlemen is eminently distinguished for his self-respect. He values his character ... as he respects himself, so, by the same law, does he respect others' (372).

We see in Smiles's writing the non-negotiability of the English conception of 'gentle' behaviour: 'Gentleness is indeed the best test of gentlemanliness. A consideration for the feelings of others, for his inferiors are dependents as well as his equals, and respect for their self-respect, will pervade the true gentleman's whole conduct' (380).

This ethic of 'earnestness' restrained by 'decorum' became embodied in the British Victorian monarchy. The new courtesy practices and the idealization of family and propriety had created an aura of perfection in Victorian England, one shared by the Queen herself. Victoria and her husband Albert had maintained a model middle-class marriage, setting an example for the rest of the population. The Queen was not averse to publicizing the domestic side of her life – it was perhaps the first time that the British monarchy had taken middle-class values and replayed them to the public. This confirmation had a profound influence on the working classes, giving them access to a collective morale that transcended issues of wealth and title. Ironically, this common social denominator was made possible precisely by the fact that class differentiation had been accepted as a given.

Paralleling 'tact' and an appreciation of 'gentleness' was a very strong belief in the efficacy of rules. Rules helped define an orderly way to achieve personal and civilizational competence. John Stuart Mill and Harriette Taylor ([1869] 1912), worrying about the spirit of the times, wrote that the English were alienating themselves from emotion by adhering to so many rules. They warned that Victorian values were alienating the English from nature. Despite their warnings, work, thrift, and a steadfast observance of rules became the hallmarks of a 'reputable family.' That Victorians had such a horror of deviance, non-conformity, and bad reputation is understandable when viewed from the perspective of rules and the manner they were equated to social harmony and social health.

Despite the self-help movement, the certainties of nineteenth-century rationalizations of science were being shaken by a growing sense of futility at the end of the 1800s. A series of bad harvests created social unrest, precipitating the second Reform Bill of 1867. The bill gave the working classes of the towns voting privileges and forced upper- and middle-class Victorians to face the fact that a new class was emerging, one that had already demonstrated its power through a series of strikes and riots.

By adopting ideal values and categorical explanations of reality, the Victorians had set themselves up for disappointment – observable reality did not conform to the ideals of the self-help movement. The social optimism of a writer like Smiles and the moral fury of a Wilberforce were based on a mono-directional view of social economics. An ethical and disciplined life was seen as the best path to individual happiness. Yet, what was not sufficiently considered was that varying motivations could produce the same beneficial results. A man buying a dog for his wife was contributing to the creation of jobs no more and no less than another buying the same dog for his illicit mistress. There are echoes of Kant's thinking in the Victorian attempt to establish a categorical moral imperative. Yet, the times required a commercialism unshackled by conservative restrictions.

Confronted with these dilemmas, Victorians took to doubting the viability of their moral project. If there seems to be any hypocrisy in the Victorian era, as has been retrospectively suggested by many historians, novelists, and cultural critics, this hypocrisy does not lie as much in an act of bad faith or a consciously adopted double standard as it does in the fact that conservative Victorians were trying to make ideal declarations in spite of an economic juggernaut that required a tempering of social idealism.

Certainly, the old art of gentlemanly conduct went through a transformation during this period. In 1935, Henry Dwight Sedgwick was already mourning the passing of the gentleman in his book *In Praise of Gentlemen* ([1935] 1970). Yet, Sedgwick was ignoring a very important development in English courtesy. Certainly, the formality of aristocratic gentlemanly behaviour was suffering with the demise of the British Empire, but England had preserved Smiles's ideal of *gentleness*, the ministering to the comfort of the other. Both mechanic and lord had somehow managed to internalize the functional properties of Hume's and Smith's conceptions of *sympathy*. This very important development in English civility should inform current observations of English interaction style.

## The Dangers of Impropriety: Romanticizing Family Life

One idea that survived and prospered as a consequence of the cult of sensibility was that marriage should be contracted out of love and mutual attraction rather than as an economic or political alliance. The high valuation that the Victorians placed on spiritual union between men and women was already in vogue in the novels of the late eighteenth century (Stone 1977:284). The Victorians formalized this view of relationships in a standard public morality.

In fact, something remarkable occurred during the Victorian era. As a consequence of a variety of factors, there occurred a further *domestication* of the male – masculinity was redefined in terms of home life. During the eighteenth century men had spent a great deal of their time in the enormously popular coffee houses. They did their socializing there, met their business contacts, and drank without much thought to their domestic responsibilities. The problem was serious enough for English women to band together and call for the coffee houses to close (Lillywhite 1963). The bringing of the male back into the household set the stage for an idealization of marriage and romantic union.

In 'The Subjection of Women' ([1869] 1912), Mill and Taylor referred to the growing influence of moralists on the behaviour of men:

> The association of men with women in daily life is much closer and more complete than it ever was before. Men's life is more domestic. Formerly, their pleasures and chosen occupations were among men, and in men's company: their wives had but a fragment of their lives. At the present time, the progress of civilization, and the turn of opinion against the rough amusements and convivial excesses which formerly occupied most men in their hours of realization – together with (it must be said) the improved tone of modern feeling as to the reciprocity of duty which binds the husband towards the wife – have thrown the man very much more upon home and its inmates, for his personal and social pleasures: while the kind and degree of improvement which has been made in women's education, has made them in some degree capable of being his companions in ideas and mental tastes. (540)

Work was now more than a means for paying the basic expenses of a family. It was also a means for the fulfillment of moral duty and the accumulation of economic and social status. Moreover, the home became the place where qualities and feelings not allowed in a competitive commercial world could be learned and practised. This walled garden brought the man back into the folds of the family, promising him that he would find a peace not readily available in the outside world. The idealization of the Victorian woman as the caretaker of the home followed from this nostalgic conception of the home as the last bastion of a former more idyllic existence. It also permitted the idealization (romanticization?) of the man as the 'hero' who was capable of seeing to the material comforts of his family in a contingent world: making sure that his wife had the means to be well-dressed in public, ensuring that her status vis-à-vis other women was protected, enrolling his children in the best schools, and maintaining a circle of friends that could provide him with professional advancement as well as the consolations of friendship.

The idea of the woman as a 'submissive and pretty creature,' put there to minister to her husband's comfort and pleasure, is the simplified retrospective version of the Victorian conception of womanhood. In actuality, women were regarded as important socializing agents for their husbands as well as their children. John Ruskin's 1865 lecture of *Queens' Gardens* expressed very well the moral and emotional valuation of women as spiritual guides of their husbands:

> His intellect is for speculation and invention; his energy for adventure, for war, and for conquest, wherever war is just, wherever conquest is necessary. But the woman's power is for rule, not for battle – and her intellect is not for invention or creation, but for sweet ordering, arrangement, and decision. (1902–12, 1:111–12)

The suggestion that the woman possessed socializing powers beyond those of the male was quite a radical idea for the mid-nineteenth century. It was one thing to affirm that a woman lacked the talents of a man, but quite a different thing to suggest that she possessed qualities that a man did not. It was this idealization of a woman's power to be a tempering force in the family that led to the myriad civility rituals intended to 'protect' women from 'danger.' Even feminist writers, such as George Eliot and Beatrice Potter Webb, who passionately argued for women's suffrage, were careful to affirm the moral influence of women and the vital role they played in the family.

A culture's attitude towards sexuality is always noticeable in its courtesy practices. Since courtesy is a practice that involves contact between two or more people it also involves the human body and its subtle language. As soon as an act of courtesy is exchanged between two people there is awareness on the part of both that they have come into *personalized* contact with each other. A courtesy practice based on deference to propriety and a stiff gravity says as much about its practitioner's attitude towards sensuality as it does about his or her relationship to morality. *There may be a connection between sensual inhibition (or sensual privatism) and formalism.* Certainly, what is kept unstated in conversations (of the verbal and bodily sort) points to what is considered inappropriate, or even shameful.

The moral triumph of the Victorian middle class had important consequences on the practice of sexuality. What has come down to us as the 'prudish' Victorian attitude to sex was really the attitude of the middle class. The upper and lower classes initially followed their own freer and less shame-imbued codes (Porter and Hall 1995). But even they became influenced by Victorian sexual codes by the end of the nineteenth century.

The education of the upper-middle-class and upper-class male became an arduous process, requiring segregation from girls within all-boys' schools. Discipline was strict – the goals of these schools were not, as in the French system, to produce intellectuals, but men able to fit in and conform to the standards of 'gentlemen of breeding.' Paxman (1998) explains the aristocratic schoolboy attitude (something later imitated in public schools) as a particularly male mentality that fuelled patriarchal dominance:

> What the Breed represented was a certain ideal, a carefully selected number of the strengths and weaknesses of the male taken and raised to Platonic heights. They were bold, unreflective and crashingly pragmatic, men you could trust. It has been the misfortune of the English male that, just as he found himself living in a country different to the one he imagined himself to be living in, so the so-called English ideal excluded most of the population from the identity with which they had been born. (177–8)

Building such a restrained character required considerable discipline. Eton's reputation for forming young men of character was not built without pain:

> The champion flogger was the Reverend Dr. John Keates, appointed headmaster of Eton in 1809, who beat an average of ten boys each day (excluding his day of rest on Sundays). On 30 June 1832 came his greatest achievement, the thrashing of over eighty of his pupils. At the end of this marathon, the boys stood and cheered him. It says something about the spirit of these places that he was later able to tell some of the school's old boys of his regret that he hadn't flogged them more often ... In the circumstances, is it surprising that the products of these schools were skilled at hiding their emotions? (179)

What was also being sought was a sexual ethic that would facilitate and preserve the strength and longevity of the family by restraining the sexual impulse. School sports, for example, were a means of keeping the minds of youth off sensual temptations by exhausting their libidinal urges through tiring physical exertion. Just as importantly, sports taught them fair conduct, discipline, and the understanding and respect of the 'rules of the game,' abilities that could be applied to the demanding area of diplomacy and commerce. The civility required of the English in sports – such as cricket – hearkened back to the early Christian values of *justice, concern for the dignity and comfort of the other, and the avoidance of taking extreme cruel pleasure in victory.*

The English constitutional monarchy and the religious institutions of England helped bring forth a new civility philosophy: the right to enjoy personal liberty could not be achieved in a socially isolated setting; freedom required discipline of the kind acquired through sports such as golf, tennis, and cricket – sports requiring a civil submission to the referee and the ethic of fair play. While it was the objective of the player to win, he was not to do so at all cost nor fail to honour his or her opponents for courageous performances during the play. Thus, complex rituals of face-saving and ministering to others in victory and defeat made the English of the nineteenth-century world authorities in sports etiquette.

It was an educational system that moved Ford Madox Ford (1907) to comment: 'That a race should have trained itself to such a Spartan repression is none the less worthy of wonder' (147–8). This high valuation of discipline at the best schools certainly appealed to many upper-middle-class and middle-class families who sent their children to boarding and finishing schools, hoping that they would emerge with good breeding. Certainly, this separation between parents and children placed in boarding schools created some additional reserve in parent–child relations. The development of an individualistic and disciplined young man or young lady required absence from home; the youth was in the tutelage of teachers who were not kin and less disposed to be informal. It was not surprising that by the late nineteenth century, kissing between fathers and sons had been prohibited because it was considered not manly enough. It was perhaps thought that too much physical affection would undo the discipline that had been instilled through great effort. Manliness required stoicism, and stoicism required a restraint of the emotions, even when one was experiencing a painful flogging. Paxman (1997) reminds us that social certainty fares better in England than in some other countries because England continued to possess an aristocracy: 'Once such a master-class existed everyone else knew their place in the pecking order' (265). And the values of the aristocracy did provide the rising middle classes with rationalizations for stoicism, discipline, and moderation, in sexual as well as domestic matters.

No culture that does not hold the family as an ideal institution will seek to establish repressive sexual mores that prohibit premarital sex. The limitation of sexual experience outside marriage is a tool by which men and women are motivated to accept legalized co-habitation and its accompanying duties. Young men and women who are able to enjoy the emotional and physical rewards of marriage without limiting themselves to one partner may not be motivated to enter a contract meant for life; they certainly might be motivated to prolong their sexual experimentation and delay marriage before committing to it. So the connection between the rise of the middle-class nuclear family and the restriction of sexuality is profoundly deliberate. So are changes in fashion. Victorian fashion ensured that the entire body of a woman was covered without the accentuation of those parts considered provocative. The 'hourglass' figures of Victorian women were constructed to project the image of a sexually modest and morally conscientious gender. Similar standards were imposed on the male; the dressed-up 'dandy' was considered a dangerous exhibitionist, an irresponsible social parasite (Yeazell 1991).

This high valuation placed on behavioural and sensual modesty, the precondition for marriage, was evident in the life of Queen Victoria. Unlike Elizabeth I, who had chosen to remain celibate despite her affections for one man, Queen Victoria had contracted a marriage that turned out to be quite affectionate. Prince Albert's love letters to the queen reveal that they had a very loving relationship. The deep feelings that she held for him drove her into a protracted mourning following his death in 1861. Her withdrawal from social life left the middle classes in a quandary. What sort of sexual ethic were they to embrace when the queen herself was now celibate? She had already distinguished herself as a strict and efficient queen capable of obtaining extraordinary global success for her country – that she was imitated and respected went without saying. Her withdrawal into dour self-pity had its effects on middle-class attitudes towards sexuality. Her model marriage had acted as a confirmation of the middle-class idealization of marriage and the family. Her withdrawal now left a vacuum that was quickly filled by a Church that revived the Christian value of sexual moderation and abstinence.

Frustrated with the queen's protracted mourning and withdrawal from public life, the upper classes turned to Prince Edward, the Prince of Wales, for leadership. And he provided it obligingly considering that he loved being in the company of beautiful women, many of them readily available singers and actresses. Using his lifestyle as justification, the upper classes adopted a liberal attitude towards sex, one more in keeping with that of their eighteenth-century predecessors. Sexual promiscuity in the upper classes was tolerated as long as it was not discussed outside aristocratic circles. As for the lower classes, they also lived relatively free from the sexual restraints of the middle class. In the East End of London, where adolescents slept as many as six or eight to a bed, there were plenty of opportunities for sexual intimacy. Incest was present, and no properly enforced legislation existed against it. The young girls selling matches in Trafalgar Square and around Piccadilly Circus were very often child prostitutes. Certain brothels even specialized in providing young virgins to men. The Victorian propensity to depict middle-class and aristocratic children in scenes of innocence stood in stark contrast to the lot of lower-class children left free to roam the streets at the mercy of strangers (Walkowitz 1980, Marcus 1966, Mason 1994, Porter and Hall 1995). Fyodor Dostoevsky ([1862] 1955) and Hippolyte Taine ([1863] 1957) were both horrified by the poverty and prostitution they witnessed in the Haymarket sector of London. Taine wrote:

> I recall Haymarket and the Strand at evening, where you cannot walk a hundred yards without knocking into twenty streetwalkers; some of them ask you for a glass of gin, others say 'it's for my rent, mister.' The impression is not one of debauchery but of abject, miserable poverty. One is sickened and wounded by this deplorable procession in those monumental streets. (31)

Despite the fact that London had no less than 50,000 prostitutes on the street, summary declarations regarding the Victorian middle-class family and its sexual mores need be tempered by recognitions of exceptions. There were enough deviations from the strict preservation of marriage and the social stigma attached to co-habitation to indicate that many were unpleased with the prudery of their own class (Jackson 1994, Hammerton 1992, Bland 1995, Johnson 1979). Charles Dickens, who supported the morality of his period, left his wife and co-habited with a young actress named Ellen Terman, who, in deference to Dickens's reputation, agreed to remain virtually invisible. Mary Ann Evans, a well-known moralist who published under the male pseudonym of George Eliot, lived with a man who was unable to get a divorce. So to say that all middle-class Victorian men and women were hapless sexual partners would be almost like saying that they had managed to extinguish the sexual impulse. Even so, many Victorian men remained ignorant of a woman's sexual needs. Some men reported in their personal journals that upon hearing their wife have an orgasm for the first time they concluded, with considerable alarm, that she was having a fit; some called in a physician (Hall 1991). This was not surprising considering that many women were conditioned into believing that a 'good' woman distracted her mind to non-sexual thoughts during the act of intercourse in order not to fall into the type of behaviour ascribed to a licentious woman. They certainly had frightening advice from Dr William Acton, who catalogued the many medical ills supposedly caused by sexual desire (1857 [1968]). Moreover, many Victorian husbands would have been sorely worried had they seen their wives actually enjoying sex, for that might have meant that a woman was sexual enough to be attracted to extra-marital adventures. The ideal that a good woman 'does not move in bed' was the unspoken rule in many Victorian families. A man 'took his pleasure' from a woman. Many women even considered the sexual act as an unpleasant experience and submitted to it in order to satisfy their husbands' conjugal 'rights' or their mutual need to have children. This double standard originated from the 'classical' idea of sexuality which posited that men had a much more active sex drive than women. Nevertheless, a 'moral' man was expected to control his sensuality for the sake of 'gentlemanly conduct' (Comfort 1967).

Yet, there were also bedrooms where these rules were being ignored and where men and women were constructing a romantic view of marriage that very much rejoined the words of the courtly writers who had advised that periodic abstinence and the development of a mind–heart spiritual affinity could only make sexual union that much better when it did occur. The frequency of sexual activity might have been lower compared with what it is in contemporary times, but there is no guarantee that passion was lacking. In fact, if one refers to the romantic love stories of the period, one is impressed with the heartfelt sensuality of Victorian love and its ideas of devotion and loyalty. So, ironically enough, paralleling the association of sexuality with shame and moral lassitude was a rise in the idealization of romantic courtship and love.

Also paradoxical was the existence of so many prostitutes and brothels in a country in which the integrity of the family was being promoted as a non-negotiable social ethic. That there were so many prostitutes does not indicate how many married middle-class men visited them. The accusation made against the Victorians that they held a hypocritical double standard does not take into account that there existed different factions with varying sexual mores and thresholds of tolerance – so the practice of looking at the English of the period collectively as 'the Victorians' is misleading. One thing is certain: there was concern shown in middle-class circles as to how much vice should be tolerated. The middle-class Victorian matron who was passionately against prostitution and pornography was not hypocritical at all; she was found working on projects that were committed to rescuing 'fallen women' from their profession (Mahood 1990). Different social classes faced different problems and turned to different solutions.

Members of the socially active middle class did not lack compassion for the 'fallen woman.' A woman seduced by a man who had proposed marriage to her and subsequently broken his promise to her was held in considerable sympathy (Frost 1995). The mid-eighteenth-century Foundling Hospital was already admitting illegitimate babies mothered by women who had good cases regarding the circumstances surrounding their impregnation (Barret-Ducrocq 1991). In *The Making of Victorian Sexuality* (1994), Michael Mason has calculated that there were nearly 300 institutions (asylums) for prostitutes by the end of the nineteenth century. Different institutions specialized in different levels of rehabilitation, ranging from those that took in girls who needed to be protected from resorting to prostitution to those that housed unrepentant prostitutes under guard. Yet, the existence of institutions should not in any way give the impression that the Victorian family washed its hands of an errant daughter and sent her away pregnant and destitute. The family's honour counted as much as the girl's virtue. In most cases, a stay away from home was arranged and the child subsequently disposed of. Even the staunch, sexually conservative moralist Dr Acton, who headed a commission investigating prostitution, was careful to distinguish between housemaids who had been seduced by a member of the household staff (or by a member of the employing family) and those women who charged for their services. He recommended that the unfortunate housemaids be employed as wet nurses ([1857] 1968). While from a retrospective position we may find these facilities as little else than places of incarceration that put citizens under the increased control and surveillance of the state, they were, nevertheless, a better alternative than condemnation to utter destitution in the streets.

The moral worry over unwed mothers was related to two positions taken by middle-class Victorians: (1) a woman had to be a virgin upon marriage, and (2) marriage was the ideal state for a woman wishing to be protected from the dangers of society. These two positions, when put together, did not leave much of a middle-class future for either a single mother or a woman who remained single and experimented sexually. Middle-class feminists, for their part, were not struggling for sexual freedom outside marriage as much as they were seeking rights to equal education and work. They continued to uphold the values of the family even while arguing that women did possess sexual needs (Maynard 1993, Russet 1989, Dyhouse 1989). Those who were part of the 'sex reform' movement, although they argued against the idea of a 'classical sexuality' (which concurrently rationalized prostitution by stating that men's and women's sexual needs differed substantially), remained committed to the idea of a monogamous marriage, albeit one in which sexuality was not repressed (Bland 1995).

This fear of the sexually active woman was reflected in the precarious status of the woman of marriage age who had no husband. In *The Spinster and Her Enemies: Feminism and Sexuality 1880–1930* (1985), Sheila Jeffreys describes the limited opportunities available to a woman without a husband. If she was at all attractive she had to live under the suspicious gaze of 'respectable' women who wondered if her celibacy was not an excuse for sexual promiscuity. She was either relegated to a position without status in her own family or had to accept a position as a governess or maid. The entry of women in the teaching and nursing professions in the latter part of the century was the first instance in which spinsters were able to meet their own subsistence needs while holding a relatively acceptable position in society.

Some of the Victorian rules of etiquette between men and women in public reveal this penchant for keeping the woman in an asexual role and decreasing the male's opportunities for making sexual advances on her. They also reveal the extent to which the woman has been idealized as a sensitive being in need of protection. The following rules were embedded in the novels of the period, especially those of Jane Austen:

- Walking along the street, the lady always walks along the wall. (*This kept the lady away from the danger of the street and away from other men's physical proximity.*)

- Meeting a lady in the street whom a man knows only slightly, he must wait for her to acknowledge him. Only then may he tip his hat to her. A man never speaks to a lady unless she speaks to him first. (*This excluded the possibility of a man verbally flirting with a strange woman on the street.*)
- If you meet a lady who is a good friend and who indicates that she wishes to talk to you, you must turn and walk with her if you wish to talk to her. You must not keep her standing on the street. (*This was to prevent the woman from appearing as if she were habituated to being on the street along with 'loose' women.*)
- When they are going up a flight of stairs, the man must precede the lady. (*This allowed the man to clear the way for the woman and defend her from all possible harm.*)
- If alone in a carriage, a man does not sit next to a woman unless he is her husband, brother, father, or son. (*The privatization of body space was connected to an increasing distancing between men and women.*)
- If unmarried and under thirty, a woman is never to be seen without a chaperone in the company of a man. Except for a walk to church or a park in the early morning, she may not walk alone, but should always be accompanied by another lady, a man, or a servant. (*The rule existed in order to diminish amorous encounters as well as vulnerability to crime.*)
- A woman must never call on a man when she is alone, unless she is consulting that man on a professional or business matter. (*Again, the motive is sexual distancing and the exclusion of possibilities of damaging gossip.*)
- At a public exhibition or concert, the man is expected to go in first in order to find the lady a seat. Leaving a carriage, he is expected to help the lady out while making sure that her skirts do not become soiled. At a social function, it is always the man who is introduced to the lady and never the other way around – this, because it was considered an honour for a man to meet a woman who was considered the morally superior gender. Nor is a man allowed to cut someone verbally. This privilege is reserved for a woman who feels her dignity has been slighted or a moral imperative transgressed.

The campaign against sexual enjoyment received the support of a considerable number of medical professionals. Themselves of middle-class backgrounds, they accelerated the middle-class project of chastity by publishing articles and books stating that frequent sexual enjoyment led to senility and an early death. Some of them, citing cases from the lunatic asylums, helped rationalize the denial of the natural drives of the body. Ornella Moscucci (1990), in *The Science of Woman: Gynaecology and Gender in England, 1800–1929,* and Cynthia Eagle Russett (1989), in *Sexual Science: The Victorian Construction of Womanhood,* have discussed the collusion of the medical sciences in the promotion of an asexual female. In the 1860s, Dr Isaac Baker Brown even suggested that many female medical problems were related to masturbation. He caused a scandal when he suggested that clitoridectomy be performed on such women. The public outrage was caused not only by the barbarity of his suggestion, but by the fact that many middle-class women took offence to the accusation that they were practising self-gratification in considerable numbers.

Some companies even manufactured special corsets for men to wear so that they could not reach their sexual organs without undressing first. When medical practitioners announced that masturbation would have serious mental and physical consequences for men, some young men castrated themselves. Venereal disease was considered such a shame that many of those who contracted it avoided consulting a doctor. As for young women, many were taught that a single act of intercourse would produce a baby. That some young women committed suicide after succumbing to temptation was understandable.

Predictably, sexual instruction of the young was almost non-existent. There was silence in the schools, and any sexual knowledge was acquired on the sly and shared in hushed voices. This led to a socialization process that taught that sex was a nasty necessity of life, best kept silent. In the upper classes young women servants were sometimes expected to provide sexual initiation to the young master of the house, but in middle-class circles, silence was often maintained regarding anything to do with sexuality. It was even forbidden to refer to a woman's legs as legs – the word used was 'underpinnings,' the same words used for the legs of an armchair. In many of the conduct books, parents were advised to never speak of sexuality with their children. Such books warned that knowledge would lead to curiosity and curiosity to experimentation. This silence may partially explain Victorian art representations of children and youth in impossibly innocent surroundings and activities. Children were taught to see women as 'angelic' beings and to look upon women as they looked upon their sisters and mothers. The tendency in some Victorian literature to compare a beloved mate with the memory of a mother may be connected to this transference of love for the mother onto other women who are then idealized as pure reproductions of the uncorrupted feminine sex. That much of this literature was male-generated seems to indicate that sex was not a top priority for many ambitions men who were busy building the empire (Hyam 1990).

It is understandable that Victorians, such as Hannah More, reacted indignantly to the popularity of a bold, sensual, and seductive French literature. Enough Continental works of literature argued against marital fidelity and in favour of passionate bonds consummated for the sake of passion alone that there arose a fear that English society was in danger of losing its moral centre because of the licentiousness of a growing part of the Continental population. This fear of sexual compromise was expressed by Tennyson in his epic poems *Guinevere* and *The Passing of Arthur*. Tennyson wrote that it was Guinevere's infidelity towards the king that brought discord to the holy round table and caused a civil war that delivered the realm into the hands of the barbarians.

Over-riding sexuality was a profound respect for romantic love. Mainstream Victorian romance novels did not emerge in order to sexually titillate their readers, but to express their authors' belief in love as the ultimate grace. In his poems, Browning was not shy to suggest that if a person were to meet his or her true love and recoil for any worldly reason he or she would have turned life into a failure. It is easy to discount these writings as the musings of Romantic poets. But that would be an error, for English literature became a major force in the moulding of an English consciousness and lifestyle. In fact, one of the telling autobiographical writings of the period was Charles Kingsley's (1877) *Letters and Memoirs of His Life*. Kingsley confessed to having lived a youth during which he was taken in by sexual proclivity only to awaken later in life and realize that he was beset by doubt. He solved his crisis by giving himself to love with childlike simplicity. And it was a woman who saved him from his disbelief by managing to promise him that eternity was love itself (164).

The Victorian restraint on sexuality and the resulting high valuation of romantic love was a substantial return to the classic notions of chivalry and *fin' amour*. By idealizing the woman as a romantic object it became possible to separate passion and virtue from outright expression of sensuality. This Romantic idealization of soul love – the idea that one must live one's whole life in hopes of meeting that special soul mate – was ingrained in Western society long before the appearance of Romanticism in the nineteenth century. Perhaps influenced by classical writers, Victorian novels glorified love and the exciting passions of attraction, fear of rejection, and the joy of reciprocated love. A person 'fell into love,' which virtually meant falling out of a rational state. And, falling into love, he or she fell out of the body and its animalistic needs and into some realm that was poetic and tender.

While marriages of convenience had been tolerated prior to the Victorian restraint of sexuality, there now developed a literature that denigrated arranged marriages because they did not fulfill the highest aspirations of men and women: the joining of two souls in a life-long relationship that had love at its central motive. For the Victorians, the love of home, the strict respect for family and the authority of that family, and the important roles accorded to the mother and father became legitimized and imbued with the cementing ideal of romance. That the parents rarely exhibited affection towards each other openly in front of their children does not indicate what took place during their private moments together, and we should hesitate before labelling the Romantic movement a hypocritical one. But we can safely say that the circumspection of sex must have had the opposing effect of stimulating the imagination of the young.

The ideal of pure love is expressed in the lines of Tennyson's poem 'Guinevere' (1898). King Arthur meditates over the type of love that prevents discord and corruption:

> I knew
> Of no more subtle master under heaven
> Than is the maiden passion for a maid,
> Not only to keep down the base of man,
> But teach high thought, and amiable words
> And courtliness, and the desire of fame,
> And love of truth, and all that makes a man. (474–90)

The campaign against sensuality affected all walks of life, including art, theatre, and dress. For a painting to include a nude it had to demonstrate that it had a good reason to do so, a reason that went beyond titillating its viewer. A play that contained a scene referring to sex was considered a threat to public decorum and good manners. The music halls were the only places that brazenly defied the Victorian censorship; naturally, attendance at these ribald shows was considered unfit for members of polite society. It was only at the end of the century that some of the avant-garde began attending such shows for distraction, and, even then, they were careful to register moral dismay through nervous giggles.

The restrictions placed on overt sexuality and the idealization of romance led to the adoption of circumspect and indirect codes of courtesy between men and woman. Many young men who took these moral codes seriously must have rationalized in their minds that attraction to a woman meant that they were feeling love for her. The erotic impulse and the romantic feeling became merged for many and love became a rationalization for sexual arousal. Guilt was avoided in this way, for love was considered noble while lust was not. As shown in some of the manners prescribed for men and women in public, the male related to the female in an ambivalent way when it came to being in her proximity without the presence of chaperones. Being a 'gentleman' in the presence of a woman meant not making overt sexual advances, not with a woman of 'good breeding' at least. That was the meaning of modern chivalry – the gentleman was expected to protect a lady not only from other men but from his own self. So ingrained became the middle-class notion of 'gentlemanly conduct' that it carried over into the twentieth century, and we see it practised in America right through the 1950s before the arrival of the 'sexual liberation' movement. So, what the Victorians made of sexuality is extremely important to our understanding of contemporary relations between men and women in Anglo-American cultures, for the sexual revolutions of the twentieth century were acts of resistance (and undoing) against these previous restraints. Victorian views of sexuality were not restricted to English society but managed to spread to many other countries, including those frequented by colonial missionaries.

The preoccupation with 'danger' during the nineteenth century had a seminal influence on the manner in which people interacted with one another. Much of the 'reserve' of the Victorians may have been connected to such cautiousness. A person who deviated from the norms of propriety was considered a 'danger to society.' For middle-class Victorians seeking propriety, it was a comfort to know that 'danger' was being eradicated or, at least, being put out of view. Evasion of the unpleasant and concern for public spaces became connected. Silence stepped in to 'hush up' disconcerting realizations.

Indeed, anything that did not confirm with their cultural and political ideals might have been considered dangerous by zealous upholders of middle-class values. The woman who lit a cigarette when most women did not was dangerous. The spinster was dangerous. Street boys were dangerous. Authors writing in favour of free love were dangerous. Meetings without chaperons between young men and women who might become lovers were dangerous. This pervasive obsession with danger was the result of a society attempting to place itself within the boundaries of a set of practices that it could believe in and replay to itself as the best of all possible worlds. Having first restrained their own selves, middle-class Victorians set out to restrain their social environment.

The Victorian restriction of sexuality was particular to the nineteenth century, however. During the eighteenth century, although a woman had to be a virgin upon marriage, unmarried youth were allowed to 'bundle' together – a board was placed between the two in bed but they were free to enjoy whatever they could within that limitation. Nearly 10 per cent of women getting married were already pregnant. As for romance, it was considered sufficient that the two partners have a basic liking for each other, thereby justifying marriages arranged for reasons of convenience. This liking was considered to stand apart from sex, thereby allowing for a sexual ethic that was far more liberal than that of the Victorians. There was already a separation between liking/loving and sex – the Victorian denigration of sex in favour of love was not prevalent in the eighteenth century, certainly not among the working classes and the nobility. Aristotle's *Masterpiece* (1725), a sex manual, was freely read in the 1700s. Aretine's *Postures* was also freely circulated, despite Daniel Defoe's personal crusade against the frequency of sexual intimacy.

Certainly, the Victorians were influenced by the consequences of the demographic situation of the eighteenth century. In London, where there were ten men for every twelve women, marriage was always in a man's favour. Upon marriage a wife's identity merged with that of her husband. It would seem, therefore, that the beginnings of the Victorian sex ethic are found in the 1700s; they are as much connected to declining rates of marriage as they are to a movement seeking to restrict sensuality for purely moral reasons. Since young men were delaying marriage in the interests of acquiring professional stability, it became important to preach against readily available sex to provide such men with the incentive to speed up their decision to become married. In desperation, catalogues appeared listing debutantes and other women of good standing who were available for marriage. The problem was considered so serious that a campaign was launched against 'Onania,' or the 'Heinous Sin of Self-Pollution.' Some of the rigid corsets found in Victorian catalogues were invented a century before.

So there seems to be a functional transformation occurring in the late 1700s that is then picked up by the Victorians and to which are assigned moral meanings. By investing so many of their useful habits with moral imperatives, the Victorians lost sight of the fact that some of these practices could be dispensed with when the social situation no longer called for them. And this revision did begin at the end of the nineteenth century, when a body of literature began to question strict moral and social regimes. John Stuart Mill and Harriette Taylor's ([1869] 1912) *The Subjection of Women*, written three years after Mill argued for a parliamentary amendment giving women the right to vote, was a passionate statement against the idealization of women and their containment in the supposed safety of the patriarchal home:

> If the family in its best forms is, as it is often said to be, a school of sympathy, tenderness, and loving forgetfulness of self, it is still oftener, as respects its chief, a school of willfulness, over-bearingness, un-bounded self-indulgence, and a double-eyed and idealized self-indulgence. (142)

What did unite the genders was the immutable belief that discipline, order, and the proper distancing between individuals would maintain a satisfactory civil society. No work has expressed this sense of devotion to tradition and order better than *The Remains of the Day* (1989), the novel by Booker prize winner Kazuo Ishiguro. The film version, starring Anthony Hopkins as Mr Stevens, the impeccable English butler, won eight Academy Award nominations. Stevens is the perfect embodiment of the restrained English gentleman whose sense of propriety prevents him from demonstrating any sentiment that might compromise his unstinting commitment to moral and spiritual order; he remains stoic, gentle, and self-effacing right to the end.

If the Victorian patriarchs and matriarchs were sometimes categorically intransigent about their ideas, reluctant to consider opposing views, it was because of their practised ability to label and judge their opposition. The more morally conservative factions considered opposition to their values as a threat to the continuance of the social project that they were engineering. The Victorian penchant for general theories which sought to set universal standards regarding human behaviour and the evolution of races and countries was a product of the synthesis that occurred between the middle class's search for a reliable and permanent value system and the ambitions of scientists who sought to rationalize an evolutionary view of the world. If the world was on a path towards perfection, then the 'civilizing process' brought in by the Victorian revolution was a high point of evolution. Hence, the ease with which Victorians transferred their moral mission onto international turf.

No account of the Victorians that is under 500 pages in length and profusely illustrated can communicate the paradox of moral propriety living side by side with ornamental splendour. Evangelism and Romanticism came together to produce a culture which favoured the consumption of products that a century ago would have been considered extravagant. When all is said, the paradox may be a superficial one, for rationalism produced social order, while piety produced the Romantic aspects that favoured a celebration of individuality and inventive genius (Campbell ([1987] 1993:219).

The celebration of the modern was most observable in the glamour years of London (1919–1939), when English high society had its finest moments. The appearance of a moneyed class mingling with the aristocracy contributed to a certain amount of deformalizing of social relations. While the notion of 'distinction' did not lose its social value in a culture where royal blood continued to afford special privileges, the behavioural rituals attached to distinguished behaviour were partially deformalized to reflect a more contemporary and democratic society. At a party attended by the king of England, the pianist Arthur Rubinstein kept on playing a song that the king clearly disliked. In any other era, this breach in etiquette would have been sorely received. Yet, the king managed to unobtrusively shift to another part of the house until something more to his liking was played. Lady Colefax, who was hosting the party, was flustered by the king's displeasure, not because she feared retaliation but because she was eager to maintain the cohesion of her social circle.

Much seemed to have changed since the days of Henry VIII; Locke's interpretation of liberty had not fallen on deaf ears – the English had found a way to reconcile a monarchy with a parliamentary democracy. As for the struggle between the constrictions of 'sense' and the impulsiveness of 'sensibility,' a workable solution had been found: 'tact' communicated to the other that the speaker was not without feelings but rational enough to know that emotional restraint was a symbol of emotional maturity as well as a confirmation of a sense of communal responsibility achieved through communicating respect for the biographical and emotional privacy of the other. This made the English, despite their history of mercantile and colonial forcefulness, a nation that held considerable regard for gentle interactions, especially between strangers. This has perhaps helped England maintain one of the lowest national murder rates in the world.

One would think that the English civility tradition would have been adopted in the new American republic. After all, both countries shared common Protestant religions and the same language. But that was not to be the case. The American experience differed greatly from the experience of the French as well as the English. No theory of civility that does not take into account the unique origins of the American republic and the subsequent development of a distinctly American civility tradition can manage to explain the manner in which societies that favour independence are so different from those that favour interdependence. These differences are so remarkable that they affect every aspect of life including political philosophy, education, courtship, and friendship. An understanding of the American civility tradition is necessary if we are to successfully build a topology of civility that allows us to compare the practices of various cultures in meaningful and reliable ways.

# 7 The American Experience: Democracy and Informal Civility

> Private and public life are subject to the same rules; and truth and manliness are two qualities that will carry you through this world much better than policy, tact, or expediency, or any other word that was ever devised to conceal or mystify a deviation from the straight line.
> – General Robert E. Lee

**America as a Manifest Destiny**

In previous chapters we have described how the development of centralized monarchies gave rise to a civility ethos that served to legitimize the privileges accorded to aristocrats. As we will argue in our comparison of contemporary civility practices in France and England (chapter 10), this background has had a salient influence on the manner in which individuals interact with one another. In this present chapter we will describe the formation of a civility tradition that was not the outcome of aristocratic society, but a reaction to it. The American experience not only shows us the roots of American civility, but allows us to appreciate the opportunities and limitations of a society based on a high valuation of independence, a subject which we develop further in chapter 8.

Revolutionaries have a way of committing their citizenry to a long-term project. By calling for a new constitution, they bring forth a reformed society that must adapt to the principles of the revolution. Slogans and fervour must be supplemented with concrete social policies addressing the infrastructure of the nation. Compromises become unavoidable. This was the case in France. Although the French Revolution was a rebellion against despotism, the preservation of the republic ended up requiring a highly centralized government.

As for Britain, citizens of the Isles had to maintain some sense of national identity even though their colonial influence was waning. They had to remain loyal to an ideology of personal liberty for which they had fought hard during the seventeenth and eighteenth centuries, even though they accepted to preserve a modified monarchy capable of protecting their small territory from continental ambitions.

The early Americans, on the other hand, took upon themselves to create a political and economical identity that would protect them from the type of rule from which they sought liberation and from the religious conflicts that had left Europe economically and politically enfeebled.

Thus, the American penchant for the *new* was born on the day the first Pilgrims set foot on the Atlantic shore. Although the later philosophy of American pragmatism would remain mistrustful of continental idealism, America itself was originally built on an idealistic notion of personal and political freedom. And, despite hundreds of years of intellectual, political, and social debates, this early idealism is very apparent in the way Americans relate to one another and the manner in which they periodically question the state of their union.

Emerging from the American Declaration of Independence was a Bill of Rights and a series of amendments that differed considerably from the various declarations of rights drafted in France during the years following the French Revolution. The American bill had a particular amendment for which no specific provision had been made in other constitutions, even in the English Declaration of Rights. An important feature of the American document was the Ninth Amendment, which stated: 'The enumeration in the Constitution, of certain rights, shall not be construed to deny or disparage others retained by the people.'

This amendment recognized that American citizens were not only free to enjoy the specific rights being given to them then and there, but additionally free to make future legal arguments for rights not clearly specified in the bill. This made the American Bill of Rights an open-ended document that served to prevent some future tyranny from refusing new rights to the people. This was the major innovation of the American Revolution, and it facilitated an ongoing evaluation of personal and collective values.

Self-interest, a topic that had been hotly debated in English politics and literature during the late seventeenth and the first half of the eighteenth century, was accepted in America as the unavoidable consequence of a multicultural democracy. It was assumed that lifting the restraints on ambitions would help build a strong and self-regulating nation (Taylor 1997:27–8). It is in the shadow of this democratic promise of a social 'equality' that can be continuously updated at the local and national level that we begin our search for the American civility ethos and a particularly American conception of selfhood and self-expression. We hope that the study of the American experience will not only help us better understand European approaches to civil interaction but yield some important information on the social psychology of civility, not contained in Norbert Elias's seminal work, *The Civilizing Process* ([1939] 1978, 1982). This aspect will be further developed in Part III of this book.

In *Founding Father: Rediscovering George Washington* (1996), Richard Brookhiser has remarked that even George Washington, whose ambition was to free America from the political limitations of the Old World, remained somewhat influenced by the civility rules of Europe. Although the French ritual of the *leveé* continued to be practised during George Washington's presidency, Washington himself had to break from the Old World by favouring a more simple civility ethos. In *110 Rules of Civility and Decent Behaviour in Company and Conversation* (c. 1640) he listed what he considered important rules of social interaction. It is interesting to note that certain of the rules that the young Washington learned from the French Jesuits exclude the possibility of aristocratic privilege. Brookhiser describes Washington's rules as the beginning of a particularly American egalitarian courtesy ethic free from Continental court protocols:

> Manners in the western world were originally aristocratic. *Courtesy* meant behaviour appropriate to a court; *chivalry* comes from *chevalier* – a knight. Yet Washington was to dedicate himself to freeing America from a court's control. Could manners survive the operation? Without realizing it, the Jesuits who wrote them, and the young man who copied them, were outlining and absorbing a system of courtesy appropriate to equals and near-equals. When the company for whom the decent behaviour was to be performed expanded to the nation, Washington was ready. Parson Weems got this right, when he wrote that it was 'no wonder every body honoured him who honoured every body.' (1996:130–1)

This active *honouring* of the other was different from the civility ethos of Europe, an ethos based on a 'hands-off' politeness. According honour in France was determined by the status of the speakers in the social hierarchy; similarly, in England, praise was faint and reserved. The American ethos, however, seemed to permit the 'complimenting' of the other with enthusiasm and without understatement. When General Robert Lee spoke of the moral benefits of avoiding mystery and tact in favour of the 'straight line,' he was expressing a very American view of civility, one founded on a rejection of the complex understatements and sentimental *sous-entendues* of European civility practices and one based on the affirmation of an open-door 'populism.'

Tracing the origins of American civility ideals is not as easy as it may first appear. When one refers to the 'early settlers' one is referring to a variety of religious groups that occupied different geographic regions requiring different social and political responses to communal organization. America's egalitarian Bill of Rights should, therefore, not predispose one to conclude that all Americans subscribed to the same social values or styles of discourse. The original settlers were there for adventure and profit as well as the manifestation of providence. This divergence of purpose is noticeable in the marked difference between the New England and southern settlements. The northern Puritans had never broken with their Calvinistic roots. The Bible they used was the Geneva Bible, and its 1560 translation was the official scripture of those of them who eventually moved to New England and Pennsylvania in search of freedom from religious persecution. The southern settlements, on the other hand, were founded on the English values of a landed gentry; their ideologies and civility practices were very different from those of the simpler-living northern Puritans. Each group managed to have a hand in the formation of an American ethos: religious purity and opportunism became the founding pillars of American territorial and industrial development, setting the stage for a paradox that would continue to complicate moral and political discourse in America for centuries to come.

The Puritan writings affirmed the importance of worshipping God and remaining constantly vigilant of the moral dangers facing the new society. Lacking the assurance of a guaranteed salvation, Puritans considered work and personal success a religious duty. It was this concept of 'duty' that moved those in the north to become mistrustful of the forces of liberalism emerging in other parts of the country, notably the aristocratic south. As late as the mid-eighteenth century, Jonathan Edwards – most remembered for *Sinners in the Hands of an Angry God*, his hell-and-brimstone lecture of 8 July 1741 during the evangelical revival

– felt justified to deliver the following frightening words to his congregation in Enfield, Massachusetts:

> If God should let you go, you would immediately sink, and sinfully descend, and plunge into the bottomless gulf ... The God that holds you over the pit of hell, much as one holds a spider or some loathsome insect over the fire, abhors you, and is dreadfully provoked ... he looks upon you as worthy of nothing else but to be cast into the bottomless gulf. (cited in Reid 1988:66–78)

Hearing his words, his congregation took to fitful weeping, for the fear of hell and damnation was very vivid in the evangelic imagination. The first settlers who arrived on the shores of Massachusetts Bay brought with them this long-standing fear of damnation and the visual representations associated with the devil's persona. Their conception of evil, however, was gradually transformed by the realities of the new world. America was vaster than the cramped, polluted cities of Europe. While the European landscape was spoiled and ravaged by what Europeans considered to be the work of the devil, America was unspoiled territory, a Garden of Eden with no visible traces of evil. Convinced that they had been guided to a corner of the world reserved for them by God, the early settlers took to stressing the primacy of 'good works.' The Manichean paradigm, assigning equal strength to good and evil, was replaced by an ideology of good. The devil was recognized as a threat but only insofar as he was a leftover from the Old World, a world that had been racked by numerous famines, wars, and every conceivable private and public brutality.

One of the early settlers, Thomas Tillam (cited in Meserole 1968), wrote a poem upon his arrival in Massachusetts. While the poem demonstrates fear of the devil, it reveals that the new Puritans were not quite certain what form the devil would take in this new, unspoiled world:

> Methinks, I have the Lambe of God thus speake
> Come my deare little flocke, who for my sake
> Have lefte your Country, dearest friends, and goods
> And hazarded your lives o'th raginge floods
> Posses this Country; free from all anoye
> Here I'le bee with you, heare you shall Injoye
> My sabbaths, sacraments, my minestrye

216   Civility: A Cultural History

> And ordinances in their puritye
> But yet beware of Satans wylye baites
> Hee lurkes amongs yow, Cunningly he waits ... (397–8)

Accepting the 'good' as an active force requiring communal participation, the Puritans could not revert to a Manichean conception of life that left room for chance occurrences. The theologian Thomas Cooper sermonized that the thing 'which seems Chance to us, is as a word of God acquainting us with his will' (quoted in Thomas 1619:79; cited in Delbanco 1995). All events, regardless of their nature, were governed by God's will. So, while the Puritans recognized the devil as an ever-present force, they held that their ultimate business was with God; the responsibility for that relationship rested squarely on the shoulders of the individual and, by extension, the community.

The early Puritan religion, therefore, was a religion of transformation rather than initiation. The transformation of the soul required a major overhaul of sentiments and actions. Puritans were not as much concerned with the medieval idea of 'cardinal' sins as they were with the soul's existing tendency to sin. The sinner was not the victim of specific deficiencies but of an overall deficiency. Bainton (1952) explains the uncompromising Puritan conception of human nature: 'Sins cannot be treated singly because the very nature of man is so perverted that he needs to be drastically remade' (29). Calvin had indeed specified that everyone was guilty coming into the game of life; corruption could just as easily reside in the soul of a churchgoer. Deprived of any guarantee that he was doing well in the heavenly realm, the Puritan had no recourse but to evaluate himself in the worldly one (Weber 1930). Did a person keep a clean home? Were the children dressed properly? Was business taken care of with integrity and diligence? Was the seeking of profit tempered by acts of charity? These were the questions that preoccupied the Puritans, who believed that meticulous attention to worldly affairs was the best way of gaining God's favour.

While medieval Catholicism had favoured abstention from ambitious mercantilism, the Puritans adopted industriousness as the highest good. This distinction is an important one because when Catholics spoke of 'natural laws,' they recognized that these included important prohibitions against excessive greed. In the new country, however, two of the cardinal sins of Christianity became amplified into major vices: the sin of sloth (laziness) and the sin of lust (desire). The traditional notion of the devil as a proud, ambitious, and greedy entity was changed into one that showed the devil abhorring work and loving pleasure. He became an almost comic character, pitiful and undeserving of respect, more of a nuisance than a worthwhile adversary of God. While Puritan preachers spent some portion of their sermons identifying the ways in which the devil could weave his way into human affairs, many of their sermons were actually civic discourses on issues of debt payment and honest living in a close-knit community where communal development required frequent exchanges of contracts and cash. When the ministers did preach against sin they did not warn of the devil as much as cautioning about the primordial bank of sin residing in the human soul.

By distancing themselves from Manichean dualism, the early Puritans fell into a 'monism' that positioned God as the central actor in human history. Darkness was not seen as a power in itself but a state characterized by the absence of light. And 'the light' was a human community tirelessly working to establish itself and accomplish the mission assigned to it by God; 'darkness' was the avoidance of that mission. In such a worldview, the individual was continuously subjected to what Paul Ricoeur (1967) has called 'the fear of not loving enough' (45). To Ricoeur's statement we might add, 'the fear of not working enough.'

The sheer geographical space of America also influenced the formation of a particularly American morality of optimism. The American did not have to conform due to cramped quarters. If a person did not like the status quo of a given community, he could pack up and move. Until the 1900s, a considerable portion of America's interior remained unexplored, providing adventurous spirits with a 'huge experimental theatre of liberty' (Johnson 1997:47).

The Puritan outlook did not, by any means, govern all of the American settlements. Southern American society was quite different from its northern counterpart. While many of the northern settlers had left Europe in search of religious and political freedom, the southern settlers had come to the south attracted by its economic opportunities. They were certainly more at ease with the Old World values of a 'landed gentry' than they were with the Calvinistic work ethic – in fact, plantation owners even restricted the authority of preachers by having them appointed for short, fixed terms (Tindall and Shi [1984] 1999:132–3). Freed from labour by a slave population and profiting from the service of indentured workers from the Old World, the southern gentry followed a modified version of European aristocratic ideals. The northern Puritan virtue of hard work was balanced in the south by the search for a 'genteel' life of leisure. William Byrd II, a gentleman farmer who was well educated in the classics and owned no less than 3,600 books, writes in a letter of 1726 to his English friend, Charles Boyle, Earl of Orrery:

> Besides the advantages of pure air, we abound in all kinds of provisions without expenses (I mean we who have plantations). I have a large family of my own, and my doors are open to everybody, yet I have no bills to pay, and half-a-crown will rest undisturbed in my pockets for many moons altogether ... I live in a kind of independence on everyone but Providence. (cited in Fox-Genovese and Genovese 2005:118)

Like many other Southerners, Boyle did not consider the use of slave and indentured labour a social evil but as a gift from providence.

Hector St John de Crèvecoeur, a French aristocrat who wrote *Letters from an American Farmer* ([1782] 1957) and *The Meaning of Being American* ([1782] 1978), conveyed back to the Old World the opportunities and identity dilemmas of the Americans:

> What then is the American, this new man? He is neither European, or the descendant of a European, hence that strange mixture of blood, which you will find in no other country. I could point out to you a family whose grandfather was an Englishman, whose wife was Dutch, whose son married a French woman, and whose present four sons have now four wives of different nations ... Here individuals of all nations are melted into a new race of men, whose labors and posterity will one day cause changes in the world. ([1782] 1978)

Americans shared de Crèvecoeur's conviction that America would act as a catalyst for world change. This conviction provided American patriots with the ideology they needed to adopt a common, dynamic, participatory patriotism. Thomas Paine's pamphlet *Common Sense*, published anonymously in 1776, became a best-seller for it gave Americans a justification for their presence in a land that was not originally theirs. Paine ([1776] 1976) sincerely believed that the 'cause of America' would eventually become the cause of all mankind.

Like many intellectuals in Europe, St John de Crèvecoeur ([1782] 1957) worried about what effects such unstrained national optimism would have on personal character:

> They grow up a mongrel breed, half civilized, half savage ... You cannot imagine what an effect on manners the great distance they live from each

other has! ... Europeans who have not the sufficient share of knowledge they ought to have, in order to prosper; people who have suddenly passed from oppression, dread of government, and fear of laws, into the unlimited freedom of the woods ... Is it then surprising to see men this situated, immersed in great and heavy labours, degenerate a little? (48)

So, it was perhaps unavoidable that the American personality would become internationally alienated. How was one to explain to people living in congested London or Paris one's experience of crossing open plains on which rode tribes of Natives? And how was one to explain the sensation in one's chest as one stood on one's porch, sipping on a mug of coffee, breathing unspoiled air, and gazing with satisfaction at hundreds of miles of open and unspoiled land? Americans could not have easily duplicated European forms and practices had they wanted to. The face of the land they occupied was immense and changing rapidly. It was understandable that Europeans would have some trouble understanding this new nation that resisted categorical definitions by Old World norms. The formation of the American republic was a watershed event of no less importance than the rise of Renaissance society.

Moreover, the large trans-Atlantic distance between America and the Old World made Americans turn inwards. If they did experience sentiments of nostalgia, it was towards their own land and the great changes it had gone through as untouched wilderness had been transformed to accommodate demographic and economic expansion. James Fennimore Cooper's novels, collectively known as *The Leather Stocking Tales*, trace the massive changes that occurred between 1740 and 1830 as the first adventurous working-class settlers displaced the Indians and then were themselves displaced by a more sedate middle class. Cooper focused on the contradictions faced by Americans. The vanishing wilderness was a tragedy that placed Americans in a precarious moral position – they were the agents of change, yet the changes required the destruction of a landscape that they had come to appreciate and love (Spiller, 1968). Cooper's *The Last of the Mohicans: A Narrative of 1757* ([1826] 1986) was not only a biography of a transformed Native civilization but also an admission of the moral conundrum faced by Americans. Cooper's heroes are the antithesis of ambitious colonizers. They are the predecessors of the upright, individualistic gentlemen, the rugged cowboys of later frontier romances – although placed in a world that is rapidly industrializing, they manage to keep a clear conscience by remaining loners and staying clear of industrial barons.

This association between purity and aloneness is also present in the character of Hester Prynne in Nathaniel Hawthorne's *The Scarlet Letter* ([1850] 1923), in Melville's Captain Ahab in *Moby Dick* (1967), and in Edgar Allan Poe's haunting stories of alienated aristocrats searching for meaning ([1875] 1946). What is characteristically American about these heroes and anti-heroes is that they have to invent themselves in the absence of a reliable hierarchical society founded on aristocratic bloodline.

The American hero is saddled with a double duty: to restrain himself from being absorbed into a common fate that negates his personal identity, while remaining of upright moral character in order to protect the purity of the collective democratic experience. These heroes differed considerably from those in English novels, who were, for the most part, representing the aristocratic aspirations of the rising English middle classes.

Not only did Americans rebel against the allegiance demanded of them by the Old World, they also rebelled against the manifestation of that Old World within their own borders. A growing antipathy towards the aristocratic privilege of the south, which many northerners considered a residual relic from Europe, facilitated the rise of an important anti-slavery literature. Harriet Beecher Stowe's *Uncle Tom's Cabin*, the most influential anti-slavery novel of the period, showed how slavery had disrupted and twisted the black American family (Oakes 1998:195). Frederick Douglas's (1855) autobiographical work, *My Bondage and My Freedom*, equally contributed to the growing unrest that led to the American Civil War of 1861–5.

The Civil War was a watershed in American history. It questioned the values of the south as well as the old Puritan certainty in a common divine providence (Linderman 1987). An exhausted and shaken population was faced with the moral incertitude unleashed by the fact that citizens sharing a common heritage had to go to war with one another. Which side God chose to help on a given day was a matter of 'luck' rather than providence, for the combatants were all Christians. The carnage at the Battle of Gettysburg in 1863 caused 50,000 casualties in just three days. The American poet Walt Whitman observed that some of those returning from the war deserved more pity than the ones who had died on the battlefields.

The Puritan belief that all events were manifestations of God's will had already been shaken by the arrival of the Enlightenment in America. Moreover, the Great Evangelic Awakening of the mid-1700s had contested both the severe preaching of the Puritans as well as the libertinism that had spread in the wake of new prosperity. New preachers were arguing for heartfelt piety, loosening the hold of Puritan dogma in favour of an evangelical emotionalism (Tindall and Shi [1984] 1999:156–61). Seeking religious justifications for their military actions, both sides in the Civil War found comfort in evangelism. There were frequent references to divine help in the correspondence of generals from both camps (McPherson 1988, Rose 1994). In his Second Inaugural Address of 1865, Abraham Lincoln framed the military victory in religious terms:

> If we shall suppose that American Slavery is one of those offenses which, in the providence of God, must needs come, but which, having continued through His appointed time, He now wills to remove, and that He gives to both North and South, this terrible war, as the woe due to those by whom the offense came. ([1865] 1953:332)

Although the rebuilding that followed the end of the Civil War brought economic prosperity to many regions, it was the north that benefited most from industrial development. The exploitation of previously untapped resources (gold, iron, silver, oil, and coal) and the new intercontinental railway of 1861 gave American business the distribution facilities it needed to build what has since become known as the 'American marketplace.' The continuing influx of inexpensive immigrant labour further facilitated the acquisition of sizeable fortunes. In 1860, there were 100 millionaires in America; fifteen years later, there were over 1,000. The country's population increased from 31 million in 1860 to 76 million in 1900. By the First World War, America was a major world power well on its way to becoming the world's richest nation.

Writers were quick to note the social and personal costs of the rapid development that followed the Civil War. One sees in their work the emergence of a distinct American civility ethos, one based on a delicate balance between communalism and rugged individualism. There emerged, for example, in the works of Samuel Clemens (Mark Twain) the hero who manages to survive the social regimentation of massive industrial development by steering clear of it and maintaining his rural individuality (Kaplan 1974). Although books such as Twain's featured characters who were considered lazy according to middle-class American standards, a point was being made about American mainstream culture: sometimes dishonourable characters seemed to have hearts of gold. Bret Harte's ([1869] 1984) *The Outcasts of Poker Flat* presented gamblers, prostitutes, and petty robbers, who, although living on the margins of respectable society, had no small amount of integrity when put to the test.

The doubtful characters in these novels were vindicated by the discovery in the late 1800s that many of the tycoons, although respected in society, had acquired their fortunes through dishonourable means. The Romantic naturalism of a literature reacting to the utilitarianism of the period gave voice to a distinctly American literature of 'social conscience' that persists right through the twentieth century. At the core of this literature is the demand that the original democratic promises made to the individual be honoured. And, quite frequently, this search for democratic purity is represented through sympathy for the rebel.

American writers thus increasingly affirmed the value of individual liberty in a homogenized society cut off from its agricultural heritage. Walt Whitman's ([1855] 1971) *Leaves of Grass* exalted the human body and sexual love. Ralph Waldo Emerson's essays (1940) argued for social justice, respect for the freedom of the individual, and a social ethos that would remain free from the courtly values of Europe. Emerson believed that 'self-reliance' and 'non-conformity' were noble qualities that would contribute to personal and communal excellence. Similarly, Henry David Thoreau ([1849] 1967) argued in *Civil Disobedience* that actions against the state were perfectly justified if they were meant to fight social ills. Their work indicates the conflict residing at the centre of the American experience: the need for personal purity resists and critiques the necessary expedience of industrial progress and the mandates of capitalism. The scholar-writer becomes an enemy of private and public avarice (Wilson [1987] 1989:212).

Such social introspection led to a psychological form of the novel best exemplified by the work of Henry James, perhaps the greatest American novelist prior to the twentieth century. James's early work addressed America's relationship with Europe. In *The American* ([1877] 1970) he recounts the story of Christopher Newman, a self-made American millionaire who goes to Europe to find a bride, only to be refused by the woman's family because he is not an aristocrat. Newman, nevertheless, demonstrates his moral worth by refusing to take revenge on her family when he has the opportunity of doing so. James's novels are based on their characters' talents of psychological perception. There is a moment of insight during which the characters understand themselves as they never have before. For James, self-awareness was the only reliable path to wisdom and compassion; such acute referral to 'self' placed communalism and the inner identity of a person in a state of tension, revealing a conflict that was to be repeatedly represented in American fiction and social philosophy.

Thus, deprived of the social hierarchies of Europe, Americans were forced to forge an identity that was at once innovative as well as cognizant of the accumulated forces of American communalism. This dualism in the American psyche is observable in the American conduct books and etiquette manuals that were written prior to the twentieth century. *On one hand these books value an almost ascetic commitment to religious and communal values, while, on the other hand, they encourage the development of an independent personality given to welcoming imaginative and daring action.*

## American Conduct, Etiquette, and Action-Oriented Individualism

Difficult questions needed answering within the context of a constitution that approved of the sanctity of self-interest. How were manners to be perceived in a democracy? And how were they to be reconciled with religious asceticism and devotion? Was there to be an elite, and, if so, what qualifications should determine the composition of that elite? Did European etiquette and the artifice of style endanger the American democratic standard? And what was to be the relationship between religion, ethics, and civility in a mercantile society that was developing far more rapidly than expected?

Although there remained, even before the revolution, considerable consensus that America required a system of civic membership suited to its particular geographic realities, numerous debates occurred between those who wanted to preserve a European form of gentry and those committed to the development of a 'natural' American conception of gentlemanliness not dependent on either theocratic or aristocratic standards. In *The Gentleman in America* (1949), Edwin Harrison Cady traces various streams of thought that were involved in the creation of the ideal American gentleman. He notes that the predominant ideal was 'intellectually rigorous and morally strenuous' (30). In the New England region, the art of gentlemanly conduct was religiously defined. The Puritan theocracy made service to the community contingent on service to God and one's calling. This theocratic standard was broadly applied. On 27 September 1631, Josias Plastowe was caught stealing corn. He was sentenced 'thereafter to be called by the name of Josias, & not Mr., as formerly hee use to be' (town council judgment cited in Miller and Johnson 1938:378). While citizens of aristocratic backgrounds were allowed to use 'Esquire' at the end of their names and the gentry did enjoy the appellation of 'Mr,' these titles could be permanently lost for a petty or major misdemeanour. The Christian gentleman was expected to be not only civil but also moral according to specified Christian rules of behaviour. John Winthrop (1588–1649), governor of Massachusetts, successfully fulfilled the role of the New England Christian gentleman, not only defending the state from the meddling of politicians in England but spending nearly his entire fortune on the welfare of the community.

So strong was the association between honour and godliness that when Samuel Sewall (1652–1730), magistrate of the Salem witch trials, issued his apology for his role in the misguided trials, he couched his penitent remarks as an apology towards God as well as the community. Sewall had accepted to be magistrate out of a duty to God and he made his apology as a duty to God.

Although the New England theocratic experiment did not survive the rising mercantilism of the region, the ideal of the 'Christian gentleman' did survive and became a thorny issue in the ensuing debates regarding ideal American civility.

In contrast to the Christian ideal of gentlemanly conduct was Lord Chesterfield's ([1774] 1969) conception of the gentleman of all seasons. Chesterfield rationalized self-interest in a mercantile world by advising that good manners and a calculating spirit would take a man far in competitive mercantile society while keeping him immune to its corruptive influence. He approved of 'putting on a face' and advised that this was a necessary measure of prudence in civil society. The 'fine gentleman' was removed from the New England conception of religious civility. Chesterfield's utilitarianism fell short of the American need to develop a moral justification for a particularly American form of civility. The 'fine gentleman' was parodied in the American press as a pretentious dandy. Americans needed to make a distinction between the 'fine gentleman' and the 'well-bred gentleman' (Rubinstein 1995).

The debate over ideal gentlemanly conduct was very much connected to political debates between those favouring a democracy led by aristocrats and those supporting a completely republican government. Federalists and Jeffersonians disagreed on what was to be the role of the gentry in America. Affected by events in France, the federalists feared that complete egalitarianism would produce anarchy. Jeffersonians, on the other hand, considered the American population mature enough to remain civilized despite being allowed to live in an entirely democratic setting. Fearing the oppressions of European aristocracy, Thomas Jefferson (1743–1826) believed that simplicity and humility would help protect and manage a government that offered complete liberty. He remained dismayed with the elaborate etiquette rituals in Washington and considered them remnants of a corrupt world. When he took over as president he immediately simplified those protocols.

Jefferson's ideal of gentlemanly conduct posited that a person possesses an innate moral sense that can flourish despite the absence of an aristocratic elite. Arguing against a federalism that would limit social mobility, he stated:

> I hold it to be one of the distinguishing excellence over hereditary successions that the talents which nature has provided in sufficient proportion, should be selected by the society for the government of their affairs, rather than this should be transmitted through the loins of knaves and fools. (1904–5, 8:405)

This belief in the inherent goodness of men who are left free was to become a central ideal of American civil society. Implicit in this rejection of theocracy and aristocracy was the belief that intellectual and moral integrity would liberate the 'natural gentleman.' Jefferson thought that such a gentleman would be civil as well as magnanimous:

> It is the practice of sacrificing to those whom we meet in society all the little conveniences and preferences which will gratify them, and deprive use of nothing worth a moment's consideration; it is the giving of a pleasing and flattering turn to our expression, which will conciliate others, and make them pleased with us as well as themselves. How cheap a prize for the good-will of another! (cited in Randolph [1871] 1939:273)

Writing to Dr Benjamin Rudy, Jefferson revealed his affection for democratic social census:

> For thus I estimate the qualities of the mind: 1. Good humor; 2. integrity; 3. Industry; 4. science. The preference of the first to the second quality may not at first be acquiesced in; but certainly, we had all rather associate with a good humoured light-principled man, than with an ill-tempered rigorist in morality. (1904–5, 11:413)

Taking note of the code of the duel still in force in the south, Jefferson stated, 'I never saw an instance of one or two disputants convincing the other by argument. I have seen many, on their getting warm, become rude and shooting one another' (12:199).

Jefferson worried considerably about the aping of European manners. He advised Americans to forgo the Grand Tour of Europe, remaining convinced that a 'well-bred' gentleman could be successfully formed right on American soil. 'Be good, be learned, and be industrious,' Jefferson advised, 'and you will not want the aid of traveling to render you precious to your country, dear to your friends, happy within yourself' (6:262). Predictably, he favoured an American system of universal education free from the influence of foreign models (5:188).

All told, Jefferson's conception of egalitarian civility was not entirely anti-aristocratic. Rather, he favoured an aristocratic bearing that would emanate from the individual instead of from association with a caste. His meditations on civility were considerably utopian. Jefferson's gentleman could be religious as well as refined – what determined his worth as a man was whether his demeanour was profoundly *natural* and *truthful*.

This search for a universal gentleman capable of transcending the trappings of partisan interests is also present in James Fennimore Cooper's *The American Democrat* (1838), his major work of social analysis. Cooper managed to provoke the ire of the clergy as well as the plutocracy with his uncompromising credo of agrarian integrity. Cooper's gentleman was a proud and uncompromising character:

> He is truthful out of self-respect, and not in obedience to the will of God; free with his money, because liberality is an essential feature of his habits, and not in imitation of the self-sacrifice of Christ; superior to scandal and the vices of the body, inasmuch as they are low and impair his pride of character, rather than because he has been commanded not to bear false witness against his neighbour. (cited in Cady 1949:119)

Cooper was trying to idealize the 'natural American gentleman' as a sort of knight of the wilderness, possessed of an integrity that could not be corrupted by religious, economic, or political privileges.

This search for an ideal republican gentleman, capable of weathering the contingencies of a changing geographical and economic landscape, was no less ambitious than Baldassare Castiglione's meditation regarding the ideal courtier. Cooper would have found Oliver Wendell Holmes's satisfaction with the 'fine gentlemen' quite disturbing. Holmes wrote:

> Good dressing, quiet ways, low tones of voice, lips that can wait, and eyes that do not wander – shyness of personalities, except in certain intimate connections – *be light in hand* in conversation, to have ideas, but to be able to make talk, if necessary, without them – to belong to the company you are in, and, not to yourself. (1891–5, 11:139–40)

Cooper's predisposition towards naturalism is also present in the writings of Ralph Waldo Emerson (1803–82). Emerson's scholar-gentleman remains unaffected by the pretensions of the moneyed crowd: 'He always means what he says, and says what he means, however courteously ... for he is truth's man, and will speak and act the truth until he dies' (1909–14, 8:75–6). This was a civility ideal that would have sorely tested French and English interaction rituals. It was simply too direct for European tastes and the manner in which Europeans related to 'time, context and space.'

Emerson's gentlemen possessed considerable power and magnetism precisely because of their refusal to compromise themselves. They were prime movers of men: 'The will of the pure runs down from them into their natures, as water runs down from a higher into a lower vessel. This natural force is no more to be withstood than any other natural force' (3:95). Emerson reconciled the saint and the gentleman by referring to the purest ideals of American democracy: 'Everything that is called fashion and courtesy humbles itself before the cause and fountain of honour, creator of titles and dignities, namely, the heart of love. This is the royal blood' (3:153–4).

The progression from religious civility to a patriotic and communal notion of civility was, consequently, a unique contribution of American political and social thought. While it complicated relations with Europeans who were habituated to a less direct civility code, it allowed Americans to maintain a distinctly American cultural identity. The civility ethos of simplicity and directness could apply to all Americans, whether they were religious or not, born in America or freshly off the boat. Herein lay the roots of American secularism. It was developed not out of outright rebellion against the various religious creeds of America, but in reference to a deeply personal and individualistic civility standard that all creeds could share. This transition from Puritan religiosity to an American Christian moral propriety and then to action-oriented civility is observable in the conduct manuals of America.

Americans embarked on a bold experiment: to adopt a courtesy ethic not slavishly patterned on what had been inherited and imported from Europe, but, rather, based on what was needed to fulfill American migrational, economic, political, and religious realities. Benjamin Franklin ([1746] 1750) noted this need for a particularly American civility ethos in *Reflections on Courtship and Marriage*: 'If class relations change, so also must the canon of breeding or else forfeit every vestige of authority; and it follows that the more violent the change, the more imperative is the need for compromise and adjustment' (15).

By the mid-1800s, when the anonymously penned *How to Behave* (1856) appeared, Franklin's prophecy had been realized in a slew of conduct books that presented a distinctly American approach to civility. The writer of this particular book affirmed a social standard that was a particularly American development, quite different from the notions of liberty and egalitarianism that had arisen in France and England. The author of *How to Behave* declared without any reserve that 'true republicanism requires that every man shall have an equal chance – that every man shall be free to become as unequal as he can' (124). No better representation of American capitalism could have been made.

This hostility towards aristocratic privilege and its attendant restriction of social mobility contributed to a high valuation of personal success. Despite the fact that both America and Europe were affected by Victorian morality, Americans had less of a need to justify economic activity, precisely because America did not have disappointing memories spanning centuries of despotic rule. The rising middle classes were able to 'heartily' accept prosperity without worrying that they risked falling into the heartlessness that had characterized the earliest European elites. This liberated a certain 'enthusiasm' in social relations, an enthusiasm that had to be maintained even when there was considerable underlying mistrust. If there has been a social uneasiness to American civil relations it has been in some measure due to this contradiction between the need to demonstrate outright communal enthusiasm and the need to advance personal interests.

This preference for egalitarian interaction is present in most of the American conduct books published prior to 1900. While it would be impossible to review the majority of them, there are sufficient examples of varying themes to provide a reliable understanding of how American civility became uncoupled from its Old World origins. A dedicated compilation of these conduct manuals has been provided by Sarah E. Newton (1994) in *Learning to Behave: A Guide to American Conduct Books before 1900*. Newton has catalogued major conduct books published before 1900 and listed 196 books for children, 142 for men, 188 for women, and a further 57 for both genders (even more titles can be found if one takes into account the hundreds of books published for use in Sunday schools). Also useful is a previous and historically informed study by Arthur M. Schlesinger ([1946] 1968), *Learning How to Behave: A Historical Study of American Etiquette Books*.

For the purposes of our own work, we have selected some books addressed to children, men, and women to help show the development of an American civility standard that increasingly valued 'directness' and 'ease.'

*Children's Conduct Books*

Three various movements are noticeable in children's conduct books, and they seem to reflect the social changes that occurred in America as Americans proceeded from Puritanism to evangelicalism and then to a more secular mercantile morality.

The early American children's conduct books were based on the belief that the human species was an imperfection of nature. Even children were considered marked by Adam and Eve's primal transgression against God. In a poem entitled 'Childhood' the Puritan poet Anne Bradstreet ([c. 1660s] 1967) viewed the child as an innately corrupt being:

> Stained from birth and Adam's sinful fact,
> Thence I began to sin as soon as act:
> A perverse will, a love to what's forbid,
> A serpent's sting in pleasing face lay hid:
> A lying tongue as soon as it could speak
> A fifth commandment do daily break (54)

Bradstreet's fear of the evils that supposedly resided in a child was also shared by many Puritan preachers, including Cotton Mather (1663–1728), who believed that a good whipping was better than damnation in hell. This mission to exorcise evil tendencies and preserve Christian virtues forms the foundation of Puritan children's literature. In *The Pu-*

*ritan Family* (1966), Edmund Morgan writes this enlightening account of the constricted life-world of the Puritan child:

> Children were ignorant and children were evil, but their ignorance could be enlightened and their evil restrained, provided the effort was made soon enough. The pious parent was faced with two tasks, instruction and discipline. He had to fill his children's minds with knowledge and he had to make them apply their knowledge in right action ... There was no question of developing the child's personality, of drawing out or nourishing any inherent qualities which he might possess, for no child could by nature possess any desirable qualities. He had to receive all good from outside himself, from education – and ultimately from the Holy Spirit ... The problem of discipline was to make an evil-natured but at least partly rational animal act against his nature and according to his reason. (97)

Heimert and Delbanco (1985) present a similar view of a religious society that devoted considerable energy to questioning its relationship with evil. The saying 'to beat the *hell out* of someone,' may have originated in a period when socialization was considered to have a dual purpose: to drive out what was bad and preserve what was good. Rarely were physical affection and the notion of free and unconditional love mentioned in the Puritan writings. Instead, early conduct book writers recommended a good dose of strict discipline supplemented by arduous lessons in religious purity. These works used children's fear of damnation (and their fear of having God punish their parents for their children's bad deeds) to instill desired attitudes and behaviour (Sloan 1955).

Such unwavering confidence in Biblical teachings informed Cotton Mather's approach to conduct. In *Addresses to Old Men, and Young Men and Little Children in Three Discourses* (1690), Mather advised children to become 'sons of Christ' and reject any bad behaviour equated with the dominion of sin. He used the poignant story of his own dying son to help make his points. So dependent were works such as Mather's on the religious ideas of damnation and salvation that there emerged the genre of 'the dying joyful or angelic child' who turned to his or her contemporaries to impart some final words of advice before moving on to a well-deserved place in heaven. Mather's other conduct works included *A Family Well-Ordered, or an Essay to Render Parents and Children Happy in One Another* (1699). In this particular work, Mather reminded parents that they were ultimately responsible for teaching their children piety;

he advised that the best way for achieving such piety in the family was to insist on *absolute obedience* on the part of the child. A rebellious child was seen as a manifestation of evil, an echo of Lucifer's original rebellion against a divinely ordered universe. The child was, therefore, not to be reasoned with but given commands that would bring forth positive, dutiful behaviour.

James Janeway's ([1672] 1822) *A Token for Children, being an exact account of the conversion, holy and exemplary life and joyful deaths of several young children* was another Puritan tract that attempted to frighten children into believing that any lapse in their behaviour would lead to a loss of salvation. Recounting the stories of thirteen children, Janeway creates composites of children who, although they come from morally disadvantaged backgrounds, manage to find their way to heaven through an almost angelic consideration for others and an unwavering belief in God's goodness. One of the girls in the stories, Sarah Howley, delivers herself into God's hands and, thereafter, consecrates herself to sharing her understanding of the gospel with family and friends. The girl exhibits no less that thirty-four saintly traits by the time she closes her eyes and meets her saviour in heaven (Example 1). In another story (Example 7), a notoriously wicked boy is saved from begging in the streets; he reforms himself by abandoning his naughty, manipulative ways and adopting Christian piety. His transformation consists of painful confessions and remorse; his reward is ascension to heaven at the age of nine. Janeway describes the boy's ordeal with considerable self-righteous satisfaction: 'He was made to cry out of himself, not only for his swearing and lying, and other outwardly notorious sins; but he was in great horror for the sin of his Nature, for the vileness of his heart, and original corruption' (Example 7, Section 8).

Another widely read Puritan writer, John Bunyan, used a slightly more conciliatory tone in *A Book for Boys and Girls; or Country Rhymes for Children* ([1686] 1889). Rather than issuing frightening warnings regarding what happened to children who strayed from the paths of faith and duty, Bunyan tried to convince his readers with pleasing rhymes that spoke of the 'joys' reserved for children who agreed to be faithful and obedient.

There is an unmistakable streak of coercion in these early Puritan conduct books that seems to accord well with the severity of the early Puritan communities. These religiously oriented conduct books favoured a hierarchical model of authority extending from God, down to the father, and further down to the wife and the children. Ensuing social relationships were vertical, with influence transmitted from the elders to the young. The early communities, often made up of various Protestant sects, shared the common belief that men, women, and children had to be constantly vigilant in order not to regress into sin. Such personal and communal vigilance was made that much more anxiety-provoking by the fact that salvation seemed always out of reach. Religious doubt, the one thing that could lead to a loss of religious heart and liberate personal desire, was a private and public danger. Preachers sermonized that communities needed to remain sober and vigilant if individuals were to find personal and collective salvation. So passionate was this communal self-surveillance that the Methodists of New England even banned Christmas because it involved partying and frivolity; they replaced it with the festival of Thanksgiving, which they found more appropriate to their faith.

It was understandable that, in such a vertical system, the proposed mores were not up for discussion by the children who were commanded to adopt them. This vertically oriented social ethic was most easily applied during the early settlement period, when sons were not allowed to acquire property from their fathers unless they had reached middle age; economic dependence on the father assured a certain amount of moral subservience. It was not until later, in the eighteenth century, that sons began acquiring land at an earlier age or simply moving away from home to acquire their own homesteads (Tindall and Shi [1984] 1999:138). Self-reliance, the most dangerous threat to the fixity of vertical authority, became a valued personality trait.

A similar attempt to communicate with children through the glorification of qualities considered holy was embedded in the genre of children's lyric poetry. Isaac Watts ([1715] 1972), perhaps the most prolific children's lyric poet, managed to side-step the fire-and-brimstone lectures of the more severe preachers; he tried to convince his young readers that there were plenty of 'natural delights' waiting to be discovered by children, provided they behaved with utmost virtue. Promising joy and salvation in return for goodness, he wrote poems addressing religious as well as family matters:

*Heaven and Hell*
There is beyond the sky
A heaven of joy and love;
And hold children, when they die,
Go to that world above. (cited in Demers and Moyles, 1982:65)

*Love between Brothers and Sisters*
Whatever brawls disturb the street
There should be peace at home;
Where sisters dwell and brothers meet,
Quarrels should never come. (67)

*Against Idleness and Mischieve*
In books, or work, or healthful play,
Let my first years be past,
That I may give of every day
Some good account at last. (68)

Despite these severe tracts, there was a countervailing movement in childrearing. John Locke's ([1693] 1989) *How to Bring Up Your Children* had considerably influenced American intellectuals. Locke argued that children were born with natural talents that, if left unhampered, would lead them to value curiosity and moral action. Along with Rousseau, who wrote *Emile* ([1761] 1979) (a treatise on ideal childhood), Locke became the forerunner of the 'rational moralist.'

While rational moralists did not deny the existence of God, and even made frequent references to the presence of a divine being, their advice on conduct was framed within reasoned arguments rather than on Biblical commands. They believed that a child should be socialized to understand that his behaviour would have important effects on the cohesion of the whole family. The consequences of this transformation in views of childhood is noticeable not only in the conduct books of the nineteenth century but also in the rise of a new vehicle for stimulating children's imagination, the book of fiction written specifically for children (Hunt 2000).

So, nearing the 1800s, an important change began occurring in the manner in which children were viewed by those writers who favoured the 'rational morality' approach. The child was now seen as an impressionable and tender being who needed to be taught positive virtues without being excessively berated for his evil nature. Bernard Wishy (1967) attributes this change to the rise of a republicanism that secularized (and softened) the original Puritan ethic. Specific reasoned examples, rather than threats of damnation, were now used to encourage children to adopt a 'good disposition.' C.G. Salzmann's (1796) *Elements of Morality, for the Use of Children* used anecdotes to provide children with concrete examples of what was to be considered 'good' and 'bad' behaviour. Salzmann used a fictional family to ground his description of an exemplary family. So did Charlotte Sanders (1799) in *The Little Family*, a story of a family prospering through the practice of faithful obedience, industriousness, and grace.

A proliferation of conduct books were published between the years 1820 and 1870, a period during which the American middle class acquired considerable power. These books tried to reconcile the realities of a rapidly changing social and economic landscape with the need to preserve a democratic morality that could transcend differences in religious disposition. Following the Civil War there was a considerable need to maintain religious tolerance in a land where a plethora of denominations were suddenly living in mixed communities. This need for a common-denominator civility had effects on the conduct literature of the time. Some books, such as *Mentor, or Dialogues between a Parent and Children; on Some of the Duties, Amusements, Pursuits, and Relations of Life* (1828), covered a range of practical topics such as play, vanity, work, truth, lying, effective use of time, cursing, and deference. The warning of hellfire was replaced with reasoned arguments that tried to show the effects of good and bad behaviour; the advice was written in such a way as to be applicable to children of all religious denominations.

A further interesting shift occurred in these later American works. The conduct books went beyond preaching in favour of religious devotion and took into account the contradictions inherent in a society that had to balance spiritual devotion with capitalist expansion and its competitive imperatives. The religious virtues were listed, as they had always been, but there occurred a change in the methods used to enlist the interest and imagination of young readers. The ideal of salvation became complemented (and often eclipsed) by the ideals of industriousness, unselfishness, and loyalty towards communal values. Good conduct (obedience, pleasantness, industriousness, and lack of egotism) was now enlisted in favour of a functional familial and communal harmony. Mary Lystad (1980), in *From Dr. Mather to Dr. Seuss: 200 Years of American Books for Children*, has reviewed children's books during a 200-year period of American history and also finds that, in the eighteenth and nineteenth centuries, practical behavioural tips came to predominate over religious dictums. With the broadening of the educational system, books appeared teaching children their responsibilities towards their school, their teachers, and their schoolmates.

The children's conduct books of the nineteenth century were additionally gender-specific. Such gender-specificity is found in Reverend

Harvey Newcomb's work, published as two separate books – *Anecdotes for Girls* (1849) and *Anecdotes for Boys* (1860). The boys were encouraged to be patriotic, restrained in their desires, fond of knowledge, and adept at self-help and hard work. They were to desist from gambling, using bad language, and reading immoral books. As for the girls, they were encouraged to be pious, learn the arts of cooking and tidiness, develop a benevolent attitude, and desist from being irresponsible and lazy. Catherine Sedgewick's (1857) *Morals of Manners, or, Hints for Our Young People* made similar distinctions; many of the ideal behavioural traits recommended to the boys were very different from those prescribed for the girls. Nevertheless, Sedgewick affirmed a democratic notion of civility, reminding her readers: 'It is not here as in the old world, where one man is born with a silver spoon, and another with a pewter one, in his mouth. You may all handle silver spoons, if you will. That is, you may all rise to places of respectability' (61). Although gender distinction and role-assignment existed long before the nineteenth century, what appears as a distinctly nineteenth-century development is the preparation of the young girl to one day act as a moral stabilizer in the absence of her work-bound husband.

Good 'behaviour' was now posited as a pathway to happiness for the child *and* the family. Lydia Sigourney's (1833) *How to Be Happy, Written for the Children of Some Dear Friends* taught that happiness was the ultimate reward for the child who showed amiability towards parents, siblings, and other children while resisting egotistical impulses. This was an important change, for it placed the child at the centre of the conduct book and offered rewards in exchange for good behaviour. This had the effect of increasing individual responsibility; while the child had previously been asked to fulfill God's desire because that was the law of life, he was now asked to develop precisely those qualities that would serve best his own place in the new world. By appealing to the child's own desire for success, the conduct writers legitimized individuality and the idea of personal fulfillment. Belief in predestination was paralleled by a belief in self-reliance and success. Characteristics commonly applied to adults were now being presented to children of young age.

Admonitions delivered to boys focused now on what a boy was to choose as a profession. William A. Alcott's (1844) *The Boy's Guide to Usefulness* reveals in its title this movement towards an applied work ethic that becomes its own justification rather than an act of service toward God. Alcott, who was a prolific writer of conduct books, advised his readers that 'it is a melancholy and highly alarming fact, that most wicked men, who have come to a miserable end, began their career in idleness' (49). Alcott's advice was remarkably free from class considerations: 'There is nobody in the world – no class of person, I mean – from whom you may not, in one condition or another, learn something' (100). Particularly interesting was his advice on how the young were to relate to their elders. He rejected servile reverence while admonishing his readers to learn the art of 'respect' (103). In *The Young Man's Guide* (1846), Alcott again warned that 'nothing is more essential to usefulness and happiness in life, than habits of industry' (38). Temperance (62), cleanliness (88–9), and keeping a balanced disposition (177) were promoted as the principal qualities that would keep a young man out of the company of those who might lead him astray. On the matter of relations with women, Alcott advised his reader: 'Whatever advice may be given to the contrary by friend or foes, it is my opinion that you ought to keep matrimony steadily in view' (244).

Similarly, *Advice to a Young Gentleman on Entering Society* (1839) explained that in a rapidly changing world a young man had to be cautious when entering the company of others. The author argued: 'Any one who hopes to get on at all in life, will find it frequently necessary to treat men very differently from what he actually feels – to talk pleasantly with those he hates, and behave respectfully to those he despises ... preserve your equanimity as long as you remain in company, and after you have retired, review the circumstances, and decide what is best to do' (135).

Yet, reasoned arguments did not satisfy the religious requirements of the American communities. Americans faced a dilemma similar to the one faced by English Victorians who had to reconcile etiquette with morality. A new institution, the Sunday school, emerged in America to compensate for the rising moral secularism of industrial society. Although the Sunday school movement was the creation of English evangelists who sought to educate and convert poor orphans in England, it found its way to America and became a strong national heritage. Comprehensive studies of the Sunday school phenomenon have been published by Margaret Cutt, *Ministering Angels* (1979), and Anne M. Boylan, *Sunday School: The Formation of an American Institution, 1790–1880* (1988). Cutt suggests that Sunday schools filled a vacuum left by the disappearance of the early Puritan preachers. Faced with a religiously diverse society, Sunday schools attempted to give religious and moral instruction to children and youth to supplement what they were learning in common schools burdened with the teaching of the new sciences.

David Nord (1984) has suggested that the rise of the Evangelic Sunday School at a time when industrialism and print communications were expanding in America provided the emerging mass media with an evangelical origin and helped harmonize early American religiosity with industrial achievement. Sunday school publications numbered over six million per year as early as 1830 (1–30). Nathan O. Hatch (1989) also explains that the early media were given to replaying the themes of conduct books while promoting a Christian industrial democracy. According to his estimates, during the period 1800–80 America was flooded by millions of pamphlets, hymn books, conduct books, journals, magazines, newspapers, and Sunday school books published by the American Tract Society.

Sunday school teachers thus had to lecture on 'usefulness' as well as 'piety.' They had to caution against the moral dangers of industrial society without invalidating the principles on which industrial progress was based. The title of Rev. Charles B. Haddock's (18–?) *Christian Education: Containing Valuable Practical Suggestions in the Training of Children for Usefulness and Heaven* demonstrates this dual purpose of Sunday school instruction. Haddock warns parents of the dangers of over-reliance on the rewards of work in the new society: 'While others, then, are seen studying, and toiling, and denying themselves, that they may leave their children a *name* or an *estate*, remember, Christian Father, Christian Mother, remember, that the richest legacy you can bestow on your children, is a *pious education*' (5).

Yet, in keeping with the increasing rationality of industrial life, he warns that reasonable discussion and the giving of example should precede punishment during the socialization of children: 'Appeal first to the approbation of God, to the sense of duty, to the generous feelings – gratitude, love, kindness – and to the happiness of virtue and miseries of vice. In the last resort, and then only, have recourse to punishments' (10).

Another guide to parenting, *Early Piety* (1834), by Rev. Jacob Abbott, strictly differentiates between the ability to reason and the capacity to have religious faith. Abbott cautions that only religious instruction will nurture and maintain faith (33). This effort to preserve an appreciation of how the 'soul' differs from the 'mind' is also forefront in *Easy Lessons for the Little Ones at Home* (American Tract Society, c. 1855): 'Is it your soul which thinks. When you love your dear mother and father, what is it that loves them? Is it your head, or your eyes, or your ears? No. You cannot love with these. You love with your soul ... God made your soul and put it in you, so that you could love him' (15).

In S.C. John Abbott's (1833?) *The Child at Home; or, The Principles of Filial Duty Familiarly Illustrated*, love of family and God is grounded in a rational happiness. Abbott reasons with his readers that 'there can be no real happiness when there is not an amiable disposition. You cannot more surely make yourself wretched, than by indulging in an irritable spirit' (153). There is no mention of evil. A few pages later, Abbott tells his young readers: 'You must have an opinion of your own. And you must be ready, frankly and modestly, to express it, when the occasion requires, without being intimidated by the fear of censure. You can neither command respect nor be useful without it' (163).

This seeming conflict between agreeability, faith, and piety on one hand and self-assertion on the other is a frequent paradox that appears in nineteenth-century conduct books and Sunday school books. The child is required to maintain an active imagination that moves him to positive action while avoiding those distractions that might lead him into vice.

*The Polite Boy* (18–?) by Uncle Madison exhorts its young readers to 'cease to do evil, learn to do well' by rejecting bad habits and adopting good ones (13). The author reasons with children, explaining that life is like the keys of the piano – whether the music will be pleasant or not will depend on which keys are hit (13–14). The writer also gives considerable attention to the question of tolerance, no doubt with America's multicultural landscape in mind: 'All men belong to one family; the good and the bad, the wise and the ignorant, the strong and the weak. One God created them all ... Would we not have a happy world if all would really exercise this love?' (54). Regardless of these pious and compassionate statements the ideal quality being promoted is one of action: 'Be punctual and methodical in business and never procrastinate ... Rather set than follow an example ... Practice strict temperance ... Rise early and be an economist of time ... Never acquiesce in immoral or pernicious opinions ... Be not forward to assign reasons to those who have no right to ask them' (85).

The entire argument is embedded in fetching stories of famous men who learned their lessons and succeeded despite difficulties; the reader is given a set of rules to follow as well as models to admire and emulate. Timothy Shay Arthur's (1850) *Advice to Young Men on Their Duties and Conduct in Life* similarly tries to set a balance between deference to

## The American Experience: Democracy and Informal Civility 239

elders and the development of self-respect (115). A distinctly independent personality is being promoted.

One interesting text is *Etiquette for Little Folks* (1856?) by Mrs Henry S. Mackarnass. In a fifty-two-page tract the author provides one-line rules for children to follow in a variety of situations in life: with parents, at table, among other children, in school, at church, in the street, with superiors, with equals, and with inferiors. In addition to the usual admonitions given about table manners and not eating too loudly or stuffing one's mouth full of food (advice already current during the Renaissance) (12–14), the book advises children to do the following:

> Always bow to your parents if they are in the company of others (6); Dispute not, nor delay your parents' commands; never make faces or contortions, nor grimaces, while anyone is giving you commands (8); Never take another's chair; never quarrel with your brothers and sisters; use respectful and courteous language towards all domestics; never be domineering or insulting (9); Sit not down [at table] until your parents are seated (10); Find no fault with anything that is given you; speak not at table. If others are discoursing, meddle not with the matter, but be silent except when spoken to (11); Never speak to your parents without some title of respect, as Sir, Madam, &c.; Dispute not, nor delay to obey your parents' commands; Go not out of doors without your parents' leave, and be sure to return by the limited time. Never grumble, or show discontent at any thing your parents appoint, speak or do (7); Bear with meekness and patience, and without murmuring or sullenness, your parents' reproofs or corrections, even if it should sometimes happen that they are undeserved (8); Let your countenance be moderately cheerful, neither laughing nor frowning. To look upon one in company, and immediately after whisper to another, is unmannerly. Whisper not in company. Be not froward [sic] and fretful among your equals, but gentle and affable. (19)

Undoubtedly, few children were able or willing to fastidiously follow the above rules. Yet, the fact that such advice was being dispensed indicates the extent to which the child was expected to defer to hierarchical figures who played a predominant role in determining his status as a child of good breeding.

Such a demanding childrearing ethic was attracting opposition, however. Mocking the severity of such conduct books, Mark Twain ([1867] 2001) dispensed some tongue-in-cheek counsel in *Advice for Good Little Girls*:

Good little girls ought not to make mouths at their teachers for every trifling offense. This kind of retaliation should only be resorted to under peculiarly aggravating circumstances. If you have nothing but a rag doll stuffed with saw-dust, while one of your more fortunate little playmates has a costly china one, you should treat her with a show of kindness, nevertheless. And you ought not to attempt to make a forcible swap with her unless your conscience would justify you in it, and you know you are able to do it ... Good little girls should always show marked deference for the aged. You ought never to 'sass' old people – unless they 'sass' you first.

## Men's Conduct Books

Conduct books addressed to American males also preached a philosophy of 'action.' While in the seventeenth century Americans had welcomed Continental conduct books such as Richard Alstree's *The Whole Duty of Men* (1658) and *The Gentleman's Calling* (1660) and Henry Peacham's (1627) *The Compleat Gentleman*, the few Continental books that were of much interest to Americans in any sizeable numbers in the nineteenth century were personal motivation books such as Samuel Smiles's best selling *Self-Help* (1859) and *Thrift* (1875).

This movement away from religious virtue in favour of secular ends is already noticeable in the eighteenth-century American conduct literature addressed to males. In 1796 Mason L. Weems produced *The Immortal Mentor: or, Man's Unerring Guide to a Healthy, Wealthy, and Happy Life* in which he included Benjamin Franklin's popular essays 'The Way to Wealth' and 'Advice to a Young Tradesman.' Without directly contradicting Cotton Mather's religious Puritanism, Franklin managed to produce a body of conduct advice that, without apology, sanctioned the pursuit of monetary profit. Understandably, Franklin appealed to the ambitions of males who were excited by the financial opportunities of a rapidly expanding economy.

Franklin's *Autobiography* of 1771–88 (1950) provided an exemplary story of how a person could survive and prosper through times of considerable change provided he combined ambition and mercantile common sense. Franklin's appeal lay in his open admission of his own mistakes (affectionately referred to by himself as *erratum*) and how he had managed to learn from them by not indulging in self-blame. He wondered how a God who had created humans could blame them for occasionally erring. Franklin was promoting the virtue of ambition and the acquisition of profit through the thoughtful management of life choices. He was also transcending the categorical dividing line between 'good' and 'evil.' The recognition of error (as opposed to sin) encouraged self-forgiveness; and self-forgiveness encouraged experimentation, for an error made could be corrected without undue self-mortification. The roots of an action-oriented American pragmatism are found in Franklin, for, although he did not preach against idealism and altruism, he did judge the value of an act by the usefulness of its outcomes. The enduring effect of his life philosophy was confirmed in *Time* magazine's special issue on Franklin, 'The Amazing Adventures of Ben Franklin' (7 July 2003:26–49).

Other conduct writers stepped in to dispense advice on how young men were to behave in the new industrial towns and cities. Rev. John Todd's (1841) *The Moral Influence, Danger and Duties Connected with Great Cities* advised a young man to make every effort to preserve his religious faith and observe the Sabbath even though he would be living in a city where he would be unknown and unobserved by kin and clergy. The dangers confronting a young man in a large city included gambling, reading of immoral books, the theatre, the company of loose women, and the unprofitable use of time. Echoing Franklin, Todd believed that any man could rise to the highest of offices and fortunes, but he cautioned that reputation of character was the only protection in a world where the influences of religion and family associations were on the decline.

In *Manhood's Morning* (1896), Joseph A. Conwell similarly idealized American individualism and exhorted young men to go forward and embrace lives of action that remained loyal to America's greatness. This greatness was based on certain characteristics designed to keep the male concentrated on his work. Rising early, remaining focused, finishing what was started, and being forthright and civil were presented as the building blocks of a dynamic personality capable of prospering in the new industrial society. The book's subtitle, *Go It While You're Young*, shows this growing tendency to encourage the young to take risks and break away from the family.

The American development of a 'manly' character, efficient and honourable, became the ideal of conduct manuals. Although they did link work and religious values, these conduct manuals left the male free to be aggressive during his explorations of opportunity. Predictably, this placed the American male in a moral bind. In doing so, the writers of these conduct books created a tension between the qualities of action/self-affirmation and Christian sentiment. A Christian gentleman would defer to the sentiments of others; the manly achiever, however, had to conquer and build by being acquisitive and competitive. This 'heroic' manliness would have a salient influence on the manner in which the American male achieved feelings of self-worth.

To reconcile the contradiction between Christian ethics and competitive self-assertion, there emerged further books speaking out against crass materialism and reminding that personal accomplishments had to be acquired through honourable means: self-restraint, honesty, and honour pertaining to all matters including relationships with the opposite sex.

Thus, work became the connecting bridge between morality and prosperity. Reverend J.W. Kasey's (1858) *The Young Man's Guide to True Greatness* singled out idleness as the principal cause of poverty and loss of self-esteem. This American belief in the sanctity of effort – and its sure rewards – was elevated to a quasi-religious duty. Women were even enlisted to testify in favour of manly ambition. In J.R. Miller's (1893) *Young Men: Faults and Ideals* a group of women are surveyed and asked what they find most regrettable about some men. In reply, they cite lack of motivation and absence of clear purpose. It would seem that, although women were simultaneously being cautioned not to adopt the manly ambitions, they were being enlisted to confirm those same male attributes as qualities they desired in partners.

The conduct writers of the eighteenth and nineteenth centuries managed somehow to link character, religiosity, and marketable ambition in such a way as to teach the American male that being American required the integration of qualities which, although they were contradictory, would help support the American mission. The male was required to be ambitious, action-oriented, and decisive, but not to the point where he would not care about the consequences of his commercial forwardness. He was required to restrain his aggression but also be ready to defend the honour of his country. He was to achieve financial success but restrain his passion for the enjoyment of the fruits of that success. That not all men succeeded in remaining committed to this demanding standard is understandable. But what did become ingrained in the American male, as a result of this socialization, was the ability (and the preference) to be emotionally restrained in the gentler emotions that might have interfered with the energy required for determined action and achievement. This restraint, however, did not have a similar dampening effect on the more violent emotions.

There seemed to be a marked difference in the works of literature that appeared in England, France, and America during this same period. The emotional constitution of the male was depicted differently in each country. In England, the male in the novel was given to making tender, amorous declarations; this was a legacy of the Age of Sensibility and the Romanticism that followed it. A similar high valuation of male sentimentality was present in the French literature. In the American novel, however, the male seemed locked up in an image of himself as a strong being able to tolerate a woman's emotions without revealing his own.

A particularly American phenomenon emerged from this high valuation of independence and commitment to work: a peculiar tension developed between fathers and sons. Fathers tried to control the work of their sons while insisting at the same time that the sons make successes of themselves. A son's work was to be independent while also satisfying the ambitions of the father (Rose 1994:167). This paradoxical combination of self-affirmation and conformity created considerable tension in families, especially at the end of the nineteenth century and the beginning of the twentieth. If a list of words or value statements were to be selected to represent themes most frequently appearing in over 150 men's conduct books of the period they would be: self-reliance, self-government, self-restraint, disciplining of desires, power of the will, and patriotism towards a common national project. Increasingly, the old rituals of deference were being softened and informalized in order to allow the emergence of a social ethos based on individualism. Yet, that ethos was not removing existing restraints on the body; an action-oriented self was requiring the limitation of the finer emotions (Hemphill 1996).

A further condition that favoured American 'directness' was the co-existence of groups of various ethnic backgrounds that felt threatened by one another. During and following the Civil War hundreds of different accents were heard in New York as migrants congregated and competed for social and economic benefits. The conflicts between these various groups were serious enough to cause considerable social hesitancy. The ambiguities that often result when elaborate courtesy rituals are practised towards those who do not know the codes of those rituals can have serious consequences. A gesture that is meant to signify friendliness or deference can very well be misinterpreted as an insult. 'Directness' assured that what was meant was rapidly communicated with a minimum of misinterpretation. Simplicity and directness became a common denominator for civil interactions in a multicultural society.

## Women's Conduct Books

Although books addressing the moral education of the family were originally intended for a male audience, the governance of the family (together with the teaching of manners and the efficient keeping of a house) were the subjects of hundreds of tracts and books addressed to women. And, here again, arriving in the nineteenth century, we see a concentrated effort to define what was believed to be a woman's 'natural' character and how it differed from that of a man.

While the gender-definition project was similar to the one undertaken in England, there was a marked difference due to the manner in which early American communities were organized. An American household was a work unit contributing to the prosperity of the community. An exaggerated need for privacy would have weakened the community. Faced with an undeveloped frontier, Americans always needed to maintain a communal sense of town and village organization to provide security in a vast land in which towns and cities were separated by considerable stretches of wilderness. The church and town hall were places of worship as well as assembly. Many important decisions regarding legislative changes were made in these halls with the participation of families that had equal rights to speak and vote. The work of women was not private but even subject to admiration and criticism by other women. Privacy was a luxury being acquired on the industrializing eastern coast; in more agricultural parts of the country, communal cooperation was the essence of survival.

This ethos of cooperation and mutual reliance accorded a special status to women. While the early settlers believed in the Puritan tradition of the male's dominance in all matters pertaining to the family, a shortage of women in the new colonies eventually allowed women to obtain advantages that they might not have possessed in the Old World. Dowries were made obsolete and women acquired the right to choose a husband for themselves. Moreover, following the violence and disorder experienced in the all-male Jamestown settlement, women became highly regarded as stabilizing forces, for it was observed that their presence in a community helped establish order and decorum.

In a frontier settlement, where disease was rampant and medical aid scarce, women became front-line participants standing alongside men, facing the dangers of early colonial life. Women also acquired considerable importance and status during the Civil War, when they not only took care of estates left unmanaged by men who had gone off to war, but also became prolific commentators on the social issues emerging in postwar America. This gave women in America a special status of 'partnership' with the male, for they were, in effect, co-creators of a new nation (Wertenbaker 1927:280–90).

Conduct book writers first set about trying to secure agreement from women to play specifically defined roles within the community. Predictably, this was originally accomplished through the citing of religious scripture. Cotton Mather's (1692) *Ornaments for the Daughters of Zion* was perhaps the first women's conduct book to appear in America. Mather used Biblical references to justify his advice that a woman should accept her role as keeper of the house and remain a devoted wife, desisting from using ornaments of beauty or passing time reading romances. Mather advised his female reader to submit to the will of her husband as she would to the will of God. Citing Biblical precedents, he explained that acceptance of God meant acceptance of the husband's authority and wisdom. Idleness and a quarrelsome disposition were deemed to be the habits of an ungodly woman. A woman who sought to please God was industrious and capable of bringing comfort and harmony to her family by turning away from vanity and fashion. Such a woman would read the Bible every day and avoid all frivolous activities. She would reject dancing and idle gossip and devote her time to the study of 'housewifery.' Mather also encouraged women to learn arithmetic and accounting to help in the management of the household.

Noteworthy about Mather's writing is that he is asking the woman to obey her husband yet expecting her to be ready to reason with him should he be on the verge of making unwise decisions. She is supposed to submit to his will but also have influence over him and keep him pious and virtuous. She is to apply God's will – first to herself and then to her family. She is, in a manner, being given the role of moral caretaker.

By the middle of the eighteenth century, there was a marked change in the manner in which religious belief was used to convince women to restrict themselves to domestic duties. God was no longer presented as a wrathful being whom a woman had to fear but a benevolent protector who would reward her plentifully if she did not stray from her path. The benefits of housewifery, although still couched in the religious language of 'virtue,' were presented as rational outcomes of a well-adjusted family capable of taking advantage of the natural gifts bestowed on the American people.

Benjamin Franklin, in *Reflections on Courtship and Marriage* (1746), even argued against the encouragement of weakness in women. He attributed these weaknesses to faulty education as well as the negative influence of men who encouraged women to be vain and pleasure-seeking. Franklin was proposing an education for females that went beyond housewifery, perhaps hoping that a woman who was educated in worldly subjects would rise above the supposed 'weakness' of her sex.

By the late eighteenth century, conduct books, such as John Bennett's (1788, published in England) *Strictures on Female Education*, were going beyond religious scriptures and using examples from nature to rationalize women's duties. Bennett explained that, like the animal species, the human species had its superior members. According to him a woman was considered to be physically and emotionally inferior to her mate and needed to control her emotions and desires. On one hand, the woman's superior ability to keep harmony in the home was being praised while, at the same time, that same virtue was being attributed to her inability to take on manly tasks requiring sustained thought and emotional restraint.

There was a further change in tone in American women's conduct books published after the eighteenth century. While prior to the Industrial Revolution they had focused on keeping the woman within very limited duties, they now responded to the improved education of women and rising calls for women's suffrage by taking the side of the new woman and affirming her rights to an educational and political voice. Just as had the books addressed to men, women's conduct manuals began fervently addressing the dangers that confronted a woman who might become affected by the wrong public influences in the emerging urban centres.

A.J. Graves's *Girlhood and Womanhood* (1844) and Daniel C. Eddy's *Lectures to Young Ladies on Matters of Practical Importance* (1848) provided specific warnings to women regarding the dangers of the city and how they were to protect their reputations when surrounded by temptation. Eddy meticulously differentiated between 'good' and 'evil' companions, warning his readers to learn to distinguish between the two. For Eddy, even attendance at an amusement park was risky. Graves lectured that a woman's character had to be properly formed in girlhood – such a strong foundation would help protect her from the 'dangers' faced by women in a mobile society. But he also warned that such protection would evaporate and be replaced by corruption were the woman to begin idealizing some of her learning and to forget that she was being influenced by other mortals capable of writing convincing prose favouring vice. Romantic fiction was singled out as a dangerous genre capable of making a woman live in a fantasy world at the expense of her real identity.

Despite the use of natural and religious explanations to justify women as the 'weaker sex,' some conduct book writers began arguing for improved education for women. The subjects suggested as 'appropriate' reading for women were history, religion, geography, biography, and a limited number of classical authors. Many conduct book writers warned that too much reading could lead to a pedantic woman no longer able to infuse her home with warmth and simple joy. Rev. John S.C. Abbott's *The Mother at Home: Or The Principles of Maternal Duty, Familiarly Described* (1833) provided mothers with a long and detailed explanation of how they were to raise socially conscientious children. Abbott addressed many difficulties that a mother could encounter with her children and then proceeded to remind the reader that it is 'maternal care' that determines whether a child will grow up to have a good or weak character (13–14): 'Never give a command which you do not intend shall be obeyed (29). Never punish when the child has not intentionally done wrong (53). Guard against too much severity (61). One great obstacle is the want of self-control on the part of the parent (64). Parents must have deep devotional feelings themselves' (113).

What is noteworthy about this particular tract is that the mother is being warned to maintain a rational control of her children in order to be able to maintain her credibility and influence when her husband is away. The task of dispensing a moral education is now being assigned to the woman, in tandem with the dislocations of industrial society and the frequent absences of the father.

What was the reward offered to women if not a place in heaven? T.S. Arthur, in *Advice to Young Ladies on Their Duties and Conduct in Life* (1848), suggested that a woman's duty was to be fulfilled through a sharing of a non-deistic love for others. Through the use of rationality a new proposition was being presented to women: that their duties were their 'rights.' It was their 'right' to make a paradise of their homes, comfort the sad, heal the sick, save others from vice, and teach the young. That this was a deft manipulation borrowing catchy terms from the literature on women's rights is evident. Yet, this framing of duty as a 'right' gave women considerable authority over those functions that were assigned to them.

In *The Young Woman's Guide* (1840) William Alcott reminds women that, although they are the 'weaker' sex, they should remember that the weak govern the strong, provided they remember to remain modest and wise (98–9). In *The Young Wife* (1842) Alcott advises his reader to 'do everything for your husband which your strength and a due regard to your health will admit' (76). He presents a sustained explanation for why a woman should do everything possible to avoid conflict with her husband, going far enough to suggest that the best way to bring back an erring husband into the folds of the family is to remain stoic and allow him to realize the errors of his ways. To accomplish this, the woman is to make her home as agreeable as possible, rise early (142), and take complete responsibility for her children, never leaving infants in the care of another (7). In matters of her own education she is to remain independent of her husband's personality but not become arrogant and pedantic; she must even be ready to drop a topic of study that does not interest her husband and adopt one that does. According to Alcott, education is not meant to give pleasure regarding a specific topic but is intended to help the development of the mind (301). While he encourages independence he does so within the limitations of a womanly 'sphere of influence' in which the management of the stability of the household is given prime importance (358–60). A philosophy of consensus between genders was being presented here and would have substantial effects on twentieth-century American gender relations and civility between men and women, especially during the 1940s and 1950s.

So, by the arrival of the nineteenth century, conduct writers had assigned a particular 'mission' to the American woman. It was a mission very much based on the original American democratic patriotic promise. She was to play an active role in the creation of a strong and stable America by properly raising and instructing morally aware children capable of responding to the challenges of a rapidly developing American society. The woman was no longer just the maker of the home but, in a manner of speaking, also the moral caretaker of the nation.

Despite her important role as a primary agent of socialization, she continued to be asked to restrain her intellectual interests. In *The Young Bride's Book* (1849), Arthur Freeling stressed the powerful influence of a woman on her husband, while exhorting her to select her reading material with great care:

> While proper reading furnishes the mind and matures the judgment, there is a class of books which has a tendency directly to the contrary; I refer to works of imagination, novels and the like ... The indiscriminate reading of novels is one of the most injurious habits to which a married woman can be subject ... it produces contempt for ordinary realities. (57)

Like Alcott, Freeling believed that men had a deep appreciation for modest women with endearing qualities and that they would be motivated to treat a woman with respect and love provided the woman took care to project the proper qualities of 'amiable temper' and a 'cheerful smile.' Freeling remained convinced that a woman possessed stronger resistance against worldly corruption than did the male (16). He also advised his readers to remember that 'a woman may be of great assistance to her husband in business, by wearing a cheerful smile and continually weave her countenance' (6).

Two anonymous books written by women dispersed similar advice regarding the importance of sacrifice for the sake of family cohesion: *Young Wife's Book; A Manual of Moral, Religious and Domestic Duties* (1838) and *The Young Lady's Book: A Manual of Elegant Recreations, Exercises, and Pursuits* (1830). The author of the first book reminds women that once they have vowed to obey, serve, love, and honour their husband, they should stick to these vows as 'inalienable' conditions of their family life. 'No longer seeking *individual* enjoyment, her pleasures must spring from *participation*, and her [happiness] be the reflected bliss arising from the peace of another' (1838:12). Thus, the matrimonial duties are to be based on reciprocal understanding: 'They consist of mutual forbearance and mutual offices of love and kindness' (12). And what is to be the education of a woman? The author warns against acquiring knowledge and then turning it into pedantry (206). The reader is cautioned that a man enjoys a rational companion able to speak of a variety of topics without appearing vain. The woman is encouraged to read, but also exhorted to evaluate the ultimate function and use of what she is studying. As in most conduct books of the era, the 'domestic duties' of the household are given into the charge of the woman, and she is to ensure that they stay in her charge if she is to take responsibility for pleasing her husband (210). In addition to taking care of household matters, she is to remain 'industrious' at all times and avoid all idle moments. The benefit of such constant action is no longer rationalized as an act that pleases God but as a pleasant personal sensation: 'Activity of body produces activity of mind; and again, activity of the mind quickens the feelings of the heart, and makes us more alive to happiness; while slothfulness of body causes sluggishness of mind and heart' (221).

The author of the second anonymously penned book, *The Young Lady's Book* (1830), preaches a similar combination of fortitude and obedience, strong-mindedness and agreeability, moral development and intellectual humility. The author presents an interesting conception of the mental capacities of the ideal American woman:

> Mental improvement should always be made conducive to moral advancement: to render a young woman wise and good, to prepare her mind for the duties and trials of life, is the great purpose of education. Accomplishments, however desirable and attractive, must always be considered secondary objects, when compared with those virtues which form the character and influence the power of woman in society. (23–4)

Needless to say, many dissenting responses appeared in the wake of such literature. An anonymous woman published the following lyric in *Harper's Weekly*:

> Useless, aimlessly, drifting through life,
> What was I born for? 'For somebody's wife,
> I am told by my mother. Well, that being true,
> 'Somebody' keeps himself strangely from view.
> ... My brothers are, all of them, younger than I,
> Yet they thrive in the world, and why not let *me* try? (29 August 1863)

Thus, both men and women were being solicited to fulfill their particular 'callings' within a larger national project that spanned a 4,000-mile-wide country. The male was entrusted with the outside world and the woman with the inner world of the family. They were both being enlisted in the service of a common American society in which work and prosperity were to be considered the ultimate good.

It was this common project and its division of labour that transformed the original American promise of 'equality' and 'liberty' into a project of 'collective conformity' that problematized the pure application of the idea of 'liberty.' The 'All-American Boy' and the 'All-American Girl' were prototypes that emerged from early specifications of what it meant to be an 'American' male or female. And the meanings were very gender-specific: James Bean (1856) writing in *Advice to a Married Couple* took great care to remind both partners that they were to excel in what they did best but not encroach on the domain of the other (14). Despite one's reservations about the long-range effects of such a gender-specific national ethos, one notices when reading these conduct books that what was being prepared was a family unit capable of contributing within a nation whose productivity was about to become the highest in the world. Max Weber's *The Protestant Work Ethic* could have very well been entitled the *American Work Ethic* without losing its empirical or theoretical validity.

**Being at Ease: The New American Civility**

What differentiated the nineteenth-century English and American conduct books was that the American ones focused on the ideal of community and equality without making extensive references to social class. In a post–Civil War era, unification was very important to Americans. So, although at first glance the American and English projects may appear similar, there are important differences even though both nations maintained substantial 'regimes' for behaviour. While both referred to moral principles rationalized by a limitation of sexual pleasure, the American mission had an additional component: *the furthering of the original American mission of equality and patriotism through 'populist' philosophies.*

The open (and often informal) friendliness of the American – a characteristic often criticized by more reserved Europeans – has been substantially connected to America's early frontier mentality and the nomadic ethos that arose out of Americans' high mobility. It has also been connected to the American ideal of 'populism' and the social psychological effects of such a national philosophy. An American who arrives in a group and exclaims, 'How'ya all doin'?' is expressing the same warm, conforming friendliness that a new arrival on the prairie was expected to express to signify that he was willing to act in the common interests of the community. The ideal of social consensus continues to inform public and private discourse, even at the institutional level.

Thus, the community was very much a self-help group. Establishing a mining facility, building a town despite limited capital, establishing a legislative judiciary and executive, were all done through the use of public assemblies with little recourse to central authority. This localization of decision was an important factor in the formation of an American individualistic democratic spirit based on relationships of association rather than formal rituals of hierarchical deference.

Three streams of courtesy practices emerged in America: one in the Puritan north, one in the aristocratic south, and another one at the time of the development of the western frontier. The settlements in the south continued to subscribe to courtesy practices brought in from England and France. Tact and honour were prime requisites in social dealings. The slightest insult could provoke a confrontation. And at the time of the early settlement, when single men outnumbered single women by seven to one, it became extremely important that a man defend the honour of the woman he was courting. The traditional demurring style of the southern belle, immortalized in such films as *Gone With the Wind*, had its roots in this demographic imbalance. The southern woman, her presence at a premium due to the shortage of females, was able to set courtesy and delicacy standards which were less in vogue in the communities of the north. If America ever venerated style, as did the French, it did so in the south, where the terms 'southern gentleman' and the 'southern lady' came into vogue.

The north and the west were reticent to adopt 'extraneous' stylistic distinctions: The American notion of 'manhood' was based on action and movement rather than tact. Tact requires a censoring of thought and emotional expression. It does not encourage forceful, self-affirmative behaviour. There is a certain gentleness to tact, even a quality of pleading, that softens the edges of expansionism. Americans navigating in uncharted territory required an adventurous, forceful American ethos and had to circumnavigate around etiquette rituals in favour of more immediately functional discourse practices. Travelling through unknown territory sometimes occupied by hostile groups (Native Americans included) did not require tact and courtesy as much as it did raw courage and direct, quick, and efficient interpersonal communications.

That the English (and French) reacted with dismay towards American directness was understandable. They could not accept why Americans were so possessed by their own national project of equality and independence to break ties with European culture. Although there was regular traffic between the east coast and Europe, most Americans were preoccupied with building America according to their own republican fervour. While American elites looked to Europe for inspiration, the American working classes continued to consider European habits a threat to American ways. Ironically, the antipathy was reversed on the European side: the elites mistrusted the Americans while the working classes admired their brash ambition.

Reactions from the English came in the work of Fanny Trollope, who produced a 300-page attack on American manners in 1832. Having tried her hand at establishing a business in America without much success, she turned her three-year experience in America into a travel book in which she mercilessly dissected Americans and their practices. She wrote without reserve and with very little tact: 'I speak ... of the population generally, as seen in town and country, among the rich and the

## The American Experience: Democracy and Informal Civility    253

poor, in the slave states and the free states. I do not like their principles. I do not like their manners. I do not like their opinions' (321).

The book was a sensation in England. Attempting to understand the functional causes of American manners, Trollope questioned the entire American psyche:

> Where there is no court, which everywhere else is the glass wherein the higher orders dress themselves, and which again reflected from them to the classes below, goes far towards polishing in some degree, a great majority of the population, it is not to be expected that manner should be made so much a study, or should attain an equal degree of elegance; but the deficiency, and the total difference, is greater than this cause alone could account for. (131)

Agreeing, albeit with tongue in cheek, that America was a creative place, she nevertheless considered Americans well on their way towards cultural nemesis:

> To doubt that talent and mental power of every kind, exist in America would be absurd; why should it not? But in taste and learning they are woefully deficient; and it is this which renders them incapable of graduating a scale by which to measure themselves. Hence arises that overweening complacency and self-esteem, both national and individual, which at once renders them so extremely obnoxious to ridicule, and so peculiarly restive under it. (263–4)

The Frenchman Michel Chevalier possessed a more useful understanding of American culture. In *Society Manners and Politics in the United States* ([1839] 1983), he explained that Americans could not easily copy the etiquette of the Europeans because their particular environment required them to learn through living examples rather than traditional principles (348).

Perhaps the most perceptive conclusion regarding American civil society was reached by Harriett Martineau (1837). In the final pages of her insightful three-volume study of America, she warned against categorical summaries of American culture. Noticing the paradoxical nature of American republicanism, she wrote:

> I offer no conclusion of my subject. I do not pretend to have formed any theory about American society or prospects to which a finishing hand can be put in the last page :... the Americans may fall short, in practice, of the

professed principles of their association, they have realised many things for which the rest of the civilised world is still struggling; and which some portions are only beginning to intend. They are, to all intents and purposes, self-governed. They have risen above all liability to a hereditary aristocracy, a connexion between religion and the State, a vicious or excessive taxation, and the irresponsibility of any class. Whatever evils may remain or may arise, in either the legislative or executive departments, the means of remedy are in the hands of the whole people: and those people are in possession of the glorious certainty that time and exertion will infallibly secure all wisely desired objects.

The civilisation and the morals of the Americans fall far below their own principles. This is enough to say. It is better than contrasting or comparing them with European morals and civilisation: which contrast or comparison can answer no purpose, unless on the supposition, which I do not think a just one, that their morals and civilisation are derived from their political organisation. A host of other influences are at work, which must nullify all conclusions drawn from the polities of the Americans to their morals. Such conclusions will be somewhat less rash two centuries hence. Meantime, it will be the business of the world, as well as of America, to watch the course of republicanism and of national morals; to mark their mutual action, and humbly learn whatever the new experiment may give out. To the whole world, as well as to the Americans, it is important to ascertain whether the extraordinary mutual respect and kindness of the American people generally are attributable to their republicanism: and, again, how far their republicanism is answerable for their greatest fault, their deficiency of moral independence.

No peculiarity in them is more remarkable than their national contentment. If this were the result of apathy, it would be despicable: if it did not coexist with an active principle of progress, it would be absurd. As it is, I can regard this national attribute with no other feeling than veneration. Entertaining, as I do, little doubt of the general safety of the American Union, and none of the moral progress of its people, it is clear to me that this national contentment will live down all contempt, and even all wonder; and come at length to be regarded with the same genial and universal emotion with which men recognise in an individual the equanimity of rational self-reverence. (297–301)

The anti-aristocratic sentiment of the American civility tradition, however, was sorely tested at the end of the nineteenth century and the beginning of the twentieth when a new culture of etiquette emerged from the prosperity that followed the Civil War and the period of reconstruction (Soltow 1975). In the long peace that followed the Civil War, the wealth of Americans multiplied to undreamed-of levels. Railroad builders, copper barons, gold miners, bankers, stockbrokers, realty speculators, ironmasters, and war profiteers formed a new aristocracy. Excess and extravagance became the marks of social distinction in this new *gilded age* (Kasson 1991).

Mary C.W. Sherwood ([1884] 1907) included the following nostalgic observation in her conduct manual, *Manners and Social Usage*: 'The war of 1861 swept away what little was left of that once important American fact – a grandfather. We begin all over again' (6). And, indeed, a new crop of men was emerging in a newly prosperous society. Matthew Josephson (c. 1935) observed in *The Robber Barons* that 'the modern nobility springs from success in business' (315). These new men of wealth were the 'haute-bourgeoisie' of America. Although some of them appended the numbers 'III' and 'IV' to their names in a bid to imitate European aristocrats, they remained anomalies in a populist nation.

As Thorstein Veblen ([1899] 1925) explained in *The Theory of the Leisure Class*, middle-class reputation in American industrial society became determined through ownership of property rather than family pedigree. As for the upper classes, they maintained reputations of superiority by consuming time in unproductive ways. Having the luxury of wasting time in elaborate leisure events served to show, quite conspicuously, that a person had the ability to afford such a life. The ultimate status was having so much money that one could live on its interest without having to work at all. In a manner of speaking, some of the old standards of the feudal aristocracy became adopted by the American financial elites to distinguish themselves as a special group. Some even had family shields and heralds prepared. American high society remained a conglomeration of imitators, trans-Atlantic voyagers, and upstarts trying to present themselves in the image of European aristocracy.

Rituals of etiquette allowed members of this class to remain distinct from the rising middle classes (Hall 1982, Trachtenberg 1982). As for the middle classes, they read in the newspapers about the Four Hundred most important families and came to learn, albeit vicariously, of the manner in which they lived. This had a certain top-down influence. The names of self-made millionaires, such as John D. Rockefeller, Cornelius Vanderbilt, Andrew Carnegie, and Colin P. Huntington served to remind Americans that they too could achieve social distinction and wealth through personal effort; this predisposed some middle-class families to keep up with changes in etiquette rituals being practised at the higher levels of American society.

As the centre of social life moved from the political circles of Washington to the business circles of New York, etiquette manual writers stepped in to service the new mercantile aristocracy. Their etiquette advice merged French traditions regarding table manners and entertaining with the rules of interaction developed by the English Victorians. Much of the advice dispensed to the genders in these late nineteenth-century books reproduced advice very similar to the advice dispensed on the European Continent (Allen 1915, Schlesinger [1946] 1968:31–48).

The bulk of the advice was dispensed in women's magazines. Magazine columns and articles were then compiled into books. *The Bazar Book of Decorum*, *The American Code of Manners*, *Social Life*, *Amenities at Home*, *Manners and Social Usage*, and *The Art of Entertaining* were some of the titles sponsored or written by magazine staff writers between the years 1870 and 1892 (Schlesinger [1946] 1968:33). Schlesinger estimates that no less than five or six major titles emergd every year between 1870 and 1917 (34). Due to the large circulation of magazines across class boundaries, it could be reasonably assumed that the new etiquette advice was being read by many who neither had the means nor the social position to practise the rules being proposed. The magazines did serve, however, to have an effect on the manner in which people related to one another in more modest circumstances. While a family of modest means may not have had the required finances to organize a debutante ball, the rules of etiquette were noted and many of them adopted.

The term '*de rigueur*,' associated with old-world European etiquette, came into vogue during this period. Schlesinger has observed that many of the new interaction rules contradicted the older American conduct manuals:

> As etiquette authorities now saw their mission, it was to instill a more aristocratic behaviour, one more consonant with the improving fortunes of the middle class. To persons who flinched at the thought of greater formalism *Appletons' Journal* said, 'Are not over-refinements better than under-refinements?' (34)

This tension between prosperous innocents and the rituals and protocols of the entitled was dramatically expressed in Henry James's ([1979]

1995) *Daisy Miller*. The heroine of the story travels to Europe with her mother and is caught in a web of misunderstandings precisely because she is not aware of (nor anxious to adopt) the complex interaction rules of the aristocracy. James's book was reminiscent of Jane Austen's ([1811] 1965) *Sense and Sensibility*: civility seemed complicated by the tension between decorum and sincerity, outright expression of sentiment, and deference to rituals of propriety and emotional restraint. Schlesinger ([1946] 1968) observes astutely that socially ambitious readers must have taken note of Daisy Miller's errors and learned what not to do if they wished to gain a footing in European polite society (47).

There was a typically American reaction against this new cult of etiquette. E.L. Godkin (1896) warned that democratic American civility was in danger of being eroded: 'Is it possible that we are about to renew on this soil, at the end of the nineteenth century, the extravagance and follies of the later Roman Empire and the age of Louis XIV?' (328).

This reaction against the imitation of European etiquette may have moved C.F. Beezeley, writing under the name of Daphne Dale (1895), to compose a substantial text entitled *Our Manners and Social Customs: A Practical Guide to Deportment, Easy Manners, and Social Etiquette*. As the title of the book suggests, a new style of discourse was being formalized in America: that of 'ease.' Courtesy was no longer the privilege of those of good breeding who could practise its prescribed verbal and bodily rituals, but a communal activity in which anyone could participate. The anonymously written *The American Book of Genteel Behavior* (1875) summarized the new American public ethos in its long subtitle: *A Complete Hand Book of Modern Etiquette for Ladies and Gentlemen. Embracing the Customs and Usages of Polite Society in All Places and at All Times. Being a perfect guide to all about to enter either public or private life, showing how to act under all circumstances with ease, elegance and freedom*. The keywords here are 'ease, elegance, and freedom.' Similarly, Nathaniel P. Willis (1857), an authority on social graces, declared: 'We shall be glad to see a distinctively American school of good manners, in which all useless etiquettes were thrown aside, but every politeness adopted or invented which could promote sensible and easy exchanges of good will' (cited in Schlesinger [1946] 1968:21).

This civility ethos of 'ease' and the ready exchange of 'good will' would remain a distinct aspect of American civility, despite the rise of an American 'high society' that claimed special distinction for itself. This combination of unlikely characteristics – ease, elegance, and freedom – resulted in a civility style that was informal and readily congenial – in other words, at ease and open to variation. Lillian (Eichler) Watson (1922) and Emily Post (1922) would attempt a reformulated version of turn-of-the-century etiquette in their widely promoted twentieth-century conduct manuals. While courtship rules would change in these latter conduct manuals, the ideal of an American civility ethos based on simple friendliness would remain a constant.

The high society of New York might have continued to attract public fascination if it were not for the great wave of immigration that hit that city at the turn of the century. As fascinating as were the goings-on of the 'Four Hundred,' a second generation of working-class Americans competing for a piece of the golden calf took the attention of the media (Blunin 1989). Moreover, socialist ideology questioned the legitimacy of a wealthy elite claiming special badges of social distinction. William Dean Howells (1870–1920), one of America's outspoken socialist writers, questioned the usefulness of high society. According to Cady (1949), 'the question Howells and more and more Americans were to raise was the intensely American "So what? What does all this come to in the end?" Stripped of all but glitter, Best Society eventually stripped itself of all significance for the American mind' (155).

What did survive from the gilded age was a considerable valuation of 'social skills.' Although the 1920s saw a proliferation in slang (e.g., 'you're swell,' and 'damn') as the formal social functions of the wealthy gave way to smaller and more informal gatherings, there remained a common-sense respect for a standard code of manners. Americans had experienced a certain social dysfunction during the Civil War when northern and southern manners had come face to face. It is not unreasonable to suggest, as has Schlesinger ([1946] 1968), that, at times, northerners and southerners had trouble understanding each other's meanings (69). America required a civility ethos that could transcend ethnic and political differences. As north, south, east, and west became increasingly involved with common economic and political projects, including the two world wars and the depression, there was a corresponding homogenization of manners and civility ideals. A common republican civility ethos also helped individuals to move from one part of the country to another without experiencing (or causing) social perturbation. In a country of rapid change, a common and manageable civility ethic became a reassuring constant. High mobility caused considerable 'imitation,' thereby lessening (although not eliminating) differentiations connected to wealth (70). As for immigrants from Europe, even though they maintained their own interaction standards within their own families, they adopted the American ethos of an informal civility in order to adapt to their new home and the values of an action-oriented culture. And, as second- and third-generation children of immigrants adopted American ways from their school friends, the ways of the Old World were substantially modified.

## Reflections on the Meanings and Consequences of a Civility of 'Ease'

In his seminal work *Democracy in America* ([1884] 1994), Alexis de Tocqueville offered some useful (and timeless) insights into the nature of American democracy and the effects it has had on the construction of American culture:

> As distinctions of rank are obliterated and men of different education and birth mix and mingle in the same place, it is almost impossible to agree upon the rules of good manners. The code being uncertain, to contravene it is no longer a crime in the eyes of those who do know it. So the substance of behaviour comes to count for more than the form, and men grow less polite but also less quarrelsome. (568)

The French and English could count on the practices of their aristocracy on which to base their courtesy customs. Even revolutionary France had preserved the proverbial French values of 'style' and 'refinement.' The Americans, however, anxious to begin anew and avoid the hierarchical restrictions of the Old World, were hesitant to replicate European etiquette. Tocqueville might have agreed with such an analysis, for he associated a country's courtesy practices with its prevalent political organization:

> In the United States distinctions of rank are slight in civil society and do not exist at all in the world of politics. An American therefore feels no call to pay particular attention to any of his fellows, nor does he think of expecting anything of that sort himself ... Scorning no man on account of his status, it does not occur to him that anyone scorns him for that reason, and unless the insult is clearly seen, he does not think that anyone wants to offend him. (568)

He also equated the expediency of American manners to the elevation of ambition to a moral duty:

Everyone living in democratic times contracts, more or less, the mental habits of the industrial and trading classes; their thoughts take a serious turn, calculating and realistic; they gladly turn away from the ideal to pursue some visible and approachable aim which seems the natural and necessary object of their desires. (598)

According to Tocqueville, the absence of an aristocracy that can be emulated renders public manners bereft of the refinements (as well as the coarseness) of manners in a multi-tiered class society. The motivation for refinement, itself a tool of social distinction, becomes weakened. The absence of a ruling class also eliminates the reactive vulgarity of an underclass, resulting in a relatively standard and narrow spectrum of public mannerisms. Tocqueville observes that the result of this absence of contrasts results in a public congeniality which he terms 'sincerity' (607). Decorum (symbolic representation) is replaced by authenticity (directness). Tocqueville takes care to distinguish between 'manners' and 'dignity,' mentioning that the Americans he observed excelled at individual dignity, even in the absence of elaborate civility rituals. He interprets such dignity as the 'gravity' of Americans, a sort of self-defensive restraint: 'This disposes them to measure their words and their behaviour carefully and not to let themselves go, lest they should reveal their deficiencies. They imagine that to appear dignified, they must appear solemn' (610).

Finally, he provides another possible reason why Americans did not possess enough fear of losing their public reputations and were, consequently, not overly concerned with adopting extremely restrained codes of manners and speech based on non-imposition and a minimum of self-disclosure:

> One is astonished at the imprudent suggestions sometimes made by public men in free countries, especially democracies, without their being compromised, whereas under absolute monarchies a few casual remarks are enough to ruin a man's reputation forever, without hope of recovery ... When a man addresses a large crowd, many of his words are not heard, or if heard, are soon forgotten. But where the masses dwell in silent stagnation, the slightest whisper strikes the ear. (611)

The proverbial 'openness' of the American may be based on this absence of fear of serious communal sanctions against lapses in protocol. As Tocqueville observes quite astutely, in a society where everyone can speak, the value of words takes on less importance, for speaking is not restricted to those of title; by the time one has spoken, others have started speaking in their own turn.

The Victorian upper middle classes, ready to emulate the English aristocracy, considered the flaunting of wealth as bad taste. But in a democracy where wealth was recently acquired and national pride was based on entrepreneurial accomplishment, the flaunting of wealth became a means for making social-status claims that would have otherwise been impossible to make in the absence of an aristocratic hierarchy that dispensed titles to individuals. 'What a person did,' therefore, was most often more important than 'who' his ancestors were. This standard is still somewhat prevalent – many Americans who fall into a first conversation will ask about the other's means of gaining a livelihood quite early on in the conversation. In France and England, such immediate curiosity might be interpreted as lack of discernment and lack of respect for the privacy of the other. The critique, however, would be a hasty and ethnocentric one; it would be based on a particularly European hierarchical conception of identity. A multiculturally informed civility theory, however, must take into account how each culture relates to conceptions of authority, deference, time, context, and space – important facets of civil interaction which we will discuss in Part III of this book.

## Summary to Part I: Comparing the Cultural Histories of American, English, and French Civility

Based on the historical evidence presented so far and the cultural values and interaction dimensions noted in our discussions, we find that England, France, and America have managed interaction and impression management in considerably different ways. We do not find that we can speak of a standard Western modernity when noticing these differences. The civilizing process is no longer a homogeneous evolution towards increased restraint as much as it is a process of national habitus formation subject to the specific geographic, economic, political, and philosophical realities of the nation. These local realities play a major role in determining how social interactions are organized and interpreted.

The historical evidence does not provide sufficient cause for envisioning an eventual convergence of a global American or even European culture. While we find that certain common denominators will create a standard public sphere that can be shared by people of different nationalities, we feel that there will be enough cultural variation to preserve important differences. And we hope to test this proposition in the second part of this book, when we observe civility and interaction in these three countries in a contemporary setting.

History has certainly had an important influence on courtesy codes. We have seen how America deviated from England and France in forming a conduct book tradition that was progressively less given to regulating etiquette and more inclined to specifying the qualities of an ambitious person. Freedom and ambition took precedence over style and formalism. In the first paragraph of *Common Sense* ([1776] 1976), Thomas Paine reveals what was to eventually become a flexible American attitude towards social change:

> Perhaps the sentiments contained in the following pages, are not yet sufficiently fashionable to procure them general favor; a long habit of not thinking a thing *wrong*, gives it a superficial appearance of being *right*, and raises at first a formidable outcry in defense of custom. But the tumult soon subsides. Time makes more converts than reason. (63)

So, although all three countries were headed for a common industrial future, they followed rather different philosophies of interaction due to their differing notions of ideal citizenship. While the Americans had sought to be 'at ease' and 'open,' the English preferred a standard code of politeness heavily dependent on 'tact' which left much unsaid in the interests of not causing embarrassment to self and others. This sense of 'propriety' became linked to the notion of moral worth and a national tradition rationalized by the continuity of a stable monarchy. In England, what came to matter as much as the sentiments of the actors was their ability to maintain a pleasant and non-confrontational exchange. Thus, the routine of public interactions was *humanized* (as opposed to mechanized or bureaucratized) through a broadening use of a simple courtesy standard that could be followed by different classes. Values of 'tact' and 'consideration' were maintained as common cultural traits, even in the presence of class-related differences. This 'cult of politeness' and 'tact' has led to a certain 'reserve' in interactions that has maintained a separation of public and private personas. 'Modesty' becomes a parallel social ideal in this culture of politeness. Perhaps its influence has been prolonged by England's fear of being overwhelmed by the American penchant for exhibitionism and self-promotion and the French love of flair and drama. On the whole, Britons have taken care not to blow their own trumpets and have reacted with uneasiness when someone else blows it for them.

This more formal and discretionary delineation between the public and the private provides rich opportunities for communal cohesion. But there is a cost to be paid: decreased self-revelation and intimacy. The putting on of a polite and accommodating face – although a socially comforting practice that greatly decreases interpersonal tension in public – often keeps out of view the private sentiments necessary for real intimacy. Some may consider this a curse, others a blessing. For some, such emotional privacy can even become a habitual state that becomes carried into intimate relations. One can 'chat,' but does one really talk about what matters deep inside? Emotional restraint is the opportunity cost paid by extremely polite societies. Stoicism and mental discipline become by-products of such restraint. One simply does not make a scene, not if one can help it. And having an arm's-length relationship with one's emotions, one learns to consider the actual gravity of a situation before reacting. And when things become heated, one does not have a 'fight' but has a 'row.' So, the putting on of a 'brave smile' is a distinctly English characteristic.

In America, there has been a particular correlation between what is privately thought and felt and what is publicly expressed, making Americans more 'open' with one another and, consequently, more vulnerable to mutual tensions, angers, and hurts. In effect, Americans have increasingly been given to searching for 'authentic relationships' in their public and private dealings. The opportunities for intimacy are greater in such authentic environments, but so are the risks of conflict and loss of communal cohesion.

In France, a post-revolutionary compromise was reached between deferring to the other and deferring to the self. That compromise involved a balancing of style, sentiment, and mutual deference; paradox was accepted in France in the interests of balancing the need for equality with the need for a distinct hierarchical civilization capable of resisting Anglo-American assimilation.

The French have never been satisfied with a simple routine politeness. Their valuation of 'style' and 'aesthetics' has given particular importance to the presentation of self in the front stage of life. This legacy from French court society is a major factor in the maintenance of a sense of 'francophone' identity. The monarchs may have been beheaded, but their subjects continue to value distinction. Pride plays a visible role in French culture. Actors are not relying on a national ethic of restraint as much as they are on the talents of the opinionated self. A delicate relationship exists between modesty, self-admiration, and cultural coherence. Like the Americans, the French value individualism; but their individualism is not posited as a self-referential kin-opposed introversion. Being French requires deference to communal as well as personal values.

Thus, artifice and rituals provide the French with a subtle social-distancing mechanism. This much has survived from France's rich courtly tradition. No matter how agreeable or disagreeable the exchange, it can be done in style and with wit. The Frenchman can bow and say, 'Go to hell sir, and may your journey there be a pleasant one.' And he can do so with the anger-restraining use of a strange mixture of courtesy and irony. This allows for the indirect expression of feelings of anger and hatred. A plethora of metaphors allow the French to disagree but with a relative lack of emotional violence. Being French and civilized entails the use of a variety of adaptive talents: courtesy, some artifice, and a continual affirmation of the poetic characteristics of the French language and the potential of human drama. Moreover, the desire for precision, at the public and private levels, predisposes the French to favour rich dialogue. There is an enjoyment of complexity. Ironically, this complexity can complicate the love of precision because it can lead to multiple explanations for a given mood or statement, thereby creating doubt and the need for further specification. This is the price paid for the coupling of emotional and linguistic complexity. A competent social actor must become adept at reading hidden meanings and interpreting the poetic metaphors casually thrown into mundane conversations. Facial expressions (moods) take on added importance in the speech decoding process.

So, the French are not free to use the English imperative of 'tact' and 'politeness at all times' because *that would contradict their expressive needs.* The value of 'tact' is too minimalist to accommodate the particularly French requirement of cultural complexity and dramaturgical flair. Nor are the French free to adopt the American love of 'openness.' The French are sometimes rude with one another and even secretive in their declarations. They do not feel that it is a universal law to like everyone; they are comfortable with that notion. *That is their definition of authenticity.* They may even feel that it is not even natural to like everyone, citing the saying that 'a man who is friend to all is a friend to none.'

Because of this high valuation of acts of passion, the rationality of what is being expressed is not always the issue. What is also valued is the *manner* of expression and the intellectual persona of the speaker. The effects of disagreements are, therefore, less spectacular and less socially disheartening than they might be if suddenly imported into a culture of agreeability or strong mistrust of artifice.

French emotionalism, therefore, is distinctly different from American emotionalism. It is more romantically inclined, whereas American emotionalism seeks to create immediate results that eliminate emotional dissonance. In emotional exchanges between Americans a specific American trait is observable – the emotion is expressed in order to create a specific immediate benefit for the self through a change in the ecology of the relationship. The emotion is purposive.

In a culture such as France, where a romantic predisposition leads to considerable emotionalism, a very different social reality comes into being than the one observed in England and America. The French do not have a history of emotional suppression, especially not following the French Revolution. This does not mean that some lid has been lifted off a Pandora's box – only that, as long as traditions are respected, the French give each other the right to be emotional, for they consider sentimentality part of cultural homeostasis. Emotions become commonly understood dramaturgical tools to make points within discussions that claim to be rational.

For the purposes of this first part of the work we have tried to follow the civility traditions of France, England, and America over a common time period (1200s to 1900) in order to familiarize ourselves with the seminal political, economic, philosophical, religious, and moral transformations that affected each country. These developments may help explain why each country has managed to maintain a civility ethos and practice that is very particular to it. We hope, in the following parts of this work, to further explain how late-modern developments have not altogether managed to have a levelling effect on these cultures even when we take the universal social psychology of human interaction into serious account. Since the idea of a 'global civil society' has yet to be manifested (Armstrong 2006:349–57), we do not err on the side of caution if we avoid generalizations about supposedly 'regional' or 'continental' cultures. We will be arguing that levels of individualism and communalism, together with the different politeness rituals that accompany them, play a salient role in the maintenance of distinct national civility traditions.

# Part II

# The Rise of the Late-Modern American Self

> Our desire becomes an oracle we consult. It is now the last word, while in the past it was the questionable and dangerous part of us.
>
> – Harold Bloom

# 8 Conformity, Opposition, and Identity

> Until the old world dies out utterly, the 'abnormal' individual will tend more and more to become the norm.
>
> – Henry Miller (1949)

## Introduction

In Part I we tried to show how France, America, and England developed different civility preferences due to the manner in which each nation was affected by a variety of factors, including political philosophy and system of government, religion, intellectual history, geography, economy, familial norms, and the manner in which emotions were restrained and expressed. By the close of the nineteenth century each nation possessed its own civility and interaction ethos. The industrialization of the West did not have a substantial levelling effect over national identity or national ideology.

A similar partiality towards cultural ideology seems to have held during the twentieth and twenty-first centuries – each of the three nations included in our study has responded to late modernity (or as some would have it, postmodernity) in characteristic fashion. This is not to say that historical precedence has dwarfed contemporary developments, but, simply, that the manner in which each nation has responded to the contemporary world has been biased by its biography.

In this part of this book we would like to focus on the American experience during the twentieth and twenty-first centuries even though previous and forthcoming sections of the book pay equal attention to France, America, and England. This break with the preferred method of comparative studies (to keep the comparison steady and even) has a methodological purpose. Since this study has up to this point attempted to show how the settlers in America broke away from the cultural ideologies and practices of the countries from which they originated, it is appropriate that we test this hypothesis by seeing whether America's contemporary experience has differed from that of its two European allies in a way that may be considered characteristically American.

So, while Parts III and IV of the book return to a tri-nation comparison in order to construct a cross-culturally valid understanding of the 'anatomy of civility,' we have decided in this part of our discussion to focus on the various developments that have led to what some consider is a very noticeable crisis in American civility.

We are interested, once again, in asking the question 'Why?' Why is it that contemporary cultural norms and expectations in America have developed in a certain way rather than another?

It is our thesis that American constitutional ideals, together with increasing diversity in America, predisposed Americans to become considerably critical of their society; this self-critique weakened generational continuity and facilitated the expression of impulses and emotions that had previously been kept muted. This cultural transformation provides us with a valuable point of departure for understanding the mechanisms that are operant during acts of civility and incivility. It allows us to go beyond Elias's theory of state formation and address issues directly connected to the formation of identity and emotional expressiveness. Changes in civility and emotional freedom have been observed not only in the degree to which pain and anger are restrained or expressed, but also in the manner in which citizens relate to duty, identity, guilt, shame, embarrassment, and pride – major factors that affect civil and uncivil acts and sentiments.

Debates over civility and the ideal civil society during the twentieth century and the beginning of this century have not been as much related to issues of manners as they have been to a series of questions addressing the possibilities and limits of self-interest and individual and group identity. At stake in America (and increasingly in other countries) is a difficult question that might have to be eventually faced as rapid changes are experienced in demography, family organization, economics, immigration, and social philosophy: *Can morality, diversity, and the personal psychological and sexual freedom promised by a technologically fuelled conception of consumer-oriented capitalism co-exist without creating alienating contradictions?* (Bell 1976). It is a particularly American question, reflecting back on the long-standing ideological tension between American altruistic communalism and American self-interested capitalism. It leads to yet another question: How can a society that has always championed human rights retain its cohesion when faced with competitive interests that force individuals to frame their requirements within a dialogue of competing claims? Can there be an ideal ethics of discourse in a field of troubled emotions and unsettled claims (Habermas ([1987] 1989)), 1994, Taylor et al. 1994)?

## Rudeness and Civility in the American Late-Modern Democracy

Predictably, considerable changes in social norms and behavioural rituals have caused concern over uncivil behaviour. While rudeness has always been part of civil society, many commentators are now worried that a threshold has been crossed and that much of late-modern incivility is not simply rudeness but purposive antisocial behaviour emanating from sentiments of aggression, bitterness, alienation, smugness, selfishness, entitlement, cultivated stupidity, and moral indifference.

The worry over uncivil behaviour seems to be most urgently expressed in America. While commentators in France and England are also noticing a rise in uncivil behaviour, there seems to be less concern being shown over those daily private and public interaction rituals not involving acts of hooliganism and violence. Our observations indicate that these two countries, for reasons that continue to intrigue us, have managed to maintain a civility tradition that is fairly similar to the one practised by previous generations, even though some British journalists are following the lead of their American counterparts and bemoaning the loss of traditional British manners. It would seem that the cultural ethos of France and England has managed to survive the dislocations of modernity more than has the social ethos of America, an ethos that has been politically, economically, and religiously predisposed to change, transformation, and a continuing affirmation of an authenticity in need of constant revival.

The American concern over rising incivility is not unfounded. By incivility, we are referring not only to a lack of manners but to a communicative style that is energized by a sentiment of non-cooperation, an exaggerated absorption with one's own self, or an uncaring attitude towards the welfare of others. In a broader sense, we are referring to the degree to which individuals remain respectful of those habituations most valued by their culture.

When we began writing this part of the book, we found over 350,000 articles and sites on the Internet directly addressing the topics of discourtesy, incivility, and social cynicism. A great number of these concerned the perceived and documented lack of civility in schools, families, and public settings. A methodical search revealed to us that the overwhelming majority of the sites carrying these articles were of American origin.

Briana Cummings, writing in the Harvard web periodical *Digitas*, calls rudeness the 'silent killer.' Quoting a *U.S. News and World Report* survey, she reminds us that 'nine out of ten Americans think incivility is a problem; half call it "extremely serious."' She goes on to write: 'Ever since the sixties, social niceties have been derided as hypocritical. Yet Americans also value peace, cooperation, community, and respect. In their typical schizophrenic fashion, Americans are trying to have it all' (2001). Cummings locates the core of the American social dilemma. The search for authenticity and the need for communal cohesion, usually antagonistic traits, have been adopted by Americans as the founding pillars of an evolved postmodern society.

Researchers at the Public Agenda Organization, in *Aggravating Circumstances: A Status Report on Rudeness in America* (a national study funded by the Pew Charitable Trust) (2002), have discovered that a majority of Americans consider rudeness a pressing national problem: 88 per cent of Americans have come across rudeness in their daily lives and 79 per cent consider lack of respect a serious issue; 64 per cent report that it bothers them a lot; and 41 per cent admit to occasionally being rude themselves. Among the reasons cited for such rudeness, 84 per cent believe that it is the outcome of parents not teaching their children manners, 62 per cent believe that it is connected to a decline in values and morality, and 60 per cent believe that, despite efforts by families, negative role models are increasing the rudeness of youth. In the area of business service, 41 per cent report that they have found service sometimes so lacking that they have walked out of a store and 77 per cent report having suffered from salespersons who act as if the customer were not there; 84 per cent consider company phone recordings an insult.

An interesting finding of the survey is that 69 per cent of respondents feel that respect and politeness are contagious and that they could spread if practised more; 49 per cent believe that a respectful person will be better treated. They similarly consider rudeness contagious, with 41 per cent believing that people stop being nice when surrounded by rudeness. Also of note is the finding that 42 per cent of respondents believe the best thing to do when someone is rude is to walk away, while 36 per cent say the solution is to be 'especially polite' to the person in question; there seems to be a marked unwillingness to confront the rude person.

Jessica Reaves, a columnist for TIME.com, responds to the above survey in a 3 April 2002 column, 'In Defense of Rudeness.' In her satirical piece, Reaves makes some interesting points about America's obsession with social agreeability. Reaves herself reveals a typically American need for 'authenticity.' She confuses French rudeness with American rudeness and fails to see their varying meanings. Referring to the survey, she states:

> This just in: a lot of people think Americans are rude, obnoxious and badly behaved ... Super. I say this is a very, very good thing. It's time for Americans to feel the joy that is rude. Rudeness is something Americans have taken far too long to master. For two centuries we've been considered a stupidly cheerful nation, the land of opportunity, the folks who always reside on the sunny side of the street ... millions of immigrants came because they didn't like their treatment at home. But now think it may be time for us to reevaluate our place in the world ... Take France. The French are self-satisfied in a way that makes most Americans uncomfortable. They love everything about themselves: their cheese, their art, their little cars. They don't give a flying figue what anyone else thinks of them, and they're perfectly happy to tell all of us precisely what they think of us. Sure, they're rude, but they're comfortable with their rudeness. They embrace it. They cherish it. It's part of their identity.
> Or take the English, a special breed at once almost totally irrelevant and yet utterly convinced of their own superiority to the rest of the world. This allows them to treat the rest of the world's inhabitants shabbily without ever once acknowledging that we exist.

The above article provides considerable insight into the American psyche. Although Reaves's disparaging remarks towards the English do not represent the sentiments of Americans, she is very American in her search for 'authenticity.' The English are criticized for presenting a courteous face while treating the world 'shabbily.' The double standard seems unacceptable. The French are singled out as being a self-satisfied population that accepts rudeness as an essential part of being French and are, therefore, given credit for at least being forthcoming with their misanthropy. Yet, what Reaves does not consider is that rudeness for a country such as England or America can be quite psychically traumatizing because it entails a profound reversal of habitus. For a nation in which 'popularity' and the need to be accepted have always been valued, the act of rudeness can be personally devastating and socially demoralizing. French rudeness has its roots in complex historical processes of democratization; a French person can be rude one moment yet extremely courteous and refined the next. It is an accepted practice, and its socially corrosive effects are, by consequence, much less extreme than they would be in America and England, where rudeness is as frightening as unrestrained anger.

Thus, the degree to which a nation requires codes of courtesy in order to maintain its sense of social harmony is affected by *how* it feels about discourtesy. A proverbially courteous nation that experiences a sudden discourtesy epidemic will fall into moral panic. A simplified comparison, therefore, does not suffice. Shared meanings and the social psychology of 'habituation' have to be taken into account.

Sentiments regarding civility are fairly grim in America, the one country that was certain it would build its own civility tradition free from Continental influence and meddling. We searched in France and England for general surveys similar to the American Public Agenda survey on rudeness. Most studies of incivility, however, were connected to studies of crime and hooliganism. The majority of Web articles posted in French on the topic of civility (a mere 3,470 in April 2007) addressed issues to do with extreme public discourtesy such as driver behaviour, crime on public transport systems, and juvenile delinquency. In England, on 29 April 2002, the prime minister of the United Kingdom was quoted by Sky News television as welcoming the idea of posting 'coppers' (police) in certain schools to control troublemakers. There has been a toughening of laws directed at persons indulging in criminal or disruptive behaviour in England, but there still does not seem to be as widespread a concern over face-to-face interactions within the non-criminal population as there is in America.

In a series of polls taken in France in 2006, the following were universally considered by the French to be unacceptable acts of incivility. They are listed in order of importance:

- Not to offer one's seat on the metro or bus to an elderly person (67 per cent).
- Enter a room or shop without saying 'Bonjour' (61 per cent).
- To use gross words in public (53 per cent).

- Jump one's place in line (49 per cent).
- Call someone by the familiar 'tu' (you) when unwarranted (48 per cent).
- Arrive late at an appointment (45 per cent).
- Interrupt someone in mid-speech (44 per cent).
- Call an acquaintance after 21h30 (36 per cent).
- Yawn without covering one's mouth (34 per cent).
- Smoke at the dinner table (34 per cent).
- For a man: not to give the right of way to a woman (34 per cent).

It is interesting to note that screaming at other drivers, arguing with the grocer, and never speaking with one's neighbours are not included in the above list. The French have their definition of what is acceptable and unacceptable incivility. It would seem that what particularly traumatizes citizens of a given culture is when their top-priority civility rules are ignored.

In the United States, a country more habituated to social consensus, many Americans point to the country's unique legal system as contributing to a spirit of litigation and social confrontation. While the system is serving to protect the rights of the individual against powerful professions and interests, the state included, the American 'lawsuit' seems to be creating much social hesitancy. The story of the American doctor who drives past an accident because he is afraid of being held liable if something goes wrong as a result of his intervention is legendary.

Writing in the *Wall Street Journal*, Hilton Kramer (1999) has called this litigious spirit 'the Second Cold War.' Deborah Tannen calls America 'the argument culture' (1998) and suggests that citizens are at the end of their tether and ready for a more conciliatory style of discourse. Martin Golding (1980) has pointed out that the proliferation of interest groups and the struggle for 'rights' have created a confrontational situation in which the universal meaning of rights has been eclipsed by sentiments of entitlement (53–64). Stuart Taylor, Jr, and Evan Thomas report in *Newsweek* (2003) that the American civil-jury litigation system, while protecting individuals from corporate and institutional irresponsibility, is making professionals overly cautious and damaging the medical and educational systems. Taylor and Thomas explain that public trust can weaken as a consequence of a litigious spirit: fearing litigation from parents, educators become hesitant to enforce standards of behaviour and achievement; similarly, medical practitioners avoid admitting errors (and correcting them) out of fear of patient lawsuits. Some practitioners even give up performing risky surgeries. A 'disclaimer' society emerges out of the remnants of a civility culture founded on mutual recognition and communal cooperation.

Philip K. Howard, a legal reformer, believes that nothing short of rewriting tort law will lift this inhibitory pressure. In *The Collapse of the Common Good: How America's Lawsuit Culture Undermines Our Freedom* (2002) he estimates that laws facilitating litigation and the protection of individual rights are having the opposite effect and damaging the right of free expression.

Mark Caldwell also expresses concern over rising social confrontations. In *A Short History of Rudeness: Manners, Morals and Misbehaviour in Modern America* (1999), he admits that Americans cannot return to old standards of courtesy that were based on hierarchical relationships, but reminds us, nevertheless, that there is a pressing need for some social ethic that promotes and sustains mutual sympathy. Michael J. Meyer (2000) believes that civility should be considered a communal virtue; he proposes that a return to coherent public ideals would have a positive influence on personal behaviour (69–84). Peter N. Stearns (2001) notes a decline in political civility and participation in voluntary associations and wonders if Herbert Mead's conception of a stable American consensual national character is not due for revision (65–79). Robert D. Putnam (2000) also recognizes that there has been a decrease in American communalism but believes that a revival might be in the making. Kate O'Beirne (2006), in *Women Who Make The World Worse*, a scathing critique of three decades of radical feminism, contends that the American family and American educational system have been disoriented by radical feminist rhetoric that thrives on a culture of gender mistrust and blame.

There seems to be considerable concern over the necessity of agreeing on a workable late-modern civility standard. This project, however, is more easily imagined than actualized. As Adam B. Seligman (1998) warns, the affirmation of group rights and sanctions has weakened the generalized trust that was a prerequisite for secular individualism. Seligman argues that the bridging of trust between the public and private spheres, a consequence of the co-existence of a multiplicity of interests, has weakened trust in the private spheres and affected civility standards (2000:79–111). Equally concerned with the issue of trust is Piotr Sztompka (1998), who, in a study of post-communist societies, has found that arbitrariness, ineptitude, secrecy, and monocentrism have a devastating effect on trust and civility (191–210). Ronald E. Jones

(2002), referring to Shils's theory of social structure and solidarity, has similarly warned that, as balance between the centre and the periphery disintegrates, there is increased incivility between the young and the aged as a consequence of a failure of tradition to accommodate change (409–25).

Addressing the issue of civility in a diverse nation, Robert W. Hefner (1998b) views the demise of vertical associations and the preference for horizontal egalitarian relations as key topics that should preoccupy civility researchers. Stephen L. Carter (1993) wonders if the mixture of democracy, the rule of law, and liberal politics has 'trivialized' the entire notion of religious devotion and the civilities that used to arise from it. In *Integrity* (1996), Carter argues for a civil society based on the valuation of deep honesty and caring. In a subsequent book, *Civility: Manners, Morals and the Etiquette of Democracy* (1998), Carter discusses whether the lack of civility instruction in schools has created a moral vacuum in which the sensational and the rude are held up as worthy of admiration and as signs of personal power and competence. He affirms with considerable conviction that the reconsecration of a civil society will require the teaching of civility to children at a young age.

Martin E. Marty (1998), the renowned American writer on religion and ethics, argues that a considerable contradiction has developed between the notion of a common good and the multiplicity of political and social interests. Edward Shils (1998), recalling his previous studies of centre and periphery in social structure and solidarity (1975), maintains that civility is a vital aspect of liberal democracy; the survival of that social system depends on such civility, an important safety valve that allows for the co-existence of liberty within a diversity of individual rights. Maria Renata Markus (2002) refines the distinction between political and personal behaviour by suggesting that a distinction should be made between 'decency' and 'civility,' since civility is connected to the preservation of multiple rights, while 'decency' tries to assure that no one is put in a shameful or humiliating predicament. She explains that, while civility contributes to social cohesion, it is decency that creates morale within a population (1011–30). In a more ironic vein, David G. Myers (2000) questions why there is so much spiritual hunger in an age of plenty. Charles Edgley and Dennis Brissett (2000) find that the consequence of a heightened sensitivity to rights is 'a nation of meddlers.' Much of behaviour in such a society is defined by prohibition rather than positive pro-social behaviours. This theme of prohibition and 'self-control' is the central thesis of historian Peter N. Stearns's *Bat-*

*tleground of Desire: The Struggle for Self-Control in Modern America* (1999). Stearns disagrees with those who criticize Americans for having become hedonistic and bereft of emotional discipline. On the contrary, he argues, Americans have become more controlled and repressed than were the Victorians.

Focusing on the workplace, Lynne M. Andersson and Christine M. Pearson (1999) ask whether corporate workers are not stuck in a prisoner's dilemma that pits competitiveness and civility against each other. I. Maitland (2002) also wonders if self-interest in business dealings does not conflict with ideals of empathy. Robert Bly (1994) passionately questions the effects of 'bottom-line' capitalistic thinking on public civility and family harmony. As for the recipients of consumer culture, it would seem there is enough tension in public places to make shopping mall administrators post instructions regarding acceptable behaviour (Wilson 1998, Williamson 2002:486–99).

Another source of worry in the United States is the effects corporations are having on civil interactions. Robert F. Murphy (1971) points out that the principal task of late-modern sociology is the study and explanation of the 'unintended consequences' of social actions. This applies to studies of contemporary organizations, which, although originally rationalized by ideologies of social improvement, are now substantially uncoupled from concerns over social problems and are having considerable influence on civility in private and public circles.

The traditional view of corporate culture which assumed that corporate owners and workers come together in a relatively equitable 'exchange relationship' (Homans 1958, 1961, Gabriel 1993, Thibault and Kelley 1959, Blau 1964) may no longer be reliable. While the early industrialists had rationalized capitalism in terms of patriotism and social improvement, the new late-modern corporation has used 'bottom-line' profitability as the ultimate measure of rational action. Bly (1994) quotes a vice-president of Colgate-Palmolive who responds to the growing worry over the exportation of American jobs in the following manner: 'The United States does not have an automatic call on our resources. There is no mindset that puts this country first' (156).

That the contemporary corporation has had a profound influence on the emotions of the population is evident to anyone who has read studies of contemporary families. Policies of downsizing and restructuring have caused considerable worry and stress. A parallel strain has also been imposed on service personnel, who have been required to 'manufacture' appropriate emotions of congeniality towards demanding customers even in the absence of job security. In a classical study of 'emotion work,' A.R. Hochschild (1983) observed that service personnel, such as flight attendants and debt collectors, have had to manufacture emotions to get their jobs done properly. Gouldner ([1954] 1981) considers the long-range ability of an organization to achieve its goals dependent on the effective 'emotion work' of workers. Such emotion work becomes a form of commercialized civility and acts to energize workers to be efficient and respond credibly to the needs of clients. What effect such managed workplace civility has on the private life of the worker has yet to be properly determined. This has required personnel to repress normal reactions, creating an extraordinary level of stress. Studs Terkel (1972) similarly observes that those employees who do not 'play act' the emotions expected of them risk being branded as 'insubordinate through manner' (82–3). It seems little has changed since Terkel's warning.

This emotional pressure increases dramatically in 'strong culture corporations' whose success depends on high levels of 'enthusiasm' on the parts of sales personnel, who are expected to retain a continuing 'faith' in the products they are asked to sell (team players). A group leader's efficacy is measured by his or her ability to keep workers within a zone of ideological and emotional belief or 'corporate faith.' The salesperson who begins questioning the viability of the project creates a perturbation in the 'culture' of the organization and is shunned or eliminated in the interests of protecting the 'morale' of remaining staff (Hopfl and Linstead 1993).

Terkel identifies *fear* as the central mechanism in organizational emotional conformity. Such fear seems to increase in direct proportion to the scarcity of employment (Baumol, Blinder, and Wolff 2003). Predictably, job insecurity creates additional social hesitancy and civility issues between workers and also between workers and their managers, not to mention between workers and their families. Hochschild (1983) notes that job scarcity and the fear of the power possessed by management hierarchy to affect one's life chances contribute to submissive *play-acting* and *feigned obedience* (102). The integrity of authentic sentiments of loyalty becomes corroded by stress and worry. The worker, noticing that the corporation is reneging on its original promise of social improvement while continuing to demand peak performance, becomes resentful and cynical (Crenson and Ginsberg 2002). This cynicism decreases the willingness to be involved with the needs of the corporation and has a negative influence on productivity (Manson 2000).

Overall, the emotional competence of parents and their children is considerably affected by the degree of stress experienced by parents during the hours they spend at work (Googins 1990, Warren and Johnson 1995). In a survey conducted in 2002, CCH Human Resources Group (2003), a leading consultancy on employment law in the United States, found that while personal illness accounted for 33 per cent of absences from work, 'reasons other than illness accounted for 67 percent of unscheduled absences. Specifically, these reasons were: Family Issues (24 percent); Personal Needs (21 percent); Stress (12 percent); and Entitlement Mentality (10 percent).' Similar findings had been reported by Goodman, Atkin, and Associates (1984) two decades previously.

In fact, a parent who is stressed at work may resent the additional stress of family life and suddenly flare up in response to the demands of a child. Time that should be ideally devoted to family matters is spent worrying about work already done, work to be done, or work that may suddenly no longer be available. Children, sensing the contingency of their parents' availability, become more anxious and more demanding or else become inured to minimal contact with parents. Parenthood becomes, in Hochschild's words, the 'second shift' ([1989] 1997). Torn by the role conflict caused by demanding families and corporations competing with each other for their attention, some parents turn to work as an escape. Some others leave the work market in a bid to eliminate an infernal circle of obligation and guilt. Both find no escape from what Hochschild terms the 'time bind' (1997), a direct consequence of technological development and the hegemony of corporate competitiveness.

While statistical studies can reveal one side of corporate life, conversation analysis can contribute to an understanding of the discontent that is being expressed in indirect ways. Instances of 'subversive humour,' for example, are additional indicators of discontent. Through the use of biting humour, workers preserve a sense of personal discrimination while contesting the perceived power of their employers (Holmes 2000; Rodriguez and Collinson 1993:744). Such humour differs markedly from person-to-person humour connected to personal affection and playful competition. Scott (1990) identifies such reactions as consequences of indignation triggered by forced submission and humiliation (111–12). Humour and gossip about the organization and its powerful members, however, does not guarantee radical change in management attitudes. At best, it provides 'partial consolation' and a temporary release from anger, boredom, and tension (Gabriel 1993:137).

Conformity, Opposition, and Identity   281

All in all, the 'self-referential' corporation creates self-referential employees who measure their life chances not only according to their position within a given organization but in relation to opportunities offered by sudden job changes. The cynical desire to make the best of the system replaces the idealism of loyalty. This does not necessarily represent the preference of workers; surveys indicate that more than 50 per cent of Americans would accept lower pay for better treatment at work (World Values Survey 1999–2001). Books have been written to advise the disenchanted on how to protect themselves in this contingent environment. One title warns workers to *Control Your Destiny or Someone Else Will* (Tichy and Sherman 1994); another title gives advice on *Job Shift: How To Prosper in a World without Jobs* (Bridges 1994).

Yet, this corporate culture of expediency and bottom-line justifications may not be in accord with the inner temperament of Americans. The Baylor Institute for Studies of Religion released a national survey (2006) investigating how Americans felt about mixing religion with law. The survey found that although 94 per cent of Americans believed in God, there were different visions regarding the nature of that 'god' and whether prayer should be allowed in schools:

- 31 per cent of Americans believed in an authoritarian God who is an integral part of human affairs and given to punishing sin; of these 91 per cent believe prayer should be allowed in schools.
- 23 per cent believed in a benevolent God who, although very much part of human affairs, is reluctant to punish human short-comings; of these 79 per cent believe prayer should be allowed in schools.
- 16 per cent believed in a God that is detached from worldly affairs yet unhappy about the way in which they are being managed; of these, 69 per cent believe prayer should be allowed in schools; and,
- 24 per cent believed in God as a force in the universe neither active in the world nor angry with it; of these, 47 per cent believe prayer should be allowed in schools.

So, a considerable part of individual self-centredness may be the result of the diminishing paternalism of corporations and the ambiguous status of religious ethics. Feeling powerless to change the system in which they spend so much of their working days, individuals adopt a self-centred approach to reality. Deprived of a safe harbour favoured by all groups, they are forced to shore up the self and protect it from uncertainty and humiliation. Yet, this is not the complete picture; while corporations have a major effect on civility, there is also the issue of interpersonal communications, the hotbeds of civil and uncivil behaviour. It would seem Americans are now searching for a moderate spirituality. In a recent survey conducted by the Pew Organization (2006) on Americans' sentiments towards religion and politics, 69 per cent of respondents said that the liberals had gone too far in keeping religion out of the schools and government, while 49 per cent expressed reservations about attempts by Christian conservatives to impose their religious ideas on American culture. It would seem Americans are seeking some spiritual space that can prosper between the two extremes of the cultural divide.

One of the dangers of hypothesizing about courtesy/civility and planning civility research along the lines of dissonance study, however, is that one might be tempted to study antisocial behaviour at the cost of ignoring pro-social behaviour. We know what percentage of the population resorts to violence, but know very little about how many people smile at one another and open doors for one another. This can only be discovered through assiduous field research. It is the degree and type of pro-social behaviour in the law-abiding sector of a culture that substantially defines a society's interaction ethos and civility practices. Moreover, we need a reliable understanding of the social psychology of civility and the emotions that are involved in civil and uncivil behaviour. A comprehensive sociology of civility must cross over disciplinary, ethnic, and national boundaries if it is to provide a reliable explanation of the anatomy of courtesy. We do this in Part III of this book.

Abbot L. Ferriss (2002) has noted this dearth of pro-social civility studies. Defining civility as 'consideration for others in interpersonal relationships' (376), Ferris notes that the measure of violent crime such as robberies, muggings, and assault does not indicate the 'vast amount of civility' for which there are yet no objective measures (381). He does suggest that the degree to which anger is restrained has a positive correlation to rates of civility, and recommends that measurement of anger restraint should be an integral part of future studies (389–91). Even here, one has to proceed with caution: the extent to which anger is restrained is not a reliable indicator of the extent of friendliness and care shown in private and public; a person could be very calm and forbiddingly cold. Social bonds can be threatened by corrosive expressions of anger as well as freezing detachment.

Moreover, some cultures welcome passionate anger as a mark of integrity and sincerity, while others consider it a mark of emotional weakness and loss of personal control. One has to be careful not to construct ethnocentric measures and indexes that apply to one culture but collapse into incoherence when transported and tested in another region. What is important is not only the act but the meaning behind the act as understood within a given culture. So, the worry over 'rudeness' will tend to depend on what a given culture normally considers 'polite.' People from one culture may find the practices of another culture quite rude, just as they may experience considerable worry when a long-standing civility practice of their own culture is suddenly suspended. If speaking loud in a restaurant has been a long-time habit, then no moral worry will be shown over it; but in a culture used to speaking in low voices, the appearance of loud restaurant talk may signal imminent social decay. Habituation is the means for legitimation, and it plays a major role in the determination of what is to be cause for worry and what is to be accepted as innocuous. There are certain universals that transcend cultural preferences, and we discuss these in a later section.

It would seem that many of those caught in the web of competition and self-interest that is contributing to the complaints of rising rudeness seem to be seeking a revised social contract. The following letter was written by an unnamed American high school student. It has been making the rounds of Internet chain emails since 1999, over thirty years following the 'cultural revolution' of the 1960s. The disillusioned teenager writes:

> The paradox of our time in history is that we have taller buildings, but shorter tempers; wider freeways, but narrower view points; we spend more, but have less; we buy more, but enjoy less. We have bigger houses and smaller families; more conveniences, but less time; we have more degrees, but less sense; more knowledge, but less judgment; more experts, but more problems; more medicine but less wellness. We have multiplied our possessions, but reduced our values. We talk too much, love too seldom, and hate too often. We've learned how to make a living, but not a life; we've added years to life, not life to years.
>
> We've been all the way to the moon and back, but have trouble crossing the street to meet the new neighbour. We've conquered outer space, but not inner space; we've cleaned up the air, but polluted the soul; we've split the atom, but not our prejudice.
>
> We have higher incomes but lower morals; we've become long on quantity, but short on quality. These are the times of tall men and short char-

acter; steep profits, and shallow relationships. These are times of world peace, but domestic warfare; more leisure, but less fun; more kinds of food, but less nutrition.

These are days of two incomes, but more divorce; of fancier houses, but broken homes. It is a time when there is much in the show window and nothing in the stockroom.

The letter could have been written in the 1960s, yet what differentiates it from the documents of that decade is the helplessness of the author; no prescription for change is provided. The teenager is making an eloquent plea for some compromise between consumerist bottom-line self-interest and communal cooperation. One wonders, however, how this same teenager, raised in a pluralistic democratic society of values and lifestyles that favour individualism and an a priori self-esteem, would react to Allan Bloom's (1987) suggestion that 'it is necessary that there be an unpopular institution in our midst that sets clarity above well-being or compassion, that resists our powerful urges and temptations, that is free of all snobbism but has standards' (252). Like Robert Bly (1994; cited in Davetian 1998), who believes that many late-modern Americans are stuck in a perpetual adolescence which renders them extremely centred on their own needs, Bloom is not optimistic about the viability of a democratic culture based on a generalized system of rights that includes no specification of communal responsibility. Stephen H. Wirls (1996) also argues that the disparity between liberal democracy and the moral requirements of a civil society may actually require new policies that might be in considerable tension with ultra-liberal ideals (31–48). João Teixeira Lopes (2005) cautions about the 'symbolic violence' contained in civility and etiquette rituals that are constructed by one social group at the expense of another (43–51).

Many of the critiques of contemporary 'rudeness' and 'lack of consideration for others' seem to subscribe to the premise that previous eras possessed a better conception of civility and the ethics required for mutual consideration. Narratives regarding the passing of 'traditional' respect for manners and communal solidarity are dependent on such hindsight wisdom. They are also linear accounts, not paying enough attention to how civility and incivility appear in the form of 'waves' in response to social conditions. So we fondly look back to the benefits of communal cultures in which conformity to specified social rituals provided social certainty. Yet we forget that many of these rituals were

Conformity, Opposition, and Identity   285

adopted not only to promote harmony but also to restrict mobility between classes and provide the privileged with a powerful tool for the social exclusion of those they wished to keep out of their own circles of association and obligation.

Agreeability is not necessarily synonymous with an emancipated society. While it can promote social equity, it is influenced by many other factors, the political, institutional, and emotional awareness of the population not being the least of them. We have found, for example, that highly despotic societies can continue to favour extremely polite behaviour between citizens, just as nations governed by democratic bureaucracies can tolerate considerable injustice. We also remain aware of the role played by residual emotional pain in the negotiation of interactions. Certainly, Ferriss's (2002:389–91) suggestion that 'anger' be factored into civility research deserves serious consideration. We have made the same point in a paper delivered at a sociology conference (Davetian 1996) and specified in an article arguing for an 'emotionally-informed social theory' (2005) that 'pain' and 'loneliness' measurements should be part of a reliable social theory, for civil behaviour often depends on a person's self-concept, which itself is affected by their emotional state.

These alarm bells, however, distract us from an important, albeit frightening, question: Can a culture eliminate a crisis in civility just by willing it away? Or is such a crisis the unintended outcome of a long history of development in which political, economic, moral, religious, and psychological factors have somehow intersected to produce the crisis? Is a change of heart, without a substantial revision of institutions, sufficient medicine?

The premise that we live in an uncivil age begs argument. The private and public cruelties of past eras may have been far more wrenching than anything we have experienced in our own lifetimes. The world wars of the twentieth century and the atrocities of the Nazi nightmare and other regional dictatorships could be (and have been) offered as evidence of a 'terrible century.' But at least these atrocities have been followed by seminal improvements in our conceptions of human rights and the dignity and rights of the person ('Never again!' is, after all, the determined cry of an awakened civilization). While the idealistic writings of the Enlightenment philosophers were the work of a minority of concerned thinkers, our own age has brought forth a virtual explosion of works addressing ethics, social justice, and economic equity. What has distinguished the twentieth century and these first few years of the twenty-first century is a considerable amount of self-reflection and social reappraisal.

## The Oppositional Self and the Search for Authenticity

Many scholars and mainstream writers have located the 1960s as the 'turning point' in Western civility. The great unrest unleashed by the cultural revolution of the 1960s is seen as a watershed event that led to a deformalization of manners and a rise in public and private incivility. The 1960s was certainly an important decade, and its effects are still with us: so much of our social equity programs emanate from the protest movements of that decade. Even so, while the youth of the 1960s verbalized what may have previously been kept silent, few of the social changes that followed in the wake of this cultural uprising would have been possible without the discontent that had been building in the latter 1950s. These conditions would make the 1960s and the decades that followed in the United States as particularly American as the events following the American War of Independence.

Certainly, the experiences of Europeans and Americans were different before and after the Second World War. The Europeans who initially faced the Third Reich's fury unaided learned the meaning of living with considerable restraints. Although the United States eventually joined the struggle against the Third Reich, the majority of Americans lived far away from the scenes of battle. England and France had an opportunity to test their long-standing approaches to adversity and emerged even more stoic than before. In the postwar period, while Europe set about rebuilding its infrastructure, America managed to surge forward into a period of prosperity and political dominance that made it the most powerful and most influential nation in the world. Yet, it retained a continuing fear of what could happen to its democracy if forces such as those of Hitler or Stalin were to be let loose on America. As a protective measure, it adopted a corporate culture that restated the American narrative of freedom, but within a communally and economically rationalized patriotism (Johnson 1997:760).

This corporate culture had been long in the making. Social scientists who study American society without focusing on the particular cultural and industrial history of New York City in the late 1800s and early 1900s will miss the unique modern break between America and Europe. While earlier settlers had spread across the United States into communities that were distinguished from one another by the ethnic origins of their settlers, the later immigrants who arrived in New York congregated in the most congested part of the world. Different ethnic groups rubbed elbows on the busy streets of New York from dawn until the late evening, frequenting the more than 25,000 produce and merchandise carts that lined the sidewalks and streets of the city. One takes so much of the present global industrial landscape for granted, not realizing how much of it originated in New York City. In order to survive and succeed in this megalopolis of multiple languages and diverse civility codes, the new American had to learn to leave enough of the Old World behind to find common ground with others with whom he might otherwise have fallen into conflict. What united people of different ethnic, religious, and national backgrounds was the new American work ethic: to work hard in order to achieve a chosen goal and to not stop until that goal was achieved. It was this unwaveringly optimistic ethic that distinguished America, provided it with a common egalitarian civility ethic, and set the stage for later disappointment.

The 1930s was perhaps America's most important decade in the twentieth century. The Great Depression left the core of American civilization, New York, in economic shambles. The uncaring federal government, headed by President Herbert Hoover, was replaced by a socially concerned administration under the leadership of former New York governor Franklin D. Roosevelt. Roosevelt's 'New Deal' economics was a turning point in American contemporary history. The entire notion of a citizen's rights to government help originated in this era. Under the leadership of men like Roosevelt, Fiorello H. LaGuardia, and Robert Moses a major change in American government occurred, a change that revitalized early American ideals of communalism. Their public works programs, originated and tested in New York City, set the stage for a new American corporatism based on expansion.

The rise of such a corporate culture, built on narratives of optimistic conformity and solidarity, did not silence dissenters on the fringe. It even helped energize them and gave them new social purpose. Artistic style changed radically following the war, moving away from traditional forms and searching for 'originality.' Many of the novels were given to delivering nostalgic critiques of American culture. John Steinbeck's ([1989] 1939) *The Grapes of Wrath* mourned the ruin of the land by corporations, banks, and dubious commercial interests. While Steinbeck's novel championed the fate of migrant workers in the vineyards of California, it sent an angry warning to Americans about U.S. society in general and its penchant for unbridled development. Steinbeck's other works of fiction were equally critical of American capitalism. This emerging social conscience energized groups which had become disturbed by a rising bigotry against African Americans. While black Americans had been integrated in the various neighbourhoods of the big cities, new government and banking interests ghettoized them in the newly mapped urban landscape. By the late 1950s Harlem in New York had become a ghetto from which blacks could not easily escape. While there were numerous white-owned businesses, none of them would employ an African American.

The black Americans endured even worse conditions in the south, despite the fact that white southerners continued seeing themselves as privileged American aristocrats. In nine full-length plays and over a dozen shorter ones, Tennessee Williams catalogued a suffering southern aristocracy that was dangerously close to savagism were it not for its veneer of civilized decorum (Longley, Silverstein, and Tower 1960:212). And Margaret Mitchell (1936) explored the psyche of a vanishing southern aristocracy in *Gone With the Wind*. In this novel, the heroine Scarlett O'Hara seemed to be lacking in virtue but was an exciting portrayal of the potential energy of a woman not dominated by turn-of-the-century Victorian Puritanism. *New York Times* reviewer J. Donald Adams described the novel's heroine as 'lacking in many virtues – in nearly all one might say but courage – alive in every inch of her, selfish, unprincipled, ruthless, greedy and dominating, but with a backbone of supple springing steel' (cited in Longley, Silverstein, and Tower 1961:249). America was searching for heroes and heroines who counterbalanced a culture of standardization, and it was willing to admire personages who had qualities contrary to what centuries of conduct books had preached to be the ideal virtues. Predictably, there was a countermovement to this new libertarianism in Hollywood movies: Will H. Hays, a former Republican national chairman, was selected to lay down a code of behaviour for artists and studios. Hays began by trying to drive out of Hollywood those he considered of loose morals and then laid down a code of behaviour that survived (on screen at least) well into the 1950s. Some of Hays's rules of comportment stipulated that directors should avoid:

> kissing that lasted for more than seven feet of film, clergy in comic or villain roles, the 'explicit,' 'the attractive,' or 'justified' treatment of adultery and fornication, nudity under any circumstance, sympathy for 'murder, safecracking, arson, smuggling etc in such detail as to tempt amateurs to

try their hands,' and 'all low, disgusting, unpleasant though not necessarily evil subjects' ... Hays went into considerable detail: if an actor or an actress were seated or lying on a bed, albeit fully clothed, one and preferably both should have one foot on the ground. (Johnson 1997:711)

The combined effect of this literature of reappraisal was to disconnect avant-garde Americans from many of the reassurances of American patriotism. Describing the new literary generation in America, Edmund Wilson wrote with wonder: 'Those years were not depressing but stimulating. One couldn't help being exhilarated at the sudden, unexpected collapse of the stupid gigantic fraud. It gave us a new sense of freedom; and it gave us a new sense of power' (1952:498). Wilson noted that while American intellectuals had previously championed individualism, they now called for a planned economy (Johnson 1997:760).

The moment was now seen as a unique experience, not requiring connection to historical precedent. This severance from the authority of customs also entailed a change in established standards of public civility; that which was 'old-fashioned' was increasingly viewed as suspect, as not 'modern' enough (Davis 1972). In the United States, this penchant for the modern became accelerated and validated by the proliferation of a new manufacturing sector that provided Americans with convenience and luxury products that still remained out of the reach of many working- and middle-class Europeans. While Europe also admired modernity and welcomed U.S. products, it continued to look to America as the affluent society, economically and psychologically less inhibited than the Old World. On one hand Europeans yearned for the political freedom enjoyed by Americans, while, on the other hand, they rested secure in knowing that they possessed a long history that included extended periods of economic and political hardship. They had survived numerous tyrannies and were, therefore, less given to the type of uncompromising idealism that leads to later disappointment. In America, corporate culture stepped in to assure Americans that their country's special mission remained intact. It was a promise that many members of the 1960s generation would find ludicrous.

What must be considered in comparisons of American, English, and French industrial and corporate cultures are the differences in the size of the countries. England and France are smaller countries and able to maintain administrative cores that act as unifying forces for their populations. The high mobility of Americans across spans stretching 4,000 miles and more did not afford them with the unifying conditions enjoyed by countries such as England and France. In addition, a series of civility traditions came to be practised in America: one in the south, another in the west, and still others in the midwest and the north, where migrants were doing their best to develop a common interaction ritual that would cause minimal ethnic conflict.

The one unifying value that transcended regional differences was the ethic of consumption, a carefully engineered social practice intended to convince Americans to overcome their fear of another Great Depression and begin buying the many new manufactured goods that were flooding the market after the Second World War. One of the leading architects of the new American consumer society was a public relations expert, Edward Bernays, a nephew of Sigmund Freud. During the 1920s he became the master-builder of the American public relations machine. He was the innovator of a psychological public attitude control system that stimulated people's 'desires' and then offered to satisfy them through the purchase of products. Using what was known of crowd psychology, Bernays succeeded in adding to the democratic citizen the character of the 'consumer.' Calling this 'the engineering of consent,' this magician of the new consumer society proceeded according to the premise that most people possessed destructive irrational and aggressive drives which had to be distracted with the fulfillment of artificially created 'wants' and 'needs.' The influence of Freud's writings regarding a 'death instinct' are noticeable in Bernays's philosophy (Tye 2001, Bernays 1936). 'Born to shop,' 'shop till you drop,' and 'when the going gets tough, the tough go shopping' became American catch phrases, the consequences of Bernays's astute use of psychological manipulation in the services of pleasurable (and profitable) consumption. Ernest Dichter ([1960] 1985) extended Bernays's work by creating the 'focus group,' a tool of market research designed to uncover the hidden motivations of the female consumer and her resistance to the new convenience products. Like Bernays, Dichter believed that masses were fundamentally irrational and that a marketing elite should be entrusted with controlling such irrationality in the interests of a prosperous, democratic culture. While England and France continued to believe that civility standards were the prime determinants of social order, America turned to organized business and the retail sector for cultural assurance. American civility took on a 'managerial' tone, efficient, clipped, bravely optimistic.

If Americans now needed assurance that capitalism, consumption, and religious devotion were not at odds with one another, they received it from Norman Vincent Peale's (1952) *The Power of Positive Thinking*, which, next to the Bible, became the best-selling book in America. Peale deftly managed to convince his readers that faith in God and salesmanship was totally compatible. His message was devoid of notions of sin or atonement. He preached that man's subconscious mind possessed great powers to manifest desired realities (wealth included) and he equated that mental powerhouse to Christ's 'Kingdom of God.' This was a key development in American culture, a development that has had a massive influence on contemporary U.S. consumer and popular culture. If God and 'making a buck' could be unabashedly accepted as mutually compatible values, then an accelerated capitalism, accompanied by its natural consequence of greed and the commoditization of life, could co-exist with religious fervour. This problematized standing notions of civility and ethics as a communion with another world at the expense of material gain. Moreover, the rearrangement of the relationship between 'godliness' and 'commercialism' freed Americans from the cautions of early Protestantism and Catholicism: by compartmentalizing what were previously incompatible practices, mainstream Americans were able to continuously demonstrate that they were the most religious nation in the West while also being the most materialistic.

A new status was accorded to American youth in this society of consumption that was increasingly becoming uncoupled from the classical Protestant notions of asceticism. Despite the original sobering effects of the Great Depression, Americans had succeeded by the mid-1950s in transcending their fear of scarcity and creating a new American familial environment in which 'teenagers' occupied a central place in the new society of consumption.

A few factors contributed to this emergence of a vocal youth subculture distinctly set off on its own with its own rituals and codes: prosperous parents who took to giving their children 'pocket money,' thereby increasing their ability to socialize among themselves in shopping districts, restaurants, and amusement places; an expansion in the economy which permitted teenagers to get jobs while in school and acquire their own cars and circulate far from the surveillance of parents and relatives; and a steady decline in the extended family and decreased contact between teenagers and members of their family outside their own households.

While the extended family had motivated children to want to become adults as early as possible (for adults seemed to have more freedom than children and were frequently criticizing children), the emergence of a 'teen culture' now gave children a far more attractive goal to aim for: 'teen-hood,' a state which accorded freedom to youngsters to enjoy activities separate from those of the family while sparing them the sobering demands made on adults. Teen culture became a rehearsal ground for adulthood and a profitable marketing ground for corporations. European youth watched American films and marvelled at the freedom and affluence of American youth. Experts tried to explain the 'wildness' of some youth by stating that adolescence was a time of metabolic turbulence. Yet, as early as 1928, Margaret Mead had warned in *Coming of Age in Samoa* ([1928] 1961) that the American hypothesis that puberty and adolescence were stressful due to chaotic hormonal changes was without universal foundation. She attributed the problems of American youth culture to the imperative of 'free choice': 'A society which is clamouring for choice, which is filled with many articulate groups, each urging its own brand of salvation, its own variety of economic philosophy, will give each new generation no peace until all have chosen or gone under, unable to bear the conditions of choice' (235).

So, although the rebelliousness of the youth of the 1960s was not yet observable in the youth of the 1950s, they were, nevertheless, establishing their place in a society that was becoming increasingly youth-centred and less tied to vertical authority relationships. 'Father' became 'dad' and 'mother' became 'mom.' The terms 'sir' and 'ma'am' got dropped some time at the beginning of the 1960s. Intimacy between parents and their children in the absence of extended kin led to further informalization and a consequent increase in permissiveness. What had previously been learned in the extended kin group now became learned in the domain of school grounds and public places. 'Hanging out' became a way of leaving the house and being with one's own peers. And media became a part of the new extended peer network, helping form new attitudes and facilitating the reformation of old ones. And the status quo was the one thing that worried those American youth who wanted to test the limits of experience. Submission to parental precedents meant loss of new freedoms and pleasures, certainly a decrease in the prestige of their new 'unique' identity. A new 'teen' identity cut through intergenerational continuity.

Corporations contributed to the break-up of the family circle by regularly transferring their employees to where they needed them. The majority of corporate employment application forms included the question 'Are you willing to relocate?' The question seemed to be a test of loyalty to the corporation. Tindall and Shi ([1984] 1999) explain that the women's clubs and associations of the 1950s were intended to serve as hospitality units for families arriving in new communities. American communal hospitality has always been based on this recognition of mobility and the need to integrate new arrivals in order to strengthen the community. The 'settler' is recognized as a sort of kin as long as he or she is willing to fit into the circle and live by its codes (1443). 'Fitting in' became the mantra of the mobile. Frequent relocations created this need for anchoring in unknown towns and cities and contributed to a rise in conformity and standardization. This, in turn, led to a 'populism' that required simplified, friendly, and unaffected exchanges. While in England and France eccentricity was tolerated and even admired, in America it was the 'regular guy' and the 'regular gal' that became the highly valued symbols of 'all-Americanism.'

This conformism created enough strain to bring about its own antithesis. Although in the previous century the truant was subject to shunning and ridicule, American media in the late 1950s and 1960s began denigrating the straight-living teenager as a bore who had no passionate commitments. This sudden reversal must have put considerable pressure on youth, forcing teens to evaluate the social opportunity costs of conformity and rebellion. As late as 1939, Elias ([1939] 1978) had observed that the behaviour of children was controlled through references to abnormality and normality:

> The censorship and pressure of social life forming their habits are so strong, that young people have only two alternatives: to submit to the pattern of behaviour demanded by society, or to be excluded from life in 'decent society.' A child that does not attain the level of control of emotions demanded by society is regarded in varying gradations as 'ill,' 'abnormal,' 'criminal,' or just 'impossible' from the point of view of a particular caste or class, and is accordingly excluded from the life of that class. (141)

'You're so crazy!' was no longer a negative judgment but a compliment affirming the originality of the other. Searching for the 'weird' seemed to have a salutary effect in combating the emotionally deadening effect of 1950s' conceptions of normality. As this steady affirmation of liberty (and independence from small-town communal ties) occurred, social competence became as important as academic excellence. The degree to which someone could be 'wild and young' seemed to bring with it the social approval of peers. Being 'popular' became the religion of this new youth movement. This was an instance in which long-standing values of American moral propriety became reversed: the body and its presentation became a source of power; reputation based on communally known acts became supplemented by 'look' and 'image.' A teenager could gaze with admiration at a passing peer without knowing the least bit about his character. The pressures put on the American teenager were enormous. Success no longer depended on learning lessons or fixed rules of behaviour; popularity consisted not only of imitation but the self-generation of trendy speech and action. Ironically, the old aristocratic requirement of 'wit' became a prime vaunted quality of democratic youth culture. Media programs became the new conduct manuals and took on a socializing function.

Adult culture was under similar pressures. Examining the newsreels, television programs, and magazines of the period, one has the impression that public commentators were little concerned with people living outside the comfort zone of the middle class. Yet, there was an undercurrent of spiritual doubt and social anxiety despite this up-beat tempo and the sunny smiles of Americans shown close up in television commercials. Frequent relocation and suburban architectural uniformity were robbing middle-class Americans of their individuality. A family that moved away from its kin was that much less a part of a supportive network and that much more vulnerable to having its identity transformed. Tindall and Shi ([1984] 1999) confirm this unexpected consequence of American industrial mobilization: 'The traditional notion of the hardworking, strong-minded individual advancing by dint of competitive ability and creative initiative gave way to the concept of a new managerial personality and an ethic of corporate cooperation and achievement' (1440).

Eventually there was a backlash against such conformity in a culture that had always prided itself in being original. This resistance emerged in artistic and literary circles. In their search for new values to counteract the levelling effect of middle-class conformity, the writers and artists of the 1950s established experimental genres that often used shock methods to awaken their audience to new possibilities. Art took on a spontaneous and organic form, sometimes adopting minimalism to counter the overstatements of traditional forms. 'Beat' poetry, for example, attempted to return to the original promises made to Americans: a coherent culture that respected the individual. Beat poets used incoherence to mirror the conditions of the new consumption-driven society. The beat of the poem was the beat of the human heart in relentless protest. Whether the protest was coherent or not was less of an issue than the fact that the heart was still alive. Allen Ginsberg's ([1956] 2001) poem *Howl* was a cry of pain and rage against the manner in which America had, through unbridled development, abused its human and natural resources:

> I saw the best minds of my generation destroyed by madness,
> starving hysterical naked,
> dragging themselves through the negro streets at dawn looking
> for an angry fix.
> angelheaded hipsters burning for the ancient heavenly connection
> to the starry dynamo in the machinery of night ...

Writers were reacting to (and dramatizing) the growing alienation in the 1950s culture of plenty. Men who worked in the corporate world now had the opportunity of enjoying the benefits of a secure life, but on condition that they demonstrate a quasi-spiritual devotion to corporate objectives. As for women, they were required to be 'optimistic' guardians of the household, cheerfully administering to the needs of their husbands and their children, enjoying the time they spent in their kitchens surrounded by their 'ultra-convenient,' 'time-saving' appliances. Not all men and women succeeded in this Herculean task, as poignantly dramatized in Arthur Miller's ([1948] 1998) play *Death of a Salesman*. Miller succeeded in eliciting sympathy for the American common man caught in a world not of his making.

The literature of the period suggests that what was alienating was not industry itself but the manner in which industry had been elevated to the most important human activity and owners of industry posited as models of society. The problem was that this elevation of technology and salesmanship to a quasi-divine status had not resolved issues of moral laxity, corruption, and injustice. Nor had the emotional needs of citizens been addressed. A slew of sceptical works questioned this incongruence: Sloan Wilson's (1955) *The Man in the Gray Flannel Suit*, David Riesman's (1950) *The Lonely Crowd: A Study of the Changing American Character*, William Whyte's (1956) *The Organization Man*, and Vance Packard's *The Hidden Persuaders* (1957) and *The Status Seekers* (1959). In the social sciences, C. Wright Mills investigated the new wealth owners with works such as *White Collar* (1951) and *The Power Elite* (1956), and economist J.K. Galbraith (1958) offered up *The Affluent Society*, an uncompromising critique of short-term economic thinking.

Emerging works by psychologically concerned writers were equally unforgiving of the prevailing ethic of the 1950s. Commenting in 1961, Philip Roth, author of the best-selling *Goodbye Columbus* (1959), said: 'The American writer in the middle of the twentieth century has his hands full in trying to understand and then describe, and then make credible much of American reality. It stupefies, it sickens, it infuriates, and finally it is even a kind of embarrassment to one's own meagre imagination' (cited in Tindall and Shi [1984] 1999:1451).

The social ethic of the time was the 'mastery of passion' and the cultivation of a well-rounded personality. 'Adjustment' to 'reality' was supposed to be the consequence of such mastery. Regrettably, not enough consideration was given to the legitimacy of the reality itself and its consequent effect on personal happiness. The great salesman became the hallmark of American corporate society. And he was a new breed of American, combining business acumen, unabashed enthusiasm, and a down-to-earth quasi-invasive friendliness. If Americans have a feeling that certain of their civility rituals are simply extensions of the American penchant for 'deal promotion,' they are not far from the truth, for managerial efficiency somehow managed to affect relationships within and outside the family. As part of our research we listened to hundreds of hours of audio and television soundtracks of conversations in documentaries and in encounters between family members, and then compared the tones of voices to those of managers discussing projects. We find very similar cadences of speech. This similarity is less apparent (to us, at least) in English and French familial conversations.

An American public previously exposed to optimistic films that sang the praises of progress and suburban bliss was now exposed to films showing disordered mental states. Women, who had been presented as paragons of family virtue, were featured in films that showed the disturbed side of their lives (Barbara Stanwyck's and Elizabeth Taylor's films stand out as prime examples of this new cinematography of discontent). These films used a minimalist method that did not overtly reveal the director's intention; the 'oblique' method of cinematography allowed directors to subtly introduce new ideas to their audiences without triggering their resistance. What might not have passed in the declarative statements required for print communication now passed in the visual medium through the showing of stories. Action filled in for dialogue that might have been rejected; facial expressions represented changed inner states, whereas an outright confession of the inner state might have elicited objection and shock. Hollywood was not only entertaining its audiences but beginning to play an important role in directly and indirectly reflecting *and* forming the needs, ideals, and dreams of Americans (Walker 1970). Especially in the 1970s and 1980s stars acquired the power to compensate for the decline in local culture by building a virtual culture in which they occupied positions of privilege and influence; this had an important effect on mainstream behavioural norms and the shame threshold (Jarvie 1970).

This new culture of 'disappointment' and 'disagreement' was an unexpected development in a society that had maintained that 'being agreeable' was proof of good citizenship. Yet, it was perhaps necessary. Disobedience to the unacceptable required a certain measure of uncivil expression (Zwiebach 1975). The enthusiasm and conformity of the 'yes man' was demeaned because of the nature of those things to which he had been agreeing. In her philosophical novels *The Fountainhead* (1945) and *Atlas Shrugged* (1957), the American writer Ayn Rand, founder of the American 'objectivist' movement, made uncompromising criticisms of American collectivism and the moral corruption of citizens who pretended to be altruistic while being morally and philosophically unworthy due to mindless conformity. Certainly, the heroes in her books were very direct, to the point of what some might consider unapologetic bluntness. On a political level, Rand was fiercely opposed to Dewey's action-oriented progressivism and felt that it had encouraged moral irresponsibility. Her mistrust of instrumentalist action was shared by Hannah Arendt ([1954] 1972), who held Dewey responsible for infantilizing American students and making them feel 'that you can know and understand only what you have done yourself' (182).

For those living in the 1960s the 'flower-power' and 'protest' movements may have seemed like totally original movements, even though the pressures had been building through the 1950s: civil rights, women's rights, minority rights, and environmental concerns had all been treated by the intellectuals of the period. And there had been a growing feeling that many of the well-adjusted and cheerful parents of the 1950s had been playing a role, one based on well-polished acts of conformity. The stage was set for a reversal. The 1960s was the point of saturation when the above issues found a broader audience. And that audience was passionate and, at times, hostile (Viorst 1979).

Some American youth turned against their parents with uncompromising disobedience and discourtesy. Although these actions also swept through many European countries and even as far east as Japan, their effects in America were particularly disturbing and long lasting.

The discourtesy shown by these youth was quite 'subversive.' It was not a case of thoughtless discourtesy because many of the members of the cultural revolution came from middle- and upper-class families and were sufficiently familiar with the standard American code of manners. They willingly turned against the restraints that they had been taught to internalize, claiming social and political rationalizations for their run-away generation (Isserman and Kazin 2000). Comedy programs on television stepped in to soften the blow; they represented the validity of the claims of an increasingly anti-racist, anti-authoritarian youth cohort but imbued the generational debate with comic scenes that made the acceptance of new points of view less jarring than they might have been in a dramatic genre.

On many of the American ivy-league university campuses, students purposely and gladly abandoned rules of decorum. Professors were jeered, food riots started, fire alarms set off in the middle of the night. American youth voiced their protests while discovering the immediate pleasures of giving in to impulse. At first, the militant students tried to reason with the administration for changes, then, receiving little accommodation, turned to the derision and ridicule of school authorities. Many American campuses were literally under psychological and political siege (O'Neill 1971). Some of it was done with softening humour, creating bonds of sympathy between liberal teachers and students; some of it, however, was violent and led to numerous ruined careers and the firing of many campus student journalists (Hoffman 1991).

Arthur Marwick (1998), director of the Open University Centre for Research into the Sixties (UK), has examined the many issues that were involved in this massive cultural reappraisal. He concludes: 'The consequences of what happened in the sixties were long-lasting: the sixties cultural revolution in effect established the enduring cultural values and social behaviour for the rest of the century. This had not been a transient time of ecstasy and excess, fit only for nostalgia or contempt' (806). A great deal of social legislation occurred in America during that period: the Civil Rights Act (1964), Equal Opportunities Act (1964), Voting Rights Act (1965), Medicaid Act (1965), Older Americans Act (1965), Head Start Act (1965), and the Higher Education Act (1965).

Allen J. Moore's (1969) analysis of the period similarly identifies the American youth of the 1960s as a socially concerned generation. His analysis of this generation and their parents is worth considering in the interests of understanding what followed later:

Conformity, Opposition, and Identity 299

In previous generations young adult rebellion took the form of frivolous activities, such as swallowing goldfish, panty-raids, and sitting on flagpoles. The purpose of most youthful rebellion was to get attention or to playfully provoke adults. In fact, rebellion seldom became more serious than the expected *every-generation* crusade on behalf of free love ... Although the present generation can be very fun-loving and playful, their rebellion tends to be deeply serious, and is directed not so much toward parents or authority figures as against the basic structures of society. For the most part they have selected those concerns which are already big issues for the larger society and have succeeded in turning some low-key social debates into explosive issues. In a society that has been in the habit of expecting playful pranks from its young people, it was a surprise when young adults took up the big causes of education, politics, and international affairs. (49)

The Vietnam war, highly unpopular with most of America's youth, drove an additional wedge between parents who continued to favour conservative American politics and those youth determined to get across to their elders that authentic American patriotism needed to be applied to daily living and that a war fought for nebulous reasons thousands of miles away was not proof of any real public moral integrity. We may suspect in retrospect that the Vietnam war served to weaken the rising influence of the totalitarian Soviet regime; but, at the time, many Americans, especially those being conscripted into the armed forces, had difficulty understanding why the war was being fought. Some sons who opted to avoid the draft were stunned to see their parents turn them in to the military authorities. A.D. Horne's (1981) collection of essays by survivors and observers of the war, *The Wounded Generation*, analyses the lasting scars left by the war on American patriotism and communalism.

Pop stars achieved legendary status and political power during the war because they became the mouthpieces of a generation in protest. John Lennon's wistful song 'Working Class Hero' struck at the heart of the Western ideal of equality by rejecting the claim that class differentiation was being eliminated by rising affluence. His song 'Imagine' acted as a banner for the peace movement and reflected the idealism and optimism of a new generation willing to ask 'What if the system were to operate differently?' In their own turn, The Rolling Stones released one of the most influential music albums of the twentieth century, *Beggar's*

*Banquet*. One of the songs, 'Sympathy for the Devil,' tore into a complacent, older generation. During six minutes and twenty seconds of lyrics, Mick Jagger confronted the one subject that had become forgotten in the culture of plenty: corruption. Taunting his audience to 'Guess my name,' Jagger hinted that the devil may very well have found his way into the new world.

One of the most telling works to appear in this period of protest was a novel by Ken Kesey, *One Flew Over the Cuckoo's Nest* (1962). The film version directed by Miloš Forman (1975) became a cult classic. Acted by Jack Nicholson, the incorrigible protagonist of the movie is a man who becomes interned in a psychiatric hospital. Unrestrained by middle-class ideas of decorum and discipline, he proves saner and more compassionate than the people managing the asylum. Kesey was criticizing the mechanical morality of a society that adhered to principles of restraint and punitive discipline at the cost of empathy. He was also idealizing the character of the straight-talking anarchist.

This making of moral points through black comedy and poignant drama became an important genre in the 1960s and 1970s and contributed to a rising sense of 'irony.' It was ironic that the madman seemed saner than his keepers – ironic that the teenager demonstrating for civil rights was more worldly and less prejudiced than his parents, who urged him to remain 'adjusted' to social norms. Irony followed from disappointment. And irony liberated a generation from conditioned automatic behaviour. The ironic individual once believed in an ideal but has become disappointed by its non-fulfillment. Irony becomes a way of distancing oneself from the disappointment while retaining some sense of the original ideal. And this distancing became a political tactic of the counterculture, cutting into the long-standing belief in 'agreeability.' It was an important tactic enlisted in the development of an anti-authoritarian self-awareness. Imaginative acts became a means by which moral and political points could be made (Klinkowitz 1980).

By the mid-1970s, a variety of television programs were satirizing the contradictions of American society. *Saturday Night Live* became an American institution; what gave the show legitimacy was the appearance of actors of solid mainstream reputation. The program satirized nearly every facet of American society, sometimes with considerable malice. A large portion of the American public seemed to be becoming less formal and less attached to the ritual of patriotic rhetoric.

In many respects, the movement of the 1960s and the early 1970s was a movement against 'social adjustment.' Many were feeling that American society – in its existing form – was not worth adjusting to because it produced a debilitating lack of critical awareness. Martin Luther King, Jr, had himself affirmed in a speech that 'maladjustment' to certain social realities and prejudices was an effective and noble tactic of resistance. The cultural movement of the 1960s in America was, therefore, as much against mechanical social behaviour as it was in favour of political and sensual liberty. This dual agenda of the movement cannot be stressed enough. The downgrading of the supposedly upright citizen as an 'uptight square' was not a frontal attack on decency as much as it was a rejection of adjustment to social conventions that were seen to be producing destructive consequences. The Victorians suppressed 'misanthropy' in the interests of social harmony; the cultural revolution of the 1960s welcomed it in some measure as a liberational tactic.

Yet another social conflict had been brewing. The generation of the 1960s had grown up viewing films from the 1940s and 1950s that promoted successful romantic liaisons as the foundation of family life. Even the film *The Graduate* (1967), a sceptical indictment of capitalism and suburban moral expediency, ended with a scene of the two young protagonists running away to find monogamous bliss. Members of the flower generation, raised on a steady fare of Hollywood romance, may have turned critically on their parents for not having lived up to the summit of this romantic ideal. Relations between genders and between parents and children also came under considerable scrutiny during this time. Daughters became increasingly allergic to the roles played by their mothers. The conflict continued into the late 1970s and was aptly expressed by Nancy Friday's ([1977] 1984) best-selling book, *My Mother, Myself: The Daughter's Search for Identity*. What might have motivated the young women of this generation to discount the moral and role preferences of their mothers was the low status enjoyed by those same mothers. The status of the 1940s and 1950s housewife had been considerably high even though it was held that men and women were basically different and had to make the best of their differences. But the mothers of the teenagers of the 1960s were in a mood of discontent. Although they had not yet developed the power to fully assert themselves within their families, they were certainly complaining. The daughters simply formalized and gave voice to a movement already in germination.

Television programs took the cause of women and packaged it in sitcoms. *All in the Family* featured a despotic, bigoted father who kept ridiculing his hapless wife as a know-nothing. He was always berating her for this or that, eyebrows raised in amused exasperation whenever she offered her conciliatory wisdom. The series was meant to provide the new society with a target for ridicule: the bigoted, all-American father and his American wife who was always pretending to be less intelligent than she really was. This series, along with other sitcoms such as *Maude*, served to sensitize sons and daughters to the plight of some of their mothers and the alternatives offered by a new American feminism not at all averse to self-affirmation through civil disruption. Yet, despite this new wave of the feminist movement, while America may have led the world in female emancipation in the 1920s, it began lagging in the latter half of the century in comparison with Europe. Cass Wouters (2004) believes that this may have been due to the fact that American dating rituals were established quite early on, before the arrival of second-wave feminism, and remained entrenched in a male-dominated conception of gender.

As far as sexuality was concerned, many of the youth of the 1960s went a step further than their parents and accepted total sexual intimacy prior to marriage. 'Necking' and 'petting' between teenagers had already existed in the 1940s and 1950s; yet there had been considerable sexual anxiety. The young woman of the 1950s was torn with guilt about her sexual desires. The imperative of preserving virginity until after marriage was still an American social more. Many of the Hollywood film actresses were embodiments of the sexually ambivalent woman, prim and proper according to 'wholesome' American standards but periodically out of breath with sexual excitement, much to her own consternation. This tug of emotions between the strong male and the demurring but tempted woman was a common theme in postwar American cinema. It is doubtful that this theme would have found a ready audience in France. The French were ahead of the Americans in sexual liberation and were exploring the existential angst that *both* women and men felt when confronted with the contingency of late modernity. Topless and nude public bathing on the beaches of the Côte d'Azur was common long before American youth took off their clothes at rock concerts in defiance of American codes of public decency. America was late liberating itself from sexual prudery, and the acceleration of this liberation within a narrow historical time frame created a double standard: defiant sexuality to counteract lingering sexual guilt and playful purity to soften the embarrassment still felt in the presence of desire. This struggle between purity and lust is a persistent issue in American culture.

One development that has often been overlooked by cultural sociologists was the invention of the birth control pill. Before the advent of the pill if a woman became pregnant it was generally accepted that the father of the child would marry her to avoid the cultural stigma attached to having a child out of wedlock. The pill now allowed couples to experiment with sexuality without necessarily making a deeper emotional commitment. This had a salient effect on relationships between men and women. The sexual political will of this generation might have remained mute without the existence of effective and discreet birth control methods.

The permissiveness of the 1960s (and post-1960s) provided youth with the space they needed to take the inhibited bodies inherited from a culture of restraint and dance till they had reclaimed the natural grace and energy of those bodies. So, what occurred during this period was a rebalancing between the mind and the body. The Protestant ethic had subjugated the body in the service of goals created by the mind; this restraint of physical impulse was at the root of Puritanism and later Victorianism. The Romanticism of the years 1850 to 1950 created the preconditions for bodily pleasure by permitting an initial phase of restrained yearning. The 1960s and 1970s turned the longed-for into the experienced. Conduct books that appeared during the middle of the century also focused heavily on gender relations. In the United States, in particular, efforts were being made to level inequalities between genders while continuing to extol the virtues of sexual modesty (Wouters 2004). This is particularly noticeable in the 1990s, when conduct books began advising members of both genders to be 'sensitive and flexible in all relationships' (150).

Did the 1960s resolve America's continuing struggle with its Puritan sexual past? Perhaps not – although decades have passed, the subject of sexuality is still very much at the core of the American dialogue. In a documentary broadcast by the History Channel as part of its series *The Sexual Century*, Helen Gurley Brown, long-time chief editor of *Cosmopolitan* magazine, the same magazine which years ago preached that a young woman should hold out on sex in order to secure a suitable mate, now declared: 'The fact that we have now given ourselves permission to feel these wonderful feelings; that's the most fabulous thing that's happened ... We have learned to enjoy it and glory in it ... I'm fond of saying that sex is one of the best three things we have; I don't know what are the other two.'

It seems many Americans continue to turn to their media advisers for advice. The cover of the August 2003 issue of *Cosmopolitan*'s American edition announces the following features: 'Our Most Shocking Sex Survey 15,000+ Men Tell What They're Aching For. Girl, the Power's in Your Hands Now ... Beyond Kama Sutra ... We Teach You How to Give Him the Most *Intense* Pleasure Possible ... Get Naked! Does Stripping Down Stress You Out? How to Feel *Sooo* Sexy in the Buff.' To this day, the features remain similar: the female is being coached on how to be equal in sexual prowess to the most accomplished courtesans of antiquity.

What stands out in the cultural revolution of the 1960s and the social changes that decade inspired was the sudden need for 'authenticity.' While the 'creative extremism' of some of the youth of the 1960s tested the limits of many social paradigms, what mattered equally was whether an ideal was morally justifiable and emotionally ethical. These youth were not fighting against American ideals as much as they were bringing attention to their corruption. What mattered to them was whether something was 'real' or 'bullshit.' The exclamation 'that's unreal' was heard repeatedly in the daily interaction of youth. Like their forefathers, they sought perfection. The early Americans, by resisting tyranny and embracing change, had established a democracy predisposed to frequent self-critique. And enough issues were criticized and debated during the 1960s for Isserman and Kazin (2000) to refer to the social movement as the 'civil war of the 1960s.' Richard Sennett (1977) also noticed these major changes in the meaning of citizenship in his book *The Fall of Public Man*.

A disoriented generation of elders had little power to stop the spread of this new 'Renaissance.' Yet, this Renaissance was not brought about without the use of irony. Oddly enough, the ironical observations of members of the counterculture were motivated by a contemporary commitment to purity. This was reflected in some of the terminology used by the new generation. The struggle with the establishment was sometimes equated with the Roman-Palestinian conflict of 2,000 years ago. There were frequent references to the hippies as 'Jesus freaks,' and many hippies took to calling members of the establishment 'the Romans.' It was, as Farber and Foner (1994) have stated, an 'age of dreams'. It was also an age during which many of the young generation sought purity of motive and action in literature. Nietzsche's *Thus Spoke Zarathustra* ([1883] 1969) and his other works, notably *Beyond Good and Evil* ([1886] 1996), appealed to the 1960s generation because of the author's merciless critique of the contradictions of nineteenth-century

Christian morality. Berating Christianity's self-congratulatory asceticism and abnegation of physical desire, he railed against the 'despisers of the body': 'Behind your thoughts and feelings, my brother, stands a mighty commander, an unknown sage – he is called Self. He lives in your body, he is your body ... There is more reason in your body than in your best wisdom' ([1883] 1969:62). This was tantamount to saying 'trust your feelings' and stay free of ideology. The strong streak of idealism in Nietzsche's writings appealed to this generation. Going 'beyond good and evil' required assiduous personal reflection.

This search for sensual and moral purity soon overtook Hollywood. In the late 1960s, old-guard studio executives were overpowered by a cultural revolution for which they had made few provisions. Young talent moved in to fill the vacuum and produced a series of daring independent films that not only represented the mood of the times but changed the entire mission of cinema (Biskind 1999). Films became the new novels of America, presenting believable characters capable of evoking emotion just as had the characters of eighteenth- and nineteenth-century novels. Directors, writers, and actors took on a new role, that of social moralists. They became the new models of a generation in search of believable and morally courageous heroes. The artist in America, thirsting for justice in the midst of capitalist expediency, found a voice in the mainstream through the medium of cinema. And that medium permitted the expression of what had previously been kept silent, namely the wistful melancholy of the young generation and its thirst for meaning.

What Elias has considered a long process of evolution of manners was cheerfully reformed within a few months by the bolder members of the 1960s cultural movement. The restraint of bodily functions, described by Elias as a *sine que non* of the civilizing process, was substantially abridged. At the dinner table, fork and knife were handled more casually than before; people ate food while talking; nudity became accepted as a good; breaking wind among friends was occasionally tolerated with the semi-embarrassed humorous exclamation, 'You're so gross!' What counted was being 'free' and 'natural.'

That certain segments of culture dared become less inhibited – and consequently more spontaneous – may not have been an indication of a decivilizing process but of how secure (or bored) Americans had come to feel with their rational approach to reality. The rational dared now act irrationally, believing that they would not lose their bearings. It was an act of faith which history might prove not wholly justified.

Cass Wouters (1986:1–18) suggests that this deformalization and 'decontrolling' was made possible by the efficiency of previously imposed restraints. His view accords with that of Elias ([1939] 1978), who maintained that the abandoning of controls was possible 'because the level of habitual, technical and institutionally consolidated self-control' was previously established. Elias considered the reversal a 'relaxation within the framework of an already established standard' (140). The implication here is that a person is behaving in a new way because he is still anchored in the old way. The argument may be based on an unwillingness to part with historical continuity. It is a little like saying that Johnny dares to be bad because he is basically good. If Johnny was not basically good then his bad behaviour would ruin the social order. But what both Elias and Wouters may be ignoring is that the decade of the 1960s was not controlled by those who authored the cultural revolution. A tremendous resistance was mounted by the establishment, especially by those of its members who controlled business interests that were totally in opposition to the notion of communalism. A decivilizing process did not occur not only because the notion of civilized behaviour was sufficiently anchored in the human psyche, but because many continued to remain inhibited and in control while the spontaneous went on their freedom trip. While a certain number tuned in and dropped out, the majority continued doing their work, fixing the plumbing, carrying the garbage to the dumps, putting out fires, and so on. The economic survival imperative, together with the absence of a clear communalistic plan, prevented the cultural revolutionaries from taking their wishes and needs to their limit. So to look back and say that some of the wild and unrestrained behaviour was due to hyperefficient previous restraints is to reveal a need to preserve theoretical consistency at all costs. We still do not know at what point a substantial decivilizing process is set in motion.

The price paid for this social reformation was a mistrust of rules. A rule must be grounded in a cultural meaning that goes beyond the rule itself. And that meaning must be felt and revered as a social good that extends across generations. Otherwise, the rule becomes culturally meaningless or, at best, the limited codex of a subculture. What occurred in the 1960s and 1970s was that, due to the special time frame in which they found themselves, youth observed that the rules of justice, equality, and communal caring had become demeaned by a culture of rapid change and expediency. While their complaint was against expediency and its moral lapses, they made an associative error and concluded that the concept of a rule was to be met with suspicion. Not only was the outcome of the American ethical tradition put in question but also the national spirit and emotional discipline that had traditionally been used to uphold that tradition. Lasch-Quinn (1999), in her study of race relations in America, has reviewed these changes in behaviour and believes that the rebellion against formality and authority, and its linking with human rights, problematized subsequent efforts to associate morality with manners. This uncoupling did not facilitate understanding between liberal and conservative factions. As Suzanne Staggenborg (1999) has observed, social conservatives interpreted the actions of the counterculture as an 'abdication of social responsibility in favor of self-interest' (60). Mistrust of motives was rampant on both sides of the culture divide.

Human awareness increases in periods of dissonance; the existence of contrasts and contradictions between ideals and reality makes self-reflexivity and the calculation of risks particularly urgent (Giddens [1991] 2001:182). In such times, no formulas can be easily applied to all groups and ages. Contingency follows from greater personal awareness and increased choice. Early Americans had to resist the aristocratic customs of the Old World that they had left behind. The new frontier environment demanded new reactions. Similarly, the youth of the late 1950s, 1960s, and early 1970s became a modern version of the early pioneers. Reacting to what America had become, they asked for a renewed social contract. The burning of flags and the guerrilla discourtesy should not make us blind to the fact that many of their ideas were similar to the ideas of those who drew up the original American Declaration of Rights.

We notice in this critique of American bourgeois society a deep disillusionment that contains the same elements of Romanticism that appeared in England during the Industrial Revolution. Robin Campbell ([1987] 1993) goes so far as to locate the rise of a distinct modern personality in the intersection of eighteenth-century sensibility and nineteenth-century Romanticism. The act of willing emotion according to preference rather than externally determined propriety standards gave individuals a fairly rudimentary 'autonomous control of emotional expression' (75). Romantics contributed to the growth of a separation between personal preference and social norms by assigning special moral worth to a 'belief-dependent emotionality' quite different from a moral sensibility that conforms to external moral standards. *Passion*, especially when connected to indignation over social conditions, became legitimized in this growing movement towards individualism and was considered part of the reformation of social conscience rather than a purely self-interested egoism. Whether the Romantic was passionately working to improve social conditions or withdrawing from the world in order to preserve his creative and moral character, he could consider his social role as one of heightened commitment to long-term civilizational progress.

Ernest Bernbaum (1962) has astutely located the logic underlying the character of the Romantic, a character given to viewing the private and public worlds as separate (and often irreconcilable) realms: 'One was the world of ideal truth, good news and beauty: this was eternal, infinite, and also absolutely real. The other was the world of actual appearance, which to common sense was the only world, and which to the idealist was so obviously full of untruth, ignorance, evil, ugliness and wretchedness, as to compel him to dejection and indignation' (91). Lionel Trilling (1971) has similarly described the Romantic personality as harbouring an 'intense and adverse imagination of the culture in which it had its being' (ix). J. Gaudefroy-Demombynes (1966) also describes turn-of-the-century Romanticism as an oppositional passion: 'a way of feeling, a state of mind in which sensibility and imagination predominate over reason; it tends towards individualism, revolt, escape, melancholy and fantasy' (138).

The passionate belief in humankind's ability to transform social reality through the use of personal imagination and genius leads to a high valuation of heroic action. It also renders the Romantic vulnerable to sudden disappointment. The revolution in manners and morals set in motion after the the First World War and again in the 1960s was not simply a consequence of the desire for hedonistic experiences, but the manifestation of the high expectations of a generation raised on Romantic idealism.

When all the various factors that caused the cultural revolution of the 1960s and 1970s are considered, what is singularly striking is that many young Americans were experiencing strong emotional pain and anger *and* showing it. The 'unrestraining' of emotion in America played a paramount role in the rise of present-day American civility. It might not have been as easily achieved in a society not founded on the principles of individual autonomy and a Declaration of Independence that provided for the continual renegotiation of individual rights. It would also have been difficult to achieve in a society habituated to the deferential protocols of vertical associations founded on the traditions of aristocratic caste distinctions and/or strong intergenerational continuities.

The radical Scottish psychiatrist R.D. Laing, highly popular in America, expressed this generational disjuncture in his various works that challenged conventional psychiatry's definition of schizophrenia. In *Politics of Experience and the Bird of Paradise* (1967) he expressed his conviction – acquired through years of work with the mentally ill – that mental illness was the consequence of abnormal communications rituals taking place in disordered families and societies that had legitimized psychological disorder. What was considered normal by majority consensus was not necessarily normal from the perspective of individual sensibility and need. Many 'normal' social practices were precisely what drove sensitive people who could not adapt to social abnormality into the safety and protection of madness. While Laing did not give enough attention to the biochemical roots of certain forms of schizophrenia and psychosis, he had a profound influence on how psychiatry and psychotherapy were to be practised in the latter part of the twentieth century. He authored the idea of the 'innocent victim' and had a profound influence on the way Western courts would handle offenders. Family psychological history became an important consideration in the judicial process. In chapter three, entitled 'The Mystification of Experience,' Laing condemned the 'normal' family as a 'mutual protection racket,' whose primary purpose was to create 'a false consciousness of security; to deny death by avoiding life ... to promote respect, conformity, obedience' (55).

At no time in history had there been so much change as occurred during the period 1850 to 1960. The 1960s was the point of culmination. Demographic and technical changes radically altered human relationships. The 'generation gap' initially appeared not only due to moral disagreement but because different generations with different experiences came to occupy the same time frame in history. Members of the new generation realized that their parents had not experienced youth in the same way they were experiencing it and, consequently, could not offer relevant and reliable advice. A new environment made some of the advice they were receiving seem outdated. Moreover, they took to resisting their influence because some of the practices they wished to adopt stood in direct opposition to the established ways and ideas of their elders.

This spirit of 'opposition' was also noticeable in corporations. Many of the younger executives began 'talking back' and arguing with the older guard in the name of a new management paradigm. Nowhere was the corporate struggle between the late baby boomers and their parents more visible than in the advertising industry, many of whose members were now making vocal demands for 'creative freedom.' Agencies became split between those who took creative risks and those who preferred to remain with 'tried and proven' hard-sell methods (Goldman 1997). The one ad that aptly symbolizes the revolt in the corporate world and the search for emancipatory communications was Jeremy Sinclair's ad created for the British Family Planning Association. The ad shows a pregnant man in profile. Above the picture is a headline: 'Would you be more careful if it was you that got pregnant?' (29). Although the creative movement in advertising was a distinct outcome of English pop art, it soon arrived in America and was adopted by a new breed of copywriters and art directors who considered the creative integrity of the ad sometimes more important than its ability to sell the advertised product. Ironically, the creators of the engine of capitalism were nonetheless affected by a Romantic neo-Marxism that made them at once supporters of capitalism as well as reformers of it. Many advertising writers and art directors began producing public service advertisements that moralized about social issues. The idealism of the counterculture is apparent in the ads that appeared in the late 1960s and early 1970s. One ad, which won an award for public service in advertising, showed a graveyard under a headline that read, 'Peace: It can work with live people too.' Humour, hard-hitting drama, and social commentary were combined to sensitize consumers. When a young copywriter came up with the original slogan for the Volkswagen Beetle, drawing a pencil outline of the car with the headline 'Think small,' he was not only selling the car but bringing attention to the intelligent use of natural resources. Not being the owners of the capital invested in the products they advertised, advertising agencies played a seminal role in altering corporate conceptions of the consumer.

That the rebellion of the 1960s would lose its edge was predictable considering that the leaders of the movement did not resort to violent revolution and remained dependent on the cooperation of the establishment. Nevertheless, a major transformation in society had taken place; although the elders resisted at first, they eventually heeded the complaints of the youth protesters. The systemic nature of this development is demonstrated by the fact that by the mid-1970s many of the parents' generation had adopted some of the fashions and mores pioneered by their children. A partial mutual colonization had taken place.

Thus, an important outcome of the 1960s was an increasing tendency on the part of parents to recognize the emotional issues affecting their children. This increased intimacy also freed parents to reveal their own emotional issues. Prior generations had done their best to ensure that unpleasant adult topics did not reach the ears of children and teenagers. A Victorian parent did not readily admit to having conflicts with his or her own parents. The adage 'Children should be seen not heard' was designed not simply to make children invisible but to keep them from claiming the right to critically participate in adult discussions and, eventually, criticize their own parents.

In the 1960s, however, many youth, in a bid to rationalize and share their own preferences and insights, took on the role of family 'psychoanalysts' trying to 'liberate' their fathers and mothers from the restraints that had supposedly constricted their lives. 'Loosen-up, mom' would have been considered presumptive advice and provoked the ire of elders in former times. In the America of the 1960s such familiarity appealed to some of the younger parents who were also beginning to suspect that America had indeed become 'uptight.' The young were referring to two characteristics of Americans who were over thirty: a tendency to be 'square' – to try and categorize everything according to unbending conceptions of good and bad – and an observable 'tightness' in their demeanour that revealed that the restraints that they had been made to internalize had stunted their spontaneity and emotional expression. When the hippies arrived on the scene many all-American fathers were still shaking hands with their sons rather than giving them a hug; a pat on the back was sufficient indication of affection.

Some of the most heated arguments occurred between new mothers of the 1960s and 1970s and their own mothers concerning the manner in which they had been raised and the different manner in which they wished to raise their own children. Threatened by a more liberal childrearing ethic, the older parental generation remained ambivalent towards the new permissiveness, thereby driving a further wedge between the generations.

Theodore Roszak (1979) understood the full brunt of the meaning of this period: 'We live in a time when the very private experience of having a personal identity to discover, a personal identity to fulfill, has become a subversive political force of major proportions' (xxviii). This generalized confrontation with tradition had multiple effects: (1) a steady rejection of authority through the mocking of precedent and the use of authority-demeaning shock tactics (some of the youth of the

1960s revelled in being called 'freaks' and deliberately tried to offend the well-heeled members of the establishment); (2) a peculiar aura of 'pleased defiance' in media representations of individuals seeking new 'experiences' and new 'moral and emotional frontiers' (in video clips from the period we notice not only the public exhibition of new forms of behaviour but a defiant pleasure in such exhibition); and (3) a doubt-based intellectual debate regarding the origins and nature of 'fixity' and its ultimate reliability and legitimacy. A culture of historical retribution had come into being, one that has survived to this day.

Many social historians who describe the 1960s as a generalized Western phenomenon minimize the fact that the issues facing American youth were considerably different from those facing their European counterparts. American youth embarked on a substantial re-evaluation of their heritage, contemplating social issues as varied as America's race problem (a problem that dated back to a society that had used slaves on its soil), the Vietnam war (a war that was killing thousands of American youth, especially those with no funds to stay in college and receive a draft deferral), the claims of Native Americans, the rising powers of American corporations, and the ambitions of an expansionist government. European youth were not saddled with such a complicated history of social injustice. Britain, for example, had already decided to play a limited role in world affairs after its involvement in the Suez Canal crisis in 1958 (Briggs 1987:358). Moreover, the British parliament had passed a series of bills that distinguished between the realms of 'public and private morality,' deciding that private morality was not to be the business of government legislation. This conciliatory spirit may have helped contain the hippie movement as a minority movement – when one of the members of the Rolling Stones was sentenced to imprisonment for drug offences, a national poll indicated that 85 per cent of British teenagers either agreed with the sentence or thought it too lenient (361). Reaction in America to the court judgment was considerably more hostile. Meanwhile, when Charles Manson was convicted of masterminding the August 1969 killings of actress Sharon Tate and others in her entourage, some American youth took to protesting that one of their idols was being framed by the government (Bugliosi and Gentry 2001).

All this is not to say that the cultural revolution of the 1960s did not radically affect European nations. Far from it. We are only suggesting that it affected the United States in a manner that was particularly American. Tilly (2004) demonstrates that social movements are not restricted to an age or geographical region but are necessary and reoccurring vehicles for social change. Contrary to 'new social movement' theorists, such as Alain Touraine, Claus Offe, and Jurgen Habermas, Tilly demonstrates, as did Craig Calhoun (1993), that what are termed 'identity movements' had roots that went back long before the 1960s, even as far back as the nineteenth century (Tilly 2004:69–71). Yet, a comparison of the issues that preoccupied the youth of the 1960s in various countries reveals that although American youth shared many issues in common with their European counterparts (e.g., educational reform, peace, economic justice), they went beyond those issues to address the core nature of the self. This was a new development that would have far-reaching consequences.

One of those consequences, most observable in the United States, was the discovery and expression of considerable personal emotional pain. Although Elias [1939] 1978) did not underestimate the long-range traumas of socialization when, in deference to the Freudian model, he admitted that certain individuals carry scars from the restraints they have been forced to internalize, he maintained that most individuals fared quite satisfactorily in the end (243). We question this conclusion because much personal pain has been expressed during the last four decades. As we will argue later, a generation that attempted to reform society discovered at the eleventh hour that it did carry the scars of the past, not only the scars of its own childhood but the accumulated scars of American history. This emotional awakening had far-reaching effects on social norms, civility, and social philosophy. It certainly pointed Americans in a direction that was not at all imagined by the French youth who managed to bring the French economy to a standstill in 1968.

**The Freeing of the Expressive Body**

Social scientists who focus on textual research (as we have done in chapters 1 to 7) run the risk of ignoring ongoing developments in popular culture. What C. Wright Mills (1959) termed 'methodological inhibition' has prevented many serious scholars from considering the intimate relationships between popular culture, individual psychology, and social structure. American sociologists have particularly been vulnerable to ignoring the massive effects of popular media. Aghast at some of the 'easy fixes' offered up by media inspirational speakers, they have discounted the substantial influence these speakers have had on social norms and outcomes. For example, TV personality Oprah Winfrey, commanding a daily audience of over 60 million viewers, has as much influence on the social standards and behaviour of a population as any politician or social philosopher – in the short run at least.

Anthony Giddens has taken into account the close connections between social change and popular culture. In *Modernity and Self-Identity* ([1991] 2001) he has listed the major 'dilemmas' of the self in late modernity as it faces the demands of ideological, psychological, and systemic changes. The rise of the late-modern concept of selfhood has occurred in the intersection of four basic mutually antagonistic forces: 'unification versus fragmentation, powerlessness versus appropriation, authority versus uncertainty, and personalized versus commodified experience' (180–201).

These contraindications have led to a culture of increasing 'risk.' Contingency and the eclipsing of authority by a market-driven economy have broadened the field of human experience and caused fragmentation within previously unified local habitats (189). Yet, this fragmentation has also had unitary effects, for it has released aspects of personal and collective existence that may have been previously repressed. As markets have expanded and ignored 'pre-established forms of behaviour' they have promoted an individualism that has become entrusted with servicing the problematic of its newborn identity and responsibilities (197). The resulting (and necessary) 'self-reflexivity' has been a peculiar characteristic of the late-modern self which has been forced to construct its identity in a fragmented world in which the authority of tradition and elders has become replaced by the multiple and conflicting views of 'experts' (195).

In such a contingent culture, the individual is forced to anchor himself in a self-referential piecing-together of 'meaning.' Scepticism is an outcome of such uncertainty. As the control of a central political and moral authority decreases in the face of rival minority groups, the individual is given more responsibility to control his own life. And that control is made possible only when there is a life plan available, a process through which the person can keep track of where he is in the narrative of his life at any given moment. An individual has to ask questions that are often intensely personal: Where am I in my own existence? How am I feeling? Am I satisfied or not? How can I help myself to feel more satisfied? To whom do I belong?

And these were, indeed, the questions that emerged from the American cultural revolution of the 1960s. When members of the counterculture came up against the formidable military policing power of the American state during their failed protests at Kent State in 1970 and the Democratic National Convention in 1968, they realized that social change would have to be brought about through alternative means. It was rationalized that if one could not directly change society then one could change it by changing oneself. The self that had been manipulated by social forces and the interests of elites could be liberated from the controls imposed on it. It was hoped that this liberation would ultimately transform society. Direct political activism was supplemented by the *discovery and reformation of the self*. The transformation of the self became a form of social protest.

The 'socialization' of the American consumer had been based on the premise that it was best to form the consumer's behaviour in order to save him from self-destructive tendencies. New therapies emerged in the 1960s, however, claiming exactly the opposite. Many therapists were deeply influenced by the work of Wilhelm Reich, a member of Freud's circle. According to Reich ([1950] 1964, 1973), human nature was not a cauldron of destructive primitive instincts. On the contrary, it was the repression of normal drives and their bio-physical energy that twisted human personality. Reich maintained that the 'libido' could be repressed only at great cost to human society. He held that a person whose bio-energetic integrity was left intact would not react in destructive ways. Reich's contribution to our understanding of the 'civilizing process' was enormous. According to him, excessive restraint was anything but civilizing.

Reich's ideas inspired a new school of psychotherapy and personal growth work that gave considerable attention to the body and to emotions. An institution that attracted a considerable number of the therapists and seminar leaders who contributed to the 'self-transformation movement' was the Esalen Institute in California. Fritz Perls ([1959] 1980), who had been trained by Reich, developed a 'gestalt-oriented' therapy that sought to liberate self-expression in the interest of creating a whole person. Perls insisted that the liberation of emotions and repressed thoughts would empower the individual and make him whole. In countless encounter groups participants learned to 'take responsibility' for the unknown part of their innermost thoughts and feelings, become familiar with them, and learn to express them. 'Honesty' of feeling and the recognition of the body as a memory bank of trauma (and intuitive wisdom) became the common denominator of a variety of therapies (Rothschild 2000). This was perhaps the first time in the post-Victorian era that the body was seen as an acting, feeling, *and* thinking entity. While Spinoza ([1677] 1959) had heroically attempted to reverse Descartes's splitting of the mind and the body in his passionate plea that mind and body were one and under the dominion of God, it was the Cartesian view of the body as a mechanism apart from the mind that had dominated much of early twentieth-century thinking.

Thousands of practitioners became influenced by the ground-breaking work done at Esalen. Workshops were offered in psychotherapy, body-awareness training, and massage. It was thought that liberation of feeling would increase a person's capacity to feel joy (Schutz 1967). It was further thought that the reclaiming of the emotional self could become a political means for resisting the conformist values of a corporate and political environment built on the moulding of a narrowly defined, repressive national character.

This new 'therapeutic movement' put a tremendous amount of pressure on the individual to take responsibility for his own psychological and spiritual growth. Conformity to communal values became paralleled (and frequently contraindicated) by personal growth and the need to discover and build the 'authentic self.' This reversion to emotional authenticity had considerable social consequences. It established an irreconcilable tension between a presentation of self that was focused on the comfort of 'the other,' the central pillar of courtesy, and a presentation of self that remained loyal to personal desire and emotion. While the Victorians had believed that excessive sincerity could create embarrassment in social discourse, the American therapeutic culture agreed to pay the cost of unease despite the nineteenth-century American consensual ideal of being 'at all times at ease' and 'agreeable.'

American corporations responded to this new diversity by heeding the writings of Abraham Maslow (1962, 1975), who had developed a hierarchy of 'types' and 'needs.' Corporate marketing researchers now focused on the most important need of the new consumer: *self-actualization*. The resulting marketing, named 'values and lifestyles,' was made possible by the development of varied and smaller manufacturing runs that allowed corporations to service a variety of preferences. Diversity – what had begun as a direct frontal attack on the corporation – became corporate America's greatest ally. By encouraging 'individualism' the corporation began servicing the varied desires of individuals and remained a central player in cultural tastes.

The etiquette books of the 1980s and 1990s reflected this growing emotional expressiveness and the belief that authorship of the self was a personal undertaking. Letitia Baldridge's (1987) *Complete Guide to a Great Social Life* contained considerable advice on matters such as self-esteem and the art of becoming comfortable with one's aloneness. Baldridge offered advice that went beyond etiquette and good manners. Reassuring her reader that self-improvement needed not be dependent on wealth or social position, she advised: 'The fact that any kind of improvement – physical, spiritual, or intellectual – is *completely up to you* should give you a certain sense of power' (121–2). In all sections of the book, including chapters on entertaining, making friends, and being a success at work, parallel advice was dispensed on how to handle insecurities, fears, and uncertainties connected to personal issues. No assumption was made that the reader would not require such advice. The book was a good example of how the therapeutic mentality of self-healing and self-creation had become integrated into literature on conduct.

We are suggesting that 'self-referentiality' is not only the consequence of a democratic social ethic that recognizes the claims of the individual, but also a direct cause of an American 'therapeutic mentality' that treats personal feeling and desire with extreme seriousness. *'What do I want to be?'* – a question more appropriate to a career decision – has been transformed into: *'Who do I want to be?'* a question that, by its very nature, requires decisions about the manner in which one relates to oneself and others beyond assigned roles and responsibilities. This orientation towards self is even noticeable in the manner in which American evangelical religions have used faith in therapeutic ways (Rieff 1966).

Although he does not substantially refer to the American therapeutic movement, Giddens (1991) distinguishes between the 'feeling real self' and 'unfeeling unreal self.' According to him, the search for personal integrity becomes at once a search for 'authenticity':

> To be able to act authentically is more than just acting in terms of a self-knowledge that is as valid and full as possible; it means also disentangling – in Laing's terms – the true from the false self. As individuals we are not able to 'make history' but if we ignore our inner experience we are condemned to repeat it, prisoners of traits which are inauthentic because they emanate from feelings and past situations imposed on us by others (especially in early childhood). The watchword in self-therapy is 'recover or repeat.' (79)

This search for emotional authenticity is accompanied by the desire not to repeat precedent or, at least, drive its reverberating effects out of one's system. The past comes to represent a disintegrative and limiting experience for certain individuals – their reactions to that realization greatly affect their private and public behaviour. Certainly, some become cynical of any communally proposed project, preferring to adopt a 'live and let live' philosophy.

The American movement towards an emotionally expressive person was slow to take root in Britain. English growth therapies followed softer approaches that did not require extensive emotional expression. The English preferred to restrain their emotions while using more talk-oriented methods of personal growth. The French, who had been used to expressing their emotions frequently, saw no need to go in search of the 'well' from which their emotions emerged.

A social standard can last for a long time as long as it is perceived as 'legitimate' or 'inevitable.' But when certain practices and standards are perceived as incompatible with other valued ideals and practices, then a period of uncertainty follows as old practices are shifted to the background and new ones brought to the fore. The luxury to demand such correlation between ideal and actual practice is an outcome of prosperous democracies, especially those that are pressured by competing interests to revise older systems of subjugation, or those, such as the United States, that have assigned a premium to the quality of 'sincerity.'

America was highly vulnerable to the type of social critiques that emerged from its own shores as well as from Europe. Europeans had a long history of subjugation. They also possessed long-standing traditions that assured national and cultural identity based on a continuance of customs balanced by measured innovations in style. There did not exist a strong enough antipathy between the old and the new as there did in America, a country that had purposefully rejected the Old World in order to create itself in its own image. The 'politeness' of the English (together with their emotional restraint) and the 'style' of the French (together with their honouring of individualism and their acceptance of occasional and quickly forgiven outbursts of emotion) were deeply ingrained. Continental disbelief in historical justice did not immediately or necessarily require a remarkable degradation in social relations. Europeans therefore could integrate the onslaught of the postmodern European social critiques without throwing their own codes of interpersonal discourse off-balance. Furthermore, intellectual dissent (and philosophical discussion) was a long-standing practice of European society and accepted as a necessary social activity. Radical groups were tolerated by the mainstream and considered part of social discourse. Members of the bourgeoisie adopted whatever ideas they wanted and left the rest. They were habituated to having philosophical discussions about life and society, ideas that were not immediately measured by their social usefulness. So, philosophizing about the futility of things did not immediately render actual personal and private behaviour dysfunctional. Counteracting this intellectual nihilism was a strong sense of national identity based on a long-standing pride in European civilization and its aesthetic accomplishments.

The social critiques emanating from Europe found their way into U.S. universities, dealing a considerable blow to American certainty. Only history will tell whether the European philosophers of the twentieth century helped America emancipate itself or caused excessive doubt and guilt. Many American intellectuals took the premises of the 'poststructuralist' and 'postmodern' writers and applied them ruthlessly to their own cultural history, causing a considerable disenchantment with established American values and practices.

The French were able to integrate Michel Foucault's ([1966] 1970, 1979) merciless commentaries on the structures of power and knowledge while still believing in the age-old sanctity of individual freedom, a privilege that they attributed to the French Revolution. Not much was being said that already had not been said by French writers of the Enlightenment. The French were singularly conscious of the trade-off that they had accepted between the ideals of the revolution and their need for social order. French intellectuals had always published in mainstream newspapers, and their presence was normalized by such public exposure.

Similarly, in Britain, a population given to valuing 'liberty' of speech was not overly perturbed by iconoclasm; members of the British aristocracy have always reminded the population of the meaning of 'liberty' through their own outrageous acts. Eccentricity in Britain was not associated with misanthropy towards the community. English intellectuals were less given to searching for radical re-evaluations of modernity. While the humanist portions of Marx's writings had appealed to members of the English New Left, the country had respected Marx's socialism while steering clear of radical Soviet Marxism. French writers, on the other hand, had to deal with Marxist writer Louis Althusser's insistence that humanism and Marxism were quite unrelated. As far as Althusser was concerned, any observable coherence in history was the product not of individual actors but of the systems of influence and power in which they were placed (Marwick 1998).

While England managed to respond to those parts of the postmodern writings that it found useful, American intellectuals chose to consider the totality of their implications; America's social and political environment at the time, one of 'rights affirmation,' predisposed it to become substantially self-critical and considerably categorical. Ontological uncertainty was the ultimate product of such unforgiving scrutiny of the human psyche. English social theory later made up for lost ground, but, in the period when the original 'postmodern' literature appeared, American academics were particularly ready for a decentring project. In America, a generation emerging from public schools that did not properly teach American history, let alone European history, was suddenly made to read the intellectual products of European countries out of context. Most American youth starting university, unfamiliar with what Voltaire had meant by *the infamous thing*, or with the writings of their own American pragmatists, were suddenly waddling through the abstract and maddeningly elegant writings of thinkers such as Kierkegaard, Foucault, and Sartre. The Europeanization of the American academy was a jarring change that further destabilized American moral fixity. For a young nation like America such dislocation, doubt, and disagreement had unbalancing consequences, for many of its hopes for a just society were based on early pre-industrial American communalism and the sanctity of populist consensus.

That many American academics responded favourably to the European theorists was understandable considering the rising American intellectual discontent with the authoritarian consequences of fixity and tradition. The new claims of minority groups and a growing awareness of the injustices of past American racial, gender, political, and economic policies motivated academics to be open to the new social critiques. Moreover, these critiques gave them an opportunity to become socially active. The social sciences had been late responding to the social issues that plagued U.S. society; they now galvanized to make up for lost time.

What also facilitated the entry of European social theory into the U.S. academic market was a precedent set by the American philosophy of pragmatism. Pragmatists did not regard 'practice' as an automatic consequence of a fixed reality, but as an opportunity to develop procedures that could potentially lead to positive social benefits (Dewey 1910, 1929; James 1890, [1897] 1977, 1909; Peirce [1869] 1931–58, [1877] 1986). These pragmatists held that the search for truth should not eclipse the search for human happiness. In fact, they remained sceptical of the entire idea of searching for a Platonic convergence of truth and reality.

This ambivalence towards an essential truth capable of standing above human action required a continuing suspicion of dogma as well as the categorical dualities often necessary for the categorization of 'truths.' For William James (1909), one of the principal strengths of pragmatism lay in its ability to depart from a priori dogma in favour of empirical investigation. James questioned any body of foundational 'truth' that could not (or would not) allow proper empirical verification. Similarly, Pierce ([1877] 1986) held that the understanding of an idea is an interpretative act because it is inexorably tied to the observation of effects. In his essay 'On the Grounds and Validity of the Laws of Logic' (1869, 5:416–34) he argued that 'logic' was an outcome of human meaning and the only referent that could be successfully used in the analysis of various relationships between various signs. According to Peirce, the function of pragmatic inquiry was to shed light on how conceptions of 'the real' (that which we believe exists regardless of interpretation) play a constraining role on the inquiry process (5:433–4). In stating this, Peirce stood in transformative relation with Darwinism – logic was the one element that permitted a rationalization of a human progress not limited to species-specific evolution.

Pragmatism was a bold move against American traditionalism. Loyalty to tradition implies the acceptance of discomfort and even dissonance. Tradition is maintained for reasons that sometimes require the rejection of change and abstention from the enjoyment of novelty. Sometimes even the search for happiness must be tempered in favour of a lesser but more lasting contentment. Instrumental thought is anathema to the traditionalist because it transforms hierarchical knowledge in favour of a more horizontal, pluralistic social mentality. Robert L. Duffus, writing in the *New York Times* (3 May 1925), welcomed Dewey's philosophy: 'It is natural, in a sense, for such a vigorous and life-loving faith to develop on the soil of a new and youthful nation' (cited in Longley, Silverstein, and Tower 1960:212).

Cornell West (1989), in *The American Evasion of Philosophy: A Genealogy of Pragmatism*, reminds us that pragmatism, regardless of its particular hue, is not given to favouring grand theory or philosophizing for the sake of philosophizing. Any intellectual activity that stands outside practice becomes suspect. At its best, it provides the means for a cultural critique that furthers individual rights and individual growth within a culture of tolerance.

This allergy towards idealism and vertical associations has had a salient effect on the degree to which intellect is valued. In *Anti-Intellectualism in American Life* (1963), Richard Hofstadter states that democracy has a levelling effect on elitist intellectualizing: 'Again and again, but particularly in recent years, it has been noticed that intellect in America is resented as a kind of excellence, as a claim to distinction, as a challenge to egalitarianism, as a quality which almost certainly deprives a man or woman of the common touch' (48–50).

Surveying a variety of late-modern (and postmodern) social theorists (Marcuse 1964; Marcuse, Wolff, and Moore 1969; Foucault [1966] 1970); Derrida 1967a, 1967b, 1967c), we find a series of characteristics common to postmodern social philosophy: (1) it is anti-epistemological; (2) it distrusts essentialism; (3) it negates the accuracy of 'realism'; (4) it is anti-foundationalist; (5) it does not accept 'knowledge' as a reliable indicator of reality; (6) it rejects the idea of 'truth' as representation of reality; (7) it questions the habitual terminologies of disciplines; (8) it suspects 'grand narratives' and does not believe in systemic structural homeostasis; (9) it considers 'reason' anything but neutral or objective; (10) it shows scepticism towards 'words' that have come to take on fixed ideological connotations; (11) it is sceptical of the idea of an autonomous subject; (12) it is reluctant to accord great value to the project of the Enlightenment.

Allan Bloom (1987) has made the useful observation that European philosophy became Americanized when it reached the U.S. academies. While it was used to re-examine American social values, it was also edited to extract what appealed to American critics in the European literature of 'despair' (147–8). This distinction is important, for much of European literature, especially French literature, had made an art form of existential despair. Readers were able to read these works and feel inspired by them; however, the literature had quite a different effect on idealistic Americans raised on a civility diet of directness and optimistic practicality.

**The Therapeutic Society**

The sense of contingency and relativism promoted by the postmodern debate has had considerable effects on social interaction. A culture of rights and entitlements has emerged from the uncompromising critique of tradition, considerably affecting standing notions of communal bonds.

While every culture in history has caused pain to its children through the imperatives of the socialization process – a process considerably reliant on the impositions of prohibitions, restraints, and roles that contradict the child's need for unlimited pleasure and unconditional love – these pains have been compensated for through the consolations of a network of supportive kin. In extended family networks, a youngster who has been castigated by his parent can turn to an uncle or aunt or grandparent for distraction and consolation. Similarly, a spouse who is having marital difficulties can receive encouragement and strength by talking to a trusted cousin or uncle or sibling. Such advice received from kin is different and usually more conciliatory than advice received from friends, who may not have an investment in keeping the extended family intact.

Émile Durkheim (1953) took note of how social bonds play a seminal role in social organization. He found that the desires of the self and its need for communal associations should be balanced: 'The human personality is a sacred thing; one does not violate it nor infringe its bounds, while at the same time the greatest good is in communion with others' (37). Giddens (1991) has issued a similar warning to late-modern Western society: 'The inability to take a serious interest in anything other than shoring up the self makes the pursuit of intimacy a futile endeavour' (173).

Yet, 'self-centredness' – one of the traits least favoured by courtesy conduct writers – has been the unavoidable outcome of a culture that seeks 'authentic' social bonds to satisfy the emotional needs of the self. It has also been a consequence of rapid change – thrown into an anonymous crowd whose tastes and practices are constantly and rapidly changing, the individual has been saddled with the onerous task of imitating those in the crowd who have developed a reputation or 'fame' capable of withstanding change. The worship of celebrity culture, so prevalent in America, not only is an obsession with gossip, but also indicates the desire of individuals to find some measure of 'fame' (familiarity between themselves and others). The meteoric rise of American websites such as MySpace and YouTube have responded to this need by allowing individuals to create their own profiles and manage their own public identities. The outrageous names and profiles posted on these sites attest to the individual's desire to outdo others who are saddled with the same social burden: how to exist and be original in a culture that prizes originality and bravado over depth and substance.

Expectedly, the search for personal satisfaction has led to a certain deformalization in civil interactions. Such decrease in 'formality' between genders – a consequence of a variety of economic, ideological, and emotional factors – has contributed to the release of thoughts and emotions which in previous eras, such as the Victorian period, might have been referred to obliquely but kept under restraint. Couples have come to expect that a true loving bond requires the maintenance of passion, love, and mutual kindness over a long period of time. Positive emotional expression and 'open sharing' become the new standard, confounding many who used to content themselves with performing their marriage duties without considering the complexity and contingency involved in maintaining romantic love over the period of a lifetime.

A major issue in relationships has been the emerging identity of women. As early as 1965, Betty Friedan had questioned women's acceptance of their traditional role as homebound nurturers. In *The Feminine Mystique* (1965) she wrote of her own search for a 'purpose' in life that went beyond caretaking. While men were given to asking themselves professional questions such as '*What* do I want to be?' Friedan asked, '*Who* do I want to be?' The question addressed not only the division of labour in marriage, but a woman's search for validation in the creative arena of work in a male-dominated culture. Additionally, it addressed the emotional needs of a woman who managed to liberate herself from the constructed mysteries that had kept femininity within bounded definitions. Germaine Greer (1970) took up the same theme in *The Female Eunuch*. Gloria Steinem, co-founder and editor of *Ms* magazine, became another dynamic activist for women's rights. Steinem's website still carries a quote from one of her interviews given a couple of decades ago: 'I have yet to hear a man ask for advice on how to combine marriage and a career.' Her more recent works include *Revolution from Within: A Book of Self-Esteem* (1992). The feminist project has tried to address a variety of issues, including career management, family planning, choice of lifestyle, and sexual preference. Men have also been faced with similarly complex role conflicts even though the men's movement has lost some of its impetus.

Giddens ([1991] 2001) explains these new romantic liaisons as 'pure relationships' that are considerably different from former duty-bound relations. In a 'pure relationship' participants frequently measure their level of happiness and wonder if they are receiving feedback that coincides with their needs and their image of themselves:

Yet, pure relationships, and the nexus of intimacy in which they are involved, create enormous burdens for the integrity of the self. In so far as a relationship lacks external referents, it is morally mobilised only through 'authenticity': the authentic person is one who knows herself and is able to reveal that knowledge to the other, discursively and in the behavioural sphere. To be in an authentic relation with another can be a major source of moral support ... But shorn of external moral criteria, the pure relationship is vulnerable as a source of security at fateful moments and at other major life transitions. (186–7)

This search for authenticity and personal satisfaction complicates the imposition of restraints based on traditional notions of 'duty' and 'function.' The prolific breadwinner who is emotionally unresponsive is rejected; so is the meticulous mother and keeper of the house who is satisfied measuring her worth by whether or not she has performed her duties competently. Freed a little from the restrictions of traditional gender-role definitions, the male–female relationship has fallen into considerable contingency. Bereft of the type of courtship codes used by the Victorians, late-modern women and men are left with their emotions as reference points. They not only must try to be authentic and loyal to their own inner feelings, but must also read the feelings of a potential or existing mate in order to ensure that both will not emerge from the contact less integrated than before.

Due to this search for emotional equity, many men and women have tried helping each other resolve issues that involve topics as diverse as childhood experience and the pressures of overwork. The new male–female relationship has become a heroic attempt to include in the relationship a therapeutic project that tries to heal centuries of alienation between the genders. This new 'familiarity' has had a profound influence on the practice of 'tact.' Tact permits the silencing of certain thoughts and feelings. The 'emotionally honest' relationship, however, requires the revelation of what might otherwise be kept silent. There is considerably less artifice – and considerably more opportunity to give and receive hurtful criticism.

Relationships have also come under the influence of the standards of a society of consumption. Roger Scruton (1999) believes that the subordination of relationships to a commodity culture has served to commodify sex, thereby turning love into an abstraction; such exchanges of companionship according to the rules of mutual consent and carefully measured value-exchange demeans the spiritual side of love and creates a void that, ironically, fuels further unproductive attempts at acquiring love as a commodity (57–63). Ironically, the act of measuring benefits acquired for the self prevents 'the losing of the self' in the act of romance.

Can the self find an ideal place of emotional balance when faced with the demands of competitive corporations and isolated nuclear families? Can there ever be enough time to sit back and take stock of one's feelings? In *The Second Shift* ([1989] 1997), her groundbreaking study of the dilemmas faced by working women, sociologist Arlie R. Hochschild observes that we are experiencing nothing short of a social revolution due to the massive entry of women into the workplace. Hochschild's study shows the two-way interactive relationship between economy and cultural values and habituations. The end result of economic pressure and continuing dissonance between the genders is a stressed family environment in which both fathers and mothers pay an emotional cost. The stress level seems higher in women:

> As the main managers of the second shift, women become the 'heavies,' the 'time and motion' persons of the family-and-work speed-up. They hurry children through their daily rounds – 'Hurry up and eat ...,' 'Hurry and get into your pajamas ...' – and thus often become the targets of children's aggression. (262)

Children's reactions to this hurried, time-hungry environment are usually extreme. They either withdraw or become excessively emotional and over-activated in order to gain attention or drain off the tension of pain. As Hoschschild observes wryly, a parent who has two children, each of whom has adopted a different coping mechanism, is stuck with a double stress and is forced into 'drawing the one out and calming the other down' (262).

Despite the glamorization of 'busy-ness,' this continuing race against the clock has important effects on civility. As Hochschild argues, home life becomes a stressing work environment, while, ironically enough, work outside the home becomes a respite. It is not surprising that such acute family stress leads many partners to separate from each other, in spirit if not in body.

It would seem, then, that the degree of expectation in a relationship affects the consequent degree of disappointment. In serial monogamy, both outgoing and incoming partners are vulnerable to the forces of emotional disagreement. A man and woman trying to have a successful relationship must do so within a culture in which cynicism and doubt regarding relationships is rampant. Few of the assurances given by the Victorians of the 1800s and the Americans of the 1950s are there to console and reassure potential partners. Moreover, a hyper-romanticizing of relationships in the media has contributed to a sentiment of deprivation since reality can never equal fiction. Even a relationship that might in other eras have been considered emotionally satisfying is measured against the models of romance and love emanating from storytellers and advertisers.

The American reversion to the naturalism of emotional expression has also had important consequences for the socialization of children. A review of American films from the 1960s to the present shows that the 'emotional volume' of interactions has been on a continual rise. 'Self-expression' has become the mantra of the post-1960s generations. Within this emotionally and ideationally vocal culture, there has been a parallel broadening of the range in which permissible child and youth 'talk-back' occurs. Childraising experts of previous eras would be shocked by the new American parenting, just as American parents would be stupefied by the comments of Dr John B. Watson ([1928] 1972), the American founder of behaviourism, who wrote the following advice to mothers in 1928:

> There is a sensible way of treating children. Treat them as though they were young adults. Dress them, bathe them with care and circumspection. Let your behaviour always be objective and kindly firm. Never hug and kiss them, never let them sit on your lap. If you must, kiss them once on the forehead when they say good night. Shake hands with them in the morning. (81–2)

Watson's view of childhood was not at all marginal in his era. This mechanized view of human behaviour (and the human body) paralleled the regimentation occurring in industry and American labour management methods. The obsession with 'functionality' as a prime evaluator of personality and action was a direct outcome of a philosophy of action that left emotions sorely neglected. While this repression of sentiment might on the surface appear as emotional restraint, it was actually emotional denial, for there is a difference between holding back known emotions in the interests of social order and denying those emotions that form an important part of the human constitution of 'primal needs.' The denial of an a priori consciousness by American behavioural psychologists was, in fact, a reversal of Victorian and American sentimentalism and romanticism. This materialistic view of human consciousness was the outgrowth of a high valuation of methodological efficiency and not connected to an idealistic meditation on human emotional happiness. It caused an outright neglect of the depth of human emotion and required a later easing of restraints.

The new respect for emotional sensitivity and a 'therapeutic' relationship between parents and children has had its opportunity costs. It has required considerable permissiveness, a consequence of which has been the development of a quasi-peer culture between some parents and children. As early as the 1940s, Geoffrey Gorer (1948) was observing that American parents were experiencing a strong desire to be loved, so strong that they would be willing to purchase that love by agreeing with their children's desires even when they knew that the immediate gratification of some of those desires may not be good for the children in the long run. This desire for consensus made parents open to the emerging anti-authoritarian popular philosophies. It also made them vulnerable to what could be commercially marketed in the name of 'personal emancipation,' 'responsible parenthood,' and the 'rights of the child.' And, most certainly, it made them unaware of the manner in which a child consumer culture was being installed in society and the power that this culture would have in placing additional stresses on the family.

This new liberalism in childrearing should also be seen in light of the 'ideologies' and 'self-interest' of the parents who subsequently reached child-bearing age in the 1960s and 1970s. John Rothschild and Susan Berns Wolf (1976) ask a disturbing question in their book *The Children of the Counter-Culture*. They wonder whether the flower children did not unintentionally neglect their children thinking this would give them the freedom that they themselves had not possessed and for which they had fought so bitterly and relentlessly. Their children, however, not having experienced the moral and political issues for which their parents had fought so passionately, might have interpreted the new 'laissez-faire' parenting as a lack of interest or lack of love. So one is left wondering about the opportunity costs of this new permissive American parenting. The consequences of the loosening of parental authority were not quite clear at the time; even today, it is a politically volatile issue, for each negative consequence seems to also have a positive side when compared with the parental cruelties of former eras.

Traditional cultures did not promise to understand their children; it was up to the child to understand adult society, appreciate the functional properties of its customs, and learn its codes of behaviour. Such cultures, although severe, at least provided the child with a continuing extended family and clarity regarding the behaviour expected of them. The codes kept parents restrained from seeking personal fulfillment at the cost of family solidarity. In post-1950s American society, however, adults had to increasingly learn what bedevilled them as well as their children. Children took to testing limits in a bid to see how far they could go in satisfying their own desires before receiving sanctions from their parents. In the presence of change, limits became negotiable and differed from family to family. It became current belief that youth itself was a troubled period, like some sort of medical disease that would hopefully cure itself over time. What was not seen, however, was that constant social negotiation of rights and permissions has an agitating effect on interactants, regardless of their age.

Such uncertainty put considerable pressure on individuals not to appear illegitimate in their claims of rights. There was a consequent fear of 'being judged.' 'Who are you to judge?' became the defensive reply of one who did not want to be assimilated by non-negotiable behavioural imperatives. That this reply has been sometimes delivered to the parent indicates how far the codes of restraint and deference have changed. It was always the parents' role to judge and evaluate the behaviour of their children; now this is considered by some as an abnormal desire for 'control.' This 'self-centred' attitude is further expressed through the popular belief (probably acquired as a result of failed confrontations in marriages) that a person should 'never try to change another.' The project of moral development becomes a personal one; missionary zeal, even that of a parent, becomes contraband, for it is based on faith in absolute values.

In late-modern American nuclear families, parents and children are asked to empathize with the needs of each other. The child takes on a parental duty and is asked to recognize that the happiness of his parents is as important as his own needs for an intact family. While in traditional cultures many children sought to please their parents by being 'good' (without having to think too much of their parents' emotional issues), many contemporary children have taken to measuring their interests against the demands of an inconsistent adult society.

Notwithstanding the novel solutions devised by parents for 'quality time,' it would seem that children who are left for long periods on their own because of the heavy work schedules of their parent(s) acquire an acute introspective space. In *Talking with Teens: The YMCA Parent and Teen Survey Final Report* (Global Strategy Group 2000) researchers found that for the 39.7 million American youth between the ages of 10 and 19 the foremost problem reported by them was insufficient time spent with their parents. In another report entitled *The Teens and Their Parents in the 21st Century: An Examination of Trends in Teen Behaviour and the Role of Parental Involvement* commissioned by the Council of Economic Advisers (2000), 'parental involvement' is singled out as the major deterrent for risky teen behaviour. In yet another report, entitled *Teen Risk-Taking: A Statistical Portrait* (Duberstein et al. 2000), the authors report that over 25 per cent of teens had seriously contemplated suicide.

Some other thought-provoking works that include even more worried views regarding the effects of a time-bound culture of self-fulfillment include: Jane M Healy's (1990) *Endangered Minds*, Joseph Chilton Pearce's (1992) *Evolution's End: Claiming the Potential of Our Intelligence*, Edward F. Sigler and Meryl Frank's (1988) *The Parental Leave Crisis*, and Ken Magid and Carole A. McKelvery's (1988) *High-Risk: Children without a Conscience*.

In our review of the conduct books of the fifteenth to seventeenth centuries we have observed a predisposition to treating the child as a functional necessity of a larger social world, and less often as an emotional being with his or her own rights and needs. Only when conduct books began suggesting that children be taught through stories that featured them as central players in family dramas did the status and rights of children increase.

This shifting standard of parenthood seems to indicate a change in human awareness and a new recognition of what might have gone unrecognized (or, faintly understood) in prior eras. Certainly, narratives of the 'damage' done to children are less observable in societies of slow change because one generation resembles the other in substantial ways. There is not enough disequilibrium for the younger generation to suddenly review its position and take to complaining about it in public; lack of alternatives makes people compliant to the socialization they have received. Similarly accepted is the restraint of emotion. Complaints are muted during childhood itself or kept at the level of silent tears. If the child wants to contest a rule, he does so with a considerable tact that borders on hedging. The child does not dare overpower the parent with emotion, because a host of socialization agents forbid such imposing expressions.

Comparing America with Europe, Tocqueville ([1884] 1994) realized the inherent contradiction between 'authenticity' and 'duty' and seemed to be partial to the former.

The struggle against 'authority' and 'formality' has opened a window of opportunity: the private self has been given a chance to evaluate its relation to social norms according to standards of personal fulfillment. Yet, such evaluation has had a profound influence on civil interactions and the classical definitions of civility and the concern for the comfort of the other. The movement against self-denial has had somewhat of an 'anomic' effect on social bonds. Psychoanalysis opened the first door to the regions that had remained suppressed in the interests of social cohesion; the American feeling therapies that followed from Freud's ideas opened subsequent doors. Whether a person was inner-directed or experiential, the goal was self-actualization. At first, the concept of self-actualization was based on a communion with the inner self and regulated by intense work on personal biography. Later, it became abridged to signify any claim made in the name of the self. While the original participants in the growth movements had sought to exteriorize the claims of the inner self, the cohorts who followed them responded to the corporate idea of lifestyle as an emblem of selfhood. The way a person lived became as important as how he felt. The experiential mode of self-definition coincided with the 'practice' of lifestyle, and its efficacy was measured by whether or not a person was able to project an 'image' that coincided with the identity he wished to possess. While 'distinction' could no longer be obtained through noble title it could be obtained through the types of clothes worn, the restaurants frequented, the activities pursued, and the cars purchased. In a democratic society built on an ideal of equality, 'standing out from the crowd' became the new emblem of distinction.

**The Risks and Opportunities of a Culture of Entitlement**

The label 'the me generation' would have been more descriptive had it been called 'the identity generation.' The combined effects of the therapeutic movement, the identity movement, and the rise of a self-centred mentality made cutting-edge Americans not only originators but consumers of a repackaged form of their original ideologies. And this packaging was particularly American and influenced by America's long-standing self-image as a 'country with a universal mission.' Bloom (1987) states that 'once Americans had become convinced that there is indeed a basement to which psychiatrists have the key, their orientation became that of the *self*' (155). It was thought that this self, although always 'mysterious' and out of reach, could be symbolized and nurtured through the taking on of positions that went beyond loyalty to community. Discussing America's particular reaction to European nihilism, Bloom defines American nihilism not so much a 'lack of firm beliefs but ... a chaos of the instincts or passions' (155). He minimizes, however, the fact that disbelief in existing forms creates a need for discovering new forms; humans are not capable of managing without a certain degree of stability and custom. Even informality can become formalized into a form of its own (Wouters 1986).

One of the consequences of a society populated by individuals who are allowed to accept and/or reject portions of the social norms of their society is the rise of a 'culture of entitlement.' Identity then requires giving to the self those rights considered to be *owing* to it. This sense of entitlement is not solely connected to expectation but also to the fact that the individual is allowed to 'choose' from a variety of permissive attitudes and behaviours. No longer limited by a strict code of personal and public behaviour, the individual is free to construct his identity based on personal preferences and personal evaluations of what is considered taboo and shameful.

It would seem that there is a correlation between the number of behaviours that are considered shameful and the degree to which personal impulses are restrained and refined in the interests of public decorum and solidarity. Social and political conditions in the latter part of the twentieth century have produced a new cultural environment in which the specifications for good behaviour are diminished in favour of personal choice. This change in habituation and rules of conduct has occurred at the primary (parental) and the secondary (educational and political) levels.

In an issue of the British daily *The Independent*, columnist Anne McElroy compares today's bureaucratized, permissive educational system with the schools of her childhood: 'In my primary school we were taught for two years by a deranged woman who so obviously disliked children that it could only have been a sadistic streak that kept her in the job. We grew up unprotected from the lazy, bad and cruel teachers, in a culture that assumed that the teacher was always right.'

McElvoy voices a complaint often heard in youth culture in the 1960s against an authoritarian educational system that was not being held accountable. Since then, the teaching profession's self-surveillance and bureaucratization have provided students with much-needed protection. It has also transformed the school. The purpose of education itself has been put into question. The study of precedence, custom, and established 'facts' has been supplemented by a revision of attitudes. The schools have, in effect, attempted to resocialize society by addressing the issues that divide identity groups: racism, ethnocentrism, gender discrimination, child abuse, and environmental degradation. The school has become an institution of the therapeutic society, a means for developing personal awareness, sometimes at the cost of academic competence.

The consequence of this democratization in schools is considerable. Permissiveness is demanded of the teacher as well as a simplification of curriculum. Critics of education have called this a 'dumbing-down' process (Bloom 1987:336–47). The liberalization of teacher–student relationships, combined with an academic agenda pressured to include the issues of minority groups, has complicated the entire notion of a standard educational canon. The purpose here is not to argue for the merits or demerits of the post-1960s educational project but to point out that the liberalization of the school has facilitated incivility in certain cases. Traditionally, the status of the American teacher helped preserve decorum in the classroom. Today, the relationship between teachers and students undergoes similar changes undergone by gender relations. 'Purity' of feeling and democratization of opinion overshadow 'respectful duty.'

Parallel transformations have occurred at the level of the state and the corporation. As Habermas (1994) has explained, the neutrality of the law in matters to do with the preservation of rights requires the state to maintain 'moral' facelessness: 'political questions of an ethical nature must be kept off the agenda and out of the discussion of "gag rules" because they are not susceptible of impartial legal regulation' (123).

A *government of tolerance* posits that by remaining neutral the state can best assure the protection of a variety of rights that may be in opposition to each other. While Rousseau might have insisted that free speech be preceded by some 'moral vocabulary,' the purely liberal state does not see morality as a general state project. Its purpose is to define what is not permitted, not to preach about what should be practised.

The population is to construct its own meanings with that which is not prohibited to it. Habermas ([1987] 1989) has discussed this empowerment of the individual to reach his own moral conclusions and called the individual 'the bearer of rights' (121).

These rights go beyond the right to appear equal before the law, the basic requirement of a society of free individuals. Additionally required is that the law recognize the differences between various identities. Expectedly, the competition for rights diminishes tact. Not only is a citizen concerned for his own rights but is prone to criticize those behaviours that contradict his own interests. In response to this conundrum, social policies are adopted that facilitate a consensus achieved within a broad definition of tolerance; this requires that a specific national ethos of morality be reformulated within a definition of civil rights rather than civil cohesion.

A state that lays claims to rational democratic legitimacy loses the luxury of making informal decisions based on moral sentiments. Paradoxically, the more the population demands the satisfaction of local rights negotiated in minority settings, the more the state is forced to adopt a formal position in regards to rights and their protection. Weber's 'faceless bureaucracy' is a product of such democratization. The cost of this 'impartiality' is a loss in the state's authority to 'pursue any collective goals beyond guaranteeing the personal freedom and the welfare and security of citizens' (Habermas [1987] 1989:123).

So, in democratic countries the state becomes the legitimate source of rights claims. While it is constitutionally prevented from dominating civil society, it provides the legislative means for ensuring that the rights of civil society are preserved. In effect, the state becomes a dispensing machine for rights. Rights are no longer determined by majority consensus but by the ability of groups to lay claim to legislative benefits. Naturally, this increases the opportunities for litigation and has a salient effect on public civility. It also has a corrosive effect on a welfare system that has been decades in the making (Osborne 1997:6–8).

In such a culture of entitlement, even the notion of majority consensus is challenged because majority rule is considered a means of keeping minority issues underrepresented. Schudson (1997) suggests that democratic conversations between citizens based on a recognition of rights is an outgrowth and not a cause of democracy; so it would seem that the mutual dependence between a state that guarantees rights and a citizenry affected by its own needs for recognition releases the potential for a general concept of civility that may withstand perturbations between the interests of the public and private spheres. The only price required is a decrease in spontaneity in the interests of mutual recognition (297–309). Peter Wagner (1996) points to the paradox created by such diversity. A mentality comes into effect that welcomes 'diversity and singularity, on the one hand, and resists universal statements, on the other, except that one that no well founded universal statements are possible' (109). The erosion of boundaries requires the construction of a special boundary against hyper-coherence, a precondition for authoritarian ideology.

Robert W. Hefner (1998a) offers some reassurance, explaining that the democratic basis of civility is heterogeneous and is dependent on free speech and associations based on modern values, diversity included (16–27). Similarly, Charles Taylor (1994) tries valiantly to reconcile the tensions that are inevitable consequences of a politics of entitlement. He explains that while the individual needs recognition at the personal level, he also requires recognition within the group in which he was born and socialized. The individual asks for recognition as a citizen possessing the right to advance in life without being stereotyped with the identity marks of a given group, yet he also wishes that the group to which he belongs be respected. The multiplicity of rights that can be claimed by any one person puts the state in a difficult position in which it is bound by democratic duty to recognize 'difference' while affirming itself in favour of a neutral, unbound citizenship. Yet a segmented recognition is sometimes the best way to protect members of a group from total exclusion from significant jobs in the mainstream culture; the absence of a politics of recognition may cause a prolongation of discrimination and exclusion (Davetian 1994).

Worry over the actual specification of the conditions and contradictions of a politics of pluralism misses its 'systemic' consequences. Habermas (1994) brings attention to the fact that the dialogues of political interest groups have a democratic effect that surpasses the specific claims that are being made:

> Citizens who are politically integrated in this way share the rationally based conviction that unrestricted freedom of communication in the political public sphere, a democratic process for settling conflicts, and the constitutional channeling of political power together provide a basis for

checking the illegitimate power and ensuring that administrative power is used in the equal interest of all. (135)

Habermas is searching for an approximation of an 'ideal speech situation' in which the mere act of communication produces consequences that enhance emancipation. This search for a 'constitutional patriotism' is an abstract ideal in a liberal state that no longer has the right to legislate the loyalty of its citizens. Few countries possess laws requiring all citizens to vote in national elections. What Lionel Trilling (1955) aptly termed the 'oppositional self' is given the right to use its personality to perturb the habits of a culture but not required to ground its demands in a larger politics of national cohesion. Habermas's (1994) hope is that the combined effects of perturbations emanating from varied claims for distinction will create a stream of discourse that will approximate Rousseau's ideal of a social contract free from humiliation and dependence. Taylor phrases this ideal as the affirmation of distinct identities that are shared within a framework of rights that accords universal importance to each identity (39). Both explanations, however, do not adequately take into account the competition for scarce cultural and economic resources.

So, from the point of view of the state, the individual (and the group in which he claims membership) is at once sacred but also to be held faceless in the interests of overall justice. The state is at once required to be dynamic as well as restrained, concerned as well as detached. This conflicted reality complicates the adoption of a civility ethos that is proactive as well as all-inclusive.

The politics of tolerance imposes a new restraint on the open expression and admission of prejudice, while releasing the tensions that invariably occur when differing groups suddenly find themselves united by an officially imposed code of tolerance (Beckwith and Bowman 1993; Renzetti 1993; Johnson 1992). Nat Hentoff (1992) considers the political correctness and rights movement to constitute a censoring process. In *Free Speech for Me – But Not for Thee* he accuses the U.S. left and right of playing a mutual game of censorship at the detriment of communal solidarity. If there is one thing on which both friends and foes of political correctness seem to agree on it is the fact that it champions a 'transformative' view of education and society. Whether that transformation should be welcomed is the big bone of contention (Beckwith and Bowman 1993; McCormack 1992). That the affirmations of rights and the practice of civility are competing values cannot be denied (Russell 1996). On a short-term basis, the politics of recognition has entailed a loss of consensus and social solidarity, but it has produced a more abstract social civility, one based on the much-needed recognition of civil rights (Peck 2002).

The long-range effects of a politically correct culture may include the emergence of a new sentiment of social cohesion and solidarity despite a culture of plural interests; on the other hand, as suggests Parthasarathy (2001), it may lead to the less desirable alternative of taking a position of 'indifference' (neutral tolerance) as a means of tolerating differences (104–6). Certainly, it places extraordinary pressure on individuals to distinguish themselves in a cult of individualism while restraining themselves in order not to offend other voices and interests (White 2006).

The notion of political tolerance in America does not accord enough importance to the mounting tension between those who favour a secular society and those who believe that the excesses of the 1960s and the rise of a society of individual rights have detached America from its Judeo-Christian heritage. The rise of the Christian right and its increasing influence in social philosophy and political outcomes has certainly been neglected by sociologists who are at ease studying the sociology of religion but reluctant to admit that a great majority of Americans are governed by their religious convictions. While Europe, particularly France, has adopted a thoroughly secular social and political ethic, the United States continues to be torn between its long-standing affirmation of self-discipline in the name of religious and national purity and a pleasure-oriented individualism which overrides many of the practices previously considered taboo. An across-the-board comparative study that attempts to determine the 'extent of liberalism' in the cultures being compared will not yield reliable insights, for what needs be understood is not the degree to which a culture is liberal in comparison with another but the extent to which (and in how short a time period) a culture has undone or transformed its previous norms. The extent of change and the length of time taken for that change to be implemented are directly related to the degree to which a culture is perturbed or anomic. History indicates that the American experiment since the 1960s has been a brave one, certainly one that has created strong divisions that have affected civility. Certainly, the 'culture wars' in America are not settled, considering that the forces of moral modesty and those of moral liberalism continue to be at odds with each other. We were stunned during our field research of contemporary America (described in the concluding chapters of this book) to observe the important role played by religion in the lives of Americans and how much this set America apart from its European allies.

**Conclusion**

We have tried in this chapter to restrict our discussion of late modernity to the United States because it is the one nation that has tested the limits of novelty and change in such a short period of time. It is also, regardless of world sentiment, an extremely powerful and influential civilization. We generalize when we speak of Western civilization as if it were a standard culture to which a number of nations belong. We question the generality of world systems theorists, such as Immanuel Wallerstein (1974), who consider modern American capitalism as a mere continuation of a centuries-old colonial capitalistic project that began in Europe. Such an over-arching systems theory fails to consider those aspects of American capitalism that are connected to uniquely American interaction values (more on this in Part III).

Alexis de Tocqueville's ([1884] 1994) analysis of American democracy continues to provide a plausible explanation for why societies that lack an aristocratic heritage tend to favour individualism and tolerate persons who have a deep need to stand out from the crowd (568, 598, 610–11). A nation founded on the ideal of minimizing hierarchical relationships and favouring change and mobility is in some way predisposed to placing a high valuation on personal rights (as opposed to communal duties). If it were otherwise, it would risk having a population in which all personal distinctions are levelled in the name of community. In fact, the constitutional nature of a democracy that lacks an aristocratic heritage requires citizens to continuously recreate themselves to fulfill the ideal type of citizen incorporated in the U.S. constitution. This creates preconditions for the tempering of generational continuity and has a weakening effect on social philosophies that call for restraint and caution. It certainly affects how 'liberty' and 'freedom' are defined and practised.

Here we would like to return to our observation of fundamental differences in how the United States, England, and France defined 'liberty' in their particular geographic, economic, and philosophical contexts. Two conceptions of freedom emerge in this comparative study, sug-

Conformity, Opposition, and Identity 339

gesting that liberty, in itself, is not an absolute generic reality. While 'individual freedom' specifies that the person must stay free of unwanted social influences that might prejudice his political and creative rights, 'communal freedom' means that the community must exist in a state of cohesion in order to resist and prevent domination from some outside force, including the destructive impulses of its own citizens.

Each of the three countries in our study has experienced social movements that seek individual as well as collective freedom. But the time periods and conditions in which these movements occurred have differed from one country to another. As we have argued in previous chapters, the French conception of liberty was considerably defined by the need to avoid a return to monarchical despotism, while the English notion of liberty was connected to the need for liberty of political and religious diversity. As for the American liberty movement, it was a movement for freedom to remain independent of the rule of empires. And, as America arrived into the twentieth century, the empire it feared the most was the empire of its own accumulated heritage. It is understandable that many Americans set to deconstructing their past in search of new amendments to the original vision of their founding principles. The ninth amendment had promised them that the constitution would not prevent the claiming of rights not already enumerated. A permissive society took the amendment literally and called in additional rights for itself in the twentieth century, the right to be discourteous being one of them.

One issue stands out in our reconsideration of that important decade when many Americans abandoned the easy assurances of traditional conformity. In the 1960s the one thing that had distinguished America and made it admired across the world suffered a great blow. That thing was American patriotism. From the day Americans declared their independence from the colonies, one American generation communicated to each successive generation the meaning of being American. The 1960s and the decades that followed questioned the legitimacy of that pride. Americans, searching for authenticity and human rights, agreed to deride the legacy left them by their predecessors. It was a decision that transformed the United States from a functional capitalistic enterprise into a socially engaged and socially conscious nation in which its citizens were willing to step out of centuries-old isolation to address issues as far-reaching as the spiritual teachings of monks in Tibet and the freedom of other peoples in the world. This was a quantum increase in civilizational worth despite the rude protests that had been necessary to bring about such an awakening. What worries this writer, however, is the effects of a weakened patriotism on the daily values and interaction rituals of Americans. We discuss this further in our comparative field study of contemporary America, France, and England.

# Part III

# The Multifaceted Anatomy of Civility

It is incredible how necessary an ingredient shame is to make us sociable; it is a frailty in our nature; all the world, whenever it affects them, submit to it with regret and would prevent it if they could; yet the happiness of conversation depends on it, and no society could be polished if the generality of mankind was not subject to it.

– Bernard de Mandeville

# 9 Towards a Cultural Sociology of Civility

> ... concepts such as 'individual' and 'society' do not relate to two objects existing separately but to different yet inseparable aspects of the same human beings, and ... both aspects (and human beings in general) are normally involved in structural transformation. Both have the character of processes, and there is not the slightest necessity, in forming theories about human beings, to abstract from this process character.
> – Norbert Elias

## Introduction

The study of the historical background of a culture is vital to one's understanding of its civility practices as well as its ongoing present. Yet, there are other equally important factors that must be considered. Although they may in some measure be the outcomes of historical and moral forces, these factors need to be studied on their own merit because the manner in which they intersect makes for an 'anatomy of civility' that is sociological as well as psychological. In this part of the book we will discuss these various factors and show how a 'cultural sociology of civility' needs to study these factors within an interactive model. These factors include the manner in which individuals are socialized, the degree to which a given culture favours independence or interdependence, the way a culture relates to time/context/space, the specific manner in which politeness is expressed, and, very importantly, the coping mechanisms used in instances of embarrassment and shame. So in this part of the book we would like to discuss each of these various aspects in order to share with the reader the variables that we took into account during our research of contemporary civil interaction in France, England, and America (part IV). These variables allowed us to construct a 'topology' of civility that proved invaluable during our field research. So we will discuss these different aspects, each according to its own merit, in order to illustrate how the complex subject of civility can be studied with a fair amount of methodological rigour. Civility is no longer a topic limited to the interests of journalists and conduct/etiquette book writers; it is a topic that can inform a cross-culturally and emotionally competent sociology of culture and produce insights in a variety of areas including relations between nations.

**Towards an Emotionally Informed Social Science**

Any sociology of culture that is not emotionally informed about the subject of its study risks reaching conclusions at the expense of the actual human processes of its subjects. To arrive at a workable theory of courtesy/civility – and a parallel understanding of discourtesy/incivility – we are going to have to guard against sociology's tendency to avoid topics that it considers the proper domain of psychology or anthropology. Being an integral component of human interaction, civility is best understood through a deliberate study of human social psychology. A civil or uncivil experience immediately generates sentiments in all participants in the interaction. Even those who remain cold-blooded in the face of abrasive discourtesy are choosing one emotional state rather than another.

Fortunately for those of us working on the elusive connections between private lives and social outcomes, an encouraging amount of work has been done of late on the 'sociology of emotions.' While it is regrettable that the study of emotions should be a specialty rather than a body of knowledge informing all sociological specialties – historical, political, and economic studies being not the least of them – it is an encouraging start.

One work that seems most helpful in our task of reconciling human personality and social organization is Jonathan H. Turner's (2000) *On the Origins of Human Emotions*. Turner prepares the ground for his subsequent *The Sociology of Emotions* (Turner and Stets 2005) by providing a detailed discussion of primary and secondary emotions and the neurological apparatus that connects emotions and thoughts. Turner's Darwin-inspired narrative provides an affective as well as biological map of what is involved in the creation of a social environment. Of particular interest are two sections: 'The Emotional Repertoire of Humans' (66–84), in which Turner presents research done in various disciplines on a typology of primary and secondary human emotions, and 'The Neurology of Human Emotions' (85–118), in which he presents convincing evidence on the neurological connections between thought and feeling processes. He concludes that language cannot in itself explain human behaviour: 'True, learning is the key to activating humans' innate potential for using and understanding emotional syntax and to invoking the relevant emotionally ordered stocks of knowledge but learning alone cannot explain humans' incredible facility with emotions' (133).

Turner's work indicates that certain emotions are socially influenced (of the secondary order) and certain ones (of the primary order) are wired into the neurological apparatus of the person. His discoveries suggest that social theories that focus exclusively on socially constructed social norms and actions gloss over the deeper solar plexus regions of social identity and social outcomes. It would seem that emotions do not need words in order to exist.

Jack Barbalet (1998), another important contributor to the growing literature on the 'sociology of emotions,' has similarly argued that although emotions can be culturally affected, they possess a social structure of their own and play an important role in determining the type of actions taken in response to social events. P.E.S. Freund (1982, 1989, 1990) also cautions that an exclusively social-constructionist view underestimates the bodily reality of emotions, thereby producing a further split between organic and social explanations of society. R. Harré (1991), on the other hand, argues against an overly physiological view of emotions; he cautions that a 'bodily feeling is often the somatic expression to oneself of the taking of a moral position' (143). Unable to completely deny the existence of bodily reactions, the social-constructionist viewpoint attempts to claim that it is the language game or moral position that sets in play an emotional reaction; certainly, this view leaves no room for the possibility that emotions may be stored in the body and accumulate over a period of time, thereby rendering an individual prone to one word game or moral position rather than another.

Also instructive is the rich body of work done by Thomas J. Scheff, who has examined the phenomenon of *shame* and its role in the development of functional and dysfunctional social bonds. He is one of the few theorists who attempts to show how 'failure to grieve' in childhood has consequences on later adult behaviour and how 'humiliation' and 'anger' are intimately linked in personal and political acts.

It is not the purpose of this discussion to list all the work being done in the sociology of emotions but to indicate the considerable progress that is being made. This growing body of work includes Simon Williams's (2001) excellent review of the philosophical, theoretical, and empirical issues embedded in a sociology of emotions and Nicholas Rose's studies of how power, personhood, and the governing of the social self are incalculably linked. Particularly noteworthy is the anthropologist Richard H. Wills's *Human Instincts, Everyday Life, and the Brain: A Paradigm for Understanding Behaviour* (1998). Starting with the concept that much of human behaviour involves the exchange of emotional and material resources, Wills has produced an atlas of human behaviour that shows the varieties of situations that result from emotion management. The work contains no less than 2,272 documented observations of interactions and conversations, many of which reveal the nature of civil interaction and the emotional repertoire that is enlisted in the process of 'face-preservation.' Other primary works arguing for a re-embodiment of social analysis include: Arlie H. Hochschild (1975, 1979, 1983, [1989] 1997, 1997), Nick Crossley (2001), Richard Sennett (1990), Bendelow and Williams (1997), Theodore D. Kemper (1977), Tangney (1992, 1995), Williams (2001), Baumeister and Wotman (1992), Juliette Greco (2001), Chris Yuill (2004), Anthony Synnott (1993), and David Howes (2004).

The inclusion of 'emotion study' in civility theory is crucial since civil and uncivil behaviours are not 'acts' detached from emotional involvement, but are very often affected by the emotional dispositions of the actors and their sentimental reactions towards their inner selves, towards one another, and towards their culture. Cultural habituation and personal biography, therefore, play mutually affecting roles. So, to arrive at a useful theory of civility that can be used as part of sociological studies we need to go beyond the categories of 'individual' and 'society' and address the topic of 'human relational processes' that are embedded in the institutional and personal *sensoriums* that are involved in personal and public relations.

## Restraint and the Civilizing Process – Reconsidering Norbert Elias's Theory of the Civilizing Process

Norbert Elias understood the methodological problems of theorists who took sides between the 'individual' and 'society' paradigms. He shied away from studies such as those of Talcott Parsons that focused on the health and homeostatis of the social system (Parsons 1968:310), while remaining equally sceptical of an inflexible Marxist determinism that located human alienation in the process of wealth production and wealth ownership. Neither approach seemed to assign enough power to individuals who were, regardless of their political and economic situations, creating shared meanings and realities with one another. Perhaps unintentionally echoing Herbert Mead's (1934) conception of an interactive social order, Elias believed that actors had considerable power of agency even though they remained vulnerable to the effects of systemic forces and their surprising consequences. In *A Society of Individuals* (1991) he demonstrated this commitment to a process sociology that did not separate individual and social forces: 'The structures of the human psyche, the structures of human society and the structures of human history are indissolubly complementary, and can only be studied in conjunction with each other. They do not exist and move in reality with the degree of isolation assumed by current research' (36).

Thus, although he accorded individuals considerable power, Elias placed them within networks that were continuously shifting and being renegotiated:

> People stand before the outcome of their own actions like the apprentice magician before the spirits he has conjured up and which, once at large, are no longer in his power. They look with astonishment at the convolutions and formations of the historical flow which they themselves constitute but do not control. (62)

This recognition of mutual *relationism* makes the dichotomy between 'individual' and 'society' redundant. Elias ([1969] 1983) suggests that even a notion of 'we-ness' must take into account the geodesic effects of multi-directional influences. He calls these multi-directional changes 'shifting balances of tension' (145). Even domination becomes a two-way process best studied in a long-range developmental framework: 'In one form or another the constraints that more powerful groups exert on less powerful ones recoil on the former as constraints of the less powerful on the more powerful and also as compulsions to self-constraint' (265).

Elias's work provides a valuable starting point for the development of a *part-whole* sociology that transports insights between the micro and macro levels in the manner preferred by C. Wright Mills (1959) in his definition of the sociological imagination: 'the capacity to range from the most impersonal and remote transformations to the most intimate features of the human self – and to see the relations between the two' (7).

Thomas Scheff (1997a) proposes a similar part-whole approach, especially for the analysis of social processes that involve emotive exchanges (528–38). Scheff explains in his model of the 'social bond theory' that authentic mutual relationism requires a mutual awareness and continuing interest in the points of view of the other (1997b:76–8). Following Durkheim's idea of social integration (1951), Scheff proposes that the social bond between parent and child cannot be too tight or too loose; the first bond leads to a self-debilitating engulfment by convention and the latter to a sentiment of detachment and isolation (77). Both types of bonds seem to have a reverberating effect on social relations.

Yet even a theory of mutual relationism can run into empirical problems if turned into a meta-theory that takes little account of cultural variations. Zygmunt Bauman (1979) has criticized Elias for concentrating too much on the idea of process and relation while minimizing the active powers of the individual or 'collective subject of knowledge' (120). Dennis Smith (1984) has also criticized Elias for not stressing enough the power humans possess for choosing and evaluating (370). This exercise of choice can occur even in periods of considerable transnational technical and cultural standardization. Certainly, while trying to avoid the argument that the individual is free or that society determines all human action (Elias and Scotson 1965:172), Elias does not adequately investigate the primary needs of the individual and how the expression of those needs is routed by the specific socialization standards of the culture in which the individual is born. Even though he focuses on the manner in which human relations are composed of power shifts that are mutually balancing ([1970] 1978:75), he does not provide a detailed account of what makes people act in the way they do. So, while his study attempts to bridge the gap between the categories of 'individual' and 'society,' his explanations remain, nevertheless, predominantly systemic, focusing on how civility developed in the West as the result of the centralization of political and economic power. Certainly, his study would have been more substantial had he focused more on the depths of human social psychology and developed a comprehensive theory of shame and pride that was based not only on manners and etiquette but also on the psychological needs of individuals of all social classes.

Additionally, Elias seems to have exclusively based most of his conclusions on those medieval and Renaissance texts emanating from Italy and France. His study of court society is mostly based on the court in France. Had he extended his study to England as well as a nation (such as America) that had broken free of an aristocratic system, he might have been able to provide a more comprehensive discussion of personal psychology within cross-cultural differences. A cross-cultural study including countries governed by varying political systems would have provided Elias with the opportunity of seeing how different people have adopted different ways of constructing their civility tradition. This would also have provided an ideal opportunity for studying the universals of civility and those aspects of civil interactions that are purely nationally bound social constructs. We have tried to do this in this present work and hope to achieve our goal in the remainder of this book.

Despite some of these omissions, Elias has provided a magisterial review of the manner in which certain bodily and emotional expressions were muted through the manipulation of 'shame' ([1939] 1978). His theory of 'restraint' is a strong starting point for the study of civility. His reading of over 450 literary texts revealed to him how practices considered 'socially unacceptable' were revised through the eras in tandem with developments in economic and political conditions. The general tendency was towards increasing restraints. Along with the raising of the shame threshold – the definition of the forbidden – came an internalizing of shame so that it became automatic and increasingly unconscious. So strong was the shame emotion that it even became unsettling to refer to shameful topics. This made the study of shame particularly problematic, because any mention of 'shame' risked triggering 'shame' in the listener or reader. While the German and French languages have different terms for different severities of shame (thereby facilitating the discussion of milder forms considered socially beneficial), the English language has only one all-encompassing term, and any discussion of it can imply reference to its most grievous type. So, ironically, the imposition of taboos brings a parallel taboo regarding the discussion of the forbidden topic, especially in anglophone cultures.

Elias demonstrates this growing tendency to remain silent regarding practices considered shameful in his discussion of a conduct book written by a well-known pedagogue, W. Von Raumer. In *The Education of Girls* (1858; cited in Elias [1939] 1978), Von Raumer advises mothers to make every effort to keep sexual knowledge from their girls. The purpose of this secrecy is to create a sense of shame in the girls in order not to inhibit them from broaching the subject:

> Children should be left for as long as is at all possible in the belief that an angel brings the mother her little children. This legend, customary in some regions, is far better than the story of the stork common elsewhere. Children, if they really grow up under their mother's eyes, will seldom ask forward questions on this point ... not even if the mother is prevented by a childbirth from having them about her ... If girls should later ask how little children really come into the world, they should be told that the good Lord gives the mother her child, who has a guardian angel in heaven who certainly played an invisible part in bringing us this great joy. 'You do not need to know nor could you understand how God gives children.' Girls must be satisfied with such answers in a hundred cases, and it is the mother's task to occupy her daughters' thoughts so incessantly with the good and beautiful that they are left no time to brood on such matters ... A mother ... ought only once to say seriously: 'It would not be good for you to know such a thing, and you should take care not to listen to anything said about it.' A truly well-brought-up girl will from then on feel shame at hearing things of this kind spoken of. (180)

Elias's commentary on the above passage illustrates his intuitive understanding of how modernity (at least up to the 1930s when he was writing) had been paralleled by a quantum raising of the shame threshold:

> In the civilizing process, sexuality too is increasingly removed behind the scenes of social life and enclosed in a particular enclave, the nuclear family. Likewise, the relations between the sexes are isolated, placed behind walls in consciousness. An aura of embarrassment, the expression of a sociogenetic fear, surrounds this sphere of life. Even among adults it is referred to officially only with caution and circumlocutions. And with children, particularly girls, such things are, as far as possible, not referred to at all. Von Raumer gives no reason why one ought not to speak of them with children. He could have said it is desirable to preserve the spiritual purity of girls for as long as possible. But even this reason is only another expression of how far the gradual submergence of these impulses in shame and embarrassment has advanced by this time (180).

Elias further notes that von Raumer himself is having difficulty coping with the notion of shame. He does not explain why the young girl should be kept ignorant of a natural function that she will eventually have to discover and accept. Not only is he uneasy about causing embarrassment in his reader; he is also avoiding his own embarrassment about the topic. Typical of the gentry of the time, he approaches the subject with 'delicacy,' leaving much unsaid.

Elias's conception of the internalization of repression is based on his observation of such texts as von Raumer's. To support his argument regarding shame internalization, Elias remarks that, as one proceeds from one decade to another, subsequent editions of the same conduct book eliminate mention of a practice that has been adopted in the interim. The social prohibitions and resistances within the subjects themselves have made them now remain silent about the forbidden practices; thus, the shame mechanism has set in motion a 'compulsive silence' (181).

The criticism could be made that conduct books do not reveal the interaction ethos of a culture. However, we question this criticism because of two facts: (1) educated men and women do not write about ideal conduct unless there exist living examples of it, otherwise, their works would be utopian and of little immediate practical relevance; (2) conduct book writers reveal the nature of ongoing practices by suggesting their improvement; an existing practice must be specified if an argument is to be made for its modification. In fact, one could even suggest that contemporary media, such as film and television, continue to fulfill the original functions of the printed conduct books and etiquette manuals. One studies them aware of the powerful role they play in the representation as well as reformation of social practices.

This said, there is a problem in Elias's work: the translator took the German word *'scham'* and translated it to 'shame' in English, not taking into account that English has no provisions for distinguishing between larger and smaller shames. Such a distinction exists in German. *Schande* refers to *disgraceful shame* while *scham* refers to the more mundane shameful experiences that, in English, are more appropriately represented by the word *embarrassment*. Ideally, the translator should have used both English terms, strictly depending on whichever term was most appropriate in a given passage of Elias's text. Elias himself did not explain in detail the anatomy of shame. While he used the word quite frequently, he did not explain how and why a person could be made to feel shameful or whether the emotion of shame was a primary emotion or a derivative of a deeper emotion that shame was intended to push out of view.

Despite some of the above problems, Elias's theory of restraint (if not internalized shame) seems to hold right up to the middle of the nineteenth century in America, England, and France. According to Elias's definition of the 'civilizing process,' post-medieval Western history has been characterized by a steady increase in the sophistication and complexity of the restraints imposed on persons and institutions through increasing rationality. Certainly, the period between 1200 and 1800 was a watershed period in European and American history, representing a profound transformation in society as well as in the manner in which individuals thought of social relations. Within the paradigm developed by Elias, the long 'civilizing process' of the West had two defining features: (1) an ever-increasing control of public violence by the state, and, (2) increased delineation between the private and public spheres with an accompanying intensification of controls imposed on behaviour. This process involved the diminution of those acts and behavioural traits considered 'dangerous' and potentially socially 'disruptive' and 'disagreeable.' According to these measures, it could be said that a relatively high level of behavioural restraint was achieved in England and France by the time of the mid-Victorian era and, a few decades later, in America.

When reading Elias's work, we are additionally faced with a problem peculiar to our own epoch. The mere words 'civilizing' and 'civilization' seem to set off alarm bells reminding us of the colonial abuses of evolutionary theory. The title of Elias's work (*The Civilizing Process*) might give the impression that he was presenting a prescription for what is to be considered 'civilized.' This was not his primary intention. He certainly was not a conduct book writer, even though he reviewed conduct books, as we have also done in portions of this present work. He was investigating a *process* that had been used by Westerners to define civilization in the West. The word 'process' in the title of his work reveals his sociological purpose and method. He considered the development of manners and standards of politeness to be intimately connected to a multitude of forces, the centralization of power and the control of violence by the citizenry being not the least of them. The empirical evidence he presented was not intended to argue for a fixed definition of the meaning of being civilized but to exemplify the practice of a 'relational' sociology capable of studying the 'individual' and 'society' as interactive agencies that are subject to the vicissitudes of historical forces. Consequently, his work is as much a treatise on systems theory and sociological method as it is a study of a specific aspect of social life.

Realizing the methodological limitations of evolutionary nineteenth-century theory, as well as twentieth-century disembodied studies of short-term social change, Elias specified that the ultimate purpose of reviewing history was to reveal 'the intractable problem of the connection between individual psychological structures (so called personality structures) and figurations formed by large numbers of interdependent individuals (social structures)' (225). Anthony Giddens (1984, 1990) has located similar relationships between agency and structure in his 'structuration theory.' So have Charles H. Cooley (1909, 1922), George Herbert Mead (1934), and E. Goffman (1959) in their studies of the interactive relationship between the formation of *self* and the organization of *society*.

Despite the wisdom of Elias's ([1939] 1978) argument for an inclusive sociology, he does not sufficiently take into account the 'cumulative effects' of psychological and bodily restraints. Observing Western civilization as 'it has been,' he equates the outcome of a variety of interactive processes (and the subsequent control of what was considered dangerous or distasteful) with a 'civilizing process.' Man is leaving nature behind or, at best, learning to dominate and gentrify it. Elias admits that at any given time the 'civilizing process' can also entail a lifting of restraints, but he keeps such an eventuality within the confines of the same notion of 'civilizational continuum' by suggesting that restraints are lifted only after they have been sufficiently internalized. The lifting of the restraints seems to confirm to Elias the original efficiency of their internalization:

> It is not uninteresting to observe that today [in the 1930s (the translator)], when this standard of conduct has been so heavily consolidated that it is taken for granted, a certain relaxation is setting in, particularly in comparison to the nineteenth century, at least with regard to speech about the natural functions. The freedom and unconcern with which people say what has to be said without embarrassment has clearly increased in the postwar period. But this, like modern bathing and dancing practices, is only possible because the level of habitual, technically and institutionally consolidated self-control, the individual capacity to restrain one's urges and behaviour in correspondence with the more advanced feelings for what is offensive, has been on the whole secured. It is a relaxation within the framework of an already established standard. (140)

Important questions remain unanswered in this explanation. We are not told at what point the imposition of restraints and shame stops contributing to social cohesion and begins perturbing social solidarity – we are no closer to having a more reliable accounting of the 'depersonalizing' costs of repression. Although Elias ([1939] 1982) admits that 'the civilizing of the human young ... always leaves scars' (244), he has not had the opportunity to observe the social dialogues (and conflicts) that occur when those scars are made conscious as they were during the twentieth century. He warns that while it took many long centuries to develop states capable of restricting the acceptance of physical aggression and outright cruelty, 'the civilizing process' can be rapidly reversed through a collapse of those violence-regulating institutions that exercise authority over clearly marked territories ([1939] 1978:191–205). Yet his consideration of a possible collapse of the long-term 'civilizing' project is limited to the collapse of violence regulation and the sudden appearance of a tribal 'free trade' zone of violence such as the one fictionalized in William Golding's (1954) *Lord of the Flies*. One has the impression that Freud's (1930) explanation of civilization and its innate destructive discontents left an indelible impression on Elias, one that predisposed him to think that the lifting of restraints could return humanity to a primeval state of interminable conflict similar to a collective death wish.

Such scenarios of irreversible degeneration distract us from less spectacular, but consequential, transformations in the management of restraints and self-identity. In any case, civilized people do not easily revert back to pre-civilized times (assuming that we ever lived without civil networks), especially not if an economic system remains in place that does not pit small groups against one another in outright tribal battle for nearly non-existent resources. For instance, although the German Third Reich committed unspeakable atrocities, its highly disciplined military and bureaucratic apparatus maintained strict social order. This was not a case of chaotic barbarism but methodical and focused cruelty, a process that can be achieved against a victim group while 'civilizational' restraints between members of the offending group are meticulously and decorously maintained. That the members of the German SS were attending opera performances and addressing one another with elaborate codes of etiquette while unspeakable horrors were going on in the concentration camps tragically illustrates how a society can maintain dual identities of decorous restraint and unlimited aggression. The 'bureaucratization' of evil and the rendering 'banal' of evil (Arendt 1977) occurs due to this co-existence of sophisticated levels of civilizational restraint and merciless cruelties practised within highly rational purposive institutions.

Similar restraints and bureaucratic order were maintained in Stalinist Russia, where millions were sent to their deaths in the Gulag Archipelago. The perpetuators personalized their own identities while depersonalizing the identities of those whom they liquidated – a total social depersonalization did not occur. Similar processes have been observed in contemporary civil wars, pogroms of ethnic cleansing, and military dictatorships (Davetian 1996). Michel Foucault (1979) has also convincingly reminded us that horrendous tortures and public executions were being practised precisely by the same people who were considered of noble birth and upright social standing. So we are better off viewing civility as a bilateral process involving restraint on one hand and aggression and tactical behaviour on the other.

The suggestion that a substantial easing of restraints can suddenly set off an escalating, regressive 'de-civilizing process' is a non-productive idea and one that diminishes our understanding of the meanings and consequences of the late-modern era. It is based on the idea that a society could actually exist without shame and its restrictive influences. Although strong shame can lead to violent behaviour, as we will explain in a later section, most shame leads to renewed attempts to eliminate dissonance and re-establish social harmony. The apocalyptic vision of civilizational degeneration prevents us from noticing how a given culture *re-civilizes* itself without going through any period of outright barbarism. It also draws attention away from the fact that incivility can be used as a moral weapon to transform social values, as was done in the 1960s and during other social movements of the twentieth century.

History shows that the human tendency towards conformity has permitted moral movements to define the permissible and the forbidden, thereby establishing a relative degree of social consensus. Persuasion, coercion, and appeals to conscience have allowed the maintenance of coherent civility traditions, even in the presence of major conflicts. Yet, there is a point where the human being is no longer satisfied with speaking the unspeakable only when permitted to do so; benefiting from a more critical awareness, he begins to demand the right to speak regardless of the constrictions of tradition. This, in effect, is a characteristic of 'high individualism,' a consequence of late modernity, a time when the parameters of 'embarrassment' and 'shame' have been substantially altered. Such sudden reversals in value systems and habituations make us question our understanding of the 'civilizing process' as conceptualized by Norbert Elias. That is why we prefer to call developments in contemporary culture a *new civilizing process* or a *re-civilizing process*. So, one hesitates to fully agree with Elias's proposition that as a practice is controlled externally the restraining force becomes internalized and no longer in need of external surveillance. Embarrassment in public and private does not disappear when a restraint has been internalized. Rather, it disappears when the restraint and its accompanying prohibitions are deregulated and considered no longer worthy of moral censure; this deregulation actually follows from a gradual elimination of the internal repertoire of shame-triggering thoughts and emotions and is indicative of a process already ongoing due to a human agency that is operating alongside institutional change.

For example, if people are no longer embarrassed to mention the word 'nude' it is not because they have become internally habituated to their unease. As long as unease is internalized it continues to have an inhibitory effect on behaviour; at the very least, it creates an aura of silence around the prohibited thought or action, leaving it locked up within the individual's repertoire of shame issues. The mention of the forbidden elicits nervous smiles and giggles of embarrassment. Representations of the nude and mentions of nudity were no longer considered a social problem worthy of moral panic when the conception of nudity itself became normalized due to a new social habituation. The change happened at the external level and then had a liberating effect on internal control levels.

So there are specific moments of social awakening during which a particular restraint is banished and can be re-established with great difficulty because a fundamental shift in human awareness and emotional disposition has occurred. To bring back the restraint one would have to struggle against the new awareness and impose the old restraint as an edict rather than a habit. A long process of persuasion spanning more than one generation would be needed. Such a forced attempt to 'regenerate' a past practice or order – at the root of fascist philosophies – is more easily imagined than accomplished in a secular democracy, where political figures no longer have the mandate to speak with passionate authority regarding cultural transformation.

Reversals of influence (from restraint to permissiveness) also occur when a prohibition that has driven a pleasurable practice into the private realm becomes meaningless or no longer useful; the forbidden behaviour is brought out in public on purpose and demands are made for it to be recognized as a norm rather than an aberration. Until it is publicly accepted it may even be practised provocatively in order to speed up its normalization in public. Acceptance is gained through an initial 'perturbation' of the public conscience followed by the 'desensitization' that accompanies familiarity.

All this is said in order to argue that we may be dealing with a social self that is undergoing an important transformation. This transformation has been liberated by considerable changes in social organization, political and institutional values, and levels of human awareness. The eras prior to the mid-twentieth century, observed by Elias as well as by us, although they were periods of considerable change, had three fixed characteristics that linked them to one another and facilitated a workable narrative of a civilizing process always in development:

1. *A political system that played a pivotal role in the formation of a public ethos.* The medieval courts, the Renaissance city-states, the courts of Europe, the Victorian monarchy, and the founders of the American republic put forward political leaders entrusted with explicitly setting down moral norms that then became integrated into the daily practices of their populations. Political leadership contributed to the formation of social philosophy. In our own epoch, while the state can influence behaviour through legislative measures, state leaders are not as given to taking on the personal role of moral philosophers. Our fear of a strong leader with the capacity of becoming a dictator limits the moral rhetoric we are willing to hear from politicians.
2. *A continual search for either a religious or a secular moral standard that helped ground the changes that were occurring.* The search for a common morality was of continuing concern. Even the American frontier, which welcomed novelty, did not easily tolerate substantial moral transgressions. Paradoxically, the same society that had formed itself around an ideal of democracy and freedom was quite morally conservative and strict. The 'hustler' was the exception rather than the rule; so was the 'libertine.' Similar searches for a collectively defined moral standard existed in England and France.
3. *Family-rearing practices whose main purpose was the teaching of norms followed by adults.* The authority of elders was central to every era and supported by the prestige and influence of extended kin networks operating according to the principles of vertical association. This verticality was embedded in the school system and the extended family network.

Elias ([1939] 1978) was able to count on the above fixity to ground his narrative. Although he stated that the 'civilizing process does not follow a straight line' and that change is brought about through 'diverse crisscross movements, shifts and spurts in this or that direction' (186), he nevertheless concluded that the story of Western civilization was a journey towards increasingly complex restraints within a political and economic system that itself was becoming more centralized.

Thus, Elias did not adequately anticipate the phenomenon of 'reversal' or 'reactance' and the boomerang effect of nonconformity. Discussing the liberalization of the use of bathing costumes in public, for example, he explains that the revealing of the human body would not have been possible without the prior controlling of the sexual impulse (187). The implication here is that restraint of the sexual impulse became ingrained enough at some point not to be threatened by the sudden appearance of half-dressed women and men. Elias failed to consider, however, that, while the sequence of 'sexual restraint followed by bathing costumes' was correct, the appearance of bathing costumes could then have had the effect of re-stimulating sexual interest and weakening and reversing old restraints. Victorians who preferred to keep silent about prohibitions were afraid that the mention of the forbidden would lead to an activation of the desire mechanism. They might have understood quite well the social psychology of sudden reversal and the physiological nature of human emotion and desire.

Anticipating the possibility of a reversal in restraints, Elias recognized that many words and ideas that had been rendered 'silent' and 'private' would, at some point, have to be brought out into the open, particularly the 'thick wall of secrecy' on sexual matters built between parents and the adolescent (182). His prediction was accurate to a certain degree; such a dialogue did occur, beginning in the 1920s and reaching epidemic proportions following the 1960s. We are now dealing with the consequences of that dialogue and a new set of developments in late-modern Western societies. Lifting the restraint of silence has brought forward new, unexpected practices that now require their own analytical frameworks.

Thus, the history of the twentieth and the twenty-first centuries seems to involve intense questioning of former certainties. 'Restraint' was a suitable existing definition of a civilizing process based on the above-listed classical parameters. In contemporary culture, however, the entire notion of 'restraint' – as it has been known – becomes highly contingent and subject to deconstruction and reformation. Sometimes, the philosophy of restraint is even considered to have contributed to a proliferation of automated behaviours that have dampened critical awareness and personal satisfaction. This was one of the premises of the cultural revolution of the 1960s and much of the postmodern writings. The struggle for 'democratic rights' complicates the search for a standard ethic of civility based on restraint; likewise, the accelerating search for 'emotional freedom' complicates the meaning of civilized behaviour as hitherto defined.

Ironically, what Elias refers to as an 'internalization' of restraints has, in fact, helped liberate individuals from previous 'surveillance' agents that were active when people could not be trusted to manage their own self-regulation. This easing of surveillance (e.g., gender-segregated schooling and chaperoned dating) has not only put tremendous pressures on the individual for self-surveillance, but also given the individual space in which to evaluate whether certain restraints are desired or not. Similarly, the expansion of 'lifestyle choices' has allowed for revaluations of existing norms. Elias's 'process sociology' model continues to hold, except now *it holds in a two-way relationship between individual actors and social configurations in which individuals hold more discretionary power than ever before.*

In conjunction with the 'coming out of the body' in late modernity (Shilling 1993, Synnott, 1993), a distinct story can be extracted from the historical evidence presented so far. The story of Western civilization is not only the search for economic and political stability, but also the search for an optimal level of individual freedom of thought and emotional/sensory experience and expression. Sometimes, this progression has been the limited project of isolated thinkers and artists, while, at other times, it has been carried forward at the grass-roots level. The reclaiming of the body, together with its emotions and sensations, seems to have occurred not by the grace of restraints, but in spite of them.

The taming of chaotic forces (such as the forces of early medieval violence) and the 800-year journey towards an industrialized state should, therefore, be examined not only from the point of view of restraints, but also from the point of view of the freeing of a critical human awareness and the development of institutions. We are proposing that the 'civilizing process' has not been solely a one-way process involving the monopolization of violence by the state but, rather, the outcome of a two-way relationship between a state seeking to preserve order and a population seeking to preserve human liberties. As Tilly (1986, [1995] 2005, 2003b, 2004) has demonstrated, this relationship has been energized and regulated by a 'contentious politics' that has both limited and regulated the impulse towards chaos; such chaos can occur when a state is excessively powerful and also when a population has little political discipline.

What we are suggesting here is that institutions of the private and public type play as important a role in the regulation of violence as do the state's policing apparatus. The recognition of the important role played by the citizenry in the establishment of a culture in which violence is limited and regulated problematizes the 'civilizational perspective,' which sees civility as the outcome of the civilizing effects of democratization. Gary Lafree (2006) makes this distinction in his studies of crime. His study of homicide rates in forty-four countries from 1950 to 2000 does not fully support the civilizational perspective. He shows that homicide rates are highest in transitional democracies (25–49). In another perceptive work, *Losing Legitimacy: Street Crime and the Decline of Social Institutions in America* (1998) Lafree notes that between 1948 and 1998 street crime rates in America increased eightfold. He shows how these increases were historically patterned: since much of the crime explosion took place in the form of a 'crime wave' during the period 1960–70 and had an expected disproportionate impact on racial minorities, LaFree argues that social institutions are the key to understanding crime waves. He explains that crime in America increased along with political distrust, economic hardship, and family disintegration. He also notes that crime rates should be understood in historical context; interracial income inequalities can explain rises in crime rates even in periods of economic growth (1996). Moreover, decreases in crime rates (possible even in eras of recession) are possible, as happened during the 1990s when the 'crime bust' occurred in tandem with massive investments in criminal justice institutions (1998). This moves us to conclude that crime rates are responses to institutional situations but not necessarily indications of the authentic social integration of a given society. If, for example, increased surveillance decreases crime, we are no further ahead in understanding the civility ethos of the population, since repressive measures complicate observations of true motive.

Can we achieve a sufficient understanding of incivility by focusing solely on religious or moral accounts of societies? Or do we need to combine our understanding of a culture's moral and religious history with the history of its institutional development? What role do institutions play in the preservation of civility and the limitation of crime and violence?

A.R. Gillis (2004, 1989) similarly focuses on the institutional factor in civilizational development. In two groundbreaking articles that study state institutions and crime in nineteenth-century France, Gillis shows that educational and policing institutions had an important influence on crime rates. Gillis (1989) uses time-series analysis to show that the long-range effect of France's establishment of two national police forces was a decrease in major crimes between 1865 and 1913. Controlling for the fact that the sudden increase in police does correlate with increased reporting of crime, Gillis shows that, despite rises in reporting of lesser crimes, major crimes decreased as a direct result of increased state surveillance. He further proposes that it was not the crime rate that led to increased policing but the broader interest of the state to repress 'dangerous classes' and limit political challenges to the state. Gillis (2004) has also discovered in his studies of schooling, moral education, literacy, and crime in nineteenth-century France from 1852 to 1913 that the establishment of educational institutions given the mandate to produce conformity through a moral curriculum had a salient influence on crime rates. He specifies, however, that the defining factor in change in crime rates was 'literacy.' Just as crime rates decreased in the literate population, they increased in those portions of the population that remained illiterate. He suggests that public education and, importantly, literacy contributed to the idea that society was being threatened by 'dangerous classes.' Literacy was also essential to the development of complex state bureaucracies capable of recording, storing, and processing information about their populations. As Jack Goody (1989) has argued in his seminal work on the connection between the development of writing and the organization of strong-state bureaucratic societies, writing was as important to the formation of the central state as was the restraint of violence; it also played a seminal role in the organization and communication needed for the French Revolution (Markoff 1986:323–49).

Agreeing with LaFree's and Gillis's institutional approach to civilizational development, we remain additionally sceptical of narratives that ignore the complexities of interactions and how these are made contingent in eras such as ours when a multiplicity of voices increases consensus on certain levels while creating dissonance on others. We remain aware that many social trends and mentalities occur in 'waves' and that a multi-directional analysis is the only way in which we can safeguard against the muddling of causes and effects or the reductive dangers of nostalgia that occur as a result of studies that are limited to a short historical span.

In view of the above, we propose an alternate way of describing periods in which long-established restraints are substantially altered or abandoned. The changes are best considered a transformation of the 'civilizing process' rather than a dismantling of it. The 'reactance' to which we have brought attention through our review of the period 1930–2004 has created a variety of forms of discourtesy. We can no longer speak in terms of the 'well-mannered' and 'ill-mannered' or the 'well-bred' and 'ill-bred' individual. More is at stake than simply learning how to appear as a respectable and caring member of society. Sometimes, the social conditions of the society require reactionary behaviour that abridges politeness and the social graces in order to make a passionate point regarding the need for social change. We see this practised during the 1960s and after. So there are two ways of analysing uncivil acts: on one hand they can be lapses in protocol or acts of impoliteness due to oversight or due to the fact that society no longer provides clear-cut guidelines; on the other hand, they can be quite *purposive* and represent the actor's conscious desire to cause social change or get the upper hand in a social situation which he believes has the potential to diminish his rights and well-being as a person. Culpepper (1996) has studied such intentional impoliteness and considers it a tactic of 'intentional social agitation.' Certainly, the emotional charge is different in acts of unintentional and intentional discourtesy. Purposive acts of discourtesy can be observed in a variety of situations, ranging from family conflict to international negotiations between governments. They need to be considered as part of the civility process of a society.

We would not suggest that discourtesy did not exist in previous eras when elaborate courtesy codes required a certain formalism in social interactions. There were plenty of opportunities for discourteous behaviour and these involved purposive insults designed to attack the well-being, reputation, and honour of the adversary. This 'purposive discourtesy' was not limited to members of a given social class; the elites, the middle classes, and the working classes have had their distinctive ways of purposefully causing another person to lose face; how the impoliteness has been delivered has been dependent on what would normally pass as politeness and rudeness within that particular social class (Kleiner 1996:155–75).

**Socialization, Civility, and the Presentation of Self**

A macrological view of civility takes into account institutional and historical processes. Yet it does not adequately explain what makes people agree to control their thoughts, emotions, and acts in order to conform to culturally constructed norms. Regardless of whether a civility ritual is being followed, forgotten out of thoughtlessness or lack of training, or purposely omitted in order to cause dissonance, the process of civility is something learned as part of the socialization process. Not only does our development of our personal identity teach us the norms and rituals of our culture, but it instills in us emotions that may later on predispose us to be civil or uncivil. Civil identity is socially constructed and is dependent on a culture's definitions of pride, shame, and embarrassment and the conditions in which they are to be experienced. It is also dependent on personal biographical experiences.

The history of the human race consists of one generation teaching a subsequent generation the symbols and rules of social conduct they have received and learned to live by. The need to survive physically and socially makes an individual choose behaviours that will contribute to social cohesion, for it is known in some inner core of the self that complete social chaos would threaten the well-being of all, the self included.

The limitation of desire, therefore, is a universal phenomenon, essential if children are to learn and adopt the symbols and practices of their culture. Whether a system of socialization is founded on punishment and extinction of unwanted behaviours or the rewarding of desired characteristics, what motivates the child to agree to learn the code of his culture is his need to (1) gain love, approval, and acceptance in the social world within and beyond the confines of the family, and (2) achieve the competence and relative freedom already possessed by adults.

George Herbert Mead (1934) has provided an excellent preliminary understanding of how a child becomes a functioning adult capable of responding to others in society through a shared understanding of the meanings and practices that constitute socially accepted behaviour. While Mead does not delve extensively into the emotional nature of socialization (Robinson and Powell 1979), he does outline a useful system for analysing the development of role adoption, shared meanings, and common social values, which are universals in all social communications.

Mead explains that a child learns to see himself as an individual both separate from the social as well as intimately affected by its codes. For Mead, a child is not born with a personality but, rather, with the *ability to form one* during his exchanges with the world of *significant others* (parents and kin) and *generalized others* (the larger social arena of actors and institutions lying outside his immediate experiences in his personal circle). As the child grows older he begins participating in *games* and learns that his position in a given game is 'defined' in relation to positions and roles occupied by the other players in the game. By observing the rules and procedures of group action, the child learns the taking on of 'roles' and, eventually, the nature and function of symbols. Although he may, while play-acting, take on the roles of his parents or an admired person, it is through participating in games with peers that he learns the meaning of situating himself in the world beyond the family. By 'anticipating' the requirements of various roles, he rehearses for the day when he will have to choose a set of adult roles. This interactive experience with the world creates a personality that is both an expression of the 'I' as well as the 'Me,' which Mead considers the internalized repository of the codes of the *generalized other* – in brief, the social order (135–72). The 'I' is socialized through a 'we-ness' process and begins seeing itself as a 'Me,' a product of social interaction in a culture in which certain practices and norms are held in higher regard than are others. The 'game' is, therefore, one of the child's earliest introductions to the concept of civility and civil (cooperative) behaviour.

Symbolic interactionists, heirs to Mead's legacy, further specify that the taking on of roles that are foreign to the child helps him develop the ability to *define a situation*. He evaluates himself as the player of the role and in relation to the role itself and its requirements (i.e., the *situation*). Such overall evaluation that goes beyond the immediate and narrow needs of the self leads to the *objectification of the self*. An important part of this experience of objectification rests in observing the behaviour of others and *imagining* what must be their inner experience. Mead locates the development of understanding and sympathy between subjects within this imaginative and projective act. It is a perfectly rational explanation of a complex socialization process that could apply to every culture. Whatever the codes, they are learned in this manner, even though they may be subject to the forces of later reversal or rebellion.

Mead's theory is highly dependent on cognitive normalcy. His project was one of cognition and perception rather than critical evaluation of emotional interaction and conflict. Seeking an understanding of the process that permitted an intelligent being to reflect on himself, he used role models to explain how a child learned to become aware of himself. Although he concentrated on studying cooperative action, he did not give sufficient attention to the unequal power ratios that might predispose one party to adopt the meanings of another but with extreme reluctance; nor did he take sufficient notice of situations of conflict in which the very idea of shared meanings becomes distasteful and requires defensive and subversive actions. In brief, Mead minimized the conflict aspect of relationships, believing that 'no hard-and-fast line can be drawn between our own selves and the selves of others, since our own selves exist and enter as such into our experience only insofar as the selves of others exist and enter as such into our experience also' (196).

He recognized that the child himself had a certain socializing effect on the adult, but saw this interaction as part of the overall building of 'consensus.' His conciliatory sociology was better suited to an era less given to questioning the idea of *consensus*. Unfortunately, it does not fully explain occurrences in an emotionally expressive, media-populated, child-centred, parent-centred, capital-driven, pluralist society. Certainly, the French monarchs and their children had shared meanings prior to the arrival of Louis XVI – the children were seen with the queen and king as seldom as possible; their bedrooms were even located far away from the bedrooms of their parents. This was a shared meaning and a definition of roles in the pure sense of Mead's sociology. But one thing missing was an interview with the children to determine how they felt about the arrangement.

Despite the above-mentioned weakness, Mead's theory of socialization is invaluable to our understanding of social interactions because he explains how shared meanings are dependent on shared symbols. If there is to be social attunement there must be a certain common understanding *and* acceptance of symbols and the values to which they are attached.

Similar to Mead, Charles Horton Cooley (1909, 1922) considered socialization as a process of role adoption. He explained that a person becomes a social being by virtue of the fact that he is dependent on others for a worthy sense of self. Cooley's 'looking-glass self' makes the mirror (or the other) a direct point of reference in the identity of a social actor who must construct a sense of personal identity by *imagining* what others may be thinking of him: 'A self-idea of this sort seems to have three principal elements: the imagination of our appearance to the other person; the imagination of his judgment of that appearance; and some sort of self-feeling, such as pride and mortification' (1909:184).

More so than Mead, Cooley (1922) recognized that mutual interdependence in social relations creates emotional reactions (264). A person 'monitors' himself in order to be able to 'read' the mind of others and, thereby, receive necessary feedback on his self. Cooley ventured into new territory by using the words 'pride' and 'mortification' to describe the reactions available to an individual during his appraisals of his position vis-à-vis other social actors. Although he did not explain the anatomy of these emotional states and what primary emotions may have been at their foundation, he did remind repeatedly in his writings that the central motivation for cooperative social action was self-esteem and social inclusion.

Erving Goffman (1959, 1963, 1967) developed Cooley's conception of human interaction further. While he did not use the word 'shame,' he did explain that much of social interaction was constructed to avoid sentiments of 'embarrassment.' Goffman's social individual is intensely aware that his acceptance in society will depend very much on the 'impressions' he leaves on others. In Goffman's social system, the individual is an *actor* in a true theatrical sense. It is his desire to be adjusted to the social world that causes him to care about the reactions of others. Embarrassment, a momentary indication of maladjustment, is a normal aspect of interaction and serves to re-establish interactive order:

> One assumes that embarrassment is a normal part of normal social life, the individual becomes uneasy not because he is personally maladjusted but rather because he is not ... embarrassment is not an irrational impulse breaking through social prescribed behaviour, but part of this orderly behaviour itself. (1967:109, 111)

According to Goffman, what facilitates social harmony is the fact that social 'attunement' is a mutual need of all social actors. The 'management of impressions' is a relational process that binds all actors in 'performances' designed to represent each actor in the best light (1959:20–30). If an actor is to present an acceptable 'front,' one which his 'audience' accepts as legitimate and desired, he must to a certain degree accept the duties connected to his social role as well as the values which his audience holds in high esteem.

This 'dramatic realization' (30) is accomplished through the communication of information about the actor via verbal and non-verbal cues. These cues are used by an actor's audience to evaluate the authenticity of his social performance (35). While the actor may indulge in aberrant behaviour or thoughts and emotions that contradict the 'front' he is presenting to society, his acceptance or rejection by others will, nevertheless, depend on whether he is able to convince his audience that his identity and personal characteristics are socially sanctioned.

The necessity of maintaining an acceptable 'front' is what decreases the possibility of conflict between individuals and between groups. The pressure on individuals to conform to the standards of their 'reference' groups creates the potential for the 'discrediting' and 'stigmatizing' of a given actor (1963:42). Once a person is stigmatized due to a failed frontal presentation, he must regain entry into the social group by exhibiting behaviours that disassociate him from the impression formerly given (44). This can be done through apology, self-justification, or by showing that the audience was also to blame for the failure of the interactional exchange.

Goffman's view of social interaction is vital to our understanding of civility. All civil interactions (and also uncivil ones) consist of presenting a 'face' to others and helping others 'preserve' or 'lose' face. That is why civility is a 'collaborative' phenomenon that confirms the social value of those who are involved in the civil interaction. The arrival at a 'working consensus' is dependent on mutual caretaking of face or front. A certain amount of trust and effort is needed in order to avoid 'embarrassing predicaments.' Such predicaments occur when an actor's 'line' or 'front' is put in question either by a 'loss of poise' or by a challenge emanating from his audience. An actor, therefore, is dependent at once on 'reparatory' help from his audience as well as guidance from his own judgment of his 'performance.' Goffman, like Cooley, believes that the evaluation of one's performance often involves an imaginative act that can work for or against oneself: 'He may ... add to the precariousness of his position by engaging in just those defensive maneuvers that he would employ if he were really guilty. In this way it is possible for all of us to become fleetingly for ourselves the worst person we can imagine that others might imagine us to be' (1959:236).

Civility, therefore, consists not only of helping the other realize that our judgment of his performance is favourable but also of helping the other avoid the need for morbid introspection. Much of this mutual reassurance is delivered through non-verbal cues (1967:4) learned through ritualized symbolic action appropriate to the given culture.

Goffman rarely uses the word 'shame' in his theory of social interaction. Although it is somewhat implicit in his discussion of 'embarrassment,' it remains ambivalent and prevents his theory of interaction from taking comprehensive account of different gradations and types of embarrassment and shame. For example, his explanations do not sufficiently specify how embarrassment can be other-directed or self-directed, dependent on whether one is trying to live up to publicly or personally generated expectations. We will discuss this distinction further in our section on the emotional nature of shame.

A person has two alternatives when confronted with an embarrassing situation that makes him 'lose his footing.' How he reacts will depend very much on whether he receives reparatory help from his audience. If he wishes to acknowledge his loss of poise, he can admit wrongdoing and make apologies, he can claim to have been misunderstood and try to change the audience's appraisal of him, or he can deny that he cares what the audience thinks of him. If he receives little encouragement or help from his audience, he may even deny that he feels embarrassed or diminished in his self-esteem. He may develop a thick skin. This denial can be accomplished through aggression directed at those who have caused his loss of face and/or the decision to conquer future unnerving situations through the maintenance of an unflustered front that hides emotional perturbation or awkward sentiments. Although most individuals do not develop a thick skin, they do prefer to conceal their unease during socially threatening situations or during moments when their self-evaluation suffers a setback (Edelman 1987). As Helen Block Lewis ([1971] 1974) has demonstrated in her extensive analysis of conversations between psychotherapists and their clients, even in the therapeutic trust environment individuals are prone to not making direct references to their sentiments of embarrassment, preferring to use dialogue that represents these emotions indirectly.

So it would seem that the subject of 'embarrassment' or 'shame' not only involves the bypassing of taboo subjects but is also a form of taboo in itself, for facing the issue may release painful sentiments. It is, therefore, understandable that many writers who have referred to shame have failed to explore it deeply. Elias's study of the civilizing process in the West possesses considerable psychological insight because he shows how the experience of shame and embarrassment becomes internalized and hidden from view in tandem with the development of rationality. The rising valuation of 'delicacy,' 'discretion,' and 'propriety' not only serves to identify unwanted behaviours, but also has a dampening effect on emotional expression, including the disclosure of painful sentiments such as embarrassment and shame, especially in cultures that do not have a variety of words to differentiate between major and minor embarrassments. So, part of social propriety becomes the concealment of sentiments that might create mutual unease ([1939]

1978, 1982). This propensity to deny shame has been discussed at considerable length by Kaufman (1989), Kaufman and Raphael (1984), and Keltner and Buswell (1997).

It would seem then that the manner in which civility is practised in a given culture is not only dependent on its historical traditions but also on the manner in which guilt, shame, self-esteem, empathy, and emotional expression are handled. In fact, manifestations of courtesy and discourtesy are, very often, affected not only by the emotions of guilt, embarrassment, shame, and pride, but also by the extent to which a culture allows forthright demonstrations of emotions.

It is unfortunate that few of the above-mentioned writerse use their theoretical work to go deeper into the subject of emotions. As a result, they present a dramaturgical conception of society that leaves much unsaid regarding the emotional nature of personal and public interaction processes. Yet, we need to better understand the emotional basis of the socialization process and how emotional reactions can have a considerable effect on civility. We hope to complete the paradigm in the remainder of this part of the book while continuing to build a descriptive sociology of civility that takes cross-cultural differences into account.

As we have argued throughout this book, the study of civility requires an interest in a variety of subjects. History, economics, politics, philosophy, religion, cultural norms, sexuality, gastronomy, and emotions all play a vital role in the formation of civil and uncivil behaviour. In the following sections we hope to explain the emotional as well as cross-cultural aspects of civil interaction. We hope that this will deepen our understanding of civility. We begin with the cross-cultural dimension before proceeding to the emotional dimension because, more often than not, the form and extent of emotional expressions will be affected by the 'mentality' of a given culture.

## The Cross-Cultural Dimension

We must first make an important distinction between 'communal' cultures that favour restraints in the interests of social cohesion and 'individualistic' cultures that tolerate the removal of certain restraints (or the imposition of new ones) in the interests of personal freedom and identity. The two have different rules, produce different personal identities, and create different conundrums in civility practices. Naturally, these tendencies are not either/or categories, but, rather, tendencies (or ideal types) that can be found in varying combinations in all cultures.

In most cultures, however, one trait or mentality will predominate over the other.

Taking such cross-cultural differences into account not only helps us understand other cultures, but, additionally, deepens our insights into our own practices. There is no better way to notice and understand why one does things in a certain way than to see others doing them differently. Understanding the complexities of cross-cultural factors also allows us to minimize the misunderstandings that appear when practices of one type of culture are imposed on another type of culture. William G. Rosenberg (1998) has studied the effects of superimposing individualistic Western notions of freedom and the pursuit of material well-being on post-Communist societies habituated to a traditional communal view of relationships; he cautions that this sudden tension between two habituations forced to share the same public and private space may actually be creating resistance to democracy itself (518–40). Similarly, Eisenstadt (1998a,b) argues for a civilizational understanding based on a recognition of the different streams of historical, moral, religious, and economic developments that produce differing private and institutional identities.

In fact, just as conception of selfhood differs from culture to culture, so do the rules governing emotional expression. What is considered a 'positive' or a 'negative' emotion will differ from one culture to another, depending on the interaction values of the culture and what is considered desirable at the personal and collective levels (Ellsworth 1994:45). *By consequence, what is openly said – and what is kept implicit and ambiguous – will vary across cultural lines and according to specific interaction situations involving factors as varied as the relationship of the speakers, their relative power in relation to one another, and their culture's values regarding intimacy, distancing, and imposition.* Such variations can also exist in the same society where different ethnic groups follow different interaction values.

We experienced an instructive case of cultural dissonance during a voyage to the former Yugoslavia when it was still under Soviet influence. We entered a store that had very few goods left on the shelves. This was due to the poverty and political instability of the region. Our travelling companion remarked with ironic humour that the store must have been doing very well since everything seemed to be sold out. The clerk laughed. Encouraged by the laughter, our companion continued making ironic comments about the empty shelves, thinking that the clerk would understand that he was showing dismay at the consequences of Sovietization. The clerk laughed even harder. We suddenly noticed, with considerable alarm, that the clerk's eyes were blazing with rage. We excused ourselves and retired to our hotel where we looked up 'anger' in the index of our guidebook to Yugoslavia; we learned that people in that region of the world sometimes start laughing gaily whenever feeling extreme contempt for another person. The clerk had responded with very strong anger, but according to the manner of her culture. In an Islamic country, the same scene might have led to the withdrawal of the clerk into a coldly respectful silence and a subsequent exaggerated politeness. In America, the offence taken might have been expressed by a threatening stare or a direct put-down of our own persons. The sentiment of distaste and the taking of offence are universal; the manner in which it is expressed, however, is culture-specific.

Peter B. Smith and Michael Harris Bond (1998) caution that the search for reliability in studies that cross cultural boundaries and habituations must take into account the fact that particularly Western conceptions of human behaviour are often used to design surveys that are then applied to non-Western cultures. Referring to the findings of various anthropologists during the 1950s and 1960s, Smith and Bond differentiate between 'etic' and 'emic' studies, specifying that 'etic' studies try to locate what is universally common while 'emic' studies focus on how an activity or meaning is represented in a specific local social setting (57). The problem of 'etic-oriented' studies is that they may use dimensions for a meta-analysis that are not appropriate to all of the cultures being studied. For example, to ask respondents in two countries 'how' they express anger towards their employer may be the wrong manner of framing the question, considering that one of the cultures may not favour showing aggression to begin with. Malaysia, for instance, happens to be the top-ranked country in the world in which relationships involving power are very distanced and formal (47); it would be expected that a Malaysian would not be disposed to speak without deference to a superior and might find the question embarrassing or even baffling.

Furthermore, there are variations within a culture that become lost when we refer to survey results that are calculated according to a measurement of 'means' (41–2). When speaking of violence in America, for example, it is useful to specify that rates of murder and violent confrontation are remarkably higher in those regions in the south and the west where climate is hotter (Cohen and Nisbett 1994) and/or where more formal codes of honour and courtesy predispose citizens to be sensitive to insult. In a study of southern Americans, Cohen et al. (1999) discovered that while southerners restrained themselves more than northerners during the initial stages of conflict, they were far more given to sudden bursts of anger as the conflict advanced and entered the stage of insults. Appropriately, the authors entitled their article, 'When You Call Me That, Smile!'

Smith and Bond (1998) suggest that a harmonization of 'etic-emic' views should be the goal of studies including more than one culture (41, 67–8). This delicate feat is accomplished by taking the cultural background and values of each group into account prior to arriving at more universal comparisons. We have tried to do this in the preceding chapters by giving considerable weight to the biographies of each of the cultures included in this book and the different streams of 'mentality' that have developed as a consequence of a variety of interactive factors.

Further comparative studies of Western countries that share common technical environments would even further improve our understanding of how civility varies across cultural boundaries. Although Smith and Bond provide extensive references to cross-cultural studies, the majority of the studies they quote compare Western and East Asian countries. There remains a considerable need for separate regional research on the Middle East, Europe, and North America. Studies that would set out to compare 'emotional expression' and 'individualism' in various Western countries, as we have tried to do in this section, would yield interesting results and might show that the traits of 'individualism' and 'emotional expressiveness' are not always positively correlated, as we have found in our own study (more on this shortly).

Certain cross-cultural standards and measures have been successfully located by researchers who have taken 'etic-emic' distinctions into account. Aware that general survey results do not necessarily explain differences in temperament at the local level, these researchers have studied cultures individually prior to developing broader cross-cultural measures and comparisons. Mursy and Wilson (2000), for example, have explained in a study of Egyptian complimenting that the manner in which a compliment is accepted in Egypt is very much based on the values of the communal group; the recipient of the compliment accepts it in the name of the group rather than as a recognition of an achievement due solely to personal talent.

Lorenzo's (2001) study of compliment responses among British and Spanish university students has found notable differences. The British tend to deflect the compliment by withdrawing slightly, while the Spaniards use it to aggrandize themselves, but not without an appropriate measure of self-deprecating humour. Both tactics serve to communicate the deferential message that the beneficiary is not altogether worthy of the compliment.

So, it would seem that although the need for civil reaction and the psychological process of 'preserving face' is a universal phenomenon, the manner in which civility is practised is affected by the beliefs and values of specific cultures (Ingelhart, Basanez, and Moreno 1998). We, therefore, question the notion that technology has a globally levelling effect on culture, for we see no overwhelming evidence of this even in nations that share common technologies and religions. The McDonaldization perspective of globalization (Ritzer 1993) is far too reliant on economic explanations and the consumption of pop culture and not sufficiently balanced by studies of interaction and moral valuation (Davetian 2001b). Globalization theories that posit that the sharing of capitalism and its products will level local cultures are overly reliant on the idea that people with various cultural histories will react in the same way if placed in the same marketing environment. The behaviour of a Frenchman, an Englishman, and an American, however, remain considerably different even though they may consider themselves technical, political, and economic allies.

A traditional communal culture needs two conditions in order to live up to its name: social customs designed to favour the continuance of the culture with as little cultural dissonance as possible and a morality standard that stabilizes relationships according to codes of duty and obligation. While technical changes are welcomed in such societies, changes in behaviour and beliefs are regarded with some suspicion because they are thought to possess the potential for destabilizing existing cultural consensus regarding the culture's core identity. Thus, a communal society that has maintained its customs for centuries can very well adopt technology exported by 'individualistic' societies without necessarily abandoning its own interaction code. So, the distinction between 'agricultural' and 'industrial' societies is a superficial distinction and no longer useful to studies of late-modern cultures. In Japan, for example, the goals of Western technical progress were achieved through the substantial preservation of long-standing communal Japanese social values and interaction styles (Smith and Bond 1997:203). We cannot stress enough that when we speak of 'communal' we are not speaking of technically underdeveloped cultures, but, rather, of cultures that value communal continuity and vertical associations. Equally troublesome is the notion that communalism dissipates as smaller towns are replaced with large urban centres (Moser and Corroyer 2001:611–25). In countries where religious ethics, and/or a strong national identity, continue to have a strong influence on public morality, civility practices are fairly standard whether one is in a small town or a city setting. While the anonymity of the city does provide opportunities for the breaking of moral codes, the civility ethos remains broadly applied. It may become abridged in an urban setting, but it does not become redundant.

Émile Durkheim ([1897b] 1997) noted the difference between communalistic and individualistic societies when he described how a complex division of labour had facilitated the transition from 'mechanical' to 'organic' solidarity in social relations, the latter permitting more variance between individual preferences while, nevertheless, creating a new form of interdependence. Our own perspective is slightly different, for we find that 'mechanical' and 'organic' solidarity can co-exist in a given society even though it may have achieved a complex and specialized division of labour. In some cultures, rituals dating to an era of 'mechanical' solidarity will be preserved even after a society has entered an 'organic' phase in which there is considerable specialization and anonymity. This is especially noticeable in cultures that suddenly move from agrarian to industrial modes of production in a short span of time due to the importing of technology from cultures that took a long time to develop the technology in the first place.

In general, the communal social ethos will favour the 'social or group personality' of the individual. Personal identity here will be defined in terms of a person's adaptation to the codes of the community. The community, for its part, will be reluctant to encourage the development of a self-centred personal identity that is given to departing from communal standards. Because of this, definitions of 'honourable' and 'shameful' behaviour will be specified with a fair amount of clarity. The *idea* of community will be maintained despite mobility and urban centralization – even in large cities, strangers will relate to one another based on their mutual awareness of a standard communal interactive code. The replaying of specified civility rituals will help confirm communal identity while creating sentiments of harmony between individuals.

Predictably, communal societies slow down the development of self-referential identity. 'Obligation' and 'duty' towards a variety of social hierarchies temper the development of an independence-oriented consciousness. In addition, restraints placed on emotions assure the expression of those emotions that favour group solidarity and the suppression of those that might threaten such (Tajfel 1972).

The 'individualistic' social ethos has its own opportunities and limitations. While it allows considerable opportunities for the development of a self-directed life, it complicates the maintenance of a communal personality based on conformity to homogenized codes that go beyond specifications of individual talents. As personal choice increases, an uncoupling takes place between the individual and the community.

Jurgen Habermas (1990) has addressed this issue of 'uncoupling' or 'alienation' in individualistic societies by arguing that the passing from formal to informal society has required radical transformations in moral conventions. He stresses that the 'social world of legitimately regulated interpersonal relations, a world to which one was naively habituated and which was uncritically accepted, is abruptly deprived of its quasi-natural validity' (126). Using a different viewpoint, yet noticing the same crisis, Giddens ([1991] 2001) observes that readily available public information has made individuals become aware of problems that they themselves may not possess. A person entering marriage, for example, is eerily aware of the high rate of divorce (14). This certainly has the effect of creating two parallel anomies: one that is personally experienced and another that is felt through one's imagination of the predicaments of others. Both of the above writers point to an increasingly complex society in which there is great potential for social hesitancy. Philippe Breton (2002) cautions that this complexity translates into 'fear of others' and becomes a precipitating factor during acts of confrontation and violence.

The distinction between 'communal' and 'individualistic' societies is not a categorical one. Much variation can exist within a culture, as well as between cultures that are classified as 'communal' or 'individualistic.' We are speaking of traits rather than categorical states of consciousness. These traits require a more assiduous analysis that distinguishes between 'formality' and 'informality,' for an informal culture can continue to adhere to formal moral values, provided those values are so taken for granted that they do not need to be openly demonstrated through formal regulatory interaction rituals.

Whether a given group or culture favours communal or individualistic standards will have a considerable effect on its civility rituals. In 'conventional' cultures, manners, politeness, and deference are mutually connected and imply acceptance of the authority of standard codes linking morality and courtesy. The literature of the medieval era, the Renaissance, and the Victorian era established a strong link between propriety, virtue (morality), and deference. Social membership involved a noticeable amount of 'moral obedience' and 'deference' to rank. In contemporary times, however, due to a decreased tolerance of authoritarian codes, we are forced to make a distinction between manners, politeness, and deference. The three involve different emotional investments and compromises. Deference – more than manners and politeness – implies a submission to the non-negotiable power and influence of another person or institution. One can have impeccable manners but not defer to other people's wishes and remain quite self-determined. So a distinction needs be made between the ways in which the self is represented and negotiated in conventional communal and post-conventional individualistic cultures.

In fact, much of 'inter-civilizational conflict' may be connected to the moral disagreements that occur when communal and individualistic societies come face to face. Seeking to find present and human causes for their differences, members of such diverging cultures may resort to demonizing each other's customs and social values. Sometimes, passionate references are made to differences in religious belief, but these differences are only part of the answer. On other occasions, when détente is sought, references are made to their common technical cultures in order to minimize the differences that are value-oriented rather than technical (Davetian 2001b). Neither narrative leads to authentic intercultural understanding.

A fairly instructive system of classification of social values has emerged from the work of Geert Hofstede. In a seminal study, *Culture's Consequences* (1980), Hofstede uses survey data from forty studies of 'national characters,' each one comparing five or more nations. These studies supplemented his own study of 117,000 IBM workers in various countries. By 1983, Hofstede had accumulated data on value differences in fifty countries. His study debunked the belief current in the 1950s and 1960s that corporate management style was a universal reality. He found that management styles and values varied from country to country. Similar observations have been made by Inglehart and Baker, who have analysed the data produced as part of the World Values Survey (WVS) (1999) and developed 'Inglehart's Map,' in which a series of variables have been condensed into two dimensions representing cultural variation ('traditional v. secular-rational' and 'survival v. self-expression'). Hofstede (2001) agrees in a recent edition of *Culture's Consequences* (2001) that the dimensions developed following the WVS data accord with his own mapping: 'Inglehart's key cultural dimensions were significantly correlated with [my] dimensions. Well-being versus survival correlated strongly with individualism and masculinity; secular-rational versus traditional authority correlated negatively with power distance' (33–4).

Hofstede's findings move us to continue questioning whether economic globalization and transnational corporate projects will eliminate cultural distinctions. Hofstede's study shows considerable statistical variations between respondents from different cultures. While the results cannot be used to typify all members of a culture, they can be used to show that considerable variation exists in the 'values' generally favoured by cultures. So although the results indicate that the Japanese value authority more than do the English, there are no guarantees that a minority of English might not value authority more than their Japanese counterparts. What is being sought is a general typology of cultural preferences.

In order to locate value tendencies in various countries, Hofstede constructed four 'dimensions' (or criteria) that functioned independently of one another and occurred in differing combinations. These dimensions were: (1) individualism versus collectivism (the degree to which a person's identity is defined by personal achievement and personal preferences, or, on the other hand, by the imperative of maintaining the profile of the community to which the individual belongs); (2) large or small power distance (the degree to which respect and deference are exhibited towards those in positions of authority); (3) strong or weak uncertainty avoidance (the degree to which planning aims at decreasing uncertainty and increasing stability, and, conversely, the degree to which risk is welcomed or avoided); and (4) masculinity versus femininity (the importance given to achievement [masculinity] as opposed to interpersonal harmony [femininity]).

Hofstede then gave each of the countries a rating by averaging the responses that concurred with each dimension. From the data compiled by Hofstede (1983), we have extracted a summary of the ten most individualistic and ten most collectivist societies, based on three dimensions which interest us: *individualism-collectivism, power distancing*, and *uncertainty avoidance* (see tables 9.1 and 9.2). The differences between America, Britain, and France reveal some startling facts that reawaken our interest in their historical differences.

Hofstede's data suggest a consistent negative correlation between individualism and the valuation of power distance and uncertainty

Table 9.1
Overall ranking across three dimensions for the ten 'most individualistic' nations (numbers indicate rank out of 51)

| Country | Individualism | Power distance | Uncertainty avoidance |
|---|---|---|---|
| United States | 1 | 38 | 43 |
| Australia | 2 | 41 | 37 |
| Britain | 3 | 43 | 47 |
| Canada | 4 | 39 | 41 |
| Netherlands | 4 | 40 | 35 |
| New Zealand | 6 | 50 | 40 |
| Italy | 7 | 34 | 23 |
| Belgium | 8 | 20 | 5 |
| Denmark | 9 | 51 | 51 |
| France | 10 | 15 | 12 |

Table 9.2
Overall ranking across three dimensions for the ten nations 'most favouring power distance' and 'uncertainty avoidance' (numbers indicate rank out of 50):

| Country | Individualism | Power distance | Uncertainty avoidance |
|---|---|---|---|
| Malaysia | 36 | 1 | 46 |
| Panama | 51 | 2 | 12 |
| Guatemala | 53 | 3 | 3 |
| Philippines | 31 | 3 | 44 |
| Venezuela | 50 | 5 | 21 |
| Mexico | 32 | 6 | 18 |
| Arab region | 26 | 7 | 27 |
| Ecuador | 52 | 8 | 28 |
| Indonesia | 47 | 8 | 41 |
| Africa (west) | 40 | 10 | 34 |

avoidance. *Yet, France stands out as an exception to this rule.* Although rated in the top ten for individualism it also rates unexpectedly high in power distance and uncertainty avoidance:

*France:* Individualism (10), Power Distance (15), Uncertainty Avoidance (12).
*United States:* Individualism (1), Power Distance (38), Uncertainty Avoidance (43).

*Britain:* Individualism (3), Power Distance (43), Uncertainty Avoidance (47).

Hofstede did not note or explain this anomaly. Yet, it is one of the landmarks of cross-cultural studies. Here we have a French culture that possesses strong individualistic *as well as* collectivist tendencies. Remarkably, France, although 10th out of a field of 53 on the individuality trait, scores nearly equally high on the power distance trait (15th) as well as the uncertainty avoidance trait (12th). We would expect it to score somewhere around 35th or 40th on these two last traits. We will attempt to explain this paradoxical finding later on. As for the negative correlation between power distancing/uncertainty avoidance and individualism for other countries ranking top in power distancing, the correlation remains predictable and with few noticeable exceptions. It is interesting to note that Belgium, a country that has substantially adopted French civility practices, also scores high in individualism (8th) as well as power distance (20th) and uncertainty avoidance (5th).

We are moved to wonder why France would value individualism *as well as* power distancing. *Could it be that something in its emotional socialization system requires the co-existence of what might initially appear as opposing tendencies?* If so, what can this tell us about French civility practices and social norms, as well as those of England and America?

It should be noted that the valuation of power distance and uncertainty avoidance entail a certain adherence to vertical authority. In order that distance be preserved, certain codes of deference are required, and these codes are implicitly founded on the premise that certain individuals are of more worth and possess more wisdom and experience than others. In a parenting situation, the maintenance of power distance would require that considerable authority – and perhaps even special knowledge – be assigned to the parent.

Hofstede's study is particularly convincing because it was undertaken in a corporate environment in which one would expect relative homogeneity of attitude across national boundaries – it would seem that even IBM's bureaucracy and standard corporate values were not able to neutralize cultural differences.

A similar measure of values has been developed by Shalom Schwartz and collaborators (Schwartz and Bilsky 1987, 1990; Schwartz 1991). Their findings confirm the negative correlation between values ascribed to self-direction, stimulation, hedonism, achievement, and power on one hand, and security, conformity, tradition, benevolence, and universalism on the other. There seems to be a negative correlation between agreeableness-achievement (–0.37), agreeableness-power (–0.36), and agreeableness-hedonism (–0.40). There is also a positive correlation between extroversion-stimulation (0.25) and extroversion-benevolence (0.24), and a negative correlation between extroversion-tradition (–0.25). It would seem that the restraint of affect and the preservation of collective stability are correlated, or at least have been until now. An interesting finding of this study is the positive correlation between conformity and conscientiousness (0.23) (cited in Smith and Bond, 1998:3; 84:table 4.1).

Whether a culture subscribes to communal or individualistic values – and the degree to which it values authority and uncertainty-avoidance – will affect the manner in which it relates to 'time, context, and space' and, by consequence, the type of politeness rituals that it employs. Again, we are reminded that America could not have developed anything but an individualistic culture (high in voluntarism, but low in authority-deference) by the sheer fact that its jewel city, New York City, was built by the grace of sheer personal grit.

**Time, Context, Space, and Cultural Ideology**

In *Dance of Life* (1983), the celebrated anthropologist Edward T. Hall explains that every culture is affected by the manner in which time, context, and space are experienced. It is stunning that his discoveries are not included in most introductory social science texts. He and Mildred Reed Hall further elaborate on these measures of cultural difference in *Understanding Cultural Differences* (1990), a book that analyses differences between American, French, and German notions of ideal interaction and best business practices. While Hofstede's (1983) measures of individualism and communalism provide a strong departure point for understanding civility differences between cultures, Hall's analysis allows us to further refine our understanding of these differences.

Hall identifies important differences between 'low-context' and 'high-context' cultures based on an analysis of how a culture relates to time, context, and place. High-context societies tend to be partial to complex communal rituals, while low-context societies tend to be more individualistic. Expectedly, the former include richer communications networks than the latter and require deft manoeuvring in social and civility practices.

Hall (1983) differentiates between *monochronic time* and *polychronic time*, explaining that a considerable amount of bitterness between people of different cultures occurs due to different conceptions of time (179). Monochronic time is characterized as linear use of time and is understood in terms of quantifiable segments. In monochronic time (M-time), events are planned to occur one at a time; the importance of preventing extraneous events from interrupting a set schedule takes precedence over interpersonal relationships. Efficiency takes on extreme importance and is measured through the 'use' of time. How time is 'spent,' 'saved,' 'wasted,' or 'made' reveals the quantitative nature of linear time. Polychronic time (P-time), on the other hand, is characterized by the simultaneous occurrence of many things and by a great involvement with people. People act differently, depending on which conception of time is prevalent in their culture.

Monochronic people:

- do one thing at a time
- concentrate on the job
- are low-context and need lots of information
- are committed to the job
- adhere religiously to plans
- are concerned about not disturbing others
- show great respect for private property; seldom borrow and lend things
- emphasize promptness
- are accustomed to short-term relationships

Polychronic people:

- do many things at once
- are highly distractible and subject to interruptions
- are high-context and already have information
- are committed to people and human relationships
- change plans often and easily
- borrow or lend easily
- base promptness on the type of relationship
- have a strong tendency to build lifetime relationships (1990:14)

Although these patterns cannot be applied with rigidity to all cultures, a given culture will have a tendency to lean more towards one mode than the other. Additionally, ethnic groups within a culture may have predispositions towards one mode even though the interaction ideals of the majority culture are in the opposing mode. Hall categorizes northern European and American cultures as monochromic and Mediterranean cultures as polychronic.

The manner in which people relate to time is correlated to whether a culture is *high-context (HC)* or *low-context (LC)*. High and low context refers to the amount of information that a person can manage without feeling that he is being overloaded or not being given all the facts he requires. People from a high-context culture often convey information implicitly and maintain larger networks of personal contacts and sources of information. People from low-context cultures tend to verbalize background information to a considerable degree and tend not to be fully informed of what is not within their immediate interest (1976:7).

Hall specifies that a major distinction between HC and LC modes of communication is the degree of interpersonal involvement as well as the amount of information exchanged:

> A high-context (HC) communication or message is one in which *most* of the information is already in the person, while very little is in the coded, explicit, transmitted part of the message. A low-context (LC) communication is just the opposite: i.e. the mass of the information is vested in the explicit code. Twins who have grown up together can and do communicate more economically (HC) than two lawyers in a courtroom during a trial (LC), a mathematician programming a computer, two politicians drafting legislation, two administrators writing a regulation. (1976; cited in Hall and Hall 1990:6)

It would seem that cultures that value complex information networks in families and with friends and close colleagues are of the high-context type. HC individuals 'do not require, nor do they expect, much in-depth, background information. This is because they keep themselves informed about everything having to do with the people who are important in their lives' (Hall 1976:7). According to Hall's topology, America would be classified as a low-context culture while France would qualify as a high-context society. We would add that England is neither, falling into a category that Hall does not use: *moderate context*. We will explain this further.

Generally, Hall and Hall's (1990) definition of HC (high-context) and LC (low-context) cultures can be summarized according to a series of characteristics or outcomes:

HC  Many covert and implicit messages (metaphoric; read between the lines)
LC  Many overt and explicit messages (plain and literal meanings)
HC  Internalized messages (inner focus of control; self-blame)
LC  plainly coded messages (focus on outer control; blaming of external sources for failure)
HC  Much non-verbal coding (considerable body language)
LC  Verbalized details (restrained body language)
HC  Reserved reactions (react more inwardly than outward)
LC  Reactions on the surface (react more outwardly)
HC  Distinct in-groups and out-groups (closely knit groups of affiliation: families)
LC  Flexible in-groups and out-groups (open and public groups of affiliation)
HC  Strong social bonds (relationship is more important than the task; long-term relationships)
LC  Loose social bonds (task more important than relationships; short term relations)
HC  High commitment
LC  Low commitment
HC  Open and flexible time (process more important than product)
LC  Highly organized time (product more important than process)

Hall further explains that the manner in which time and context are used has a telling effect on the use of *space* 'proxemics' (10–12). He defines space as the 'visible boundary ... [that] ... is surrounded by a series of invisible boundaries that are more difficult to define but are just as real. These other boundaries begin with the individual's personal space and terminate with her or his "territory"' (10).

The delineation of space involves all the senses, including the olfactory and auditory. In some cultures, speaking loudly is considered an invasion of personal space (11). Each sphere of space – 'personal social space' and 'public social space' – has varying rules regarding the use of body mannerisms as well as the use of familiar forms of address.

So it would seem that the 'physical distance' one maintains between oneself and another is determined by cultural habituation as well as psychological predisposition. And this cultural habituation has a salient influence on the manner in which one uses one's 'sensorium' during one's relations with others. If a person is habituated to 'keeping his distance' then someone who stands too close to him will make him feel that his 'space' is being invaded; this may move him to judge the other as being 'too forward' or even 'shameless.' Conversely, someone used to standing close to others might interpret distance as a sign of alienation or disdain. The sentiments will be registered without conscious understanding of why there is such an immediate visceral reaction.

*The misunderstanding and conflicts that occur from mismatches in conceptions of context, time, and space can create considerable dissonance in civility, understanding, and sympathy.* As Hall elaborates in his comparisons of German, American, and French business cultures, much of the alienation felt between the French and the Americans and the French and the Germans may be connected to the fact that they follow different contextual, time-use, and space-delineation standards. Conflict and incomprehension result not only from what is being said and done but from *how* it is being said and done.

Expectedly, the stability of the above-listed values and dimensions will be greatly determined by the manner in which subjects 'appraise' situations and react to them. Varying appraisals of an identical situation will trigger different emotional responses. Moreover, not all cultures assign the same values to universal emotions. Ekman (1972) and Ekman et al. (1987) have experimented with photos showing the human face experiencing a variety of emotions. While respondents in various countries managed to identity the photographed faces as experiencing emotions such as 'enjoyment, anger, sadness, fear, surprise, and disgust,' their appraisal of which emotions they considered desirable or not varied according to their own cultural habituations (Matsumoto 1992 and Schimmack 1996, cited in Smith and Bond 1998:75). Particular attention, therefore, needs be paid to the manner in which the citizenry of a nation manages its emotions, for there can be considerable variation even between cultures that are considered individualistic and self-referential.

The potential antagonism between 'communal' and 'self-referential' mentalities (at least as understood in Anglo-American society) was observed during the protracted tensions between the late Princess Diana and the Windsors. A queen who had reigned for nearly half a century using duty and restraint of emotion as her guiding principles was suddenly confronted with a self-referential person who insisted that the monarchy be 'humanized' and brought down to the level of the people. Elizabeth II may have been surprised (and perhaps even embarrassed) by the claims of the princess. A monarchy was supposed to act as a reminder of duty, harmony, restraint, and honour. Its function was not to resemble the people but to give the people some stable model to emulate, a model that stood above the contingency of emotion and the vicissitudes of change. The emotional restraint adopted by the queen in favour of duty required some distancing between her and her people. The distancing was not necessarily an act of self-aggrandizement but one of presenting a grave countenance to symbolize a collective commitment to British institutions and norms.

The queen's commitment to her role was mentioned by her son Charles, Prince of Wales, during a short speech delivered at the end of the Jubilee celebrations of 2002. The prince remarked that the queen had steadfastly held to her duty and been a reminder of 'continuity' in an era of 'perilous change' (BBC 2002). Princess Diana, however, had been an agent of change, a considerably self-referential woman who considered emotional interaction, familiarity, informality, and open mutual recognition as important as the preservation of the protocols of a long-standing British institution. She was the outcome of an individualistic therapeutic mentality. Graham Turner, a British court journalist and author of *Elizabeth: The Woman and the Queen* (2002), has stated that a major difficulty between the princess and the queen was that the princess desired to be 'recognized' by the queen for her efforts whereas the queen may not have understood why the performance of duty, being that it was a duty, would need extraordinary recognition (ITV 2002).

**Politeness Theory: The Various Faces of Civility**

One thing that communalistic and individualistic, and low-context and high-context cultures, have in common is the need to maintain personal esteem and social harmony through the preservation of face. 'Face' is defined as *the impression that a person desires to give off to others, and also the person's own conception and experience of his or her self and its worth.* It is interesting to note that many cultures will use the word 'face' in its literal translation to refer to the person's reputation. In English, we refer to 'losing face.' The same usage occurs in French. And, similarly, in a country such as Iran, the process of losing face is referred to as 'having one's face dissolved' (*abeh-rooh-as-bein-raftan*).

The manner in which citizens of a given culture help each other preserve and save face indicates a culture's social organization (vertical or horizontal, hierarchical or egalitarian), the manner in which its youth are socialized, its standards of emotional expression, and its views regarding personal achievement and the assignation of status. Certainly, anyone who undertakes civility and cross-cultural communications research will, early on in the field study, come up against a primal fact of human communications: there are two ways of expressing something, one direct and the other indirect. Each culture tends to favour one of the two forms over the other, depending on its accumulated heritage, its political ideals, its socio-economic organization, and its moral philosophy. So, while all cultures attempt to govern communications according to the civility rule of not causing offence to others, the actual means used to convey such consideration of the other can be diametrically opposed as one travels from one culture to another. Embarrassment, therefore, occurs in two situations: when there is a specific cause for embarrassment due to loss of face of one or more parties, and one in which an embarrassing unease occurs because a usual ritual of communication is omitted or replaced with one to which the interactants are not habituated.

Penelope Brown and Stephen C. Levinson's ([1983] 1987) seminal study, *Politeness: Some Universals in Language Usage*, provides an efficient model for the study and interpretation of civility rituals and modes of reaction. Brown and Levinson view politeness rituals according to Erving Goffman's explanation of how individuals remain vulnerable to one another's reactions and negotiate to preserve coherence and personal/mutual esteem. According to Goffman:

> The human tendency to use signs and symbols means that evidence of social worth and of mutual evaluations will be conveyed by very minor things, and these things will be witnessed, as will the fact that they have been witnessed. An unguarded glance, a momentary change in tone of voice, an ecological position taken or not taken, can drench a talk with judgmental significance. Therefore, just as there is no occasion of talk in which improper impressions could not intentionally or unintentionally arise, so there is no occasion of talk so trivial as not to require each participant to show serious concerns with the way in which he handles himself and the others present. (1967:33)

Like Goffman, Brown and Levinson consider civility a process that involves the mutual caretaking of face needs:

> Face is something that is emotionally invested, and that can be lost, maintained, or enhanced, and must be constantly attended to in interaction ... normally everyone's face depends on everyone else's being maintained,

and since people can be expected to defend their face if threatened, and in defending their own to threaten other's faces, it is in general in every participant's best interest to maintain each other's face, that is to act in ways that assure the other participants that the agent is heedful of the assumptions concerning face. ([1983] 1987:61)

Face, therefore, is defined as the public *self-image* that a person wishes to maintain. 'Losing face' means being put in a humiliating or embarrassing situation vis-à-vis the other or in the presence of the other and/or in relation to oneself.

Face-preservation is of two types: (1) *negative face: the basic claims to territories, personal preserves, rights to non-distraction – for example, freedom of action and freedom from imposition*; and (2) *positive face: the positive consistent self-image or 'personality' claimed by interactants (the desire that this self-image be appreciated and validated by those whose opinions are valued)* (61).

The interactions necessary to preserve negative and positive face are negotiated through the exercise of rational faculties that include the appraisal of the motives of each interactant. These appraisals are energized by a certain awareness of the 'cost benefit' of face saving and are related to a 'hierarchy of politeness' (17). Interactants, therefore, not only deal with one another to preserve positive and negative face but do so remaining aware that certain situations are more crucial than others when considered in relation to personal interest (61).

The limits of personal territory and the types of personalities valued may vary from culture to culture. Yet, the imperative of maintaining face or public self-image remains a universal in human interaction. This is not to say that all interactions are meant to preserve face – some are intentional manoeuvres designed to create sentiments of inadequacy in the other. Nevertheless, whether the motive underlying the interaction is face preservation (cooperative civility) or face loss (incivility), certain rules of face work apply and are indicative of the type of politeness hierarchies and values of a particular culture.

Stated more simply, the preservation of face is a 'need' or 'want.' *Negative face preservation* involves the 'want of every "competent adult member" that his actions be unimpeded by others' (62). *Positive face preservation* involves 'the want of every member that his wants be desirable to at least some others' (62). Thus, every interaction, by virtue of its participant's need for negative and positive face preservation, contains within it the potential for a 'face-threatening act' (FTA) (65).

Preservation of negative face involves 'non-imposition' or the making of an imposition in such a way as to make it appear as slight as possible. The negative face of the other can be threatened through requests that the other perform an action or service in the present or future; suggestions, reminders, and advice addressed to the other; threats, warnings, and dares; offers of actions or services that would obligate or indebt the recipient; compliments, expressions of envy, or statements of admiration that would threaten the other's material and spiritual independence by making him feel that some of what is valued by him may have to be shared with the speaker; and expressions of strong negative emotions that might imply harmful intent (66).

The positive face of the other can be threatened through a negative evaluation of that which the other considers to be a valuable aspect of his personality or public self-image. Such threats can be delivered through statements of disapproval, criticism, contempt, ridicule, complaints and reprimands, accusations, insults and challenges of the other's belief or desires, and any statement that suggests (covertly or overtly) that the other is wrong or incompetent. Outright demonstrations of lack of concern for the face needs of another include the expression of violent emotions, the showing of irreverence or lack of respect, the thoughtless or purposeful mention of topics taboo to the other, reminders of weaknesses or deficiencies in the other, the mention of emotionally divisive subjects, outright non-cooperation in an activity, interruption of the other's conversation or non-attention to it, and a host of other statements and acts that make the other feel as if his desired identity is remaining negligently unrecognized or being intentionally denied (66–7).

In addition to having to endure the complexities of ministering to the face of others, *every speaker also runs the risk of losing face whenever expressing courtesy towards another person*. Statements and acts that threaten one's own negative face include: expressing thanks, since gratitude implies a debt; accepting thanks or apology from the other, since this implies that one now has to help minimize the other's loss of face; accepting offers and gifts from the other, since this entails going into financial or emotional debt towards the other and having to reciprocate in the future (68). Those situations that threaten one's own positive face include apologies that imply error or wrongdoing; acceptance of compliments because they require one to appear humble and downplay one's image; loss of control over a bodily function; confessions and admissions of guilt; the giving of compliments that are not welcomed by the addressee (68).

Face-threatening situations can, therefore, be classified according to whether they have the potential of damaging the positive and/or negative face of the interactants. The same risks apply regardless of whether the interaction occurs between two individuals, more than two individuals within a group, or between local or international groups.

The types of interactions possible in face-threatening situations have also been documented by Brown and Levinson. Three main interactive rituals are possible: (1) *on-record*: a statement or act that is clear enough not to leave doubts about its meaning and intention; and (2) *off-record*: a statement or act that is ambiguous enough to allow for more than one interpretation of meaning and intent. In this case, the actor cannot be held accountable for the outcome or perception created in the other. Off-record statements and acts include hints, demonstrations of distress without outright requests for help, statements softened and made ambiguous through metaphor or irony, rhetorical questions and understatements; (3) *without redress*: a statement or act presented clearly and directly enough to indicate that the actor is not worried about retribution from the addressee.

Such lack of concern regarding the potential danger of the FTA is possible in any of three circumstances: (1) when there is agreement between interactants that face-saving rituals will be dispensed with in the interests of efficiency, or in order to respond to the urgency of a situation; (2) when the danger to the face of the addressee is so small as to be negligible, or when all statements and acts are perceived by both interactants as being in their mutual interest; (3) when the power of the speaker is incontestably superior to that of the addressee, or when the speaker feels that he can secure the support of others to invalidate the addressee's face without causing damage to his own (69).

Parallel to the above interaction ritual are *redressive actions*. These consist of 'attempts to counteract the potential face damage of the FTA by doing it in such a way, or with modifications or additions that indicate no face threat is desired or intended' (69–70). Redressive actions are central components of politeness and civility, softening and reversing face-damaging interactions.

Whether an act of politeness will be of the *negative* or *positive* type will depend in great part on whether it is the *positive* or *negative face* that requires attention. *Positive politeness* indicates to the other that his image of himself and his wants are valued and accepted. The potential threat of loss of positive face is minimized by communicating to the addressee that a certain reciprocity is shared with him (70). The predominant sentiment here is one of implied solidarity and intimacy or, in the case of the unequal power-ratio involved in acts of one-way deference, admiration or the paying of homage. *Negative politeness* is directed at the negative face of the other and his need to maintain his claims of territory and self-determination. As such, negative politeness is avoidance-based and 'characterized by self-effacement, formality and restraint':

> Face-threatening acts are redressed with apologies for interfering or transgressing, with linguistic and non-linguistic deference, with hedges on the illocutionary force of the act, with impersonalising mechanisms (such as passives) that distance ... [the actors] ... from the act, and with other softening mechanisms that give the addressee an 'out,' a face-saving line of escape, permitting him to feel that his response is not coerced. (70)

Brown and Levinson observe that negative politeness has a built-in tension. On one hand, the actors have to go 'on record' that they are ministering to the face of each other, while, on the other hand, they have to remain 'off record' in order to give the impression that they are not imposing. The authors identify *conventional indirectness* as a solution to some of this tension – a compromise is reached through the use of statements that have become conventionalized enough to be broadly recognized as non-intrusive face-preserving devices (70). The use of conventionalized statements allows interactants to know that face is being saved without the need for prolonged on-record face-saving exchanges. For example, the conventionalized statements 'Would you please pass the salt?' or 'Would you please excuse me while I answer the phone?' are processed without complications because all actors are habituated to recognizing the deference embedded in the words: 'Would you please ...,' a phrase that automatically implies that the addressee remains free to accept or refuse the request. Such indirectness would be more frequent in high-context cultures where complex social relations limit the amount of directness an actor can exhibit without attracting censure for over-stepping the boundaries of intimacy.

The functional benefits or 'pay-offs' of the different strategies of politeness are varied. *On-record* politeness allows the speaker to appear direct, non-manipulative, honest, and trustworthy (due to the mere fact that the speaker trusts the addressee enough to speak with directness). This is a prevalent attitude in low-context cultures that are dependent on actors who reveal enough information about themselves and their motives to balance out the minimal information that circulates in the larger social circle. By avoiding the risk of being misinterpreted, the speaker can later call on public support to contest any unjust complaints on the part of the addressee. *Off-record* politeness, on the other hand, allows a speaker to be known as tactful and not given to coercing others. It also serves to keep the speaker free from being held responsible for any face-damaging consequences. By using off-record politeness a speaker can also test the addressee's feelings towards him by gauging the friendliness or reserve of the responses he receives (71–3). Both on-record and off-record strategies are used in negative and positive politeness interactions. Whether the objective is the creation of distance or intimacy, the manner in which the objective is achieved requires an astute measurement of the required directness or ambiguity.

How an FTA is evaluated depends on a variety of factors: (1) the symmetric relation, or *social distance* between interactants; (2) the asymmetric relation, or the *power* of the interactants in relation to one another; and (3) the absolute ranking of the *imposition* being made according to the values and interaction codes of the particular culture (74).

The determination of *distance, power*, and *weight of imposition* requires mutual relational understanding. They are not factors that can be analysed and then assigned to the interactants; the interactants themselves must also be aware of them and be influenced by them (75–6). So the calculation of the potential dangers of a face-threatening situation is largely dependent on the interactants' own calculation of risk to their faces. The calculation of that danger is determined by the symmetric relation, the asymmetric relation, and the estimation of the gravity or weight of the imposition. These values do not remain fixed but diverge as each person takes on various roles in different social settings.

The factors of *power* and *distance* (Hofstede 1980, 1983), therefore, play a major role in determining the degree of 'ambiguity' and 'directness' in social relations. They also affect the extent to which *deference* is demonstrated. 'Excuse me, but would you by any chance have the time' implies a greater power and distance ratio than the statement 'Do you have the time?' Particularly deferential are statements that embed requests within long, drawn-out sentences such as: 'I know this is an imposition and a terrible bother for you, and I would not trouble you if I had any other choice, but would you mind terribly if I asked you to give me a lift home?'

Implicit in all politeness rituals is the belief that *the person of the one being addressed is worthy enough to be treated with deference and caring*. This deferential view of human personality can be the result of a hierarchical secular system that defines worth by status, reputation, wealth, and accomplishment or by an ideological position (secular or religious) that posits that every individual is worthy of deferential (and/or friendly) treatment and is to be considered sacrosanct in all social interactions, regardless of group affiliation.

Both secular and religious rationalizations of negative politeness have a common denominator: *the preservation of distance*. In aristocratic societies, those of non-noble birth were expected to keep their distance when in the presence of the nobility. The same self-effacement was a central part of caste systems, in which certain groups of people were considered 'untouchable' or impure. So it is useful to differentiate between *discriminatory distancing between unequals* and *respectful distancing between equals*. It is also worth keeping a sharp eye out for the manner in which societies with aristocratic backgrounds begin using the same deference shown to their former aristocracies in their face-to-face interactions within a republican setting. This is nowhere more observable than in France, where citizens treat one another either with very cautious and elegant deference or with outright and linguistically elegant and creative self-affirmation.

Ministering to positive face may have greater risks than do negative face strategies. An actor may try to confirm the positive face of an addressee, but nothing guarantees that the addressee himself will appreciate or welcome the effort. If the speaker is not considered important enough to be a point of validating reference then the addressee might consider the compliment as irrelevant, irritating, and even mercenary, thereby causing the compliment giver to lose his own face. A study of positive politeness rituals indicates that the establishment of commonality, reciprocity, and mutual interest requires considerable psychological forethought. Not all positive politeness statements are direct declarations such as 'I love the shirt you are wearing' or 'You're such a smart lawyer.' Many positive politeness interactions involve considerable dramaturgical manipulation and a balancing of on-record and off-record statements.

Pomerantz (1978) has also explained that in the practice of compliment giving conflict must be delicately avoided. The compliment must not be rejected, so as not to insult the other; yet, it must be partially rejected in order to avoid exaggerated self-praise (87). Tact requires gestural hesitancy as well as linguistic competence. A shy smile and the words 'Well, I owe it to my editor' become an appropriate response to the compliment, 'You wrote a great book.' Of course, someone adept at positive face work would not necessarily say 'You wrote a great book' but would show consideration for the negative face needs of the other (e.g., the tension the other has to go through to diminish the compliment) by saying something less obligating such as 'I hear your book is being well received.' This type of subtlety is observable in societies in which citizens exhibit considerable respect towards one another's privacy (e.g., England and France).

So, positive face ritual, whether it is direct or indirect, is based on three premises: (1) the implication that common ground will be established between the two parties; (2) the unspoken or spoken agreement that interactants will cooperate with one another; and (3) an implicit understanding that there will be a sharing of sympathy, empathy, and mutual encouragement (Brown and Levinson [1983] 1987:fig. 3, 102).

Such *common ground* is established through the minimization and avoidance of disagreement. This is achieved through: (1) statements and gestures that communicate to the other that the other is admirable and interesting. This is accomplished through the demonstration of interest towards the plans and accomplishments of the other, through expressions of approval and sympathy, and a showing of interest towards the declarations and ideas of the other; (2) claiming in-group membership with the other by using statements that remind the other that he and the speaker possess mutual affinity; (3) claiming common points of view, attitudes, and opinions. Such *mutual cooperation* (actual or feigned) is established by indicating to the other that his wants are known and taken to heart and that the speaker is ready to enter a bond of reciprocity and mutual inclusion. Such optimistic mutual identification is necessary for the maintenance of an ongoing transpersonal *empathy*. The calculation of the extent to which something needs to be said in order to establish mutuality is also a central mechanism of both negative and positive politeness rituals (103–25).

Politeness strategies may seem quite simple when neatly listed on paper. But, in reality, they require overt or intuitive knowledge of the linguistic and gestural codes of a culture. The simple phrase 'sort of' is a very effective dampener of conflict. 'I sort of wish ...,' 'I sort of didn't like what you did ...,' or 'I sort of wish you would ...' are statements based on a desire to avoid explicit complaint. Knowing the meaning and use of the phrase 'sort of' is crucial for the construction of tentative declarations. A person who wishes, for example, to avoid disagreement with another's views while remaining true to his own ideas may start by 'sort of' agreeing with the other before adding his own differing opinion once some mutuality has been established. The entire process of *social manipulation* requires such linguistic and gestural dexterity. The exact choice of words and gestures will depend on the given culture and the peer group involved, but the anatomy of agreeability will remain constant and involve the use of subtlety to decrease the potential for conflict – that is, of course, if civility, rather than incivility, is the goal of the interaction. So, although positive politeness rituals speed up intimacy, they must convey just the right dose of interest and commitment within the context of the particular social situation. It goes without saying that there is considerable social manipulation involved in the practice of positive face rituals. And, certainly, those raised on a steady fare of negative politeness may find the hedging and moving into position of practitioners of positive politeness as ambiguous, invasive, and even somewhat insincere and manipulative.

The degree to which *softening* strategies are used will depend on factors already mentioned (such as power and distance) as well as on how a given culture views emotional and ideological conflict. A population that values agreeability at all costs would be aghast at abandoning some of the softening strategies and redressive actions of positive politeness; it might even consider the distancing of negative politeness an indication of social misanthropy. Similarly, a culture that values individual privacy would not be given to abandoning negative face work.

Whether one is practising negative or positive politeness, conversations require considerable attention to the need for 'correction' at moments of potential embarrassment. 'Self-correction' (self-repair) and the revision or retraction of a statement that suddenly threatens another's face is a frequent mechanism of civility management and requires both speaker and addressee to sometimes negate and alter the expression of what they really think and feel (Schegloff, Jefferson, and Sacks 1977). The speaker may state, 'I hate people who are lion tamers.' The addressee may respond with unease: 'My husband is one.' Then the speaker may retract his statement by altering his meaning to 'I'm sorry I guess I don't like my brother-in-law and he happens to be a lion tamer.' The addressee may help the reparation along by offering his own compromise: 'Well, some lion tamers are a little overbearing.' In reality, the speaker may have a problem with all lion tamers and the addressee may be very partial to her husband, lion tamer or not.

*Negative politeness* has its own strategies and subtle rituals. Although the basis of the negative politeness ritual is non-imposition, a form of avoidance, it involves a variety of tactics that require insight and forethought. Some situations involving negative face work require anabridged and economical statement of civility, since a more elaborate presentation might be interpreted as an imposition or a ruse. Here, the most minimal assumptions are made about the other's wants; the objective is to show that one has no intention of imposing on the other. Requests are made with a certain 'pessimism' in order to communicate to the other that he retains the right of refusal. This does not at all mean that the speaker will not subtly press for what he wishes to acquire from the other. It simply means that a minimization of presumption will be communicated through a momentary depersonalizing of the pronouns of both parties, with minimal references to the persons of the speaker and addressee (Brown and Levinson ([1983] 1987:fig 4, 131) (e.g., 'It would be nice if someone drove me to the airport').

So, a delicate balance must be struck between not imposing on the other and not creating the feeling that he is being rejected or that he is not needed. In certain cultures, where negative politeness rituals are meticulously followed, there are parallel positive politeness strategies that are used to maintain a sentiment of respectful association. In Iran, for example, a person will pay particular attention not to overstay his welcome in someone's presence. Yet, he will never depart abruptly. When ready to leave he will ask the other for permission to depart (*ba ejazeyeh-shomah*). The addressee will most usually respond with a protest that the other is leaving too early and, in turn, receive assurance that the other is leaving only not to be a bother (*mozahemeh nasheem*). Those who cannot understand why in certain cultures visitors and hosts stand at the door for a considerable time conversing before finally saying their final goodbyes may wish to consider the practice as a politeness tactic intended to avoid abrupt endings. At one dinner party in a first-generation American-Italian family in New Jersey we counted goodbyes said by the same people seven times before the guests finally departed. Each goodbye was followed by somewhere between five and ten minutes of conversation. The second-generation children, more habituated to less elaborate civility rituals, continued watching their favourite television program, undoubtedly aware that they would be able to finish watching the show in peace before having to really put their coats on.

In their own cross-cultural research, Brown and Levinson specify many other refinements of negative and positive politeness strategies (101–228). For our purposes, we have concentrated on providing a general view of how people use sentiments, statements, and gestures to avoid conflict and promote harmony.

In contrast to Brown and Levinson, H.P. Grice (1975) presents an instrumental theory of politeness that minimizes the subtleties and complexities of interaction. Grice's maxims encourage considerable directness in conversation, specifying four components of effective communications: *quality* – clarity and sincerity; *quantity* – not saying any less or more than required; *relevance* – remaining relevant and focused; *manner* – avoiding obscurity and multiple meanings (45–6). Grice favours a particularly American instrumental definition of effective conversation based on a normative ideal of equality. He does not take power and distance factors into sufficient consideration. His model is based on the optimistic assumption that the intended and perceived meaning of a statement will remain identical. The maxims prove quite insufficient, however, when applied across cultural boundaries.

Brown and Levinson's ([1983] 1987) analysis provides us with a more balanced and realistic description of the various interaction rituals that are the foundations of civility. Their model also allows us to take into consideration the emotional predispositions of interactants. The degree to which negative or positive politeness will be practised in a given situation will depend not only on the factors mentioned above but also on the levels of self-esteem of the interactants and the valence of their need for recognition and approval. Power and distance factors, therefore, are complicated by the emotional states of the interactants and the biographies of the social bonds that they have already experienced. Therefore, it becomes important to differentiate between social hesitancy that emanates from a desire to show respect and social hesitancy caused by a lack of personal confidence or lack of interactive experience.

Brown and Levinson do not go into great detail regarding discourtesy. A simple extrapolation can be made, however. The same mechanisms that apply to politeness also apply to acts of incivility. In cultures or situations requiring negative face rituals, discourtesy can be practised through the negation of negative face; conversely, in cultures practising positive face civility, negations of positive face can effectively communicate discourteous intent.

Acts of *negative incivility* consist of denials of the other's desire for autonomy and space, either as a tactic of insult or out of overwhelming personal need for the presence of the other. Rather than communicating to the other that one has no intention of imposing on the other's autonomy, one takes the other for granted and invades the other's intimacy without reassuring the other that his privacy is valued and respected. Such imposed acts of obligation can be carried out in a dominating or in a manipulative way designed to charm the other while denying the other's rights to self-determination.

Acts of *positive incivility* consist of acts and expressions designed to deny or question the worth of the other and communicate a lack of intention or willingness to establish a mutual common ground that permits mutual recognition. Here, the act of discourtesy can be either *covert* or *overt*. A covert act of incivility may consist of making indirect remarks that put the other's worth in doubt or else force the other to have to affirm his worth in competition with that of the instigator. An overt act of incivility, on the other hand, is a *bald, on-record* statement or emotional expression that forcefully puts the other's worth in question and forces the other into a position in which he must react to preserve face. The other is left with the option of withdrawing (an admission of loss of face), defending his worth (also a humiliating experience because self-justification implicitly gives the other the right to act as a judge or evaluator), protesting by citing the injustice of the other's remark (the admission of received injustice being a disclosure of emotional vulnerability), or attacking the other with an equalizing statement or emotional expression. Thus, the statement 'You salespeople can never do anything right!' can be counter-attacked with a response such as 'With customers like you it's a wonder we manage at all.'

The manner in which an act of impoliteness will be delivered will depend on: (1) the degree of anger or contempt felt by the speaker, (2) the level of intimacy in the relationship, (3) the speaker's evaluation of the reaction of the other and whether the other will submit to the discourtesy or retaliate, (4) the degree to which the speaker wishes to maintain future common ground with the other, and (5) the degree to which overt abrasive competition is being expressed between the parties.

The manner in which a person reacts to an act of discourtesy will depend on: (1) the degree of insult or hurt felt, (2) the degree to which the person expects others to be polite towards him, (3) the respondent's desire to maintain future common ground and his evaluation of the offender's possible reaction to any counter-attack, and (4) the person's own relationship to his own biography and self-image. Whether the reaction will be tame or highly disturbing will depend considerably on a variety of factors such as the person's existing stress level; his tolerance level (whether or not he is already overloaded with anger and pain waiting to be released and whether he has frequently suffered insults and taunts); the degree to which he fears or welcomes confrontation; the extent to which he is willing to empathize with the other and heal his own hurt by forgiving and forgetting the insult; and, finally, whether he judges the insult a random occurrence or a portent for future hurts.

Beyond the above two forms of incivility is a third form which is quite insidious. This incivility takes the form of *mute negation*. Here, the uncivil person does not overtly show his incivility, but takes on a silent stance which communicates to the other that there is something wrong about the other or with the situation that they share in common. Silent negation can be an extremely powerful way of establishing dominance over the other, because it puts the other in a position where he has to evaluate whether future common ground with the offending party is wanted or not. If it is, then the offended party needs to draw out the other and try to heal whatever is wrong. This in itself is an act of submission or, at the very least, deference towards the silent party. Hence the phrase 'He was given the silent treatment.' Whether an act of incivility is motivated by anger or the desire for interpersonal or political power, it will be expressed in one of the above ways.

Some examples of *negative* and *positive* impoliteness might help explain how the most minute acts can become interpreted as uncivil behaviour depending on the current civility standards of a city, region, or country. Examples of *negative discourtesy* include: creating a scene in a classroom, thereby denying the autonomy of the teacher and students; calling someone at an inopportune time when there is no real emergency; calling someone by their first name when the other is a total stranger; stealing a parking space from another or cutting in front of them in traffic; entering someone's home in order to steal; failing to thank the other for a service rendered; failing to be courteous when asking the other for a service; making noise to an extent that leaves the other with diminished autonomy in his own environment. Examples of *positive discourtesy* are: calling the other names; criticizing work done by the other of which the other is proud; criticizing the other's way of handling things; making statements that are hurtful to the other; siding with an enemy of the other; making statements that communicate to the other that his happiness is of no importance; making statements to the other that indicate readiness to lose any possible future common ground; and making demands on the other for recognition (sentimental or material) without offering exchange in value.

One thing that Brown and Levinson do not take into account is the manner in which both *positive* and *negative* politeness can exist in the same culture, with one being used to temper the other. The co-existence of these traits can confuse the keenest observer. A case in point is

England. While the English demonstrate a tremendous amount of amiability in public (a positive politeness trait) they are also, beneath the friendliness, extremely reserved (a negative politeness trait). As we will make clearer in the chapter discussing our field research in England, France, and America, this bipolar civility ethos can have both opportunities for excellent social bonds as well as risks to those same bonds, risks which can result in considerable and surprising biting humour and even anger.

The number of interactants in a given social situation will have considerable influence on civility rituals, even though the rituals themselves may remain of the negative or positive type. Dyads, in which two people are face to face with each other with considerable knowledge of the contents of their interaction, differ considerably from triads, in which three people must maintain face with one another without being certain of whether two of them are privy to information not enjoyed by the third. The complexity of maintaining face increases as more people are added to a social interaction or network.

Indeed, as George Simmel ([1908] 1950) has pointed out, the number of interactants has a great effect on the nature and quality of interactions. The compression of large numbers of people in urban areas necessitated a transformation in face-to-face relations, which were multiplied for each individual; emotional restraint increased in direct proportion to the need for friction-free encounters in anonymous settings where a minimal measure of trust (achieved through emotional disengagement) was necessary. Mennell (1974) has observed, meanwhile, that recognition of this fact does not guarantee coherent sociological explanations. Sociologists continue to have difficulty carrying over discoveries made at the level of small groups to analysis of larger 'social systems' because they find it difficult to 'conceptualize the appearance of "emergent properties"' (81). This is partially due to the difficulty involved in ascribing to larger social systems the emotional properties of dyads, triads, and small groups.

Thus, an insightful micro/macro sociology may need to risk personalizing complex systems and seeing how they, like individuals, are affected by emotional as well as systemic constraints. Such a preliminary effort was made by Elias in his theory of 'game models' ([1970] 1978). Elias showed that as participants in a social network increase, the number of possible interactions increases due to the appearance of different possible configurations. A group of 10 people, for example, would potentially be able to have 1,013 different interactions with one another, with no two of them being identical. Forty-five of those would be the different dyads that could be formed within a group of 10 people; proceeding to interactions involving 3, 4, 5, 6, and more individuals, we end up with over 1,000 different configurations, each contributing to a change in the social ecology and in the power differential between participants (cited in Mennel 1974:86). Certainly, the degree of 'connection' or 'dispersal' in the network (88) (or formality or informality of the network) will have a distinct effect on the consistency or ambiguity of the civility rituals. If civility suffers in urban settings where many people are in constant contact with one another, it is perhaps partially due to the fact that the myriad permutations of social contact make it difficult to apply a standard civility ritual. In such cases, only a strong national civility ethos can minimize the effects of such disjunctions. In highly individualistic societies the differences in civility between urban and smaller communities is greater than in societies that possess a clear and broad national civility ethic. In highly individualistic societies, the anonymity factor of urban areas is compounded by the lack of a portable civility ethos.

**Guilt, Shame, Embarrassment, and Civility**

*Guilt*

One of the problems in Norbert Elias's study of civility is the fact that he leaves the issue of 'guilt' relatively unexplained. While he discusses shame towards the bodily functions in great detail, he does not discuss how guilt and shame can become linked in the moral construction of civility or how the relationship between these two emotions undergoes radical transformation as we proceed from medieval, through Renaissance, and into modern times.

It is our own hypothesis that the manner in which a culture relates to 'time, context, and place' and whether it favours 'individualistic' or 'communalistic' interaction values will affect its relationship to duty, guilt, shame, embarrassment, and pride. While the universal definitions of the words remain fairly constant, the manner in which they are experienced and the degree to which one sentiment rather than another is experienced will vary according to cultural norms.

'Guilt' is considerably different from shame even though the two are often mistaken for each other. The feeling of guilt requires the discomforting admission that a moral or sentimental code *accepted by the person himself* has been transgressed. The sociopath has no guilt because he does not feel obliged to follow the moral codes of his community.

Guilt is a fault committed by the individual in a foreseeable situation. Something that should not have been done has been done or something has not been done that should have been done. Within intimate relationships, a situation of guilt is often caused by a 'sin of omission,' with one party complaining that another has failed to do something expected of him, be it the fulfillment of a duty or the giving of recognition and affection. The 'guilt trip,' whether it truly represents the actual suffering of the aggrieved or dramatizes and falsifies it, seeks to influence the offender to accept fault and make reparations. If repentant, the guilty party expresses regret for having acted in the manner he did and seeks to make the offended one feel consoled in the interests of repairing the relationship. If asked by a third party about the nature of the conflict he may even argue in favour of the offended person and take responsibility for having caused the offence. All this, if he accepts that he is at fault (or at least pretends to) in order to diffuse the situation (Baumeister, Stillwell, and Heatherton 1995).

Guilt is more readily accepted (and more frequently assigned) in societies where there is a fairly clear understanding of emotional and moral duty between family members and between individuals and the norms of their community. It is felt particularly strongly in nations where religion as well as politics guide social action, thereby increasing the number of behaviours that are guided by notions of sin, atonement, and/or punishment. The feeling of guilt serves two functions: it demonstrates to the aggrieved party that the offender is suffering and that the need for retribution is, therefore, less. It also shows that the offender cares enough about the relationship to feel bad about his deed. This serves to increase 'hope' between parties regarding the future of the relationship as well as the community in which the relationship is embedded. In certain instances, the emotion of guilt is necessary for the preservation of social order and solidarity within smaller and larger groups.

Quite a different impression is left, however, when both parties withdraw from each other due to a suspicion of motives. This impasse is noticed in interpersonal situations as well as negotiations between groups and nations. The party who has done the offending is usually unwilling to avow his guilt due to his need to appear legitimate – conflict increases as each party accuses the other without avowing his own role in the situation.

When felt in moderate doses, guilt serves to teach a person the moral and sentimental standards of the human community located within and beyond the family. A person who accepts to feel guilt is accepting to question his behaviour and is prepared to make adjustments in favour of the interests of others. Yet, an interesting phenomenon occurs in individuals who are made to frequently feel guilty by their primary socializers. They have one of two reactions: they become either guilt-bound and suffer loss of energy (and sometimes loss of heart) due to the heavy weight of imposed blame; or they begin turning against the whole notion of guilt and rebel against it; or they develop the habit of laying guilt and blame on others as a compensation. Whether or not they will dare rebel against the process depends on whether a social 'window of opportunity for change' presents itself. Although this reaction of rebellion may not be observable within one or a few generations, the continued pressure of substantial amounts of guilt, without the co-presence of credible cultural justifications and meanings, begins to wear down the ability of a population to maintain an overall sense of communal responsibility. The result of this contingency is an 'emotionally defensive' population composed of individuals who avoid avowals of wrongdoing at all costs. The 'yes, but ...' syndrome appears only after a period of protracted pressure.

It is worth noting that one of the most frequent criticisms of the American establishment during the 1960s was aimed at its supposedly 'uptight Protestant guilt ethic.' Hedonism required a transformation of long-standing conceptions of guilt, thereby considerably affecting the practice of civility. The struggle does not seem to be over. In July 2007, there were 43,100 websites that included the phrase 'guilt-free,' promoting everything from guilt-free parenting, to guilt-free soldiering, to guilt-free cooking, to guilt-free guilting.

Guilt is one of the most ancient sentiments of our species. It is the means by which individuals are kept loyal to collectively affirmed moral standards. Obedience is the guiding principle and guilt is the alarm mechanism used by a conformity imperative that threatens the offender with social exclusion. Alexander Mitscherlich (1969) reminds us in *Society without the Father* that obedience 'is imposed by fear of the strength of the party that imposes it. Anticipation of a threat that has been really experienced leads to the habit of obedience. But the continuous reiteration of the sense of impotence and fear of punishment is required if obedience is to develop into an "attitude"' (167).

In Nathaniel Hawthorne's ([1850] 1923) *The Scarlet Letter* what is remarkable is not only the social exclusion of the adulteress; the branding of her person with the scarlet letter 'A' as punishment for adultery also serves other members of the community to affirm their own adherence to the code transgressed by the offender. Their sentiment of abhorrence is in itself an act of moral solidarity. The onlookers are comforted by the fact that it is not they who are being chastised in public; simultaneously, their fear of similar social exclusion is awakened by the punishment dealt to the adulteress. Similar example-setting punishments are used by dictatorships to maintain their totalitarian control.

We are not suggesting that there is no innate sense of right and wrong in the human being that would exclude the need for coercive socialization. Rather, the maintenance of a collective sense of conscience requires a certain amount of social solidarity and consensus. The mechanism that facilitates a collective adherence to a principle or code is the fear of being excluded from the community and falling into the pain of isolation. Thus, the mechanism used for securing compliance with social norms is 'anxiety.' Elias ([1939] 1978) mentions this in his explanation of the psychic foundations of restraint:

> Society is gradually beginning to suppress the positive pleasure component in certain functions more and more strongly by the arousal of anxiety; or, more exactly, it is rendering this pleasure 'private' and 'secret' (i.e., suppressing it within the individual), while fostering the negatively charged effects – displeasure, revulsion, distaste – as the only feelings customary in society. (142)

The tactics enlisted to control behaviour through anxiety-provoking non-acceptance of undesired behaviour lose some of their effectiveness in eras when the social codes are not sufficiently and clearly specified. When parents and educators follow inconsistent standards and shift the boundaries of the permissible, obedience weakens and a self-referential judgment mechanism steps in and diminishes the motivation to feel guilt. Moreover, the valuation of 'independence' and 'personal excellence' counterbalances the more assiduous applications of moral codes that restrain excessive personal interest. The valuing of 'getting ahead,' 'making it,' and 'making something out of oneself' creates a resistive force that moves the ambitious person to remain vigilant and protect himself against the intimidating effects of strong guilt. A particular allergy develops towards the judgmental person, as well as the person who preaches duty over personal preference – such persons may even come to be considered archaic or intolerant. This is a crucial development in the easing of restraints within a liberal society and why we feel that a new conception of 'civilizing' is required in a highly individualistic (and independence-valuing) society where a politics of 'rights' complicates the search for a national civil ethos.

Interestingly enough, in considerably individualistic societies, guilt becomes less connected to collective moral codes and more to emotional demands made by people within one's closer circle of influence. Stanfield and Stanfield (1997) feel that such intense search for self-gratification is disturbing nurturance relationships that require reciprocity or a generous distribution of material and emotional resources; they question whether an 'exchange theory' of relationships can produce fulfilled individuals. It is this personalizing of guilt between actors who are known to one another that makes the carrying of guilt particularly burdensome. It certainly makes the party who is feeling the guilt want to avoid whoever is creating such discomforting feelings of obligation.

The manner in which a given culture relates to and responds to guilt has a salient influence on the manner in which citizens manage their civil interactions. It would be expected that a culture that allows considerable blame laying will tend to gravitate towards the disavowal of fault. We notice this in societies in which demands of patriotism and/or religious obligations are very high. Constrained by the continual exhortations of their socializers, individuals in such societies will tend to be equally demanding themselves when put in socializing roles and cause guilt in others while themselves avoiding the admission of personal fault.

*Embarrassment and Shame*

Embarrassment and shame are considerably different from guilt and require a different set of insights. Brown and Levinson's ([1983] 1987) study of politeness rituals suggests that politeness emerges from a mutual recognition of the potential for embarrassment and shame and, by consequence, is a contract to engage in practices that decrease the possibility of 'loss of face' (13–14). Goffman (1967) has similarly defined such embarrassing incidents as situations in which 'facts at hand threaten to discredit the assumptions a participant finds he has projected about his identity' (107–8).

Yet, a more specific understanding of shame is needed for the design of reliable civility theory and research. While guilt is experienced as a feeling of specific indebtedness towards the external world, shame is often felt as a personal failure. This feeling can be experienced in one of two situations: (1) It can be felt because a moral code or custom (e.g., do not burp at table; do not have sex before marriage) has been transgressed and the individual made to look incompetent or unworthy due to a judgment rendered on him by other social actors. In this case, we could say that the shame is *organic*. (2) Shame can be felt because the person concludes that he has failed to live up to his own personal expectations of himself. In this case, the shame is *self-referential* and much more resistant to communal healing rituals.

What is important to realize is that the levels of guilt and shame in a given culture are not positively correlated. *A person who feels little guilt can be disposed to feeling shame quite frequently.* So we question the notion that a late-modern guilt-eased culture can be free of shame; in fact, the level of self-referential shame may actually be on the increase in such cultures.

So, a person who does feel relatively guilt-free when it comes to breaking collective norms may be very disposed to feeling shame at failing to live up to his own code of behaviour. The amount of shame in such an instance will depend on the degree of perfectionism desired and/or existing sentiments of inadequacy. As we will argue later in this section, the observation of frequent shame or embarrassment in a given individual gives us no indication of the ultimate social integrity of that person, for shame, in and of itself, may be a defence mechanism used in order to avoid more profound painful sentiments of personal failure.

We are suggesting here that in a highly individualistic society the avoidance of shame (and the need to conceal it when it does occur) involves much more than conformity to social customs and values. More is at stake than the simple following of precedent. Much of Elias's argument in *The Civilizing Process* ([1939] 1978, [1939] 1982) was focused on shame of the 'organic' type. While a feeling of shame or embarrassment was felt when a commonly prescribed ritual was not observed, it was experienced in relation to the cohesion of the group or the community; the motive for the establishment of rituals was not the promotion of a self-sufficient personal identity but the preservation of collective standards of decorum. When the Victorians decided that sexual permissiveness was immoral, individuals internalized shame towards sex not because they wanted to build a self-referential identity but because they did not wish to endanger their membership in a social habitat that possessed considerable power to validate or discredit their communal personality. Eventually, the shame became unconscious ([1939] 1978:140), making the person resistant to accepting deviations that did not accord with the internalized norm. A person who successfully internalized such shame was considered someone with 'personal conscience.' But such conscience towards collective values did not immediately assure that the person was also in touch with his own needs. This was precisely the point made by some of the members of the 'counterculture' in the 1960s (Rothschild and Rothschild 1976).

In instances of self-referential shame, however, a person is not simply conforming to the behaviour (or standards) of others, but measuring them against his own ideal and deciding how much of the social standard he wishes to adopt. The liberty to choose one's own ideal personality is greater in societies that favour individualism and disfavour power distancing; equally great are the risks of experiencing a sense of personal failure. This pressure on the self can, in fact, become quite intense; Goffman (1967) has even suggested that in many instances the expression of shame (which he refers to as 'embarrassment') itself must be concealed, because to appear flustered is considered a sign of weakness, moral fault, low status, defeat, and guilt (101–2). If anything, 'modesty' gives way to self-affirmative exhibitionism. Thus, in order to avoid the shame associated with being in a situation of shame, the individual must take great care not to reveal that he feels ashamed. The result is a habitually defensive personality. This is a consequence of a society that holds the individual considerably responsible for his own self-determination.

The difference between 'organic' and 'self-referential' shame is, therefore, an important one. A person can be highly conscientious regarding the preservation of communal codes of shame, yet substantially unconscious about the injustices embedded in those codes. The desire to conform to external norms and avoid exclusion can suspend critical awareness. Yet, in 'self-referential' shame there is, in fact, a heightening of personal awareness and self-critique. At risk is the person's own evaluation of himself vis-à-vis his own conception of competence and worth. So, Cooley's (1909) *looking-glass self* seems transformed in a society that encourages competitive self-development – the person responds not only to what he imagines others think of him, but also *according to what he expects of himself*. The individualist has less of a margin to avoid dissonance and uncertainty because of the high valuation put on 'self-affirmation' (Heine and Lehman 1997:389–400). The opportunities for self-justification increase in such competitive environments, along with the potential for uncivil exchanges.

While the root sentiments involved in shame may be universal, the conditions under which they are experienced, and the manner in which they are expressed or denied, are culturally determined. They seem to depend to some degree on the extent to which 'interdependence' and 'independence' are valued (Markus and Kitayama 1991). It would seem that there is an important difference between an 'independent' and 'interdependent' self-concept. The independent person acknowledges that his or her social world comprises relationships with others, yet the interdependent person sees these social relationships as a process of mutual inclusion (Myers [1994] 2004:24).

In a study of emotions requiring self-conscious evaluation in the United States and Japan, S. Kitayama, H.R. Markus, and H. Matsumoto (1995) made interesting comparisons between the manner in which Americans and Japanese viewed 'selfhood' and the conditions under which a person felt 'shame' or 'pride.' They found that the Japanese valuation of 'interdependence' predisposed Japanese to value the opinion of others as a central measure of self-worth (445). Shame (*haji*) for the Japanese meant not being able to live up to the 'expectations of others.' This same high valuation of dependence on the good opinions of others (*amae*) caused Japanese to consider feelings of 'superiority' as 'negative' emotions (446). The Americans, however, valued their self-worth according to whether or not they succeeded in becoming independent of others (445). The researchers found that what is judged as a positive emotional state in one culture can very well be considered an undesirable one in another. Additionally, they found that Americans differed from the Japanese in that they reported feelings of happiness in situations in which they were not socially engaged with others, while the Japanese considered their happier moments as those spent with others:

> In Japan, all the generic positive emotions consistently had very high correlations with the socially engaged positive emotions, but the corresponding correlations with the socially disengaged positive emotions were much weaker. This pattern was completely reversed in the United States. This can be interpreted to mean that in Japan generic happiness is more clearly associated with social engagement. (453)

A correspondingly 'pro-interdependence' attitude was found in Japanese respondents who were asked questions intended to measure their self-esteem. Their answers revealed that their self-esteem was dependent on the appraisal of others. American respondents, on the other hand, measured their self-worth through self-appraisal. The researchers concluded that 'what the esteemed inner attributes of the self are to independent selves may be what the esteemed social relationships are to interdependent selves' (454). The Japanese sentiment of self-respect (*jison-shin*) was dependent on satisfactory social relationships. But 'self-esteem' itself, the positive valuation of the self for its own merits independent of social interaction, was relatively weak in the Japanese sample. Americans, on the other hand, were much more given than were the Japanese to appraising their failures based on personal valuations of themselves (455). A surprising finding of the survey was that Americans were almost three times more likely to experience positive emotions than were the Japanese. Although the rate of 'negative' emotion experiencing was also higher in the United States, there seemed to be considerably more frequent experiences of 'authentic' personal happiness and liking for others (457). Kitayama, Markus, and Matsumoto concluded that 'in independent cultures, these engaged emotions may also arise as a result of one's own positive appraisal of others without reciprocal response from the others; thus, they may be a matter of primarily personal and private experience' (458).

They also speculated on whether a particular interpretation of the meaning of a given emotional experience 'may in turn transform the nature of the experience itself' (449). This is an important observation because it suggests that the manner in which a reality is perceived will have a considerable effect on the emotional reaction triggered by the reality. *Whether a given practice is considered hurtful or not, civil or uncivil, will have a considerable effect on a person's reaction to its presence or absence.* This may seem evident and not worthy of further discussion, but it does imply that two people experiencing the same reality could have different reactions to it. In an LC culture, for example, multitasking may be perceived as a brutal invasion of personal space. In an HC culture, multitasking may even be considered a confirmation of personal competence and worth.

Another factor affecting reactions to civil and uncivil behaviour is a person's emotional biography. This cannot be stressed enough. Sociologists often ignore the depth of a person's emotions and the influence of those emotions on the person's social interactions and social behaviour (Davetian 2005).

## Pain and Civility

Repeatedly we have cautioned that any sociological study that does not take serious account of the role played by human emotions in social outcomes impoverishes its ability to produce durable insights. In this section we would like to provide some empirical support for this viewpoint.

So far, we have discussed the manner in which embarrassment and shame play a central part in the civility process. We have also discussed how cultural habituations affect the manner in which people relate to one another and to the environments in which they live. This is only part of the explanation. The remainder of the 'civility puzzle' can be found in a profound understanding of the nature of human emotional needs and the consequences of their denial. The majority of sociological studies describing 'civilizing processes' are focused on pro-social civil behaviour. Yet, there is much we can learn about civility by studying its counterparts: incivility, aggression, and rudeness.

In the past forty years or so a relatively new phenomenon has emerged in the offices of counsellors and psychologists. A helping profession that previously was focused on behaviour modification through the use of 'talk therapy' has come to realize that a box of tissue paper should be a staple on the desk of every psychotherapist. We have finally accepted that people carry within them deep emotional pains connected to childhood issues that remain unresolved and which contaminate their adult behaviour.

We now have substantial empirical evidence suggesting that people are as much influenced by their personal biographies and unresolved emotions as they are by their cultures. This evidence comes from one researcher-therapist who, more than any other mental health professional, has come so close to explaining the psychogenesis of human discontent. His discovery occupies a central role in our own argument regarding the necessity of differentiating between 'manners' that come from social training and 'civilities' that are connected to more profound psycho-emotional processes.

Dr Arthur Janov has gone beyond the limits of psychoanalysis as well as the bio-energetic theories of Wilhelm Reich (1950) and Alexander Lowen (1967). He has taken on the project of explaining the nature and sources of emotional pain. His discovery allows us to address the social costs of restraint and repression. Particularly, we are given an opportunity to see how emotion and behaviour are dialectically connected; the restraint of the non-social impulses does not always bring about pro-social effects; in fact, the opposite can occur, as the energy of denied emotions rebounds against repressive restraints and moves the individual to particularly uncivil behaviour.

While traditional psychotherapies have tried to help the adult remain grounded in the present based on the assumption that regressive behaviour would be disintegrative, Janov has discovered that the opposite is true – it is the Herculean effort to repress out of consciousness memories and emotions connected to childhood that makes adulthood elusive.

References to memories of childhood are found in the literature of every country. One of the classic examples of how present events can trigger memories (pleasant and unpleasant) from the past is to be found in the pages of Marcel Proust's remarkable *Remembrance of Things Past* ([1954] 1983), an autobiographical novel in which the narrator recounts the present while also being reminded of scenes and emotions from the past. Proust brilliantly accomplishes a 'time-travel' in which associations, emotions, and memories are used to lift the veil of forgetfulness that separates the adult from the young child. The rich use of detail, sound, and nuance in Proust's work is like a neurological map of the human psyche.

Janov has similarly shown that memories are located on a bedrock of emotion. In his first work, *The Primal Scream* (1970), he documented a therapeutic process that seemed to be helping adults release emotional pain supposedly originating from childhood experience. The book struck a chord in a generation that wondered why it felt so much frustration and yearning; it became an instant best-seller and was soon translated into over twelve languages, triggering a worldwide movement in feeling-oriented therapy. While Sigmund Freud and Wilhelm Reich had written extensively about 'emotions' and the 'compensatory' character structures that arise due to emotional repression, they had stopped one step short of discovering the full extent of a person's feeling self and the consequences of the suppression of that self.

Janov developed a process of clinical psychotherapy that helped a client remember and regain access to feelings that he may have kept suppressed. Access to these feelings was gained through tapping into upsetting situations in the present as well as through direct reflections on past experience. This process differed radically from conventional psychoanalysis and behaviour modification therapy. Instead of being asked to embark on an analytical conversation with a therapist, the client was encouraged to 'let go' and feel his emotional reaction to events that had occurred in his life. This 'reliving of trauma,' along with the expression of the emotions that had been restrained at the time of the trauma's occurrence, seemed to have a healing experience. The feeling-experiencing of previously registered but repressed sadness, grief, loss, anger, humiliation, rejection, neglect, and fear seemed to have a positive effect and liberated the person to express positive feelings in the present with greater clarity and honesty than before. There was a marked decrease in anger and uncivil reactions in post-primal clients who had terminated a substantial portion of their feeling work. They were less defensive, less self-seeking, and more able to minister to the needs of others. They came to understand that being 'uptight' was nothing else than being physically constricted against feelings that needed to be felt.

What was remarkable about Janov's work with his clients was that when a client regained his composure after experiencing deep wrenching pain he or she did not look any worse off for having had the feeling experience. Janov's work debunked the centuries-old belief that loss of control over strong emotions would lead to mental illness. Feeling an emotion in connection to the original event that caused it seemed to actually heal mental and emotional disturbance. Emotional expression seemed anything but dangerous, provided it was done in a safe environment with the help and support of a competent and compassionate therapist.

Janov's approach went against the entire idea that 'restraint' and 'civilized behaviour' are functionally correlated within a closed and reliable system of checks and balances. The totality of the evidence we have presented, from medieval times right into the Victorian era and even into the twentieth century, has shown one predominant tendency: the imposition of restraints on aggression, sexuality, bodily functions, and emotions has steadily increased in tandem with increased specialization, technical development, and state centralization. This general picture of an accumulation and sophistication of restraints is also the major empirical discovery of Elias's own comprehensive analysis of conduct over a long period of time ([1939] 1978, [1939] 1982). Janov, however, reversed the process and helped his clients to remove the restraints that had been placed on their emotions and their bodily expressions. Since no de-civilizing effect was observed (not as long as the person expressed his or her feelings *in connection* to their real source rather than 'acting them out' or 'taking them out' on others), we feel it important to give some consideration to Janov's discovery as part of our study of how emotions and civil/uncivil reactions are intimately related. Janov's discovery has been supported by neurological research on the human mind's ability to store memory and emotion out of consciousness (Penfield and Roberts 1959:45, 50–1; Melzack and Wall 1965:971–9; Melzack and Scott 1957:155–61; Herrick 1926:91; Janov and Holden 1975).

Janov's explanation of emotional transference demonstrates that an emotion that is being restrained is not necessarily being sent out of existence. Denied direct expression, it can become rerouted and cause symbolic and inappropriate behaviour. The process of 'sublimation' is one example of such redirection; that of 'reaction formation' is another. So while restraints can become sufficiently applied at the external level they are not as securely controlled at the internal, individual level. An exaggeration of restraint can produce reactive behaviour through the process of impulse redirection, for the sum total of the restraints can produce an overload situation that requires relief. Giddens ([1991] 2001) also refers to the social implications of the process of transference when he writes that 'feelings of personal impotence may become diffused "upwards" towards more global concerns' (193).

Janov's (1970, 1975) work confirms this *privatization* of negative and positive emotions and the manner in which it affects shame and self-esteem. By recognizing that certain individuals carry with them an overload of unfulfilled need and its attendant pains, Janov makes us question the validity of the traditional behavioural psychology model that evaluates a person's mental health by whether or not he or she is able to 'adjust' to society. His work demonstrates that expression of primary repressed emotions has a positive effect on a person's social identity and his interactions with others (1970:152–3). What has concerned Janov during his clinical work with functional adults undergoing pain-expression therapy is not whether an individual is able to conform to and adjust himself to cultural norms, but whether he is being 'expressive' (real) or 'defensive' (unreal) at the level of personal feeling. Thus, he does not define normalcy according to behaviour*al adjustment* but according to what a person *feels* during his interactions with others (31). In fact, following his seminal discoveries, we are moved to wonder whether the restraint of emotion is not in reality a process that produces pathological societies, perhaps genteel on the surface in the short run but conflicted in the long run.

Janov uses the word 'neurotic' to refer not to pathological personalities but to anyone who has repressed his pain and adopted ideas and behaviours that help keep such pain repressed. He simply defines neurosis as repression of feeling (24). According to his dialectical hypothesis, many individuals who struggle for satisfaction in their lives are vulnerable to suffering from discontent because, even when the im-

Towards a Cultural Sociology of Civility 413

agined object of affection is attained, they are left suffering from the original 'primal' feeling of absence of fulfillment (39–41). Thus, he differentiates between 'wants' and 'needs,' explaining that, very often, individuals want what they do not need because they are afraid to feel their primal needs and be overwhelmed by the pain of unfulfillment.

Extending Janov's discovery to the study of social restraints and civility we see that in a reflexive society, in which the rewards for conformity are less obvious than in an organic environment, *the early internalization of restraints against the expression of pain may be weakened and the potential for social dissonance increased as actors 'act' our their pain with one another. This acting out is, in a manner of speaking, a means for avoiding loss of face and the emotional pain that would be released by such loss of face. In that case, 'loss of face' is loss of the defensive personality, the presentations of the unreal self – presentations intended to ensure that others do not manage to expose the vulnerability of the self. In fact, the emotion of shame itself could be considered a defence against the more primary and fundamental emotion elicited by the pain of rejection: the infinite and inconsolable sentiment of deep, heart-wrenching sadness.* This may explain why young children are so willing to please and why they can be made to feel disconcerted and embarrassed at the slightest provocation. The embarrassment is the outward manifestation of the anxiety that is provoked by the potential loss of social approval and acceptance.

It would be useful to say, then, that the emotional valence of interactions among citizens will be dependent not only on what courtesy codes they have learned but also on how they handle their emotions according to past biography. A person who is engulfed in anger is going to be less disposed to being courteous than someone who is relatively at peace. Equally, a person who is depressed due to an accumulation of repressed sadness may not be able to find the energy required to minister to the face needs of another.

Janov has subjected his discoveries to the most rigorous tests. Individuals who have experienced primal therapy have been followed by medical doctors and neurologists. Profound and lasting changes have been measured in core body temperature, blood pressure, EEG activity, and other measures of physical health. It would seem that the release of emotion has a lasting effect on the homeostasis of the body. It is not the goal of this book to present a detailed rationalization of Janov's discovery. And, indeed, we remain aware of the fact that the release of repressed emotion, if not done with the proper guidance of a competent therapist, can have disintegrative effects and overload the individual with unmanageable amounts of pain that have serious behavioural consequences. Our purpose here is not to argue for or against the 'curative' powers of primal therapy but to confirm that primal therapists have helped us observe the tremendous well of emotional pain that exists in certain individuals and the manner in which it affects their interactions in the present. Those interested in investigating Janov's discoveries in more detail can do so by examining some of Janov's own comments and the comments of his clients at http://www.primaltherapy.com/.

It is interesting that this discovery of the depth of emotional repression occurred in America. Perhaps the long-standing American mistrust of anger and its imagined antisocial qualities had run its course and citizens required a more emotive social environment (Stearns and Stearns 1986). One cannot say that England was similarly disposed. The English have restrained emotion. Perhaps that is not exactly the same as repressing it.

Thomas Scheff (1987) also suggests that shame and embarrassment can be studied from the emotional perspective. Although he does not substantially discuss the anatomy of personal pain, he suggests that an *accumulation* of shame can lead to a 'humiliated fury' that becomes directed at that which the person conceives to be the cause of his shame (109–49). This anger is explained by the fact that the usual reaction to shame is to want to conceal it (Tangney 1992; Lewis [1971] 1974; Elias [1939] 1978). The need to conceal is an automatic defence against the experiencing of the self as inadequate or unacceptable. That sense of inadequacy can be rooted in childhood biography or in the sentiment that one is not living up to present public and/or private standards. We hesitate to even make this distinction, since many people continue seeking social approval as an adult because such approval keeps a previously denied pain at bay (Davetian 2005).

Whatever the cause, the frustration felt in reaction to an exposure of shame can be directed at the self or at someone who is thought to be the instigator of the negative appraisal. The witness is not welcomed in an instance of shame because he is seen as 'the dealer or instigator of pain.' Expectedly, there is more of a tendency in individualistic, emotionally expressive cultures to preserve loss of face through 'rebutting' rather than compromise (Smith and Bond 1998:140). In an organic culture, the admission of embarrassment is made in relation to a code that is inherited from a bank of collective values; in a self-referential culture, however, admission of personal shame is also an admission of a personal failure to achieve a personally created goal or, at worst, an admission that the usual defence mechanisms against pain are about to fail. While an admission of shame serves to repair the communal personality of a person who admits to having transgressed against a communal code, such admission on the part of a self-referential person may serve only to further damage the legitimacy of the identity he has authored for himself. Such pressure to appear unflustered may lead to considerable defensive action; the personal emotional distress emanating from such pressure may even energize ideational activism, for the need to rationalize one's dissatisfaction can be temporarily assuaged through engagement with many volatile political issues (Milburn and Conrad 1996:4–5).

When shame and its underlying pain are denied, a secondary emotional process emerges to keep the awareness of the shame out of consciousness. Helen Block Lewis ([1971] 1974) has suggested that the redirection of anger towards other parties is a balancing mechanism that allows the shamed (hurt) person to regain his composure, since shame (hurt) is such an unsettling experience. Such denial can also occur in male–female relationships in which shame is experienced differently due to gender socialization (Lewis 1977). Building on Lewis's research in psychotherapy, Scheff (1994b) suggests that, in certain people, the consciousness of shame may become so acute that it predominates their lives:

> Under the whip of repressed shame, thoughts, speech and action are repetitive and compulsive. In a typical episode, patients will report obsessing about a scene in which they felt injured and ridiculed, or in error. They repeatedly replay the scene in their imagination, thinking about what they might have said and done. (289)

The compulsion to redress a situation that has already occurred abridges the time span required for the conscious realization that shame has been registered. If the shame were felt, there would be less of a need for retribution. Scheff comes close to locating the emotional nature of shame when he states that the expression of anger can act as the 'motor for continuous conflict, an infernal machine which can run for the whole lifetime of an individual' (293). He explains this as a consequence of the refusal or inability to 'acknowledge' shame:

> The outward form involves a cycle of honour, insult, and retaliation by

one party, which triggers the same cycle in the other, and so on, *ad infinitum*. Since unacknowledged shame and alienation go hand in hand, this proposition locates interminable conflict in civilizations in which relationships within and between groups are mostly alienated. Persons with zero bounds, if their alienation is completely unacknowledged, like Hitler, can go only one of three ways: madness, suicide, or homicide. (292)

Similarly, J.P. Tangney et al. (cited in Tangney 1995:125) confirm in their study of anger that 'shame-prone' individuals are more subject to experiencing anger and the need for retaliation than those who are relatively free from shame:

Across individuals of all ages, shame-proneness is associated with maladaptive and nonconstructive responses to anger, whereas guilt-proneness is associated with constructive means of handling anger – strategies that are likely to strengthen and enhance interpersonal relationships. (129)

A similar argument has been presented by Kaufman (1989) and Kaufman and Raphael (1984). Wicker, Payne, and Morgan (1983:25–39) have also demonstrated that the desire to 'punish' is reported more frequently by people who discuss their responses to shame than those who discuss their reactions to guilt. This externalization of responsibility makes the observation of shame quite difficult, because the manner in which blame is transferred to the external world (or the manner in which the entire shame reaction is concealed) will often enlist words and behaviours not readily associated with shame. One may see the reaction as a rational expression of anger rather than what it actually is: *a self-preserving tactic triggered by sudden panicked concern for the cohesion of the self*. Yet, is the self that is being protected the 'real feeling self' or, as Janov contends, the 'unreal self' constructed to keep the pain of the real self out of consciousness?

Predictably, the consequences of pain denial and shame denial are damaging to social relationships because they lead to arguments that have little to do with the actual sentiments of the parties. *They also strike at the heart of the authenticity imperative.* The pained or shamed person may resent the witness and react in a way that prevents conciliation and honesty. This reaction may require him to employ distracting tactics designed to cloak the truth.

The point being made here is that the existence of unresolved emotional pain adds a new dimension to the analysis of civility. Individualism can no longer be the sole measure of a culture's attitudes towards shame, pride, and civility. Nor can individualism be an accurate indicator of emotional responsiveness. *A culture can be individualistic and libertarian without encouraging substantial emotional expression.* Its individualism can be based on the practice of rational logic rather than emotional self-disclosure. Authenticity and social compassion can be achieved through a philosophy of tolerance and justice as readily as it can through an ethos of unrestrained, open-hearted friendliness. Civility, therefore, needs be studied not only in relation to conceptions of individuality but also in context of a culture's emotional ethos. This requires a sociology that is emotionally informed (Davetian 2005, Scheff 1994a, 1994b). It also requires an analytical framework that takes into account how different cultures have different emotional valences and how these affect the management of face preservation.

The role of embarrassment and shame in instances of courtesy and discourtesy – as well as their connection to emotional distress – is thus of considerable importance. If shame is deflected in the form of blaming external causes, then manners alone cannot guarantee positive civil interactions. Even a well-mannered individual can become disposed to expressing the anger that results from shame, especially if he lives in a culture that encourages emotional expressiveness or that has little patience for the social faux pas. In a culture that lacks the rituals of wit inherited from aristocratic cultures given to avoiding violence through pointed understatements, expressions of anger can be quite abrasive. In such cases, rather than being 'put in his place,' the offender is 'blown off his feet.'

Janov has repeatedly mentioned in his various books that the unfulfilled individual seeks to compensate for his unfulfillment by seeking substitute gratifications. This is especially noticeable in the narcissist personality, a personality that continues to trouble conduct book writers who worry about the social effects of self-obsessed individuals whose sense of entitlement causes them to be mindless of the face needs of others (Truss 2005, Twenge 2008).

Whether the narcissism is felt at the personal level ('Gee, I am so great!) or at the communal/cultural level ('Gee, my nation is great!) the end result is the same: the conviction that one occupies a privileged self. This sentiment acts as an effective social anaesthetic against sentiments of pain, unworthiness, or unbearable social contingency. Youth who seem inordinately confident with their own performance in the absence of actual competence may in reality be coping in the best way they can with the tremendous pressures put on them by a society given to demanding achievement at all costs while forgetting that the most basic fundamental need of the human being, beyond the need for shelter and food, is love and recognition.

Caught in the trap of proving himself to the outside world in order to avoid facing the pain of his inner world, the narcissist falls prey to sentiments of entitlement. 'It is my right,' 'I deserve this,' and 'I am great' are the defence reactions of a person unable to admit lack of personal integration. Whether they are made on the basis of legally established rights (such as the right to have equal opportunity regardless of skin colour, gender, or sexual preference) or whether they emanate from a private evaluation of self-worth, these claims have quite different behavioural implications. Legal entitlement is a mark of collective citizenship, defined by extensive discussions at the legislative level. Self-ascribed entitlement, however, is contingent on personal sentiment and requires substantial and repeated validations of a fragile personal image that remains continually under the threat of emerging pain.

So, when speaking of narcissism we are not referring to a self-esteem that is based on actual worth and accomplishment. A person with authentic self-esteem would not need the spurious satisfactions of narcissism. In the strictest sense, a person of authentic self-esteem who seeks the approval of others for qualities that he possesses and admires in himself should not be considered narcissistic, but, rather, as someone who has the justifiable desire to have his authentic self appear visible to others. Very different from this authentic self-esteem, however, is the sentiment of 'vanity.' The vain person cannot let pass a slight of his imagined worth; in order to preserve his imagined competence and worth he must immediately defend his person and position – expectedly, this increases the possibility of argumentation and incivility.

The pressure on individuals to 'market' themselves through 'image management' is particularly heightened in cultures where considerable innovations in education, technology, arts, and fashion demand continual upgrading of work and social skills. The fear of potential humiliation in such competitive environments sets in motion a compensatory movement in the direction of a 'brave' and 'daring' presentation intended to camouflage ongoing insecurity.

Whether a person's self-confidence is rationally justified or based on fantasy further depends on the actor's relationship with his own biography and the collective image of the culture he inhabits. The amount of 'unfulfilled need' for love and recognition that a person carries within him will also determine the extent to which he is vulnerable to narcissism, for the alternative to the compensatory comfort of self-love could be depression, the precursor to being flooded by unresolved grief (Janov 1970:23, 31, 36, 153–4, 273–5). Certainly, *modesty*, a facilitator of civility, is weakened in the presence of narcissistic need, for modesty requires a moderation of the demands made on others as well as claims made on behalf of the self or one's culture. Self-absorption, like ethnocentrism, limits the potential of a universal 'we-ness.' The narcissist must continuously guard against taking on the position of others because mutual consideration would require self-restraint and a diminution of acquisitive presentations of self (Lasch 1980).

Ironically, due to his strong need for self-validation, the narcissist is at once manipulative of social relations as well as substantially dependent on the moods and reactions of others (by virtue of his need for validation). While his 'individualism' is founded on a belief in independence, his emotional vulnerability corrupts his self-sufficiency and makes him actually quite other-oriented. If he stops seeking frequent external validations of his opinions of himself, he risks sinking back into the silence and emptiness of an unadorned and unrecognized self. This strong need for self-validation through approval-seeking behaviour can lead to numerous acts of manipulation and 'in-your-face' performances that may leave an observer with the impression that the person is 'shameless.' That would be an erroneous conclusion, for, very often, it is the fear of an existent (or imagined) pain or shame that drives the narcissistic personality.

'What's in it for me?' is the fundamental question that motivates the narcissistic personality. The question emerges when the narcissist is asked to consider a value, philosophy, or act meant to benefit the collective. The emotional poverty of this question lies at the root of many contemporary acts of discourtesy and lack of civility.

The manner in which the body is enlisted in the development of the narcissist is also of interest. The body becomes a means for negotiating attention and recognition in an anonymous society in which citizens are already habituated to the spectacular. This 'commodification' of bodily identity is referred to by B.S. Turner (1984), who explains in *The Body and Society* that the management of impressions becomes transformed as a result of citizenship in a mass market founded on the ethic of consumerism: 'The self is no longer located in heraldry, but has to be constantly constituted in face-to-face interaction, because consumerism and the mass market have liquidated, or at least blurred, the exterior marks of social and personal difference' (109).

A. Frank (1991) and Anthony Giddens (1990, [1991] 2001) also explain that awareness of the body becomes heightened in an age of contingency. Frank presents a historically informed typology of bodily identity, proceeding from the 'disciplined body,' which derives its security from 'regimentation' while denying its desires, to the 'mirroring body,' which derives its security through the satisfaction of desires via acts of consumption, to the 'dominating body,' which resists ontological insecurity by dominating other bodies through force, and the 'communicative body,' which creates itself through ongoing interactions with others (1991:51, 89). Late modernity puts the narcissism of the 'mirroring body' and the relationalism of the 'communicative body' in an interesting conjunction. The 'disciplined body' (and its physical and moral constraints) loses popularity. The communicative person resists restraint in the name of emancipation, while the narcissist resists constraints, suspecting that they might limit his search for gratification.

At the centre of such intense presentations of personality is the 'dread' of embarrassment and failure (Goffman 1959, 1967). An omnipotent personality defends against feeling this dread by taking on an a priori bodily identity that conveys an image of physical superiority and power. Rather than risk relating to others through a 'mirroring' or 'communicative' process he chooses a 'dominant body-personality' image to avoid the anxiety of inadequacy. The narcissist adopts a similar defence, albeit in softer form: his need for 'omnipotence' (avoidance of criticism and compromise with others) is not as dependent on the conquering of the other as it is on the containment of his own imagined or real sentiments of deprivation and deficiency through the seduction of the critical faculties of others. Shame is the price the narcissist pays for excessive ministering to the self, a project that is futile because it can never resolve the emotional pain that continues to reside within the body of the narcissist.

Giddens suggests that sensual communicative interaction with others is weakened by this narcissistic search for personal gratification (1991:70). He links narcissism with imagined power: 'Narcissism is a defense against infantile rage, an attempt to compensate with omnipotent fantasies of the privileged self' (172). The keyword here is 'privileged' – the fantasy that the self is 'entitled' to being 'welcomed' by the external world because of something special about it. And, indeed, the need to be special is the need of the child-adult who exhibits a heightened need for intimacy:

> Individuals demand from intimate connections with others much greater

emotional satisfaction and security than they ever did before; on the other hand, they cultivate a detachment necessary to the maintenance of the narcissistic ego defenses. The narcissist is led to make inordinate demands on lovers and friends; at the same time, he or she rejects the 'giving to others' that this implies. (173)

This preoccupation with self at the exclusion of the needs of other social actors is a major cause of interpersonal tension and mutual non-recognition. Yet, it is the trap that anyone with unresolved childhood needs can fall into without blame. It affects intimate relations, family organization, work environments, and just about every situation in which people come face to face with one another. Certainly, the search for personal satiation complicates acts of mutual recognition or, at best, brings forth a situation in which individuals exchange recognition with the implicit contract that their own individual agendas be recognized and accepted without disorienting criticisms. This exchange type of recognition, however, does not increase intimacy and may even create an infernal circle of benefit evaluation leading to a demoralizing climate of psychological isolation. The speakers may be 'full of themselves' but considerably bereft of satisfying social communion.

The history of a nation plays a substantial role in the proliferation or control of personal narcissism. In a social system that has experienced aristocracy and built a national heritage and pride based on its aristocratic traditions, there is a certain amount of cultural narcissism that tempers the need for private and isolated presentations of self. One can be a citizen and retain the sense of personal confirmation that comes from being a member of an 'accomplished' culture that offers itself up as a model for emulation.

The English and French have had the benefit of enjoying a cultural narcissism based on a long and varied history. Although the French and English lost much of their colonial influence, they continued to define the meaning of 'being English' and 'being French' according to established civility traditions. Americans, however, had to build their national pride according to the accomplishments of free people supposedly possessing equal status; no aristocratic tradition was present to soften and temper the search for personal identity. Tocqueville ([1884] 1994) noted the consequences of such similarity and mass representation: 'In ages of equality, all men are independent of each other, isolated and weak. One finds no man whose will permanently directs the actions of the crowd' (439).

It would seem that the weakening of the aristocratic standard, while serving to abolish ascribed privileges, created a new problem: competitiveness not only required the self to be differentiated, but placed that differentiated self in opposition to the populism and conformity that are part and parcel of a national ethos based on the honouring of the 'uniform crowd' (537). Self-centredness was the paradoxical consequence of this belief in equality among people; a person needed only understand himself to understand how to deal with others, since it was assumed that individuals thought and felt in similar ways in a democracy (565).

The degree of self-absorption also affects the degree of 'empathy' that is shown in social relations. In principle, a courteous person would be able to practise empathy by showing concern towards others and act in ways that increase or maintain the comfort of others. But this process is affected by the degree to which a person suffers from raging unfulfilled needs. Batson et al. (1988:52–77) have discovered that individuals who are capable of forgetting their own needs are able to empathize with another person through the taking on and imagining of the other's predicament. Certainly an individual who is made to feel shame frequently is in no position to minister to the needs of others; analysing the data presented by Batson et al., Tangney (1995) also observes that shame complicates the practising of social empathy: 'Shame is a very painful reaction that involves a marked self-focus ... It seems likely that instead of promoting other-oriented emphatic concern, the acute self-focus of shame would foster self-oriented personal distress responses' (130).

Thus, a loop is created in which the need to withdraw and hide from the judgment of others produces the conditions for further avoidance behaviour even when social situations require the showing of real empathy. Such failures in empathic communications may lead to a collective loss of heart; they may even explain why some people, although living privileged lives in wealthy nations, feel isolated and alienated even when in the company of others.

Self-ministry would be emancipatory in a morally conscious society populated by individuals who have managed to heal themselves of lingering sentiments of pain and unworthiness. However, in a social environment in which the private and public demands made on a person are increasingly paradoxical (e.g., honesty and accommodation in personal relationships despite relentless competitiveness in public dealings, and personal optimism despite rising social risks), the communicative act becomes a restless one, given to frequent contradictions, shocks, and disappointments. Incivility and social hesitancy become the outward manifestations of these unresolved paradoxes and tensions, leaving an indelible effect on social bonds.

In preceding sections we have frequently stated that sociology needs to take emotions and pain into consideration and have attempted to give some examples of how exclusively behavioural explanations provide an incomplete view of personal identity and agency. Yet, distinctions have to be made between emotions that strengthen the social bond and those that weaken it. We are not arguing for a free-floating emotionalism, but trying to understand how emotions are involved in the making or unmaking of trust and intimacy.

Following from Durkheim, Thomas Scheff (1997b) has hypothesized that 'threats to a secure social bond can come in two different forms: the bond may be either *too loose* or *too tight*' (77). An understanding of this difference provides useful insights into the opportunities and opportunity costs of *solidarity* and *isolation*. Scheff explains that relationships in which the bond is too loose are *isolated* and hampered by mutual misunderstanding (or a refusal to understand) on the part of interactants. Relationships in which the bond is too tight are *engulfed*: at least one of the parties in the relationship, usually the subordinate party, understands and embraces the priorities and standpoints of the other (willingly or reluctantly) at the expense of his own desires and ideas.

In 'engulfed' families (and cultures) certain members are always trying to be on their best behaviour through obedience and conformity, thereby limiting their curiosity, intuition, and feelings (77). The submission is not limited to children but can also involve spouses deferring to the wants and wishes of their families, even when their feelings tell them to do otherwise. Similar inhibitions apply to citizens living in authoritarian political systems or devitalized democracies. This sort of social bond creates a feeling of alienation on the part of all, regardless of whether they occupy dominant or submissive positions. The denial of the inner sentiments of the various parties excludes the possibility of open and authentic sharing, since that which is not avowed cannot be expressed. Roles are acted out, but with little self-disclosure. The dramaturgical frontstage of behaviour becomes uncoupled from the inner sentiments of the actor and gives rise to a substantial backstage in which authentic thoughts and sentiments are protected from public disclosure; when the uncoupling between what is said and what is kept silent is disturbing enough to create unbearable ambivalence in the individual, that which is kept silent becomes archived in the subconscious, where it is kept out of conscious awareness. A child or teen who is placed in an engulfing situation is faced with a no-win situation: if he complies with the emotional limitations set by his family, he loses his sense of self; if he withdraws into isolation to maintain his independence, he risks not benefiting from some of the accumulated knowledge and experience of his elders (78).

Scheff explains that social bonds that force their members into a *no-win* situation are often heavily focused on discussions of material topics such as chores, money, schoolwork, work, renovations, and so forth. Secure social bonds, however, include discussions of the relationship itself and the feelings of all participants (80). A weak (or deconstructed) social bond, however, keeps interactants distanced from one another. They may consider themselves 'free' but they run the risk of becoming emotionally detached and depersonalized (Laing 1976). Nor does mundane interaction provide long-term solace. Nothing guarantees that individuals who converse for hours about mundane subjects feel any closer to one another than they did before conversing.

Referring to Martin Buber's (1958) seminal and elegant treatise on the sanctity of the 'I-Thou' relationship, Scheff (1978b) warns that without the recognition of the mutual human worth that is implicit in the 'I-Thou' relationship, individuals are left with two very unsatisfactory alternatives. These are the alternatives of 'I-It' relationships, in which the other is considered simply an object to be manipulated and/or dominated to satisfy one's own desires; or the 'It-Thou' relationship, in which one's own needs are submerged by the imperatives of the other. Scheff considers that no good can come of either alternative since both cause considerable alienation (79). We would add that both extremes bring about considerable shame, non-recognition, and an accompanying seething reaction of discontent waiting to be released at the right moment when the power ratio between the interactants is altered.

A fourth interactive mode, one that needs be considered in the context of a late-modern society in which the recognition of a multiplicity of personal rights is equated with social democracy, is the 'I-You and Our Mutual Deal' relationship. Participants overtly engage in a balancing process designed to achieve self-preservation through mutual recognition. They may even openly declare to each other that they expect fair exchange. This is the 'up-front' pragmatic relationship. While the 'I-You' relationship solves emotional issues in an equitable way through a balancing of the power-ratio, it does not pretend to contribute to the type of 'I-We' awareness that energizes communities to feel that there is a solid bond between the actions of community members and the civic morale of the community. Interactants may do quite well with one another at the level of small groups while remaining relatively impoverished at the level of communal involvement. As Pierre L. van den Berghe (1963) has pointed out, an individualistic consensus to live and let live does little to sustain collective morale.

# Part IV

# Contemporary French, American, and English Civility and Interaction

> The reason man does not experience his true cultural self is that until he experiences another self as valid he has little basis for validating his self.
> – Edward T. Hall

# 10 A Comparative Field Study of France, America, and England

> I don't trust Americans. They behave as if they've known you all their life although they've just met you.
>
> – a French person, Paris

> I don't trust the French. You never know what they mean. They never come out and say what they have to say.
>
> – an American person, New York

> The French are the masters of complexity ... as for the Americans they are rather naive.
>
> – an English person, London

## Introduction

In the preceding sections we have repeatedly spoken of civility 'habituations' in broad and ideal terms. Of course, this does not mean that an entire population is going to behave in a standard fashion. For example, when we speak of an American civility ethic that favours informality we remain aware that there are many Americans who do remain impeccably reserved in their dealings with others. Equally, when we speak of the French being emotionally expressive, we remain aware that there are emotionally restrained individuals in France who would find even the amiable reserve of the English rather maudlin. Thus, we are simply observing 'tendencies' that occur more often than do others. One thing we have learned during the preparation of this work is that nothing short of a multi-disciplinary approach can reveal complex nuances in a culture; furthermore, the more kaleidoscopic one's angle of view the more difficult it becomes to categorize reality within fixed frames.

We have also been trying to map out those factors that should be examined during a comprehensive study of civil society, especially any study that compares the civility practices of two or more countries. These factors include *individualism; communalism and degree of deference to authority and tradition; interdependence and independence; low- and high-context orientations; manner of expressing and/or deflecting shame; type of politeness rituals; and differing levels and types of emotional expression.*

Keeping these factors in mind, we travelled through America, France, and England wondering if the historical and theoretical work that we had developed would prove useful to informal and formal observations of civil interaction in those countries. While we did not wish to reduce all observations to an a priori template, we were interested in seeing if our explanations could hold up during field research. To facilitate our work we constructed a 'research template' that took account of the above-mentioned factors.

**A Framework for Comparative Field Research in Civility**

Understandably, in the space available in this volume, it would be impossible to present a verbatim ethnography of a field voyage that took us to a variety of cities and towns in America, France, and England over the span of many years, the last six of which were funded by the Canadian Social Sciences and Humanities Research Council and the British Commonwealth Association of Universities (1998–2004).

The guidelines we developed for our research were intended to allow us to study those social processes that have the major influences on those social interactions which constitute the core of civil society: (1) family and childrearing; (2) the notion of self and self-esteem; (3) education; (4) conversation; (5) friendship; (6) courtship; (7) work ethic; (8) state bureaucracy and citizenship; (9) politeness rituals.

For our field research we chose to be participant and observer. We lived and travelled in the countries, not as a researcher on a structured mission but as someone going about daily life while participating and observing. We reminded ourselves to use our eyes and train them to see afresh what may have previously been taken for granted; to use our hearing, again with the desire to listen as completely as possible; to actively participate in the life world of our subjects and allow that participation to be authentic and as minimally manipulative as possible; to converse with our subjects about their lives and our own and, thereby, put them at ease to converse about many aspects of civility, including topics that are remotely connected to it; to readily engage in self-analysis in relation to our interpretation of that which is observed; to take note of the visible as well as the invisible, the said as well as the not-said.

We find that this method of field research, the method of the 'flaneur' (the wanderer), best suited our own temperament as well as the nature of the topic chosen for research. As Charles Baudelaire said, the flaneur has the privilege of 'botanising on the asphalt' (cited in Walter 1973:36). He does more than observe the crowd. The fact that he walks in the crowd prevents him from remaining detached. He is in the midst of it and a vital part of what he is observing and describing. This allows him to see what he might not see were he to remain aloof in the interests of 'objectivity.' Moreover, participant observation allows one to see both what people say they do and what they actually do, something that is not possible with the survey or the structured time-bound interview. We also purposefully chose to study our subjects over a long period of time, aware that the schedule-bound 'field trip' risks remaining a trip rather than an in-depth longitudinal experience. Thus, we chose to observe 'social frames' in succession and interconnection rather than in isolation.

Specifically, we made it a rule never to approach an individual by stating the topic of our research at the onset. We have learned through years of travel that confidences and confessions are shared spontaneously in a climate of trust but come forward less easily in response to direct questions. This is especially true in societies that favour non-imposition. Thus, we interacted with our subjects according to whatever social opportunity was at hand, only later describing our project and, even then, in a casual way. This helped put others at ease and freed them to speak not as subjects being interviewed but as individuals sharing a space of global co-citizenship with us. This revealed much that might otherwise have remained hidden if the 'interview question' was our principal method of interaction. Thus, we were confidants as much as we were researchers. We accomplished this by never being in a hurry, by always accepting to 'waste time' going off-topic, for we considered any and all conversations useful to our understanding of the people who were our hosts. And we did accept all invitations for interacting with individuals in private and public settings. We did not discriminate according to dress, social or economic position, or education. We learned as much from the homeless as we did from those living in upscale suburbs. When it came to the study of formal settings such as offices, government services/agencies, and schools, we did reveal the nature of our study and conversed with relative openness, not shy to ask direct questions about practices (e.g., asking French human resources personnel why the offices of managers were more frequently than not located in the centre of the floor plan, asking American managers where on earth the statement 'kill the competition' originated from, or asking English managers why English business meetings were based on consensus-seeking rather than rule by majority vote). Needless to say, our study of bureaucracies, media, public spaces, educational institutions, and public interactions required us to spend long stretches of time 'hanging around' while watching others conduct their business. We categorically made it a rule to be more often on foot than in a car, for, unlike Baudrillard (1998), who toured America by car observing from behind a windshield, we were interested in being in the midst of what we studied and, in a sense, being 'contaminated' by our subject.

Our conclusions result from living in, observing, and studying all the above-mentioned aspects and processes in the following locations. *America*: New York (Manhattan, Queens, Brooklyn, Long Island), Vermont, New Jersey, Connecticut, Maine, Utah, North Carolina, Texas, Virginia, Nebraska, and California; *England*: Central, West, and East London, Wimbledon, Croydon, Brighton, Eastbourne, Southampton, Worthing, Canterbury, Littlehampton, Birmingham, Manchester, Glastonbury, and Liverpool; *France*: Central Paris and surrounding districts, Calais, Dieppe, Versailles, Lyon, Marseilles, Boulogne, Lille, Grenoble, Bordeaux, Rouen, Aix-en-Provence.

Throughout the field study we remained conscious that since civility was a face-to-face interactive practice and involved a variety of emotions, it would require a research template that took into account various key indicators of civility, incivility, and various emotions.

Three sets of guidelines were used to ground our observations and separate them from the realm of fiction. The first set allowed us to define the various faces of civility and incivility. We call these *definitive indicators*. A second set of guidelines included varying factors of which a researcher should remain conscious while making observations. They included indicators of habituations that differ across culture boundaries. We call these *categorical indicators*. The third set allowed us to apply a fairly reliable template for the identification and observation of emotions. We call these *emotional indicators*. As we have argued previously, emotions play a central role in civility and incivility; so, it is important to have some idea of how various emotions are to be recognized.

*Definitive Indicators*

CIVILITY
*Associated words:* politeness, pleasantness, agreeability, gentility, deference, empathy, good manners, propriety, pleasing disposition, consideration, caring, delicacy, empathy, tactfulness, hospitality, altruism, amenity, diplomacy, ceremony, refinement, modesty, gallantry, correctness, grace, friendliness, gratitude, accommodation, artifice. *Associated gestures and behaviours:* smiling, shaking hands, nodding, graceful movements towards the other, waving, bowing, relaxed brows, bodily composure, lowered shoulders.

DISCOURTESY
*Words associated with discourtesy:* rudeness, thoughtlessness, impudence, rudeness, tactlessness, disregard, lack of consideration, undiplomatic, indelicate, coarseness, churlish, exclusive ceremony that has a freezing effect, crass, aggressive. *Gestures and behaviours associated with discourtesy:* frown, aggressive movements towards the other, cold stare, brows lowered and taut, obscene gestures, sarcastic laughter, harsh voice, glaring, pointing at the other, puffed out chest, turning of the back on the other, non-observance of known rules of manners, cold demeanour signifying unfriendliness or lack of desire for consensus.

*Categorical Indicators*

*Individualism and communalism:* the degree to which a person's identity is defined by personal achievement and personal preferences (independence) or communal cooperation and cohesion (interdependence).

*Power distance:* the degree to which the person feels obliged (or willing) to show deference to those in positions of authority or in positions deemed worthy of respect and deference (Hofstede 1983).

*Uncertainty avoidance:* the degree to which a person prefers to avoid uncertainty and risk (Hofstede 1983).

*Reflexive vs. communal morality:* personal moral valuation versus adherence to communal moral evaluations.

*Cultural narcissism:* the tendency for members of a culture to think of their cultural values and interactive styles as excellent or more excellent than those of other cultures (nationalism).

*Personal narcissism*: the tendency for a person to have a very high opinion of himself and the readiness to promote that self without disinterested consideration for the selves of others.

*Positive or negative politeness rituals:* the degree to which civility rituals establish mutual identification and/or non-imposition (Brown and Levinson [1983] 1987).

*High- or low-context cultural communications*: the manner in which interactants relate to time, context, and space (Hall and Hall 1990).

*Emotional Indicators*

Since many of the above factors require the observation of sentiments, it is wise to go into the field with a certain amount of forethought regarding actions and reactions that are energized by emotions:

1. All emotions must first be evaluated from the subject's own 'appraisal' of the situation. The degree to which a subject cares about the outcome of a situation (i.e., the emotional investment) will greatly affect the charge of the emotion as well as its appraisal. 'Motivational relevance' is an important part of emotional reaction. This relevance applies to all emotional reactions (Smith and Lazarus 1993). So, the same emotion of 'anger' may be triggered by two different events, each representing varying degrees of other-blame and/or self-blame. Smith and Lazarus offer a useful *core relational theme* in their mapping of the emotions: happiness (success), hope (potential success), sadness (loss), fear (danger), anger (other-blame), guilt (self-blame). It should be specified that anger can also lead to self-blame, depending on the extent to which guilt or shame is felt. These emotional reactions can be identified across cultural boundaries. P. Ekman and his collaborators have identified principal emotions expressed across cultural lines, based on observations of facial expressions. They include: *enjoyment, sadness, anger, disgust, surprise,* and *fear.* He and his collaborators showed photographs of faces depicting the above emotions in ten countries and obtained consistent agreement from respondents as to the emotion being depicted in each photograph (Ekman et al. 1987).
2. Emotions also serve the function of communicating appraisals to

those with whom one is communicating. Because of this they can become dramaturgical tools that sometimes involve exaggeration and falsification.
3. The appraisal of the person regarding a generalized feeling of anxiety will influence its reshaping into a specified emotion that is then considered reality. Thus, appraisal can add a 'qualitative' or 'meaningful interpretation' to what begins as a 'visceral enervation' (Schacter and Singer 1962). So, it would seem that the level of irritation of a population depends very much on the manner in which individuals 'perceive' events in their lives. Abramson, Seligman, and Teasdale (1978) have shown, for example, that people who explain misfortune in terms of factors that they cannot control are prone to depression; similarly, a hopeful outlook helps minimize the effects of disappointment and loss.
4. 'Action readiness factors' have been mapped out by Fridja (1987) and Fridja et al. (1989). Anger, happiness, love, desire, confidence, interest, energy, elation, and contentment promote action or action readiness. On the other hand, feelings such as sadness, depression, desperation, fear, and anxiety inhibit action and may lead to withdrawal. So, it is just as important to observe those who are withdrawn and not attracting much attention as those who are socially active and expressive.
5. Facial expressions do not always demonstrate the primary emotion being felt. A person may have a hangdog facial expression but the emotion that may have been experienced prior to the taking on of the 'look' may have been one of anger. Expressions can, therefore, communicate actual emotional states or be communicative devices that cover an emotion in order to hide or deny it or alter its effect on others (R. Buck 1984).
6. Behaviour in dyads, triads, and groups differs. Allowances have to be made for group influence, groupthink, social influence, and a variety of emotional processes that are activated when group behaviour is involved. It is, therefore, important to observe members of a culture in private as well as public settings (Myers [1994] 2004).

Once these factors are taken into consideration and noted it becomes possible to design a template for the active study of emotions during interactions. In fact, there are certain linguistic and gestural guidelines that help us define an emotion in the context in which it is occurring.

## Linguistic and Gestural Guidelines for Emotions

During past studies of interactions we have been able to construct a series of words and expressions/gestures that identify particular emotions. Our guidelines accord in many instances with those developed by Suzanne Retzinger, who has done a study on emotions of violence (1991). These associated words and gestures/behaviours include:

ANGER
*Associated words:* pissed off, mad, ticked-off, furious, put out, irritable, indignant, teed off, enraged, fuming, bothered, resentful, bitter, spiteful, murderous, cold and distant, hot temper, frustrated, incensed, wrathful, outraged, fierce, flaming, heated, furor. *Associated gestures and behaviour:* Brows lowered and taut, narrowed eyelids, glaring, sarcasm, bodily threats through leaning forward, cold stare, clenched fists, chopping motion of hands, obscene gestures, sarcastic laughter, fluctuating tone to denote sarcasm, hitting objects, throwing objects, hitting another, shouting, screaming, speechlessness, taut lips, downturned mouth, pointing at the other, harsh voice, loud voice; in certain cultures, rapid laughter.

SADNESS
*Associated words:* gloom, dejection, despondency, grief, blues, tearful, weepy, sighing, depressed, despondent, glum, dispirited, disconsolate, forlorn, heartbroken, doleful, miserable, dejected, rueful. *Associated gestures and behaviour:* Crying, weeping, pouting, lowered shoulders, caved-in chest, knotted brow, tears, shuffling of feet, slow body movements, listlessness, far-away look, touching the other pleadingly, broken voice, inarticulated words, frequent irony; in certain cultures, a brave smile or forced laughter.

SHAME
*Associated words:* embarrassment, mortification, regret, abashed, chagrin, remorse, discomposure, quandary, confusion, disgrace, loss of face, rebuffed, deserted, distant, hollow, inadequate, unworthy, worthlessness, trivialized, demeaned, offended, incapable, incompetent, stupid, simple-minded. *Associated gestures and behaviour:* vagueness and obliqueness, sarcasm, defensiveness, self-justification, withdrawal/silence, indifference, lowered gaze, slouch, hesitant smile, self-censoring, mumbling, tense laughter, blushing, crying, turning head away, turn-

ing gaze away, bowed head, covering face with hands, anger at an object or person.

In preceding sections of this book we have discussed a variety of factors that need to be taken into account during the study of the civility ethos of a given culture. In addition, our preliminary understanding of the various emotions involved in civil interaction suggests that civility research should consider the following premises and postulates:

- *Saving face* is a universal need. The manner in which face is saved, however, is socially constructed and subject to regional variations. In Iran, for example, where courtesy practices and codes of public decency are formally prescribed under the general appellation of *ta'arof* (to behave with meticulous concern for the comfort of others) (Vivier-Muresan 2006:115–38), a person can lose face (*abeh-rooh az bein raftan*) if he is made to fall into a shameful state (*khejalat*). The concept of shame and embarrassment (*khejalat*) is an extremely potent social reality for Iranians, even those of secular temperament. The word is even used to describe displeasure towards the behaviour of another (e.g., 'I felt ashamed at what he did'). Mutual responsibility triggers frequent instances of shared shame. One commonly hears 'he took away my face' (*Abeh-rooh man-roh bord*) when a relative causes embarrassment to the family. In instances of embarrassment, the offender says 'Forgive me' (*bebakhshid*), and the other replies, in order to minimize the loss of face (through the denial of the right to judge), 'May God forgive' (*khoda bebakh-sheh*).
- Whether a *negative* or *positive* politeness strategy is employed in interactions will depend not only on the given situation but also on the degree to which a culture (1) favours *communalism* and/or *individualism*, (2) favours or disfavours *power distancing* and *vertical* (as opposed to horizontal) status assignations, and (3) encourages or discourages the expression of primary emotions (anger and pain). Thus, the amount of emotional repression or expression in a given culture plays a seminal role in the type of civility rituals used by its members.
- Hierarchies are of two types. The first is attached to title and functional status. The other is attached to talent, ability, and popularity within the community. Thus, an individual can possess a privileged place in the social hierarchy through adherence to the rules applying to his function in the hierarchy and/or via personal charisma and competence.

- Whether an individual is bound by *communal* or *self-referential* norms will have a marked effect on the manner in which *guilt* and *shame* are experienced and processed. Thus, early socialization, as well as ongoing codes of adult interaction, will have a major influence on the manner in which an individual maintains composure and assists others in maintaining theirs, and also on the manner in which he attempts to regain his composure when *face* is threatened.
- Whether or not adjustments to personal behaviour and presentations of personal image can be made without resorting to confrontational denials of failure depends on the degree of directness in the discourse of individuals. The degree to which citizens of a culture practise discretion in their relations with one another affects the degree to which shame is defended against. In a culture that values 'telling it like it is,' the need for reacting against shame with immediate defensive behaviour increases, for one's neighbour prefers authenticity to the insincerity involved in the mutual concealment of fault. Such risks of being engulfed by shame are also high in cultures where citizens, for some reason or other, feel compelled to frequently criticize one another.
- A lack of balance between *cultural narcissism* (patriotism and pride in national heritage and one's communal personality) and *personal narcissism* (pride in one's personal identity) can have corrosive effects on social solidarity and civility. Similarly, excessive cultural pride can impinge on the personally generated identity of an individual. So, strong social bonds can be as problematic as loose ones.
- Since various cultures use *positive* and/or *negative* politeness rituals, a study of the predominant interaction rituals of a given culture tells us much about its civility rituals and the ideals that lie at the foundation of that culture's moral, emotional, and behavioural development. These rituals tell us much about the historical background of the culture and its preferred system of governance and status assignment.

*A General Template for Multi-Dimensional Observation*

The above factors were incorporated within a template. We were keen to observe the following dimensions of each of the three nations of our study:

| Quality/practice | Type or rate | Outcome(s) |
|---|---|---|
| Governance | | |
| Independence values | | |
| Interdependence values | | |
| Public relations | | |
| Private relations | | |
| Predominant politeness ritual | | |
| Distinction boundaries | | |
| Emotionalism in public | | |
| Emotionalism in private | | |
| Impoliteness ritual | | |
| Cultural narcissism | | |
| Personal narcissism | | |
| Shame management | | |
| Face-redress method | | |
| Anger expression | | |

## Understanding the French, Americans, and English

In the remainder of this chapter we summarize our observations in a manner that takes into account the various categories of analysis we chose for our study while providing a manageable account of our understanding of how and why civility standards are different in the three countries chosen for our comparative study.

In addition to learning from the observations and insights produced as part of our field study we have referred to some respectable and methodologically reliable surveys which provide us with instructive comparative data that complement our own field research. The data reveal the attitudes of French, English, and Americans on a variety of topics, the principal ones being family, courtship, and childrearing; religion; work; and citizenship. The most interesting and multi-dimensional of these surveys is the World Values Survey (WVS), which has emerged from the European Values Survey (EVS), which originated in 1981 and was originally limited to European countries. The present WVS is conducted in almost eighty countries. Led by a group of social scientists from leading universities, the survey is performed on nationally representative samples. We will be referring to the survey whenever appropriate during this chapter and use its results within our own narrative. Whenever citing percentages and other information emerging from the study we indicate such data with the abbreviation (WVS). Most of the data we will quote come from the 1999–2001 wave, the latest available results. Although the English responses are categorized under the appellation 'Great Britain,' the survey does separate Ireland in a nation category of itself. These data as well as data on other countries can be found at http://www.worldvaluessurvey.org.

Some other sources that we have found useful and fascinating are: Polly Platt's *French or Foe?* (1994) and Raymonde Carroll's *Cultural Misunderstandings* (1987), two leading texts that explore why the French and Americans have particular difficulty understanding each other's cultural practices. Equally instructive have been the following texts on cultural differences: Edward T. Hall and Mildred Reed Hall's *Understanding Cultural Differences* (1990), a seminal comparison of business and cultural practices in America, France, and Germany; Gilles Asselin and Ruth Mastron's *Au Contraire! Figuring Out the French* (2001); Jean-Benoit Nadeau and Julie Barlow's *Sixty Million Frenchmen Can't Be Wrong* (2003); Mark Caldwell's *A Short History of Rudeness: Manners, Morals and Misbehaviour in Modern America* (1999); and Michèle Lamont's *Money, Morals and Manners – The Culture of the French and American Upper Middle Class* (1992). Although a few of these works were not written by conventional academics, the fact that their authors are professionals working in the burgeoning field of 'cross-cultural communications' makes their work empirically reliable and valid.

In the narrative that follows we have felt compelled to keep in mind the question of 'social ethics': What are we to do about our own understanding of 'moral behaviour' and 'sincerity' when studying civility? We are faced with the same conundrum that confronted Victorian writers who had to somehow chart a middle course between personal ambition, communal solidarity, and etiquette/manners. So, we remain aware that a courteous person can also be manipulative and even disturbingly corrupt. Being 'two-faced' is not a phenomenon limited to any one country but a universal occurrence in all social situations where truth cannot always be told without causing embarrassment or even conflict. We have had to ask ourselves how we would reconcile differences in civility practices considering that various cultures have different tolerance levels for 'social lying.' For example, preserving one's face as well as the face of another requires us to sometimes lie to each other (and ourselves). How are we to judge *lying* when we encounter it in our observations? Should we define it as immoral and/or amoral behaviour or as an inevitable aspect of social life? Nancy Sherman (1991) suggests that the 'aesthetics' of manners and civility somehow manage to train the individual to access his or her inner virtue; she argues that hiding one's feelings can sometimes contribute to virtuous action. In our own case, we decided to treat the phenomenon of 'insincerity' with an open mind, for, every so often, the same individuals who show a tendency of a certain sort can also show its exact opposite as a balancing regulator or remedy. In short, we decided to beware against typecasting our subjects.

Early on in our fieldwork we noticed that we would have to provide particular explanations for French civility codes because they differed so remarkably from Anglo-American ones. We were already intrigued by Geert Hofstede's (1980, 1983) study showing that the French paradoxically value individualism and authority/power distance (hierarchy) almost equally, whereas England and America seem to have a non-paradoxical preference for the individualism traits. We were also aware that, due to its language, France has been set off and protected from assimilation by Anglo-American cultures; in fact, an adequate understanding of the variations between English and French expressions and sayings (and the rich use of metaphor and nuance in the French language) is required if one is to fully appreciate the complexities and paradoxes of French culture.

As argued in previous chapters of this book, we find that the 'national histories' of a culture and the biographies of its institutions play a central role in affecting its cultural norms and the manner in which individuals of various social classes select their ideal values and behavioural traits. These influential biographies emanate from the intersection of a variety of social systems: political organization, economic system, moral and philosophical dispositions, psychological and emotional factors, and the ways in which ideal manners are explained and practised. One important study which partially confirms our own thesis is Michèle Lamont's (1992) study of how upper-middle-class men define personal and cultural worth, *Money, Morals and Manners – The Culture of the French and American Upper-Middle Class*. Lamont has shown how cultural boundaries and class differences are reproduced through the idealization of certain traits over others. In the process, she has made a valuable contribution to the sociology of culture by showing that economically developed Western countries do continue to be culturally different from one another. Her study consists of semi-structured interviews with upper-middle-class men in France and America who were given an opportunity to reveal their conceptions of 'their sort of folk' (1). Lamont observes that this conception of worth affects 'an intrinsic part of the process of constituting the self' (11).

Lamont classified the responses she received along three symbolic boundaries: socio-economic, moral, and cultural. The socio-economic boundary was defined by the importance accorded to wealth and the process of acquiring it and using it to have power over others; the moral boundary was defined by personal integrity, sincerity, honesty, and consideration for others; the cultural boundary was defined by the possession of education and intelligence, refined taste, a cosmopolitan worldview, manners, taste, and an appreciation of high culture.

What distinguishes her comparative study is the fact that she compares across national boundaries as well as between cosmopolitan areas (e.g., Paris and New Jersey) and provincial areas (e.g., Clermont-Ferrand in Auvergne and Indianapolis in Indiana); additionally, she takes note of differences between capital and provincial areas within the same nation. Although her interviews number only 160 (40 in each area) she does manage to make a credible case for the fact that Pierre Bourdieu's ([1979] 1984) conception of class reproduction may be too limited to economic explanations. While the concepts of 'worth' and 'distinction' are vital parts of class reproduction and, as Bourdieu perceptively points out, are a form of 'symbolic violence,' the standards used to define such distinction are varied and dependent on national histories and 'cultural ideology.' Our own study similarly demonstrates this nuanced nature of culture.

Not surprisingly, Lamont (1992) discovers that although both American and French members of the upper middle class tend to favour inclusion and exclusion – by the mere fact that they select certain traits as more desirable and admirable than others – they do differ in the priorities they assign to the various symbolic boundaries: 'Moral boundaries are as important in France as they are in the United States, the socio-economic boundaries are the most salient in America, and [the] cultural boundaries emerge most sharply in France' (130). Echoing Tocqueville, Lamont concludes:

> While some indicators could be interpreted as suggesting that high culture is slightly more democratized in the United States than in France, cultural boundaries are not very salient in the boundary work of New Yorkers or Hoosiers: Americans who are culturally sophisticated seem to be less likely than their French counterparts to believe that they can legitimately expect to draw prestige from their cultural sophistication because

the principles of cultural egalitarianism and cultural laisser-faire mitigate against this belief. In contrast, we saw that French participants more often make cultural distinctions as a way to gain socioeconomic status; i.e. to improve their social position; that they frequently draw socioeconomic boundaries on the basis of cultural status signals (e.g., rejecting working class people as 'vulgar'); and that signals of high culture status play a more central role in the French workplace. Also, evidence suggests that Americans are more likely than the French to believe that cultural standards of evaluation should be subordinated to moral ones (i.e. to 'what kind of person you are'). (130)

Lamont observes another telling difference between the manner in which Americans and French view money and the making of money:

These national boundary patterns are manifested in the ways Parisians, New Yorkers, Hoosiers, and Clermontois criticize the different form of boundaries: the French prove to be much more likely to oppose socioeconomic boundaries than Americans, whereas the latter more often oppose intellectualism and cosmopolitanism ... Also, moral and socioeconomic purity more frequently go hand in hand for the Hoosiers, who often take moral purity to be reflected in socioeconomic success by deducing honesty and moral character from success. This is less true for the Parisians who tend to presume that money is corrupting and that moral and socioeconomic purity are incompatible. (120–31)

Here one runs into a little difficulty with some of Lamont's interpretations of the differences. Is the French search for cultural distinction a consequence of mistrust of the capitalist imperative, as implied in Lamont's discussion? Or could another explanation hold true: those preferring moral rather than socio-economic boundaries may mistrust capitalism not because they are convinced that there is an incompatibility between money-making and moral/cultural distinction, but because they fear being colonized by a particularly American brand of populism that is the outgrowth of a particularly American capitalist market. In that case, populism, rather than capitalism, would be the alienating factor. One wonders about this because France has managed to be one of the top ten economic powers of the world – it would not have achieved this status had it categorically mistrusted capitalism.

Lamont's study would have been even more excellent had she included members of the British upper middle class, since the United

Kingdom is both strongly capitalistic as well as aristocratic, given to favouring individualism and personal liberty while continuing to adhere to class-oriented boundaries. The British would have made an excellent control group and contributed to a multi-dimensional understanding of nuances that may not be readily apparent in a bilateral study. That is why, in this present work, we have found it important to not only compare an anglophone and francophone culture but to include a second anglophone culture as a safeguard against explanations that are too facile. Certainly, it allows us to understand the role played by intervening variables in the development of a cultural norm or practice – for example, did Protestantism facilitate capitalism or was there an intervening variable (such as romanticism) that emanated from Protestantism but without which the conspicuous consumption required for a successful capitalist market would not have been possible?

What distinguishes Lamont's interviews is her ability to allow her subjects to speak in their own voice and reveal without much apology that they do favour cultural exclusivity. The fact that they do not agree with the exclusivity standards used by their counterparts (and even openly criticize them) reveals just how 'taste' and 'cultural ideology' can divide nations and even regions.

In *French or Foe?* (1994) Polly Platt, an American francophile and cross-cultural expert who provides orientation seminars for Americans and other foreigners settling in Paris, has observed similar differences and repeatedly warns Americans to ready themselves for the following surprises when they arrive in France:

> The public French face is closed. The grim-looking passport control policeman probably ignores your 'hi.' The taxi driver and the hotel concierge may look stern or grumpy. That doesn't mean you look or talk funny, or that they hate Americans, or Britons, or Asians, or that their mother has just died. Nor does it mean they'll cheat you. They're just being French (23) ... Our cult of friendliness has made the reflection-smile seem like a fundamental right. You may not think so until it's happened to you, but smiling at someone who doesn't smile back can be catastrophic for Americans. (25)

Platt's advice seems very useful. Over 140,000 copies of her book have been sold through twelve editions. We ourselves have noticed important differences in the way citizens of different cultures 'contextualize' their interactions and social experiences. So far in this volume we have agreed with Edward Hall's (1983; Hall and Hall 1990) observation that cultures usually fall into *high-context* or *low-context* frameworks of perception and behaviour. Although we remain faithful to Hall's theory throughout most of this chapter, we find it too expedient to classify England as a low-context culture alongside America. We have noticed too many important differences between American and English interaction practices and are moved to question whether England would not be better classified separately. Throughout our historical review we have noticed that the English have adopted a middle road between American and French practices. Certain of the English practices are very much high-context practices while others are low-context ones. We hope to make this clearer as we proceed and will suggest that a new term needs to be added to Hall's topology: the category of a 'moderate-context' culture.

Our historical review indicates that the civility practices of America, England, and France have been affected by politics and state organization, economics, moral philosophy, literature, and national myths. *But do these differences continue to exist in a contemporary context?* During a social theory conference in England in 2001, an eminent American sociologist responded to a paper we presented on the 'sociology of civility' by commenting that, as far as contemporary comparisons of America, France, and England are concerned, the deformalization of the world and the pervasive influence of global media no longer permit fruitful cross-cultural comparisons. We categorically disagreed with our colleague. Our field research indicates that these nations continue to differ in substantial ways despite predictions of a levelled cultural field (Davetian 2001a). A few nights spent watching television in England, America, and France should sufficiently show the inadequacy of such reductions.

In fact, the cultural differences are so remarkable that one continually notices irritation and bafflement when citizens of these three countries come face to face with one another. The dissonance is most observable between the French and Americans. These are a small sampling of the comments made to us during our discussions with citizens of these two countries:

- The French talk interminably and say nothing. Their conversations are meaningless. They just love to hear themselves talking.
- The Americans say little or deliver monologues. They are unaware of what it means to have a real conversation.

- The French consume great amounts of food. They force you to eat every morsel, except for the cheese.
- The Americans waste so much food. It is an insult to the hostess and such a waste of well-prepared food.
- The French raise children as if they were raising slaves.
- The Americans raise children as if they were training delinquents.
- American friendships are superficial.
- The French take too long to become friendly.
- The French are never on time.
- The Americans value time too much.
- The French state is a dictatorship.
- The American state is a chaotic free-for-all.
- America is controlled by capitalists.
- France is controlled by bureaucrats.
- The French always blame everyone else except themselves.
- The Americans have this cowardly habit of apologizing for their errors.
- French managers take forever to decide.
- American managers make hasty decisions.

Witness also just a few preliminary observations of differences between French, American, and English civility practices:

- France: Never ask to use the washroom of your hosts while dining at their house even though the dinner may last six hours.
- America and England: Make sure your washroom is clean and pleasingly arranged for your guests.
- France: Never address someone you have just met by their first name(s).
- America: Establish intimacy right away in the name of friendliness.
- England: Establish a cautious friendliness without invading privacy.
- France and England: Do not pry into the profession of someone when you first meet them.
- America: Ask what the other does for a living very early on to show interest in their life.
- France: It is all right for a man and wife to argue in public.
- America and England: Desist from revealing marital conflict when in the company of anyone, sometimes not even closest friends.
- France: It is necessary to teach children the rules of behaviour by criticizing them whenever necessary.

- America: It is necessary to teach children by setting an example that does not demean their self-esteem.
- England: It is necessary to teach children discipline and rational behaviour by teaching them emotional restraint.

*State System*

One of Norbert Elias's ([1939] 1978, 1982) important contributions to the social sciences was his carefully presented thesis that civility practices and interaction ethics are closely correlated to changes in the governance powers of the state. A similar observation was made by Alexis de Tocqueville in *Democracy in America* ([1884] 1994); he convincingly argued that America's rejection of the aristocratic system of government was a major factor in the development of 'horizontal' (as opposed to hierarchical) relations between citizens. Our own historical review has similarly noted historical variations between the American, English, and French notions of liberty and ideal governance. These variations, more than partiality or aversion to capitalism, determine the manner in which individuals in each country distinguish themselves.

Moreover, the degree to which the state is involved in the management of the nation has a salient influence on the nature of face-to-face interactions and the general 'cultural ideology' that is used in a given era. France is governed by a socialist state that stands between the ruthless laws of the free market and the welfare of its citizens. The American state is less given to such socialist sentiment. The English state is, similar to the one in France (albeit less proficiently), extensively involved in the social welfare of its citizens. The minimalist social safety net in America may explain why Americans are more concerned with 'job security' than are the French and English. When asked about whether job security was important, 46.3 per cent of the French replied in the affirmative, compared with 71.8 per cent of Americans and 65.1 per cent of the English. As far as the importance of pay was concerned, the French again seemed to demonstrate less concern than the Americans and English: French 68.2 per cent, Americans 88.9 per cent, English 81.2 per cent (WVS).

The effects of these divergences in state systems are remarkably noticeable in relations between parents and children and in the ecology of extended family life. State systems also have a major influence on whether a culture values 'vertical' as opposed to 'horizontal' relationships, and whether it favours individualism, communalism, and power distancing or, as in the case of France, a paradoxical combination of both.

Louis XIV's reputation as the 'Sun King' was partially based on the fact that he had managed to establish a centralized state in which he acted as the absolute arbiter, controlling even the most minute of court expenses. The 'Sun King' was the centre of France, and his decisions *irradiated* outwards to the various regions of the country. The geographical shape of France, a *hexagon*, facilitated this centrally located bureaucratic apparatus. Paris became the centre of France, and its civil servants held considerable authority over the rest of the country. Napoleon Bonaparte took advantage of this geographical reality by appointing regional *prefects*, who reported directly to him, thereby providing him with a political control not less than that possessed by the monarchs who preceded the revolution. It is only recently (since 1982) that France has begun to cautiously experiment with decentralization. Predictably, there is much duplication at the national, regional, and municipal levels as a result of such decentralization efforts. In a country of 36,500 municipalities the short- and long-term future of this transition is being hotly debated even as we write.

The American system, however, has been anything but centralized. At the inception of the American state, citizen assemblies very often made decisions free from the interference of Washington politics. The American ideal of 'self-governance' referred not only to the country's break from colonial rule but to the retention of considerable independence by the various American states. The continuing absence of consensus among these states regarding the death penalty is only one example of this lack of totalizing federal influence. It also reflects Americans' willingness to welcome change at the communal level – the idealization of continual improvement (progress) has facilitated and preserved such decentralization. It may also explain why, despite less-than-stellar turnout at federal elections, Americans continue to exhibit a strong commitment to civic duty through strong volunteer participation in local social welfare initiatives.

Such decentralization has also made America the least socialist of the major industrial countries. America's corporate cultural mentality is noticeable in a variety of situations: most American university graduates do not enter the public sector but seek positions in private enterprise; public utilities are for the most part privately owned; corporations contribute sizeable amounts of money to public programs and educational institutions; and government policies are considerably influenced by the interests of major corporations. The relative weakness of the American 'social safety net' is, on the other hand, partially compensated for by the high rate of volunteerism among Americans (19.8 per cent of Americans report being engaged in non-paid social services, compared with 4.8 per cent in France and 2.8 per cent in England) (WVS). Also, 21.4 per cent of Americans report belonging to groups, compared with 6.9 per cent of the French and 5.1 per cent of the English (WVS).

The English system of governance is also fairly centralized due to the fact that the British parliament remains part of a state system in which most of the bureaucratic functions are standardized across the nation. No state or provincial taxes are levied. Major moral issues such as the death penalty, as well as laws on tolerance and hate, are all national laws not subject to local revision. The difference between France and England lies in the fact that the English bureaucracy tends to avoid confusing and complicated procedures; it is perhaps the user-friendliness of the system and the politeness of public officials that give the impression that England is less centralized than it actually is. In reality, it is a nation in which surveillance is at an all-time high, with one surveillance camera for every fifty citizens.

These differing systems have not only had an effect on political organization but also influenced how individuals live their private and communal lives: how they raise children, how they manage friendships, how they conceive of courtship, how they converse, and how they organize their work and home environments. Not surprisingly, these were the responses given to the suggestion, 'Democracies are not good at maintaining order': 55.4 per cent of the French agreed, compared with 33.5 per cent of the English and 22.3 per cent of the Americans. The French preference for a high-profile government is also observable in the responses given to the statement, 'In democracies, the economic system runs badly': 49.9 per cent of the French agreed, compared with 28.7 per cent of the English and 22.5 per cent of the Americans (WVS).

*Family and Childrearing*

As Philippe Ariès (1962) has argued in *Centuries of Childhood: A Social History of Family Life*, childrearing practices are highly influenced by political, economic, and moral ecosystems. Whether a child is born in Atlanta or New York, Paris or Calais, or London or Liverpool will have a great effect on the type of life he is going to have and the type of family, education, and friendships he is going to enjoy. Particularly, his life

450  Civility: A Cultural History

Table 10.1
Behavioural and personality qualities most desirable in a child
(percentages)

|  | France | England | America |
|---|---|---|---|
| Obedience | 35.6 | 49.1 | 32.0 |
| Independence | 29.3 | 53.3 | 61.1 |
| Imagination | 18.3 | 38.3 | 30.0 |
| Unselfishness | 40.4 | 60.1 | 39.0 |
| Manners | 68.6 | 92.1 | N/A |
| Religious faith | 7.8 | 18.2 | 52.1 |

is going to be intensely affected by how his culture defines the meaning of childhood and the duties of parenthood.

It is not surprising then that even the definition of a parent's function should vary from one culture to another. When the French refer to parental obligations towards the child they do not use a phrase such as 'raising a child' but, rather, *éduquer l'enfant* (to educate the child). The raising of the child is defined in terms of teaching him to learn how to behave (*apprendre à être sage*) and do things the way they 'should' be done (*faire comme il faut*). In America, the emphasis is placed on the personality of the child, while in France the emphasis is on the norms of the society and the behavioural rules attached to those norms. The goal of French socialization, therefore, is *adaptation* while that of American parental supervision is *innovation*. This difference helps explain differences in a variety of areas, including management techniques, conversation structures, courtship, and friendship. It also helps explain variations in the emotional profile of each culture. This variation is noticeable in the WVS results. Respondents in France, England, and America were asked what behavioural and personality qualities are most desirable in a child (table 10.1). The qualities mentioned by respondents demonstrate important cultural differences in conceptions of the ideal child and ideal parenthood.

These varied responses tell much about views towards independence and interdependence. While all three nations value obedience, the English value it the most. The English also value manners (92.1 per cent) and unselfishness (60.1 per cent) highly. And while America and England favour independence (61.1 per cent and 53.3 per cent respectively), France considers it of secondary importance (29.3 per cent), just as it does imagination (18.3 per cent). On matters of religious faith, predictably a majority of Americans (52.1 per cent) consider it an important quality to nurture in a child, compared with only 18.2 per cent in England and even less in France: 7.8 per cent.

The World Values Survey seems to point to a particularly strong valuation of restraint in England. Not only do the English come first in valuing 'obedience,' they also value the qualities of 'unselfishness' and 'manners.' Can these qualities be attained without unintended negative effects? One wonders because of the increasing press devoted to a supposed wave of rudeness and cynical rage in England since 2004. The Scottish writer A.A. Gill (2004) contends, in a scathing diatribe entitled *The Angry Island*, that the English have proverbially been polite because politeness has been the means by which they have kept the lid on seething anger. Why do the English queue up in such an orderly fashion, asks Gill? He states that all hell would break loose if they did not; unresolved anger dating way back in history would erupt to cause chaos. Whether his hypothesis regarding the emotional profile of the English is true or not is less important than the fact that his book received widespread reviews in the English press. So did Lynne Truss's best-selling complaint about rudeness in England, *Talk to the Hand – The Utter Bloody Rudeness of the World Today, or Six Good Reasons to Stay Home and Bolt the Door* (2005). It would seem that despite the long-standing sacrosanct position occupied by English civility, there are strong signs of strain appearing in public and in private.

Across the Channel, it is interesting to note that, despite the high rate of secularism in France, the ideal qualities associated with a good child are similar to those valued in traditional religious communities: a low valuation of independence and imagination, and a high valuation of unselfishness. French families – as well as those in other high-context cultures – favour a clear demarcation between the adult and the child. Parenthood is a communal responsibility. Parents do not seek to have 'independent' children but children who are well educated regarding the norms of their culture. Whether or not one's child is *bien élevé* (well-bred or well-educated) reflects back on the family. That is why it is not uncommon for strangers in public who are being irritated by a child or youth to remark that the child is *mal élevé* (badly bred). The criticism is directed at the parent because the child is not solely in the care of the parent, but of society in general.

Soon the child learns that there is to be a proper balance between appearance (conformity to social expectations) and personal sentiment. He also learns that aiming for behavioural perfection is not the exception but the generalized expectation of the adults with whom he comes into contact. Here we note fundamental differences between the priorities imposed on American and French children. American children are encouraged to be innovative and creative; French children are asked, above all else, to do things competently.

It is understandable, then, that in communal societies parent–child relationships are not primarily intended to establish friendships between the two parties (although friendly feelings are always present) but to allow the parents to have considerable say over the emotional and intellectual education of the child. Although the friendship is a welcomed by-product, amiability is not sufficient reason for the suspension of parental judgment. A French parent is, thus, much less likely than an American or English parent to ask his child to participate in decisions related to his upbringing. The American approach is supposed to help the child develop independence at an early age; this tendency to ask the child to be both obedient and innovative is noticeable in the American conduct literature of the eighteenth and nineteenth centuries as well as in the contemporary American parent–child relationship.

The French would find such democratic equality between parent and child patently absurd (Asselin and Mastron 2001:69). They would even consider horizontal relations in the family as a threat to social cohesion and moral continuity, for French families are located in a society replete with complex interdependent relations that fall on various levels of a vertical social hierarchy. In return for the freedom to discipline and socialize their children according to communally specified norms (a 'high-context' practice), French parents are willing to risk being unpopular with their children. This luxury may not be as readily available to families in low-context cultures where extended kin networks and friendship circles are limited; in such cases, parents are noticeably dependent on the approval of their children because their own support networks are limited. Being less able to count on relatives to help in the socialization of their young, such parents are vulnerable to the objections of children who disagree with the parental rules.

While the American parent is given to continually negotiating with his child, hoping to avoid dissonance in the name of harmony and mutual esteem (prime ideals of the American civility ethos), the French parent does not feel obliged to provide explanations in every case for the duties and obligations he imposes on the child. While the French might agree with Lord Acton's dictum, 'All power corrupts and absolute power corrupts absolutely,' when it comes to protecting their individuality from the potential tyrannies of the state, they would bristle at the suggestion that parental authority should be subject to the opinions of the child. Agreeing to such egalitarianism would be tantamount to isolating themselves from their communal ties and responsibilities and delivering centuries of civilizational development into the care of uninstructed children. We suspect this explains why, in the study conducted by Geert Hofstede (1980, 1983), France ranks fifteenth out of fifty nations in favouring 'power distance' (deference to authority) even though it ranks tenth in favouring individualism. Platt (1994) similarly summarizes the differences between American and French parenting:

> Where an American mother would hesitate to bruise the child's ego, the Frenchwoman, with all those centuries of unbroken tradition behind her, does not hesitate to call attention to stupidity, bad taste, bad manners, boring comments, inappropriate reaction and any lapses in impeccable appearance. (129)

During hundreds of hours spent in French families, observing, discussing, and asking questions regarding French parent–child relations, we noticed that the French child lives a seemingly paradoxical life. On one hand he is required to conform to predetermined and firmly imposed social rules, while, on the other hand, he is required to develop originality, wit, and a critical spirit. These requirements appear paradoxical at first glance to those habituated to the American system of childrearing in which it is believed that considerable freedom is required in childhood in order to produce a self-reliant and innovative adult. French family organization, however, demonstrates that there may be an optimum level at which restraint and freedom become mutually complementary (and quite non-paradoxical).

So, the French child faces a twofold pressure. On one hand he must not disappoint the parent, while, on the other hand, he must not compromise the parent's public reputation as a parent. Any failure of his to be a child worthy of acceptance (and admiration) reflects back on the parent, for parenthood is a communal responsibility and the carrying out of that responsibility is judged based not on the degree to which the parent has helped the child achieve independence, but on the extent to which he has successfully transmitted French cultural values to the child.

This complex burden of responsibility makes the child become involved in his culture at an early age, for he sees his culture uncompromisingly represented in the person of his own parent. He must learn the complex codes of his culture if he is to succeed in decoding the statements made to him, many of which are quite implicit and understated. And the parent reinforces the child's 'no-exit' predicament by allowing himself to criticize the child in private as well as public: this not only communicates to the child that appropriate behaviour is expected of him inside and outside the home, but, additionally, signals to strangers or acquaintances that the parent is a devoted and responsible parent and is living by the codes of the community. It is, therefore, not surprising that strangers permit themselves (and are permitted) to gently criticize or console a child whom they do not know personally. Such benevolent interference is acceptable in a country where communal solidarity counts as much as personal privacy and freedom. It is also a means of keeping the child habituated to dealing with the adult world outside the confines of the family – a requirement for mature, interdependent citizenship. We have observed this same practice in high-context cultures as varied as Iran, Italy, and Lebanon.

A consequence of this rich and intense socialization process is the liberal use of body language. At an early age, the child understands that commands and expectations can be relayed to him through the parent's bodily expressions. Raised eyebrows, sharp looks, and purposive silent treatments sensitize the child and train him for future membership in a culture where everything is not overtly verbalized (Wylie and Brière 1995:81). Moreover, French parents allow themselves to be emotional with their children whenever they feel the situation calls for it; this is facilitated by the fact that French husbands and wives are not particularly averse to having disagreements with one another in front of witnesses. Quarrels are, therefore, accepted as part of communication and not cause for excessive worry. While the Anglo-American family (especially the English one) attempts to teach the child that rational behaviour requires a repression of emotion and a tempering of body language, the French see no contradiction between mercilessly mathematical Cartesian precision and the expression of deep sentiments on an ongoing basis. One culture sees quarrelling as an inevitable part of the mystery of life, while the other considers it a symptom of social failure. The American parent blows up at the child not because he is using a dramaturgical tool to make a point, but because he is at the end of his tether ('Okay! That's it!'). The blow-up follows in the heels of repeated emotionally restrained failed negotiations rather than as part of an ongoing emotional discourse. This may explain why it is so distressing.

During the time we spent in American, French, and English families we noticed that the French parents were quicker to voice objection towards a given behaviour of their child than were the English and, especially, the Americans. This absence of inhibition contributed to the avoidance of the type of blow-ups that result when reactions are delayed, compounded, and then suddenly released with pent-up fury.

The foundation of the French cultural habitus rests on five tenets that are introduced to the child very early in his life: (1) there is a specified way for doing things properly; (2) logic is at the foundation of reasonable behaviour; (3) language is of paramount importance in the formation of a proficient member of society; (4) solidarity and commitment in family and friendship circles are as important as work and passing short-term social interactions; (5) membership in the community requires an abiding respect for the accumulated accomplishments of French civilization. These five requirements for social membership are not negotiable and are further reinforced by the public educational system. For twelve long years the child will be repeatedly taught the accumulated accomplishments of French civilization and the unique contributions made by French writers, philosophers, artists, statesmen, and scientists.

The life of the French child is, consequently, driven by the French penchant for a healthy respect for conformity (civilizational continuity) *as well as* individualism (personal originality) (Hofstede 1983). Meanwhile, the parent is in firm charge of the child's development and has considerable say regarding the extracurricular books that the child will read at home, the friends the child will have, and the clothes the child will wear (and the way he will treat those clothes). Unlike in low-context cultures where family solidarity takes a back seat to personal achievement, few children in traditional French families are allowed to leave the table before the meal is completed. The meal itself is an important social function permitting parents to teach children their place in the wider social circle and within the family itself. Exhortations to sit up straight, to eat properly, and to not interrupt adult conversations are learned at an early age at the dinner table. Few French parents would take seriously a child's request that he be allowed to eat his food in front of the TV. Agreeing to the request would not only contribute to the child isolating himself from the community but also negate the importance of the meal and its deeply symbolic function as a means by which social relationships are developed and deepened. Thus, French families – in the traditional or ideal-type sense – seem to operate according to the rules of the 'tight social bond,' while leaving considerable room for freedom once the youth reaches adolescence, which for the French is a period of respite from a demanding childhood.

Moreover, French parents teach their children that their social universe needs to include continuing contact with members of the extended family. The Sunday meal with grandparents and other family members in traditional families, and the frequent holidaying with family members, teach children and youth that the family (and the community) have priority over their other contacts. We were stricken by how often we observed one youth cheerfully (or stoically) tell a friend that he or she would not be able to attend a peer-organized social function because of a family gathering. One thing is certain: frequent interactions with members of the extended family predispose children to become habituated and comfortable with interactions with people of all ages. We observed this same facility among English youth, but were saddened to see that American teens continue to remain uneasy and disaffected when face to face with someone considerably older than themselves. We observed this particularly with Generation X; the present cohort of youth seems to be more able to bridge the generational gap, probably because it is less pronounced than before in a culture so broadly concerned with the worship and preservation of youth.

The acceptance of a strong parental presence is made that much more possible by the fact that the French parent is intensely involved in the education of his child and often participates in the completion of his homework. Few children would succeed in the demanding French educational system without parental coaching. A child's future is immensely determined by his performance at the primary and secondary levels; helping with homework is not just a sign of parental love, but a pressing necessity, especially at the start of the school year when parents are given long and exacting lists of supplies to purchase for their children: the size of the ruler, the type of book cover, the number of pens are specified in uncompromising detail. The American parent does not enjoy this a priori privilege. So often we heard a parent ask his child if his homework was done and then let the matter drop when the child assured (somewhat vaguely and impatiently) that it was. Few parents asked to see proof of completion, even though they must have sensed that the homework could not have possibly be done if the youth was on the phone or in front of the computer or television for most of the evening.

The French sense of interdependence is also noticeable among siblings. In families where there are a few children, the eldest child (especially if it is a daughter) is given the right to help in the socialization of the younger children; there is a sort of hierarchy in the family according to age grade; children learn from each other that they can only get along by being alert and witty. Whereas American children prepare one another for a competitive world by bickering and competing for the attention of their parents, French children see themselves as allies in a demanding adult world in which solidarity with one another will be of mutual benefit. Repeatedly, we have been impressed with how French siblings cover for one another with parents while American siblings are so often complaining about one another.

An important aspect of French socialization involves teaching the child to develop the ability to participate in conversations with wit and originality. Repeatedly, he is forbidden from interrupting the conversations of adults or butting in with ill-considered thoughts. Raymonde Carroll (1987) notes the useful effect of such prohibition: 'Thus, by ordering the child "not to speak if he has nothing to say," "not to act cute" or "not to say silly things," I force her or him to discover the best ways of retaining my attention' (51).

The child, therefore, learns to pause and think before speaking. He learns from the wit of practised adults. Arriving in puberty and adolescence, he has already developed considerable linguistic and emotional maturity. *He has developed individuality and the ability to be independent because premature independence has been denied him.* Laurence Wylie (1981) notes some of the positive effects of this French obsession with the art of *se conduire bien* (to behave well):

> By age ten, the French children have become *bien élevés* (well reared). They have learned about limits, boundaries, delineation, and appropriate behaviour ... They have learned control over themselves, over their bodies. They have acquired tremendous inner psychological independence, I think, that American children do not have. I think they have not learned what American children do learn, that is, the emphasis on striking out for themselves, venturing out, trying new things. (58)

> ... And when verbal expression is not permitted, there is the expressive power of the eyes, the body, the importance of mime. And finally, there is fantasy. I think that the French children have an inner personality, an inner independence, an inner life that American children lack. And they illustrate and embellish it in a way that gives French literature and cinema

a particular and very beautiful cast. Each individual is surrounded by his own wall, enclosed in his own circle, but through these escape mechanisms, he can exist even though there are social controls. (62)

Wylie astutely identifies the paradoxical nature of restraint and freedom as well as the opportunity costs of each. One thing stands out in our own analysis: French parenthood is built on the need for solidarity and conformity while American parenthood is built on the need for diminishing dissonance and encouraging self-reliance. The American child from very early on is taught that he is a performer in a society in which being original, trendy, and comfortable with change is appreciated and lauded. He becomes an actor seeking love and approval prior to possessing the sophisticated tools required for pulling off the project with excellence. Early on he learns that not much effort will be required for success. This is the first lesson the child receives in dealing with reality in a low-context manner. The lesson is further taught in a media given to featuring the sensational and the hyper-real.

In short, French children are the apprentices of society; American children, on the other hand, are given extraordinary power at an early age. This at once empowers them as well as robbing them of the opportunity of rehearsing adult behaviour before they reach adulthood. Achievement and originality stand in for emotional maturity and worldliness. As Platt (1994) has observed, the French are indebted to their civilization, while the 'American parental contract is with the child' (127). It should come as no surprise that successive generations of Americans are so remarkably different from one another that they warrant their own names (e.g., the Baby Boomers, the Lost Generation, Generation X, Generation Y). Generational continuity is weak even though the structures of capitalism are not.

During hundreds of hours spent in American families observing parent–child interactions we were stricken by how much stress is created by a parental childrearing ethic that seems divided against itself. The American parent is attempting to socialize the child to function in a culture that has historically mistrusted tradition and hierarchy while attempting to preserve his parental authority over the child.

The American child is taught early on to be independent of family circles. He is encouraged to be sociable in the world, to 'make friends,' to be 'popular' and seek harmony in his social relationships. He is being prepared to 'make it for himself' in the world. He must seize every opportunity and learn to choose from a myriad of choices offered up to him at the educational as well as the extracurricular level. The mobile nuclear American family, while it offers its children myriad opportunities for developing self-reliance and openness to innovation and change, produces considerable discord between parents and children. Used to a geography and history favouring large allocations of space to each citizen, the American parent provides considerable 'space' to his child but then ends up complaining that the child is no longer sharing the family space. Many studies have shown that American teenagers spend no more than a few minutes of conversation with their parents every day. It would seem as if sympathetic identification with the parent is very low. The American mother says goodbye to her children at the door with, 'Have fun,' encouraging their independence. The French mother sees her children off with *'Soyez sage'* ('Be good'), reminding them of their interdependence.

It is instructive to note that it is not lack of will on the part of the American parent that causes confusion in the child but the readiness to keep critiquing a given behaviour almost mechanically, without insisting on its suspension. The child does something. The parent objects. The child does it again. The parent objects again. The child continues doing whatever he was doing, now coming up with justifications for his behaviour. One has the impression that the parent is nagging rather than educating the child. The exchanges are emotional, but not in a purposive way that leads to a clear demarcation between acceptable and unacceptable behaviour; it would seem that the parent is not quite sure of what is to be the actual limit. Constant negotiation and 'deal making' energize such unsure exchanges. The search for efficiency and expediency ('low-context' habituations) makes the parental experience a managerial rather than moral experience. Repeatedly the child is left with the impression that he is conforming to the whims of an individual rather than the ethos of an entire culture, especially so because he encounters a completely different social ecology in school, one of permissive tolerance even in the face of lax performance.

Whether all this is due to indecisive parenting or to America's historical preference for socializing its young to be self-affirmative and daring (the 'go-getter' personality ideal) is open to speculation, depending on whether one's orientation is historical or psychoanalytical. Either way, it would seem that the uncertainty has increased in direct correlation to the growing influence gained by the media in post-1950s America and the rise of a 'culture of entitlement' and 'rights negotiation.' The same litigious mentality that has caused two-thirds of all the lawyers in the world to be based in America – a direct consequence of America's long-standing search for rights equity between citizens – seems to be perturbing the confines of the American family.

We would expect French children to harbour considerable resentment towards their demanding parents. Platt, however, observes that 'when these children [French] grow up, they *are* pals with their parents, perhaps more than American children' (128). The *high-context* relationship with the parent seems to build strong social bonds that survive into adulthood.

In our own observations we were continually confronted with American pre-teens and teens who seemed to have developed a knee-jerk defence towards their parents. This attitude was most observable between mothers and daughters. Eyes turned upwards in exasperation, sneering mouths, threatened foot stomping, and shrieks of protest were some of the many body gestures we observed in a society in which the child seems to be in continual dissatisfaction. Although French children also exhibit considerable protestation, the usual response of the parent is to put aside the issue at hand and address the civility of the child or youth (or the lack of it).

This, however, does not mean that the American child is emotionally independent of his parents. Quite the opposite seems true. He is emotionally vulnerable to the judgment of the parent. Any conflict in values or wishes is a conflict between him and the parent because he lives in a multicultural society where conservatism and liberalism are in perennial conflict. There is, therefore, no clear indication that the parent is exercising the will of the culture since there is no formal declaration of the necessity to preserve that culture. In a deconstructed America in which a variety of rights are always in competition with one another, the parent is left with no alternative but to tell the child, 'It is so because I said so,' whereas what would free the parent from excessive resentment from the child would be the freedom to say, 'I didn't make up this rule. America did.' Apart from the standing American high valuation of originality, financial independence, and creative nerve, the parent has few cultural markers on which to depend. Having chosen a civility ethos of 'ease' and 'informality,' Americans are left with no choice but to trade in a certain amount of parental authority and competence in return for children who are able to take considerable initiative in their own socialization. The opportunity cost of this is that during heated conflicts the parent falls into an emotional state that renders exchange with the child a little like a fight between siblings. Dealing heart to heart provides ample opportunities for abrasive and damaging mutual discourtesy as well as opportunities for authenticity and intimacy. We were left with the impression that while 'in-fighting' is a common occurrence in all families, regardless of the culture in which they are placed, in-fighting in American families leaves interactants particularly disappointed.

Possessing a certain amount of self-determination puts the American child under great pressure, especially when he reaches adolescence. French children have the luxury of blaming their shortcomings on society (e.g., 'I did what I was told. Don't blame me for the results'). The American child, however, forever saddled with the duty to prove himself through his own wits, while making a success of himself in the social world lying outside the family (as opposed to the extended kin network), often ends up blaming himself for any mishaps and shortcomings. The pressure increases as the youth enters adolescence.

While adolescence for the French child is a period of newfound freedom and a relative release from the first relentless phase of behaviour formation carried out by parents and teachers, American adolescence is a training ground for responsible adult life. Not only is the American adolescent suddenly required to demonstrate his competence as a budding adult by demonstrating that he is emotionally independent, original, inventive, popular, interesting, competent, and able to become financially independent; he is also required not to completely break free of parental influence. Adolescence is reserved for this 'halfway house' of teenhood. If there is a phase of the child-adult that many Americans never quite pass through with complete success it is the phase of American adolescence. The American youth wishes to be accepted for 'who I am' yet, more often than not, is resistant to receiving some competent help in the construction of his or her identity.

While the French adolescent is allowed a period of respite before adulthood, the American youth is suddenly asked to live by a new set of rules upon reaching teenhood. While prior to adolescence he was intensely dependent on parental approval, he must now seek the approval of a wide variety of acquaintances who, similar to him, inhabit a culture in which agreeability, a tailgaiting pace of life, and the hegemony of financial success and image-making comprise the dominant themes by which performance is judged. So much depends on his initiative and so little on specified civility rituals and cultural markers. In short, the life of the American youth becomes public property, with little demarcation between the 'frontstage' and 'backstage.' While the

French youth remains protected by a large family circle on whom he can count for support, the American youth swims in public space unable to retreat to the temporary safety of a large familial network. A wide variety of adult initiations are suddenly offered him in the guise of 'teen culture,' the most notable ritual being the high school prom and the prom date symbolizing courtship, entry into the work world, and marriage. In recent years, these rituals have been expanded by savvy marketers who have packaged 'pre-teen' and 'teen' culture, giving American youth the impression that they can remain longer than usual in these privileged categories as long as they are able to spend money to acquire their emblems of membership.

It is not surprising then that American adolescence, so aptly caricaturized in Hollywood teen films, is a time of frenzied searching for approval, honorifics, and inclusion. Ironically, the child who was left free to develop according to his own needs (as opposed to rigid social dictates) is now forced to become a conformist and play by the rules of a large youth tribe that requires him to maintain an image even in the absence of emotional certainty and stability. The frequent American smile and grin (vital aspects of American civility) are not simply products of a national ethos of friendliness, but also the outward manifestations of approval-seeking behaviour.

Thus, while the French learn when to be forward and when to deal in nuances, the American, favouring a direct form of communication, has no recourse but to minimize the space between his backstage and frontstage. The risks of loss of face are, therefore, considerable, because, in the absence of nuance, one cannot easily change one's position without causing personal or mutual loss of face. Lack of reserve puts the self in the way of interactional harm, a danger against which the French and English have ample defences, understatement being the principal one.

The socialization process has a profound influence on the amount of information the future adult will need in order to be able to function ('high' or 'low' context). The French child grows up with few explanations and justifications for the imposition of the social code; he is left to figure out the social code for himself and, therefore, becomes able to read nuances and discover the meaning of missing information through observations of his social environment. The American child, habituated to endless explanations and negotiations, grows up requiring considerable guidance and information. Ironically, what begins as an ethos of independence ends up producing individuals who require a great amount of input. The American seeks approval not only as a sign of membership in the community but also as an emblem for a self that is continually under pressure to perform. He is given to mistrusting elitism while, at the same time, seeking recognition for his own performances.

English children, like their French counterparts, are born into a society that has been ongoing for nearly two thousand years. There is a sense of discipline that ensues from two centuries of colonial dominance and a successful passage through two world wars. In short, the English possess a quiet confidence that is noticeable in their socialization rituals. Our observations indicate that the English parent is given to understatement much more than his French and American counterparts. So much of the English sense of propriety, civility, and fairness is based on the implicit assumption that certain aspects of life – consideration for the privacy of the other and the imperative of not causing undue embarrassment to the other – are non-negotiable hallmarks of English civilization. Very early on the child is taught to be extremely polite towards strangers. Repeatedly, we observed English mothers and fathers surveying even their toddlers to ensure that they say 'Thank you' and 'Please' when in contact with strangers. This heightened sensitivity to civil interaction affects the English notion of 'fair play.' Even though bullying is increasingly becoming a problem in schools and workplaces, the majority of the English continue to maintain a surface civility that is authentic and economical. The English child benefits from this training in polite interaction. Implicit in the politeness taught the English child are a variety of social ideals: obedience, modesty, unselfishness, humility, emotional temperance, and restraint of exhibitionistic impulses.

The English child inhabits a cultural milieu that is at once 'high context' as well as 'low context.' The economy of emotional expression is a considerably HC practice, for the English child (and parent) must read into meanings (stated and unstated) in the absence of outright emotional expression. At the same time the economy in communication creates a sense of time and space that is considerably LC due to its proficiency and economy. Repeatedly, we had difficulty trying to pin English families down to HC and LC standards. We concluded after countless experiences with families that the English were a 'moderate-context' culture. Moderation, the hallmark of English civility standards, has affected the English to such a degree that their socialization and interaction practices are frequently in the middle of extremes. English children are taught to respect elders (HC), yet they are also required to be independent and mature; they are taught to be extremely punctual yet also socialized to be comfortable in social situations in which time takes second place to warm and friendly conversations. We were repeatedly impressed with the fact that the English seem rarely in a hurry yet have managed to be one of the most productive nations in the world. The pace of life in London may even be quicker than the one in New York. We noticed this confident relation to time in upper-class, middle-class and working-class circles.

Comparing English 'proxemics' and 'contextualization' to those of Americans, we concluded that the English and the French seem more comfortable with human interaction than are the Americans. We found American youth and adults in a hurry when it came to interactions, of both the social and business types. At the risk of sounding particularly critical of American socialization practices, we were too frequently left with the feeling that Americans, even in their friendly contacts, exhibited a tense body language that indicated that they were in a rush to get away from the people with whom they were in contact. We observed this in family situations as well as in interactions between strangers. We had no alternative but to speculate that this uneasiness was not so much due to the presence of isolation but to the presence of distracting emotional energy. Whether additional factors, such as reticence to take time away from the self in order to be completely in the presence of others, are involved is anyone's guess.

We also observed that submission is a frequently observed phenomenon in English socialization. While English philosophy is based on the ideal of 'liberty' and 'rights,' this idealism is tempered by English stoicism. The inevitable is accepted. And even today the English class system places certain families in inevitable categories. The child's socialization, therefore, is influenced not only by the imperative of 'fair play,' but by the English stoic realization that things do not always work out with fairness. This creates a civility ethic that places a high valuation on moderation, sometimes at the cost of individual self-affirmation. It did not surprise us to discover that 49.1 per cent of the English favour obedient children (WVS).

One noticeable consequence of the American independence-oriented socialization process is the manner in which American youth construct an 'emotional style' for themselves and use this as an emblem of distinction. During years of travel in the three nations included in this study we were repeatedly struck by the emotional affectation of American youth. The need to be 'cool' and original seemed to have required stylized ways of representing emotions. While emotions are universals, Americans have managed to construct a particularly unique emotional style that changes from generation to generation. Peter N. Stearns (1994) discusses this at length in *American Cool: Constructing a Twentieth Century Emotional Style*. What is involved is not simple style of speech but the manner in which facial expressions, figures of speech, and amount of emotional activation are calibrated to match representations in media.

*Conceptions of Self-Esteem*

The above differences in socialization standards have a salient influence on the manner in which the 'self' is defined and experienced. The Americans define the self as some inner part of the person, a bank of thoughts, emotions, and preferences that stand apart from those of others. The ideal American is independent, self-reliant, and able to act in his own best interests. A great part of his sense of worth is based on what he is capable of 'doing' or 'achieving.' Alexis de Tocqueville noted that, coming from a society where his 'space' (physical and emotional) is extremely important, the American not only has to defend his turf but also protect his image from any disparaging remarks. Tocqueville ([1884] 1994) perceptively understood that the loosening of filial obedience ties had a profound influence on the manner in which the self was presented and defended from second-party interference:

> But as soon as the young American begins to approach man's estate, the reins of filial obedience are daily slackened. Master of his thoughts, he soon becomes responsible for his own behaviour. In America there is in truth no adolescence. At the close of boyhood he is a man and begins to trace out his own path. (585)

The French conception of self, on the other hand, is based not only on doing but on 'being.' In fact, the French do not speak in terms of a 'self' as a sort of repository of personal feeling but, rather, of a *personalité* (personality), more appropriately a dramaturgical composite of traits and practices. The emphasis is not on the private self but on the character and behavioural front that the person presents to the world. This more communal (outward) view of personhood affords considerable dramaturgical freedom to the individual. Although the person is expected to maintain solidarity with others, he is equally expected to demonstrate originality and wit and stand out from the crowd. The

French *personalité* is a paradoxical celebration of the conventional as well as the original and extraordinary.

The rationalization for disobeying a parental request, delivered by the Anglo-American teen in the name of 'being like everybody else,' falls on deaf ears in France. Being like the others is the last thing that French parents want of their children. They want them to be original within the dictates of logic. It is not surprising then that the corporate media have not been able to colonize teen culture in France as completely as they have done in America. After all, it was France that coined the phrase 'Vive la différence!' This may explain why, despite a healthy respect for tradition, when asked how readily they follow instructions on the job, 40.2 per cent of French respondents said they had to be convinced first, compared with 20.2 per cent of Americans who gave the same response (WVS); 65.1 per cent of Americans reported that they easily follow instructions on a job (WVS), a surprising response when considered vis-à-vis America's high valuation of independence, although understandable when considered in relation to American low-context (minimal information) organizational procedures.

As for the English, although they favour individualism, their respect for the individual is not based on brash affirmation of personal style, but, rather, on a collective stoicism that requires the individual to be able to weather the storm and not lose his bearings. Modesty stands in for exhibitionism. The English sense of liberty is one bounded by decorum, behavioural as well as emotional. English liberty is a communal as well as personal privilege. This preference for stoic calm (and the restraint of personal dramaturgical exhibitionism that results from such emotional stoicism) was evident in the English response to the terrorist attack on London in July 2005. It was interesting to compare the coverage of the event on CNN and the BBC (the British Broadcasting Corporation). British announcers remained extremely controlled; so did the individuals they interviewed. Within the first few hours, however, the American coverage sought every opportunity to reveal the 'emotional reaction' of the English. The world took note that, despite the deformalization spearheaded by former prime minister Tony Blair that has in great measure modernized Britain and had an important role in releasing the English from their pre-1960s sense of reserve and formality, citizens of all ages reacted to the attack with remarkable calm. Emotional restraint is an ingrained English quality.

So, while the American affirms his self by referring back to a heroic tradition in which the hero surmounts obstacles in order to affirm his special worth as a person, the French individual proves himself within an interdependent society by being *débrouillard* (capable of 'untangling' himself and finding his way through a complex society favouring high-context interactions requiring considerable interpersonal acuity). There is an important difference in the two modes of individualism: *one is based on accomplishment and obtaining approval for 'performance,' while the other is based on the ability to represent a long-standing culture in appropriately original ways. Approval in France is most generously given when an individual contributes to the glory of the Republic.*

Such difference is also observable in the manner in which the French speak of *honneur* (honour). What matters to the preservation of a satisfactory public personality is not the possession of broad popularity or material things but the preservation of 'face.' While the American can save face through 'spin management,' the French person occupies a complex social system in which a faux pas (wrong move) on his part is noted and ascribed to his personality. To this day, well-mannered, destitute aristocrats receive more respect in France than a self-impressed member of the nouveaux riches.

It is, therefore, understandable that the French are taught at an early age to exercise *pudeur* (caution in interpersonal communications). It is considered bad taste to share intimate information with a stranger or to be too exhibitionistic in the early stages of a relationship. This caution or *negative politeness* in interpersonal relations makes for a society in which immediate friendliness with strangers is not a priority; what matters is relating to the other with dignity and showing consideration for the emotional and biographical *privacy* of the other. That is the essence of 'French formalism.' It is a sort of 'hands-off' policy between interactants who are not yet on a familiar basis. It is not an accident that the French have two words for 'you' (the formal, respectful *'vous,'* which signifies non-imposition and respectful distance, and the more familiar *'tu,'* reserved for friends and close acquaintances). It has not been uncommon in France for a couple to continue calling each other by the honorific form *'vous'* even though they are in the initial phases of a courtship. Some children are even required to call their parents by the *'vous'* appellation even way past puberty. Certainly, the *'vous'* form is often used by youth when addressing their grandparents. This is a classic example of 'negative politeness,' a form of politeness that cannot exist in a society that does not respect the aged as elders. Even though, following the student rebellion of 1968, the French have tolerated less formal relations between students and teachers, they are now wondering whether a law should not be passed insisting that students and teachers go back to addressing each other with the formal *'vous.'*

By the time a French child has passed through the initial stage of his socialization he has become acutely aware that there is a definite dividing line between strangers and intimates. He has experienced enough instances of rudely delivered critiques of his behaviour and had enough alliances with his siblings against the authority of parents and educators to know three important things about surviving and prospering in his culture: (1) a stranger need not be automatically accorded the status of a friend; in fact, it is perfectly all right to be confrontational with strangers whenever they are irritating you or whenever you need to protect your turf or wishes; (2) individuality can be preserved only by affirming it and resisting authority (the French child waits for the day when, freed from parental prohibitions, he can exercise his own free will and critique others as he himself has been); (3) one's own face and the face of others must be preserved through the use of anachronisms, sayings, and nuanced understatements; thus, a good command of the language is necessary. The degree to which a person masters the grammar of the language (and the rich compendium of sayings and aphorisms – over 2,000 at the most basic level) will more often than not reveal both his placement in the social class system as well as the anticipated degree of his future success in social interactions and the employment market. The English openly have admitted that a 'colloquial accent' can limit life chances; such admission, however, is made within a society still affected by a continuing monarchy. In the French Republic such admissions of inequality are made subtly and always rationalized by 'educational competence.'

We have implied in this section that American conceptions of the self are based on personal achievement. Does the above conclusion hold when one considers actual responses to surveys? When asked 'How important is it in a job that you can achieve something?' these were the responses given in the affirmative: Americans (83.7 per cent), English (57.0 per cent), French (50.3 per cent).

*Education*

Difference is valued in France inasmuch as it takes *form* into account and reaffirms French civilizational pride. Nowhere is this more noticeable than in the French education system and its insistence on preserving the canon of French civilization. The French have managed to design an educational system that demands utmost conformity while providing assiduous training in the development of critical thought. And language plays a central role in this system. So important is language to the French that chances in life are substantially determined by how well a person can use the language in social and professional activities. Eloquence is highly valued and admired. Every Thursday afternoon, eight months out of the year, members of the Académie Française (founded in 1635 by Cardinal de Richelieu) meet to discuss the French dictionary in a bid to preserve the purity of the French language. If anything has helped keep France from becoming assimilated by an anglophone global capitalism it is the rigorous demands of properly spoken and written French. Platt (1994) has similarly observed the love of language in France: 'The French talk about their language as if it were a person, a living marvel who is their mistress and whose delicious qualities they're continually discovering anew' (155).

Education in France is not intended to build self-esteem – not directly at least. There are arduous rites of initiation:

> In school, this nation of celebrated individualists is taught early on that it's knowledge which is important ... not what they happen to think about it. The moment they write, 'I feel that ...' on a term paper, they get a zero. What they worry about is France 'losing its identity,' in the new Europe, or in the floods of immigrants. (127)

Thus, considerable emphasis is placed on philosophy, literature, and mathematics. Ideas are valued for their own sake rather than measured against a bottom line of usefulness. The preservation of a coherent national identity requires this. The French consider their classics as the foundations of civilized knowledge and believe that mastery of the French canon will equip a student to succeed in whatever profession is chosen later on. This is different from the American preference for 'practical' knowledge. Nowhere but in France would 18 per cent of adults watch a television program during primetime every Friday that features four or five writers discussing their most recent books. Bernard Pivot's program *Apostrophe*, first aired in 1975, managed to retain the attention of the French for years until Pivot himself stopped the program due to personal exhaustion. In a nation that elects presidents who have written books (Charles de Gaulle, François Mitterrand, Giscard d'Estaing), the *word* is sacred. Equally sacred is the role of the state in the education of citizens; the majority of schools (85 per cent) are run by the state (*école publique*). Private schools (*écoles privées*), often Catholic, are partially subsidized yet surveyed by the state.

The French continue to consider the development of the intellect as a rite of initiation, a fact that moves cross-cultural writers such as Asselin and Mastron (2001) to state:

> The French think of themselves as supremely rational beings – logical and intellectual. They have a high regard for reasoning, and their schooling, particularly secondary education, places a premium on philosophy regardless of the student's area of specialization. Unlike the United States, where intellectualism is vaguely suspect, it is a high compliment to refer to a French person as an intellectual, and the realm of ideas for their own sakes is valued and respected. (13)

Rigour and inflexibility assure that most students (the serious ones at least) have little time for extensive extra-curricular activities. Many French parents enrol their children in pre-school education as early as the age of three. Those who eventually go on to university experience twelve years of formal schooling, the last three of which are devoted to preparation for the university entrance program, the *baccalauréat* or *le bac*. How well one does in the *baccalauréat* degree courses determines the type of university one will be admitted into as well as the kind of job one can hope to have. If France ever did replace the aristocracy of the bloodline it replaced it with an aristocracy of education. An elitist educational system, committed to excellence rather than the maintenance of the 'self-esteem' of slacker students, is the new aristocratic tradition. The best students are discovered early on, rewarded, and encouraged to maintain their excellence. While American schools have been known to promote an under-achieving student from one grade to another for 'social' reasons, French schools are not at all averse to making students repeat a year if they perform poorly. Thus the French child grows up knowing that there is a certain 'justice' to the world: excellence leads to success while mediocrity ends in failure. The American philosopher-novelist Ayn Rand once wrote that the best way to demoralize the excellent is to treat them the same way as the not-so-excellent. American educators who believe in pushing all students along from one grade to the next may benefit from Rand's excellent perception of human social psychology. Certainly, American educators have been doing everything possible to make learning 'fun.' The French and English, on the other hand, realize that the learning of certain subjects entails some pain, mathematics being one of those subjects.

Another striking difference between French and American schools is the amount of homework assigned. French educators and parents are in agreement over the fact that the evenings of a child should be spent practising what has been taught to him during the day. The child is expected to go beyond a summary understanding of the material; equally, he is expected to know details but not attempt to use them to camouflage a lack of critical understanding. Thus, there are few multiple-choice exams in the arts and humanities. Pure memorization will lead to failure, for exam questions require a demonstration of knowledge as well as the ability to apply and critique it. What is additionally required of the student is clarity and the ability to demonstrate knowledge in grammatically acceptable form. The *dictée* (dictation) occupies a great amount of time in French schools. Students are taught the complex rules of their language and then expected to use them in papers that are free from spelling and grammatical errors. Out of a grading scale of 1 to 20, a grade of 19 or 20 is rarely given. One of our French informants remarked to us, 'I am not at all sure that even God would qualify for a 19 or 20.'

Perhaps the system would not survive if it were not for the cooperation of the French parent. The school is the property of the educational system. A parent has little say in the nationally established curriculum. He or she can either help his child succeed within exacting standards set by the system or face the consequences: limited life chances. As for the French teacher, he or she is not out to gain the love of the students but to discipline and instruct them in competent scholarship. It is not unusual for a teacher to risk unpopularity by calling on students at random. It is a form of friendly misanthropy that earns the mute ire of the lazy and the respect and admiration of the committed.

In the French system, therefore, error is not kindly regarded. To err is to let down the community. It is not simply a matter of personal preference. While low-context cultures encourage the admission of error (as a learning experience), high-context cultures aim for error-free performance and are, therefore, more given to demanding and allowing in-depth thought before action. It is understandable that the French, being socialized by a strict educational system not given to rewarding mediocre work, become adults who are uneasy to admit error (more on this tendency later, for it plays a central role in the way embarrassment and shame are managed).

The French penchant for training students in deductive reasoning, however, tends to produce students who are conformist, theoretical, and sometimes afraid to head in creative directions. Despite assiduous intellectual training and considerable linguistic talent, they prefer to remain with the theoretical roots of a problem until they feel justified to pass on to its practical solution. The American student, habituated to giving opinion even in the absence of reliable information, learns to 'turn on a dime' and proceed from empirical observation. So while the French system produces excellence at the secondary level, some of that excellence remains undeveloped at the university level, where American and English students excel in research-oriented environments.

What awaits the French student who completes the *baccalauréat*? If the pass is a normal pass the student can count on automatic admission to one of the regular universities. But if the performance is extraordinary he or she then qualifies for entry into one of the five most prestigious universities (*grandes écoles*). The lucky student will then attend a two- or three-year preparatory course and then pass entrance exams for admission into any of the following: École Polytechnique (X), where the highest civil servants are trained, École Nationale d'Administration (ENA), École Normale Supérieure, and two universities specializing in business administration and management: École des Hautes Études Commerciales (HEC) and École Supérieure des Sciences Économiques et Commerciales. Americans who mistrust elitism need only imagine the feeling that would be triggered in them were Harvard University to suddenly change its name to Harvard Superior University.

With most of these select schools recruiting their students from Paris, it is easy to see why a student's life chances are affected not only by actual performance but by the reputation and location of the *lycée* that he attends. Sadly, only 10 per cent of students in elite schools are from working-class families. Only 5 per cent of all students end up in the *grandes écoles*. Success at these schools assures a top post in the government or the corporate sector. France is literally run by graduates of X and the ENA. Tuition at the regular universities is about $100 a year and free at the *grandes écoles*.

Once the student is admitted into one of the elite schools he is faced with a harrowing work schedule that leaves little time for employment. While many students in America choose to go to university far away from their homes, the majority of students in France cut expenses and remain at home in order to be able to meet the demands of their curriculum without having to work. This has the secondary effect of deepening kin and friendship ties.

A similar standard-bound system exists in England, where secondary students have to pass Ordinary Level and Advance Level exams

## A Comparative Field Study of France, America, and England 473

in order to qualify for university. Admission is based on the number of A-levels passed. More A-level passes are required for admission to the top-ranked universities. Moreover, studies indicate that students living in more affluent areas are five to six times more likely to gain admission into university. Presently, only 30 per cent of high school leavers go on to university studies. While English students are not subjected to as much homework as their French counterparts, they do have considerably more than American students, who are expected to learn through hands-on work in the classroom.

As for America, it possesses more universities per capita than any other country in the world. The mix of private, state, and city universities makes the application of a national standard virtually impossible. While prospective college students are asked to take entrance exams (SAT, LSAT, etc.) to determine their aptitude, each school has a different admissions cut-off point. In addition, high school grades do not reflect actual performance. After decades of experimentation in literacy training, American schools are graduating cohorts still incapable of writing clear, grammatically sensible sentences. Despite the Head Start program, which requires student skills to be tested across a nationally imposed standard, there is growing fear that some schools have abandoned teaching for the sake of inspiring a love of knowledge and adopted a test-preparation mentality instead. Once again, American pragmatism limits the imagination of its supposed beneficiaries.

Many factors have contributed to what some call the 'dumbing-down' or 'closing of the American mind' (Bloom 1987). Our own observation of classes in primary and secondary schools in the United States left us saddened and, we dare admit, outraged. We found that the excessive use of the multiple-choice exam had paralysed the abilities of students to think critically. Rote memorization and ticking of boxes on answer sheets have robbed students of the opportunity of developing their writing and expressive skills. At the university level, long course outlines detailing the most elaborate explanations of how many points would be lost for how many hours the paper was delivered late did not compensate for the above weaknesses despite the repeated use of commanding exclamation marks.

Robert Bly (1994), who has written an uncompromising critique of American culture in the late twentieth century (*The Sibling Society*), believes that the deconstruction movement in American education has had serious consequences: 'Our society has been damaged not only by acquisitive capitalism, but also by an idiotic distrust of all ideas, religions, and literature handed down to us by elders and ancestors. Many siblings are convinced that they have received nothing of value from anyone' (163).

Bly believes that loss of admiration for the accumulated wisdom of Western culture has caused American youth to hesitate to speak from 'the centre of their beings.' Although accorded considerable freedom as children, they arrive in their early teens with no point of admiration but those located in their own peer culture or the media products deftly marketed to their age group. To speak to them of pride for America's civilizational accomplishment and obtain knowing nods is the exception rather than the rule. The opposite is true in France; oddly enough, despite the French post-structuralist writings that had such a decentring effect on the American academy, the French continue to revere leaders (dead or alive) who have had the ability to exercise personal power and act as inspirational models.

The question of what motivates a person to strive for great and worthwhile things is one of Bly's central preoccupations. He maintains that contemporary American culture provides no incentive outside of material reward. And he asserts that this is because the culture no longer values 'the invisible rewards' that are a part of initiation. He attributes this to a regression to a 'literal state' that excludes the possibility of mythical inspiration (81–4). As far as Bly is concerned, both ends of the political spectrum find initiation unnecessary for the production of culture: 'The left regards initiation as silly, and the right as an impediment to production' (86).

According to Bly, a disturbingly large proportion of primary and secondary students are *actively* resisting learning. One of Bly's principal complaints is that the American educational system has lost its classical liberal curriculum and been overwhelmed by a utilitarian, job-oriented menu of courses that does not foster critical thought (45–6). If a given lesson is not fun, requires some difficult work, or is thought to not be useful for a career, many of the students are tempted to reject it. Bly has little faith in the ability of youth to catch up with the learning they have missed during their childhood; he sees the educational problems of American youth as a by-product of the popular culture to which they have become addicted. He predicts a 'drop in coherence all across the board' and foresees a lengthy recovery period (139).

Throughout our field research we followed every academic and research guideline in order to come up with a sociological explanation for the manner in which the American educational academy has come to increasingly expect less of its students. In the end, our efforts to turn away from the truth staring us in the face were unsuccessful. The truth is perhaps so simple that it eludes educational theorists. Perhaps the human being does not like to go through the discipline required for progressive learning through many years of school. Perhaps the motivation collapses if the strict exhortation of teachers is silenced and replaced with a laissez-faire attitude. Certainly the cooperative link between parents and schools has become broken as a result of overworked parents and a liberal childraising system in which, ironically enough, many parents would object if educators were to impose stricter standards on their children. Both parents and educators look with despairing cynicism upon the massive laziness and near-apathetic expediency that pervades the American student body without realizing that they are directly to blame for not taking a stand. What does this have to do with civility? We would suggest that civility towards oneself and one's country requires some readiness to suffer discomfort (as one does in learning) for the sake of the continuance of one's culture. American students who marvel at how their Asian-American counterparts study so hard misunderstand the reason for this motivation: namely, the self-discipline that is habitual in individuals raised according to standards of 'interdependence.'

*Conversation and Politeness Rituals*

Whether a culture is 'polychronic' or 'monochronic' and 'low-context' or 'high-context' has a significant influence on the manner in which individuals engage in conversations with one another. The facility with which they start conversing and the degree of commitment they exhibit during conversations also indicate whether they favour qualities of interdependence/power distancing or independence (Hofstede 1980, 1983). These preferences can vary between public and private interactions, but there will be a general tendency towards one type of practice since private and public interactions occur in a common cultural, ideological framework. These variations are observable in conversation styles and conversation ethics in France, America, and England.

  The French do not readily talk to strangers. Just because two people occupy the same space, such as a subway car or an elevator, does not mean that they feel obliged or inclined to begin a conversation to fill the silence. But when the French do converse they do so with verve. Unlike Americans (and to a lesser degree the English), who see time as a commodity to be measured, saved, and used, the French have no qualms about devoting considerable energy and time to conversation. It is in conversation that they celebrate their language, practise their wit, and establish and strengthen social ties. Time becomes pliant during a good conversation. So while they may stare blankly in the subway or bury themselves in a book to avoid locking eyes, they will heartily plunge into a conversation provided the situation calls for one. In short, the French see no reason why strangers should talk to each other just to show politeness. Their definition of civility does not consist of immediately establishing mutual interest with the other (*positive politeness*) but, rather, of showing respect for the private space of the other (*negative politeness*). Smiling at a stranger on the street (as is the case in smaller British towns) or smiling and saying 'Hi, how are you today?' (as is the case in some American towns where *positive politeness* can be observed in its purest form) would be considered an imposition and invasion of privacy by the French. Even in small French towns there is an observable demarcation between the private and public self.

In keeping with this spirit of non-imposition (*negative politeness*), the French will restrict their initial conversation with a new acquaintance to topics that do not require prying into the private life of the other. They will not immediately ask about the profession of the other as will Americans, who quickly try to show interest in the activities of the other (*positive politeness*). While they will look directly into the eyes of the person with whom they speak (a habit that continues to make Americans uneasy), their comments will be restricted to topics that do not require excessive self-disclosure.

Another salient difference between Anglo-American and French culture is the manner in which physical space is handled during an interaction (*proxemics*) (Hall and Hall 1990:12). In France, the physical space left open between conversants is much less than the space required by Americans and the English. Concurrently, the French abhor being loud, for they feel it a sign of ill-breeding to be overheard by strangers. The English are similarly inclined. During our field research in England we had to listen very carefully while eavesdropping on conversations in restaurants. We had a difficult time in England piecing together conversations that occurred at tables very close to our own. Americans, however, consider a relatively high voice volume as a sign of enthusiasm. Although the volume of conversations varies as one passes from region to region, there is a general tendency not to worry about being overheard in the United States.

Additional differences are noticeable in American, English, and French conversations. Once a French conversation is in high gear, the conversants will think nothing of interrupting one another. What is important to them is not the speaker but the conversation itself. Each conversant is free to contribute his thoughts to the conversational process that encloses and nourishes the group. Interruption, therefore, is a contribution to the face of the other rather than an attack of face. Quite different from American and English conversations, in which speakers take turns speaking, French conversations are rapid and energetic and allow participants to jump from one topic to another almost as if the talk were a process of free association. For the French, a conversation represents a network energized by various intellects cooperating with one another to push the conversation to new euphoric heights. Punctuated by frequent laughter and wit, conversations are the lifeblood of French society.

Whether a culture is *high-context* or *low-context* will also affect the degree of nuance in a conversation. Low-context cultures tend to favour a conversational style that has a minimum of ambiguity. While the Americans will speak with some hesitation in their voices to indicate that they are not taking the time or space of another for granted, they do favour fairly direct talk. 'Talking straight,' 'Laying it on the line,' and 'not mincing words' are American phrases that indicate this preference for non-ambiguity. Even though a culture of 'political correctness' is rendering American speech less direct than before, there continue to be unmistakable indications of preference for as little ambiguity as politically possible. French talk, however, is filled with nuance and metaphoric sayings. Anyone who has not mastered the language and its extremely rich archive of metaphoric sayings (transmitted from generation to generation) may have a hard time following a truly energized French conversation. Being direct at all times is not a priority. The French favour a certain amount of ambiguity, not only as a civility practice that signals to the other that the speaker does not wish to impose on him through undue familiarity, but also as a means for making rich use of the language. *Parler bien* (to speak well) is not only a sign of good breeding for the French but a testament to how well the speaker has managed to use and profit from the knowledge offered up to him during years of arduous schooling. The French love of conversation as an end in itself, as a way of representing the drama of human life, is noticeable in small-budget French films in which directors successfully place a small cast in a creative plot and then allow the conversations of those characters to become the film. There is little dependence on special effects and sumptuous sets.

Just as the English enjoy the 'understatement,' an effective linguistic tool for conveying displeasure without outright rudeness (or deflecting a compliment out of politeness), the French favour the *sous-entendue* (the underlying, implicit meaning) as a sign of elegance and conversational-intellectual competence.

What struck us during the many conversations we had with the French was the frequency with which they peppered their talk with philosophical sayings and musings; in a country where great ideas are held in such esteem, the conversation is a sacred vehicle for the preservation and creation of ideas. Talk is never a waste of time, not in a community that favours interdependence.

The English, on the other hand, although they also have an aristocratic heritage that favours conversation as a pastime of the leisured classes, are more reticent to have the type of open-ended, free-flowing conversations favoured by the French. There is an inescapable orderliness to English conversations. Here one notices great efforts to communicate using *positive politeness* rituals. While the English will use *negative politeness* in the initial stages of a relationship in order to assure the other that they respect his privacy and do not wish in any way to cause discomfort, they will switch to *positive politeness* as the conversation and relationship progress and will make every effort to communicate their readiness to avoid saying something that might make the other person uncomfortable. Contrary opinions are delivered with caution and delicacy (the directness of English academics at conferences being the exception rather than the rule). Preserving the face of the other, therefore, is an important element of English conversation rituals and defines the particularly English habit of 'discretion.' The English have managed to maintain their politeness ethic as they have passed from being a fairly formal to an informal culture by following the simple values of tolerance and amiability. Both these qualities stand in for the traditional English reserve and serve a similar function: to avoid abrasive confrontation whenever possible and to keep emotions restrained in the interests of preserving interactive dignity. The qualities of tolerance and amiability have helped the English to restrain emotional energy without losing the ability to feel deeply. Anyone who doubts this need only think back to the massive outpouring of grief that accompanied the death of Princess Diana in 1997. The world looked on with surprise as the British people showed their sadness in public without embarrassment. And they also took note of the dignified way in which the queen diffused, at the eleventh hour, the embarrassment that had swept over the country following her silence in regard to the loss of the princess. Duty first, self second was the credo followed by the queen. But a new England, for a while at least, asked the queen to reveal herself. And she did so in a televised speech, perhaps signalling the start of an era in which stoicism and emotional disclosure could attempt to co-exist in a state of mutual sympathy.

It is such 'mutual sympathy' that is so noticeable in conversations between strangers and between friends in England. While the English love humour and are not averse to teasing one another, they take considerable care to enfold their humorous comments in gestures and looks that convey kindness and lack of misanthropy.

Both France and England possess a rich arsenal of statements designed to communicate to the stranger that the speaker has no intention of taking him for granted. This affirmation of dignity precludes the possibility of easy instant friendship. A country such as France, which has over thirty choices for the way a letter should be addressed according to sex and rank, does not suffer instant familiarity gladly. While Americans will favour whatever civility method that saves time and maintains harmony, the French continue to be willing to devote whatever time is necessary to showing one another that they know how to behave. As for the English, privacy is a cherished ideal, and their acts of civility are always tempered by the need not to impose on the other. It is, therefore, understandable that the English will always say 'Sorry' to each other when accidentally touching in public. Repeatedly, we were amazed that those whom we ourselves accidentally brushed in public did not hesitate to say 'Sorry!' first.

Yet the extreme horror of the English towards embarrassing situations should not make us blind to the positive consequences of such fastidious preference for dignified outcomes. One notices the positive effects in the smallest details. For example, English television networks continue to broadcast a warning before showing a program or film that contains stroboscopic light effects. They do so because such effects can trigger seizures in those who suffer from photosensitive epilepsy. Is this due to the fear of litigation from a sensitive viewer? No, it is because of the English notion of fair play and mutual consideration. In America, where litigation is rampant, no such warning is broadcast. One notices many other such courtesies in England; for example, giving the right of way to a car coming onto a main road from a side road. Despite reports of 'road rage' in a sensation-hungry media in England, English drivers remain some of the most competent and courteous in the world. It would be rude to be otherwise.

This same attention to etiquette is observable in France in mundane activities such as entry through doors and into elevators; who enters first is still regulated by age, sex, and rank, making for what the French affectionately call *la bataille de la porte* (the battle of the door). Approaching a stranger in public is always preceded by *'Excusez moi de vous déranger ...'* (Excuse me for bothering you ...). When walking into a store to make a purchase, a customer will say *'Bonjour,'* addressed as much to the owner as to the others who are present, with the departure punctuated by *'Au revoir.'* Arrival at the office is still often accompanied by hellos and handshakes; Americans and English who value physical space frequently feel ill at ease with the proximity and implied commitment of frequent handshakes (and ceremonial kisses).

*Friendship*

One of the abiding myths of North American sociology is that longer work hours, increased commuting times, and a rise in extra-curricular activities are cutting into the time that people have left over for friendships. This hypothesis implies that all cultures are subject to the same rules governing the establishment and maintenance of friendships. It is thought that the more time one has, the more friends one will have – a dubious proposition when put to the test.

We find another hypothesis more plausible: American culture became work-oriented precisely because American friendships were low-context to begin with and left individuals free to focus on their work. A culture that valued high-context friendships might have had trouble building the type of hyper-capitalism that is enjoyed in America. Relationships would have come before work and slowed down the economic engine. If there is one factor that complicates the maintenance of friendships in America it is the concept of multi-tasking in a low-context and monochronic culture in which the overburdened worker may find the maintenance of friendships an 'additional task' that overloads his strained system.

The French (as well as citizens of Latin and Middle Eastern countries) are proof that the first hypothesis does not have cross-cultural validity. While the citizens of those countries do not make friends easily and defer to their own family circles, they do invest considerable time and loyalty in the friendships that they do develop. In many countries they manage to do so even while working two shifts to make ends meet. The saying 'He who is a friend to all is a friend to none' summarizes the French sentiment regarding friendship. A friendship is not to be taken lightly and is to be cultivated over the long term *regardless* of other commitments. The French would even find it ridiculous to call someone they had just met 'a friend.'

Nor are French friendships built on a bedrock of agreement. A friendship is meant to be a complementary experience. Heated disagreement and quarrel are sometimes accepted as healthy aspects of an honest exchange of ideas and opinions, certainly a test of the worth of the relationship. While the American child turns to his playmate and declares 'You are no longer my friend' simply because the friend is disagreeing with him, the French learn to reserve such reactions for acts of outright betrayal.

Depth rather than agreeability are, consequently, the ideals of intimate French liaisons. Disagreeing with a friend is not equated with attacking his face or rejecting his worth as a person; it is simply a disagreement with an idea that is not automatically attributed to the personality of the friend. This is made possible by the fact that the French are frequently discussing ideas and also frequently changing opinions as new logical explanations become available to them. Since they defer to logic, they are as willing (if not always comfortable) to change their own viewpoint if new information becomes available.

Friendships for the French seem to follow from habits acquired at the familial level. The French friendship circle is a sort of family circle of its own. Unlike in America, for example, where marriage often entails the loss of friends, the French maintain their friends within overlapping friendship circles. It stands to reason that the absence of the feeling that one is a friend in a transient fashion (until the other finds a mate) allows for friendships in which considerable effort is invested in the development of intimacy and permanence. In America, high mobility and the nuclear nature of the family (and the marriage) complicate the development of such in-depth, long-term alliances. Americans take their friendships on the go, unlike the French, who carefully select their friends and then make them a central part of their lives. While the French are not given to joining 'public groups' (WVS) and will rarely pressure each other to do so, they do take their friendship circles very seriously.

This preference for serious, in-depth alliances makes the French quite averse to being 'neighbourly' just for the sake of it. They consider automatic friendliness with strangers, neighbours included, as an aberration rather than a virtue, a sign of superficiality and meddling. This explains why they mistrust automatic smiling and grinning and refer to such niceties as a *sourire de circonstance* (a contrived, situational smile). This French 'suspicion' of others plays a very important role in French civil relations and the manner in which people deal with one another in various social situations. Françoise Maintenon, the Marquise d'Aubigné, warned the French in 1772 that a good dose of suspicion in social relations was good for building a person's moral fibre. Her words seem to have had an effect. English 'reserve' and the French 'closed face' achieve the same goal: to maintain distance and a climate of non-imposition (*negative politeness*).

Another factor differentiating French, English, and American friendships is the degree of 'approval' sought in interactions. The Americans, habituated to being responsible for their own self-formation, are in constant need of exhibiting their accomplishments. The approval of the other is not only a guarantee of civility and avoidance of discord but also a reward bestowed on individual accomplishment. Automatic smiling, generous grinning, and frequent nodding are some of the ways in which mutual interest and agreeability are established quickly and clearly. The English, on the other hand, are less given to displaying their accomplishments and find too much talk about oneself a sign of boorishness. This has been a major point of contention between America and England; the Americans find the English inordinately restrained and self-effacing while the English marvel at the American penchant for self-disclosure and self-aggrandizement.

Hall and Hall (1990) describes the consequences of this search for approval in friendships: 'The American drive to be liked, accepted and approved by a wide circle of friends and associates means they must inevitably sacrifice some of their individuality. The French are less likely to hide their real selves, and hence the French are equally less likely to be good team players in business or elsewhere' (152).

And this is the abiding contradiction of low- and high-context cultures. In an ironic way, the drive for independence and expedience has its price; it seems to create the opposite effect. Nowhere is this more observable than in the area of helping. High-context individuals take great care not to impose on others although they are capable of enjoying in-depth relationships. When they do need help they only have to describe their predicament; the friend steps in and insists on helping. In a low-context relationship, however, independence is the ideal. Agreeability is not only a way of giving and securing approval, but of communicating to others that one does not presume to interfere in their life beyond a certain limit. When the other needs help one waits to be asked for the help, not wanting to offer it out of turn and risk offending the other's sense of competence and independence. The result is a loss of intimacy; the same individuals who try to seek approval based on their competence as independent agents remain relatively alone in a crisis.

The English may seem as disposed as are the Americans to have friendships that are abridged and emotionally economical. Yet, there is a difference in the manner in which Americans and the English view independence in friendships. Americans seem to wish to preserve their autonomy while the English seem to value their privacy, their right to have a space free from intrusion. But they will leave that space on a moment's notice to help a friend or a neighbour before retreating back into privacy. The existence of so many 'pubs' in England is a testimony to the fact that the English have managed to differentiate between 'liberty' and 'isolation.'

*Courtship*

A culture that is not shocked by nudity is bound to favour courtship rituals that are different from those of a sexually conservative culture. Marianne, one of the official national symbols of France, has one breast exposed; French sunbathers (along with Italian ones) were going topless on the beaches long before American movie stars were allowed to kiss on screen without reserve. The rapid rise of an American pornography industry and the easing of sexual restraints following the 1960s should not predispose one to categorically assume that American romantic relationships are not much different from their European counterparts.

We began our research by attempting to determine if we could learn anything about each nation's views towards relationships through the study of its divorce rate. We quickly found that divorce rates are no longer reliable indicators because many people are co-habiting and when these do separate it is not counted as a divorce. We have to refer, instead, to the results of attitude surveys. When asked 'Is marriage outdated?' 36.3 per cent of French replied yes, compared with 25.9 per cent of the English and 10.12 per cent of the Americans. Yet, when asked 'Is a long-term relationship necessary to be happy?' a majority of the French

(65.4 per cent) replied in the affirmative compared with 26.9 per cent of the English (Americans were not included in this question) (WVS). So while over one-third of the French may no longer favour marriage, the majority of them believe in long-term commitments. Moreover, 86.1 per cent of the French believe that 'a child needs a home with mother and father,' compared with 66.8 per cent of the English and 64.4 per cent of the Americans (WVS). And when the question is asked, 'Does a woman have to have children to be fulfilled?' the French answer 67.1 per cent in the affirmative, compared with 20.8 per cent of the English and 15.0 per cent of the Americans. So, it would seem that traditional conceptions of courtship and family life are highly valued in France.

More striking than the actual marriage and divorce rate is the variety of courtship practices among different cultures. One thing that quickly comes to the attention of a cross-cultural ethnographer in France is the fact that French teens do not date in the same manner as their American counterparts. Friendship circles in France are not designed to encourage teens to pair off and leave the group. While pairing-off is not prohibited, the friendship circle consists of young men and women in continual interaction with one another. This is perhaps because the French do not consider friendship and romance as part and parcel of the same reality. In fact, the French still use different expressions to classify various types of marriages: *mariage d'argent* (marriage for money), *mariage de convenance* (marriage for social position), *mariage de raison* (arranged marriage), and *mariage d'amour* (marriage of love).

Americans, on the other hand, do not conceive of romance as something different from friendship. While it includes intimacies that go beyond what friends would do together, it is assumed that 'one's romantic partner is also one's best friend.' Whether this mutual dependence is due to the nuclear nature of the American family or the fact that many friends are lost after marriage (e.g., the wife or husband ends up playing many roles, including that of primary confidant) is not clear. The French are more given to accept that males and females are different from each other. A considerable amount of gender-specific humour is bantered around even in polite circles. Also, since they do not categorically seek harmony and agreement in their friendships, the French do not require their romantic liaisons to be trouble-free. While Americans try to normalize (homogenize) relations between genders, the French continue to prefer a more primordial view of sexual relations. No doubt the writings of the early French writers on courtly love have left an indelible impression: the French do not consider that a good relationship has to be built on agreement or the same list of interests. By consequence, there is considerably more independence between women and men.

Repeatedly during our conversations with the French we were told that romance involves *séduction* (seduction) and that the rules of seduction (the art of pleasing and attracting the other) often require intrigue. Moreover, they questioned the supposed gender-neutral sexual politics of the Americans. Seduction was considered a normal part of presenting an attractive and original personality, even in friendship circles. One informant told us: 'Romance is a fever. A friendship is not a fever. It is ridiculous to think that lovers can be total friends.' Perhaps this sentiment explains why the French feminists of the 1970s affirmed that there were significant universal differences between men and women (Badinter 1989).

Because they maintain a clear cut-off point between platonic and sensual relationships, Americans seem to need extraordinary amounts of information in order to determine whether a platonic contact has the potential for developing into romance. The dating 'game' is designed to provide that information. The two individuals 'go out together' and 'sense each other out' to see if they are compatible and mutually interested in proceeding into a romance. Often, at the first date, there is a great amount of hedging and cautious conversation designed to give off the impression that neither will feel humiliated if the other does not show further interest. This seemingly gender-neutral and non-committal contact has the potential of creating misunderstandings; surely many contacts that could develop further are discontinued because the interactants misread each other's cues. We were continually amazed to observe that many American youth are continually asking their friends if they think that so-and-so is interested in them. It would seem that the indicators are unclear.

The French, on the other hand, seem to have a high-context command of the gender situation. By the time two people have agreed to see each other outside the friendship circle (or meet as strangers in a public place) they know whether the meeting will be a deepening of friendship or the beginning of a romance. The French are not necessarily 'faster' than the Americans, simply more informed of the possibilities and, consequently, less in need of a protracted time period to initiate romantic behaviour. One of the reasons why the French have additional information is their different relationship with space (proxemics) (Hall and Hall 1990:12). French friends are much more given to touching one another than are American ones. By the time there is potential for romance they have already felt it through their gestures and touch. Americans, on the other hand, require more space between bodies in public; friends do not touch each other as much, and, by consequence, extraordinary information is required to proceed into the romantic stage, which does involve touching. The French have also learned to differentiate between playful flirtation and serious attraction:

> The unstated assumption – not shared by Americans – is that men and women will want to please and charm each other, but that such mild flirtatiousness is harmless and essentially playful as long as the participants remain in the category of friends. Thus, a Frenchwoman may go out to a restaurant, for example, with a man other than her husband without necessarily raising eyebrows. For Americans, the lack of clear category boundaries means that in many cases such a situation is suspect, at best. (Asselin and Mastron 2001:94–5)

Another factor that deeply influences courtship practices is the degree of hesitancy (and fear) which men and women experience towards each other. It would seem that the gender wars of America have had a profound influence on courtship. Considerable care is taken not to start off on the wrong foot. This is markedly different from the gender behaviour of the 1960s and 1970s when men and women felt more at ease to signal their sexual or romantic interest in each other. Elisabeth Badinter, an American-trained French philosopher and feminist, has written extensively regarding gender issues in France and America. She states: 'I have the feeling that French men are less afraid of women (than British and American men are) and have always wanted to preserve their tenderness' (cited in Platt 1994:169).

What strikes one during comparisons of what is considered 'civil behaviour' in courtship is the different manner in which the French and the Anglo-Americans define a successful relationship. The Americans consider harmony and agreeability sacred goals of a relationship. Just as they look on friendships as networks of mutual support and agreeability, they seek similar consensus in their romantic liaisons. In a manner, the other is supposed to reflect one's own self and confirm the validity of the image that one wishes to project about oneself. Discord is considered a sign of a troubled relationship. And when discord does occur, Americans try to smooth over the tensions that come in its wake by 'having a talk' about the relationship. The talk is designed to improve mutual understanding through self-disclosure; the objective is further harmony (agreement). One has the impression that American couples consider their liaison a 'corporate body' that must be protected from internal and external conflict. And when the conflicts surpass their standing definition of a harmonious relationship, steps are taken to improve the relationship, emotionally disengage from it, or terminate it. There is a strong strain of conformity in American relationships, conformity towards the desires and preferences of the other. So, while the Americans equate the existence of affection with the actual emotional effects of conduct, the French are comfortable with the notion that there can be affection even in the absence of harmony.

One of the best summaries of coupling in France is contained in Raymonde Carroll's *Cultural Misunderstandings: The French-American Experience* (1987). Carroll bases her summary of the French romantic ethic on a French saying, *'de la haine à l'amour, il n'y a qu'un pas'* (literally 'from hate to love, there is only one step'). The point here is that harmony should not be confused with emotional indifference (68). Carroll goes on to provide a credible credo for French romantic liaisons:

> Insofar as I can never have a relationship of equality (although I can be friendly) with my parents or my children, the only relationships of equality I can have are with my brothers and sisters (if there isn't too great an age difference) or with my friends. The relationships of the first category (with my siblings) are stamped with sexual taboos, whereas those of the second category (with my friends) represent either an approved type of homophilia (in the case of the friends of the same sex) or a refusal to sexuality (as in the case of the opposite sex). In this context, the terms 'friends' and 'lovers' are mutually exclusive ... Ideally, therefore, the couple's relationship reproduces the first type (brother/sister) and the second (friends), with the addition of one distinctive element which characterizes the couple and differentiates it from these two categories: permitted and socially approved sexuality. We (French) do not expect that brothers and sisters, or friends, will never quibble (which does not cast doubt on the affective bonds). On the contrary, by showing that we can allow ourselves such behaviour, we are affirming the strength of these affective bonds. The same is true for the (French) couple. (69)

It would seem, therefore, that Anglo-American couples are less able to handle unpredictability than are French couples. Seeking stability in harmony, the Anglo-Americans are particularly vulnerable to feeling discouraged when there is conflict. This may explain why American and English couples find it necessary to conceal conflict in public; their idea of a successful relationship prevents them from arguing in public.

Two interesting insights emerge from the above. The degree of emotional dependence seems particularly high in the American romantic relationship. The French seem to be 'interdependent' rather than 'dependent.' Not wholly convinced that the 'pure relationship,' so aptly described by Giddens ([1991] 2001:186–7), is an attainable reality, they are more prone to maintaining a dialogue of selves rather than seeking a meshing of selves.

The variation in need for agreeability is once again demonstrated by the manner in which a circle of friends responds to an argument between a husband and wife. English and American friends will become extremely ill at ease if a couple start arguing hotly in their presence. The French seem better able to handle such a situation with minimal embarrassment. Although they may step in to help settle an argument, there is a remarkable absence of shock. Interestingly enough, if there is a break-up between a man and a woman, American parents will try to reason with their son or daughter in favour of their in-law (in the absence of abuse) while the French parents will automatically close ranks and attack the personality of the in-law. It is not unusual for an estranged French spouse to suddenly find herself defending her estranged mate in order to preserve her own face and sense of competence in mate selection.

## Work Ethic

The French work thirty-five hours per week and take between five and seven weeks of paid holidays per year. French businesspeople take longer to make decisions than do their American and English counterparts. Moreover, the French do not make great team players in the Anglo-American corporate sense. French corporate structure is still quite hierarchical – managers hold considerable power over subordinates and sometimes withhold information needed by their employees to get the job done. Yet, France, with a population less than one-quarter of America's, remains one of the seven largest economic powers in the world. Anglo-American business executives who are frustrated with French business practices are at a loss to explain France's high productivity.

Much of the seeming anomaly can be explained by the fact that France is a *high-context* culture. HC cultures place considerable emphasis on trust. Starting from a position of non-imposition (*negative politeness*) HC individuals need to counteract the distancing that results from negative politeness by getting to know 'the other.' Interactive 'reserve' increases the need for subsequent personal disclosure, especially if the ethics of a potential business partner are of interest.

This search for trust dominates French business practices. The attractiveness of a business deal is not the only consideration; of equal importance is whether the person or company offering the deal is considered worthy of trust over a long-term relationship. French businesspeople do not think in the short term. The same *pudeur* (caution) that prevents the French from revealing their personal details to a stranger also motivates the French to proceed with caution in business. While they welcome innovation and progress, they hesitate to reach decisions quickly. Not only do they need to get to know their possible partners and suppliers, they need to feel that they have substantial information regarding the nature of the proposed project and its long-term outcomes. This interest in the long term is a particularly high-context characteristic, for low-context cultures tend to think in the short term. It is not a coincidence that corporate performance reports are much more frequent in the United States than in France.

Business behaviour in France is, therefore, governed by 'situations' rather than standardized rules of marketing. Within companies, relations between bosses and workers are quite hierarchical even though tact and indirectness are used when a criticism is necessary. The worker, for his part, continues to depend on logic and great amounts of information in order to carry out his job. Doing a job properly according to specifications and directives will sometimes overshadow personal initiative. Before making a decision, the worker must consider a slew of questions: Will the boss be pleased or will he be critical? How will his action be received if it leads to error? Will he be able to deny the error or minimize its severity, or will he lose face? Will he be safer if he passes the project on to someone else or shows that it is under the jurisdiction of another department? These are not the questions of a slacker, but the understandable worries of a worker who is placed in a high-context situation in which it is assumed that everyone has needed information, even when bosses are purposefully withholding information from subordinates in order to retain the power to make summary decisions. Predictably, praise is not easily given in the French corporation, much as is the case in the French educational system. The employee is expected to do the job well.

The centralization of the state and its hierarchies are somewhat mirrored in the corporation. A new employee can easily identify who runs the place for, unlike in America where the most powerful executives have corner offices set away from the workers, the French manager's office is more often than not in the middle of the company floor layout. From this centre the manager can observe and stay informed of his employees's work.

American and English corporations are considerably 'low-context' and focus on completing a project according to the bottom-line imperative of profit. As long as the personality of a potential partner or supplier does not affect the competent delivery of the product, the American and English are content to let the profit imperative be the principal measure for business decisions.

This preference for abridging the various steps necessary for the conduct of business explains why Anglo-American business (and other institutional) meetings are controlled by a set agenda of topics to be discussed. The topics are selected according to whatever issues require the most urgent action. French meetings, however, are less limited by a set agenda and last longer because of frequent digressions. Disorganization is not the reason for these digressions – employees need to obtain as much information as possible before they feel comfortable to proceed with the job at hand. In short, the French do not favour the 'keep it short and sweet' business model. As previously mentioned, French employees, although they defer to authority, are not easily commanded. When asked whether they 'must be convinced first before following instructions,' 40.2 per cent of the French responded in the affirmative, compared with 32.7 per cent of the English and 20.2 per cent of the Americans.

The preference for extensive information and substance does not mean that all workers will be equally informed. It is unclear whether this is a consequence of hierarchical organization based on status assignations or a product of the traditional French spirit of *méfiance* (suspicion) (Morford 2001).

One thing is certain: Americans and English who arrive in a French corporate environment are frequently disoriented. They cannot understand why a three-hour dinner is necessary before the topic of business is even brought up and then only in an indirect way. Their preference for a *low-context* approach is based on the assumption that time is money and that it is important to be 'efficient.' How time can be saved, measured, and used constructively is the foundation of Anglo-American marketing. Americans, especially those from the north-east, where time is most at a premium, find the leisurely decision making of the French highly irritating. Many conclude, incorrectly, that the indirectness and casualness of the French are signs of an inefficient economy. The offices of cross-cultural experts in France are filled with foreign workers and executives seeking advice on how to function in the French business environment. Very soon they learn that there is a major difference between French and Anglo-American societies: people are considered subordinate to schedules in one, while workers are considered more important than schedules and agendas in the other.

It is important not to confuse the thoroughness of the French with inefficiency. French corporate culture consists of a paradox: the French seem to favour both action (individualism) as well as *risk avoidance* and deference to *authority*. Moreover, *pudeur* (suspicion and caution) assures them that they will get their facts straight before acting. But once they do act, their love of excellence and perfection makes them extremely productive. They somehow manage to accomplish this despite the existence of a hierarchy that creates considerable uncertainty among peers and between managers and subordinates. This dissonance seems somewhat counterbalanced by the fact that the French resist dehumanization and harbour considerable mistrust towards 'bottom-line' mentalities that reduce individual difference. When the Disney Corporation issued specific instructions regarding the clothing that its employees had to wear at Disneyland in France, the French unions rebelled. And when Coca-Cola indiscriminately installed public vending machines in a bid to corner the market in the 1980s, the French objected because they felt the practice was unfair to local businesses (Asselin and Mastron 2001:5). Other French objections to globalization have been numerous and include the dramatic 1999 protest against McDonald's organized by agriculture activist Jose Bové.

*Bureaucracy and Citizenship*

Richard Hill (1994) has written that the French have 'a visceral urge to assert their individuality on the other' (53). Perhaps this quality is related to the notion of *égalité* (equality), a legacy of the revolution, as well as to a childhood spent listening to the firm exhortations of parents and educators. By the time they reach adolescence, the French have been taught hundreds of rules and specifications, some to do with personal moral identity and others connected to the French way of doing things.

It is understandable that this continual experience with authority will predispose them to claim the rights that they have observed in adults and educators. As adult representatives-at-large of the community, they, in their turn, offer criticism to others. Hierarchical societies that thrive on vertical socialization systems built on a deference to authority always produce citizens not averse to being firm. Anyone who is surprised at receiving witty criticisms from a stranger in France misses the above points; the criticism is not only directed to foreigners but also traded between the French themselves; it is part of the vertical as well as horizontal social processes that guarantee free speech to all. Here is another instance where deference to authority and commitment to individualism manage to co-exist in an interdependent relationship.

This French penchant for criticism is again observable in French people's relations with their state bureaucracies. To be a citizen of France is to learn that the bureaucracy is something to be conquered and kept in line so as to avoid a quagmire of paperwork and antiquated laws that often contradict one another. When referring to their bureaucracies the French speak in terms of *se débrouiller* (figuratively, 'to manage'; literally, 'to untangle oneself'). In our own observations we noticed that creative and self-deprecating stories of one's predicament seemed to elicit the most sympathy on the part of officials.

The government is considered a service provider and is kept in check through frequent protests and citizen action groups. No nation in the West possesses a more demanding public than France. While Americans focus on issues of human rights connected to identity management, the French emphasize human rights that address not only identity but also the physical and emotional welfare of the citizen. The word *solidarité* captures the French attitude towards their roles as citizens and also describes a social philosophy that is we-oriented rather than me-oriented. It is this notion of mutual caretaking that makes France able to provide one of the world's most advanced and comprehensive universal medical care programs. It is a nation where doctors make house calls at the expense of the state, daycare and house help are provided by the state for a pittance, and citizens are willing to pay the taxes necessary so that the weakest and sickest have a decent standard of life.

The notion of less government is an anomaly to the French mentality. Less government would mean less benefits. The ideal balance lies in keeping the government on its toes and holding it accountable. The American slogan 'the less government the better' strikes the French as illogical and impractical. They feel that less government would give too much power to the private sector. Private enterprise will not and cannot replace the state as the equitable provider of social services, protection, and justice. So the French give considerable status and power to their political leaders and then expect results in return. Despite budget problems and heavy tax burdens, the central premise – that the state has certain obligations towards its citizenry – is nearly sacred in French life (Asselin and Mastron 2001:150). Judging by the French medical system, which is one of the world's top three, the French trust in a socialist state is not misplaced.

The English are similarly disposed to defer to the state. In England there is one public surveillance camera for every fifty citizens. The English are admired the world over for having unarmed street policemen; what is less mentioned is that for such a thing to be possible there needs to be a population that follows the rules. In 2007 approximately half of the banking records of Britons were compromised by a computer security breach. While citizens were dismayed, no immediate street protests against the loss of privacy were observed in the ensuing days and weeks. In France, on that same day, over ten thousand tobacco sellers flooded the streets to protest the upcoming state ban on smoking in cafés.

During the years we spent trekking back and forth between the three countries that are the focus of this study, we did our best to remain detached and to see the strengths and weaknesses of each culture. Yet, when we asked the question 'Which of the three cultures is the most family-friendly?' we had no choice but to admit that the evidence was overwhelmingly in the favour of France. Socialization rituals, education, and social benefits offered by the state were all designed to preserve the integrity of small and large collectives. While the origins of the contemporary American and English states were connected to a deep concern for communalism, we found that under the pressures of postmodern technology and capitalism, America had been faced with an unworkable choice: promote the welfare of the poor at the cost of the rich or maintain the advantages enjoyed by the rich by denying help to the poor. In large urban centres, where anonymity complicates traditional communitarian American values, the plight of individuals lacking adequate food and medical care leaves one wondering how the world's richest and most powerful nation has not found the willpower to decrease the suffering of its most unfortunate citizens.

In previous sections of this book we mentioned that a definition of civility must also involve an evaluation of the manner in which citizens treat their state and the manner in which the state treats its citizens. Total unattended freedom and a social ethic based on the sovereignty of the 'me' has not worked in America. Perhaps it helped energize the original explorers and developers of the uncharted American landscape. Yet, today, the Darwinism that accompanies unregulated capitalism seems to be producing considerable misery. It is said that a nation can be judged by the manner in which it treats its strongest and its weakest. This will be a major social issue to be faced in the coming decade as an aging population will require a society of compassion and a young generation will need some sense of what it means to be a citizen of a functional culture. Until that day arrives, millionaire celebrities will continue to pay millions for a vacation home while thousands die because they cannot afford $100 a month for medication. Will the famed generosity, sense of humour, and resolve of the Americans allow a successful outcome? We feel the answer will be yes, provided that the rift between Europe and America is healed and Americans look to their European counterparts for reassurances that a state that offers social benefits need not degenerate into a totalitarian state.

# Part V

# Summing Up

There can be no high civility without a deep morality.
— Ralph Waldo Emerson

# 11 Civilizing and Recivilizing Processes

> Today's mighty oak is just yesterday's nut that held its ground.
> – Anonymous

## Introduction

The study of civility is the study not only of the social history of a culture but of the human need for satisfactory social bonds and the problems that emerge when these bonds become too loose or too tight. When they are too tight, we are left with a collectivism that engulfs the individual, drowning out personal needs and aspirations. When they are too loose, the individual is deprived of the safety of communal norms and abandoned to a wasteland of freedom in which interactions between self and others lack meaning and depth. How a culture reacts to either extreme depends on how that culture values 'privacy.' A culture that values privacy to a fault will have great difficulty with a collectivist ethic, just as a culture that values intense public socialization will find the individualism of private cultures unbearably isolating. This does not mean that the citizens of a culture will always choose the level of social bonding that suits their temperament; historical, moral, and economic forces can propel a culture in a direction contrary to the deepest needs of its members. Periods of reformation and revolution are, in fact, corrective measures designed to bring a culture back into a sort of 'self-alignment.'

In view of the above, I took serious account of the delicacy of social bonds when planning my study of civility. I managed this by remaining as loyal as possible to cultural/emotional sociology as well as historical sociology – each stream of research yielded valuable lessons regarding the complexity and fragility of the *civilizing process* and its varied effects on social (and antisocial) interactions. Thus, I began my study with a historical review of the development of courtesy in the medieval West and progressed from there to a consideration of the social psychology of civility in the context of a contemporary society in which individual rights and communal duty have entered a tense relationship with each other.

In order to avoid the beguiling simplicity of unilateral explanations, I grounded my study in a longitudinal comparison of France, England, and America. I chose these particular countries because they have achieved comparable levels of technical development. This baseline similarity allowed me to notice those glaring differences that were influenced by factors other than technology and the globalization of markets. These differences facilitated my understanding of those elusive aspects that affect the civility ethos of a nation. Such insight was necessary for the development of a 'topology' of civility and a template for civility research, one that could be transported across cultural and national boundaries. While this template took into serious account the primordial human need for positive and successful social interactions, it did not reduce the sociological study of a culture to a priori specifications of which acts and behaviours should be considered as 'civil' across national boundaries. Certainly, my study did not posit emotional reserve as the hallmark of ideal civility; instead, I did my best to keep a keen eye on the benefits and opportunity costs of various civility traditions and the various emotional cultures that accompany them.

My work, therefore, required four streams of analysis. First, I was interested in understanding the manner in which civility had been developed and debated in the West. Second, I was interested in discovering what connections, if any, could be established between the biographies of the nations in my study and their present cultural ideologies and interaction styles. Third, I was interested in making some sense of the present state of civility and cultural ideology in each of the three nations of my study, independently of historical habituation, in order to see whether history did indeed have an influence. Fourth, I wanted to develop some reliable understanding of the social psychology of civility and the manner in which this manifests itself in cultures that subscribe to different rates of individualism and collectivism.

In fact, during the research and writing of this book, I came to appreciate how *paradox* is such an indelible part of human relations and cultural ideology. The lingering presence of contradictions may unsettle us and make us partial to narratives that minimize doubt, yet such 'pacifier logic' does not help us remain alert to the problems of certain long-standing explanations of the *civilizing process*.

During my research, I began to suspect that unilateral reliance on cause-effect types of historical evidence had its limitations. Indeed, history could be effectively used to explain the origins of a certain mentality, but not the totality of its outcomes. If one exaggerated one's preference for consistency, one risked going too far and adopting the somewhat problematic belief that, even in a period of rampant rejection of tradition, the ethos of a culture would remain untouched come what may due to its accumulated heritage. Even more adventurous would be the proposition that it was precisely this heritage that was the binding agent of the said devolution – a little like saying that even when a boat is hopelessly far offshore its anchor remains firmly grounded in familiar waters due to an anchor chain that keeps on lengthening almost by magic.

I also remained eerily aware that sudden demographic changes (remember that the baby boomers will one day pass on) could cause within the span of a single generation a massive transformation of a culture, one that might conceivably involve a wholesale abandonment of its historical, literary, and moral heritage.

In *The Dumbest Generation – How the Digital Age Stupefies Young Americans and Jeopardizes Our Future* (2008), a scathing indictment of the exaggerated hopes placed on children of a digital age, Mark Bauerlein writes that the 'progressive' notion that internet and multimedia technologies would increase the intelligence and participation of the young has turned out to be wishful thinking. Bauerlein makes the following observation about how teachers themselves have unwittingly contributed to the dumbing-down of an entire generation:

> All of them [students] expect the mentors to enter the room with credentialed authority, some know-how that justifies their position, even if some of the kids begrudge and reject it. When the mentors disavow their authority, when they let their discipline slacken, when they, in the language of the educators, slide from 'the sage on the stage' to the 'guide on the side,' the kids wonder what goes. They don't consider the equalizing instruction a liberator, and they aren't motivated to learn on their own. They draw another, immobilizing lesson. If mentors are so keen to recant their experience, why should students strain to acquire it themselves? (186)

The more variables I took into account during my study of civility, the more I became aware of some of the above paradoxical relationships and outcomes. It was one thing to investigate how the need for violence limitation in medieval times led to a courtesy ethic based on the Christian virtues of humility and altruism. Such an ethic focused on the limitation of violence, a simple enough objective with which one can have no credible quarrel. It was another thing, however, to note the paradoxical outcomes of different state systems. Why was it that states promising their citizens social equality and freedom from authoritarian rule (as had been the case in America) could somehow manage to create cultures of conformity and standardization? Conversely, how was it that states that exhorted their citizens to remain loyal to a sentiment of strong nationalism could produce cultural milieus in which strong individualism and even eccentricity were allowed and valued (as had been the case in France and in England)?

Such paradoxical effects are not fully accounted for in Norbert Elias's theory of restraint and civilization; nor are they sufficiently factored into psychoanalytical theories of repression that equate the lifting of restraints with the unleashing of a universal decivilizing process. Such perspectives do not accord enough attention to how a substantially restrained culture can abandon many of its former restraints without sliding back into an 'uncivilized' state. It is, therefore, simplistic to equate the expression of anger (historically, and perhaps incorrectly, associated with discourtesy) with a decivilizing process, and even more dubious to rest satisfied with the assertion that a polite restraint of confrontational emotions is sufficient to create and maintain an adequately civilized society. The restraint of emotion in England, for example, did not continue unchallenged – sensibility and Romanticism intervened to temper Cartesian consistency. Similarly, the ethos of 'agreeability,' so prevalent in the America of the 1950s, did not remain immune to a subsequent critical generation that demanded major changes in social values – changes that, in turn, led to a culture in which personal entitlement entered an uneasy and oppositional relationship with communal duty. Such inconsistencies and reversals explain why this present chapter is titled, in the interests of intellectual caution, 'Civilizing and Recivilizing Processes.'

These paradoxes and transformations should be cause for excitement rather than distress. Not only do they reveal the powerful force of intervening variables in social change, they assure us that paradox – although it may cause intellectual discomfort – is the unavoidable outcome of processes that change direction whenever revision is required. This is particularly observable in civility and morality movements that provoke cultural panics in the short term until the changes they call for tame and outdate the worry. They are also observable in emotional habituations: a stoic culture may reach, at some point in its history, a point of emotional rebellion, just as an emotionally expressive culture may reach a point of emotional saturation and require respite from emotional over-activation.

Because of the above, I have contextualized civility by showing its many-faceted political and social-psychological anatomy. Its earliest religious origins have given way to complex political, economic, moral, and social forces that have manifested themselves differently during various eras and in various locations. I have respected these differences and avoided presenting civility as a unidirectional evolutionary process with barbarism at one end of the spectrum and civilized behaviour at the other extreme. As I have attempted to show in my review of the contemporary American search for personal fulfillment, many of the civility rituals and moral positions that had been taken for granted during the 1930s and into the 1950s were revised by massive cultural changes originating in the 1960s. Sometimes, these revisionist forces required purposive acts of incivility, because those struggling to bring about change remained aware of how civility and emotional restraint had been used throughout history to encourage and maintain submission to the status quo. The ensuing oppositional nature of certain contemporary cultural debates is not set in stone. The recent myriad mainstream articles and documentaries on rudeness and incivility indicate that we have reached yet another point of reversal – what once served to create new forms of solidarity is now having a disintegrative effect and moving people to reflect on the meaning of civility in a complex, multicultural, electronically connected world in which cohesion is at a premium. Thus, the project of building a truly civilized society is still in the making. Certainly it is making us realize the catch-22 of civility: too much authenticity breeds rudeness and violence, while not enough breeds hypocrisy and passivity.

All this to say that we continue to be prone to the sudden appearance of what I call 'recivilizing' processes – transformations that challenge our most disciplined predictions. So, the categorization of a given culture does not necessarily indicate what hybrid forms will emerge from the tensions inherent between its habituations and emerging new properties. Even cultures that place a high valuation on authority and deference to vertical power can, surprisingly enough, temper their formal civility systems by adopting traits from less formal cultures. This is already happening in many Middle Eastern cultures, where a large youth cohort is increasingly appreciating and championing the more informal civility practices of Western nations. The converse is also true: a liberal culture can become populated by a new cohort that takes to criticizing the liberalism of its predecessors and calls for a revised, more conservative, social contract. Revisions, therefore, can be made in the direction of increased liberalism or increased conservatism. The ideology of a culture does not follow a linear pattern. The extent of revisions depends on the degree of saturation and satiation. In fact, two cultures that appear identical may appear to be so only because they are being observed in a short time frame, like a still photo taken from a moving picture – in reality, the cultures may be headed in very opposite directions.

**The Self and Others**

Where do these cautions leave us when it comes to the study of civility? Certainly, the subject is too complex for summary declarations. Even Lady Montague's benign reminder that 'civility costs nothing and buys everything' runs into complications when one considers that constant, unwavering civility may have a considerable cost: the tempering of one's own needs and/or cultural ideology. One remains aware, therefore, that in a broader social context, civility involves much more than polite treatment of the other. As I have argued in preceding chapters, many factors are involved: attitude towards modesty, self-effacement, and self-aggrandizement; notions of independence and interdependence; beliefs regarding the ideal way to use time and space; and the extent to which emotions are expressed and/or restrained.

Beyond these factors is an even more complex question: How are we to define civility in our own era? Is it sufficient to treat others with relative fairness, or are we required to question our conscience on complex and far-reaching issues such as global social and economic inequality, consumption practices, war and peace, and the right to proper education and medical care? In short, is civility a system of mannerisms, or is it a more complex process of moral evaluation and action? This question preoccupied the Victorians and it now demands our attention.

The complexity of these issues explains why, in my discussion of the various forms of politeness (the differences between individualistic and communalistic societies, and the important role played by emotions in culture), I have tried to stress the importance of avoiding tautological explanations such as 'we are uncivil because we are not civil.' The foregoing statement attempts to explain a thing through the absence of another thing. It is based on the premise that the sought-after quality (e.g., civility) is a constant and, consequently, a source of prima facie definitions. But this simplistic line of reasoning does not help us explain why those who are capable of being civil become uncivil, especially when one observes that the undesired state is sometimes accepted by its practitioner and, even, welcomed. This distinction may not seem important at first glance, but it does help us move towards more realistic and effective social policies. For example, if a given group is behaving without civility because of the presence of emerging anger, then the policies that will work best will not be the teaching of politeness but the teaching of constructive anger expression.

To develop further this line of reasoning regarding the difference between the absence of a quality and the presence of its opposite, are we correct in assuming that individualism and communal well-being are incompatible with each other or that in order to have one we must be willing to settle for less of the other? In our historical analysis of the origins of courtesy 'restraint' and 'civilization' are related; yet, do we need to hold to this paradigm indefinitely? Or is it possible that we have reached a point of awareness that now liberates us to consider other standards without endangering our social bonds? In the old paradigm, it was thought that some a priori antisocial tendency in us needed to be repressed in order to release our ability to maintain a civil society. This Hobbesian view of human nature predisposed conduct observers to conclude that society was sliding back into an 'uncivilized' state whenever their observations of rudeness became frequent. Yet this quick judgment does not help us understand why people in a given era or location become less civil than their predecessors or why succeeding generations revive the civility imperative.

After years of textual and field research, I am left wondering why we so often posit individualism and communal well-being or politeness and anger expression at incompatible and extreme ends of a behavioural spectrum that has altruistic self-denial at one extreme and the unabashed celebration of self-interest (and perhaps even cruelty) at the other. Perhaps these distinctions are in some measure illusory, being that they are based on a Judeo-Christian social philosophy that has difficulty harmonizing selfishness with commitment to the community.

Nietzsche noted this difficulty and believed that it emanated from an anemic definition of what was to constitute 'good' behaviour. Certainly we are faced with the same dilemma that confronted the warrior knights of medieval times: we are to be strong but not so strong as to threaten those weaker than us; we are to exhibit mutual consideration and speak with tact in order to ensure that as few people as possible fall into embarrassing and painful predicaments; yet, in the same breath, we are to maintain a high level of sincerity and honesty.

In the end, we are left with an important question: Why do we equate a strong sense of self-interest with 'selfishness' (i.e., the corrosive refusal to take the well-being of others into account) and associate communally ethical behaviour with the negation of the desires of the self? Could it be that our definitions of 'selfishness' and 'altruism' need to be revisited? In the classical civility paradigm, it is assumed that the person who is constantly thinking of himself at the exclusion of others is doing so because he has an excess of selfishness (i.e., he is full of himself). This we equate, perhaps hastily, with individualism. Our studies of narcissism (amply quoted in previous chapters) suggest, however, that it is a very weak sense of self that drives a person to constantly seek personal satisfaction at the exclusion of his communal duties. In such a case, the person is actually more selfless than he is selfish, for it is precisely the absence of a satisfactory grounding of the self that causes what appears to be obsessively self-oriented behaviour.

If the above reasoning has merit, then we need to probe a little deeper and ask what produces individuals with a sense of self that is so weak as to condemn them to the incessant pursuit of sensation and popularity? Could it be that some natural non-negotiable needs are not being met, or, worse yet, are being perverted?

The American novelist-philosopher Ayn Rand (1945, 1957) suggested in her novels and essays that a culture that glorifies 'altruism' strikes a crushing blow to the ability of its citizens to conduct their affairs in ethical ways. She remained convinced that 'collectivist' societies abhorred the consciousness of the individual and prohibited the development of a healthy self willing to put the interests of others alongside his own. Mindless conformity to superficial values deprived the individual of the ability to be himself, thereby leaving him no self to give to the community. Rand concluded that the selfless conformist had little to offer – she even considered this social type a danger to all creative individuals.

Rand's uncompromising critique of collectivism was delivered in the 1940s and 1950s, in the wake of a strong conformist American corporate culture and a Soviet collectivism that had degenerated into totalitarianism. Yet her critique could be applied to contemporary consumer culture. While Rand caricaturized the conformist type as a mindless cultural trooper ready to follow whatever norm was in vogue (even if it specified the shunning of the truly creative intellectual), the present fad-oriented consumer is perhaps equally manipulated by savvy 'lifestyle' marketers and expedient political interests. In the contemporary context, a similar collectivism is very much in force, not based on a substantial patriotism, but energized by an obsession with 'making choices' from among myriad possibilities. The 'chooser' becomes anything but a discriminating buyer, however, for the promise of choice offers not only the satisfaction of known wants, but the endless discovery of new ones. Wanting becomes a state of being. This sentiment of 'incompletion' comes with a host of emotional consequences: impatience, a difficulty in focusing on the needs and troubles of others, and frustration towards people and events that distract from the 'filling of the self' (self-fulfillment). The old notion of happiness, one based on sentiments of contentment, becomes unwittingly transformed into a state of endless 'becoming.'

Arthur Janov (1970, 1975) has proposed a similarly paradox-friendly theory in his study of human emotional pain and its root causes and outcomes. He distinguishes between the 'unreal self' (the pain-filled defensive self that is always seeking personal satisfaction to dull the inner pain) and the 'real self' (the feeling self that is capable of feeling its own needs and, therefore, capable of ministering to the needs of others). Rand's and Janov's work suggests that the difference between civil and uncivil behaviour may in part be connected to the degree to which an individual has developed a truly authentic sense of self, one based on the recognition of natural needs rather than the random internalization of ephemeral fads, mannerisms, and personality styles.

The suggestion that a society will remain civil in the long run provided it remains populated by restrained individuals begs argument. While the theory might hold in the short run, it runs into difficulty when we consider that there might come a point when the raging needs that have been repressed will require expression. Conformity has long-range opportunity costs. More indicative than the degree of restraint is the manner in which a given culture manages sentiments of pride, embarrassment, and shame in the wake of emotional activation. Whether or not its citizens are satisfied with the manner in which such management occurs will have a great effect on the degree of trust between citizens and the opinions they maintain regarding the state of civility in their culture. In brief, what matters in a culture is the maintenance of 'trust.' A polite society that is undergoing a period of emotional perturbation could have a level of trust far less satisfactory than that enjoyed by a culture in which abrasive rudeness is taken for granted as part of human nature.

**Trust, Risk, and Solidarity**

The one thing that various types of civility cultures require in order to remain functional is the presence of satisfactory *networks of trust*. By this I mean that interactants must feel that they occupy an environment that accords with their preconception of what is to be considered a functional and morally legitimate culture. What is in question is the degree of 'commonality' within situations involving risk. 'Trusting in trust' requires what Jean-Paul Sartre called 'the agony of trust,' a process in which one party, not really knowing in any definitive way what is to be the outcome of an interaction, allows himself to hope that the outcome will not be hurtful. A network of trust, therefore, although it can never offer complete certainty and security, must provide interaction and transaction under relatively safe circumstances.

Networks of trust also serve to provide their members with the associations needed to resist threats to their autonomy. In effect, a culture that is 'falling apart' is one in which there is little agreement regarding standards and values. Tilly (2003a) offers an interesting explanation of the connections between trust, social networks, and the rise and fall of democracies. He argues that it is not social attitudes of tolerance that make democracy viable, but the influence of 'trust networks' – religious sects, trade unions, patron–client ties, credit networks, kinship groups, mutual aid societies – which is indispensable for state rule. He states that these trust networks have been operating for over a thousand years, protecting their members from domination while setting standards of conduct. Being indispensable to the state's need to manage its population, these trust networks allow their members to have a bottom–up influence and to temper the authority of the state.

Tilly's insights can be extended to the study of behaviour at the micrological level. While a population may subscribe for a period of time to a civility ethic that leaves it vulnerable to a myriad social problems, there can come a point of reversal as dialogues between citizens take on a 'critical mass' and facilitate change. Rose-Ackerman (2001) explains why sometimes it takes a long period of time for this critical point to be reached. She observes that social problems often emanate from a 'self-sustaining system of corruption' (424). Although citizens know that a given course of action or behaviour is socially dysfunctional, they continue with it because they remain convinced that others are continuing with the behaviour and have no intention of changing it. This readiness to act in a manner that is against one's ideal or one's deepest needs for successful social bonds is a consequence of the 'bystander effect' as well as the fact that we remain uncomfortably aware that more social benefits come to those who remain in step with the majority collective. Luckily, this same desire for benefits permits a collective to change its behavioural standards when enough voices manage to create a 'trust network' in which the new behavioural forms can exist without provoking generalized anxiety regarding loss of functionality, status, or privilege.

The above insights may explain why a large number of individuals will continue with a socially corrosive practice even when it repeatedly contributes to their feelings of tension, discomfort, and alienation. A natural propensity towards the pleasure that emanates from satisfactory social bonds can, therefore, be corrupted by fads, mentalities, and cultural ideologies that diminish solidarity and cooperation among citizens. This corruption need not be permanent, however, provided there is no massive loss of cultural confidence or competence.

It would seem, then, that when all the relevant factors are taken into account, *the degree of satisfaction of a people with their civil culture will very much be affected by the extent to which they feel meaningfully connected to other members of their culture.*

Here, I would like to share with the reader the most important lesson I learned from this long-range study of civility. With the exception of a minority of individuals who remain self-sufficient and in no need of frequent social interactions, most individuals require a sense of cultural identity in order to remain on this side of frustrated (and aggressive) alienation. This sense of belonging and communion can be partially achieved through membership in a special-interest group. Yet, this cannot provide complete satisfaction if the group is placed in a culture of competing groups in which there is little sentiment of cultural or national solidarity. Even a 'live and let live' cultural ideology leads to considerable social disconnection. So, despite the abusive uses of nationalism in the past, we would do well to consider its useful functions. It provides citizens with a sense of pride in the accomplishments of their civilization as well as in the anticipated future of that civilization. Apathy, discouragement, and a frantic reliance on self are the price cultures pay for neglecting the important role played by national solidarity. This solidarity need not and should not be limited to connection to an ethnic identity. It can be a multicultural reality lived under the umbrella of a national ethos that, ideally, stands above all partisan interests and is, therefore, considered legitimate and trustworthy by all ethnic groups.

In my review of the history of the three countries of my study, I have been confronted with a glaring truth that has left me troubled. Identity in America, and increasingly in England, seems to be connected to lifestyle and personal belief systems. There is a marked absence of 'vertical' moral authority. Citizens are left on the periphery of a core that is slowly evaporating and being replaced by more local and more individualistic behavioural standards. While this has a salutary effect – protecting citizens from the debilitating hegemony of an all-powerful state or a privileged elite – it brings with it an opportunity cost: a 'live and let live' ethic that prohibits the adoption of a collective ethos that addresses substantial moral and behavioural issues.

France, on the other hand, has managed to maintain a core sense of what it means to be French, a sense that is not defined solely by personal lifestyle, interaction style, monetary standards, or technical accomplishments but through a continual awareness of the accomplishments of French civilization. This awareness is cultivated at an early age within the family circle and maintained through an educational system that respects and encourages vertical associations that act as reminders of cultural continuity. While France, like all other colonial powers, has gone through a period of self-criticism, its sense of national pride and identity has remained rooted in a consciousness of the accomplishments of French civilization. Its deft harmonization of individualism and communalism has created a culture of paradox in which civility rules are situation-specific. Yet, this paradoxical mix of privatism and collectivism has provided the French with the ability to make compensatory adjustments in their interaction values without suffering from generalized worry. Neither wholly committed to individualism or collectivism (or, if you prefer, committed to both), they are able to remain loyal to each characteristic with equal passion, without feeling that they have wandered too far offshore.

So, to speak of 'citizenship' without simultaneously speaking of 'nation' is to utter an abstraction. While revisiting narratives and slogans of our culture helps reveal those historical intrusions that have contaminated worthy ideals, the resulting cynicism should not be used to justify social, ethical, and political withdrawal. If devolution becomes an end in itself, it releases an epidemic of cynicism that only acts to empower the cunning, who then take unfair advantage of the freedoms provided by a democracy of rights; an epidemic of special interests overwhelms communalism. All we are left with then are disheartening scenarios in which individuals and institutions, in order to 'end up ahead,' deliberately and unashamedly do precisely the opposite of what they say they are doing. The white lie takes on an ominous force and actual wrongs are minimized through the use of desensitizing words, catch phrases, and mind-boggling excuses. The primal act of 'saving face,' a completely natural human response to emotional anxiety, becomes replaced with the maintenance of a 'mask' designed to conceal deliberately self-serving motives.

## Embarrassment and Shame in a Cross-Cultural Context

Can the above observations be reconciled with an actual historical as well as contemporary comparison of the civility ethos of France, England, and America? At the level of theory and observation, it would seem that the issue of national heritage and a people's relation to it is not without consequence. It plays a central role in the manner in which citizens negotiate their interactions with one another and manage the emotions that emanate from such interactions.

I have already argued that the emotions of embarrassment and shame are not 'end points' in an interaction, but interactively rooted in the more powerful emotions of anger, grief, and humiliation. These primal emotions, when left unexpressed, can create the need for later retribution and revenge. They can also make the individual very touchy towards potentially embarrassing or shame-producing situations, thereby complicating his interaction with others.

So, not only do embarrassment and shame function as powerful *prohibitions* against the expression of certain emotions, they also act, ironically, as *instigators* of emotions because frustrated and explosive expression follows from repression. At some point, the build-up of tension arising from repression requires the relief of an emotional reaction. So, while an emotionally restrained culture may prohibit the expression of outrage, this same emotional prohibition can have a humiliating effect and sow the seeds for a subsequent desire for vengeance.

Thus, what seems functional in the short term may prove to be socially disruptive in the longer run. The determining factor is the degree to which citizens remain convinced that the repressions imposed by their culture continue to have a beneficial purpose over the long run. There did come a time in American culture in the 1960s when emotional repression triggered considerable protest. Similarly, we may be witnessing the emergence of a similar emotional uprising in certain sectors of English society, where seething sentiments of anger are challenging the politeness imperative.

The connections between emotional states and cultural habituations are extremely strong, since sentiments of pride, embarrassment, and shame lie at the core of most civility rituals. I have suggested during my discussions of various aspects of life in America, France, and England that *high-context and low-context* orientations have a salient effect on politeness ethics, the manner in which ideal practices are determined, and the behaviours that are considered shameful. Generally, communal societies that place a high premium on conformity and social solidarity tend to produce an inordinate amount of *community-oriented shame*, while individualistic cultures tend to produce an inordinate amount of *self-oriented shame*. These two different types of shame tend to produce different coping strategies. There are four basic responses available to someone who has fallen into an embarrassing or shameful situation: *avowal* (self-blame), *denial* (blaming of external situations or other persons), *self-justification* (denial that the behaviour was shameful), and *deflection* (use of self-forgiving humour and distracting ruses to prevent and/or deflect or minimize criticism). The universal need to avoid a state of embarrassment or shame forces the discomforted person to seek relief through one or more of these measures. The specific measure(s) chosen will be affected by the rate of authority-deference and individualism. *Avowal* and *denial* will be preferred coping strategies in cultures where deviance from established cultural norms provokes the ire of the majority. The wrongdoer can either appease his critics through the admittance of fault or deny that the reason for the fault is his own behaviour. In a more individualistic society, where various lifestyles and cultural ideologies permit differences in outlook and behaviour, an instance of shame will be handled through *justification* of the reasons for the behaviour when considered from the point of view of personal biography or situation; the purpose of the *justification* will be the re-establishment of personal worth. Or the discomforted person will *deflect* the criticism by minimizing the fault being ascribed to him.

In both situations the coping strategies will be connected to repairing the reputation of the self as a self-contained unit rather than as an integral part of a homogeneous order that possesses authority over the person. Saddled with the responsibility of creating a self that is original, the individual will have to defend his creation by justifying its imperfections. On a deeper level, there will be an additional danger of excessive *self-blame* because the person who is saddled with the achievement imperative will not treat himself kindly when he falls below the mark he and/or others have set for him. Needless to say, inordinate amounts of self-blame cause either social withdrawal or seething feelings of aggression.

One thing that struck me about the English and aided my understanding of the French and Americans was the fact that the English are uncomfortable not only with being embarrassed, but with causing embarrassment in others. While the French and Americans are not averse to affirming themselves with strangers by use of pointed remarks and insults (sometimes placing pitiless critical pressure on the other), the English rarely go far beyond the ironic understatement, delivered with little expectation of protracted exchanges. The rising amount of 'road rage' in England should not distract us from this baseline habituation. The uniqueness of the English experience with embarrassment is noticeable in exchanges between customers and service personnel (the English are tirelessly patient customers given to avoiding the embarrassment that may ensue from confrontation) and even between police officers and the offenders whom they confront in the name of the law; the English police are given to normalizing the situation by addressing the offenders with amiable friendliness, unlike American police, who attempt to overpower suspects with an authoritarian show of their own capacity to respond violently. While the English police seek to respond to violence by helping offenders to switch over to pro-social sentiments, the Americans and French police seek to normalize the situation by repressing the antisocial sentiments of the offenders through a strong show of authority.

The English civility ethos is not one of prohibition but one of maintaining a standard of politeness and consideration for the emotional balance of the other. When faced with embarrassing situations, the English are left with no choice but to avow their predicament and then depend on their co-citizens to help normalize the situation; it is the community that provides the embarrassed person with justifications and displacements since no one is comfortable dealing with embarrassing situations. Understatement softens the process of blame and avowal. A healing process kicks in that moves all interactants past the discomforting situation. Very often, humour is enlisted to defuse the tension of the embarrassing occurrence. Criticisms are delivered with utmost tact and only if necessary; even such necessity is determined by the intimacy shared by the interactants. What matters to the English is the establishment of *common ground* inured from conflict.

I was equally impressed with the manner in which the French had managed to allow themselves periodic expressions of irritation and anger of the type that would exclude the need to pass into corrosive violence. *Soyons raisonable* (let's be reasonable) seems to be the guarantee to prevent rudeness from escalating into violence. *Ce que je voulais plutôt dire ...* (What I really meant to say ...) is an effective *redress and softening strategy* for altering one's position and retracting a statement without outright loss of face. Although they do not subscribe to the strong emotional restraint of the English, the French have the facility of responding to insult or anger with competent ripostes that keep the power between belligerents at a balance, thereby minimizing the sentiments of powerlessness that lead to the first blow. In short, they are able to put one another in a continual position of defence by delivering critical questions, suggestions, and philosophical comments that, although they do not overtly attack the face of the other, leave some safe space for differences and a balanced power ratio. Moreover, the rapidity of the French conversational style helps interactants to not dwell on a particular statement that is not to their liking; habituated to interrupting one another, they are able to override an objection with satisfactory justifications or reparations. Able to duel with words, the French seldom need to draw the sword.

Although the French are particularly given to finding reasons for criticizing one another, they seem to do so with such expert uses of *negative politeness* and understatement that it is almost a beloved national pastime, a replaying of the drama of the French child who is continually criticized to keep him on his toes. I would even suggest that a mild 'alarmism' energizes French social relations, moving them to deny embarrassment whenever they can (e.g., 'What a silly place to park a car,' said with complete seriousness after crashing into a legally parked vehicle – an elegant, albeit not outright, admission of fault). If further confronted, however, they will remain on the defensive and bypass the sentiment of personal shame that would lead to further conflict. What counts most is face-saving. Denial of blame, therefore, is rampant; even intelligent individuals will fall into irrational justification simply to avoid confessing to fault. Foreigners who have approached a store manager in France to complain about employee service have had a good introduction to this process of denial. This may explain why the French person couches his conciliatory words in a manner that attempts to avoid the humiliation of apology. The opportunities for denial of responsibility are legion. One blames the external situation or even another innocent party, but one does not blame oneself. Perhaps one's experience of blame in the parental and school system has made one overloaded with blame and not eager to take on more. This placing of blame on external situations, rather than the self, has a salient role in defusing situations. The person who feels blamed redirects the blame until the blame has achieved a third or fourth round and begun to lose force.

Contemporary Americans, on the other hand, lack to a certain degree the coping mechanisms possessed by the English and French. Habituated to a childhood in which they are expected to express their feelings in the name of personal development, they lack the stoicism of the English and are continually exposed to one another's sentiments. Moreover, favouring a culture of public and private harmony, Americans are unsettled by strong emotions, especially anger. There is a mortified speechlessness in the face of sudden anger, as if it were a taboo emotion. Observing those American interactions that escalate into violence (or an equally abrasive mute withdrawal), I noticed that interactants frequently were not able to maintain a steady stream of words that would be sharp enough to provide 'satisfaction' and exclude the need for outright withdrawal or violence. The average American may not have enough nuanced insults at his disposal to permit interactants to send each other 'to hell' without having to admit that they are doing so. American insults and put-downs have to be delivered through fairly direct statements. The abridged LC communication style in America, while it can promote quick and friendly contact, can also accelerate violent disagreement and put a particularly abrasive edge on rudeness at the public and private levels.

Furthermore, I wondered during my observations in the United States whether the American response to situations of embarrassment and shame is not connected to the American manner of viewing *the self*. I have already explained that the American sense of self is *achievement-oriented*. Although they live in an LC culture, Americans are nevertheless required to galvanize their personalities and produce considerable personal achievements, whether these be economic, intellectual, or simply connected to the 'look' or 'lifestyle' that they adopt as their emblem. Insulting an American is not so much an act of insulting the culture which he represents (for Americans define themselves before defining their relation with their culture or state), but an act of questioning his personal integrity and the 'choices' he has made for himself.

If the American is self-made, in the best tradition of the American ideal type, then a disparaging remark (or the withholding of a compliment) hits right where it hurts most: the self that is considered (rightly or wrongly) to be the creation and achievement of the person. Even if an opinion is contested, this has the potential of making the other feel as if his whole essence were being put into question, especially so in the case of people who identify with an 'issue,' take a position on it, and then identify that position with their core self. The space between public and private being abridged, the American is particularly vulnerable to suddenly 'falling out of character' or 'being shaken.' It is understandable that his response to loss of face is immediate and dependent on self-justification and self-repair. Not only must he not avow shame or embarrassment, he must shore up the self by making his audience accept that any mishaps along the way are not connected to a failure in personal competence. While the French remain defensive against the judgments of others because they must maintain a communal reputation based on their roles as caretakers of long-standing French values, the American remains defensive towards the judgment he will have to make against his private unassociated self if he considers the validity of the criticism directed at him. Entrusted with 'high achievement,' he is, oddly enough, not only an individualist in the pure sense of the word, but a person beholden to his community's high valuation of individualism and high achievement.

I particularly noticed these variations in embarrassment management when teenagers reacted to potential loss of face with parents. The French teens always sought external sources to blame in order to deflect attention away from themselves, an understandable behaviour in a nation where blame is imposed at an early age; the English teens tended to avow responsibility and apologize (unless they were of particularly hostile demeanour), an understandable reaction in a nation that has traditionally valued obedience and discipline. American teens tended to enter further confrontational exchanges designed to justify and prove that they were not at fault; rather than seeking another source to blame (itself an admission that something has gone wrong), they focused on preserving their personal image by arguing against the standard that was being used to judge their act. Face was saved not through *redressive actions* or the re-establishment of *common ground* through compromise but through a self-oriented affirmation of personal competence and an objection to external demands (*self-justification*). Members of the present youth cohort (referred to as 'Generation Me' by some social commentators) were particularly competent in the art of *deflection*. I noticed an individualistic tendency to take charge of a situation that could attract criticism and deliver the criticism of their own accord, accompanying their commentary with a slight toss of the head and a sweet, self-forgiving smile. Or the person would confess to an act that would normally attract censure and then minimize the offensiveness of the act by smiling again with a self-forgiving 'well, I couldn't help it' look. Noticeably absent was the feeling of guilt. Was this due to an indomitable desire to be free to do as one wished or was there a particular horror of admitting to fault and then facing embarrassment? One suspects it is a little bit of both, placing the person in a continually conflicted inner struggle.

In the context of contemporary American culture, I question de Tocqueville's ([1884] 1994) preference for a civility ethos that emerges more from 'natural' predisposition than from contractual obligations. He states:

> If a certain way of thinking or feeling is the result of a particular condition of life, when the conditions change, nothing is left. Thus law may make a very close link between two citizens; if the law is repealed, they separate. Nothing could have been tighter than the bond uniting lord and vassal in the feudal world. Now those two men no longer know each other. The fear, gratitude, and affection which once joined them have vanished. One cannot find a trace of them. But it is not like that with feelings natural to man. Whenever a law attempts to shape such feelings in any particular way, it almost always weakens them. By trying to add something, it almost always takes something away, and they are always stronger if left to themselves. (589)

Although his analysis may have applied to the United States in the nineteenth century, his explanation runs into some difficulties when we apply it to contemporary America. While independence from aristocratic hierarchies originally permitted Americans to be ambitious and strike out on their own, the present American scene, complicated by differing claims of independence and a less-than-stellar educational system, puts the whole notion of independence and 'individualism' in question. In the absence of a coherent, unified national pride (a form of positive narcissism) and a population dedicated to preserving its heritage in its educational system, the entire project of *being one's own person* becomes a different proposition from what it was at the turn of the century or even as recently as the 1950s, when America possessed a strong national culture in which individualism was grounded in patriotism and an unwavering belief in the viability of the American Dream.

Today, the affirmation of individualism and the freedom 'to be what I want to be' is too often an act of 'entitlement' rather than a logical extension of existing talents and support networks capable of furthering a national pro-social project involving all citizens. What replaces the old society of 'substance' is 'personal image' and 'personal power.' The individual is left to his own devices with a minimum of input. He becomes his own spin doctor; this explains why so many American conversations include extensive talk of personal psychology. Whether the self-concept that results from such a high valuation of personal achievement is earned or is a creation of his own imagination and lifestyle politics, the American must defend it because it has become his own definition of his *self*. He cannot easily fall back on the explanation, 'Look, this is what we do here in America and all of us do it, so don't go blaming me.' Since so much of American action and behaviour is subject to personal modification in the name of issues-oriented lifestyle and individuality/freedom, there is not enough free space for interactants to avoid involving their personal selves in the diatribes they exchange with one another. While in interdependent cultures the symbols of the cultures are sometimes disparaged in verbal conflict – such as derogatory references to the opponent's family or regional origins – the American diatribe gets stuck in the here and now and requires direct and immediate reparation (potentially causing loss of face to both interactants). America's litigious spirit emanates not as much from an inner American propensity for confrontation as from a dearth of *negative politeness* rituals that would provide the 'distancing' required to defuse conflict shortly after its occurrence.

Regardless of the particular culture, how can individuals in an interaction efficiently pick up on the cues they receive from one another to help determine their next comment, action, or bodily gesture? Is there a process of mind reading involved, considering that many of the indications of embarrassment and shame are subtle and may involve distracting ruses on the part of the person who is experiencing (or causing) loss of face? Goffman (1974) provides an interesting clue when he refers to 'mutual awareness.' Whether a culture is 'high context' or 'low context,' a certain amount of 'mind reading' or 'picking up on' is necessary. He explains that the act of 'being in a state of talk' implies that the interactants are focused on one another: 'A single focus of thought and attention, and a single flow of talk, tends to be maintained and to be legitimated as officially representative of the encounter' (34). This focused awareness is at work when conversants intuitively feel when a section of the talk of the other is to be followed by their own (35). This ability is universal.

In a later work, Goffman comes a little closer to explaining the dynamics of focused interaction: 'When in each other's presence individuals are admirably placed to share a joint focus of attention, perceive that they do so, and perceive this perceiving' (1983:3). The key concepts here are 'perceive that they do so' and 'perceive this perceiving.' There seems to be a 'double-decker' type of awareness at work. It is this process of *'dédoublement'* that makes human communication possible. On one level, individuals remain aware that they are talking; on another and more abstract level, they remain aware of their awareness and the manner in which they are included in each other's consciousness.

It is this mutual awareness of the shared process (a mutual in-folding) that allows for the existence of a civility ethos, for it removes the 'invisibility' or 'unawareness' that would be required for behaviour to remain unregulated. It is the place where habituations are formed and maintained through a sort of mutual surveillance. Thus, *not only are we causing emotions in one another, but we are also having emotional reactions towards the emotions that have been caused.* It is not unreasonable, therefore, to suggest that, regardless of the level of emotional repression of a culture, *a conversation of emotions* is always ongoing at the implicit as well as explicit level.

We can additionally use Goffman's model in the analysis of ethnic or national identity if we consider that a culture's 'geist' or 'ethos' resides within this region of 'mutual awareness of awareness.' This level of awareness contains not only the code for the civility rules that are current in the culture but also a sense of communal identity or nationhood.

Does this mean that different cultures have differing amounts of information in their 'mutual awareness of awareness' cultural repository? It would seem so, since some cultures are *high-context* (the rules are implicit and profuse) while others are *low-context* (the rules, although known, are minimal and require considerable additional information to be coherent in specific situations). I would suggest that *high-context cultures provide citizens with a high capacity to make use of this space of mutual awareness precisely because they offer considerable specifications of ideal behaviour, leaving members of the culture with a rich repository of behavioural information.* Nuance and understatement are made possible by the existence of this rich bank of 'implicit' experiential awareness. In fact, cultural maturity may depend on the breadth and depth of mutual awareness shared by citizens; cultural contextualization and its habituations (HC, MC, and LC) may be at the root of mutual awareness. Although Hall (1983) limits his analysis to 'high-' and 'low'-context cultures, I would suggest that England is best considered a *moderate-context culture* since it shares characteristics of high-context as well as low-context cultures. While its high valuation of time, order, and simple communication style based on amiability are LC practices, its rich bank of understatements indicates HC characteristics. It would seem that the English have managed to combine these two interaction types and fall somewhere between LC American culture and HC French (and east/south European) culture.

## A Topology of Civility and Culture

If we were to construct a classification or topology of American, French, and English civility based on the foregoing discussion, we might benefit from the following listing of correlations:

| *Quality/practice* | *Type or rate* | *Outcome(s)* |
| --- | --- | --- |
| United States | | |
| Governance | constitutional republic | central and regional |
| Independence values | very high | loose social bonds |
| Interdependence values | low | loose social bonds |
| Public relations | low-context | efficiency; independence |
| Private relations | low-context | short-term; individualistic |
| Predominant politeness ritual | positive | amiability; volunteerism |
| Distinction boundaries | financial | high valuation of career |
| Emotionalism in public | moderate-high | self-affirmation |
| Emotionalism in private | high | conflict; intimacy |
| Impoliteness ritual | positive | insult |
| Cultural narcissism | low (post-1960s) | cultural anomie |
| Personal narcissism | high | defensiveness; originality; complacency |

| Face-redress method | common ground | low-context harmony |
|---|---|---|

*France*

| | | |
|---|---|---|
| Governance | republican state | centralized bureaucracy |
| Independence values | high | social distancing |
| Interdependence values | high | social hierarchy; solidarity |
| Public relations | high-context | interdependence |
| Private relations | high-context | long-term |
| Predominant politeness ritual | negative | deference, privacy |
| Distinction boundaries | cultural | education; aesthetics |
| Emotionalism in public | moderate-high | self-affirmation |
| Emotionalism in private | high | conflict; melodrama, intimacy |
| Impoliteness ritual | negative, positive | pointed understatement, insult |
| Cultural narcissism | high | solidarity |
| Personal narcissism | moderate/high | originality |
| Face-redress method | justification; deflection | complacency |

*England*

| | | |
|---|---|---|
| Governance | constitutional monarchy | centralized bureaucracy |
| Independence values | high | loose social bonds |
| Interdependent values | moderate | moderate social bonds |
| Public relations | moderate context | proficiency, privacy |
| Private relations | moderate context | liberty |
| Predominant politeness ritual | negative and positive | tact; amiability; privacy |
| Distinction boundaries | culture/career | civic responsibility |
| Emotionalism in public | low | surface amiability |
| Emotionalism in private | moderate | reasonableness |
| Impoliteness ritual | negative and positive | pointed understatement, insult |
| Cultural narcissism | moderate | civic pride |
| Personal narcissism | moderate | modesty |
| Face-redress method | apology; deflection | compromise |

This topology indicates that LC cultures are more prone to impoliteness rituals that have the potential of escalating into serious conflicts.

A positive politeness ethic also brings with it an impoliteness ethic that involves many *bald without redress* statements, leaving interactants with no option but loss of face. Both the instigator and receiver of the act of rudeness become prone to emotional anxiety for they are both thrown into a negative emotional state from which there is no easy escape. HC cultures use the polite or pointed understatement, in keeping with their negative politeness rituals. This allows interactants to leave the critical comment where it has fallen and continue with a revised interaction; at most, the pointed understatement brings a riposte that, although it may create feelings of resentment, keeps violence at bay. It would seem that the sharper and more verbally competent the commentary, the less chance of physical violence. *This moves one to suspect that the development of linguistic competence (including a rich bank of metaphorical sayings) significantly correlates with the limitation of physical violence.*

Both HC and LC cultures have their opportunity costs, as do individualistic and communal societies. This much we have learned from Durkheim's *Suicide* ([1897a] 1951), a thoughtful treatise on the 'social bond' and its ability to integrate as well as disintegrate human personality.

It would seem that overt and unapologetic individualism at the public and personal levels necessitates the use of *positive politeness rituals*; these rituals, because they require the demonstration of overt mutual interest in the identity of the other through early demonstrations of intimacy, increase the possibility of disappointing loss of face and the necessity for immediate redress or rebuttal. In brief, their informality has a liberating as well as constraining effect. The individual is liberated from having to manoeuvre through complex presentations of self according to etiquette hierarchies while being constrained by the anxiety that surely accompanies the wearing of a transparent 'social mask.' Thus, one cannot conclude that individualistic societies offer the individual more freedom than do interdependent ones. There is a paradoxical effect that acts as an equalizer.

Communal or HC cultures, on the other hand, tend to favour *negative politeness* public rituals that assure a certain space of privacy (and civility) between strangers and between people of different ranks. In such cultures the frontstage and backstage are clearly delineated, limiting contacts that might result in premature intimacy (and conflict). One can tell a lie in the frontstage in order to save face without being thought inherently dishonest. Thus, in both England and France, considerable room is left for sincerity at the private level even though artifice and ritual are necessary at the public level. Generally, we suspect that the rate of innocuous social lying may be higher in HC and MC cultures. Yet, while HC cultures offer plenty of opportunities for avoiding the mute and furious withdrawals or attacks to which LC cultures are prone, they present their own constraints on individual freedom. For one thing, the distancing that occurs as a result of the negative politeness styles of these cultures can create considerable social distancing, contributing to interpersonal cynicism and a generalized yet muted misanthropy. John Steinbeck once spoke of the 'warmth of a fight.' He understood well the emotional opportunity costs of extreme politeness and its resultant distancing.

To sum up our observations, consider the following examples:

The French teen says to her parent, 'But I am so miserable with this rule.' The parent answers with the same explanation given him during his or her own childhood, 'Misery strengthens the personality.'

The English teen says to her parent, 'This rule is just not right.' The parent answers without a pause, supported by centuries of English restraint, 'It may not sound right to you but it is necessary and that makes it right.'

The American teen says, 'This rule sucks big time. I am so not going to go along with this!' The parent glares, searching for words: the need to raise an autonomous and self-determined person capable of living up to the American ideals of innovation/leadership and to produce an individual with an active communal conscience short-circuit the parental authority, producing mute resentment. The more the parent struggles to win over the child's admiration and respect, the more the child remains uncertain whether he should trust the accumulated wisdom of his culture. While he shares with all youth in all countries the impulse to break away from the constraints of elders, he is unique in that his experience and understanding of the history of his culture are markedly undeveloped. Trendy speech is worshipped, but vocabulary is not; exaggerated inflection is welcomed as an emblem of character without the substance required to make such inflection conceptually and morally meaningful. A case that demonstrates this desperate desire for questionably acquired accolades occurred in Lakehead, Florida, in 2008. Six teenage girls, aided by two teenage boys, lured a classmate into one of their homes and then proceeded to beat her senseless while videotaping the attack. Using a minimum of three cameras, they videotaped the thirty-minute beating and posted it on YouTube. While the rage expressed in the video seemed to indicate that some score was being settled, what stunned the media and police was the fact that the teens videotaped the event with no fear of being recognized and prosecuted. The horrified reactions of media commentators and legal experts distracted Americans from an even more troubling fact: other teens with similar free-floating anger and sensation-bound personalities roam free in communities; while they commit no physical violence, they remain similarly unconscious of the reasons behind their exaggerated obsession with the cool, the hyper-real, the rumoured, the tough, the extreme.

Each of the three countries in this study has a lot to teach us. While none of the three can put forth an ideal civility ethos, we can learn from the opportunities and constraints of each nation's cultural ideology and civic interaction. The French have been socialized to hold authority with some measure of respect because they have remained aware that the survival of French culture in an increasingly anglicized world requires a delicate balance between deferring to tradition and asserting individuality. While this serves them well in the preservation of culture, it is beginning to hinder them in a connected world in which rapid low-context exchanges are increasingly becoming the norm. The English benefit from the simple politeness ethos that has served them well for two centuries. It minimizes violent conflict and allows for orderly management of their affairs. Yet, this simplicity is bound to emotional restraint and it is having its toll. It is a simplicity that contributes to loose social bonds and creates considerable political and economic stoicism (England remains the most expensive country in the world, yet there are no public revolts and massive protests, even though the same goods can be acquired for half the price across the Channel). The Americans, for their part, are perhaps at the forefront of the rights movement. While their civility ethic favours low-context interactions and contributes to considerable personal isolation, they are able (perhaps because of the foregoing isolation) to head out in new directions on short notice. The same fragmentation that contributes to isolation offers opportunities for reorganization in new forms. Repeatedly during my field research I observed important differences in the way people worked in these three countries; the Americans were much more at ease than the French or English to change direction in midstream. If there is a loss of heart in America it is due to the idealism of Americans and the belief that America was always meant to be a universal mission even during a time of fragmentation.

In brief, both tradition and innovation come with opportunity costs. The question facing social scientists of culture, as well as concerned citizens, is the same question that preoccupied thinkers of the Enlightenment and the Victorians: *How much change can a culture integrate without beginning to disintegrate into incoherence? How much can a culture remain loyal to tradition before sliding into artifice?*

## Some Thoughts on the Future of Civility

It is an accepted rule in the social sciences that a work on some aspect of society be as detached as possible. This is especially true in the North American mainstream press, where intellectual discussion of cutting-edge social issues by academics is rare. However, for a work on civility, a topic that is receiving considerable attention in North America and Europe, the avoidance of some normative discussion on the possibilities open to us would be bizarre if not pretentious.

In the preceding sections of this book, I attempted to keep some distance between myself and the topic of research. This was beneficial because it allowed me to see how an accepted truth could have an opposite and equally useful truth. Being based in North America, however, I have not been able to avoid the widespread concern across this continent regarding the future of its civil society. While that worry may not be wholly justified, and perhaps even aggravated by a sensation-bound media, it is not completely without foundation. With the passing of each decade those who remember the meaning of the original constitutional framework of their nation become fewer as one cohort is replaced with another. In a media-dominated society where the present is glorified and sensationalized, opportunities for the remembrance and appreciation of the past have become scarce. A cohort raised by an educational system that accords little importance to history arrives in adulthood well trained in technology but seriously deficient in the humanities of its culture. It is not unreasonable to fear that this tendency will at some point leave an entire population ignorant of its past and the lessons that can be extracted from it. Individuals will then be left with the erroneous impression that only their peers can offer them anything of value, that the past is dead and unworthy of their time. This certainly was not the ethos on which the original American republic was built, nor the English one, nor the French one. Each nation affirmed that it had a mission in the world, a mission that transcended the mere accumulation of capital. That mission required citizens to remain conversant with the accumulated myths of their culture. The heroic remained valued and did not elicit derisive laughter or alarmist withdrawal.

However, in a culture where the abuses committed by historical figures have moved into the limelight of national discourse, the risks of massive loss of heart have multiplied. Irony steps in to camouflage humiliated idealism. The individual then abdicates at the first difficult signpost for, deep inside, he remains convinced that he has little control and that any effort on his part to better the world will be useless. All that is left is spurious satisfactions. Bauerlein has noticed this in his critique of the colonizing influence of a powerful digital world:

> The Enhanced Connectivity, and the indulgence of teachers and journalists, feed yet another adolescent vice that technophiles never mention: peer absorption. Educators speak about the importance of role models and the career pressures facing kids, but, in truth, adolescents care a lot more about what other adolescents think than what their elders think. Their egos are fragile, their beliefs in transition, their values uncertain. They inhabit a rigorous world of consumerism and conformity ... For many of them, good standing with classmates is the only way to acquire a safe identity, so they spend hours on the channels of adolescent fare searching out the latest in clothes, slang, music, sports, celebrities, school gossip, and one another. Technology has made it fabulously easier. (2008:133)

Certainly, the economic crisis of 2008 and a presidential campaign replete with negative attacks gave Americans additional opportunities to experience this loss of heart. Perhaps the selection of Barack Obama as president, a man who has encouraged Americans to return to the more thoughtful and caring values of the original American social contract, may indicate some emerging durable national resolve to contest the corporatizing of the public and private spheres. Certainly, his victory was seen by many foreign countries as a possible new beginning for Americans. There are also indications of change on the popular front. Books calling for a return to moral realism and civility are becoming bestsellers. Uncharacteristically, the best of them are being written by academics who are reaching beyond their cloistered disciplines to address the general public.

Yet, willing change is no guarantee that change will occur. As important as the ability to conceptualize is the ability to execute and put concepts into practice. It is one thing to call for a reform of a lax educational system, yet quite another thing to draw up the specific action plans that detail how this clean-up is to take place with the cooperation of poorly paid teachers. Equally daunting is the task of reforming the sensation-addicted media, which place outrageous 'extreme' programming above the needs of children to grow up in a morally coherent world, or calling for parental participation in an economy where time-bound lifestyles have cut into parent–child relationships. A child who realizes that her educator or parent does not have time to take an argument to completion and reiterate the adult position with quiet strength and resolve has already found the most effective method for acquiring a social 'carte blanche': keep badgering till the other tires and gives in.

Come what may, all nations are facing a daunting question: Is there a way of maintaining a workable and sincere civility ethic within and across national boundaries, despite the fact that varying interests make universal agreements problematic? Can there be a manner of regarding the other that transcends partisan political interests, ethnic and religious divisions, and the vagaries of present fashion and trends? Can we accommodate the individual while strengthening the collective?

The question is not trivial. We live in an era when the well-meaning efforts of parents and educators have produced dangerous, unintended consequences. Their attempts to raise a generation free from excessive guilt have produced positive as well as negative effects. On the upside, we now live in a culture where the rights of the individual are respected and even celebrated. Tolerance is at an all-time high, a considerable accomplishment for an increasingly multicultural society. On the downside, however, we have produced a parental and educational system that is overly permissive, to the point of outright neglect.

Jean Twenge, a psychologist at San Diego State University, has written a well-documented warning about the predicament of a generation raised on an overdose of unjustified self-esteem. In *Generation Me – Why Today's Young Americans Are More Confident, Assertive, Entitled – And More Miserable Than Before* (2008) and *The Narcissism Epidemic* (Twenge and Campbell 2009) she shows how the self-esteem movement that started in the 1970s has produced a generation characterized by excessive entitlement and unjustified self-importance. She argues that a self-esteem that is not based on actual competence and achievement produces a self-focused vanity that is disconnected from reality. A by-product of such 'narcissism' is lack of empathy for others. Encouraged to believe that they can be anything they want to be, members of this generation have developed an unjustified and simple-minded optimism that leaves them sorely unprepared for the rigours of the real world: 'One downside to this generation is that they do not take criticism well. The self-esteem ethos in schools and parenting has valued protecting young people's positive feelings over all else. Some Gen Me'ers attended schools where teachers did not correct their mistakes, and others had parents who let them do whatever they wanted. They are used to feeling important' (2002:218).

Twenge believes that the net result of this historic change in socialization standards has been a dichotomy between the actual worth of an effort and an individual's assessment of it. The 'love yourself' imperative, reinforced by indiscriminating praise, has robbed youth of the opportunity to feel justified pride in connection to authentic achievements. Too many are now convinced that they will become rich and/or famous while remaining clueless about the efforts required to become so and the formidable odds against the attainment of such a high-minded goal.

Unable (and perhaps unwilling) to be responsive citizens of a society that values real and measurable achievements, many of these youth slip into intellectual complacency. Other writers who have sounded a similar alarm include Baumeister (2003), Hewitt (1998), Myers (1992), Lane (2000), Putnam (2000), Rains and Hunt (2000), Schneider and Stevenson (1999), and Stout (2000). On the upside, Don Tapscott (1995) has recognized that the new generation raised on the internet is capable of becoming interested in knowledge, self-discipline, and social change, provided the project is presented in ways that make use of the multiple media that have formed this generation. Books alone will not do it; nor will gadgety 'fun' projects that require no additional reflection at home.

P.M. Forni of the Johns Hopkins Civility Initiative believes that a social ethic hyper-energized by uncompromising individualism weakens civility. In *Choosing Civility* (2002) and *The Civility Solution – What To Do When People Are Rude* (2008) he observes that we may no longer have a choice but to return to the old notion that civility and responsible citizenship are mutually necessary: 'Although we can describe the civil as courteous, polite and well-mannered, etymology reminds us that they are also supposed to be good citizens and good neighbours' (2002:12). He cautions that 'individuality,' while it 'certainly generates innovation, progress and prosperity ... can also be a liability' (17). Subscribing to the classic definition of civility as the withholding of those behaviours that might be offensive or hurtful to others, he concludes that 'restraint-based civility makes a civilized life possible' (18). Both Forni and Twenge have made seminal contributions to the contemporary American civility movement. Hopefully, their work will additionally act as cautions to readers in other parts of the world. Each of them call for a reformation of a culture that has become colonized by a cult of unqualified individualism; they propose a social contract that recognizes the timeless worth of socialization and behavioural standards that promote self-control and respect for others.

My own research at the Civility Institute, which supports research in civility and civil society, has similarly indicated that narcissism is at the root of many acts of rudeness. In my own analysis, I find narcissism and self-esteem to be contradictory terms; a person is a narcissist not because he has an authentic self-esteem but because he lacks a self-worth based on true achievement and self-development. A false self cannot have authentic self-esteem: it can proclaim its importance, but its delusions will come tumbling down at the slightest challenge; hence the breathless, defensive discourtesy of people who suddenly find themselves in a situation of ego-threatening embarrassment or shame. By the same token, it is not just the lack of restraint that unleashes incivility, but also the corruptive influences that move in to fill the vacuum left by the absence of self-control; unaware that self-discipline is necessary for success in life, the hyper-individualist becomes vulnerable to any shyster who moves in with promises of easy fulfillment.

So, despite the discouraging evidence that emerges in composite portrayals of generations (boomers as starry-eyed idealists, Gen Xers as slackers, and Gen Me'ers as self-obsessed techno siblings – labels which do little justice to the wild variations in temperament within each generation), can we think of a civility ethic that accommodates and transcends our generational quirks? I call the possibility of such a civility ethos *eco-civility*. Unable to satisfy all competing groups, and aware that what works for individualistic and collectivistic societies may remain different for some time, we might do well to consider a transcultural and transnational civility that is not limited to mannerisms but founded on a respect for the other, a respect that is based on what we know of the social psychology of pride, self-esteem, embarrassment, and shame. One thing is required for the practice of this civility: it is the tempering of judgment. By this I do not mean the adoption of an amoral laissez-faire neutralism or a paralysing political correctness that ends in indifference. I mean, instead, the adoption of an appreciative view of the other as a citizen of a world in which the conception, implementation, and maintenance of ethical behaviour are recognized as a difficult and imperfect enterprise. Such recognition would certainly decrease the cynicism that is an unavoidable consequence of rapid and intense judgments of the imperfections of others. It would allow some neutral zone of perception where the other is seen as a participant in a universal project that has been ongoing for over a thousand years and will continue for some time to come: the project of establishing some equitable social system despite the fact that the need to toil and labour for survival lies at the root of much of our local and international conflicts. Such eco-civility would recognize that all individuals are at once victims of this difficult process as well as its admirable helmsmen. The 'other' would then not be dissimilar to the self; she or he would be a participant rather than an adversary.

Can such civility be conceptualized in a society that has made so much progress in the attainment of individual rights? Can it be practised without a regression into vertical authoritarianism or ethnocentrism? This was the subject of an email conversation I had with Wade MacLauchlan, president of the University of Prince Edward Island, who was awarded the Order of Canada in 2008 for his contributions to law and education. He offered the following eloquent response to the foregoing questions:

> *Civility.* Civility is a rich tapestry of interactions, values and agency – both individual and communal. The following comprise the most important threads in the tapestry. We weave it on a continuous basis, day-by-day and across the generations.
>
> *Humility.* Civility requires humility. This includes listening, inclusion, deference (not to authority, but in the broadest sense of respect for the contributions and roles of others) and active curiosity. Without a desire to learn and well established practices of learning, civility can only decline.
>
> *Grace.* Civility requires grace. This begins with appreciation and acknowledgment of others, and thankfulness for our privileges (i.e., not entitlements). It involves practices of thanking others, making room for others, and enjoying humour, culture and sociability together. Common memory is important, but we have to take care that a community's shared memory is continuously inclusive.
>
> *Ambition.* Civility requires a sense of standards, and never-ceasing achievement. Without a striving for excellence, and strong practices of respectful-but-rigorous critique, it is easy for civility to drift toward compromised standards and missed opportunities, if not corruption. Civility requires change, improvement, constant striving to be our best, and a sense of communal joy in achievement.

*Confidence.* Civility requires trust. There must be a sense of belonging and place, for individuals and groups within society and community. Societal rules must be respected, by all. Information and knowledge must be reliable, and debatable. We value privacy, discretion and the right to be left alone, not as recluses but as autonomous actors/groups whose choices will be respected. And confidence includes the possibility that someone might ask you home to supper, or love you.

*Participation.* Civility requires that we step out, step forward and take part. We cannot have social cohesion or effective community without volunteers, willing leaders, and a strong, shared sense of public service. This cannot be forced, in a sense that would undermine our autonomy, and it is only useful if it is willing. But it must be encouraged. Participation requires ever-better and more effective institutions and participatory practices. New means of communication should advance participation, rather than promote withdrawal. Participation includes an active and shared engagement through the arts, community organizations, heritage, environment and humour. (28 January 2008)

If a contemporary civility ethos is to integrate the accumulated wisdom of our civilizations with our more recent commitment to human rights, it will need to possess transcendental properties and face head-on the requirement to balance civility and self-affirmation with social justice/inclusion.

Such a possibility is discussed with remarkable eloquence in the work of Paul Woodruff, the University of Texas classicist. In a thought-provoking book entitled *Reverence: Renewing a Forgotten Virtue* (2001), Woodruff presents an erudite argument for the positive role that authentic *reverence* can play in the healing of uncivil society. What distinguishes Woodruff's proposition is that his conception of reverence is not connected to religious belief and is completely workable in secular circles. Reverence includes manners, but goes beyond them. It presupposes ethics and justice, but takes us into even more meaningful territory, past the interest politics and belief systems that so easily divide populations. Reverence is not an antidote to corrosive selfishness. Nor does it try to take away self-interest. Instead, it adds a quality of thought and feeling that contributes to our need for being whole and connected to one another. We are not asked to give up something; we are given the opportunity to acquire something that would be welcomed as a 'good' by our mental, emotional, and physical self.

Nor does reverence seek to revive hierarchical codes of submission. Rather, it provides us with a way of relating to others and the world we live in despite the contingencies and breaks we are experiencing. It asks us to restrain our cynicism, look for what is good in our cultures, and not turn away and abdicate because of institutions and practices that have disappointed our expectations.

This is all easier said than done. The inspiring words give us hope, but we have to turn to the many details that have to be put into place, the strengthening of education not being the least of them. Social scientists can set an example through their own approach to a revived sociology and social psychology of culture. By remembering that human culture has a mind, a body, and a heart, we come closer to developing explanations and practices that lead not to a disembodied and alienated view of the world, but to one that remains cognizant of the fact that humanity has never destroyed itself and, most probably, never will. Such a hopeful approach to the study of culture, regardless of which country it is practised in, will have to take serious account of human emotions in cultural context. It will also have to find the means to feel inspired, even when disheartening realities come to light.

To avail ourselves of such level-headed inspiration, we will have to cross many boundaries, intellectual and national, and take advantage of insights emerging from a variety of disciplines. These insights will increasingly show us that the person and the larger society are intimately connected in an interdependent matrix in which the words 'individualism' and 'collectivism' may soon become outdated by newly emerging human interaction processes.

Where are the gentlemen and gentlewomen of our new societies? They do not wear topcoats; they appear in casual clothes, some in flip-flops, some carrying cellphones which they answer at the wrong moments (much to the horror of manners experts). I met thousands of these people during my research and travels. Some of them were shy and retiring, others were unapologetically self-confident; but one quality they shared was their unwillingness to outsource their conscience and commitment to the long-range good of their country. Perhaps, that in the end, is the meaning of a contemporary and authentic civility.

# Bibliography

Abbott, Rev. Jacob. 1833. *The Mother at Home: Or the Principles of Maternal Duty, Familiarly Described*. New York: American Tract Society.
Abbott, S.C. John. 1833? *The Child at Home: or, The Principles of Filial Duty Familiarly Illustrated*. New York: American Tract Society.
– 1834. *Early Piety*. New York: John S. Taylor.
Abramson, J.Y., M.E.P. Seligman, and J.D. Teasdale. 1978. 'Learned Helplessness in Humans: Critique and Reformulation.' *Journal of Abnormal Psychology* 87: 49–74.
Acton, William. [1857] 1968. *Prostitution*. Introduction and notes by Peter Fryer. London: MacGibbon and Kee.
– 1857. *The Functions and Disorders of the Reproductive Organs in Youth, in Adult Age and in Advanced Life*. London: John Churchill.
Adams, Christine. 2000. *A Taste for Comfort and Status: A Bourgeois Family in Eighteenth-Century France*. University Park: Pennsylvania State University Press.
Addison, Joseph. 1961. 'The Pleasures of the Imagination.' In *Eighteenth-Century Critical Essays*, vol. 1, ed. Scott Elledge, 41–76. Ithaca, NY: Cornell University Press.
Adler, Alfred. 1956. *The Individual Psychology of Alfred Adler*. New York: Basic.
Alberti, Leon Battista. [c. 1460] 1969. *The Family in Renaissance Florence. I libri della famiglia*. Trans. Renée Neu Watkins. Columbia: University of South Carolina Press.
Alcott, William. 1840. *The Young Woman's Guide*. Boston.
– 1842. *The Young Wife*. Boston.
– 1844. *The Boy's Guide to Usefulness*. Boston: Waite, Pierce.
– 1846. *The Young Man's Guide*. Boston.
Aldridge, A.O. 1949. 'The Pleasures of Pity.' *A Journal of English Literary History* 16, 1: 76–87.

Allen, Lucy G. 1915. *Table Service*. Boston: Little, Brown.
Allen, Rick. 1998. *The Moving Pageant: A Literary Sourcebook on London Streetlife, 1700–1914*. London: Routledge.
Alstree, Richard. 1658. *The Whole Duty of Men*. London.
– 1660. *The Gentleman's Calling*. London.
Amato, P.R. 1994. 'Life-span Adjustment of Children to Their Parents' Divorce.' *The Future of Children* 4: 143–64.
American Tract Society. c. 1855. *Easy Lessons for the Little Ones at Home*. New York: American Tract Society.
Anderson, R.D. 1975. *Education in France, 1848–1870*. Oxford: Oxford University Press.
Andersson, Lynne M., and Christine M. Pearson. 1999. 'Tit for Tat? The Spiraling Effect of Incivility in the Workplace.' *Academy of Management Review* 24, 3: 452–71.
Anonyme. 1793. *Secrétaire des républicains, ou Nouveaux modèles de lettres sur différents sujets*. Barba.
Anonymous. c. 1735. *The Man of Manners*. London.
Anonymous. [1755] 2003. 'Moral Weeping.' In *Man: A Paper for Ennobling the Species*. London. http://www.engl.virginia.edu/%7Eenec981/dictionary/19anonV1.html (accessed 14 July 2003).
Anonymous. 1776. *A Father's Instructions to His Children*. London: J. Johnson.
Anonymous. 1811. *A Father's Bequest to His Son*. London: Chapple.
Anonymous. 1828. *Mentor, or Dialogues between a Parent and Children; on Some of the Duties, Amusements, Pursuits, and Relations of Life*. Lexington, KY: Thomas Smith.
Anonymous. 1830. *The Young Lady's Book: A Manual of Elegant Recreations, Exercises, and Pursuits*. Boston.
Anonymous. 1838. *Young Wife's Book: A Manual of Moral, Religious and Domestic Duties*. Philadelphia.
Anonymous. 1839. *Advice to a Young Gentleman oin Entering Society*. Philadelphia: Lea and Blanchard.
Anonymous. 1840. *Female Excellence or, Hints to Daughters*. London: The Religious Tract Society.
Anonymous. 1856. *How to Behave*. New York.
Anonymous. 1856. *Talking and Debating: or Fluency of Speech Attained without the Sacrifice of Elegance*. New York: Dick and Fitzgerald.
Anonymous. 1857. *Illustrated Manners Book and Manual of Good Behaviour and Polite Accomplishments*. New York.
Anonymous. 1859. *Talk and Talkers*. London.
Anonymous. 1863. 'A Young Lady's Soliloquy.' *Harper's Weekly*, 29 August 1863.

Anonymous. 1867. *General Usage in Modern Polite Society*. London.
Anonymous. 1871. *Modern Etiquette in Private and Public*. New York: F. Warne.
Anonymous. 1875. *The American Book of Genteel Behavior: A Complete Hand Book of Modern Etiquette for Ladies and Gentlemen. Embracing the Customs and Usages of Polite Society in All Places and at All Times. Being a perfect guide to all about to enter either public or private life, showing how to act under all circumstances with ease, elegance and freedom.*
Arditi, Jorge. 1998. *A Genealogy of Manners: Transformations of Social Relations in France and England from the Fourteenth to the Eighteenth Century*. Buffalo: State University of New York.
Arendt, Hannah. [1954] 1972. *Between Past and Future*. New York: Penguin.
– 1977. *Eichmann in Jerusalem: A Report of the Banality of Evil*. New York: Penguin.
Ariès, Philippe. 1962. *Centuries of Childhood: A Social History of Family Life*. Trans. Robert Baldick. New York: Alfred A. Knopf.
Aristotle. 1926. *Nicomachean Ethics*. Trans. H. Rackam. London: Heinemann.
Armstrong, Chris. 2006. 'Global Civil Society and the Question of Global Citizenship.' *International Journal of Voluntary and Nonprofit Organizations* 17, 4: 349–57.
Aronson, Nicole. 1978. *Mademoiselle de Scudéry*. Boston: Twayne.
Arthur, T.S. 1848. *Advice to Young Ladies on Their Duties and Conduct in Life*. Boston: Phillips and Sampson.
– 1850. *Advice to Young Men on Their Duties and Conduct in Life*. Sampson Phillips.
Artz, Frederick B. 1968. *The Enlightenment in France*. Oberlin, OH: Oberlin Press.
Asselin, Gilles, and Ruth Mastron. 2001. *Au Contraire! Figuring Out the French*. Yarmouth, ME: Intercultural Press.
Austen, Jane. [1811] 1965. *Sense and Sensibility*. New York: Airmont.
Babeau, Albert. 1886. *Les bourgeois d'autrefois*. Paris.
Badinter, Elizabeth. 1989. *The Unopposite Sex: The End of the Gender Battle*. Trans. Barbara Wright. New York: Harper and Row.
Bainton, Roland. 1952. *The Reformation of the Sixteenth Century*. Boston: Beacon Press.
Baldridge, Letitia. 1987. *Letitia Baldridge's Complete Guide to a Great Social Life*. New York: Rawson Associates.
Barbalet, Jack, ed. [1987] 2001. *Emotion, Social Theory and Social Structure: A Macrosociological Approach*. New York: Cambridge University Press.
– ed. 2002. *Emotions and Sociology*. Oxford: Blackwell.
Barfield, Owen. 1954. *History of English Words*. New edition. London: Faber and Faber.

Baron, Hans. [1955] 1966. *The Crisis of the Early Italian Renaissance*. 2 vols. Princeton, NJ: Princeton University Press.

Barret-Ducrocq, Françoise. 1991. *Love in the Time of Victoria: Sexuality, Class and Gender in Nineteenth Century London*. London: Verso.

Batson, C.D., et al. 1988. 'Five Studies Testing Two New Egoistic Alternatives to the Empathy-Altruism Hypothesis.' *Journal of Personality and Social Psychology* 55: 52–77.

Baudrillard, Jean. 1998. *America*. Trans. Chris Turner. London and New York: Verso.

Bauerlein, Mark. 2008. *The Dumbest Generation – How the Digital Age Stupefies Young Americans and Jeopardizes Our Future*. New York: Jeremy P. Tarcher/Penguin.

Bauman, Zygmunt. 1979. 'The Phenomenon of Norbert Elias.' *Sociology* 13, 1: 117–25.

Baumeister, Roy F., et al. 2003. 'Does High Self Esteem Cause Better Performance, Interpersonal Success, Happiness, or Healthier Lifestyles?' *Psychological Science in the Public Interest* 4: 1–44.

Baumeister, Roy F., and Sara R. Wotman. 1992. *Breaking Hearts – The Two Sides of Unrequited Love*. New York: Guilford Press.

Baumeister, R.F., A.M. Stillwell, and S.R. Wotman. 1994. 'Guilt: An Interpersonal Approach.' *Psychological Bulletin* 115: 243–67.

Baumol, William J., Alan S. Binder, and Edward N. Wolff. 2003. *Downsizing*. New York: Russell Sage.

Bautier, Robert-Henri. 1971. *The Economic Development of Medieval Europe*. London: Thames and Hudson.

Bautier, Robert-Henri, and Gillette Laboury, eds. and trans. 1965. *Helgaud de Fleury, Vie de Robert le Pieux; Epitoma vitae Regis Rotberti Pii*. Paris: Centre National de la Recherche Scientifique.

Baylor Religion Survey. 2006. *American Piety in the 21st Century*. Waco, TX: Baylor Institute for Studies of Religion. http://www.baylor.edu/isreligion/index.php?id=40634 (accessed 10 July 2007).

BBC. 2002. 'The Jubilee.' London: British Broadcasting Company, 2 June.

Bean, James. 1856. *Advice to a Married Couple*. Boston: American Tract Society.

Beckwith, Francis J., and Michael E. Bowman, eds. 1993. *Are You Politically Correct? Debating America's Cultural Standards*. Buffalo, NY: Prometheus.

Bell, Daniel. 1976. *The Cultural Contradiction of Capitalism*. London: Heinemann.

Bendelow, Gillian, and Simon J. Williams, eds. 1997. *Emotions in Social Life – Critical Themes and Contemporary Issues*. London: Taylor and Francis.

Benedict, Ruth. 1946. *The Chrysanthemum and the Sword*. New York: Houghton Mifflin.

Bennett, John. 1788. *Strictures on Female Education: Chiefly as It Relates to the Culture of the Heart, in Four Essays*. London: T. Cadell.
Benson, Thomas W. 1996. 'Rhetoric, Civility and Community: Political Debate on Computer Bulletin Boards.' *Communications Quarterly* 44, 3: 359–78.
Berghe, Pierre L. van den . 1963. 'Dialectic and Functionalism: Toward a Theoretical Synthesis.' *American Sociological Review* 28, 5: 695–705.
Bernays, Edward. 1936. *The Growth of a Sound Idea: Public Relations and the American Industry*. New York: Economic Forum.
Bernbaum, Ernest. 1962. 'The Romantic Movement.' In *Romanticism: Points of View*, ed. Robert F. Gleckner and Gerald E. Enscoe, 00–00. Englewood Cliffs, NJ: Prentice-Hall.
Bianculli, David. 1992. *Teleliteracy*. New York: Keystone.
Billacois, François. 1976. 'La crise de la noblesse européenne (1550–1650).' *Revue d'histoire moderne et contemporaine* 23: 258–77.
Bill of Rights. 1689. *English Bill of Rights*. Constitution Society. www.consitution.org/bor/eng_bor.htm (accessed 16 October 2997).
Billy, André. 1969. *L'Abbé Prévost, auteur de Manon Lescaut*. Paris: Flammarion.
Biskind, Peter. 1999. *Easy Riders, Raging Bulls: How the Sex-Drugs-and Rock 'N Roll Generation Saved Hollywood*. New York: Simon and Schuster.
Bitton, Davis. 1969. *The French Nobility in Crisis*. Stanford, CA: Stanford University Press.
Bland, Lucy. 1995. *Banishing the Beast: English Feminism and Sexual Morality, 1885–1914*. London: Penguin.
Blau, Peter M. 1964. *Exchange and Power in Social Life*. New York: Wiley.
Bloch, Marc Léopold. [1939–40] 1961. *Feudal Society*. 2 vols. Trans. L.A. Manyon. Chicago: University of Chicago Press.
Block, Marc. [1940] 1961. *Feudal Society*. Chicago: University of Chicago Press.
– 1974. 'The Rise of Dependent Cultivation and Seignorial Institutions.' In *Cambridge Economic History*, vol. 1. Cambridge: Cambridge University Press.
Bloom, Allan. 1987. *The Closing of the American Mind*. New York: Simon and Schuster.
Blumer, Herbert. 1969. *Symbolic Interactionism: Perspectives and Method*. Berkeley: University of California Press.
Blunin, Stuart M. 1989. *The Emergence of the Middle Class; Social Experience in the American City*. Cambridge: Cambridge University Press.
Bly, Robert. 1994. *The Sibling Society*. New York: Vintage.
Borsay, P. 2000. 'From Courtesy to Civility: Changing Codes of Conduct in Early Modern England.' *English Historical Review* 115, 464: 1302–3.
Bourdieu, Pierre. [1979] 1984. *Distinction: A Social Critique of the Judgement of Taste*. London: Routledge and Kegan Paul.

Boylan, Anne M. 1988. *Sunday School: The Formation of an American Institution, 1790–1880.* New Haven: Yale University Press.
Braddick, Michael J. 2001. *State Formation in Early Modern England, c. 1550–1700.* New York: Cambridge University Press.
Bradstreet, Anne. [c. 1660s] 1967. *The Works of Anne Bradstreet.* Ed. J. Hensley. Cambridge, MA: Cambridge University Press.
Bradshaw, John. 1988. *Healing the Shame That Binds You.* Florida: Health Communications.
Brath, Stanley. 1930. *The Drama of Europe.* London: Arthur H. Stockwell.
Brathwayt, Robert. 1630. *The English Gentleman.* London.
– 1631. *The English Gentlewoman.* London.
Bredvold, Louis I. 1962. *The Natural History of Sensibility.* Detroit: Wayne State University Press.
Brennan, Thomas E. 1988. *Public Drinking and Popular Culture in Eighteenth-Century Paris.* Princeton, NJ: Princeton University Press.
Breton, Philippe. 2002. 'Violence, Acts of Speaking and the Civilizational Process (Violence, prise de parole et processus de civilisation).' *Revues des Sciences Sociales de la France de l'Est* 29L: 24–31.
Bridges, W. 1994. *Job Shift: How to Prosper in a World without Jobs.* Reading, MA: Addison-Wesley.
Briggs, Asa. 1954. *Victorian People. Some Reassessments of People, Institutions, Ideas and Events, 1851–1867.* London: Odhams Press.
– 1987. *A Social History of England.* London: Penguin.
Brissenden, R.F. 1974. *Virtue in Distress: Studies in the Novels of Sentiment from Richards on to Sade.* New York: Harper and Row.
Brookhiser, Richard. 1996. *Founding Father: Rediscovering George Washington.* New York: Simon and Schuster.
Brown, Marshall. 1991. *Preromanticism.* Stanford: Stanford University Press.
Brown, P., and S. Levinson. [1983] 1987. *Politeness: Some Universals in Language Use.* Cambridge: Cambridge University Press.
Browning, J.D., ed. 1983. *Satire in the Eighteenth Century.* New York: Garland.
Brucker, Gene A. 1962. *Florentine Politics and Society, 1343–1378.* Princeton, NJ: Princeton University Press.
– 1969. *Renaissance Florence.* Princeton, NJ: Princeton University Press.
Bryson, Anna. 1998. *From Courtesy to Civility: Changing Codes of Conduct in Early Modern England.* New York: Oxford University Press.
Buber, Martin. 1958. *I-Thou.* New York: Scribner's.
Buck, R. 1984. *The Communication of Emotion.* New York: Guilford Press.
Bugliosi, Vincent, and Curt Gentry, contributor. 2001. *Helter Skelter: The True Story of the Manson Murders.* New York: W.W. Norton.

Bunyan, John. [1686] 1889. *A Book for Boys and Girls; or Country Rhymes for Children. Being a facsimile of the unique first edition, published in 1686, deposited in the British Museum*. With an introduction giving an account of the work, by John Brown. London: E. Stock.
Burckhardt, Jacob. [1860] 1944. *Civilization of the Renaissance in Italy*. London: Phaidon.
Burke, Edmund. [1796] 1991. 'First Letter on a Regicide Peace.' In *The Writings and Speeches of Edmund Burke*, vol. 9, ed. R.B. McDowell, 187–263. Oxford: Clarendon Press.
Burke, Kenneth. 1950. *A Rhetoric of Motives*. New York: Prentice-Hall.
Burke, Peter. 1986. *The Italian Renaissance: Culture and Society in Italy*. Cambridge: Polity Press.
– 1995. *The Fortunes of the Courtier – The European Reception of Castiglione's Cortegiano*. University Park: Pennsylvania State University Press.
Burnley, David. 1998. *Courtliness and Literature in Medieval England*. London: Longman.
Bushman, Brad, and Roy F. Baumeister. 1998. 'Threatened Egotism, Narcissism, Self–Esteem, and Direct and Displaced Aggression: Does Self-Love or Self-Hate Lead to Violence?' *Journal of Personality and Social Psychology* 75: 219–29.
Cady, Edwin Harrison. 1949. *The Gentleman in America*. Syracuse, NY: Syracuse University Press.
Caillères, François de. 1690. *Des mots à la mode*. Paris: Claude Barbin.
– 1693. *Du bon et du mauvais usage dans les manières de s'exprimer*. Paris: Claude Barbin.
Caldwell, Mark. 1999. *A Short History of Rudeness: Manners, Morals, and Misbehavior in Modern America*. New York: Picador.
Calhoun, Craig. 1993. 'New Social Movements of the Early Nineteenth Century.' *Social Science History* 17, 3 (Fall): 385–427.
Calvin, Jean. 2001. *Calvin's Institutes*. Abridged edition. Ed. Donald K. McKim. Louisville, KY: Westminster John Knox Press.
Campbell, Colin. [1987] 1993. *The Romantic Ethic and the Spirit of Modern Consumerism*. Oxford: Blackwell.
Capellanus, Andreas. [1201–10] 1941. *The Art of Courtly Love*. Trans. John J. Parry. New York: Frederick Ungar.
Carlyle, Thomas. [1797] 1837. *French Revolution*. London.
– 1843. *Past and Present*. Boston: Dana Estes.
Carroll, Raymonde. 1987. *Cultural Misunderstandings. The French-American Experience*. Chicago: University of Chicago Press.
Carr-Saunders, Alexander, and P.A. Wilson. 1933. *The Professions*. Oxford: Clarendon Press.

Carter, Stephen L. 1993. *The Culture of Disbelief. How American Law and Politics Trivialize Religious Devotion*. New York: Basic.
– 1996. *Integrity*. New York: Basic.
– 1998. *Civility: Manners, Morals and the Etiquette of Democracy*. New York: Basic.
Cassirer, Ernst. 1953. *The Platonic Renaissance in England*. Trans. James P. Pettegrove. New York: Thomas Nelson and Sons.
– 1955. *The Philosophy of the Enlightenment*. Trans. Fritz Koelln and James P. Pettegrove. Boston: Beacon Press.
Castiglione, Baldassare. [1529] 1974. *The Book of the Courtier (Il Cortegione)*. Trans. Sir Thomas Hoby. London: J.M. Dent and Sons.
CCH Human Resources Group. 2003. 'Results: 2002 CCH® Unscheduled Absence Survey.' http://hr.cch.com/Default.asp?subframe=/press/releases/101602a.asp.
Chadwick, Owen. 1975. *The Secularization of the European Mind in the Nineteenth Century*. Cambridge: Cambridge University Press.
Chapone, Hester. 1778. *Letters on the Improvement of the Mind*. London: J. Walter.
Charme, Stuart Zane. 1991. 'Sartre's Images of the Other and the Search for Authenticity.' *Human Studies* 14, 4: 251–64.
Chesterfield, Lord. [1774] 1969. *Letters*. London: Dent-Dutton.
Chevalier, Michel. [1839] 1983. *Society Manners and Politics in the United States*. Boston: Weeks, Jordan.
Chrétien de Troyes. [c. 1180–?] 1967. *Perceval. The Story of the Grail*. Trans. Nigel Bryant. Cambridge: D.S. Brewer.
Cicero. 1967. *De officiis (On Moral Obligation)*. Trans. John Higginbotham. London: Faber and Faber.
Clark, Priscilla P. 1973. *The Battle of the Bourgeois: The Novel in France, 1789–1848*. Montreal: Didier.
CNN. 2003. 'Ten Commandments Deadline Passes.' 22 August. http://edition.cnn.com/2003/LAW/08/21/ten.commandments/index.html (accessed 22 August 2003).
Cobbe, Frances. 1864. 'The Nineteenth Century.' *Fraser's Magazine*, 69.
Cohen, D., and R.E. Nisbett. 1994. 'Self-Protection and the Culture of Honor: Explaining Southern Violence.' *Personality and Social Psychology Bulletin* 20: 551–67.
Cohen, Dov, et al. 1999. 'When You Call Me That, Smile! How Norms for Politeness, Interaction Styles, and Aggression Work Together in Southern Culture.' *Social Psychology Quarterly* 62, 3: 257–75.
Collinson, Diane. 1987. *Fifty Major Philosophers*. London: Routledge.

Comfort, Alex. 1967. *The Anxiety Makers*. London: Nelson.
Comfort, Alex, Charles Raymond, and Christopher F. Foss. 1974. *The Joy of Sex: A Gourmet Guide to Love-Making*. Adelaide: Rigby-Quartet.
Constitution Society. 2003. 'The Ninth Amendement.' In *Constitution for the United States of America*. http://www.constitution.org/billofr_.htm. (accessed 2 July 2000).
Conwell, Joseph Alfred. 1896. *Manhood's Morning: or, 'Go It While You're Young.' A Book to Young Men between Fourteen and Twenty-Eight Years of Age*. Vineland, NJ: Hominis.
Cooley, Charles Horton. 1909. *Social Organization*. New York: Scribner's.
– 1922. *Human Nature and the Social Order*. New York: Scribner's.
Cooper, James Fennimore. [1826] 1986. *The Last of the Mohicans: A Narrative of 1757*. New York: Scribner's.
– 1838. *The American Democrat; or, Hints on the Social and Civic Relations of the United States of America*. Cooperstown, NY: H. and E. Phinney.
Cosmopolitan Magazine. 2003. *The Hot Issue*, August 2003.
Council of Economic Advisers. 2000. *The Teens and Their Parents in the 21st Century: An Examination of Trends in Teen Behavior and the Role of Parental Involvement*. http://www.clinton4.nara.gov/media/pdf/CEAreport.pdf (accessed 15 February 2002).
Courtin, Antoine de. 1671. *Nouveau traité de la civilité qui se pratique en France*. Paris: H. Josset.
Crane, R.S. 1934. 'Studies toward a Genealogy of the 'Man of Feeling.' *ELH* 1: 205–30.
Crenson, Matthew A., and Benjamin Ginsberg. 2002. *Downsizing Democracy: How America Sidelined Its Citizens and Privatized Its Public*. Baltimore: Johns Hopkins University.
Crossley, Nick. 2001. *The Social Body: Habit, Identity and Desire*. London: Sage.
Culpepper, Jonathan. 1996. 'Towards an Anatomy of Impoliteness.' *Journal of Pragmatics* 25, 3: 349–76.
Cummings, Briana. 2001. 'Silent Killer.' *Digitas*, Harvard University. http://www.digitas.harvard.edu/~perspy/issues/2001/feb/courtesy.html (accessed 27 February 2001).
Curtin, M. 1987. *Propriety and Position*. New York: Garland.
Cutt, Margaret. 1979. *Ministering Angels. A Study of Nineteenth Century Evangelical Writers for Children*. Wormley: The Five Owls Press.
Dale, Daphne (C.F. Beezeley). 1895. *Our Manners and Social Customs: A Practical Guide to Deportment, Easy Manners, and Social Etiquette*. Chicago.
Darwin, Charles. [1859] 1995. *On the Origin of Species*. New York: Classics of Science Library.

- 1871. *The Descent of Man, and Selection in Relation to Sex*. London: Murray.
Davetian, Benet. 1994. 'Out of the Fire and into the Melting Pot. In Defense of Canada's Multiculturalism Policies.' *Canadian Ethnic Studies Journal, Special Textbook Issue* 26, 3: 135–40.
- 1996. *The Seventh Circle*. Vancouver: Ronsdale Press.
- 1998. *Reconsidering the Sibling Society*. Unpublished manuscript. Montreal: Concordia University.
- 2001a. 'The Sociology of Civility.' Paper presented at the Second Annual Conference of The International Social Theory Consortium – 5 to 7 July 2001. Falmer, East Sussex: University of Sussex.
- 2001b. 'Moral Tensions between Western and Islamic Cultures: The Need for Additional Sociological Studies of Dissonance in the Wake of September 11.' *Sociological Research Online* 6, 3. http://www.socresonline.org.uk/6/3/.
- 2002. 'Moral Dilemmas of Inter-Ethnic and Inter-Civilization Dialogue.' Paper presented at The Impact of September 11th on Racism and Ethnic Relations ESRC Research Conference, University of Kent (UK), 15 April 2002.
- 2005. 'Towards an Emotionally Conscious Social Theory.' *Sociological Research Online* 10, 2 (June).
Davidoff, Leonore. 1973. *The Best Circles: Society Etiquette and the Season*. London: Croom Helm.
Davies, Wendy. 1988. *Small Worlds. The Village Community in Early Medieval Brittany*. London: Duckworth.
Davis, Ronald L., ed. 1972. *The Social and Cultural Life of the 1920s*. New York: Holt, Rinehart, and Winston.
Davis, R.H.C. and Marjorie Chibnall. 1998. *Guilliaume de Poitier. The Gesta Guillelmi of William of Poitiers, Gulielmus, Pictaviensis*. Oxford: Oxford University Press.
Defoe, Daniel. 1725. *Minor Single Works. Some Considerations upon Street Walkers. With a Proposal for Lessening the Present Number of Them*. London.
Delbanco, Andrew. 1995. *The Death of Satan*. New York: Farrar, Straus and Giroux.
Della Casa, Giovanni. [1530] 1958. *Il Galateo (Book of Manners)*. Trans. R.S. Pine-Coffin. Harmondsworth, Middlesex: Penguin.
De Medeiros, Marie-Thérèse. [1358] 1979. *Jacques et chroniqueurs: Une étude comparée de récits contemporains relatants la Jacquerie de 1358*. Paris: Honoré Champion.
Demers, Patricia, and R.G. Moyles, eds. 1982. *From Instruction to Delight: An Anthology of Children's Literature to 1850*. Toronto: Oxford University Press.
Denis, Jeanne-Pierre. 1981. *L'honnete homme et la critique du gout*. Lexington, KY: French Forum Publishers.

De Rosa, Peter. 1988. *The Vicars of Christ*. London: Corgi.
Derrida, Jacques. 1967a. *De la grammatologie*. Paris: Minuit.
- 1967b. *L'écriture et la différence*. Paris: Seuil.
- [1967c] 1989. *La voix et le phénomène*. Paris: Presses universitaires de France.
Dewey, John. 1910. 'Science as Subject Mind.' *Science* 36 (28 January).
- 1929. *The Quest for Certainty: A Study of the Relation of Knowledge and Action*. New York: Putnam.
- 1981–90. *The Collected Works of John Dewey*. Ed. Jo Ann Boydston. Carbondale, IL: Southern Illinois University Press.
Dichter, Ernest. [1960] 1985. *The Strategy of Desire*. New York: Garland.
Dostoevsky, Fyodor. [1862] 1955. *Summer Impressions*. Trans. Philiippe Julian. London: John Calder.
Douglas, Frederick. 1855. *My Bondage and My Freedom*. New York.
Du Bosc, Jacques. 1662. *L'honnête femme*. Paris: Jean Cochart.
Duby, Georges. 1981. *The Knight, the Lady and the Priest: The Making of Modern Marriage in Medieval France*. New York: Pantheon.
Duberstein, L.L., et al. 2000. *Teen Risk-Taking: A Statistical Portrait*. Washington, DC: The Urban Institute. http://www.urban.org/family/TeenRiskTaking.html. (accessed 25 June 2000).
Duchêne, Roger. 1988. *Mme de La Fayette, la romancière aux cents bras*. Paris: Fayard.
Durkheim, Émile. [1897a] 1951. *Suicide*. Trans. George Simpson. Ed. John A. Spaulding and George Simpson. Glencoe, IL: Free Press.
- [1897b] 1997. *The Division of Labor in Society*. New York: Free Press.
- 1953. *Sociology and Philosophy*. Trans. D.F. Pocock. London: Cohen and West.
Dyhouse, Carol. 1989. *Feminism and the Family in England, 1880–1939*. Oxford: Basil Blackwell.
Eddy, Daniel C. 1848. *Lectures to Young Ladies on Matters of Practical Importance*. Lowell, MA: B.C. Sergeant.
Edelmann, Robert J. 1987. *The Psychology of Embarrassment*. Chicester: Wiley.
Edgley, Charles, and Dennis Brissett. 2000. *A Nation of Meddlers*. Boulder, CO: Westview Press.
Edwards, Jonathan. [1754] 1957. *A Careful and Strict Enquiry into the modern prevailing notion of that Freedom of the Will which is supposed to be essential to Moral Agency, Vertue and Vice, Reward and Punishment, Praise and Blame*. New Haven: Yale University Press.
Eisenstadt, S.N. 1998a. 'Modernity and the Construction of Collective Identities.' *International Journal of Comparative Sociology* 39, 1: 138–58.
- 1998b. 'The Construction of Collective Identities: Some Analytical and Comparative Indications.' *European Journal of Social Theory* 1, 2: 229–54.

Ekman, P. 1972. 'Universals and Cultural Differences in Facial Expressions of Emotion,' *Science* 164: 85–88.
Ekman P., et al. 1987. 'Universals and Cultural Differences in the Judgments of Facial Expressions Of Emotion.' *Journal of Personality and Social Psychology* 53: 712–17.
Eley, Geoff, and Ronald Grigor Suny, eds. 1996. *Becoming National: A Reader*. New York and Oxford: Oxford University Press.
Elias Norbert. [1939] 1978. *The Civilizing Process*, vol. 1: *The History of Manners*. Trans. Edmund Jephcott. Oxford: Basil Blackwell.
– [1939] 1982. *The Civilizing Process*, vol. 2: *State Formation and Civilization*. Trans. Edmund Jephcott. Oxford: Basil Blackwell.
– [1969] 1983. *Court Society*. Trans. Edmund Jephcott. Oxford: Basil Blackwell.
– [1970] 1978. *What Is Sociology?* London: Hutchinson.
– 1991. *A Society of Individuals*. Oxford: Basil Blackwell.
– 1992. *Time: An Essay*. Oxford: Basil Blackwell.
Elias, Norbert, and John L. Scotson. 1965. *The Established and the Outsiders*. London: Frank Cass.
Elias, Norbert, and Eric Dunning. 1986. *Quest for Excitement: Sport and Leisure in the Civilizing Process*. Oxford: Basil Blackwell.
Eliot, T.S. [1922] 1971. *The Waste Land*. New York: Faber.
Ellis, F. 1991. *Sentimental Comedy: Theory and Practice*. Cambridge: Cambridge University Press.
Ellis, Havelock. 1919–28. *Studies in the Psychology of Sex*. Philadelphia: F.A. Davis.
Ellsworth, P.C. 1994. 'Sense, Culture and Sensibility.' In *Emotion and Culture: Empirical Studies of Mutual Influence*, ed. S. Kitayama and H. R. Markus, 23–50. Washington, DC: American Psychological Association.
Elyot, Thomas. 1531. *The Boke Named the Governour*. London.
Emerson, Ralph Waldo. 1909–14. *Journals of Ralph Waldo Emerson*. 10 volumes. Ed. Edward W. Emerson and W.E. Forbes. Boston: Houghton Mifflin Company. Cambridge: Riverside Press.
– 1940. *The Complete Essays and Other Writings of Ralph Waldo Emerson*. Ed. Brooks Atkinson. New York: Modern Library.
Engels, Friedrich. [1892] 1952. *The Conditions of the Working Class in England*. Trans. Florence Kelley Wischnewetzky. London: G. Allen and Unwin.
Erasmus, Disederius. [1530] 1558. *De civilitate morum puerilium. A lytle booke of good maners for chyldren*. Trans. R. Whittington. London: J. Wallye.
– 1965. *The Colloquies*. Trans. C.R. Thompson. Chicago: University of Chicago Press.

Étienne de Fougères. [c. 1350] 1877. *Le livre des manières.* Paris: E. Thorin; Angers, E. Barassé.
Everett, Suzanne. 1985. *London, The Glamour Years.* New York: Bison.
Families Worldwide. 2001. 'The Numbers of Divorce.' http://www.fww.org/famnews/09182000c.htm (accessed 6 July 2001).
Farber, David R., and Eric Foner, eds. 1994. *The Age of Great Dreams. America in the 1960s.* New York: Hill and Wang.
Faret, Nicolas. [1630] 1970. *L'honnête homme ou l'art de plaire à la cour.* Geneva: Slatkine Reprints.
Ferriss, A.L. 2002. 'Studying and Measuring Civility: A Framework, Trends, and Scale.' *Sociological Inquiry* 72, 3: 376–92.
Filmer, Paul. 1999. 'Embodiment and Civility in Early Modernity: Aspects of Relations between Dance, the Body and Sociocultural Change.' *Body and Society* 5, 1: 1–16.
– 2001. 'Embodying Citizenship: Corporeality and Civility in Early Modernity.' *European Review of History* 7, 1: 109–21.
Finlay, Christopher J. 2004. 'Hume's Theory of Civil Society.' *European Journal of Political Theory* 3, 4: 369–91.
Flori, Jean. 2001. *La guerre sainte: La formation de l'idée de croisade dans l'Occident chrétien.* Paris: Aubier.
Ford, Ford Madox. 1907. *The Spirit of the People.* London: Alston Rivers.
Forni, P.M. 2002. *Choosing Civility.* New York: St Martin's Press.
– 2008. *The Civility Solution. What to Do When People Are Rude.* New York: St Martin's Press.
Fosca, François. 1935. *Histoire des cafés de Paris.* Paris: Firmin-Didot.
Foucault, Michel. [1966] 1970. *The Order of Things (Les mots et les choses).* New York: Pantheon.
– 1979. *Discipline and Punish: The Birth of the Modern Prison.* Trans. Alan Sheridan. New York: Vintage.
Fox-Genovese, Elizabeth, and Eugene D. Genovese. 2005. *The Mind of the Master Class: History and Faith in the Southern Slaveholders' Worldview.* Cambridge: Cambridge University Press.
Frank, A. 1991. 'For a Sociology of the Body: An Analytical Review.' In *The Body: Social Process and Cultural Theory,* ed. M. Featherstone, M. Hepworth, and B. Turner, 36–102. London: Sage.
Franklin, Benjamin. [1746] 1750. *Reflections on Courtship and Marriage.* London: Charles Corbet.
– 1950. *The Autobiography of Benjamin Franklin and Selections from His Other Writings.* Ed. Henry Steele Commager. New York: Newsweek.

Freeling, Arthur. 1849. *The Young Bride's Book*. New York.
Freud, Sigmund. 1930. *Civilization and Its Discontents*. Trans. Jean Rivière. New York: J. Cape and H. Smith.
Freund, P.E.S. 1982. *The Civilized Body – Social Domination, Control and Health*. Philadelphia: Temple University Press.
– 1989. 'Bringing Society Back into the Body –Understanding Socialized Human Nature.' *Theory and Society* 17, 6: 839–64.
– 1990. 'The Expressive Body – A Common Ground for the Sociology of Emotions and Health and Illness.' *Sociology of Health and Illness* 12, 4: 452–77.
Friday, Nancy. [1977] 1984. *My Mother, My Self: The Daughter's Search for Identity*. London: Harper-Collins.
Fridja, N.H. 1987. 'Emotion, Cognitive Structure, and Action Tendency.' *Cognition and Emotion* 1: 115–43.
Fridja, N.H., et al. 1989. 'Relations among Emotion, Appraisal, and Emotional Action Readiness.' *Journal of Personality and Social Psychology* 57: 212–28.
Friedan, Betty. 1965. *The Feminine Mystique*. London: Gollancz.
Frost, Ginger. 1995. *Promises Broken: Courtship, Class and Gender in Victorian England*. Charlottesville: University Press of Virginia.
Furet, François. 1988. *Revolutionary France, 1770–1880*. Oxford: Blackwell.
Gabriel, Y. 1993. 'Organizational Nostalgia-Reflections on the "Golden Age."' In *Emotion in Organizations*, ed. S. Fineman, 118–41. London: Sage.
Gaiffe, Félix. 1910. *Étude sur le drame en France au 18e siècle*. Paris.
Gailhard, Jean. 1678. *The Compleat Gentleman*. London.
Gage, John. 1968. *Life in Italy. At the Time of the Medici*. London: B.T. Batsford.
Galbraith, J.K. [1958] 1985. *The Affluent Society*. London: Deutsch.
Garrioch, David. 1996. *The Formation of the Parisian Bourgeoisie, 1690–1830*. Cambridge, MA: Harvard University Press.
Gaskell, Elizabeth. [1857] 1909. *The Life of Charlotte Bronte*. London and New York: Everyman's Library.
Gatrell, V.A.C. 1994. *The Hanging Tree: Execution and the English People 1770–1868*. Oxford: Oxford University Press.
Gaudefroy-Demombynes, J. 1966. 'The Inner Movement in Romanticism.' In *The Romantic Movement*, ed. Anthony Thorlby, 138–42. London: Longmans.
Geoffrey of Monmouth. [1138] 1973. *History of the Kings of Britain*. Baltimore: Penguin.
George, Carol V.R. 1993. *God's Salesman: Norman Vincent Peale and the Power of Positive Thinking*. New York: Oxford University Press.
Gerhards, Jurgen. 1986. 'Georg Simmel's Contribution to a Theory of Emotions.' *Social Science Information* 25, 4: 901–924.

Gerlet. 1793. *Pensées républicaines pour tous les jours de l'année, à l'usage, surtout, des enfants*. Le Petit.
Giddens, Anthony. 1984. *Constitution and Society*. Cambridge: Polity Press.
– 1985. *A Contemporary Critique of Historical Materialism*. Vol. 1. London: Macmillan.
– 1990. *The Consequences of Modernity*. Stanford, CA: Stanford University Press.
– [1998] 2000. *The Third Way*. Cambridge: Polity Press.
– [1991] 2001. *Modernity and Self-Identity*. Cambridge: Polity Press.
Gill, A.A. 2004. *The Angry Island*. London: Weidenfeld and Nicolson.
Gillis, A.R. 1989. 'Crime and State Surveillance in Nineteenth-Century France.' *American Journal of Sociology* 95, 2: 307–341.
– 1996. 'Initial and Subsequent Effects of Policing on Crime.' In *Criminological Controversies: A Methodological Primer*, ed. J. Hagan, A.R. Gillis, and D. Brownfield, 75–97. Boulder, CO: Westview.
– 2004. 'Institutional Dynamics and Dangerous Classes: Reading, Writing and Arrest in Nineteenth-Century France.' *Social Forces* 82, 4: 1202–1331.
Gilmour, Ian. 1993. *Riots, Risings and Revolution: Governance in Eighteenth-Century England*. London: Pimlico.
Ginsberg, Allen. [1956] 2001. *Howl*. Sacramento, CA: 24th Street Irregular Press.
Gisborne, Revd. Thomas. 1794. *An Enquiry into the Duties of Men in the Higher and Middle Classes*. London: Band J. White and Cadell and Daies.
– 1797. *An Enquiry into the Duties of Men*. London: Band J. White and Cadell and Daies.
Global Strategy Group. 2000. *Talking with Teens: The YMCA Parent and Teen Survey Final Report*. New York: Global Strategy Group. http:www.ymca.net/presrm/research/teensurvey.htm (accessed 3 November 2000).
Godkin, E.L. 1896. *Problems of American Democracy*. New York: C. Scribner's and Sons.
Godwin, William. [1793] 1946. *An Enquiry Concerning Political Justice*. 3 vols. Ed. F.E.L. Priestley. Toronto: University of Toronto Press.
Goffman, E. 1959. *The Presentation of Self in Everyday Life*. Harmondsworth: Penguin.
– 1961. *Encounters*. New York: Bobbs-Merrill.
– 1963. *Stigma*. Englewood Cliffs, NJ: Prentice-Hall.
– 1967. *Interactional Ritual*. Chicago: Aldine.
– 1974. *Frame Analysis*. New York: Harper.
– 1983. 'The Interaction Order.' *American Sociological Review* 48: 1–17.

Golding, Martin. 1980. 'The Significance of Rights Language.' *Philosophical Topics* 18: 53–64.
Golding, William. 1954. *Lord of the Flies*. London: Faber.
Goldman, Kevin. 1997. *Conflicting Account*. New York: Touchstone.
Goldsmith, Elizabeth C. 1988. *Exclusive Conversations – The Art of Interaction in Seventeenth-Century France*. Philadelphia: University of Pennsylvania Press.
Goodman, Paul S., Robert S. Atkin and Associates. 1984. *Absenteeism*. San Francisco: Jossey-Bass.
Goody, Jack. 1989. *The Logic of Writing and the Organization of Society*. Cambridge: Cambridge University Press.
Googins, B. 1990. 'Breaking the Hold on Corporate Denial.' *HR Magazine*, 103–4.
Gorer, Geoffrey. 1948. *The American People: A Study in National Character*. New York: W.W. Norton.
Gouldner, A.W. [1954] 1981. 'Succession and the Problem of Bureaucracy.' In *The Sociology of Organizations: Basic Studies*, ed. O. Grusky and G. A. Miller, 280–302. New York: The Free Press.
Graña, César. 1967. *Modernity and Its Discontents: French Society and the French Man of Letters in the Nineteenth Century*. New York: Harper.
Graves, A.J. 1844. *Girlhood and Womanhood: or, Sketches of My Schoolmates*. Boston: T.H. Carter.
Greco, Juliette. 2001. 'Inconspicuous Anomalies: Alexithymia and Ethical Relations to the Self.' *Health* 5, 4: 471–92.
Greenblatt, Stephen. 1983. 'Murdering Peasants: Status, Genre and the Representation of Rebellion.' *Representations* 1: 1–29.
Greer, Germaine. [1970] 2001. *The Female Eunuch*. New York: Farrar, Straus and Giroux.
Grenaille, Françoise de. 1639. *L'honnête fille*. Paris: Jean Paslé.
– 1640. *L'honnête veuve*. Paris: Jean Paslé.
Grice, H.P. 1975. 'Logic and Conversation.' In *Syntax and Semantics*, ed. P. Cole and J. Morgan, 41–58. London: Academic Press.
Groethuysen, Bernard. 1927. *Origines de l'esprit bourgeois en France*. Paris.
Guicciardini, Francesco. [1528–30] [1857] 1965. *Maxims and Reflections of a Renaissance Statesman (Ricordi)*. Trans. Mario Domandi. Introduction by Nicolai Rubinstein. New York: Harper and Row.
Guilhamet, Leon. 1974. *The Sincere Ideal: Studies in Eighteenth-Century English Literature*. Montreal: McGill-Queen's University Press.
Gurowski, Adam D.G. [1856] 1972. *America and Europe*. Freeport, NY: Books for Libraries Press.

Habermas, Jurgen. 1987. *The Theory of Communicative Action*. Trans. Thomas McCarthy. Boston: Beacon Press.
- [1987] 1989. *The Philosophical Discourse of Modernity*. Trans. Frederick Lawrence. Cambridge, MA: MIT Press.
- 1990. *Moral Consciousness and Communicative Action*. Cambridge, MA: MIT Press.
- 1994. 'Struggles for Recognition in the Democratic Constitutional States.' In *Multiculturalism*, ed. Amy Guttman, 107–48. Princeton, NJ: Princeton University Press.

Haddock, Rev. Charles B. 18??. *Christian Education: Containing Valuable Practical Suggestions in the Training of Children for Usefulness and Heaven*. New York: American Tract Society.

Haine, W. Scott. 1996. *The World of the Paris Cafe: Sociability among the French Working Class, 1789–1914*. Baltimore: Johns Hopkins University Press.

Hall, Edward T. 1976. *Beyond Culture*. Garden City, NY: Anchor Press/Doubleday.
- 1983. *The Dance of Life*. Garden City, NY: AnchorPress/Doubleday.

Hall, Edward T., and Mildred Reed Hall. 1990. *Understanding Cultural Differences*. Yarmouth, ME: Intercultural Press.

Hall, Lesley. 1991. *Hidden Anxieties: Male Sexuality, 1900–1950*. Oxford: Polity.

Hall, Peter Dobkin. 1982. *The Organization of American Culture, 1700–1900: Private Institutions, Elites, and the Origins of America*. New York: New York University Press.

Hammerton, James A. 1992. *Cruelty and Companionship: Conflict in Nineteenth Century Married Life*. London: Routledge.

Harré, R. 1986. *The Social Construction of Emotions*. Oxford: Basil Blackwell.
- 1991. *Physical Being: A Theory for a Corporeal Psychology*. Oxford: Basil Blackwell.

Harte, Bret. [1869] 1984. *The Outcasts of Poker Flat*. Oakland, CA: Star Robert House.

Hatch, Nathan O. 1989. *The Democratization of American Christianity*. New Haven: Yale University Press.

Hawthorne, Nathaniel. [1850] 1923. *The Scarlet Letter*. New York: J.H. Sears.

Hay, Denys. 1961. *The Italian Renaissance in Its Historical Background*. The Wiles Lectures given at Queen's University, Belfast. London: Cambridge University Press.

Head, Thomas, and Richard Landes, eds. 1992. *The Peace of God: Social Violence and Religious Response in France around the Year 1000*. Ithaca, NY: Cornell University Press.

Healy, Jane M. 1990. *Endangered Minds*. New York: Simon and Schuster.
Hefner, Robert W., ed. 1998a. *Democratic Civility: The History and Cross-Cultural Possibility of a Modern Political Ideal*. New Brunswick, NJ: Transaction.
– 1998b. 'Civil Society: Cultural Possibility of a Modern Ideal.' *Society* 35, 3: 16–27.
Heimert, Alan, and Andrew Delbanco, eds. 1985. *The Puritans in America: A Narrative Anthology*. Cambridge, MA: Harvard University Press.
Heine, S.J., and D.R. Lehman. 1997. 'Culture, Dissonance, and Self-Affirmation.' *Personality and Social Psychology Bulletin* 23: 389–400.
Hemphill, C. Dallet. 1996. 'Middle Class Rising in Revolutionary America.' *Journal of Social History* 30, 2: 317–44.
Hentoff, N. 1992. *Free Speech for Me – But Nor for Thee: How the American Left and Right Relentlessly Censor Each Other*. New York: Harper Collins.
Herrick, C.J. 1926. *Brains in Rats and Men. A Survey of the Origin and Biological Significance of the Cerebral Cortex*. Chicago: University of Chicago Press.
Hewitt, John. 1998. *The Myth of Self-Esteem*. New York: St Martin's Press.
Hilgard, E.R. 1973. 'Pain Reduction in Hypnosis.' *Psychological Review* 80, 5 (September): 396–410.
Hill, Richard. 1994. *Euromanagers and Martians: The Business Cultures of Europe's Trading Nations*. Brussels: Europublications.
Hilles, F., and H. Bloom, eds. 1965. *Sensibility to Romanticism*. New York: Oxford University Press.
Hincmar of Reims. [c. 806–82] 1885. *De ordine palatii, Hincmar, Archbishop of Reims*. Trans. Maurice Prou. Paris: F. Vieweg, Librairie-Éditeur.
History Channel. 2003. *The Sexual Century*. New York: History Television Channel.
Hobbes, Thomas. [1651] 1951. *Leviathan*. Harmondsworth: Penguin.
Hochschild, Arlie H. 1975. 'The Sociology of Feeling and Emotion: Selected Possibilities.' *Sociological Inquiry* 45, 2–3: 280–307.
– 1979. 'Emotion Work, Feeling Rules, and Social Structure.' *American Journal of Sociology* 85: 551–75.
– 1983. *The Managed Heart: Commercialization of Human Feeling*. Berkeley: University of California Press.
– [1989] 1997. *The Second Shift*. New York: Avon.
– 1997. 'Work: The Great Escape.' *New York Times Magazine*, 20 April, 51–5, 81, 84.
Hoffman, David, producer. 1991. 'Making Sense of the Sixties.' Video. 6 vols. Washington: WETA Washington Productions, distributed by PBS.
Hofstadter, Richard. 1963. *Anti-Intellectualism in American Life*. New York: Vintage.

Hofstede, Geert. 1980. *Culture's Consequences: International Differences in Work-Related Values*. Beverly Hills, CA: Sage.
- 1983. 'Dimensions of National Cultures in Fifty Countries and Three Regions.' In *Expiscations in Cross-cultural Psychology*, ed. J. Deregowski, S. Dzuirawiec, and R. Annis, 335–55. Lisse, Netherlands: Swetz and Zweitlinger.
- 2001. *Culture's Consequences*. New York: Sage.

Holmes, Janet. 2000. 'Politeness, Power and Provocation: How Humour Functions in the Workplace.' *Discourse Studies* 2, 2: 159–85.

Holmes, Oliver Wendell. 1891–5. *The Writings of Oliver Wendell Holmes*. 11 vols. Boston and New York: Houghton Mifflin.

Homans, George C. 1958. 'Human Behaviour as Exchange.' *American Journal of Sociology* 63, 6: 597–606.
- 1961. *Social Behaviour: Its Elementary Forms*. London: Routledge and Kegan Paul.

Hopfl, H., and S. Linstead. 1993. 'Passion and Performance: Suffering and the Carrying of Organizational Roles.' In *Emotion in Organizations*, ed. S. Fineman, 76–93. London: Sage.

Hornbeak, Katherine. 1934. 'The Complete Letter-Writer in English, 1568–1800. *Smith College Studies in Modern Languages* 15: 1–150.

Horne, A.D., ed. 1981. *The Wounded Generation*. Englewood Cliffs, NJ: Prentice-Hall.

Houghton, Walter E. 1957. *The Victorian Frame of Mind, 1830–1870*. New Haven, CT: Yale University Press.

Howard, Philip K. 2002. *The Collapse of the Common Good: How America's Lawsuit Culture Undermines Our Freedom*. New York: Ballantine.

Howes, David. 2004. *Sensory Relations: Engaging the Senses in Culture and Social Theory*. Ann Arbor: University of Michigan Press.

Huizinga, Johan. [1924] 1972. *The Waning of the Middle Ages*. Harmondsworth: Penguin.

Hulme, T. E. 1962. 'Romanticism and Classicism.' In *Romanticism: Points of View*, ed. Robert F. Gleckner and Gerald E. Enscoe, 55–65. Englewood Cliffs, NJ: Prentice-Hall.

Hume, David. [1739] 1949. *A Treatise on Human Nature*. Oxford: Clarendon Press.

Hunt, Peter, ed. 2000. *Children's Literature 1801–1902: An Anthology*. Oxford: Blackwell.

Huppart, George. 1977. *Les Bourgeois Gentilhommes: An Essay on the Definition of Elites in Renaissance France*. Chicago: University of Chicago Press.

Huxley, Thomas Henry. [1868] 1893. *The Physical Basis of Life*. London: Macmillan.

Hyam, Ronald. 1990. *Empire and Sexuality*. Manchester: Manchester University Press.

Ignatieff, Michael. 1978. *A Just Measure of Pain: The Penitentiary in the Industrial Revolution, 1750–1850*. New York: Pantheon.

Ingelhart, Ronald, Miguel Basanez, and Alejandro Moreno. 1998. *Human Values and Beliefs: A Cross-Cultural Sourcebook*. Ann Arbor, MI: University of Michigan Press.

Inglehart, Ronald, and Wayne Baker. 2000. 'Modernization, Cultural Change and the Persistence of Traditional Values.' *American Sociological Review* 65: 19–51.

Ishiguro, Kazuo. [1989] 1996. *The Remains of the Day*. London: Faber.

Isserman, Maurice, and Michael Kazin. 2000. *America Divided: The Civil War of the 1960s*. New York: Oxford University Press.

ITV. 2002. 'The Story of the Queen.' ITV (UK), 3 June.

Jackson, Margaret. 1994. *The Real Facts of Life: Feminism and the Politics of Sexuality c. 1850–1940*. London: Taylor and Francis.

Jackson, Steve. 1993. 'Even Sociologists Fall in Love: An Exploration of the Sociology of Emotions.' *Sociology* 27, 2: 201–17.

Jacquert, Louis. 1912. *L'alcool*. Paris: Masson.

Jaegar, C. Stephen. 1965. *The Origins of Courtliness. Civilizing Trends and the Formation of Courtly Ideals, 939–1210*. Philadelphia: University of Pennsylvania Press.

James, Henry. [1877] 1970. *The American*. London: Macmillan.

– [1879] 1995. *Daisy Miller*. New York: Dover Publications.

James, William. 1890. *The Principles of Psychology: The Works of William James*. 2 vols. New York: Holt, Rinehart, and Winston.

– [1897] 1977. *The Will to Believe and Other Essays in Popular Philosophy*. Cambridge, MA: Harvard University Press.

– 1909. *The Meaning of Truth: A Sequel to 'Pragmatism.'* New York: Longmans.

Janeway, James. [1672] 1822. *A Token for Children*. New Haven: J. Babcock and Son.

Janov, Arthur. 1970. *The Primal Scream*. New York: Dell.

– 2000. *The Biology of Love*. New York: Prometheus.

Janov, Arthur, and Michael Holden. 1975. *Primal Man*. New York: Thomas Y. Crowell.

Jarvie, I.C. 1970. *Towards a Sociology of the Cinema*. London: Routledge.

Jefferson, Thomas. 1904–5. *The Writings of Thomas Jefferson*. 20 vols. Monticello Edition. Ed. Albert Elroy Bergh. Washington, DC: Thomas Jefferson Memorial Association of the United States.

Jeffreys, Sheila. 1985. *The Spinster and Her Enemies: Feminism and Sexuality, 1880–1930*. London: Pandora Press.
Johnson, Paul. 1997. *The History of the American People*. London: Phoenix Press.
Johnson, Paul N. 1992. 'Politically Correct.' *Conservative Review* 2, 2: 23–6.
Johnson, Wendell Stacey. 1979. *Living in Sin: The Victorian Sexual Revolution*. Chicago: Nelson Hall.
Jones, Chris. 1993. *Radical Sensibility: Literature and Ideas in the 1790's*. London: Routledge.
Jones, E.E. 1964. *Ingratiation*. New York: Appleton-Century-Crofts.
Jones, Ronald E. 2002. 'The Collapse of Civility in Russia: The Young and Aged in a Failed Society.' *Sociological Inquiry* 72, 3: 409–25.
Jones, Sir William. [1772] 1961 'On the Arts Commonly Called Imitative.' In *Eighteenth-Century Critical Essays*, vol. 2, ed. Scott Elledge, 872–81. Ithaca, NY: Cornell University Press.
Josephson, Matthew. c. 1935. *The Robber Barons: The Great American Capitalists, 1861–1901*. New York: Harcourt Brace.
Kaplan, Justin. 1974. *Mark Twain and His World*. New York: Simon and Schuster.
Kasey, J.W. 1858. *The Young Man's Guide to True Greatness*. Big Spring, KY: J.W. Kasey.
Kasson, John F. 1991. *Rudeness and Civility: Manners in Nineteenth-Century Urban America*. New York: Farrar, Straus and Giroux.
Kaufman, Gershon. 1989. *The Psychology of Shame*. New York: Springer.
Kaufman, Gershon, and Lev Raphael. 1984. 'Shame as Taboo in American Culture.' In *Forbidden Fruits: Taboos and Tabooism in Culture*, ed. Ray Browne, 57–64. Bowling Green: Bowling Green University Press.
Kay, S. [c. 1180] 1992. *Raoul de Cambrai*. Ed. and trans. S. Kay. Oxford: Clarendon Press.
Kelso, Ruth. [1929] 1964. *The Doctrine of the English Gentleman*. Gloucester, MA: P. Smith.
Keltner, Dacher, and B.N. Buswell. 1997. 'Embarrassment: Its Distinct Form and Appeasement Functions.' *Psychological Bulletin* 122: 250–70.
Kemper, Theodore D. 1978. 'Toward a Sociology of Emotions: Some Problems and Some Solutions.' *American Sociologist* 13, 1: 30–41.
Kesey, Ken. [1962] 1973. *One Flew Over the Cuckoo's Nest*. London: Picador.
Kiernan, Victor G. 1988. *The Duel in European History: Honour and the Reign of Aristocracy*. Oxford: Oxford University Press.
Kingsley, Charles. 1877. *Charles Kingsley: His Letters and Memoirs of His Life in Two Volumes*. Ed. Fanny Kingsley. London: Henry S. King.

Kingwell, Mark. 1993. 'Politics and the Polite Society in the Scottish Enlightenment.' *Historical Reflections* 19, 3: 363–87.
– 1995. *A Civil Tongue: Justice, Dialogue, and the Politics of Pluralism.* University Park: Pennsylvania State University Press.
Kitayama, S., H.R. Markus, and H. Matsumoto. 1995. 'Culture, Self, and Emotion: A Cultural Perspective on "Self-Conscious" Emotions.' In *Self-Conscious Emotions*, ed. June Price Tangney and Kurt W. Fischer, 439–64. New York: Guilford Press.
Kleiner, Brian. 1996. 'Class Ethos Politeness.' *Journal of Language and Social Psychology* 15, 2: 155–75.
Klinkowitz, Jerome. 1980. *The American 1960s: Imaginative Acts in a Decade of Change.* Ames: Iowa State University Press.
Knowles, Caroline. 1996. *Family Boundaries. The Invention of Normalcy and Dangerousness.* Peterborough, ON: Broadview Press.
Knox, Reverend V. 1781. *Liberal Education.* London: C. Dilly.
Kramer, Hilton. 1999. 'The Second Cold War: This One Is Internal. Culture Is the Battleground.' *Wall Street Journal*, 2 April, W13.
Lacroix, Paul. 1963. *France in the Middle Ages.* New York: Frederick Ungar.
Lafree, Gary. 1996. 'The Effect of Changes in Intraracial Income Inequality and Educational Attainment on Changes in Arrest Rates for African Americans and Whites, 1957–1990.' *American Sociological Review* 61, 4: 614–34.
– 1998a. *Losing Legitimacy: Street Crime and the Decline of Social Institutions in America.* Boulder, CO: Westview Press.
– 1998b. 'Social Institutions and the Crime Bust of the 1990's.' *Journal of Criminal Law and Criminology* 88, 4: 1325–68.
– 2006. 'Democracy and Crime: A Multilevel Analysis of Homicide Trends in Forty-Four Countries, 1950–2000.' *The Annals of the American Academy of Political and Social Sciences* 605, 1: 25–49.
Laing, R.D. 1967. *The Politics of Experience and the Bird of Paradise.* New York: Ballantine.
– 1976. *Do You Really Really Love Me?* New York: Penguin.
Lamont, Michèle. 1992. *Money, Morals, Manners – The Culture of the French and the American Upper Middle Class.* Chicago: University of Chicago Press.
Lane, Christopher. 2003. *Hatred and Civility. The Antisocial Life in Victorian England.* New York and Chichester: Columbia University Press.
Lane, Robert E. 2000. *The Loss of Happiness in Market Economies.* New Haven: Yale University Press.
La Rochefoucauld, François, duc de. [1665] 1967. *Maximes.* Ed. J. Truchat. Paris: Grenier.

La Salle, J.B. [1729] 1788. *Les règles de la bienséance et de la civilité chrétienne.* Vannes: Enfans Gannes.

Lasch, Christopher. 1980. *The Culture of Narcissism: American Life in an Age of Diminishing Expectations.* New York: Warner.

Lasch-Quinn, Elisabeth. 1999. 'How to Behave Sensitively: Prescriptions for Interracial Conduct from the 1960's to 1990's.' *Journal of Social History* 333, 2: 409–27.

Laver, J. 1969. *Modesty in Dress.* Boston: Houghton Mifflin.

Lawrence, Margot. 1986. 'Tudor English Today.' *English Today* (October).

Lazarus, R.S. 1991. *Emotion and adaptation.* New York: Oxford University Press.

LeGoff, J. [1964] 1988. *Medieval Civilization.* Trans. Julia Barrow. Cambridge: Blackwell.

Leech, John. 1886. *Pictures of Life and Character.* 3 vols. London: Bradbury, Agnew.

Lees, Andrew, and Lynn Hollen Lees, eds. 1976. *The Urbanization of European Society in the Nineteenth Century.* Lexington, MA: D.C. Heath.

Lévi, Anthony. 2002. *Renaissance and Reformation: The Intellectual Genesis.* New Haven: Yale University Press.

Levi, Margaret. 1997. *Consent, Dissent, and Patriotism.* Cambridge: Cambridge University Press.

Lewis, Helen Block. [1971] 1974. *Shame and Guilt in Neurosis.* New York: International Universities Press.

– 1977. *Psychic War in Men and Women.* New York: New York University Press.

Lillywhite, Bryant. 1963. *London Coffee Houses.* London: G. Allen and Unwin.

Lincoln, Abraham. [1865] 1953. 'The Second Inaugural Address.' In *The Collected Works of Abraham Lincoln*, vol. 8, ed. Roy P. Basler, 332–3. New Brunswick, NJ: Rutgers University Press.

Linderman, Gerald F. 1987. *Embattled Courage: The Experience of Combat in the American Civil War.* New York: Free Press.

Linklater, Andrew. 2007. 'Torture and Civilization.' *International Relations* 21, 1: 111–18.

Little, Lester K. 1993. *Benedictine Maledictions: Liturgical Cursing in Romanesque France.* Ithaca: Cornell University Press.

Locke, John. [1689] 1983. *A Letter Concerning Toleration.* Ed. J. Tully. Indianapolis: Hackett.

– [1690] 1979. *An Essay Concerning Human Understanding.* Ed. P.H. Nidditch. Oxford: Oxford University Press.

– [1693] 1989. *How to Bring Up Your Children, Being Some Thoughts Concerning*

*Education.* Ed. John W. and Jean S. Yolton. London: Oxford University Press.
Longley, Marjorie, Louis Silverstein, and Samuel A. Tower. 1960. *America's Taste, 1851–1959.* New York: Simon and Schuster.
Lopes, João Teixeira. 2005. 'Reflections on Symbolic Violence and the Cultural Arbitrary: The New Etiquette Guides in the Cultural Field.' *Sociologica – Problemas e Practicas* 49 (September-December): 43–51.
Lorenzo, Dus N. 2001. 'Compliment Responses among British and Spanish University Students: A Contrastive Study.' *Journal of Pragmatics* 33, 1: 107–27.
Lougee, Caroline. 1976. *Les paradis des femmes: Women, Salons and Social Stratification in Seventeenth-Century France.* Princeton: Princeton University Press.
Lowe, Donald M. 1982. *History of Bourgeois Perception.* Chicago: University of Chicago Press.
Lowen, Alexander. 1967. *The Betrayal of the Body.* London: Colliers.
Lucas, Henry S. [1934] 1960. *The Renaissance and the Reformation.* New York: Harper Brothers.
Luchaire, A. 1902. *La société française au temps de Philippe-Auguste (French Society in the Time of Philippe-Auguste).* Paris.
Lull, Ramon. [c. 1300] 1902. *Libre del orde de cavalleria: Text original y antiga versió francesca (The Book of the Order of Chivalry).* Ciutat de Mallorca: Comissió Editora Lulliana.
Lupset, Thomas. 1529. *Exhortation to Yonge Men.* London.
Lyell, Charles. 1840. *The Principles of Geology.* London: J. Murray.
Lystad, Mary. 1980. *From Dr. Mather to Dr. Seuss: 200 Years of American Books for Children.* Boston: G.K. Hall.
Machiavelli, Niccolò. [1531] 1940. *The Prince.* Trans. Luigi Ricci. New York: Modern Library.
Mackaman, Douglas, and Michael Mays. 2000. *World War I and the Cultures of Modernity.* Jackson: University Press of Mississippi.
Mackarnass, Mrs Henry S. 1856? *Etiquette for Little Folks.* G.W. Cottrell.
Mackenzie, Henry. [1771] 1967. *The Man of Feeling.* E. Brian Vickers. Oxford: Oxford University Press.
– [1785] 2003. Untitled Article. *The Lounger* 20 (18 June 1785). http://www.english.upenn.edu/~mgamer/Etexts/mackenzie.html (accessed 14 July 2003).
MacLean, Ian. 1977. *Woman Triumphant: Feminism in French Literature, 1610–1652.* Oxford: Clarendon Press.
Magendie, Maurice. [1925] 1970. *La politesse mondaine et les théories de l'honnêteté, en France au XVIIe siècle, de 1600 à 1660.* Genève: Slatkine Reprints.

Magid, Ken, and Carole A. McKelvery. 1988. *High-Risk: Children without a Conscience*. New York: Bantam.
Mahood, Linda. 1990. *The Magdalenes: Prostitution in the Nineteenth Century*. London: Routledge.
Maintenon, Françoise. 1772. *Life and Letters of Madame de Maintenon*. London: Davis.
Maitland, I. 2002. 'The Human Face of Self-Interest.' *Journal of Business Ethics* 38, 1–2: 3–17.
Mandeville, Bernard de. [1715] 1962. *The Fable of the Bees*. New York: Capricorn.
Mankin R. 1998. 'Literature and Courtesy. The Invention of the l'Honnette Homme, 1580–1750.' *Modern Language Notes* 113, 5: 1206–8.
Manning, Brian. [1976] 1991. *The English People and the English Revolution*. London: Bookmarks.
Manson, Bonita J. 2000. *Downsizing Issues: The Impact on Employee Morale and Productivity*. New York: Garland.
Marcus, Maria Renata. 2002. 'Decent Society and/or Civil Society?' *Social Research* 68, 4: 1011–1130.
Marcus, Stephen. 1966. *The Other Victorians: A Study of Sexuality and Pornography in Mid-Nineteenth Century England*. New York: Basic.
Marcuse, Herbert. 1964. *One-Dimensional Man*. London: Routledge.
Marcuse, Herbert, R.P. Wolff, and B. Moore. 1969. *A Critique of Repressive Tolerance*. London: Cape.
Markoff, John. 1986. 'Literacy and Revolt: Some Empirical Notes on 1789 in France.' *American Journal of Sociology* 92: 323–49.
Markus, H.R., and S. Kitayama. 1991. 'Culture and the Self: Implications for Cognition, Emotion, and Motivation.' *Psychological Review* 98: 224–53.
Martineau, Harriet. 1837. *Society in America*. New York: Saunders and Oatley.
Martines, Lauro. 1963. *The Social World of the Florentine Humanists*. Princeton, NJ: Princeton University Press.
Marty, Martin E. 1998. *The One and the Many: America's Struggle for the Common Good*. Cambridge: Harvard University Press.
Marwick, Arthur. 1998. *The Sixties: Cultural Revolution in Britain, France, Italy and the United States*. Oxford: Oxford University Press.
Maslow, Abraham P. 1962. *Towards a Psychology of Being*. Princeton, NJ: Van Nostrand.
– 1975. *The Farther Reaches of Human Nature*. New York: Viking.
Mason, John E. [1935] 1971. *Gentlefolk in the Making*. New York: Octagon.
Mason, Michael. 1994. *The Making of Victorian Sexuality*. Oxford: Oxford University Press.

Mather, Cotton. 1690. *Addresses to Old Men, and Young Men and Little Children in Three Discourses.* Boston: R. Pierce.
– 1692. *Ornaments for the Daughters of Zion. Or the Character and Happiness of a Vertuous Woman: In a Discourse Which Directs the Female Sex How to Express, the Fear of God, in Every Age and State of Their Life; and Obtain both Temporal and Eternal Blessedness.* Cambridge: S. and B. Green for Samuel Phillips, Boston.
– 1699. *A Family Well-Ordered, or an Essay to Render Parents and Children Happy in One Another.* Boston.
Maynard, John. 1993. *Victorian Discourses on Sexuality and Religion.* Cambridge: Cambridge University Press.
Mazzeo, Joseph Anthony. 1965. *Renaissance and Revolution. The Remaking of Renaissance Italy.* London: Secker and Warburg.
McCormack, Thelma. 1992. 'Politically Correct.' *Society–Societé* 16, 2: 17–20.
McElroy, Anne. 2002. 'Opinion,' *The Independent*, 3 April, 3.
McIntosh, Carey. [1963] 1986. *Common and Courtly Language. The Stylistics of Social Class in 18th-Century English Literature.* Philadelphia: University of Pennsylvania Press.
McKendrick, John Brewer, and J.H. Plumb. 1979. *The Birth of Consumer Society: The Commercialization of Eighteenth Century England.* London: Europa Publications.
McPherson, James M. 1988. *Battle, Cry of Freedom: The Civil War Era.* New York: Oxford University Press.
Mead, George Herbert. 1934. *Mind, Self, and Society.* Chicago: University of Chicago Press.
Mead, Margaret. [1928] 1961. *Coming of Age in Samoa.* New York: Morrow Quill.
Melville, Herman. 1967. *Moby Dick: An Authoritative Text, Reviews and Letters by Melville, Analogues and Sources.* Ed. H. Hayford and H. Parker. New York: Norton.
Melville, Lewis. 1908. *Beaux of the Regency.* 2 vols. London: Hutchinson.
– 1926. *Regency Ladies.* London: Hutchinson.
Melzack, R., and T.H. Scott. 1957. 'The Effects of Early Experiences on the Response of Pain.' *Journal of Comparative Physiological Psychology* 50: 155–61.
Melzack. R., and P. Wall. 1965. 'Pain Mechanisms: A New Theory.' *Science* 150: 971–9.
Mennell, Stephen. 1974. *Sociological Theory. Uses and Unities.* New York: Praeger.
– 1989. *Norbert Elias – Civilization and the Human Self-Image.* Oxford: Basil Blackwell.

Méré, Antoine Gombauld, Chevalier de. [1668] 1930. *Oeuvres complètes*. Ed. Charles-H. Boudhors. Paris: Les Belles Lettres.
Meserole, Harrison T., ed. 1968. *American Poetry of the Seventeenth Century*. New York: Norton.
Meyer, Michael J. 2000. 'Liberal Civility and the Civility of Etiquette: Public Ideals and Personal Lives.' *Social Theory and Practice* 26, 1: 69–84.
Milburn, Michael, and Sheree D. Conrad. 1996. *The Politics of Denial*. Cambridge, MA: MIT Press.
Mill, John Stuart. [1831] 1942. *The Spirit of the Age*. Ed. F.A. von Hayek. Chicago.
- 1833. 'Comparisons of the Tendencies of French and English Intellect.' *Monthly Repository*, new series, 7.
- [1865] 1961. *Auguste Comte and Positivism*. Ann Arbor: University of Michigan Press.
Mill, John Stuart, and Harriette Taylor. [1869] 1912. 'The Subjection of Women.' Reprinted in *On Liberty, Representative Government, The Subjection of Women*. London: World's Classics.
Miller, Arthur. [1948] 1998. *Death of a Salesman*. Philadelphia: Chelsea House.
Miller, Henry. 1949. *The Time of the Assassins: A Study of Rimbaud*. New York: New Directions.
Miller, Perry, and Thomas Johnson. 1938. *The Puritans*. New York: American Book Company.
Miller, William Ian. 1993. *Humiliation and Other Essays on Honor, Social Discomfort and Violence*. Ithaca, NY: Cornell University Press.
Miller, J.R. 1893. *Young Men: Faults and Ideals*. New York: Thomas Y. Crowell.
Mills, C. Wright. 1951. *White Collar*. New York: Oxford University Press.
- 1956. *The Power Elite*. New York: Oxford University Press.
- 1959. *The Sociological Imagination*. New York: Oxford University Press.
Mingaux, G.E. 1976. *The Gentry*. London: Longmans.
Mitscherlich, Alexander. 1969. *Society without the Father*. Trans. Eric Mosbacher. London: Tavistock.
Mitchell, Margaret. 1936. *Gone With the Wind*. New York: Macmillan.
Moers, Ellen. 1960. *The Dandy: Brummell to Beerbohnn*. London: Secker and Warburg.
Montessori, Maria. 1971. *The Child in the Family*. New York: Dell.
Moore, A.J. 1969. *The Young Adult Generation*. New York: Abingdon Press.
More, Hannah. [1778] 1853. *Works*, vol. 6. London: Henry G. Bohn.
- 1788. *Thoughts on the Importance of the Manners of the Great to General Society*. London: T. Cadell.
- 1813. *Christian Morals*. London: T. Cadell and W. Davies.

Morford, J. 2001. 'Civility, Culture and Critical Thinking: An Interdisciplinary Approach to French Civilization.' *Contemporary French Civilization* 25, 1: 121–38.
Morgan, Edmund. 1966. *The Puritan Family*. New York: Harper and Row.
Morgan, Marjorie. 1994. *Manners, Morals and Class in England, 1774–1858*. New York: St Martin's Press.
Morrison, Andrew. 1989. *Shame: The Underside of Narcissism*. Hillsdale, NJ: Analytic Press.
Moscucci, Ornella. 1990. *The Science of Woman: Gynaecology and Gender in England, 1800–1929*. Cambridge: Cambridge University Press.
Moser, Gabriel, and Denis Corroyer. 2001. 'Politeness in the Urban Environment: Is City Life Synonymous with Civility?' *Environment and Behaviour* 33, 5 (September): 611–25.
Muldrew, Craig. 1993. 'Interpreting the Market: The Ethics of Credit and Community Relations in Early Modern England.' *Social History* 18: 163–83.
– 1998. *The Economy of Obligation*. London: Macmillan.
– 2001. '"Hard Food for Midas": Cash and Its Social Value in Early Modern England.' *Past and Present* 170: 78–120.
Mullan, John. 1988. *Sentiment and Sociability: The Language of Feeling in the Eighteenth Century*. Oxford: Clarendon Press.
Murphy, Robert F. 1971. *The Dialectics of Social Life. Alarms and Excursions in Anthropological Theory*. New York.
Murray, Venetia. 1998. *High Society: A Social History of the Regency Period, 1788–1830*. London: Viking.
Mursy, Ahmad-Aly, and John Wilson. 2001. 'Towards a Definition of Egyptian Complimenting.' *Multilingua* 20, 2: 133–54.
Myers, David. 1992. *The Pursuit of Happiness*. New York: Morrow.
Myers, David G. 2000. *The American Paradox: Spiritual Hunger in an Age of Plenty*. New Haven, CT: Yale University Press.
– [1994] 2004. *Exploring Social Psychology*. New York: McGraw-Hill.
Nadeau, Jean-Benoît, and Julie Barlow. 2003. *Sixty Million Frenchmen Can't Be Wrong*. Napierville, IL: Sourcebooks.
Nederman, Cary, J. 1995. *Policraticus: Of the Frivolities of Courtiers and the Footprints of Philosophers. John of Salisbury, Bishop of Chartres*. Cambridge: Cambridge University Press.
Newcomb, Harvey. 1849. *Anecdotes for Girls. Entertaining Narratives and Anecdotes, Illustrative of Principles and Character*. Boston: Gould, Kendall and Lincoln.
– 1860. *Anecdotes for Boys. Entertaining Narratives and Anecdotes, Illustrative of Principles and Character*. Boston: Gould, Kendall and Lincoln.

Newhauser, Richard. 1997. *The Early History of Greed. The Sin of Avarice in Early Medieval Thought and Literature.* Cambridge: Cambridge University Press.

Newton, Sarah E. 1994. *Learning to Behave: A Guide to American Conduct Books before 1900.* Westport, CT: Greenwood Press.

Newton, Tim. 1998. 'The Sociogenesis of Emotion: A Historical Sociology?' In *Emotions in Social Life: Critical Themes and Contemporary Issues*, ed. Simon J. Williams and Gillian Bendelow. London: Routledge.

Nicholls, Jonathan. 1985. *The Matter of Courtesy.* Woodbridg, Suffolk: D.S. Brewer.

Nietzsche, Friedrich. [1883] 1969. *Thus Spoke Zarathustra.* Trans. R. Hollingdale. Harmondsworth: Penguin.

– [1886] 1966. *Beyond Good and Evil.* Trans. Walter Kaufmann. New York: Penguin.

Nord, David. 1984. 'The Evangelic Origins of Mass Media in America, 1815–1835.' *Journalism Monographs* 88: 1–30.

Oakes, James. 1998. *The Ruling Race.* London: W.W. Norton.

O'Beirne, Kate. 2006. *Women Who Make the World Worse, and How Their Radical Feminist Assault Is Ruining Our Schools, Families, Military, and Sports.* New York: Penguin.

Oldenburg, Ray, and Dennis Brissett. 1994. 'The Urban Staging of Incivility.' *Research in Community Sociology* 4, supplement: 145–64.

O'Neill, William L. 1971. *Coming Apart: An Informal History of America in the 1960s.* Chicago: Quadrangle.

Osborne, Thomas J. 1997. 'Civility on Trial: Welfare in the Western World.' *Humanist* 57, 1: 6–8.

Otter, C. 2002. 'Making Liberalism Durable: Vision and Civility in the Late Victorian City.' *Social History* 27, 1: 1–15.

Ouellette, Laurie. 1999. 'Viewing as Good Citizenship? Political Rationality, Enlightened Democracy and PBS.' *Cultural Studies* 13, 1: 62–90.

Packard, Vance. 1957. *The Hidden Persuaders.* London: Longmans.

– 1959. *The Status Seekers.* London: McKay.

Pagden, Anthony. 1988. 'The "Defence of Civilization" in Eighteenth-Century Social Theory.' *History of the Human Sciences* 1, 1: 33–45.

Paine, Thomas. [1776] 1976. *Common Sense.* Ed. I. Kramnick. New York: Penguin.

– [1792] 1969. *The Rights of Man.* Ed. H. Collins. London: Penguin.

Palmerston, Lady. 1807. *La belle assemblée.* London: J. Bell.

Palmieri, Matteo. [1528] 1944. *Della vita civile.* Ed. F. Battaglia. Bologna.

Parliament of England. 1689. *Bill of Rights.* www.constitution.org/eng/veng_bor.htm (accessed 3 July 2000).

Parsons, Talcott. 1937. *The Structure of Social Action*. New York: The Free Press.
– 1968. *Sociological Theory and Modern Society*. New York: The Free Press.
Parthasarathy, D. 2001. 'The Civility of Indifference: On Domesticating Ethnicity.' *Contributions to Indian Sociology* 35, 1: 104–6.
Pasquier, Nicolas. 1611. *Le gentilhomme*. Paris: Jean Petit-Pas.
Paxman, Jeremy. 1998. *The English: A Portrait of a People*. London: Penguin.
Peacham, Henry. 1627. *The Compleat Gentleman*. London.
– 1642. *Art of Living in London*. London.
Peale, Norman Vincent. 1952. *The Power of Positive Thinking*. New York: Prentice-Hall.
Pearce, Joseph Chilton. 1992. *Evolution's End: Claiming the Potential of Our Intelligence*. San Francisco: Harper San Fransisco.
Peck, Dennis, L. 2002. 'Civility: A Contemporary Context for a Meaningful Historical Concept.' *Sociological Inquiry* 72, 3: 376–92.
Pellegrin, N. 1989. *Les vêtements de la liberté*. Aix-en-Provence: Alinea.
Penfield, Wilder, and L. Roberts. 1959. *Speech and Brain Mechanisms*. Princeton, NJ: Princeton University Press.
Perls, Frederick P. [1959] 1980. *Gestalt Therapy Verbatim*. New York: Bantam.
Pew Organization. 2006. 'Many Americans Uneasy with Mix of Religion and Politics.' http://pewforum.org'docs/index.php?DocID=153 (accessed 10 August 2007).
Picard, Roger. 1943. *Les salons littéraires et la société française (1610–1789)*. New York: Brentano's.
Pierce, Charles S. [1869] 1931–60. 'On the Grounds and Validity of the Laws of Logic.' In *Collected Papers of Charles Saunders Pierce*, vol. 5, ed. Charles Hartshorne, Paul Weiss, and Arthur W. Burks, 416–34. Cambridge, MA: Harvard University Press.
Platt, Polly. 1994. *French or Foe?* London: Culture Crossing.
Poe, Edgar Allen. [1875] 1946. *The Complete Poems and Stories of Edgar Allan Poe, with Selections from His Critical Writings*. Introduction and explanatory notes by Arthur Hobson Quinn; texts established, with bibliographical notes, by Edward H. O'Neill. New York: A.A. Knopf.
Pogrebin, Letty Cottin. 1981. *Growing Up Free*. New York: Bantam.
Pomerantz, A. 1978. 'Compliment Responses: Notes on the Cooperation of Multiple Constraints.' In *Studies in the Organization of Conversational Interaction*, ed. J. Schenken, 79–112. London: Academic Press.
Porter, Ray, and Lesley Hall. 1995. *The Facts of Life: The Creation of Sexual Knowledge in Britain, 1650–1950*. New Haven, CT: Yale University Press.
Portoghesi, P. 1972. *Rome of the Renaissance*. London: Phaidon.
Post, Emily. 1922. *Etiquette in Society, in Business, in Politics and at Home, Illus-*

trated with Private Photographs and Facsimilies of Social Forms. New York: Funk and Wagnalls.
Postman, Neil. 1985. *Amusing Ourselves to Death*. New York: Sifton.
Poulet, Emile. 1988. *Liberté, laïcité: La guerre de deux France et le principe de la modernité*. Paris: Éditions du Cerf.
Preminger, Alex, ed. 1974. *Princeton Encyclopedia of Poetry and Poetics*. Princeton, NJ: Princeton University Press.
Price, Roger. 1986. *A Social History of Nineteenth-Century France*. London: Century Hutchinson.
Priestley, J.B. 1969. *The Prince of Pleasure and His Regency, 1811–1820*. London: Heinemann.
Proust, Marcel. [1949] 1985. *Pleasures and Regrets (Les Plaisirs et les Jours)*. Trans. Louise Varese. New York: The Ecco Press.
– [1954] 1983. *Remembrance of Things Past*. Ed. C.K. Scott Moncrieff and Terence Kilmartin. New York: Penguin Classics.
Public Agenda Organization. 2002. *Aggravating Circumstances: A Status Report on Rudeness in America*. Funded by the Pew Charitable Trust. New York. http://www.publicagenda.org/ specials/civility/civility.htm (accessed 2 November 2002).
Putnam, Robert D. 2000. *Bowling Alone: The Collapse and Revival of American Community*. New York: Simon and Schuster.
Rabelais, François. [1532] 1939. *Oeuvres complètes*. Paris: Gallimard.
Raines, Claire, and Jim Hunt. 2000. *X'ers and the Boomers*. Menlo Park, CA: Crisp.
Ralph, Philip Lee. 1973. *The Renaissance in Perspective*. London: G. Bell and Sons.
Rambuteau, C.-P.B., Comte de. 1905. *Mémoires du Comte de Rambuteau*. Paris.
Rand, Ayn. 1945. *The Fountainhead*. New York: New American Library.
– 1957. *Atlas Shrugged*. New York: Random House.
Randolph, Sarah N. [1871] 1939. *Domestic Life of Thomas Jefferson*. Cambridge, MA: Harvard University Press.
Ranum, Orest. 1980. 'Courtesy, Absolutism and the Rise of the French State, 1630–1660.' *Journal of Modern History* 52: 426–51.
Reader, W.J. 1966. *Professional Men*. London: Weidenfeld and Nicolson.
Reaves, Jessica. 2002. 'In Defense of Rudeness.' TIME.com. 3 April. http://www.time.com/time/columnist/reaves/article/0,9565,221746,00.html (accessed 5 May 2002).
Reich, Wilhelm. [1950] 1964. *Character Analysis*. New York: Viking Press.
– 1973. *The Function of the Orgasm*. Trans. Vincent R. Carfagno. New York: Noonday Press.

Reid, Ronald F. 1988. *Three Centuries of American Rhetorical Discourse*. Prospect Heights, IL: Waveland Press.
Renzetti, Claire M. 1993. *Researching Sensitive Topics*. Newbury Park, CA: Sage.
Retzinger, Suzanne. 1991. *Violent Emotions*. Newbury Park, CA: Sage.
Richard, Hill. 1994. *Euromanagers and Martians: The Business Cultures of Europe's Trading Nations*. Brussels: Europublications.
Ricoeur, Paul. 1967. *The Symbolism of Evil*. Trans. Emerson Buchanan. Boston: Beacon Press.
Rieff, Philip. 1966. *The Triumph of the Therapeutic Uses of Faith after Freud*. New York: Harper and Row.
Riesman, David. 1950. *The Lonely Crowd: A Study of the Changing American Character*. New Haven: Yale University Press.
Ritzer, George. 1993. *The McDonaldization of Society: An Investigation into the Changing Character of Contemporary Social Life*. Newbury Park, CA: Pine Forge Press.
Robinson, Ira, and Evan R. Powell. 1979. 'George Herbert Mead and Emotionality – A Study in Civility.' Paper presented at the Annual Mid-South Sociological Association Conference.
Rodriguez, S.B., and D.L. Collinson. 1995. '"Having Fun": Humour as Resistance in Brazil.' *Organization Studies* 16, 5: 739–68.
Rogers, Winfield, H. 1934. 'The Reaction against Melodramatic Sentimentality in the English Novel, 1796–1830' *PMLA* 49 (March): 98–122.
Rose, Anne C. 1994. *Victorian America and the Civil War*. New York: Cambridge University Press.
Rose, Nicholas. 1985. *The Psychological Complex – Psychology, Politics and Society in England 1860–1939*. London: Routledge and Kegan Paul.
– 1989. *Governing the Soul – The Shaping of the Private Self*. London: Routledge.
– 1998. *Inventing Our Selves: Psychology, Power and Personhood*. Cambridge: Cambridge University Press.
Rose-Ackerman, Susan. 2001. 'Trust and Honesty in Post-Socialist Societies.' *Kyklos* 54: 415–44.
Rosenberg, William. 1998. 'What Is Civil? "New Russia" and the Democratic Predicament.' *Constellations* 5, 4: 518–40.
Rosenblatt, Roger. 1996. 'Where Have All the Manners Gone?' PBS. 22 October. http://www.pbs.org/newshour/essays/manners_10-22.html (accessed 15 November 2001).
Rosenwein, Barbara H., ed. 1998. *Anger's Past: The Social Uses of an Emotion in the Middle Ages*. Ithaca, NY: Cornell University Press.
Roszak, Theodore. 1979. *Personal Planet: The Creative Destruction of Industrial Society*. London: Gollancz.

Roth, Philip. 1959. *Goodbye Columbus*. London: Deutsch.
Rothschild, Babette. 2000. *The Body Remembers: The Psychophysiology of Trauma and Trauma Treatment*. New York: Norton.
Rothschild, John, and Susan Berns Wolf. 1976. *The Children of the Counter-Culture*. Garden City, NY: Doubleday.
Rousseau, Jean-Jacques. [1750] 1964. *The First and Second Discourses*. Trans. R.D. Masters and J.R. Masters. Ed. R.D. Masters. New York: St Martin's Press.
– [1761] 1979. *Émile*. Trans. Allan Bloom. New York: Basic.
– [1762] 1968. *The Social Contract and Discourses*. Trans. G.D.H. Cole. New York: Dutton.
Rouvillois, Frédéric. 2006. *Histoire de la politesse de la révolution à nos jours*. Paris: Flammarion.
Rubinstein, R.P. 1995. *Dress Codes: Meanings and Messages in American Culture*. Boulder, CO: Westview Press.
Rudé, George F.E. 1972. *Europe in the Eighteenth Century: Aristocracy and the Bourgeois Challenge*. London: Weidenfeld and Nicolson.
Runcie, Dr Robert, Archbishop of Canterbury. 1997. Lecture on the 1400th Anniversary of the Mission of St Augustine to Canterbury. 27 February.
Ruskin, John. 1902–12. *Works*. Ed. E.T. Cook and A.D.O. 39 vols. London: Wedderburn.
Russell, Dennis. 1996. *Campus Hate-Speech Regulations: The Competing Values of Free Discourse and Civility*. PhD thesis, Department of Communication, University of Utah. Ann Arbor, MI: UMI Dissertation Services.
Russell, John. 1450. *Boke of Nurture*. London.
Russett, Cynthia Eagle. 1989. *Sexual Science: The Victorian Construction of Womanhood*. Cambridge, MA: Harvard University Press.
Salzmann, Bernard. 1796. *Elements of Morality, for the Use of Children, With an Introductory Address to Parents*. Trans. Mary Wollstonecraft. Providence: Carter and Wilkinson.
Sanders, Charlotte. 1799. *The Little Family, Containing a Variety of Moral and Philosophical Matter. Written for the Amusement and Instruction of Young Persons*. Haverhill, MA: Moore and Stebbins.
Sarfatti-Larson, Magali. 1977. *The Rise of Professionalism*. Berkeley: University of California Press.
Scaglione, Aldo. 1991. *Knights at Court*. Oxford: University of California Press.
Schacter, S., and J.E. Singer. 1962. 'Cognitive, Social and Physiological Determinants of Emotional State,' *Psychological Review* 69: 379–99.
Schalk, Ellery. 1986. *From Valor to Pedigree: Ideas of Nobility in Sixteenth and Seventeenth-Century France*. Princeton: Princeton University Press.

Scheff, Thomas J. 1985. 'The Primacy of Affect.' *American Psychologist* 40, 7: 849–50.
- 1987. 'The Shame-Rage Spiral: A Case Study of an Interminable Quarrel.' In *The Role of Shame in Symptom Formation*, ed. H.B. Lewis, 109–50. Hillsdale, NJ: Erlbaum.
- 1988. 'Shame and Conformity: The Deference-Emotion System.' *American Sociological Review* 53, 3: 395–406.
- 1990. *Microsociology: Discourse, Emotion and Social Structure*. Chicago: University of Chicago Press.
- 1994a. *Bloody Revenge: Emotions, Nationalism, and War*. Boulder, CO: Westview Press.
- 1994b. 'A Theory of Ethnic Nationalism.' In *Social Theory and the Politics of Identity*, ed. Craig Calhoun, 277–303. Oxford: Blackwell.
- 1997a. 'A Vision of Sociology: 1996 PSA Presidential Address.' *Sociological Perspectives* 40: 529–38.
- 1997b. *Emotions, the Social Bond, and Human Reality*. Cambridge: Cambridge University Press.

Schegloff, E., G. Jefferson, and H. Sacks. 1977. 'The Preference for Self-Correction in the Organization and Repair in Conversation.' *Language* 53: 361–82.

Sherman, Nancy. 2005. 'Of Mannes and Morals.' *British Journal of Educational Studies* 53, 3: 272–89.

Schlesinger, Arthur M. [1946] 1968. *Learning to Behave: A Historical Study of American Etiquette Books*. New York: Cooper Square.

Schneider, Barbara, and David Stevenson 1999. *The Ambitious Generation: America's Teenagers, Motivated but Directionless*. New Haven: Yale University Press.

Schudson, Michael. 1997. 'Why Conversation Is Not the Soul of Democracy.' *Critical Studies of Mass Communications* 14, 4: 297–309.

Schutz, William. 1967. *Joy*. New York: Grove Press.

Schwartz, Shalom. 1991. 'The Universal Content and Structure of Values: Theoretical Advances and Empirical Tests in 20 Countries.' *Advances in Experimental Social Psychology* 25: 1–65.

Schwartz, Shalom, and W. Bilsky. 1987. 'Towards a Psychological Structure of Human Values.' *Journal of Personality and Social Psychology* 53: 550–62.
- 1990. 'Toward a Theory of the Universal Content and Structure of Values: Extensions and Cross-Cultural Replications.' *Journal of Personality and Social Psychology* 58: 878–91.

Scott, James C. 1990. *Domination and the Arts of Resistance: Hidden Transcripts*. New Haven: Yale University Press.

Scudéry, Madeleine de. 1680. *Conversations sur divers sujets*. Paris: Louis Billaine.
Scruton, Roger. 1999. 'Sex in the Commodity Culture.' In *Rewriting the Sexual Contract*, ed. Geoff Dench, 57–63. New Brunswick, NJ: Transaction.
Sedgewick, Catherine. 1857. *Morals of Manners, or, Hints for Our Young People*. New York: G.P. Putnam.
Sedgwick, Henry Dwight. [1935] 1970. *In Praise of Gentlemen*. Freeport, NY: Books for Libraries Press.
Seligman, Adam B. 1998. 'Between Public and Private: Towards a Sociology of Civil Society.' In *Democratic Civility: The History and Cross-Cultural Possibility of a Modern Political Ideal*, ed. Robert W. Heffner, 79–111. New Brunswick, NJ: Transaction.
– 2000. *The Problem of Trust*. Princeton: Princeton University Press.
Sennett, Richard. 1977. *The Fall of Public Man*. Cambridge: Cambridge University Press.
– 1990. *The Shaping of the Private Self*. London: Routledge.
Shaftesbury, Third Earl of (Anthony Ashley Cooper). [1714] 1964. 'An Enquiry Conserning Virtue and Merit.' In *Characteristicks of Men, Manners, Opinions, Times*. 3 vols. Farnborough: Gregg International.
Shephard, A. 2006. 'Violence and Civility in Early Modern Europe.' *Historical Journal* 49, 2: 593–603.
Sheriff, John K. 1982. *The Good-Natured Man. The Evolution of a Moral Ideal, 1660–1800*. Tuscaloosa: University of Alabama Press.
Sherman, Nancy. 1991. *The Fabric of Character: Aristotle's Theory of Virtue*. New York: Oxford University Press.
Sherwood, Mary E.W. (Mrs John). [1884] 1907. *Manners and Social Usage*. New York: Harper and Brothers.
Shilling, Chris. 1993. *The Body and Social Theory*. London: Sage.
Shils, Edward. 1975. *Center and Periphery: Essays in Macrosociology*. Chicago: University of Chicago Press.
– 1998. *The Virtue of Civility: Selected Essays on Liberalism, Tradition, and Civil Society*. Ed. Steven Grosby. Indianapolis, IN: Liberty Fund.
Sickels, Eleanor M. 1969. *The Gloomy Egoist: Moods and Themes of Melancholy from Gray to Keats*. New York: Octagon.
Sigler, Edward F., and Meryl Frank, eds. 1988. *The Parental Leave Crisis*. New Haven: Yale University Press.
Sigourney, Lydia. 1833. *How to Be Happy, Written for the Children of Some Dear Friends*. Hartford, CT.
Simmel, George. [1908] 1950. 'The Metropolis and Mental Life.' In *The Sociology of George Simmel*, trans. K.H. Wolff, 409–24. Glencoe, IL: Free Press.

Skocpol, Theda. 1979. *States and Social Revolutions*. New York: Cambridge University Press.
Skolnick, Arlene S., and Jerome H. Skolnick, eds. 1994. *Family in Transition*. New York: Harper and Collins.
Sloan, William. 1955. *Children's Books in England and America in the Seventeenth Century*. New York: Columbia University Press.
Smiles, Samuel. [1859] 1958. *Self-Help*. London: John Murray.
– [1875] 1958. *Thrift*. London: John Murray.
Smith, Adam. [1759] 1982. *The Theory of Moral Sentiments*. Oxford: Oxford University Press.
– [1776] 1979. *An Inquiry in the Nature and Causes of the Wealth of Nations*. Oxford: Oxford University Press.
Smith, C.A., and R.S. Lazarus. 1993. 'Appraisal Components, Core Relational Themes, and the Emotions.' *Cognition and Emotion* 7: 233–69.
Smith, Dennis. 1984. 'Norbert Elias – Established or Outsider?' *Sociological Review* 32, 2: 367–89.
Smith, Peter B., and Michael Harris Bond. 1998. *Social Psychology across Cultures*. London: Prentice-Hall.
Smuts, R.M. 2001. 'From Courtesy to Civility: Changing Codes of Conduct in Early Modern England.' *Continuity and Change* 16: 301–11.
Soltow, Daniel. 1975. *Man and Wealth in the United States, 1850–1870*. New Haven: Yale University Press.
Sombart, Werner. 1915. *The Quintessence of Capitalism*. New York: Harper Torchbooks.
Spacks, Patricia. 1985. *Gossip*. New York: Knopf.
Spellman, Christine M. 1985. 'Paris in the Mid 19th Century as a Screen for Urbanism, Cosmopolitanism and a Culture of the "Juste Milieu."' *Studies in Symbolic Interaction* 6: 183–212.
Spierenburg, Pieter. 2004. 'Punishment, Power and History: Foucault and Elias.' *Social Sciences History* 28, 4: 607–36.
Spiller, R.E. 1968. *A Descriptive Bibliography of the Writings of James Fenimore Cooper*. New York: Burt Franklin.
Spinoza, Baruch. [1677] 1959. *Ethics*. Trans. Andrew Boyle. London: Dent.
St Ambrose. 1984. *De officiis clericorum*. Trans. and ed. M. Testard. Paris.
St John de Crèvecoeur, Hector. [1782] 1957. *Letters from an American Farmer*. New York: Dutton.
– [1782] 1978. *The Divided Loyalist: Crevecoeur's America*. Ed. M. Cunliffe. Folio Society.
Staggenborg, Suzanne. 1999. *Gender, Family and Social Movements*. Thousand Oaks, CA.: Pine Forge Press.

Stanfield, James Ronald, and Jacqueline Bloom Stanfield. 1997. 'Where Has Love Gone? Reciprocity, Redistribution and the Nurturance Gap.' *Journal of Socio-Economics* 26, 2: 111–26.

Stanton, Donna. 1980. *The Aristocrat as Art: A Study of the Honnête Homme and the Dandy in Seventeenth- and Nineteenth-Century French Literature*. New York: Columbia University Press.

Starkey, David. 1982. 'The Court – Castiglione's Ideal and Tudor Reality.' *Journal of the Warburg and Courtault Institute* 445: 232–9.

Starzinger, Vincent E. 1965. *Middlingness: Juste Milieu Political Theory in France and England, 1815–48*. Charlottesville: University Press of Virginia.

Stearns, Peter N. 1994. *American Cool: Constructing a Twentieth Century Emotional Style*. New York: New York University.

– 1999. *Battleground of Desire: The Struggle for Self-Control in Modern America*. New York: New York University Press.

– 2001. 'On Mead on American National Character.' *Culture and Psychology* 7, 1: 65–79.

Stearns, Peter N., and Carol Z. Stearns. 1986. *Anger: The Struggle for Emotional Control in American History*. Chicago: University of Chicago Press.

Steinbeck, John. [1939] 1989. *The Grapes of Wrath*. New York: Penguin.

Steinem, Gloria. 1992. *Revolution from Within: A Book of Self-Esteem*. London: Bloomsbury.

Stone, Lawrence. 1977. *The Family, Sex and Marriage in England 1500–1800*. London: Weidenfeld and Nicolson.

Stout, Martin. 2000. *The Feel Good Curriculum*. Cambridge, MA: Perseus Press.

Synnott, Anthony. 1993. *The Body Social – Symbolism, Self and Society*. London: Routledge.

Sztompka, Piotr. 1998. 'Mistrusting Civility: Predicament of a Post-Communist Society.' In *Real Civil Societies: Dilemmas of Institutionalization*, ed. Jeffrey C. Alexander, 191–210. London: Sage.

Taine, Hippolyte. [1863] 1957. *Notes on England*. London: Thames and Hudson.

Tajfel, H. 1972. *Human Groups and Social Categories*. Cambridge: Cambridge University Press.

Tangney, J. P. 1992. 'Situational Determinants of Shame and Guilt in Young Adulthood.' *Personality and Social Psychology Bulletin* 18: 199–206.

– 1995. 'Shame and Guilt in Interpersonal Relationships.' In *Self-Conscious Emotions*, ed. June Price Tangney and Kurt W. Fischer, 114–39. New York: Guilford Press.

Tannen, Deborah. 1998. *The Argument Culture: Moving from Debate to Dialogue*. New York: Random House.

Tapscott, Don. 1995. *The Digital Economy: Promise and Peril in the Age of Networked Intelligence*. New York: McGraw-Hill.
Taylor, Charles, et al. 1994. *Multiculturalism*. Ed. Amy Gutman. Princeton, NJ: Princeton University Press.
Taylor, John A. 1997. *Popular Literature and the Construction of British National Identity, 1707–1850*. Bethesda, MD: International Scholars Publication.
Taylor, Stuart, Jr, and Evan Thomas. 2003. 'Civil Wars.' *Newsweek*, 5 December, 43–51.
Tennyson, Alfred Lord. 1898. *The Poetical and Dramatic Works*. Ed. W.J. Rolfe. Boston.
Terkel, S. 1972. *Working: People Talk about What They Do All Day and How They Feel about What They Do*. New York: Pantheon.
The Times. 1883. *The English Bobby*. London: The Times, 14 September.
Thibaut, J.W., and H.H. Kelley. 1959. *The Social Psychology of Groups*. New York: Wiley.
Thoreau, Henry David. [1849] 1967. *Civil Disobedience*. New York: Twayne.
Tichy, N., and S. Sherman. 1994. *Control Your Destiny or Someone Else Will*. New York: HarperCollins.
Tillam, Thomas. [1638] 1968. 'Upon the First Sight of New England, June 29, 1638.' In *American Poetry of the Seventeenth Century*, ed. Harrison T. Meserole, 397–8. New York: Norton.
Tilly, Charles. 1981. *As Sociology Meets History*. New York: Academic Press.
– 1986. *The Contentious French*. Cambridge: Harvard University Press.
– 1993a. *Coercion, Capital and European States, A.D. 990–1990*. Oxford: Blackwell.
– 1993b. *European Revolutions, 1492–1992*. Oxford: Blackwell.
– [1995] 2005. *Popular Contention in Great Britain 1758–1834*. Boulder, CO: Paradigm.
– 2003a. *Trust and Rule*. Cambridge: Cambridge University Press.
– 2003b. *The Politics of Collective Violence*. Cambridge: Cambridge University Press.
– 2004. *Social Movements 1768–2004*. Boulder, CO: Paradigm.
– 2005a. *Identities, Boundaries and Social Ties*. Boulder, CO: Paradigm.
– 2005b. *Trust and Rule*. New York: Cambridge University Press.
– 2006. *Why?* Princeton: Princeton University Press.
Tillyard, E.M.W. [1949] 1972. *The Elizabethan World Picture*. Harmondsworth: Penguin.
Time Magazine. 1990. 'Dirty Words: America's Foul-Mouthed Pop Culture.' *Time Magazine*, 7 May, 92.
– 2003. 'The Amazing Adventures of Ben Franklin.' *Time Magazine*, 7 July, 26–49.

Tindall, George Brown, and David Emory Shi. [1984] 1999. *America. A Narrative History*. London: W.W. Norton.
Tinker, Cauncey Brewster. 1967. *The Salon and English Letters*. New York: Gordian Press.
Tocqueville, Alexis de. [1833–5] 1958. *Journeys to England and Ireland*. Trans. George Lawrence and K.P. Mayer. Ed. J. P. Mayer. London: Faber and Faber.
– [1884] 1994. *Democracy in America*. New York: Fontana Press.
– [1856] 1995. *The Old Regime and the French Revolution*. Trans. Stuart Gilbert. New York: Anchor.
Todd, John. 1841. *The Moral Influence, Danger and Duties Connected with Great Cities*. Northampton: J.H. Butler.
Toffler, Alvin. 1983. *Power Shift*. New York: Dell.
Tompkins, J.M.S. 1961. *The Popular Novel in England, 1770–1880*. Lincoln: University of Nebraska Press.
Trachtenberg, Alan. 1982. *The Incorporation of America: Culture and Society in the Gilded Age*. New York: Hill and Wang.
Trilling, Lionel. 1955. *The Opposing Self. Nine Essays in Criticism*. New York: Viking Press.
– 1971. *Sincerity and Authenticity*. Cambridge: Cambridge University Press.
Trollope, Fanny. 1832. *Domestic Manners of the Americans*. London: Whittaker, Treacher.
Truss, Lynne. 2005. *Talk to the Hand – The Utter Bloody Rudeness of the World Today, or Six Good Reasons to Stay Home and Bolt the Door*. New York: Gotham.
Turner, B.S. 1984. *The Body and Society*. Oxford: Basil Blackwell.
Turner, Graham. 2002. *Elizabeth: The Woman and the Queen*. London: Macmillan.
Turner, James. 1990. *Without God, without Creed: The Origins of Unbelief in America*. Baltimore, MD: Johns Hopkins University Press.
Turner, Jonathan. 2000. *On the Origins of Human Emotions*. Stanford: Stanford University Press.
Turner, Jonathan, and Jane Stets. 2005. *The Sociology of Emotions*. New York: Cambridge University Press.
Tuthill, Louisa C. 1847. *The Young Lady's Home*. Boston.
Twain, Mark. [1867] 2001. *The Celebrated Jumping Frog of Calaveras County, and Other Sketches* (New York: C.H. Webb, 1867; BoondocksNet Edition, 2001). http://www.boondocksnet.com/twaintexts/frog/jf_advice_girls.html (accessed 3 July 2003).
Twenge, Jean M. 2006.*Generation Me. Why Today's Young Americans Are More Confident, Assertive, Entitled – and More Miserable Than Ever Before*. New York: Free Press.

Twenge, J.M., and W.K. Campbell. 2009. *The Narcissism Epidemic: Living in the Age of Entitlement*. New York: Free Press.

Tye, Larry. 2001. *The Father of Spin: Edward L. Bernays and the Birth of Public Relations*. New York: Henry Holt.

Uncle Madison. 18–?. *The Polite Boy, With Illustrations*. Boston: James M. Usher.

Veblen, Thorstein. [1899] 1925. *The Theory of the Leisure Class*. London: George Allen and Unwin.

Viorst, Milton. 1979. *Fire in the Streets: America in the 1960s*. New York: Simon and Schuster.

Vivier-Muresan, Anne-Sophie. 2006. 'The Iranian Code of Courtesy (*ta'arof*): The Fiction of Social Bonds.' *L'Homme* (October-December): 115–38.

Voltaire. [1758] 1992. *Candide*. New York: Knopf.

– [1735] 1999. *Philosophical Letters on the English*. Introduction by Nicholas Cronk. Oxford: Oxford University Press.

Von Martin, Alfred. 1944. *The Sociology of the Renaissance*. London: Kegan Paul.

Wack, Mary Frances. 1990. *Lovesickness in the Middle Ages: The Viaticum and Its Commentaries*. Philadelphia: University of Pennsylvania Press.

Wagner, Peter. 1996. 'Crises of Modernity: Political Sociology in Historical Contexts.' In *Social Theory and Sociology – The Classics and Beyond*, ed. Stephen B. Turner. Cambridge, MA: Blackwell.

Walker, Alexander. 1970. *Stardom, the Hollywood Phenomenon*. London: Michael Joseph.

Walker, Obadiah. 1673. *Of Education, especially of Young Gentlemen*. London.

Walkowitz, Judith R. 1980. *Prostitution and Victorian Society: Women, Class and the State*. Cambridge: Cambridge University Press.

Wallerstein, Immanuel. 1974. *The Modern World System: Capitalist Agriculture and the Origins of the European World Economy in the Sixteenth Century*. New York: Academic Press.

– 1996. 'Three Ideologies or One? The Pseudo-Battle of Modernity.' In *Social Theory and Sociology – The Classics and Beyond*, ed. Stephen P. Turner, 97–116. Oxford: Blackwell.

Walter, Benjamin. 1973. *Charles Baudelaire: A Lyric Poet in the Era of High Capitalism*. London: New Left.

Warren, J.A., and P.J. Johnson. 1995. 'The Impact of Workplace Support on Work–Family Role Strain.' *Family Relations* 44: 163–9.

Watson, John B. [1928] 1972. *Psychological Care of Infant and Child*. New York: Arno Press.

Watson, Lillian (Eichler). 1922. *The Book of Etiquette*. New York: Triangle.

Watts, Isaac. [1715] 1972. *Divine Songs Attempted in an Easy Language for Use of Children. With an Introduction and Bibliography by J.H.P. Pafford*. London: Oxford University Press.

Weber, Max. [1922] 1978. *Economy and Society*. 2 vols. Berkeley: University of California Press.

– 1930. *The Protestant Ethic and the Spirit of Capitalism*. Trans. Talcott Parsons. London: G. Allen and Unwin.

Weems, Mason L. 1796. *The Immortal Mentor: or, Man's Unerring Guide to a Healthy, Wealthy, and Happy Life*. Philadelphia: Francis and Robert Bailey.

Weitzman, Lenore J., and Ruth B. Dixon. 1994. 'The Transformation of Legal Marriage through No-Fault Divorce.' In *Family in Transition*, ed. Arlene S. Skolnick and Jerome H. Skolnick, 354–67. New York: Harper and Collins.

Wells, H.G. 1934. *Experiment in Autiobiography*, vol. 1. London: Gollancs/Cressett Press.

Wertenbaker, Thomas. 1927. *The First Americans*. New York: Macmillan.

West, Cornell. 1989. *The American Evasion of Philosophy: A Geneology of Pragmatism*. Madison: University of Wisconsin Press.

White, Melanie. 2006. 'An Ambivalent Civility.' *Canadian Journal of Sociology* 31, 4: 445–60.

Whitman, Walt. [1855] 1971. *Leaves of Grass: Selections*. Selected by Lawrence Clark Powell. New York: T.Y. Crowell.

Whyte, William. 1956. *The Organization Man*. London: Cape.

Wicker, F., G.C. Payne, and R.D. Morgan. 1983. 'Participant Descriptions of Guilt and Shame.' *Motivation and Emotion* 7: 25–39.

Wilberforce, William. 1797. *A Practical View of the Prevailing Religious System of Professed Christians*. London: T. Cadell.

Williams, Simon. 2001. *Emotions and Social Theory*. London: Sage.

Williamson, K.M. 2002. 'Civility Proxies and Social Tolerance in American Marketplaces.' *Sociological Inquiry* 72, 3: 486–99.

Wills, Richard H. 1998. *Human Instincts, Everyday Life, and the Brain: A Paradigm for Understanding Behaviour*. 2 vols. Charlottetown, PE: Emporium Press.

Wilson, Edmund. 1952. *The Shores of Light*. New York: Farrar, Straus and Young.

Wilson, Harriette. 1929. *Harriette Wilson's Memoirs*. Preface by James Laver. London: Peter Davies.

Wilson, Janet. 1998. 'Asking the Public for a Little Respect.' *Los Angeles Times*, 30 June, A1, A19.

Wilson, R. Jackson. [1987] 1989. *Figures of Speech. American Writers and the Marketplace, from Benjamin Franklin to Emily Dickinson*. Baltimore, MD: Johns Hopkins University Press.

Wilson, Sloan. 1955. *The Man in the Gray Flannel Suit*. New York: Simon and Schuster.

Winthrop, James. 1853. *The History of New England from 1630 to 1649*. Ed. James Savage. Boston: Little, Brown.

Wirls, Stephen H. 1996. The Moral Imperative: Of Liberalism's New Challenge. *Journal of Interdisciplinary Studies* 8, 1–2: 31–48.

Wishy, Bernard. 1967. *The Child and the Republic: The Dawn of American Child Nurture*. Philadelphia: University of Pennsylvania Press.

Wollstonecraft, Mary. [1790] 1970. *A Vindication of the Rights of Woman*. Farnborough: Gregg.

Woodruff, Paul. 2001. *Reverence: Renewing a Forgotten Virtue*. New York: Oxford University Press.

World Values Survey (WVS). 1999–2000. World Values Survey Association. www.worldvaluessurvey.org.

Wouters, C. 1986. 'Formalization and Informalization: Changing Tensions Balances in Civilizing Processes.' *Theory, Culture and Society* 3, 2: 1–18.

– 2004. *Sex and Manners: Female Emancipation in the West 1890–2000*. Theory, Culture and Society Series. London: Sage.

Wylie, Laurence. 1981. 'The Civilization Course.' In *Société et culture de la France contemporain*, ed. Georges Santoni, 1–63. Albany, NY: State University of New York Press.

Wylie, Laurence, and Jean-François Brière. 1995. *Les Français*. Englewood Cliffs, NJ: Prentice-Hall.

Yeazell, R.B. 1991. *Fictions of Modesty: Women and Courtship in the English Novel*. Chicago: University of Chicago Press.

Yuill, Chris. 2004. 'Emotions After Dark – A Sociological Impression of the 2003 New York Blackout.' *Sociological Research Online* 9, 3. http://www.socresonline.org.uk/9/3/yuill.html.

Zwiebach, Burton. 1975. *Civility and Disobedience*. Cambridge: Cambridge University Press.

# Index

Abbott, Rev. S.C. John, 238, 247
absolutist state (French monarchy): confronted with individualism, 51, 83; control of violence in, 38, 75; and formation of national civility practices, 16, 103, 107–8; and idea of relativity, 90; and morality of hierarchy, 24; revolutionary reaction to, 119–20; toward revolution, 98–9, 103; Voltaire's criticism of, 92, 97. *See also* Louis XIV
Académie Française, 150
Acton, William, 199, 200
address, forms of: citizen in French Revolution, 119, 128; of domestic workers in post-revolutionary France, 120; titles in early America, 223–4
aesthetics, Renaissance, 58–65
African Americans, 288
aggression: in American male, 241, 242; control and centralizing power, 26–7; control of (Renaissance), 64, 89; and courtly love, 45, 48; pacifying of (Victorian), 173; with restraint in dual identities, 354–5; tempering of (medieval), 28, 33, 35–8, 44
agreeability: American, 297; *bienséances* (France), 112; cross-cultural comparison of, 95, 379–80; English, 95
Alberti, Leon Battista, 54, 62–3, 71
Alcott, William A., 235–6, 247–8
alienation, 295–6, 375, 423, 507
Alstree, Richard, 150, 240
altruism, 177, 241, 271, 297, 433, 500, 503–4
ambition, 34, 259–60, 528
America: civility ethos free from Old World, 120; clash of northern and southern manners, 258; in comparative study, 6, 7; as culturally distinct, 445–7; field research locations in, 432; geographic influence on, 217, 219–20, 226, 448, 459; identity and lifestyle, 508; as individualistic in survey, *378t*, 378–9 (*see also* communalism and community, America; individualism, America); literature on late-modern American civility, 276–82, 284; as a low-context culture, 382, 445–7 (*see also* time, context, and

space); southern gentry, 217–18, 258; survey on religion in, 281, 282; in a topology of civility, 518–19. *See also* comparison of civility practices (France, America, England); morality, America; Puritanism; *individual concepts*

American Bill of Rights (Declaration of Independence), 136–7, 212–13, 214, 307, 308; Ninth Amendment, 212, 339

American hero, 220

American Revolution, 99, 212, 223

American Tract Society, 237

*amour propre* (self-love), 95–6

*ancien régime* feudalism, 95, 99–100, 120–1, 147

anger: American management of, 513; America's mistrust of, 414; becomes Protestant wit, 89; clamour (ritual anger), 36; as collapsed with violence, 49; cross-cultural expressions of, 370–1; in emotional biographies, 411, 413, 414; and English politeness, 451; factored into civility research, 285, 500; and medieval aggression, 35–8; to prevent violence in France, 512; to prevent violence (medieval), 36; as response to shame, 415–16, 417; as righteous, 35–8; vengeful, 36, 509; in Victorian England, 173. *See also* emotions

Anglican Church. *See* Church of England (Anglican Church)

anti-conformist movement, 158

anti-politesse movement (France), 120–1

anxiety, 403

architecture and family, 131

Arditi, Jorge: *A Genealogy of Manners*, 103

Arendt, Hannah, 297

Ariès, Philippe, 130

aristocracy: art of conversation, 114–16; behaviour as requisite for, 32, 35, 109–11; in conflict with general population, 52–3; and democratization, 75–7; English, 147–8, 149, 195–8, 209; and English reserve, 186; and feudalism, 25; French culture of, 134–5, 136; French influence on English, 150; manners and privilege of, 39–40, 42, 47; marriage of the, 45; and notions of virtue, 92–3; in personality and body, 29; pretension of, 70; and privilege, 62, 99–103; and professionals, 171; pursuit of pleasure by, 156–7; rise of courtesy standards in, 79–80, 81; and rising bourgeoisie, 123–30, 163–4, 174–5, 182; and transition from courtesy to virtue, 169

Aristotle, 207; and birth of style, 32; ideal of the *golden mean*, 32–3, 71; magnanimity *(megalopsychia)*, 63; virtue ethics, 16

arms and military power, 26–7

Arnold, Matthew, 154

art: in the Renaissance, 60–1, 70, 74

Arthurian legend, 31, 41, 44, 205

asceticism: in American context, 223, 291, 305; and capitalism, 174–5; medieval, 30; and Protestantism, 88

atheism: in France, 129

Austen, Jane: *Sense and Sensibility*, 173, 179–80

authenticity: and American para-

dox of communal cohesion, 272; American search for, 273–4; and civil behaviour, 505; and cultural revolution (1960s), 304; and denial of shame, 416; directness as American, 260; and duty, 331; French definition of, 264; and self-centredness, 323; and self-referentiality, 317–18; sentimentality and, 181; and tolerance, 417; Victorian search for, 170–1; *vraisemblance* (the act of appearing real), 181
avarice, 40

baby boomers, 310, 358, 458, 499, 527
Baldridge, Letitia, 317
Balzac, Honoré de, 132
Barbalet, Jack, 345
Baudelaire, Charles, 431
Bauerlein, Mark, 499
Baylor Institute for Studies of Religion, 281
bedroom rituals: eighteenth century and Victorian England compared, 207; Louis XIV, 108; sleeping nude, 116. *See also* sex and sexuality
behaviour: versus emotionalism, 423; English simplicity of, 150; Hollywood code of, 288–9; of ideal courtier (Renaissance), 75; as important as biography (medieval), 32; and new philosophy of efficacy (Renaissance), 62; over religion in children's conduct books, 234
Belgium, 135, 378, 379
Bell, Daniel, 270
Bernays, Edward, 290
Bill of Rights (England), 92, 142–3. *See also* parliamentarianism (British)

Blau, Peter M., 278
Bloom, Harold, 267
Blue Stocking Club, 151
Bly, Robert, 284, 473–4
Boccaccio: *Decameron*, 59
body: and courtship rituals, 483; and cultural revolution (1960s), 303; in development of narcissism, 419; manners censoring the, 116; as released from restraints (1960s), 305; Renaissance bodily functions, 78–9, 80, 81–2; Renaissance display of, 57–8, 65–6; restraints of (England), 148–9; restraints on (America), 243; self-surveillance as freeing the, 359; as servile under Protestants, 89–90; and the sociology of emotions, 345; in Victorian England, 167; Victorian restrictions on masturbation, 203, 207–8. *See also* sex and sexuality
Boethius, 33–4
Bonaparte, Napoleon, 121, 128, 448
*bon goût* (good taste), 114
Bonizo, Bishop of Sutri, 39
Borgia, Cesare, 55
Bourbon Restoration, 128
Bourdieu, Pierre, 442
bourgeoisie, America, 255, 307
bourgeoisie, England, 183–5
bourgeoisie, France: after the Revolution, 120–1, 129–30, 135; and bureaucracy, 101; café culture, 131–4; civility traditions of, 139, 153, 185; golden age of civility of the, 121, 122–5; in intellectual salons, 118–19; *la haute bourgeoisie*, 126, 128; manuals incorporating sensibilities of, 110, 112; rise of single-family households, 116; ris-

ing critical awareness of, 99–101, 113; role in central rule of, 52–3; *se distinguer*, 134; and social criticism, 319; subjugation by aristocracy of, 159; as threat to nobility, 103–4, 109, 114, 115
Brathwayt, Robert, 150
Brown, Helen Gurley, 303
Brown, Penelope, 386, 389–90, 395–6, 404
Browning, Robert, 204
Bunyan, John, 231
bureaucracy: corporate (*see* corporate culture); cross-cultural comparison of citizenship and, 18, 430, 432, 446, 491–3; as dependent on literacy, 361; in education, 332, 333; and French bourgeois, 101; French citizenship and, 491–3; government as centralized, 53, 103, 138, 446, 448, 449, 519; as oppressive, 354–5
Burke, Edmund, 148, 158
Byrd, William, II, 217–18
bystander effect, 507

café culture (France), 131–4
Caillères, François de, 114
Calvin, John, 84, 85, 87–9, 214, 216. *See also* Protestantism
Campbell, Colin, 182–3
Capellanus, Andreas: *The Art of Courtly Love*, 45–6, 75
capitalism: America's unique, 338; and civility, 278; and consumerism, 175, 283–4, 290–1; and consumption and religion, 290–1; and corporate culture, 278–9, 286–8; and counterculture, 310; cross-cultural comparison of, 443–4; fiction critical of American, 287–9; and friendship, 480; and the levelling of cultures, 373; and morality, 270–1; and Romanticism, 14; and socialism, 447, 448–9; and treatment of citizens, 494. *See also* consumer society
Caraccioli, Louis-Antoine, 129
Carlyle, 156
Carroll, Raymonde, 440, 457, 487
Carter, Stephen L., 277
Castiglione, Baldassare: *The Book of the Courtier*, 69–75, 86, 107–8, 149, 151, 226–7
CCH Human Resources Group, 280
character: and mannerism as important, 174, 189–90; manners as indicating, 9, 148; rise in importance of (Reformation), 89. *See also* national character
charm in medieval court, 34
chastity, 45, 167, 202–3. *See also* sex and sexuality
Chaucer, 148
Chesterfield, Lord, 159, 172, 224
*chevalier*, 26, 43, 213
Chevalier, Michel, 253
children: in bourgeois household, 116, 130–1; conduct books on, 330; effect of cultural definitions on, 449–51; Elias on behaviour of, 293; and family hierarchy, 452–3; naturalism in socializing of, 327; parent social bond with, 348; qualities most desirable in, *450t*; rational moralists and, 233–4; in Renaissance family, 61, 62, 64; restraint in childrearing, 327–8; and Romanticism, 182; and shifting gender relations, 326–7; sibling relation-

ships among, 457; socialization of, 363–6; therapeutic movement and raising, 328–30. *See also* education; family
children, America: childrearing, 247, 458–63; conduct books, 229–40; conduct books and discipline, 230; fiction, 233; lyric poetry, 232–3; Puritan, 216; qualities most desirable in, *450t*; sibling relationships among, 457; women's job to educate, 247. *See also* teenagers and teen culture
children, England: childrearing, 463–4; conduct books (Victorian), 166; illegitimate, 189, 200; as labourers, 152, 162; lower-class Victorian, 198; middle-class Victorian, 162, 166, 173, 194, 196, 203–4; qualities most desirable in, *450t*; in Victorian England, 162. *See also* education, Victorian
children, France: childrearing, 453–8, 460, 461–2; and paradox of individualism and deference, 453–8; politeness and revolutionary France, 120; qualities most desirable in, *450t*; sibling relationships among, 457. *See also* education, France; teenagers and teen culture
chivalry: in early American context, 213; and education of youth, 48; in medieval culture of courtesy, 43; and Victorian sexual restraint, 204–5
choice in a sociology of culture, 348
Chrétien de Troyes: *Perceval*, 23, 37, 41–2, 44
Christianity and the Church: and anger, 35–8; appropriation of the knight, 40–2, 43–4; and *The Book of the Courtier*, 74; and cardinal sins (America), 216–17; Catholic civility rituals, 83; Christian right (America), 337; and culture of courtesy (medieval), 29–31; and ethics of restraint, 16; and French tax laws, 136–7; as ideological bond, 25; infallibility of the Church, 29–31; loss of dependence on (France), 118–19, 129; loss of theological hegemony by, 53; medieval *scola*, 31; monks as 'athletes of Christ,' 30–1; and morality of social hierarchy, 24–5, 39–40; nationalization of Church lands (France), 102; and neighbourly love, 38; and publication of *The Prince*, 67; as reconciled with individualism (America), 241–2; Renaissance and medieval fatalism, 59–60; and Renaissance humanists, 60–1, 76; and Renaissance manners, 79; Renaissance resistance to the Church, 58; Renaissance wealth, 53–7, 56–7; and rise of liberalism, 53–4; Sunday school (America), 236–7; Voltaire's criticism of, 92; and women, 245. *See also* Protestantism; religion; Roman Catholic Church
Church of England (Anglican Church): formation of pious societies by, 158–9; and individualism, 146–7; and sexual moderation, 197
Cicero: *De Officiis* and *Orator*, 32–3, 58, 71
cities and urban centres: and African Americans, 288; and American communitarianism, 493; city-

states, 51, 61–2; compared to rural and small towns, 374; and development of manners, 80–1; and issues of face, 399; and medieval values, 69; and rise of bourgeoisie, 52–3; and rise of English middle classes, 147, 151; and roots of civility, 9; and standard society ethos, 400; in Victorian England, 154, 161–3, 167, 170, 172; women in, 246

citizen/citizenship: and American Bill of Rights, 212; and bureaucracy, 491–3; bystander effect, 507; in conduct books, 123; and consumerism, 290, 419; in culture of entitlement, 334–6; expanded rights to (France), 127–8; as form of address (French Revolution), 119, 128; ideal of, 96, 262; and identity (France), 508; and responsibility, 494, 526–7; rise of secular, 67; role in civility of, 9, 508–9

city-states, 51, 61–2

civic personality, 92

*civilitate*, 77

*civilité*, 77, 113

civility: anatomy of, 6, 343; cost of, 502; definition of, 6, 9, 277, 282, 494, 502, 528–9; Erasmus and the term, 77; ethnocentrism in defining, 261, 283; field study definitive indicators of, 433; need for discussion of, 19–20; origins of Western, 8; as person-centred, 16; tripartite nature of, 7; as viewed through time, 10–13. *See also* courtesy

civilizing process: and decivilizing processes, 306; and definition of aggression, 35–6, 38; definition of (Elias), 352–4, 368; and discretionary power of the individual, 359; and double standards, 49; and medieval knights, 27; and narrative of development, 357–8; not homogeneous, 261; and re-civilizing in contemporary culture, 355–6; and recivilizing processes, 18, 501–2; as role adoption, 365–6; study of, 497–9; transformations in, 362; as two-way relationship, 359–60; understanding of, 5, 7; of the Victorians, 208–9

civil society: building of, 5; and desire for self-gratification, 66

*civiltà*, 77

Civil War (America), 220–1; religious tolerance after, 234; women in, 244–5

class: and civility rituals, 285; courtesy as differentiation, 33–4; and credit networks, 145–6; and cultural revolution (1960s), 299–300; medieval, 32, 33–4, 37–8; and public civility, 79; and public good, 159; Renaissance, 61–2, 65, 76–7; reproduction of, 442–4; rise in antagonism between, 52–3. *See also* hierarchy (social)

class, America: and absence of an aristocracy, 260; compared to European, 252–5; conception of gentleman, 226–7; and cultural boundaries, 442–3; and ideal of community, 251; and magazines, 256; and property, 255–6; and socialist ideology, 258

class, England: and aristocrats, 158–9; civility ethic of, 464; growing gap in, 152–3; landed gentry, 141;

and Queen Victoria, 191; role in formation of modern state, 147–8; social compromise of Victorian, 159, 171, 174, 186–7; and Victorian sexuality, 195, 197–8

class, France: café culture and working, 131–4; and cultural boundaries, 442–3; in intellectual salons, 118–19; and language, 106, 468; and morality, 134; rise of bourgeoisie, 126

clothing, 57, 119–20, 167–8

coffee houses (England), 193

Colefax, Lady, 209

colonialization, 352

communalism and community: and childrearing, 452–3; customs of, 373–5; and emotional expression, 372–3; and family, 493; field study, 433–4, 437–8; identity in cultures favouring, 369–70; and individualism, 339, 374–5, 493, 497, 503–6; mobility and conformity, 292–3; of the 1960s, 306; and paradox of self-interest, 270–1; and personal growth, 316; positive and negative politeness rituals with, 520–1; versus self-referential authority, 384–5; survey of social values in, 376–80, *378t*; and systems of government, 447–8; and time, context, and place, 380–4, 408

communalism and community, America: as ideal, 244, 250–1; and individualism, 221–2; and litigation, 276; paradox of authenticity, 272; and rise of corporate culture, 287–8

communalism and community, France, 454–8, 471

communication: as ambiguous *(sprezzatura)*, 109; art of conversation (Renaissance), 79; as conversation of emotions, 517; cross-cultural comparison of, 475–80; dialogue (Renaissance), 70–3; directness across cultural boundaries, 396; as direct or indirect, 386, 390–1; field study, 434; high-context or low-context, 382–3; integration of genders in, 110–11; and *méfiance* (mistrust), 125; in on-record and off-record politeness, 390–1; and politeness strategies, 393–5; of rights claims in democracy, 336; shame and loss of empathetic, 422

communication, America: conversation and politeness rituals, 476–7; simplicity and directness of, 225, 227, 243, 252, 477; style of 'ease' in, 257–8

communication, England: the *art of speeche*, 148; conversation and politeness rituals, 476–80; simplicity of, 150

communication, France: art of conversation, 95, 112–15, 118–19; art of letter writing, 151–2, 479; conversation and politeness rituals, 476–7, 479–80; *pudeur* or caution in interpersonal, 467; salon culture, 116–18; wit in conversation, 492

comparison of civility practices (France, America, England): achievement, 468; agreeability, 95; attitudes to each other, 252–5; bureaucracy and citizenship, 18, 430, 432, 446, 448, 449, 491–3; childrearing, 453–8, 459; childrearing (America), 458–63; childrearing (England), 463–4; children and cultural definitions, 449–53; children's desirable qualities, 450t; children's education, 456; citizenship, 262; class, 159, 442–4; conduct books, 251, 262; conversation, 475–80; corporate culture, 289–90, 296; courtship rituals, 483–8; cultural revolution, 17, 312–13; declarations of rights, 136–7; deference, 263; democracy, 144, 259–60; as distinct, 84, 261–2, 265, 269, 373; education, 456, 468–75; education (America), 470–2, 473–5; education at university level, 472–3; education (France), 470–2; elaboration (France), 150; embarrassment and shame, 510–18; emotional expression, 318, 369–70; from etiquette to civility (France), 98; of friendliness, 444–5; of friendship, 480–3; of identity, 369–70; imitation of European practices, 255–7; individualism, 466–7; inter-generational socializing, 456; male emotional constitution, 243; narcissism, 421; politeness, 399; public and private, 263–4, 454–5; restraint, 106, 263–5; rudeness, 271, 273–4; secularism, 337–8; self-esteem, 465–8; sexual liberation (1960s), 302; sibling relationships, 457; simplicity, 150; sincerity, 316; and social critique (late-modern), 318–22, 332; study of, 6, 7, 18, 261–5, 371–2, 497–502; survey of national characters (individualistic/collectivist), 376–80, 378t; systems of government, 447–9; teen culture (America), 292; time, context, and place, 380–4; 408, 445–7; topology of, 518–19, 519–23; work ethic, 488–91. *See also* field study

compassion, 36, 41–2, 173, 176, 178–9, 222–3, 417, 494

competition and civility, 278

compliments: and politeness, 392–3; receiving of, 372–3

Comte, Auguste, 187

conduct books: for children, 234, 330; as commentary on culture, 351; courtesy books (Continental), 148–9, 240; courtesy tracts (medieval), 32–3; cross-cultural comparison of, 251; and cultural ideals, 9–10; cultural variations in, 262; and emotional expressiveness (1980s, 1990s), 316–17; on gender relations (late-modern), 303; and repression, 351; and self-obsessed individuals, 417; shame in, 349–50. *See also* literature

conduct books, America: change in, 256–7; for children, 229–40; for children (gender specific), 234–6; and dualism of American psyche, 223; equality in, 228–9; on ethos of ease, 258; for men, 240–3; for mercantile aristocracy, 256–7; moralistic Puritanism in, 229–33; rational moralism in, 233–4; social changes reflected in, 229; for women, 244–51, 247

conduct books, England: early courtesy literature, 148–53; etiquette books, 163–4, 164–6, 174; of the evangelical revival movement, 161–2; *The Galateo* as popular in England, 79; and Industrial Revolution, 158–60; moderation in, 150;

style versus morality, 160. *See also* literature, Victorian

conduct books, France: *bon goût* (good taste), 114; for bourgeoisie, 110, 112, 123; nobility as a military institution in, 109–11, 114; during the Revolution, 119, 120; on *savoir vivre*, 122–3; for women (1600s), 110. *See also* literature, France

confidence: civility requires, 529; in English socialization rituals, 463

configurational sociology, 7

conformity: and American mobility, 251, 292–4; beat poetry and American, 294–5; in children, 423, 451–2, 459; collective (America), 250, 297, 422, 487, 504; and conscientiousness, 380; consumerism and, 524; in corporate culture, 287, 316; for the courtier (France), 79; and education (France), 361, 469, 471–2; and education (Victorian), 195; of family, 309; and fear, 279; guilt and, 402; and individualism, 82, 375; and individualism (France), 453–8; industrialization and, 155, 158; and mobility restriction, 284–5; in national character survey, 379–80; and nonconformity, 358; and nonconformity (America), 222; paradox of (America), 243, 500; and patriotism, 339; and personal growth, 316; Renaissance rise of, 81; shame and, 406, 413, 510; tendency of, 355; in Victorian England, 155, 158, 167, 191

consensual society: American, 225, 276; and culture of entitlement, 334–5; and socialization of children, 365

consideration: appearance of (England), 164; Renaissance secular ideal of, 10

conspicuous consumption, 168–9

consumer society, 290–1; and capitalism, 175, 283–4; and citizenship, 290, 419; and conformity, 524; counterculture and, 310; relationships in a, 325–6; and shaping behaviour, 315. *See also* capitalism

context. *See* time, context, and space

conversation. *See* communication

Conwell, Joseph A., 241

Cooley, Charles Horton, 365–6

Cooper, Anthony Ashley. *See* Shaftsbury, Earl of (Anthony Ashley Cooper)

Cooper, James Fennimore, 219, 226–7

Cooper, Thomas, 216

corporate culture: American, 278–82, 286–8; backlash to, 294–7; and courtship (America), 487; cross-cultural comparison of, 289–90, 376–7, 379, 432, 488, 490–1; cross-cultural comparison of (France/America), 466; and idealism of counterculture, 309–10; and mastery of passion, 296; mobility and conformity, 292–4; role of New York City in, 286–7; and self-actualization, 316; survey on work absences (America), 280; and systems of government, 449; and the teenager, 292–4; use of humour and gossip, 280. *See also* work; work ethic, America

cosmetics: in post-revolutionary France, 120

courtesy: definition of, 9; *levée*, 108, 213; medieval literature on, 27;

origins of Western traditions of, 8, 23–7; shift to secular civility (Enlightenment), 90; and theology of Middle Ages, 16. *See also* civility; court society (medieval France)

Courtin, Antoine de, 111–12, 115

*courtoisie, la,* 39–40, 48, 121. *See also* court society (medieval France)

courtship. *See* marriage

court society (medieval France): courtly love in, 44–8; courtly personality, 33; criticism of, 34, 41; diplomacy in, 107; discipline in, 107; *étiquette,* 105–9; French spoken in English courts, 39; with guidance from the Church, 29–31; and legacy of grandeur, 121–2; modern civility rituals developed in, 103–9; and moral anger, 36–8; in new feudal order, 24–5, 33–5; prestige in, 104, 108; and social mobility, 39, 48

crime rates: for murder and violence (America), 371–2; and national police forces (France), 13, 361; as responses to institutional situations, 360

criminality, 274, 282

cross-cultural conceptions: field study indicators of recognition of emotions, 434–5; in field study observations, 440–1; and moral disagreements, 376; and politeness across cultural boundaries, 396; of time, context, and space, 380–4, 408. *See also* comparison of civility practices (France, America, England)

cross-cultural studies: and 'etic-emic' views, 371–2; and survey results, 371–3. *See also* comparison of civility practices (France, America, England)

crowd psychology, 290

cruelty: in feudal order, 24–5; prevention of, 4; and Renaissance humanists, 61, 63

cult of sensibility (England), 174, 175–80, 192

cultural revolution (1960s): cultural comparisons of, 17; on effect of restraints, 358–9; and misanthropy, 301; and mistrust of rules, 306–7; as response to corporate culture, 297–8; role of popular culture in, 299–300; social legislation during, 298, 312; as turning point in Western civility, 286

cultural sociology of civility, 343–4

culture of poverty, 189

cynicism (social): in corporate culture, 279, 281; and lack of civility, 272; marriage in culture of, 327

Dale, Daphne (C.F. Beezeley), 257

Damian, Peter *(Contra clericos aulicos),* 34

danger: and civilizing process, 352–3; emotions as dangerous, 190; and literacy, 361; Puritans vigilant against moral, 214; reserve of Victorians, 206; women as dangerous, 206–7; women protected from, 194, 201, 246

Dante Alighieri, *The Divine Comedy,* 52

Darwin, Charles, 184–5

Davetian, Benet, 285; *The Seventh Circle,* 4

daydreaming, 182–3

*debonereté*, 36
deception: ornamentation as, 169; and virtue, 170–1
de Crèvecoeur, Hector St John, 218–19
deference, 109; balancing with self-respect (America), 238–9; degrees of, 377; versus democratic individualism, 251; and face-threatening activity, 391–2; in field study, 433, 437; to goals of social group, 114; *indifférence* as, 110; individual accountability and, 86; and individualism (France), 124–5, 134–9, 263–4, 453–8; in individualistic societies, 376; and mute negation, 398; practices compared, 263; Renaissance value of, 64–5, 73, 74
de Gaulle, Charles, 139, 469
*délicatesse*, 107, 110
Della Casa, Giovanni, *Il Galateo*, 77–80, 150, 167, 174; English translation of, 149
Della Francesca (artist): *Flagellation*, 85
de Maistre, Joseph, 123
democracy: cross-cultural comparison of, 449; definitions of, 135; and elitist intellectualizing, 322; in need of civility, 277; and rights claims, 334, 335–6; and standard ethic of civility, 359. *See also* government systems
democratic communalism (America), 259–60; aristocrats versus republicans, 224–5; in children's conduct books, 235; and national civility practices, 16; opinion of democracy, 449; saint and gentleman in, 227; and sympathy for the rebel, 222. *See also* individualism, America
democratization of culture: effect of courtly love on, 47–8; effect of *la courtoisie*, 39, 48; and need for new specifications, 76–7; and regulation of personal desire, 67
Depression, Great, 287, 290, 291
*de rigueur*, 256
Descartes, René, 91, 95–7, 118, 316; and English culture, 153, 185
desire: change of attitude toward, 267; regulation of personal, 67
d'Estaing, Giscard, 469
devil in America, 215–17
Dewey, John, 320, 321
Diana, Princess of Wales, 384–5, 478
Dickens, Charles, 198–9
Diderot, 127
dignity, 46, 173, 260, 479; *gravitas*, 71
diplomacy, 24–5, 107
directness: applied across cultural boundaries, 396; in conversation compared, 477; in field research, 432; in relation to face, 386, 390–1. *See also* simplicity and directness (America)
*discernement*, 111
discipline: in children's conduct books (America), 230; for the courtier (Renaissance), 74; of desire in male conduct books (America), 243; in French court, 107
discourtesy: cultural feelings about, 274; field study definitive indicators of, 433
domestic workers: and class, 160; illegitimate children of, 200; in

post-revolutionary France, 120; in Victorian England, 186
Dostoevsky, Fyodor, 198
Douglass, Frederick, 220
dramaturgical artifice, 65
duels (America), 226
Durkheim, Émile, 323, 348, 374, 423
duty, 14; and authenticity, 331; in communal and individualistic societies, 374–5; communal versus self-referential authority, 384–5, 479; and gender relations, 325; and Puritans, 214; role of anxiety in, 403; and women, 247

ease, civility of (America), 257–8, 259–62, 316, 460
eco-civility, 19, 527–8; definition of, 8
economics, 8
education, 97; as central to civility, 530; and crime rates, 13, 361; democratization of behaviour in, 332–3; for girls on sex, 349–50; and lack of civility training, 277; by monastic scholars (medieval), 31–2; and standards of chivalry, 48–9; unintended consequences of, 525; universities during cultural revolution, 298; university level, 472–3. *See also* children
education, America: of children as women's job, 247; children's conduct books, 229–40; compared to French, 470–2; free of European influence, 226; lowering of standards of, 333, 473–5, 499, 515–16; parental engagement with, 475; Sunday school, 236–7; of women, 246, 247, 248. *See also* children, America
education, France, 468–72; compared to America, 470–2; parental engagement with, 456, 471; and privatization of family, 130–1. *See also* children, France
education, Victorian: as family responsibility, 162; of public, 187; of sex and sexuality, 203–4; of upper-class male, 195–7. *See also* children, England
Edward, Prince of Wales, 198
Edwards, Jonathan, 214–15
efficiency, Renaissance, 61–2
egalitarianism (America), 224, 225–6
elegance: in American ethos of ease, 257; *debonereté*, 36; as superficial and Continental (England), 160
Elias, Norbert, 305; criticism of, 348–9, 353–4; on individual and society, 343; on limiting violence, 102–3; on state formation, 143
– *The Civilizing Process*, 7–8, 11, 17, 69–75, 106, 213, 411; on abandoning controls, 306; on anxiety, 403; on children, 293; class antagonism, 52–3; configurational sociology, 7; definition of civilizing process, 7, 38; on embarrassment and shame, 368–9; on English class compromise, 171; on narrative of civilizing process, 357–8; process sociology model, 359; public and private delineations, 352; on restraints, 14, 27–8, 313, 353; on shame, 57–8, 349–51, 368–9, 405–6; on state powers, 447; theory of violence restraint, 10, 35, 49, 352; on variety in class (France), 126

Index 585

- *Court Society*, 99, 103–9, 104, 106–7, 108, 116, 347–8
- *The History of Manners*, 80–3
- *A Society of Individuals*, 347
- *What Is Sociology?* 348, 399–400

Eliot, George, 194, 199
Elisabetta Gonzaga, Duchesse, 70, 72
Elizabeth I, 142, 197
eloquence: medieval, 32; Renaissance, 58–9
Elyot, Thomas, 149
embarrassment and shame, 14, 18, 404–8; cross-cultural context of, 511–18; as crucial to social interaction, 366–8; emotional roots of, 509–11; in England, 164, 510–18; and guilt, 404–5; and internalization of restraints, 356, 405–6; management of (America), 513–16; and publican civility, 77–8; role in civility, 19; *scham*, 351; self-correction to avoid, 394; as self-referential on increase, 405; and self-reflexivity (Renaissance), 68–9; situations causing, 386; as a taboo, 368. *See also* face; shame
Emerson, Ralph Waldo, 222, 227, 495
emotional biographies: and civility consequences of restraints, 411, 413–14; connection to civility of, 17, 363; influence on social interactions, 408, 409; of medieval men and women, 28
emotions: American affectation of, 464–5; in American childrearing, 459–61; cross-cultural differences in, 370–1; cultural variation in desirable, 384; in family public/private relationships, 454–5, 488; field study parameters, 434–7;

individualism and expressiveness, 372; mutual surveillance as a conversation of, 517–18; in socialization process, 369. *See also* anger; pain in social theory; shame
emotions, restrained and expressed: American movement to express, 318; and civility practices, 16; in compared civility practices, 265; and corporate culture, 278–80; and dangers of repression, 315–16; *délicatesse*, 107; as dependent on belief, 307–8; and freedom from restraint, 359; and functionality, 327–8; in justice and politics (England), 152–3; in new republicanism (France), 126–7; and paradox of French reason, 96–7; and Protestant guilt, 90; as roots of embarrassment and shame, 509–11; self-referential versus communal, 384–5; in a sociology of culture, 344–6, 348; and Victorian compassion, 177–8
emulation (Victorian), 186
Engels, Friedrich, 155
England: British reserve, 262–3 (*see also* tact); civility roots in Locke's philosophy, 92; in comparative study, 6, 7 (*see also* comparison of civility practices [France, America, England]); as culturally distinct, 445–7 (*see also* comparison of civility practices [France, America, England]); field research locations in, 432; identity and lifestyle, 508; as individualistic in survey, 378t, 379 (*see also* individualism, England); as maintaining a monarchy, 141–2; as a moderate-context

culture, 382, 445–7 (*see also* time, context, and space); in a topology of civility, 519; Web articles about civility, 274. *See also* etiquette books (England); language; morality, Victorian; parliamentarianism (British); *individual concepts*
Enlightenment, 90–7, 123–4, 319
entitlement, culture of: in American childrearing, 459–60; and American individualism, 516; and choice of behaviour, 332; and litigation, 334; and majority consensus, 334–5; and narcissism, 417–19; and postmodern debate, 322; from the self-esteem movement, 525–6
envy, medieval, 47
equality: in childrearing, 452–3; and Christian legitimacy of hierarchy, 24; and class in England, 148; and deference (France), 134–5; and *égalité* (France), 491; self-centredness consequence of, 422
Erasmus, Desiderius, 75–7; *Colloquies*, 76; *De civilitate morum puerilium (On Civility in Boys)*, 76–7
Esalen Institute (California), 315–16
ethics: Christian ethics of restraint, 16; of discourse, 271; and field study, 440–1; as path to individual happiness, 192; and rise of Protestantism, 85; as tied to manners (Victorian), 158
Étienne de Fougères, 42
etiquette: American and European compared, 253–5; American imitation of European, 255–7; of café culture, 133–4; as distinct from civility, 78; as distinct from good manners, 150–1; and dual identities, 354–5; in early Washington, 225–6; how-to for rising middle classes (England), 163–4; practice of French court *étiquette*, 105–9, 111, 163; rules for women in public (Victorian), 201–2; and social justice (Victorian), 165; of sports (England), 196; transformed into civility, 16, 98; Victorian pretensions of, 120, 121. *See also* manners
etiquette books (England), 163–4, 164–6, 174. *See also* conduct books
exhibitionism and ornamentation: and industrialization, 175, 190; and national pride (America), 261; in Regency England, 157, 159, 169

face: in civil interactions, 367, 373; and common ground, 393; in conversation and politeness rituals, 478; and cultural context, 516–17; definition of, 385, 386–7; and face-threatening acts, 387–9, 391; field study premises of, 437; and friendship, 482; versus maintenance of a mask, 509; and management of embarrassment (France), 512–13; and number of people, 399–400; and pain of rejection, 413; and the practice of compliments, 392–3; preservation of, 388; and social distance, 391–2; strategies of politeness, 393–5; in teens across cultures, 514–15; types of preservation of, 387. *See also* embarrassment and shame
faith rift with reason, 51
family: alienating relationships within, 423–4; and boarding schools, 196–7; in children's

conduct books, 234; and corporate culture, 278–9, 280, 298–9; and counterculture, 311; cross-cultural comparison of, 493; and cultural revolution, 297–8, 301–2; and friendships, 481; and generation gap, 309; importance in Renaissance of, 62–3; and love in children's conduct books, 237–8; and marriage break-ups, 488; and narcissism, 421; in national character survey, 379; and norms, 309, 357; and parent-child social bond, 348; public/private relationships, 454; quasi-peer culture of, 328–30; and sexuality, 158–9, 197–9, 358; and systems of government, 447–8, 449; women in, 194. *See also* children; marriage

family, America: and corporate culture, 296; father-son relationship, 243; hierarchy, 232, 458; respect taught to children, 239–40; role of women in, 249; and teen culture, 291–4. *See also* family

family, France: and café culture, 133; France as friendly to, 493; hierarchy, 467–8; and post-revolutionary morality, 130–1. *See also* family

family, Victorian: conduct and the middle classes, 162; idealization of, 191; as separate from public life, 165–6; and sexual conservatism, 167; and women's sexuality, 201

Faret, Nicolas, 110–11, 112

fashion journals and magazines, 168–9, 256, 303–4

fear: in corporate culture, 279; and egalitarianism, 224; of exclusion, 403; moral (Victorian), 164–5; of others, 375

feminism: and American civility, 276; and the counterculture, 311; and cultural revolution, 301–2; and gender relations, 324–6, 486; on women and family (England), 194, 201

Ferriss, Abbot L., 282, 285

feudalism: decline of, 100–2; defending of honour in, 37–8; hierarchy of, 42; manners of, 80–1, 122, 255, 515; peasant in, 33; and restraint of violence, 24–6

field study, 18; choices in, 498; framework for, 430–3; guidelines for, 432–8; template for observations, 438–9. *See also* comparison of civility practices (France, America, England)

*fin' amour*, 48, 204. *See also* love

First World War, 221

*Flagellation* (Della Francesca), 85

Florian, 130

food: America, 239; of Regency England, 156–7, 159

Ford, Ford Madox, 196

Forni, P.M., 526; *Choosing Civility*, 5

*fortuna*, 68, 74

Foucault, Michel, 11, 103, 319, 320

France: civility rituals developed in French court, 103–9; in comparative study, 6, 7; as culturally distinct, 445–7; field research locations in, 432; as a high-context culture, 382, 445–7 (*see also* time, context, and space); as individualistic and collectivist, *378t*, 378–9, 441, 491, 492, 508; judicial system, 138; Locke's influence, 92, 95;

love of flair and drama, 263; and personality *(personalité)*, 465–6; pride in culture of, 123; survey results about incivility, 274–5; taxes, 136–7; in a topology of civility, 519; Web articles about civility, 274–5. *See also* absolutist state (French monarchy); bourgeoisie, France; café culture (France); comparison of civility practices (France, America, England); court society (medieval France); language, France; paradoxes in civility, France; *individual concepts*

Franklin, Benjamin, 228, 240–1, 245–6

free choice: and the Enlightenment, 94

freedom: in American ethos of ease, 257; American idealism of, 212; definitions of, 135, 137; and openness, 260–1; two conceptions of, 338–9 (*see also* individual freedom)

Freeling, Arthur, 248

Freemasons, 118

French Declaration of Rights, 135–9

French legacy of grandeur, 121–2

French monarchy. *See* absolutist state (French monarchy)

French National Assembly, 102, 135–6

French Revolution, 90, 96, 99–103; aftermath of, 119–25, 130–1; and centralized government, 211; citizen as form of address, 119, 128; and development of writing, 361; English anxiety over, 156; and late-modern criticism, 319; and origins of secularism, 102; tempered effect of, 134–9, 138; violence and civility after, 105

Freud, Sigmund, 290, 315, 410

Friday, Nancy, 301

Friedan, Betty, 324

friendliness: of Americans, 251, 258; of French, 468; French and American compared, 444–5

friendship: in America, 480–3, 484, 485; cross-cultural comparison of, 480–3; in England, 480–3; in France, 480–2; Victorian sentimental, 177

friendship circles (France), 484, 485

Furet, François, 101, 118

gallantry, 45, 47, 112, 433; of medieval knight, 47

Generation Me, 331, 515, 525–6

Generation X, 456, 458, 527

gentleman: American, 223–7, 224, 252; demise of, 192; education of, 195–7; in English literature, 149; *le gentilhomme*, 109; and mercantilism, 159–60; as respecting others, 150–1; restraint of, 208; and sex, 199, 206

gentleness (England), 154, 191, 192

gentlewoman, 149. *See also* gentleman

Geoffrey of Monmouth, 41

geography: and childrearing (America), 459; and ideology (America), 217, 219–20, 226; and systems of government, 448

German civility practices, 380–4

Giddens, Anthony, 102, 314, 324, 353, 375, 412, 419–20, 488; on individualistic societies, 375; on narcissism, 420–1

Gillis, A.R., 11–13, 49, 361; 'Crime and State Surveillance in Nineteenth-Century France,' 13; 'Institutional Dynamics and Dangerous Classes,' 13
Ginsberg, Allen, 295
Gisborne, Rev. Thomas, 159, 161
globalization, 6, 373, 377, 445–7, 469, 491
Godkin, E.L., 257
Goffman, Erving, 117, 366–8, 386, 404, 406, 517
*Gone With the Wind* (film and novel), 252, 288
goodness: American ideology of, 215, 225; as limiting excesses, 176; through courtly love, 46
good will, in American ethos of ease, 257
government systems: centralized bureaucracy, 519; civility as settlement between population and, 49–50; and civility practices, 447–9; English monarchy, 141–2; and formation of national civility practices, 16. *See also* absolutist state (French monarchy); citizen/citizenship; democracy; democratic communalism (America)
grace, 528; *grazia*, 71, 74–5
*grandes écoles*, 472
Greer, Germaine, 324
Grice, H.P., 396
Guicciardini, Francesco, 85
Guillaume de Poitier, 40
guilt, 400–4; in individualistic societies, 404; and punishment, 402–3, 416; role in teaching morality, 402; and shame, 400–1, 404–5; and Victorian sexual mores, 206

Habermas, Jurgen, 271, 313, 333–4, 335–6, 375
habituation, psychology of, 274, 283
Haddock, Rev. Charles B., 237
Hall, Edward T., 380–4, 427, 440, 445, 482
Hall, Mildred Reed, 380–4, 440, 445, 482
Harte, Bret, 222
Hawthorne, Nathaniel, 220; *The Scarlet Letter*, 402–3
Hays, Will H., 288–9
hedonism, 183, 189, 308; and civility, 277–8; and conceptions of guilt, 402; in national character survey, 379–80
Hemingway, Ernest, 134
Henry II, 34, 40
Henry VII, 142
hero, 305, 308; Renaissance, 59
hierarchy (social): bourgeois as threat to nobility, 104, 114; and children, 231–2, 452–3; and citizenship, 491–3; in corporate culture, 279, 316, 488, 490; of courtiers (Renaissance), 73; and democratization, 109; effects of counterculture on, 309–11; and exhibition of wealth (Renaissance), 57–8; and face, 391–2; family and quasi-peer culture, 328–30; feudal compared to Renaissance, 81; field study premises of, 437–8; in national character survey, 379; and religion, 24, 39–40, 88–90; role of manners in, 103, 115–16, 165, 421–2; in salon culture, 117; and systems of government, 447
hierarchy (social), America: as anti-aristocracy, 251, 254–5, 515–16; in

early America, 223–5; and family, 245–6, 458; ideal of minimizing, 338; taught to children, 239
hierarchy (social), England: and accents, 160; of conduct not title, 149–50
hierarchy (social), France: of court at Versailles, 101–2; in education, 470, 472; equality during Revolution, 119–21; mobility in, 111; as partial to, 138; post-revolutionary, 103–9; and rise of emotionalism, 126–7; as system of privilege, 97
hierarchy (social), medieval, 28–34, 29–31, 39, 43, 48–9
Hincmar of Reims, 31
history: and cultural class norms, 441–2; discrepancies in, 9–11; limits of, 499; understanding of, 5, 7, 523–4
Hobbes, Thomas, 68, 92, 93, 503
Hochschild, Arlie R., 279, 326
Hofstede, Geert, 135, 376–7, 379–80, 441, 453, 491
Hollywood, 462; code of behaviour, 288–9; influence on American dreams, 296–7, 301
Holmes, Oliver Wendell, 227
Homans, George C., 278
homogenization of cultures, 19
*honnête homme/femme*, 113
honour: in American south, 251–2; and godliness (America), 224; Renaissance, 70–1, 74
Howells, William Dean, 258
*How to Behave* (anon), 228
Hugo, Victor, 123
humanism and Renaissance, 58–65, 71, 75–6
human relational processes, 346

human rights, 93, 285
Hume, David, 93–4, 185, 192
humiliation: in absolutist state, 43; of apology, 513; civility as avoidance of, 9; in corporate culture, 280, 281; in courtship, 485; decency as avoiding, 277; freedom from in civility ethos, 336; linked to social bonds, 345; and loss of control, 524; and loss of face, 387, 397; repression of feelings of, 411, 414, 509. *See also* face; shame
humility, 42, 47, 528
humour in medieval courtesy, 34
Huxley, Thomas Henry, 185

identity: and American teen culture, 292–3; civility and cultural, 507–9; in communal and individualistic societies, 374–5; constructed through imagination, 364, 365–6; and the counterculture, 311–12, 313, 314–15; cross-cultural differences in, 369–70; and embarrassment, 415; European stable national, 318–19; formation in adolescence, 461–2; francophone, 263; and French nationalism, 469; and French personality *(personalité)*, 465–6; of ideal American, 465; and lifestyle, 508; as maintaining a 'front,' 366–7; and maintenance of dual, 354–5; and materialism, 65–6; and 'me generation,' 331–2; politics and rights claims, 336; and rise of oppositional self, 16–17; socially constructed civil, 363; as varying among cultures, 3–4; women's, 324–6
ideology: civility and cultural, 9;

and courtesy as differentiation, 33–4; and cult of sensibility, 179; of divine rights, 102–3; of good (America), 215, 225; and idealism of freedom, 212; of national optimism, 217, 218–19; of professionalism, 171; and rise of Protestantism, 85; of social idealism, 183–4, 187, 192; of socialism (America), 258

imagination: and American pragmatism, 473; in children, 450, *450t*; and objectification of self, 364; and Romanticism, 182–4; and social conscience, 308; sociological definition of, 347–8

immigration and migration, 258; in New York City, 286–7. *See also* multiculturalism (America)

improvement theme in Victorian England, 158, 185–8

incest, 198

incivility, 10; as affirmation of civility, 12; cross-cultural comparison of, 273–5; as current cultural obsession, 4, 285–6; examples of negative and positive, 398; as face loss, 387; French acts of, 274–5; as mute negation, 398; negative and positive, 396–9; result of paradoxical demands, 422–3. *See also* rudeness

independence and interdependence, 17–18; in children, 450, *450t*, 451–2; and conversation, 478; and friendship, 482–3; as taught to French children, 457–8

individual and social forces. *See* sociology of culture

individualism: versus collectivism defined, 377; versus communal freedom, 339; and communalism as compatible, 503–6; compared to collectivism, 493, 497; and conformity, 82; and corporate culture, 294, 316; and cultural revolution (1960s and 1970s), 308–9; and emotional expressiveness, 372; in field study, 433–4, 437–8; genesis of, 16, 49–50; identity in cultures favouring, 369–70; and late-modern identity, 314; and moral responsibility, 333–5; and new restraints of Reformation, 85–90; and political correctness, 337; and the printing press, 54; and Protestantism, 175; Renaissance rise of, 58–65; and rise of reason (Enlightenment), 91; role of Anglican Church in, 146–7; and self-control, 527; in societies with aristocracies, 338; and systems of government, 447–8; taught in children's conduct books, 235, 239–40; tempering of (Enlightenment), 94–5. *See also* individualistic societies; paradoxes in civility

individualism, America: as act of entitlement, 516; calls for planned economy, 289; and communalism, 221–2, 251; compared to French, 467; taught in men's conduct books, 241–3; for women, 248. *See also* democratic communalism (America)

individualism, England, 466; and credit systems, 145–6; and Victorian self-help, 188, 189–90

individualism, France, 466–8; compared to American, 467; and conformity in childrearing, 453–8;

and deference, 124–5, 134–9; and welfare of the nation, 135–9. *See also* paradoxes in civility, France

individualistic societies: compared to communal societies, 374–5; consensus to live and let live, 425; deference in, 376; emotional expression in, 417; and portability of civility ethos, 400; and self-referential shame, 405–6; survey of social values in, 376–80, *378t*; and time, context, and place, 380–4, 408

industrialization, 90; and civilizing process, 359–60; and conspicuous consumption, 168; dislocations of, 184–5; distrusted by middle and upper classes (England), 161–2; effect on identity and ideology, 269; in post–Civil War America, 221–2; and religious teaching, 237; resistance to rationalism of, 174; role of New York City in, 286–7; role of women in, 246; virtue and vice combined in, 188

Industrial Revolution: in England, 142, 143, 154–6; moral books in response to, 158–60; and Protestantism, 175

inequality. *See* equality

informal American civility, 258–9. *See also* ease, civility of (America)

Inglehart's Map, 376–7

insolence, 109

institutions, public and private, 360–2

integrity: linked to manners, 151; through courtly love, 46

intellectualism in America, 322

intellectual salons: civility rituals of, 121; English, 151–2; as escape from ceremony, 112; French art of conversation in, 116–18; origins in courtly love, 48

interdependence. *See* independence and interdependence

irony: and cultural revolution (1960s), 300; in face-threatening situations, 389; French legislation against, 122; and purity (1960s), 304–5; as self-critique, 89

Ishiguro, Kazuo, 208

Italy, 84–5, 87. *See also* Renaissance

Jacquerie peasant rebellion, 37

James, Henry, 222–3; *Daisy Miller*, 256–7

James, William, 320–1

Janeway, James, 231

Janov, Arthur, 409–14, 416–17, 419, 505

Japan, 373; concepts of selfhood and shame, 407–8; value of authority, 377

Jefferson, Thomas, 225–6

Jesuits (French), 213

John of Salisbury, 34, 40–1

Johnson, Dr, 176–7

Jones, William, 176–7

Judaism, 92

*juste milieu, le*, 129, 139

justice: civilized system of, 153; Enlightenment, 94; medieval, 40; Renaissance, 71

Kant, Immanuel, 94, 192

Kasey, Rev. J.W., 242

Kesey, Ken: *One Flew Over the Cuckoo's Nest* (film), 300

kindness: English, 94; Renaissance, 61; selfishness tempered with, 94

King Robert the Pious, 39
Kingsley, Charles, 204
knight (medieval): and class antagonism, 52–3; and courtly love, 46–9; gentrification of, 28, 46, 48–9; and lady's colours, 47; and restraint of violence, 28–9, 40–4
knowledge: in education (America), 473–4; in education (France), 469–70; and philosophy of pragmatism, 321; of self, 95–6; as separate from religion, 90; virtue transformed into, 31–2; women's right to, 248, 249
Knox, Rev. V., 169

lady: of American south, 252; ideal Renaissance, 75; ladylike (England), 149. *See also* women
Lafayette, Madame de, 127
Lafree, Gary, 49, 360
Laing, R.D., 309
Lamont, Michèle, 440, 441–4
language: accessibility of, 150; American slang, 258; competence and violence restraint, 520; and context and space, 383–5; in field study, 436–7; French spoken in English courts, 39; lower-class colloquial (England), 150, 159–60; and secular republicanism, 59; and sociology of emotions, 345; and Victorian sexuality, 203–4
language, France: effect of French Revolution on, 119; changes to, 150; and class, 468; and conversation, 477–8; in education system, 469; pride in, 123; as protection from assimilation, 441; and rise of middle class, 126, 128; subtleties of, 106; and use of *'vous,'* 467–8
La Rochefoucauld, François, 110
LaSalle, 115
Lasch-Quinn, Elisabeth, 307
Lateran Council (1513), 56
Lawrence, D.H., 154, 155
lawsuits as enforcing behaviour standards, 275–6
Lee, Robert E., 211, 214
LeGoff, Jacques, 29–30
Le Grand, Jacques, 148–9
Lennon, John, 299
*levée*, 108, 213
Levinson, Stephen C., 386, 389–90, 404
liberalism: of aristocratic south (America), 214; moral modesty versus moral, 337–8; Renaissance rise of, 53–4
liberty, definitions of, 135–6
Lincoln, Abraham, 221
literacy. *See* education
literacy and crime rates, 13, 361
literature: anti-slavery, 220; chivalric, 44; film as the new novel (1960s), 305; *lettre intime*, 151; medieval, 42, 43, 59, 68, 86; romantic fiction, 246–7. *See also* conduct books
literature, America: and alienation, 295–6; beat poetry, 294–5; children's, 232–3; fiction critical of capitalism, 287–9; on late-modern civility, 276–82, 284; novels on American mores, 256–7; of social conscience, 221–3. *See also* conduct books, America
literature, France: *cliché* in, 127; in intellectual salons, 118; leading up to Revolution, 96; and rise of emo-

594  Index

tionalism, 126–7; role in French culture, 469; role in revolutionary France, 124; sexuality in, 204. *See also* conduct books, France

literature, Renaissance: and chivalric honour, 69–75; on circumspect manners, 77; courtesy works, 75; on self-interest, 66–9; trust in personal judgment, 79–80

literature, Victorian, 187; criticism of morality, 208; on romantic love, 205; search for authenticity, 170; on sexuality, 203–4; sexuality compared in French and English, 204. *See also* conduct books, England

Locke, John, 91–3, 95, 162, 209, 233; *An Essay Concerning Human Understanding*, 91; *A Letter Concerning Toleration*, 91–2

loneliness in social theory, 285

longitudinal studies, 11–12. *See also* history

looking-glass self, 406

Louis XIV, 98–9, 103–4, 108, 116, 122, 128, 134, 181, 448; American distaste of, 257

Louis XV, 99–100

love: *amour propre* (self-love), 95–6; in children's conduct books, 237–8; and courtly romance (medieval), 41, 44–9; idealization of, 205–6; in marriage, 192, 199, 204–5; neighbourly, 38; origins of word, 45; relationships in a commodity culture, 325–6; theme in English salons, 151

love of justice (medieval), 33

Lowen, Alexander, 409

loyalty: in children's conduct books (America), 234; of citizens, 336, 500; to communal values (America), 234; in corporate culture, 293; courtly love and civic, 46–7; demanded by French monarchy, 98–9; in English salon, 151; in feudalism, 24, 26–8, 38; in French salon conversation, 117; to friendship, 480–1; of the medieval knight, 42, 43, 46–7; in the Renaissance, 65, 74, 76, 83; replaced by cynicism, 281; to self and others, 8, 70, 508; theme in English salons, 151; to tradition, 523; and Victorian love, 199; to virtue in industrial England, 170

Lull, Ramon, *The Book of the Order of Chivalry*, 33

Luther, Martin, 85, 87, 102. *See also* Protestantism

Macauley, Thomas Babbington, 154

Machiavelli, Niccolò di Bernardo dei: *The Prince*, 55, 66–9

Mackarnass, Mrs Henry S., 239

Mackenzie, Henry, 177, 180

MacLauchlan, Wade, 528–9

magnanimity: Artistotle's *megalopsychia*, 63

Maintenon, Françoise (Marquise d'Aubigné), 125, 181, 482

Mancini, Domenico, 148–9

Mandeville, Bernard de, 176, 188, 341

Manichean paradigm, 215–17

manners: character revealed by, 148; in children, 450t; cross-cultural comparison of, 3–4 (*see also* comparison of civility practices (France, America, England); dignity without (America), 260;

and emotion of, 19; and English class compromise, 174; etiquette as distinct from, 150–1; and the ideal of bearing, 161; integrity as linked to, 151; and knowledge, 32; as protecting social hierarchy, 115–16; Renaissance compared to medieval, 80–3; and rise in democratized culture, 76–7; role in hierarchy of, 103; roots of, 9; so as not to offend (Renaissance), 77–8; as utilitarian and simple (England), 150. *See also* etiquette

Map, Walter, 34, 148

marriage: and 'breach of promise' clause, 189; and courtly romance, 45; courtship rituals compared, 483–8; courtship rituals in England, 483–4, 487–8; courtship rituals in France, 483–8; and cultural revolution (1960s), 302; declining rates of, 207–8; and divorce, 199, 284, 375, 483–4; for love, 192, 199, 204–5; in Medieval society, 28; and post-revolutionary morality (France), 130–1; in Regency England, 157; and shifting gender relations, 324–7; women's role in (America), 245–6, 249. *See also* family; sex and sexuality

Martineau, Harriet, 3, 253–4

Marx, Karl, 155, 319, 347

Marxist theory, 8

Maslow, Abraham, 316

mass media: and American child-rearing, 458; American origins of, 237; American reliance on, 303–4; on America's litigious spirit, 275–6; on crisis of civility, 523; in cultural revolution (1960s), 298; English and American compared, 466; and information about societal problems, 375; and morality in 1960s and 1970s, 300; and teen culture, 466. *See also* popular culture

Mastron, Ruth, 440

masturbation, 203, 207–8

materialism: and change in civil behaviour, 57–8; of French aristocracy, 104–5; Renaissance, 53–7, 65–6

Mather, Cotton, 230–1, 240, 245

Mead, George Herbert, 276, 347, 363–6

Mead, Margaret, 292

Medici, Cosimo de, 56, 64–5

Medici Bank, 56

medieval popes, 29–30

melancholy, 178

Melville, Herman, 220

men and masculinity: and achievement, 377; conduct books for (America), 240–3; and conduct books for boys, 235–6; cross-cultural comparison of, 243; and directness of American, 252; domestication of, 193–4; versus femininity in society, 377; gender wars in America, 486; gentrification of the male (medieval), 48; idealization of (Victorian), 193–4; military male, 28; role of American men as public, 250; in shifting gender relations, 324; of upper-class English, 196–7; and women's sexuality, 199

mercantilism, 53, 64; as agent of civility, 145; American aristocracy of, 255–6; and the ideal gentleman, 224; and industrialization

(England), 154–6; and pragmatism (America), 240–1; and preservation of the English gentleman, 159–60. *See also* bourgeoisie; materialism
Méré, le chevalier, 112–13
Methodist: of New England, 232; social activism (England), 158
military: controlling might of, 25, 355; as institution of nobility, 43–4, 52–3, 109–11, 114
military male, 28
Mill, John Stuart, 147–8, 155–6, 187, 191, 193, 208
millennium (1000), 29
Miller, Arthur, 295
Miller, Henry, 269
Mills, C. Wright, 295, 313, 347–8
misanthrope: in cultural revolution (1960s), 301, 312; in England, 190, 319
Mitchell, Margaret, 252, 288
Mitterrand, François, 469
mobility: American, 225, 251, 258–9, 292–4; French social, 111; medieval social, 39; restricted by civility rituals, 284–5
moderation, 33, 150
modesty: English, 262, 466; and medieval priests, 31; moral liberalism versus moral, 337–8; and public politeness, 173–4; Renaissance change in, 57; and shame, 406; weakened by narcissism, 419; of women (America), 249
money: and centralized power, 26; charging of interest, 56; and networks of credit, 145; rise of economies of, 100. *See also* mercantilism
monks and monastic scholars: categorizing anger, 35–6; corruption of (Renaissance), 85; and medieval civility codes, 30–1, 34–5, 39–40, 65–6, 76, 82
monochromatic and polychromatic cultures, 381–2, 475
Montague, Lady, 502
Montefeltro, Guidobaldo, 69
Montesquieu, 92
morality: and civility, 495; Enlightenment, 94–5; in field study, 433, 440–1; French and English compared, 134; and hedonism, 182–3; innate human sense of, 176–7; *laïque*, 129; medieval, 29, 30–1; and a neutral law, 333; role of guilt in teaching, 402; search for common, 357; separation of public and private, 312; and tempering force of women, 194
morality, America: and destruction of wilderness, 219; as disassociated from manners, 307; and duty of ambition, 259–60; with etiquette, 236–7; geographic influences of, 217, 219–20; girls and women, 235; in men's conduct books, 241–3; and paradox of communalism and self-interest, 270–1, 272; and purity, 220, 305; rational moralists and children, 233–4; and 1960s and 1970s mass media, 300
morality, Victorian: and class compromise, 174; in contrast to Regency England, 156–7; and cult of sensibility, 179–80; and culture of consumption, 169; etiquette books and moral fears, 164–5; and home life, 165–6; in libertine context, 10–11; professional organiza-

tions and, 170–1; social context of, 192; style versus, 160–4; theme of improvement, 158; and useful habits, 208
moral weeping, 177, 179, 180
More, Hannah, 151–2, 158, 180–1, 182, 204
motivational habituations, 8
multiculturalism (America): and children, 234, 238, 460; directness result of, 243; and high society, 258; and horizontal relations, 277; and identity, 261; and nationalism, 508; in New York City, 286–7; and rudeness, 501; and self-interest, 212–13; and tolerance, 234, 238, 525
murder rates, English, 210. *See also* crime rates

Napoleon Bonaparte, 128, 137–9
Napoleon III, 120, 121
narcissism, 96, 97, 179–80, 417–21, 504, 525; field study, 433–4, 438; personal, 518, 519; positive, 516; and rudeness, 527; in a topology of civility, 518, 519
narrative of civilizing process, 357–8
national character, 16, 121–2, 153, 210, 276, 316; survey of, 376–80, 378t. *See also* character; patriotism
nationalism and civility, 19, 507–9, 530
Nazi period, 49
networks of trust. *See* trust networks
Newcomb, Rev. Harvey, 235
New York City, 286–7, 380, 442–3
Nietzsche, Friedrich, 304–5, 504
nihilism, 319, 332
*noblesse d'Empire, la,* 128

*noblesse oblige,* 33, 47, 104, 139
novelty and love of change (Victorian), 169

Obama, Barack, 524
observation: in French court, 107
*One Flew Over the Cuckoo's Nest* (film), 300
oppositional self, 17, 336. *See also* therapeutic movement
optimism: and geography (America), 217, 219–20; of New York City, 287; women and, 295
ornamentation. *See* exhibitionism and ornamentation
Ovid, 45, 71

Paine, Thomas, 146, 218, 262
pain in social theory, 285, 410–16, 418–20, 422–3, 505. *See also* emotions
Palmerston, Lady, 168–9
Palmieri, Matteo, 54, 65
paradoxes in civility: accounting for, 500–1; of communalism and self-interest in America, 270–2; in Victorian England, 209
paradoxes in civility, France: of individualism and collectivism, 124–5, 453–8, 508; of reason and emotions, 96–7
parenting: engagement with education, 456, 471, 475; social bond with children, 348; and teenagers, 330, 459. *See also* family
parliamentarianism (British): Bill of Rights, 92, 142–3; and formation of national civility practices, 16; history of, 123, 139–40; Reform Bill of 1867 (England), 191; and

598  Index

Renaissance networks of trust, 64; from revolution to civil protest and, 144–5
Parsons, Talcott, 346
Parsonian sociology, 8
participation, 529
Pasquier, Nicolas, 109–10
passion, 307–8
paternalism, 56, 61–2, 65, 70
patience, medieval, 36, 42
patriarchy of English upper classes, 195
patriotism: and American avant-garde (1950s), 289; in children's conduct books, 235; and corporate culture, 278; in male conduct books (America), 243; and Vietnam War, 299; weakened American, 339–40. *See also* national character
paupers and working poor (England), 152–3
Paxman, Jeremy, 146–7
Peacham, Henry, 150, 151, 240
Peale, Norman Vincent, 291
peasant fury, 37
Perls, Fritz, 315
personal fulfillment in children's conduct books, 235
personal growth movement, 315–16, 318, 331
personality *(personalité)*, 465–6
Petrarch, 59, 71
Petrus Alfonsi, 31
Pew Charitable Trust, 272, 282
*philosophes* (French), 94–5, 119, 124
Pico de Mirandola, Gianfrancesco, 51, 59–60
Pierce, Charles S., 321
pillage, 37, 44

Platonic curriculum, 31–2
Platonic Renaissance, 151
Platt, Polly, 440, 444, 453, 458, 460, 469, 486
pleasantness: *bienséances*, 112–13, 115, 124–5
pleasure: and industrialization, 175; limiting sexual (America), 251; in Regency England, 157; in sentimental interactions (France), 182
Poe, Edgar Allan, 220
policing: in America, 511; in England, 511; in France, 13, 361, 511
politeness: across cultural boundaries, 396; as appearance management (England), 169; conversation and rituals of, 475–80; definition of, 9; in definition of civility, 10; and demands for social change, 362; democratization of (England), 171; English cult of, 169–70, 262, 318; in field study, 434, 437–8; negative and positive co-existing, 398–9; negative or positive in relation to face, 389–90; off-record or on-record in relation to face, 390–1; positive and negative rituals of, 520–1; in post-revolutionary France, 120–1; preservation of distance in negative, 392; as recognition of worth (Enlightenment), 94; and restraint of criticism, 190; strategies of, 393–5, 476; strategies of negative, 394–5, 482; strategies of positive, 395, 478; as style of civil interaction, 14. *See also* civility; manners
politeness theory, 18
*politesse, la,* 114, 120, 122
political correctness, 336–7, 527

politics: centralized monarchies, 211; compromise, 145; and corruption of Catholic Church, 85; of cultural revolution, 299; English avoidance of revolution, 141–2; and formation of public ethos, 357; and idea of relativity, 90; Renaissance, 62, 64; role in culture of civility, 8; as self-transformation, 315. *See also* democracy

Poliziano, 58–9

Pope Gregory VII, 30

Pope Innocent III, 30

popular culture: and consumerism, 291; and counterculture, 310; cross-cultural comparison of, 312; effects of, 313–14; and fame, 323; and family relations (1960s), 301–2; Hollywood and local culture, 296–7; and purity (1960s), 305; role in cultural revolution, 298, 299–300. *See also* mass media

populism (America), 214, 251, 255, 293, 320, 422, 443; and corporate culture, 293; and European social criticism, 320; and self-centredness, 422

Porcari, Stefano, 56

Post, Emily, 258

postmodern and post-structuralist social criticism, 93, 319–22, 359

Potter Webb, Beatrice, 194

power: and abuse of (Renaissance), 66–9; and blind obedience (France), 99–103; centralization of, 26–31, 103–9; divine right of, 102–3; and face threatening, 391; and gender (Renaissance), 72; given to American children, 458; of individual discretion, 359; in national character survey, 377–80, *378t*, 379–80; in politeness rituals, 389–90, 396; social critiques of, 319; in socialization processes, 364–5; struggle against authority (late-modern), 331; in systems of government, 448–9; as tempered (medieval), 29

pragmatism (America), 320–1, 473

precision: *la précision*, 91; Renaissance, 59; and sentiment (France), 124–5

prestige in French court, 104, 108

Prévost, Abbé, 127

pride, 4. *See also* eco-civility

printing press, 54

privacy: and American curiosity, 261; comparison of civility practices in, 263; and English politeness, 169, 479; and friendship, 483; as luxury in rural America, 244. *See also* public

privilege, French, 98, 136

professionals and professionalism, 171, 202–3, 207, 235–6

propriety: American reversal of, 294; and embarrassment, 164, 368–9; and human spirit, 184; meaning of (England), 169, 463; Protestant conception of, 87; and restraint (England), 166; and tact (England), 262; in Victorian England, 191–2, 194, 206, 208–9; virtue and deference, 375–6

prostitution in Victorian England, 198, 200

Protestantism: and Catholicism, 89, 142; civility as religious function, 83; and cult of sensibility, 178–9; ethic of self-denial, 14; and guilt,

90; and individualism, 175; on individual responsibility, 88–90; and industrialization, 174–5; motivation for Reformation, 85–6. *See also* Calvin, John; Luther, Martin
Protestant Reformation. *See* Reformation (Protestant)
protest movements, 144, 297–300, 310, 315, 491, 492–3, 510
Proust, Marcel, 410
prudence in medieval court, 33
psychotherapy, 315–16, 331, 409–10
public: arguing in, 454–5, 488; of café culture (France), 131–4; civility (Renaissance), 79; comfort as sacrosanct (England), 173–4; comparison of civility practices in, 263; congeniality in America, 260; dangers of (Victorian), 206–7; and domestication of men (England), 193; and family life during industrialization, 161–2, 165–6; opinion (Renaissance), 62; personality in Victorian England, 187; politeness ethos of English, 169–70; and private delineation, 352; and private morality, 312; Renaissance rise of, 62; role of American men as, 250; and rule for conduct in (Renaissance), 76–7, 77–8, 81; ruling classes and good of, 159; welfare (Victorian England), 188–9; women in, 201–2. *See also* privacy
Public Agenda Organization, 272
public hangings, 152–3
public servant, Renaissance, 62
public welfare, 103
purgatory, 55
Puritanism, 182; American transition from, 228; in children's conduct books, 229–40; and cultural revolution (1960s), 303; in origins of American civility, 214–17, 220–1; reconciled with pursuit of profit, 240
'purposive discourtesy,' 362

Queen Victoria, 191, 197–8

Rabelais, 52
*raffinement* (refinement), 169
Rambuteau, Comte de, 128
Rand, Ayn, 297, 470, 504–5
*Raoul de Cambrai,* 36
rape, in medieval society, 28, 40
reason: and capitalism, 174–5; in children's conduct books, 237–8; and civic personality, 92; and clarity and precision, 91; Descartes's rationalism, 95; as English final arbiter, 153; and French blind obedience, 99–103; in French child-rearing, 455; in French education, 469–70; and French sentimentalism, 96–7; and independence for mankind, 91; rift with faith, 51; as tempering self-interest, 93. *See also* science
Reaves, Jessica: 'In Defense of Rudeness,' 273–4
recivilizing processes, 19, 501–2
Reformation (Protestant), 16, 51, 84–7, 99, 151. *See also* Protestantism
Reform Bill of 1867 (England), 191
Regency England, 156–7, 159, 169
Reich, Wilhelm, 315, 409, 410
reign of terror (Robespierre), 119–21
relationism, 347, 348
relationships and social bonds: as

isolated or engulfed, 423–4; the 'I-Thou' relationship, 424; the 'I-You and Our Mutual Deal' relationship, 424–5; as no-win situations, 424
relativity, 90, 93
religion: and children, 450t, 450–1; and culture of courtesy, 29–31; and materialism (America), 291; at odds with capitalism and consumption, 290–1; survey on (America), 281, 282; tolerance of (America), 234. *See also* Christianity and the Church
Renaissance: anger in, 37; artistic patronage, 48; attitude to shame, 57–8; mercantilism, 53–7; rise of humanism, 58–65, 75–6; rise of individual, 51–3; secularism in, 10. *See also* literature, Renaissance
Renan, Ernest, 121–2
repression: dangers of, 315–16; internalization of, 351, 353–4; of sexuality, 197–9
research template, 8, 430, 432, 435, 438, 498
respect and disrespect: civility practices to be founded on respect, 527–8; in medieval world, 38; as taught in children's conduct books, 236, 238; and a transnational civility ethic, 527–8
restraint and restraints, 14; and aggression, 354–5; of anger, 35–8, 282–3; and children, 235, 327–8, 450t, 451; and civilization, 19; and civil order, 208, 505–6; of criticism, 190; cross-cultural comparison of, 106, 264–5; and culturally constructed norms, 363; dangers of excessive, 315–16; deformalization of (1960s), 305–6; and democracies, 260; of egalitarianism, 57; and emotional transference, 412–14; in favour of social cohesion, 110; historical increase in, 352; internalizing of, 353–4, 356, 359, 405–6; Machiavelli's theory of, 67–9; medieval, 31–2; in myth of civilized behaviour, 411; and negative politeness, 390; new culture of, 27–34; and political correctness, 336–7; reason as mechanism for, 93; Reformation's new, 85–6, 89–90; and release of (1960s and 1970s), 303–5, 308–9; and reversal of, 358–9; self-control and civility, 277–8; and shame, 332; through time, 12. *See also* self-discipline
restraint and restraints, America, 212–13, 242–3, 296
restraint and restraints, England: culture of, 171, 191, 209–10, 466, 482; of reasonableness, 185; of self, 148; and sense of danger, 206–7; of sexuality, 195–6, 204–5
restraint and restraints, France, 106–7; and *sang froid*, 108
restraint of violence: in development of Western civility, 24–5, 360, 500; and language competence, 520; and refinement of anger, 35–8; as required by the medieval knight, 28–9, 40–4. *See also* violence
reverence, 529–30
Richelieu, Armand Jean Duplessis, Cardinal, 109, 469
rights, culture of, 322
rights, personal, 9
risk, culture of, 314, 377, 389–90; in

national character survey, 377–80, 378t
road rage, 480, 511
Roman Catholic Church, 84–7, 89, 123–4. *See also* Christianity and the Church
Romanovs of Russia, 39
Roman rules of good behaviour, 31
Romanticism: and capitalism, 14; and disillusionment, 307–8; and value of imagination, 182–4; and Victorian sexual restraint, 204–5
Roosevelt, Franklin D., 287
Roszak, Theodore, 311
Roth, Philip, 296
Rousseau, Jean-Jacques, 95–6, 118, 179, 183, 233, 333; social contract, 336
Rouvillois, Frédéric, 119, 123
Rucellai, Giovanni, 58
rudeness: in America, 272–3; cross-cultural comparison of, 273–4; as current cultural obsession, 4, 501; in definition of civility, 10; in France, 124–5, 273–5; late-modern American concern for, 271–3, 276–82, 283–4; narcissism at root of, 527
*ruffian*, 43
rule of law, English, 148
Ruskin, John, 194
Russell, John, 149

St Ambrose, Bishop of Milan, 31
St Augustine, 29, 54, 59, 87
St Francis of Assisi, 54
salons. *See* intellectual salons
Salzmann, C.G., 233–4
Sanders, Charlotte, 234
*sang froid*, 108, 126

*sans-culottes*, 119
Sartre, Jean-Paul, 129, 320
*Saturday Night Live* (TV), 300
*savoir vivre*, 133
scepticism, 314; *l'incrédulité*, 118
Scheff, Thomas J., 345, 348, 414, 415–16, 423
science, 179, 182, 185, 187, 191, 203. *See also* reason
Scudéry, Madeleine de, 115, 125
secularism: American, 227–8, 236–7, 276, 277, 281, 337; and children, 451; courtesy's move to, 84, 90; French, 123–4, 129, 182; and language of republicanism, 59; origin of Western, 102; Renaissance, 10, 71, 83
Sedgewick, Catherine, 235
Sedgwick, Henry Dwight, 192
self-actualization, 316, 331
self-assertion: American, 238, 241–2; France, 95
self-awareness: in courtesy and civility traditions, 82; and Descartes, 97; and dualism of American psyche, 222–3; and Rousseau's *amour propre*, 95–6
self-confidence, Renaissance, 71, 75
self-discipline: and American education, 475; medieval, 31–2. *See also* restraint
self-effacement, 110, 112, 482
self-esteem: conceptions of, 465–8; in me generation, 525–6
self-government in male conduct books, 243
self-gratification and morality, 179–80
self-help: in children's conduct books, 235; of community

(America), 251; Victorian, 185–6, 187–8, 191–2
self-improvement, 317
self-interest: and anger, 36 (*see also* anger); and communalism, 271; in democracy, 212–13; and Machiavelli, 67; and selfishness, 504; and social conscience, 308; and surveillance of self (Renaissance), 66; as tempered with reason (Locke), 93
selfishness: in children, 450t, 451; and self-interest, 504; and self-restraint, 67
self-promotion, 262
self-referentiality: and admission of embarrassment, 414–15; in corporate culture, 281; and individualism, 314; and shame, 405–6; and therapeutic movement, 317
self-reflexivity of Renaissance, 68
self-reliance as valued personality trait, 232, 243
self-restraint in male conduct books, 243
*sensibilité*, 181
sensitive heart (medieval), 32, 34
sensuality: Renaissance, 59; Victorian campaign against, 205–6
sentimentalism: compared (France and England), 181–2; and cult of sensibility (England), 174, 175–80, 192; definition of sentimentality, 178; and French bourgeoisie, 126–7; narcissistic aspects of, 180; and reason (France), 96–7, 124–5; rejection of (America), 214; and sincerity in letter writing, 152
Sewall, Samuel, 224
sex and sexuality: chastity, 45, 167, 202–3; effect of birth control pill, 303; effect of cultural revolution (1960s), 302; and gender relations, 325–6; limiting pleasure from (America), 251; reversal of restraints on, 358; and *séduction* (seduction), 485; and shame, 349–51, 405–6; of Victorian middle class, 195–204, 206, 207. *See also* body; marriage
Shaftsbury, Earl of (Anthony Ashley Cooper), 94, 176
shame: accumulation of, 414; and cultural context, 510–11; and guilt, 400–1; and internalizing of restraints, 353–4, 405–6; and lack of empathy, 422; and medieval priests, 31; organic and self-referential, 406; and pain of rejection, 413; raised threshold of, 65–6, 68–9, 81–2, 349–52; relationship to anger, 415–16; Renaissance attitude to, 57–8, 60; and self-concept, 407–8; self-referential, 405–6; and social harmony, 355; and socialization, 341, 345. *See also* eco-civility; embarrassment and shame; emotions
Sherwood, Mary C.W., 255
Sigourney, Lydia, 235
Simmel, George, 399
simplicity and directness (America), 225, 227, 243, 252, 477. *See also* directness
simplicity of English compared to French, 150
sincerity: and American therapeutic culture, 316; and deception, 170–1; in letter writing, 152; as public congeniality (America), 260; Ro-

mantics call for, 184; sentimentality as mark of, 178
slavery, 217–18, 220, 221
Smiles, Samuel, 141, 165–6, 187–8, 189, 192, 240
Smith, Adam, 176, 185, 192
social bonds, 14. *See also* trust networks
social census (America), 225, 276
social mobility: American, 225; French, 111; medieval, 39
social psychology, 6
social welfare, 152–3
Society for the Reformation of Manners, 151
sociology of culture: as effective, 4; as including emotions, 6; individual and social forces, 347; and sociology of emotions, 344–6
sovereignty of the people, 102. *See also* secularism
sports ethic of fair play, 196
*sprezzatura*, 109
Staffe, Baronne (Blanche Soyer), 122
Stearns, Peter N., 276, 277–8, 465
Steinbeck, John, 287–8, 521
Steinem, Gloria, 324
'stiff upper lip,' 172
Stowe, Harriet Beecher, 220
structuralism, 8
style: American, 252, 257–8, 294, 464–5; birth of (medieval), 32; English, 160–4; French, 113, 318; Protestant reaction to Italian, 86–7; Renaissance, 58, 71, 72–3
submission: and children, 292–3; English, 464; medieval, 64; as modesty, 34; play-acted, 279–80; and sentimentalists, 183–4; women and, 194, 199, 245

Sunday school (America), 236–7
surveillance: cameras in England, 449, 493; centralized in state, 103; and conformity (Renaissance), 81; and crime rates (France), 13, 361; of family behaviour (Renaissance), 62–3; and individual responsibility, 86; and internalization of restraints, 356, 359; mutual, 89; of self, 66, 232; of sexuality (Victorian), 200–1; and systems of government, 449, 493
symbolic interactionism, 364

tact: American, 211, 214, 251; and competition for rights, 334; conduct books on, 79; and discretion (Renaissance), 73; English, 171–4, 190, 191, 209, 262, 512; in French context, 264; as off-record politeness, 391; in the practice of compliments, 392–3
Taine, Hippolyte, 132, 198
*Talking with Teens: The YMCA Parent and Teen Survey*, 330
taxes in France, 136–7
Taylor, Charles, 271, 335, 336
Taylor, Harriette, 191, 193, 208
technology, 53, 54
teenagers and teen culture: anger and restraint in, 521–2; and corporate culture, 292; French and American compared, 461–2, 466; and parental relationships, 330, 459; and saving face, 514–15
tender heart. *See* sensitive heart
Tennyson, Alfred Lord, 154, 204, 205
Terkel, Studs, 279
theatre, and French middle classes, 127, 130

therapeutic movement, 17, 316, 325, 328–30, 385
Thoreau, Henry David, 222
Tillam, Thomas, 215–16
Tilly, Charles, 38, 49, 143–5, 155, 312–13, 359–60; *Trust and Rule*, 64; on trust networks, 506; *Why*, 11
time, context, and space, 18; definition of high- and low-context societies, 382–3; and American organizational procedures, 466; and anger management (America), 513–14; childrearing in high-context cultures, 451, 452, 454, 460; childrearing in low-context cultures, 452, 455, 458, 459; context and childrearing, 462, 463–4; context and conversation, 475, 477; context and friendship, 482–3; cross-cultural comparison of, 380–4, 408, 445–7; cross-cultural comparison of context, 517–18, 520–1; cross-cultural comparison of space, 479–80, 485–6; cross-cultural comparison of time, 464, 475–6, 489, 491; individualism in high-context society, 467; power and distance in face, 391–2; shame and context, 510; time and friendship, 480; and volume of conversation, 476; work in high-context culture, 489; work in low-context culture, 490–1
Tocqueville, Alexis de, 186–7, 259–60, 331, 338, 421, 442, 447, 465; on English individualism, 147; on filial obedience, 465; on French republicanism, 120–1; on individualism, 338; on *méfiance* (distrust), 125; on 'natural predisposition,' 515; on personal independence, 421; on systems of government, 447
Todd, Rev. John, 241
tolerance: and authenticity, 417; and Judeo-Christian heritage (America), 337; and a neutral state, 333–4; and political correctness, 336–7; rise of (Enlightenment), 92–3; as taught to children (America), 238
tradition: American and French attitude to, 473–4; and integration of change, 277, 523
Trollope, Fanny, 252–3
troubadours, 47–8
Truss, Lynne, 417, 451
trust: civility and networks of, 506–9; and French work ethic, 489; between genders in medieval society, 28; and *méfiance* (distrust), 125; secular individualism, 276
trust networks, 14–15; as roots of parliamentarianism, 64, 145–6
Turner, Jonathan H., 344–5
Twain, Mark, 153, 221–2, 239–40
Twenge, Jean, 525–6

understatement: in medieval court, 34
unselfishness: in children's conduct books (America), 234
urban centres. *See* cities and urban centres
utilitarianism: in American education system, 474; contrasting American gentleman, 224; in early America, 222; in France, 153, 185; and goodness, 176; and industrialization, 155–6; Machiavelli and, 67; in manners (England), 150; and sentimentality, 178, 182–3

utopianism and Romanticism, 183

valour in medieval court, 33
Vanderbilt, Amy, 19
Veblen, Thorstein, 104–5, 255
vengeful anger, 36. *See also* anger
Versailles clique culture, 47
Victorian England: as 'age of Improvement,' 185–6; paradox of, 209; social compromise of, 159, 171. *See also* education, Victorian; family, Victorian; literature, Victorian; morality, Victorian; women in Victorian England; *individual concepts*
Vietnam War, 299
*vilein* (peasant), 33–4
violence: and anger, 49, 513; and café culture, 133–4; central monopoly of, 7, 27–8, 359–60; and civility after French Revolution, 105; in definition of civility, 10; and origins of civility, 8; in policing, 511; and rituals of wit, 417; and self-restraint in England, 148; and the state, 38, 102–3, 143–4, 352; of state, 511; and survival, 67. *See also* restraint of violence
virtue/virtues: as foundation, 149; and knowledge, 31–2; Locke's criticism of, 92–3; medieval, 10, 33–5; as merging of sentiment and sensibility, 177–8; and moral legitimacy, 129; Renaissance discussions of, 59; return to religious (England), 158; as secular (Renaissance), 71; of sentiment and principle, 181; and vice, 188
Voltaire, 123–4, 320; *Candide*, 97; *Enfant prodigue*, 130; *Philosophical Letters on the English*, 92, 118

volunteerism, 276, 380, 449
von Oberge, Eilhart: *Tristan and Isalde*, 47
von Raumer, W., 349–51
*vraisemblance*, 113

Walker, Obadiah, 150–1
Washington, George, 213
Watson, Dr John B., 327
Watson, Lillian (Eichler), 258
Watts, Isaac, 232–3
Weber, Max, 14, 105, 174–5, 251, 334
Wellington, Duke of, 172
Wells, H.G., 155
West, Cornell, 321
Whitman, Walt, 222
Wilberforce, William, 158, 161, 192
William the Conqueror, 34, 40
Williams, Tennessee, 288
will power: in male conduct books (America), 243
Wilson, Edmund, 289
Wilson, Harriette, 157
Winthrop, John, 224
Wireker, Nigel, 34
wit: and avoiding violence, 417; of courtier, 73; French, 106, 113, 117, 122, 492; Protestant, 89
women: of American south, 252; conduct books for, 244–51; conduct books for girls, 235; and cultural revolution, 301–2, 311; as dangerous, 206–7; femininity, 377; gender wars in America, 486; intelligence of, 249–50; magazines for, 168–9, 256; medieval, 45, 46, 48; mission in America, 248; as partners in America, 244–5; in polite interaction, 110–11; in Renaissance literature, 72; rights of (America), 246, 249, 250; as

unhappy in film, 296. *See also* feminism; lady; women in Victorian England
women in Victorian England, 167, 186; as dangerous, 206–7; idealization of, 193–4, 201, 208; magazines for, 168–9; and sex, 199, 201–4; unmarried, 201; as unwed mothers, 200–1. *See also* women
Woodruff, Paul, 529
work: competition and civility, 278; cross-cultural comparison of, 488–91; in England, 186, 490–1; in France, 488–91; and friendship, 480–1; preferences in America, 281; women in public, 326. *See also* corporate culture; work ethic, America
work ethic, America, 250–1, 488, 490–1; in children's conduct books, 234, 235, 236; in corporate culture, 294, 309–10; in men's conduct books, 241–3; of Puritans, 216–17; survey of workplace absences, 280 (*see also* corporate culture); for women, 245
World Values Survey, 281, 376–7, 439–40, 466, 481, 484; qualities most desirable in children, *450t*, 450–1

*zivilität*, 77